First Philosophy

VOLUME II: KNOWLEDGE AND REALITY

First Philosophy
Fundamental Problems and Readings in Philosophy

SECOND EDITION

VOLUME II
Knowledge and Reality

General Editor
ANDREW BAILEY

Contributing Editor
ROBERT M. MARTIN

broadview press

Library and Archives Canada Cataloguing in Publication

First philosophy : fundamental problems and readings in philosophy /
general editor Andrew Bailey ; contributing editor Robert M. Martin. — 2nd ed.

Includes bibliographical references.
Contents: v. 1. Values and society — v. 2. Knowledge and reality — v. 3.
God, mind, and freedom.
ISBN 978-1-55111-972-4 (v. 1).—ISBN 978-1-55111-973-1 (v. 2).—
ISBN 978-1-55111-974-8 (v. 3)

1. Philosophy—Textbooks. I. Bailey, Andrew, 1969- II. Martin,
Robert M.

B29.F57 2011a   100   C2011-901810-1

Broadview Press is an independent, international publishing house, incorporated in 1985.

We welcome comments and suggestions regarding any aspect of our publications—please feel free to contact us at the addresses below or at broadview@broadviewpress.com.

North America   PO Box 1243, Peterborough, Ontario, Canada K9J 7H5
                           2215 Kenmore Ave., Buffalo, New York, USA 14207
                           Tel: (705) 743-8990; Fax: (705) 743-8353
                           email: customerservice@broadviewpress.com

UK, Europe, Central Asia,   Eurospan Group, 3 Henrietta St., London WC2E 8LU, UK
Middle East, Africa, India, Tel: 44 (0) 1767 604972; Fax: 44 (0) 1767 601640
and Southeast Asia   email: eurospan@turpin-distribution.com

Australia and New Zealand   NewSouth Books, c/o TL Distribution
                           15-23 Helles Ave., Moorebank, NSW, Australia 2170
                           Tel: (02) 8778 9999; Fax: (02) 8778 9944
                           email: orders@tldistribution.com.au

www.broadviewpress.com

Broadview Press acknowledges the financial support of the Government of Canada through the Canada Book Fund for our publishing activities.

This book is printed on paper containing 100% postconsumer fibre.

PRINTED IN CANADA

For Jack and Max

CONTENTS

HOW TO USE THIS BOOK

This book is an introduction to the theory of knowledge and the philosophy of science. Within this field, it is intended to be a reasonably representative—though very far from exhaustive—sampling of important philosophical questions, major philosophers and their most important works, periods of philosophical history, and styles of philosophical thought.[1] Half of the included readings, however, were published since 1950, and another important aim of the book is to provide some background for *current* philosophical debates, to give the interested reader a springboard for the plunge into the exciting world of contemporary philosophy.

The aim of this book is to introduce philosophy through philosophy itself: it is not a book *about* philosophy but a book *of* philosophy, in which more than a dozen great philosophers speak for themselves. Each of the readings is prefaced by a set of notes, but these notes make no attempt to explain or summarize the reading. Instead, the goal of the notes is to provide *background information* helpful for understanding the reading—to remove as many of the unnecessary barriers to comprehension as possible, and to encourage a deeper and more sophisticated encounter with great pieces of philosophy. The notes to selections, therefore, do not stand alone and *certainly* are not a substitute for the reading itself: they are meant to be consulted in combination with the reading. (The philosophical selections are also quite heavily annotated throughout by the editor, again in an effort to get merely contingent difficulties for comprehension out of the way and allow the reader to devote all his or her effort to understanding the philosophy itself.)

The reader can of course take or leave these notes as they choose, and read them (or not) in any order. One good way of proceeding, however, would be the following. First, read the selection (so that nothing said in the notes inadvertently taints your first impression of the piece). Then, go back and read some of the notes—the biographical sketch, information on the author's philosophical project, structural and background information—and with these things in mind read the selection again. Spend some time *thinking* about the reading: ask yourself if you really feel you have a good grasp on what the author is trying to say, and then—no less importantly—ask yourself whether the author gives good reasons to believe that their position is *true*. (Chapter 1 tries to give some helpful suggestions for this process of critical reflection.) After this, it should be worthwhile going back to the notes, checking your impressions against any 'common misconceptions,' and then running through at least some of the suggestions for critical reflection. Finally, you might want to go on and read more material by the philosopher in question, or examine what other philosophers have said about his or her ideas: the suggestions for further reading will point you in the right direction.

A word of explanation about the 'Suggestions for Critical Reflection' section: although the notes to the readings contain no philosophical critique of the selection, the questions in this section are largely intended to help the reader generate his or her own critique. As such, they are supposed to be thought-provoking, rather than straightforwardly easy to answer. They try to suggest fruitful avenues for critical thought (though they do not cover every possible angle of questioning, or even all the important ones), and only very rarely is there some particular 'right answer' to the question. Thus, these questions should not be considered a kind of 'self-test' to see if you understand the material: even people with a very good grasp of the material will typically be puzzled by the questions—because they are *supposed* to be puzzling questions.

---

1 There are two major exceptions to this. First, this book focuses exclusively on 'Western' philosophy—that is, roughly, on the philosophical traditions of Europe and of the descendents of European settlers in North America and Australasia. In particular, it does not attempt to encompass the rich philosophical heritage of Asia or Africa. Second, this collection generally ignores an important strain of twentieth-century philosophy, so-called 'Continental' philosophy, which includes thinkers such as Husserl, Heidegger, Sartre, Foucault, Derrida, and Habermas, and is characterized by such movements as existentialism, hermeneutics, structuralism, and deconstructionism.

The readings and their accompanying notes are designed to be 'modular'; that is, in general, one reading can be understood without the benefit of having read any of the other selections. This means that the selections can be read in any order. One natural way of doing the readings is chronologically; here is a list of the contents of the book arranged according to the date of the first 'publication' of the work in its original language:

The readings in this anthology are, so far as is practicable, 'complete': that is, they are entire articles, chapters, or sections of books. The editors feel it is important for students to be able to see an argument in the context in which it was originally presented; also, the fact that the readings are not edited to include only what is relevant to one particular philosophical concern means that they can be used in a variety of different ways following a variety of different lines of thought across the ages. Some instructors will wish to assign for their students shorter excerpts of some of these readings, rather than having them read all of the work included: the fact that complete, or almost complete, pieces of philosophy are included in this

anthology gives the instructor the freedom to pick the excerpts that best fit their pedagogical aims. We have also included an alternative table of contents giving suggestions for abridgement corresponding to the shortened pieces most commonly found in other introductory philosophy anthologies.

The notes to the readings in this anthology are almost entirely a work of synthesis, and a large number of books and articles were consulted in their preparation; it is impossible—without adding an immense apparatus of notes and references—to acknowledge them in detail, but all my main sources have been included as suggestions for further reading. This is, I believe, appropriate for a textbook, but it is not intended to model good referencing practices for student essays. All the material and annotations accompanying the readings were written by the editors, and none of it (unless otherwise noted) was copied from other sources. Typically, the notes for each reading amalgamate information from a dozen or so sources; in a few instances, especially for biographical information on still-living philosophers, the notes rely heavily on a smaller number of sources (and I tried to indicate this in the text when it occurred). These sources are not footnoted in the body of the text, as they should be in a student (or professional) essay. However, citations are provided at the back of the book for all direct quotations. All of the books, articles and websites that I referred to and found useful are also listed in bibliographies: Chapter 1 lists general works of reference, and the introductory material for each selection includes suggestions for further reading which include the works I looked at (when I found them helpful).

Students should make sure they are aware of the citation system that their instructor prefers them to use in their class work.

Thanks to Alan Belk, Lance Hickey, Peter Loptson, and Mark Migotti for pointing out errors and omissions in the first edition. In case of a third edition but also, more importantly, for the general good of his soul, the editor would warmly welcome further corrections or suggestions for improvement:

Andrew Bailey
Department of Philosophy, The University of Guelph
Guelph, Ontario N1G 2W1 Canada
abailey@uoguelph.ca

SUGGESTIONS FOR ABRIDGEMENT

The following version of the table of contents identifies shorter excerpts of the readings—often those selections most frequently reprinted in other introductory philosophy anthologies—as suggestions for instructors who wish to assign briefer readings for their students.

CHAPTER 1

Philosophy

WHAT IS PHILOSOPHY?

Philosophy, at least according to the origin of the word in classical Greek, is the "love of wisdom"—philosophers are lovers of wisdom. The first philosophers of the Western tradition lived on the shores of the Mediterranean in the sixth century BCE (that is, more than 2,500 years ago);[1] thinkers such as Thales, Xenophanes, Pythagoras, Heraclitus, and Protagoras tried systematically to answer questions about the ultimate nature of the universe, the standards of knowledge, the objectivity of moral claims, and the existence and nature of God. Questions like these are still at the core of the discipline today.

So what is philosophy? It can be characterized either as a particular sort of *method*, or in terms of its *subject matter*, or as a kind of intellectual *attitude*.

Philosophy as a Method

One view is that philosophy studies the same things—the same world—as, for example, scientists do, but that they do so in a different, and complementary, way. In particular, it is often claimed that while scientists draw conclusions from empirical *observations* of the world, philosophers use *rational arguments* to justify claims about the world. For instance, both scientists and philosophers are involved in contemporary studies of the human mind. Neuroscientists and psychologists are busily mapping out correlations between brain states and mental states—finding which parts of the visual

---

1   In the East, Lao-Tzu, the founder of Taoism, probably lived at about the same time in China. Buddha and Confucius were born a few decades later. In India, an oral literature called the *Veda* had been asking philosophical questions since at least 1500 BCE.

cortex play a role in dreaming, for example—and building computer models of intelligent information processing (such as chess-playing programs). Philosophers are also involved in cognitive science, trying to discover just what would *count* as discovering that dreaming is really nothing more than certain electro-chemical events in the brain, or would count as building a computer which feels pain or genuinely has beliefs. These second kinds of questions are crucial to the whole project of cognitive science, but they are not empirical, scientific questions: there simply is no fact about the brain that a scientist could observe to answer them. And so these questions—which are part of cognitive science—are dealt with by philosophers.

Here are two more examples. Economists study the distribution of wealth in society, and develop theories about how wealth and other goods can come to be distributed one way rather than another (e.g., concentrated in a small proportion of the population, as in Brazil, or spread more evenly across society, as in Sweden). However, questions about which kind of distribution is more *just*, which kind of society is best to live in, are not answered within economic theory—these are philosophical questions. Medical professionals are concerned with facts about sickness and death, and often have to make decisions about the severity of an illness or weigh the risk of death from a certain procedure. Philosophers also examine the phenomenon of death, but ask different questions: for example, they ask whether people can survive their own deaths (i.e., if there is a soul), whether death is really a harm for the person who dies, under what conditions—if any—we should assist people in committing suicide, and so on.

One reason why philosophers deal differently with phenomena than scientists do is that philosophers are using different techniques of investigation. The core of the philosophical method is the application of *rational thought* to problems. There are (arguably) two main aspects to this: the use of conceptual or linguistic *analysis* to clarify ideas and questions; and the use of formal or informal *logic* to argue for certain answers to those questions.

For example, questions about the morality of abortion often pivot on the following question: is a foetus a *person* or not? A person is, roughly, someone who has similar moral status to a normal adult human being. Being a person is not simply *the same thing* as being a member of the human species, however, since it is at least possible that some human beings are not persons (brain-dead individuals in permanent comas, for example?) and some persons might not be human beings (intelligent life from other planets, or gorillas, perhaps?). If it turns out that a foetus *is* a person, abortion will be morally problematic—it may even be a kind of murder. On the other hand, if a foetus is no more a person than, say, one of my kidneys, abortion may be as morally permissible as a transplant. So *is* a foetus a person? How would one even go about discovering the answer to this question? Philosophers proceed by using *conceptual analysis*. What we need to find out, first of all, is what makes something a person—what the essential difference is between persons and non-persons—and then we can apply this general account to human foetuses to see if they satisfy the definition. Put another way, we need to discover precisely what the word "person" means.

Since different conceptual analyses will provide importantly different answers to questions about the morality of abortion, we need to *justify* our definition: we need to give reasons to believe that one particular analysis of personhood is correct. This is where logic comes in: logic is the study of arguments, and its techniques are designed to distinguish between good arguments—by which we should be persuaded—and bad arguments, which we should not find persuasive. (The next main section of this chapter will tell you a little more about logic.)

Philosophy as a Subject Matter

Another way of understanding philosophy is to say that philosophers study a special set of issues, and that it is this subject matter which defines the subject. Philosophical questions fit three major characteristics:

1. They are of deep and lasting interest to human beings;

2. They have answers, but the answers have not yet been settled on;

3. The answers cannot be decided by science, faith or common sense.

Philosophers try to give the best possible answers to such questions. That is, they seek the one answer which is more justified than any other possible answer. There are lots of questions which count as philosophical, according to these criteria. All can be classified as versions of one of three basic philosophical questions.

The first foundational philosophical question is *What exists?* For example: Does God exist? Are quarks really real, or are they just fictional postulates of a particular scientific theory? Are numbers real? Do persons exist, and what is the difference between a person and her physical body, or between a person and a 'mere animal'? The various questions of existence are studied by the branch of philosophy called Metaphysics, and by its various sub-fields such as Philosophy of Mind and Philosophy of Religion.

The second fundamental philosophical question is *What do we know?* For example, can we be sure that a scientific theory is actually true, or is it merely the currently dominant simplification of reality? The world appears to us to be full of colors and smells, but can we ever find out whether it really is colored or smelly (i.e., even if no one is perceiving it)? Everyone believes that 5+6=11, but what makes us so sure of this—could we be wrong, and if not, why not? The branch of philosophy which deals with these kinds of questions is called Epistemology. Philosophy of Science examines the special claims to knowledge made by the natural sciences, and Logic is the study of the nature of rational justification.

The third major philosophical question is *What should we do?* If I make a million dollars selling widgets or playing basketball, is it okay for me to keep all of that money and do what I want with it, or do I have some kind of moral obligation to give a portion of my income to the less well off? If I could get out of trouble by telling a lie, and no one else will really be harmed by my lie, is it alright to do so? Is Mozart's *Requiem* more or less artistically valuable than The Beatles' *Sergeant Pepper's Lonely Hearts Club Band*? Questions like these are addressed by Value Theory, which includes such philosophical areas as Ethics, Aesthetics, Political Philosophy, and Philosophy of Law.

Philosophy as an Attitude

A third view is that philosophy is a state of being—a kind of intellectual independence. Philosophy is a reflective activity, an attitude of critical and systematic thoughtfulness. To be philosophical is to continue to question the assumptions behind every claim until we come to our most basic beliefs about reality, and then to critically examine those beliefs. For example, most of us assume that criminals are responsible for their actions, and that this is at least partly why we punish them. But *are* they responsible for what they do? We know that social pressures are very powerful in affecting our behavior. Is it unfair to make individuals entirely responsible for society's effects on them when those effects are negative? How much of our personal identity is bound up with the kind of community we belong to, and how far are we free to choose our own personalities and values? Furthermore, it is common to believe that the brain is the physical cause of all our behavior, that the brain is an entirely physical organ, and that all physical objects are subject to deterministic causal laws. If all of this is right, then presumably all human behavior is just the result of complex causal laws affecting our brain and body, and we could no more choose our actions than a falling rock could choose to take a different route down the mountainside. If this is true, then can we even make sense of the notion of moral responsibility? If it is not true, then where does free will come from and how (if at all) does it allow us to escape the laws of physics? Here, a questioning attitude towards our assumptions about criminals has shown that we might not have properly considered the bases of our assumptions. This ultimately leads us to fundamental questions about the place of human beings in the world.

Here are three quotes from famous philosophers which give the flavor of this view of philosophy as a critical attitude:

Socrates, one of the earliest Western philosophers, who lived in Greece around 400 BCE, is said to have declared that "it is the greatest good for a man to discuss virtue every day and those other things about which you hear me conversing and testing myself and others, for the unexamined life is not worth living."

Immanuel Kant—the most important thinker of the late eighteenth century—called this philosophical state of being "Enlightenment."

> Enlightenment is the emergence of man from the immaturity for which he is himself responsible. Immaturity is the inability to use one's understanding without the guidance of another. Man is responsible for his own immaturity, when it is caused, by lack not of understanding, but of the resolution and the courage to use it without the guidance of another. *Sapere aude*! Have the courage to use your own reason! is the slogan of Enlightenment.

Finally, in the twentieth century, Bertrand Russell wrote the following assessment of the value of philosophy:

> Philosophy is to be studied, not for the sake of any definite answers to its questions, since no definite answers can, as a rule, be known to be true, but rather for the sake of the questions themselves; because these questions enlarge our conception of what is possible, enrich our intellectual imagination and diminish the dogmatic assurance which closes the mind against speculation; but above all because, through the greatness of the universe which philosophy contemplates, the mind also is rendered great, and becomes capable of that union with the universe which constitutes its highest good.

Questions for Further Thought:

1. Here are some more examples of phenomena which are studied by both scientists and philosophers: color, sense perception, medical practices like abortion and euthanasia, human languages, mathematics, quantum mechanics,

the evolution of species, democracy, taxation. What contribution (if any) might philosophers make to the study of these topics?

2. How well does *mathematics* fit into the division between science and philosophy described above? How does *religion* fit into this classification?

3. Here are a few simple candidate definitions of "person": a person is anything which is capable of making rational decisions; a person is any creature who can feel pain; a person is any creature with a soul; a person is any creature which has the appropriate place in a human community. Which of these, if any, do you think are plausible? What are the consequences of these definitions for moral issues like abortion or vegetarianism? Try to come up with a more sophisticated conceptual analysis of personhood.

4. Do you think criminals are responsible for their actions?

5. Should society support philosophy, and to what degree (e.g., should tax dollars be spent paying philosophers to teach at public universities? Why (not)?)?

Suggestions for Further Reading

As a general rule, it is far better to read philosophy than to read *about* philosophy. A brief but moving work often anthologized in the "what is philosophy" section of introductory textbooks is Plato's *Apology*, which features a speech by Socrates defending the practice of philosophy in the face of his fourth-century BCE Athenian contemporaries, who are about to condemn him to death for it. Two more modern works, which are introductions to philosophy but also significant pieces of philosophy in their own right, are Bertrand Russell's *The Problems of Philosophy* (Oxford University Press, 1912) and *The Central Questions of Philosophy* by A.J. Ayer (Penguin, 1973).

Two aging, slightly idiosyncratic, but nevertheless well-respected histories of western philosophy are Bertrand Russell's *A History of Western Philosophy* (George Allen & Unwin, 1961) and the massive *History of Philosophy* by Frederick Copleston, originally published between 1946 and 1968 and recently re-issued in nine garish volumes by Image Books. Two shorter and more recent histories are *A Brief History of Western Philosophy* by Anthony Kenny (Blackwell, 1998) and *The Oxford Illustrated History of Western Philosophy*, edited by Anthony Kenny (Oxford University Press, 1994).

Of the many one-volume anthologies of western philosophical writing available, the following are among the most extensive: *Philosophical Classics: From Plato to Derrida*, edited by Forrest Baird and Walter Kaufman (Prentice Hall, 2000); *Classics of Western Philosophy*, edited by Steven Cahn (Hackett, 1999); *The Mayfield Anthology of Western Philosophy*, edited by Daniel Kolak (Mayfield, 1998); *Introduction to Philosophy: Classical and Contemporary Readings*, edited by John Perry and Michael Bratman (Oxford University Press, 1999); and *Classics of Philosophy*, edited by Louis P. Pojman (Oxford University Press, 1998).

Finally, there are a number of useful philosophical reference works. The major encyclopedia of philosophy is now the ten-volume *Routledge Encyclopedia of Philosophy*, published in 1998. This replaced the old standby—which is still a useful work, consisting of eight volumes—*The Encyclopedia of Philosophy* edited by Paul Edwards (Macmillan, 1967). Shorter philosophy reference works include *The Concise Routledge Encyclopedia of Philosophy* (Routledge, 2000); *The Cambridge Dictionary of Philosophy*, edited by Robert Audi (Cambridge University Press, 1999); the *Oxford Dictionary of Philosophy*, by Simon Blackburn (Oxford University Press, 1996); *The Blackwell Companion to Philosophy*, edited by Nicholas Bunnin and E.P. Tsui-James (Blackwell, 1996); *The Oxford Companion to Philosophy*, edited by Ted Honderich (Oxford University Press, 1995); *The Philosopher's Dictionary*, by Robert Martin (Broadview, 1994); and the *Penguin Dictionary of Philosophy*, edited by Thomas Mautner (Penguin, 1997). Online philosophy is not always very reliable and should be treated with caution, but two websites which are dependable and likely to be around for a while are the *Stanford Encyclopedia of Philosophy* (http://plato.stanford.edu/) and *The Internet Encyclopedia of Philosophy* (http://www.utm.edu/research/iep/).

A BRIEF INTRODUCTION TO ARGUMENTS

Evaluating Arguments

The main tool of philosophy is the *argument*. An argument is any sequence of statements intended to establish—or at least to make plausible—some particular claim. For example, if I say that Vancouver is a better place to live than Toronto because it has a beautiful setting between the mountains and the ocean, is less congested, and has a lower cost of living, then I am making an argument. The claim which is being defended is called the *conclusion*, and the statements which together are supposed to show that the conclusion is (likely to be) true are called the *premises*. Often arguments will be strung together in a sequence, with the conclusions of earlier arguments featuring as premises of the later ones. For example, I might go on to argue that since Vancouver is a better place to live than Toronto, and since one's living conditions are a big part of what determines one's happiness, then the people who live in Vancouver must, in general, be happier than those living in Toronto. Usually, a piece of philosophy is primarily made up of chains of argumentation: good philosophy consists of good arguments; bad philosophy contains bad arguments.

What makes the difference between a good and a bad argument? It's important to notice, first of all, that the difference is *not* that good arguments have true conclusions and bad arguments have false ones. A perfectly good argument might, unluckily, happen to have a conclusion that is false. For example, you might argue that you know this rope will bear my weight because you know that the rope's rating is greater than my weight, you know that the rope's manufacturer is a reliable one, you have a good understanding of the safety standards which are imposed on rope makers and vendors, and you have carefully inspected this rope for flaws. Nevertheless, it still might be the case that this rope is the one in 50 million which has a hidden defect causing it to snap. If so, that makes me unlucky, but it doesn't suddenly make your argument a bad one—we were still being quite reasonable when we trusted the rope. On the other hand, it is very easy to give appallingly bad arguments for true conclusions: Every sentence beginning with the letter "c" is true; "Chickens lay eggs" begins with the letter "c"; Therefore, chickens lay eggs.

But there is a deeper reason why the evaluation of arguments doesn't begin by assessing the truth of the conclusion. The whole point of making arguments is to establish *whether or not* some particular claim is true or false. An argument works by starting from some claims which, ideally, everyone is willing to accept as true—the premises—and then showing that something interesting—something *new*—follows from them: i.e., an argument tells you that *if* you believe these premises, *then* you should also believe this conclusion. In general, it would be unfair, therefore, to simply reject the conclusion and suppose that the argument must be a bad one—in fact, it would often be intellectually dishonest. If the argument *were* a good one, then it would show you that you might be *wrong* in supposing its conclusion to be false; and to refuse to accept this is not to respond to the argument but simply to ignore it.[2]

It follows that there are exactly two reasonable ways to criticize an argument: the first is to question the truth of the *premises*; and the second is to question the claim that if the premises are true then the conclusion is true as well—that is, one can critique the *strength* of the argument. Querying the truth of

---

2   Of course, occasionally, you might legitimately know *for sure* that the conclusion is false, and then you could safely ignore arguments which try to show it is true: for example, *after* the rope breaks, I could dismiss your argument that it is safe (again, though, this would not show that your argument was *bad*, just that I need not be persuaded that the conclusion is true). However, this will not do for philosophical arguments: all interesting philosophy deals with issues where, though we may have firm opinions, we cannot just insist that we know all the answers and can therefore afford to ignore relevant arguments.

the premises (i.e., asking whether it's really true that Vancouver is less congested or cheaper than Toronto) is fairly straightforward. The thing to bear in mind is that you will usually be working backwards down a chain of argumentation: that is, each premise of a philosopher's main argument will often be supported by sub-arguments, and the controversial premises in these sub-arguments might be defended by further arguments, and so on. Normally it is not enough to merely demand to know whether some particular premise is true: one must look for *why* the arguer thinks it is true, and then engage with *that* argument.

Understanding and critiquing the strength of an argument (either your own or someone else's) is somewhat more complex. In fact, this is the main subject of most books and courses in introductory logic. When dealing with the strength of an argument, it is usual to divide arguments into two classes: *deductive* arguments and *inductive* arguments. Good deductive arguments are the strongest possible kind of argument: if their premises are true, then their conclusion *must necessarily* be true. For example, if all bandicoots are rat-like marsupials, and if Billy is a bandicoot, then it cannot possibly be false that Billy is a rat-like marsupial. On the other hand, good inductive arguments establish that, if the premises are true, then the conclusion is *highly likely* (but not absolutely certain) to be true as well. For example, I may notice that the first bandicoot I see is rat-like, and the second one is, and the third, and so on; eventually, I might reasonably conclude that all bandicoots are rat-like. This is a good argument for a probable conclusion, but nevertheless the conclusion can never be shown to be *necessarily* true. Perhaps a non-rat-like bandicoot once existed before I was born, or perhaps there is one living now in an obscure corner of New Guinea, or perhaps no bandicoot so far has ever been non-rat-like but at some point, in the future, a mutant bandicoot will be born that in no way resembles a rat, and so on.

Deductive Arguments and Validity

The strength of deductive arguments is an on/off affair, rather than a matter of degree. Either these arguments are such that if the premises are true

then the conclusion necessarily must be, or they are not. Strong deductive arguments are called *valid*; otherwise, they are called *invalid*. The main thing to notice about validity is that its definition is an *if… then…* statement: *if* the premises *were* true, then the conclusion *would* be. For example, an argument can be valid even if its premises and its conclusion are not true: all that matters is that if the premises *had* been true, the conclusion necessarily would have been as well. This is an example of a valid argument:

1. Either bees are rodents or they are birds.
2. Bees are not birds.
3. Therefore bees are rodents.

If the first premise were true, then (since the second premise is already true), the conclusion would *have* to be true—that's what makes this argument valid. This example makes it clear that validity, though a highly desirable property in an argument, is not enough all by itself to make a good argument: good deductive arguments are both valid *and* have true premises. When arguments are good in this way they are called *sound*: sound arguments have the attractive feature that they necessarily have true conclusions. To show that an argument is unsound, it is enough to show that it is either invalid or has a false premise.

It bears emphasizing that even arguments which have true premises and a true conclusion can be unsound. For example:

1. Only US citizens can become the President of America.
2. George W. Bush is a US citizen.
3. Therefore, George W. Bush was elected President of America.

This argument is not valid, and therefore it should not convince anyone who does not already believe the conclusion to start believing it. It is not valid because the conclusion could have been false even though the premises were true: Bush could have lost to Gore in 2000, for example. The question to ask, in thinking about the validity of arguments is this: Is there a coherent possible world, which I can even *imagine*, in which the premises are true and the conclusion false? If there is, then the argument is invalid.

When assessing the deductive arguments that you encounter in philosophical work, it is often useful to try to lay out, as clearly as possible, their *structure*. A standard and fairly simple way to do this is simply to pull out the logical connecting phrases and to replace, with letters, the sentences they connect. Five of the most common and important 'logical operators' are *and, or, it is not the case that, if … then …,* and *if and only if….* For example, consider the following argument: "If God is perfectly powerful (omnipotent) and perfectly good, then no evil would exist. But evil does exist. Therefore, God cannot be both omnipotent and perfectly good, so either God is not all-powerful or he is not perfectly good." The structure of this argument could be laid bare as follows:

1. If (O and G) then not-E.
2. E.
3. Therefore not-(O and G).
4. Therefore either not-O or not-G.

Revealing the structure in this way can make it easier to see whether or not the argument is valid. And in this case, it is valid. In fact, no matter what O, G, and E stand for—no matter how we fill in the blanks— *any* argument of this form must be valid. You could try it yourself—invent random sentences to fill in for O, G, and E, and no matter how hard you try, you will never produce an argument with all true premises and a false conclusion.[3] What this shows is that validity is often a property of the *form* or structure of an argument. (This is why deductive logic is known as "formal logic." It is not formal in the sense that it is stiff and ceremonious, but because it has to do with argument forms.)

Using this kind of shorthand, therefore, it is possible to describe certain general argument forms which are *invariably* valid and which—since they are often used in philosophical writing—it can be handy to look out for. For example, a very common and valuable form of argument looks like this: if P then Q; P; therefore Q. This form is often called *modus ponens.* Another—

which appears in the previous argument about God and evil—is *modus tollens*: if P then Q; not-Q; therefore not-P. A *disjunctive syllogism* works as follows: either P or Q; not-P; therefore Q. A *hypothetical syllogism* has the structure: if P then Q; if Q then R; therefore if P then R. Finally, a slightly more complicated but still common argument structure is sometimes called a *constructive dilemma*: either P or Q; if P then R; if Q then R; therefore R.

Inductive Arguments and Inductive Strength

I noted above that the validity of deductive arguments is a yes/no affair—that a deductive argument is either extremely strong or it is hopelessly weak. This is not true for inductive arguments. The strength of an inductive argument—the amount of support the premises give to the conclusion—is a matter of degree, and there is no clear dividing line between the 'strong' inductive arguments and the 'weak' ones. Nevertheless, some inductive arguments are obviously much stronger than others, and it is useful to think a little bit about what factors make a difference.

There are lots of different types and structures of inductive arguments; here I will briefly describe four which are fairly representative and commonly encountered in philosophy. The first is *inductive generalization.* This type of argument is the prototype inductive argument—indeed, it is often what people mean when they use the term "induction"—and it has the following form:

1. *x* per cent of observed Fs are G.
2. Therefore *x* per cent of all Fs are G.

That is, inductive generalizations work by inferring a claim about an entire *population* of objects from data about a *sample* of those objects. For example:

(a) Every swan I have ever seen is white, so all swans (in the past and future, and on every part of the planet) are white.

(b) Every swan I have ever seen is white, so probably all the swans around here are white.

(c) 800 of the 1,000 rocks we have taken from the Moon contain silicon, so probably around 80% of the Moon's surface contains silicon.

---

3   Since the argument about God and evil is valid, then we are left with only two possibilities. Either all its premises are true, and then it is sound and its conclusion *must* inescapably be true. Or one of its premises is false, in which case the conclusion *might* be false (though we would still not have shown that it *is* false). The only way to effectively critique this argument, therefore, is to argue against one of the claims 1 and 2.

(d) We have tested two very pure samples of copper in the lab and found that each sample has a boiling point of 2,567°C; we conclude that 2,567°C is the boiling point for copper.

(e) Every intricate system I have seen created (such as houses and watches) has been the product of intelligent design, so therefore all intricate systems (including, for example, frogs and volcanoes) must be the product of intelligent design.

The two main considerations when assessing the strength of inductive generalizations are the following. First, ask how *representative* is the sample? How likely is it that whatever is true of the sample will also be true of the population as a whole? For instance, although the sample size in argument (c) is much larger than that in argument (d), it is much more likely to be biased: we know that pure copper is very uniform, so a small sample will do; but the surface of the Moon might well be highly variable, and so data about the areas around moon landings may not be representative of the surface as a whole. Second, it is important to gauge how cautious and *accurate* the conclusion is, given the data—how far beyond the evidence does it go? The conclusion to argument (a) is a much more radical inference from the data than that in argument (b); consequently, though less exciting, the conclusion of argument (b) is much better supported by the premise.

A second type of inductive argument is an *argument from analogy*. It most commonly has the following form:

1. Object (or objects) A and object (or objects) B are alike in having features F, G, H, …
2. B has feature X.
3. Therefore A has feature X as well.

These examples illustrate arguments from analogy:

(a) Human brains and dolphin brains are large, compared to body size. Humans are capable of planning for the future. So, dolphins must also be capable of planning for the future.

(b) Humans and dolphins are both mammals and often grow to more than five feet long. Humans are capable of planning for the future. So, dolphins must also be capable of planning for the future.

(c) Eagles and robins are alike in having wings, feathers, claws, and beaks. Eagles kill and eat sheep. Therefore, robins kill and eat sheep.

(d) Anselm's ontological argument has the same argumentative form as Gaunilo's "perfect island" argument. But Gaunilo's argument is a patently bad argument. So there must be something wrong with the ontological argument.

(e) An eye and a watch are both complex systems in which all of the parts are inter-dependent and where any small mis-adjustment could lead to a complete failure of the whole. A watch is the product of intelligent design. Therefore, the eye must also be the product of intelligent design (i.e., God exists).

The strength of an argument from analogy depends mostly on two things: first, the degree of *positive relevance* that the noted similarities (F, G, H …) have to the target property X; and second, the absence of *relevant dissimilarities*—properties which A has but B does not, which make it *less* likely that A is X. For example, the similarity (brain size) between humans and dolphins cited in argument (a) is much more relevant to the target property (planning) than are the similarities cited in argument (b). This, of course, makes (a) a much stronger argument than (b). The primary problem with argument (c), on the other hand, is that we know that robins are much smaller and weaker than eagles and this dissimilarity makes it far less likely that they kill sheep.

A third form of inductive argument is often called *inference to the best explanation* or sometimes *abduction*. This kind of argument works in the following way. Suppose we have a certain quantity of data to explain (such as the behavior of light in various media, or facts about the complexity of biological organisms, or a set of ethical claims). Suppose also that we have a number of theories which account for this data in different ways (e.g., the theory that light is a particle, or the theory that light is a wave, or the theory that it is somehow both). One way of arguing for the truth of one of these theories, over the others, is to show that one theory provides a much *better explanation* of the data than the others. What counts as making a theory a better explanation can be a bit tricky, but some basic criteria would be:

1. The theory predicts all the data we know to be true.
2. The theory explains all this data in the most economical and theoretically satisfying way (scientists and mathematicians often call this the most *beautiful* theory).
3. The theory predicts some *new* phenomena which turn out to exist and which would be a big surprise if one of the competing theories were true. (For example, one of the clinchers for Einstein's theory of relativity was the observation that starlight is bent by the sun's gravity. This would have been a big surprise under the older Newtonian theory, but was predicted by Einstein's theory.)

Here are some examples of inferences to the best explanation:

(a) When I inter-breed my pea plants, I observe certain patterns in the properties of the plants produced (e.g., in the proportion of tall plants, or of plants which produce wrinkled peas). If the properties of pea plants were generated randomly, these patterns would be highly surprising. However, if plants pass on packets of information (genes) to their offspring, the patterns I have observed would be neatly explained. Therefore, genes exist.

(b) The biological world is a highly complex and inter-dependent system. It is highly unlikely that such a system would have come about (and would continue to hang together) from the purely random motions of particles. It would be much less surprising if it were the result of conscious design from a super-intelligent creator. Therefore, the biological world was deliberately created (and therefore, God exists).

(c) The biological world is a highly complex and inter-dependent system. It is highly unlikely that such a system would have come about (and would continue to hang together) from the purely random motions of particles. It would be much less surprising if it were the result of an evolutionary process of natural selection which mechanically preserves order and eliminates randomness, and which (if it existed) would produce a world much like the one we see around us. Therefore, the theory of evolution is true.

The final type of inductive argument that I want to mention here is usually called *reductio ad absurdum*, which means "reduction to absurdity." It is always a negative argument, and has this structure:

1. Suppose (for the sake of argument) that position *p* were true.
2. If *p* were true then something else, *q*, would also have to be true.
3. However *q* is absurd—it can't possibly be true.
4. Therefore *p* can't be true either.

In fact, this argument style can be either inductive or deductive, depending on how rigorous the premises 2 and 3 are. If *p* logically implies *q*, and if *q* is a logical contradiction, then it is deductively certain that *p* can't be true (at least, assuming the classical laws of logic). On the other hand, if *q* is merely absurd but not literally *impossible,* then the argument is inductive: it makes it highly likely that *p* is false, but does not prove it beyond all doubt.

Here are a few examples of *reductio* arguments:

(a) Suppose that gun control were a good idea. That would mean it's a good idea for the government to gather information on anything we own which, in the wrong hands could be a lethal weapon, such as kitchen knives and baseball bats. But that would be ridiculous. This shows gun control cannot be a good idea.

(b) If you think that foetuses have a right to life because they have hearts and fingers and toes, then you must believe that *anything* with a heart, fingers, and toes has a right to life. But that would be absurd. Therefore, a claim like this about foetuses cannot be a good argument against abortion.

(c) Suppose, for the sake of argument, that this is not the best possible world. But that would mean God had either deliberately chosen to create a sub-standard world or had failed to notice that this was not the best of all possible worlds, and either of these options is absurd. Therefore, it must be true that this is the best of all possible worlds.

(d) "The anti-vitalist says that there is no such thing as vital spirit. But this claim is self-refuting. The speaker can be taken seriously only if his claim cannot. For if the claim is true, then the speaker does not have vital spirit and must be *dead*. But if he is dead, then his statement is a meaningless string of noises, devoid of reason and truth." (If you want more information, see Paul Churchland's "Eliminative Materialism and the Propositional Attitudes," *Journal of Philosophy* 78 [1981].)

The critical questions to ask about *reductio* arguments are simply: *Does* the supposedly absurd consequence follow from the position being attacked? and Is it *really* absurd?

A Few Common Fallacies

Just as it can be useful to look for common patterns of reasoning in philosophical writing, it can also be helpful to be on guard for a few recurring fallacies—and, equally importantly, to take care not to commit them in your own philosophical writing. Here are four common ones:

Begging the question does not mean, as the media would have us believe, stimulating one to ask a further question; instead, it means to assume as true (as one of your premises) the very same thing which you are supposedly attempting to prove. This fallacy is sometimes called *circular reasoning* or even (the old Latin name) *petitio principii*. To argue, for example, that God exists because (a) it says in the Bible that God exists, (b) God wrote the Bible, and (c) God would not lie, is to commit a blatant case of begging the question. In this case, of course, one would have no reason to accept the premises as true unless one *already* believed the conclusion. Usually, however, arguments that beg the question are a little more disguised. For example, "Adultery is immoral, since sexual relations outside marriage violate ethical principles," or "Terrorism is bad, because it encourages further acts of terrorism," are both instances of circular reasoning.

Arguing *ad hominem* means attacking or rejecting a position not because the arguments for it are poor, but because the person presenting those arguments is unattractive in some way: i.e., an attack is directed at the person (*ad hominem*) rather than at their argu-ment. The following are implicit *ad hominem* arguments: "You say you want to close down the church? Well, Hitler and Stalin would agree with you!" and "We shouldn't trust the claim, by philosophers such as Anselm, Aquinas, and Leibniz, that God exists, since they were all Christian philosophers and so of course they were biased." Such attacks are fallacious because they have nothing at all to do with how reasonable a claim is: even if the claim is false, *ad hominem* attacks do nothing to show this.

Straw man arguments are particularly devious, and this fallacy can be hard to spot (or to avoid committing) unless great care is taken. The *straw man* fallacy consists in misrepresenting someone else's position so that it can be more easily criticized. It is like attacking a dummy stuffed with straw instead of a real opponent. For example, it's not uncommon to see attacks on "pro-choice" activists for thinking that abortion is a good thing. However, whatever the merits of either position, this objection is clearly unfair— no serious abortion advocates think it is a positively *good thing* to have an abortion; at most they claim that (at least in some circumstances) it is a lesser evil than the alternative. Here's an even more familiar example, containing two straw men, one after the other: "We should clean out the closets. They're getting a bit messy." "Why, we just went through those closets last year. Do we have to clean them out every day?" "I never said anything about cleaning them out every day. You just want to keep all your junk forever, which is simply ridiculous."

Arguments from ignorance, finally, are based on the assumption that lack of evidence *for* something is evidence that it is false, or that lack of evidence *against* something is evidence for its truth. Generally, neither of these assumptions are reliable. For example, even if we could find no good proof to show that God exists, this would not, all by itself, suffice to show that God does *not* exist: it would still be possible, for example, that God exists but transcends our limited human reason. Consider the following 'argument' by Senator Joseph McCarthy, about some poor official in the State Department: "I do not have much information on this except the general statement of the agency that there is nothing in the files to disprove his Communist connections."

Suggestions for Critical Reflection

1. Suppose some deductive argument has a premise which is necessarily false. Is it a valid argument?
2. Suppose some deductive argument has a conclusion which is necessarily true. Is it a valid argument? From this information alone, can you tell whether it is sound?
3. Is the following argument form valid: if P then Q; Q; therefore P? How about: if P then Q; not-P; so not-Q?
4. No inductive argument is strong enough to *prove* that its conclusion is true: the best it can do is to show that the conclusion is highly probable. Does this make inductive arguments bad or less useful? Why don't we restrict ourselves to using only deductive arguments?
5. Formal logic provides mechanical and reliable methods for assessing the validity of deductive arguments. Do you think there might be some similar system for evaluating the strength of inductive arguments?
6. I have listed four important fallacies; can you identify any other common patterns of poor reasoning?

Suggestions for Further Reading

An entertaining, thought-provoking and brief introduction to logic can be found in Graham Priest's *Logic: A Very Short Introduction* (Oxford University Press, 2000); an equally brief but highly practical primer on arguing is Anthony Weston's *A Rulebook for Arguments* (Hackett, 2001). There are many books which competently lay out the nuts and bolts of formal logic: Richard Jeffrey's *Formal Logic: Its Scope and Limits* (McGraw-Hill, 1991) is short but rigorous and clear; *The Logic Book* by Bergmann, Moor, and Nelson (McGraw-Hill, 1998), on the other hand, is rather painstaking but is one of the most complete texts. An interesting book which explains not only classical formal logic but also makes accessible some more recently developed logical languages, such as modal logic and intuitionistic logic, is Bell, DeVidi, and Solomon's *Logical Options* (Broadview Press, 2001). Two somewhat older texts, which were used to teach many of the current generation of professional philosophers and are still much used today, are Wilfrid Hodges's *Logic* (Penguin, 1977) and E.J. Lemmon's *Beginning Logic* (Hackett, 1978).

One of the best introductory texts on inductive logic is Brian Skyrms's *Choice & Chance* (Wadsworth, 2000). Other good texts include Copi and Burgess-Jackson's *Informal Logic* (Prentice Hall, 1995), Fogelin and Sinnott-Armstrong's *Understanding Arguments* (Harcourt, 2001), and Douglas Walton's *Informal Logic: A Handbook for Critical Argumentation* (Cambridge University Press, 1989). Quite a good book on fallacies is *Attacking Faulty Reasoning* by T. Edward Damer (Wadsworth, 2000), while Darrell Huff's *How to Lie with Statistics* (W.W. Norton, 1954) is an entertaining guide to the tricks that can be played with bad inductive arguments in, for example, advertising.

INTRODUCTORY TIPS ON READING AND WRITING PHILOSOPHY

Reading Philosophy

As you will soon find out, if you haven't already, it is not easy to read philosophy. It can be exhilarating, stimulating, life-changing, or even annoying, but it isn't easy. There are no real shortcuts for engaging with philosophy (though the notes accompanying the readings in this book are intended to remove a few of the more unnecessary barriers); however, there are two things to remember which will help you get the most out of reading philosophy—*read it several times*, and *read it actively*.

Philosophical writing is not like a novel, a historical narrative, or even a textbook: it is typically dense, compressed, and written to contribute to an ongoing debate with which you may not yet be fully familiar. This means, no matter how smart you are, it is highly unlikely that you will get an adequate understanding of any halfway interesting piece of philosophy the first time through, and it may even take two or three more readings before it really becomes clear. Furthermore, even after that point, repeated readings of good philosophy will usually reveal new and interesting nuances to the writer's position, and occasionally you will notice some small point that seems to open a mental door and show you what the author is trying to say in a whole new way. As they say, if a piece of philosophy isn't worth reading at least twice, it isn't worth reading once. Every selection in this book, I guarantee, is well worth reading once.

As you go through a piece of philosophy, it is very important to engage with it: instead of just letting the words wash over you, you should make a positive effort, first, to understand and then, to critically assess the ideas you encounter. On your first read-through it is a good idea to try to formulate a high-level understanding of what the philosopher is attempting: What are the main claims? What is the overall structure of the arguments behind them? At this stage, it can be useful to pay explicit attention to section headings and introductory paragraphs.

Ideally during a second reading, you should try to reconstruct the author's arguments and sub-arguments in more detail. To help yourself understand them, consider jotting down their outlines on a sheet of paper. At this point, it can be extremely fruitful to pay attention to special definitions or distinctions used by the author in the arguments. It is also helpful to consider the historical context in which the philosopher wrote, and to look for connections to ideas found in other philosophical works.

Finally, on third and subsequent readings, it is valuable to expressly look for *objections* to the writer's argument (Are the premises true? Is the argument strong?), *unclarities* in position statements, or *assumptions* they depend upon, but do not argue for. I make these suggestions partly because the process of critical assessment is helpful in coming to understand a philosopher's work; but more importantly for the reason that—perhaps contrary to popular opinion—philosophers are typically playing for very high stakes. When philosophers write about whether God exists, whether science is a rational enterprise, or whether unfettered capitalism creates a just society, they are seriously interested in discovering the *answers* to these questions. The arguments they make, if they are good enough, will be strong reasons to believe one thing rather than another. If you are reading philosophy properly, you must sincerely join the debate and be honestly prepared to be persuaded—but it is also important not to let yourself be persuaded too easily.

Writing Philosophy

Writing philosophy consists, in roughly equal measures, of *thinking* about philosophy and then of trying to express your ideas *clearly and precisely*. This makes it somewhat unlike other writing: the point of writing philosophy is not, alas, to entertain, nor to explain some chunk of knowledge, nor to trick or cajole the reader into accepting a certain thesis. The point of philosophical writing is, really, to *do* philosophy.

This means that, since philosophy is based on arguments, most philosophical essays will have the underlying structure of an argument. They will seek to defend some particular philosophical claim by developing one or more good arguments for that claim.[4]

There is no particular template to follow for philosophical writing (there are lots of different kinds of good philosophical writing—lots of different ways of arguing well), but here are seven suggestions you might find useful:

1. Take your time. Spend time thinking, and then leave yourself enough time to get the writing right.

2. After you've thought for a while, begin by making an outline of the points you want to make (rather than immediately launching into prose). Then write several drafts, preferably allowing some cooling-off time between drafts so you can come back refreshed and with a more objective eye. Be prepared for the fact that writing a second draft doesn't mean merely tinkering with what you've already got, but starting at the beginning and writing it again.

3. Strive to be clear. Avoid unnecessary jargon, and use plain, simple words whenever possible; concrete examples can be extremely useful in explaining what you mean. It's also worth remembering that the clarity of a piece of writing has a lot to do with its structure. Ideally, the argumentative structure of your essay should be obvious to the reader, and it is a good idea to use your introduction to give the reader a 'road map' of the argument to follow.

4. Aim for precision. Make sure the *thesis* of your essay is spelled out in sufficient detail that the reader is left in no doubt about what you are arguing for (and therefore, what the implications will be, if your arguments are strong ones). Also, take care to define important terms so the reader knows exactly what you mean by them. Terms should normally be defined under any of the following three conditions: (a) the word is a technical term which a layperson probably won't know the meaning of (e.g., "intrinsic value"); (b) it is an ordinary word whose meaning is not sufficiently clear or precise for philosophical purposes (e.g., "abortion"); or (c) it is an ordinary word that you are going to use to mean something other than what it normally means (e.g., "person").

5. Focus. Everything you write should directly contribute to establishing your thesis. Anything which is unnecessary for your arguments should be eliminated. Make every word count. Also, don't be over-ambitious; properly done, philosophy moves at a fairly slow pace—it is unlikely that anyone could show adequately that, for example, there is no such thing as matter in three or fewer pages.

6. Argue as well and as carefully as you can. Defend your position using reason and not rhetoric; critically assess the strength of your arguments, and consider the plausibility of your premises. It's important to consider alternatives to your own position and possible counter-arguments; don't be afraid to raise and attempt to reply to objections to your position. (If you make a serious objection, one which you cannot answer, perhaps you should change your position.)

7. When you think you are finished, read the essay out loud and/or give it to someone else to read—at a minimum, this is a good way of checking for ease of reading, and it may reveal problems with your essay or argument that hadn't previously occurred to you.

---

4 The conclusion of a philosophical essay, however, need not always be something like: "God exists," or "Physical objects are not colored." It could just as legitimately be something like: "Philosopher A's third argument is flawed," or "When the arguments of philosopher A and those of philosopher B are compared, B wins," or "No one has yet given a good argument to show either P or not-P," or even "Philosopher A's argument is not, as is widely thought, X but instead it is Y." Though these kinds of claims are, perhaps, less immediately exciting than the first two examples, they are still philosophical claims, they still need to be argued for, and they can be extremely important in an overall debate about, say, the existence of God.

Suggestions for Further Reading

There are several short books devoted to helping students do well in philosophy courses. Perhaps the best of the bunch is Jay Rosenberg's *The Practice of Philosophy: A Handbook for Beginners* (Prentice Hall, 1995); A.P. Martinich's *Philosophical Writing* (Blackwell, 1996) is also very good. Also useful are: Anne M. Edwards, *Writing to Learn: An Introduction to Writing Philosophical Essays* (McGraw-Hill, 1999); Graybosch, Scott, and Garrison, *The Philosophy Student Writer's Manual* (Prentice Hall, 1998); and Zachery Seech, *Writing Philosophy Papers* (third edition, Wadsworth, 2000).

CHAPTER 2

Epistemology—Is the External World the Way It Appears to Be?

INTRODUCTION TO THE QUESTION

'Epistemology' is the theory of knowledge (the word comes from the Greek *epistēmē*, meaning knowledge). Epistemology can be thought of as arranged around three fundamental questions:

i) *What is knowledge?* For example, what is the difference between believing something that happens to be true and actually *knowing* it to be true? How much justification or proof do we need (if any) before we can be said to know something? Or does knowledge have more to do with, say, the *reliability* of our beliefs than our arguments for them? What is the difference between the conclusions of good science and those of, say, astrology? Or between astrology and religion?

ii) *What can we know?* What are the scope and limits of our knowledge? Can we ever really *know* about the real, underlying nature of the universe? Can we aspire to religious knowledge (e.g., of the true nature of God), or to ethical knowledge (as opposed to mere ethical belief or opinion), or to reliable knowledge of the historical past or the future? Can I ever know what you are thinking, or even *that* you are thinking? Do I even really know what *I* am thinking: e.g., might I have beliefs and desires that I am unaware of, perhaps because they are repressed or simply non-conscious?

iii) *How do we know that we know?* That is, how can we *justify* our claims to know things? What counts as 'enough' justification for a belief? Where does our knowledge—if we have any at all—come from in the first place? Do we acquire knowledge only through sense-experience, or can we also come to know important things through the power of our own naked reason? Do we have some beliefs which are especially 'basic'—which can be so reliably known that they can

form a foundation for all our other beliefs? Or, by contrast, do all our pieces of knowledge fit together like the answers in a giant crossword puzzle, with each belief potentially up for grabs if the rest of the puzzle changes?

The epistemological question that is the focus of this chapter is sometimes called 'the problem of the external world.' In its starkest form, it is simply this: are *any* of our beliefs about the world outside our own heads justified? Can we be sure that any of them at all are *true*? For example, I currently believe that there is a laptop computer in front of me, and a soft-drink can on the table to my left, and a window to my right out of which I can see trees and grass and other houses. Furthermore, I not only believe that these objects exist but I also believe that they have a certain nature: that the pop can is colored red; that the trees outside are further away from me in space than the window I am looking through; that the houses are three-dimensional objects with solid walls, and that they continue to exist even when I close my eyes or turn away; that my computer will continue to behave in a (relatively!) predictable way in accordance with the laws of physics and of computing. But are any of these beliefs of mine justified: do any of them cross the threshold into being *knowledge*, as opposed to mere conjecture? And if some of them are known and not others, *which* are the ones I really know? Which are the beliefs to which a rational person should be committed, and which are the ones a rational person should jettison?

It may seem that these kinds of questions should be fairly straightforward to answer. *Of course* I know that my pop can exists and is really red; it should be pretty easy just to think for a while and give my compelling reasons for having this belief—the reasons which make this belief much more likely to be true than, say, the belief that the can is a figment of my imagination, or is really colorless. However, it turns out, the problem of the external world is a very challenging problem indeed, and one which has been an important philosophical issue since at least the seventeenth century.

The first six readings in this chapter explore different aspects of the problem of the external world. First, we might ask, does the external world exist *at all*—is there any such thing as a world outside my own head, or might reality be just a dream? Descartes is the classic source for the formulation of this problem, which he raises and then tries to answer. However, in 'solving' this problem, Descartes comes to the conclusion that only some of the things we commonsensically believe about the real nature of the external world are true or justifiable. The Locke reading can be thought of as extending this insight and making it more precise through his discussion of the distinction between 'primary qualities' (which resemble our ideas of them) and 'secondary qualities' (which do not). Locke also raises a somewhat different question: what can we know about the sort of 'stuff' that the external world is made of—if it is 'matter,' then what can we say about the kind of *substance* which is matter? Berkeley seizes upon this problem and uses it as a reason to abandon the whole notion of matter: though he does not deny that an 'external' world exists, nor that most of what we normally believe about it is true, Berkeley does deny that our materialist *theory* of the external world is true: he holds that the 'external' world is really a collection of ideas in the mind of God.

Kant, faced with what by this time seemed the intractable problem of proving that mind-independent material objects exist and resemble our ideas of them, attempted to make a radical break with the philosophical assumptions which he thought had generated the puzzle in the first place. Instead of assuming that our mental representations of the world are passive pictures of reality (which, like a portrait, could either be a good likeness or misleadingly inaccurate), he argued that our minds actually *interact* with data

from the external world to *create* 'empirical reality.' For example, he claims, we cannot be mistaken in believing that external objects are three-dimensional, persist through time, and interact causally with each other, since all these features of reality are essential features of empirical experience: it is impossible, according to Kant, that anyone could experience an external reality which was not arranged in this way.

Russell and Moore represent twentieth-century approaches to the problem of the external world. Russell suggests that our belief in the existence of a material external world is justified since it is the simplest hypothesis which could explain the behavior of our 'sense-data.' However, he points out that science tells us that the real nature of this external world is radically different than the way it appears to us. Moore, by contrast, defends a more 'common sense' approach to the problem of the external world, and with great care tries to show that there are many perfectly good proofs available to show that things exist external to our minds: for example, one can solve the problem of the external world by showing that at least two hands exist, and you can do this, Moore thinks, by simply waving your hands in front of your face.

The final two readings in this section introduce two key epistemological innovations of the twentieth century. Gettier's article "Is Justified True Belief Knowledge?" presents a deep problem for the basic philosophical intuition—which in some form goes all the way back to Plato—that any belief that is both true and properly justified counts as an instance of knowledge. Meanwhile, Lorraine Code challenges another generally historically-unquestioned assumption: that the ideal knower should be as objective as possible, such that any item of knowledge should be equally justifiable no matter what standpoint one occupies. Instead, Code argues, knowers are *situated*, and what they (can) know reflects their particular perspectives (as, for example, a woman rather than a man).

There are several good introductory epistemology textbooks currently available if you want more background information. For example: Robert Audi, *Epistemology* (Routledge, 2010); Ralph Baergen, *Contemporary Epistemology* (Harcourt Brace, 1995); Jonathan Dancy, *Introduction to Contemporary Epistemology* (Blackwell, 1985); Everitt and Fisher, *Modern*

Epistemology (McGraw-Hill, 1995); Richard Feldman, *Epistemology* (Prentice Hall, 2002); Keith Lehrer, *Theory of Knowledge* (Westview, 1990); Adam Morton, *A Guide Through the Theory of Knowledge* (Blackwell, 2002); Pollock and Cruz, *Contemporary Theories of Knowledge* (Rowman & Littlefield, 1999); Matthias Steup, *An Introduction to Contemporary Epistemology* (Prentice Hall, 1996); Steup and Sosa (eds.), *Contemporary Debates in Epistemology* (Blackwell, 2005); and Michael Williams, *Problems of Knowledge* (Oxford University Press, 2001). There are also a couple of useful reference works on epistemology: Dancy, Sosa, and Steup (eds.), *A Companion to Epistemology* (Blackwell, 2010); Paul K. Moser, *The Oxford Handbook of Epistemology* (Oxford University Press, 2005); and Greco and Sosa (eds.), *The Blackwell Guide to Epistemology* (Blackwell, 1999).

RENÉ DESCARTES
Meditations on First Philosophy

Who Was René Descartes?

René Descartes was born in 1596 in a small town nestled below the vineyards of the Loire in western France; at that time the town was called La Haye, but was later renamed Descartes in his honor. His early life was probably unhappy: he suffered from ill health, his mother had died a year after he was born, and he didn't get on well with his father. (When René sent his father a copy of his first published book, his father's only reported reaction was that he was displeased to have a son "idiotic enough to have himself bound in vellum."[1]) At the age of ten he went to the newly-founded college of La Flèche to be educated by the Jesuits. Descartes later called this college "one of the best schools in Europe," and it was there that he learned the medieval "scholastic" science and philosophy that he was later to decisively reject. Descartes took a law degree at Poitiers and then, at 22, joined first the Dutch army of Prince Maurice of Nassau and then the forces of Maximilian of Bavaria. For the next decade he traveled Europe "resolving to seek no knowledge other than that which could be found either in myself or in the great book of the world."

During this period he developed an intense interest in mathematics, which stayed with him for the rest of his life. In fact, Descartes was one of the most important figures in the development of algebra, which is the branch of mathematics that allows abstract relations to be described without using specific numbers, and which is therefore capable of unifying arithmetic and geometry:

> I came to see that the exclusive concern of mathematics is with questions of order or method, and that it is irrelevant whether the measure in question involves numbers, shapes, stars, sounds, or any other object whatsoever. This made me realize that there must be a general science which explains all the points that can be raised concerning order and measure irrespective of subject matter. (from *Rules for the Direction of our Native Intelligence*)

This insight led Descartes directly to one of the most significant intellectual innovations of the modern age: the conception of science as the exploration of abstract mathematical descriptions of the world.

It was also during this time—in 1619—that Descartes had the experience said to have inspired him to take up the life of a philosopher, and which, perhaps, eventually resulted in the form of the *Meditations*. Stranded by bad weather near Ulm on the river

---

1   Vellum is the parchment made from animal skin which was used to make books.

Danube, Descartes spent the day in a *poêle* or "stove-heated room" engaged in intense philosophical speculations. When he fell asleep that night he had three vivid dreams which he later described as giving him his mission in life. In the first dream Descartes felt himself attacked by phantoms and then a great wind; he was then greeted by a friend who gave him a message about a gift. On awaking after this first dream, Descartes felt a sharp pain which made him fear that the dream was the work of some deceitful evil demon. Descartes eventually fell back asleep and immediately had the second dream: a loud thunderclap, which woke him in terror believing that the room was filled with fiery sparks. The third and last dream was a pleasant one, in which he found an encyclopedia on a table next to a poetry anthology, open to a poem which begins with the line "Which road in life shall I follow?" A man then appeared and said *"Est et non"*—"it is and is not." While still dreaming, Descartes apparently began to speculate about the meaning of his dreams, and decided, among other things, that the gift of which his friend spoke in the first dream was the gift of solitude, the dictionary represented systematic knowledge, and *"Est et non"* spoke of the distinction between truth and falsity as revealed by the correct scientific method. Descartes concluded that he had a divine mission to found a new philosophical system to underpin all human knowledge.

In 1628 Descartes settled in Holland (at the time the most intellectually vibrant nation in Europe), where he lived for most of his remaining life. His family was wealthy enough that Descartes, who cultivated very modest tastes, was free of the necessity to earn a living and could devote his time to scientific experimentation and writing. By 1633 he had prepared a book on cosmology and physics, called *Le Monde* (The World), in which he accepted Galileo's revolutionary claim that the Earth orbits the sun (rather than the other way around), but when he heard that Galileo had been condemned by the Inquisition of the Catholic Church, Descartes withdrew the work from publication. In 1637 he published (in French) a sample of his scientific work, the *Optics*, *Meteorology*, and *Geometry*, together with an introduction called *Discourse on the Method of Rightly Conducting One's Reason and Reaching the Truth in the Sciences*. Criticisms of this methodology led Descartes to compose his philosophical masterpiece, *Meditations on First Philosophy*, first published in Latin in 1641. A few years later he produced a summary of his scientific and philosophical views, the *Principles of Philosophy*, which he hoped would become a standard university textbook, replacing the medieval texts used at the time. His last work, published in 1649, was *The Passions of the Soul*, which attempted to extend his scientific methodology to ethics and psychology.

Descartes never married, but in 1635 he had a daughter, Francine, with a serving woman called Hélène Jans. He made arrangements to care for and educate the girl but she died of scarlet fever at the age of five, which was a devastating personal shock for Descartes.

In 1649 Descartes accepted an invitation to visit Stockholm and give philosophical instruction to Queen Kristina of Sweden. He was required to give tutorials at the royal palace at five o'clock in the morning, and it is said that the strain of this sudden break in his habits (he was accustomed to lying late in bed in the morning) caused him to catch pneumonia; he died in February, 1650. His dying words are said to have been, "*ça mon âme; il faut partir*"—so, my soul, it's time to part. His body was returned to France but, apparently, his head was secretly kept in Sweden; in the 1820s a skull bearing the faded inscription "René Descartes" was discovered in Stockholm and is now on display in the Museum of Natural History in Paris.

What Was Descartes' Overall Philosophical Project?

Descartes lived at a time when the accumulated beliefs of centuries—assumptions based on religious doctrine, straightforward observation, and common sense—were being gradually but remorselessly stripped away by exciting new discoveries. (The most striking example of this was the evidence mounting against the centuries-old belief that an unmoving Earth is the center of the universe, orbited by the moon, sun, stars, and all the other planets.) In this intellectual climate, Descartes became obsessed by the thought that no lasting scientific progress was possible without a systematic method for sifting through our preconceived assumptions and distinguishing between those that are reliable and those that are false. Descartes' central intellectual goal was to develop just such a reliable scientific method, and then to construct a coherent and unified theory of the world and of humankind's place within it. This theory, he hoped, would replace the deeply-flawed medieval system of thought (based on the science of Aristotle and Christian theology) called scholasticism.

A key feature of Descartes' system is that all knowledge should be based on utterly reliable foundations, discovered through the systematic rejection of any assumptions that can possibly be called into doubt. Then, as in mathematics, complex conclusions could be reliably derived from these foundations by long chains of reasoning, where each link in the chain is either a basic empirical observation or a simple and certain inference. The human faculty of *reason* was therefore of the greatest importance to Descartes. Furthermore, Descartes urged that scientific knowledge of the external world should be rooted, not in the deceptive and variable testimony of the senses, but on the concepts of pure mathematics.

That is, Cartesian science tries to reduce all physics to "what the geometers call *quantity*, and take as the object of their demonstrations, i.e., that to which every kind of division shape and motion is applicable" (*Principles of Philosophy*).

These ideas (though they have never been uncritically and uniformly accepted) have come to permeate the modern conception of science, including Descartes' influential metaphor of a unified "tree of knowledge," with metaphysics as the roots, physics as the trunk, and the special sciences (like biology, anthropology, or ethics) as the branches. One much less familiar aspect of Descartes' method for the production of knowledge is the central role played by God in his system. For Descartes, all human knowledge of the world around us essentially relies upon our prior knowledge that a non-deceiving God exists. Science, properly understood, not only does not conflict with religion but actually *depends* on religion, he believed.

Finally, one of the best-known results of Descartes' metaphysical reflections is "Cartesian dualism." This doctrine states that mind and body are two completely different substances—that the mind is a non-physical self in which all the operations of thought take place, and which can be wholly separated from the body after death. Like much of Descartes' work, this theory came to have the status of a more or less standard view for some three hundred years after his death, but at the time it was a radical philosophical innovation, breaking with the traditional Aristotelian conception of mental activity as a kind of *attribute* of the physical body (rather than as something entirely separable from the body).

What Is the Structure of This Reading?

The *Meditations* is not intended to be merely an exposition of philosophical arguments and conclusions, but is supposed to be an exercise in philosophical reflection for the reader—as Bernard Williams has put it, "the 'I' that appears throughout them from the first sentence on does not specifically represent [Descartes]: it represents anyone who will step into the position it marks, the position of the thinker who is prepared to reconsider and recast his or her beliefs, as Descartes supposed we might, from the ground up." Descartes aims to convince us of the truth of his conclusions by making us conduct the arguments ourselves.

In the First Meditation the thinker applies a series of progressively more radical doubts to his or her preconceived opinions, which leaves her unsure whether she knows anything at all. But then in the Second Meditation the thinker finds a secure foundational belief in her indubitable awareness of her own existence. The rest of this meditation is a reflection on the thinker's own nature as a "thinking thing." In the Third Meditation the thinker realizes that final certainty can only be achieved through the existence of a non-deceiving God, and argues from the idea of God found in her own mind to the conclusion that God must really exist and be the cause of this idea (this is sometimes nicknamed the "Trademark Argument," from the notion that our possession of the idea of God is God's "trademark" on his creation). The Fourth Meditation urges that the way to avoid error in our judgments is to restrict our beliefs to things of which we are clearly and distinctly certain. The Fifth Meditation introduces Cartesian science by discussing the mathematical nature of matter, and also includes a second proof for God's existence which resembles Anselm's ontological argument. Finally, in the Sixth Meditation, the thinker re-establishes the real existence of the external world, argues that mind and body are two distinct substances, and reflects on how mind and body are related.

Some Useful Background Information

1. Descartes makes frequent use of the terms "substance," "essence," and "accident." A substance is, roughly, a bearer of attributes, i.e., a thing that has properties. The essence of a substance is its fundamental intrinsic nature: Descartes held that for every substance there is exactly one property which is its essence. A substance's "accidents"[2] are all the rest of its properties, the ones which are not part of its essence.

Take, for example, a red ball: its redness, the spherical shape, the rubbery feel, and so on are all properties—or accidents—of the ball, and the ball's substance is the "stuff" that underlies and possesses these properties. According to Descartes, the fundamental nature of this stuff—its essence—is that it is extended in three dimensions, that it fills space.

For Descartes and his contemporaries there is also another important aspect to the idea of substance. Unlike an instance of a property, which cannot exist all by itself (there can't be an occurrence of redness without there being something which is red—some bit of substance which is the bearer of that property), substances are not dependent for their existence on something else. In fact, for Descartes, this is actually the *definition* of a substance: "By 'substance' we can understand nothing other than a thing which exists in such a way as to depend on no other things for its existence" (*Principles of Philosophy*). So, for instance, a tree is not really a substance, since trees do depend for their existence on other things (such as soil, light, past trees, and so on). On the other hand, according to Descartes, matter itself—all matter, taken as a whole—is a substance. Matter cannot be destroyed or created (except by God), it can only change its local form, gradually moving from the form of a tree to the form of a rotting tree trunk to the form of soil, for example.

2. Another obscure but important phrase frequently used by Descartes in the *Meditations* is the "natural light." Descartes has in mind here what in earlier writings he calls "the light of reason"—the pure inner light of the intellect, a faculty given to us by God, which allows us to see the truth of the world much more clearly than we can with the confused and fluctuating testimony of the senses.

---

2   Strictly speaking, Descartes thought of accidents as being 'modes' of the one essential property of the substance (rather than being really separate properties): shape, for example, is a mode of being extended in space.

3. Descartes, following the scholastic jargon of the time, calls the representational content of an idea its "objective reality" (he uses this term in his attempted proof of the existence of God in the Third Meditation). Confusingly, according to this terminology, for something to have merely objective reality in this sense is for it to belong to the mental world of ideas, and not the mind-independent external world at all. For example, if I imagine Santa Claus as being fat and jolly, then Descartes would say that fatness is "objectively" present in my idea—an idea of fatness forms part of my idea of Santa Claus. By contrast, the baby beluga at the Vancouver Aquarium is fat, but its fatness is not merely the *idea* of fatness but an actual property. To take another example, the objective reality of a stop sign is what it represents—the content "stop"—but its formal reality is the shaped and colored metal from which it is constructed.

4. Although Descartes' talk of a non-physical "soul" was in accord with contemporary Christian theology, his reasons for holding that the mind is immortal and non-material (largely in Meditations Two and Six) were not primarily religious ones. Descartes does not think of the soul as being especially "spiritual" or as being identical with our "better nature," for example. For Descartes the word "soul" simply means the same as the word "mind," and encompasses the whole range of conscious mental activity, including the sensations of sight, touch, sound, taste, and smell; emotions (such as joy or jealousy); and cognitive activities like believing, planning, desiring, or doubting. For Descartes the mind, or soul, is also to be distinguished from the brain: our brains, since they are extended material things, are part of our body and not our mind.

Some Common Misconceptions

1. Descartes is not a skeptic. Although he is famous for the skeptical arguments put forward in the First Meditation, he uses these only in order to go beyond them. It is a bit misleading, however, to think of Descartes as setting out in the *Meditations* to defeat skepticism: his main interest is probably not in proving the skeptic wrong, but in discovering the first principles upon which a proper science can be built. He uses skepticism, surprisingly, in order to *create* knowledge—to show that a properly constituted science would have nothing to fear from even the most radical doubts of the skeptic. Thus, for example, Descartes does not at any point argue that we should actually believe that the external world does not exist—instead, he suspends his belief in external objects until he has a chance to properly build a foundation for this belief (and by the end of the *Meditations* he is quite certain that the external world exists).

2. The "method of doubt" which Descartes uses in the *Meditations* is not an everyday method—it is not supposed to be an appropriate technique for making day-to-day decisions, or even for doing science or mathematics. Most of the time it would be hugely impractical for us to call into question everything that we might possibly doubt, to question all our presuppositions, before we make a judgment. Instead the method of the *Meditations* is supposed to be a once-in-a-lifetime exercise, by which we discover and justify the basic "first principles" that we rely on in everyday knowledge. In short, we always have to rely on certain assumptions when we make decisions or do science, and this is unavoidable but dangerous; the exercise of the *Meditations* can ensure that the assumptions we rely upon are absolutely secure.

3. Although "I think therefore I am" (or "I am, I exist") is the first step in Descartes' reconstruction of human knowledge in the *Meditations*, it is nevertheless not the first piece of *knowledge* that he recognizes—it does not arise out of a complete knowledge vacuum. Before the thinker can come to know that "I think therefore I am" is true, Descartes elsewhere admits that she must know, for example, what is meant by thinking, and that doubting is a kind of thought, and that in order to think one must first exist.

Therefore, it is best to think of "I think therefore I am," not as the first item of knowledge, but as the first *non-trivial* piece of secure knowledge about the world that a thinker can have. It's a piece of information not just about concepts or logic but actually about the world—but, according to Descartes, it's information we can only get if we *already* (somehow) possess a certain set of concepts.

4. It is sometimes supposed that Descartes thought that all knowledge could be mathematically deduced from the foundational beliefs that remain after he has applied his method of doubt. But this is not quite right. He thought that the proper *concepts and terms,* which science must use to describe the world, were purely mathematical and were deducible through pure rational reflection. But he also recognized that only through empirical investigation can we discover which scientific descriptions, expressed in the proper mathematical terms, are actually *true* of the world. For example, reason tells us (according to Descartes—and this was a radically new idea at the time) that matter can be defined simply in terms of extension in three dimensions, and that the laws which guide the movements of particles can be understood mathematically. However, only experience can tell us how the bits of matter in, for example, the human body are actually arranged.

5. Descartes does not conclude that error is impossible, even for those who adopt the proper intellectual methods of science. He argues only that *radical and systematic* error is impossible for the conscientious thinker. For example, even after completing Descartes' course of meditations we might still occasionally be tricked by perceptual illusions, or think we are awake when in fact we are dreaming; what Descartes thinks he has blocked, however, is the possibility that such errors show that our entire picture of reality might be wrong.

6. Descartes is sometimes portrayed as making the following (bad) argument to establish that mind is distinct from body: I can doubt that my body exists; I cannot doubt that my mind exists; there is therefore at least one property that

my mind has which my body lacks (i.e., being doubtable); and therefore mind and body are not identical. Descartes does seem to make an argument which resembles this (in the Second Meditation), but he later denied that this is really what he meant, and he formulates much stronger—though perhaps still flawed—arguments for dualism in the Sixth Meditation.

How Important and Influential Is This Passage?

Descartes is probably the most widely studied of any of the Western philosophers, and his *Meditations on First Philosophy* is his philosophical masterpiece and most important work. John Cottingham, an expert on Descartes, has written of the *Meditations* that:

> The radical critique of preconceived opinions or prejudices which begins that work seems to symbolize the very essence of philosophical inquiry. And the task of finding secure foundations for human knowledge, a reliable basis for science and ethics, encapsulates, for many, what makes philosophy worth doing.

Descartes' foundational claim in the search for truth—*cogito ergo sum*, "I think therefore I am"—is the most famous dictum in the history of philosophy. Although, as it happens, this actual phrase never appears in the *Meditations*—it is used in other writings by Descartes, including *Discourse on the Method* and the *Principles of Philosophy*—the *Meditations* remains Descartes' most complete account of how this principle, today simply called "the Cogito," is established.

The importance of Descartes' work to the history of thought is profound. He is commonly considered the first great philosopher of the modern era, since his work was central in sweeping away medieval scholasticism based on Aristotelian science and Christian theology and replacing it with the methods and questions that dominated philosophy until the twentieth century. This change from scholastic to modern modes of thought was also crucial to the phenomenal growth of natural science and mathematics beginning in the seventeenth century. In recent years, however, it has been fashionable to blame Descartes for what have been seen as philosophical dead ends, and many of the assumptions which he built into philosophy have been questioned (this is one of the reasons why the philosophy of the second half of the twentieth century has been so exciting).

Suggestions for Critical Reflection

1. Descartes, in the *Meditations,* has traditionally been seen as raising and then trying to deal with the problem of radical skepticism: that is, according to this interpretation, he raises the possibility that (almost) all our beliefs might be radically mistaken and then argues that this is, in fact, impossible. A more recent line of interpretation, though, sees Descartes not as attempting to answer the skeptic, but as trying to replace naïve empirical assumptions about science with a more modern, mathematical view—in particular, that Descartes is trying to show our most fundamental pieces of knowledge about mind, God, and the world come not from sensory experience, but directly from the intellect. Which interpretation do you think is more plausible? Could they both be right? If Descartes does want to refute skepticism, is he successful in doing so? If his goal is to overturn naïve scholastic empiricism, do you think he manages to do that?

2. Descartes' foundational claim "I think therefore I am" is usually called the Cogito, from the Latin *cogito ergo sum.* How does Descartes justify this claim? Does he have, or need, an *argument* for it? Is an argument that justifies this claim even possible?

3. David Hume dryly said, of the *Meditations,* "To have recourse to the veracity of the supreme Being, in order to prove the veracity of our senses, is surely making a very unexpected circuit." What do you think? Does Descartes establish the existence of God?

4. On Descartes' picture, do you think an atheist can have any knowledge? Why or why not?

5. A famous objection to Descartes' conclusions in the *Meditations* (raised for the first time by some of his contemporaries) is today known as the problem of the Cartesian Circle. Descartes says in the Third Meditation, "Whatever I perceive very clearly and distinctly is true." Call this the CDP Principle. It is this principle which he thinks will allow him to reconstruct a body of reliable scientific knowledge on the foundations of the Cogito. However, he immediately admits, the CDP Principle will only work if we cannot ever make mistakes about what we clearly and distinctly perceive; to show this, Descartes tries to prove that God exists and has created human beings such that what we clearly and distinctly see to be evidently true really is true. But how does Descartes prove God exists? Apparently, by arguing that we have a clear and distinct idea of God, and so it must be true that God exists. That is, the objection runs, Descartes relies upon the CDP Principle to prove that the CDP Principle is reliable—and this argument just goes in a big circle and doesn't prove anything. What do you think of this objection?

6. "How do I know that I am not ten thinkers thinking in unison?" (Elizabeth Anscombe, "The First Person"). What, if anything, do you think Descartes has proved about the nature of the self?

7. How adequate are Descartes' arguments for mind-body dualism? If mind and body are two different substances, do you think this might cause other philosophical problems to arise? For example, how might mind and body interact? How could we come to know things about other people's minds? How could we be sure whether animals have minds or not, and if they do what they might be like?

8. Descartes recognized no physical properties but size, shape, and motion. Where do you think Descartes would say colors, tastes, smells, and so on come from?

Suggestions for Further Reading

The *Meditations on First Philosophy* was originally published with an extensive set of objections from contemporary thinkers and replies by Descartes. A standard edition of the *Meditations* including selected objections and replies is translated and edited by John Cottingham and published by Cambridge University Press (1996). Cambridge also published Descartes' collected philosophical writings and letters in three volumes, translated by John Cottingham, Robert Stoothoff, Dugald Murdoch, and Anthony Kenny. (Volume II, which includes the *Meditations* and the complete *Objections and Replies*, was published in 1984; Volume I was published in 1985 and the letters in 1991.)

The secondary literature on Descartes is vast, but here are a few starting points. A good recent biography of Descartes is from Stephen Gaukroger, *Descartes: An Intellectual Biography* (Oxford University Press, 1995). Useful general introductions to Descartes' thought are John Cottingham's *Descartes* (Blackwell, 1986), Anthony Kenny's *Descartes: A Study of His Philosophy* (Random House, 1968), Bernard Williams's *Descartes: The Project of Pure Enquiry* (Penguin, 1978), and Margaret Dauler Wilson's *Descartes* (Routledge, 1978). *The Cambridge Companion to Descartes* edited by John Cottingham (Cambridge University Press, 1992) is helpful, and two good collections of articles on the *Meditations* are A.O. Rorty's *Essays on Descartes's* Meditations (University of California Press, 1986) and Vere Chappell's *Descartes's* Meditations: *Critical Essays* (Rowman and Littlefield, 1997). A few of the more influential (and sometimes controversial) recent books on Descartes are Harry Frankfurt's *Demons, Dreamers, and Madmen* (Bobbs-Merrill, 1970), E.M. Curley's *Descartes Against the Sceptics* (Harvard University Press, 1978), Peter J. Markie's *Descartes's Gambit* (Cornell University Press, 1986), Richard Watson's *The Breakdown of Cartesian Metaphysics* (Humanities Press, 1987), and Daniel Garber's *Descartes's Metaphysical Physics* (University of Chicago Press, 1992).

Meditations on First Philosophy

In which are demonstrated the existence of God and the distinction between the human soul and the body.[3]

Synopsis of the following six Meditations

In the First Meditation reasons are provided which give us possible grounds for doubt about all things, especially material things, so long as we have no foundations for the sciences other than those which we have had up till now. Although the usefulness of such extensive doubt is not apparent at first sight, its greatest benefit lies in freeing us from all our preconceived opinions, and providing the easiest route by which the mind may be led away from the senses. The eventual result of this doubt is to make it impossible for us to have any further doubts about what we subsequently discover to be true.

In the Second Meditation, the mind uses its own freedom and supposes the non-existence of all the things about whose existence it can have even the slightest doubt; and in so doing the mind notices that it is impossible that it should not itself exist during this time. This exercise is also of the greatest benefit, since it enables the mind to distinguish without difficulty what belongs to itself, i.e., to an intellectual nature, from what belongs to the body. But since some people may perhaps expect arguments for the immortality of the soul in this section, I think they should be warned here and now that I have tried not to put down anything which I could not precisely demonstrate. Hence the only order which I could follow was that normally employed by geometers, namely to set out all the premisses on which a desired proposition depends, before drawing any conclusions about it. Now the first and most important prerequisite for knowledge of the

---

3   First published in Latin in 1641. This translation is by John Cottingham, from *Meditations on First Philosophy, With Selections from the Objections and Replies*, revised edition, Cambridge: Cambridge University Press 1996, pp. 9–62. Copyright © 1996 Cambridge University Press. Reprinted with the permission of Cambridge University Press.

immortality of the soul is for us to form a concept of the soul which is as clear as possible and is also quite distinct from every concept of body; and that is just what has been done in this section. A further requirement is that we should know that everything that we clearly and distinctly understand is true in a way which corresponds exactly to our understanding of it; but it was not possible to prove this before the Fourth Meditation. In addition we need to have a distinct concept of corporeal[4] nature, and this is developed partly in the Second Meditation itself, and partly in the Fifth and Sixth Meditations. The inference to be drawn from these results is that all the things that we clearly and distinctly conceive of as different substances (as we do in the case of mind and body) are in fact substances which are really distinct one from the other; and this conclusion is drawn in the Sixth Meditation. This conclusion is confirmed in the same Meditation by the fact that we cannot understand a body except as being divisible, while by contrast we cannot understand a mind except as being indivisible. For we cannot conceive of half of a mind, while we can always conceive of half of a body, however small; and this leads us to recognize that the natures of mind and body are not only different, but in some way opposite. But I have not pursued this topic any further in this book, first because these arguments are enough to show that the decay of the body does not imply the destruction of the mind, and are hence enough to give mortals the hope of an after-life, and secondly because the premises which lead to the conclusion that the soul is immortal depend on an account of the whole of physics. This is required for two reasons. First, we need to know that absolutely all substances, or things which must be created by God in order to exist, are by their nature incorruptible and cannot ever cease to exist unless they are reduced to nothingness by God's denying his concurrence[5] to them. Secondly, we need to recognize that body, taken in the general sense, is a substance, so that it too never perishes. But the human body, in so far as it differs from other bodies, is simply made up of a certain configuration of limbs and other accidents of this sort; whereas the human mind is not made up of any accidents in this way, but is a pure substance. For even if all the accidents of the mind change, so that it has different objects of the understanding and different desires and sensations, it does not on that account become a different mind; whereas a human body loses its identity merely as a result of a change in the shape of some of its parts. And it follows from this that while the body can very easily perish, the mind is immortal by its very nature.

In the Third Meditation I have explained quite fully enough, I think, my principal argument for proving the existence of God. But in order to draw my readers' minds away from the senses as far as possible, I was not willing to use any comparison taken from bodily things. So it may be that many obscurities remain; but I hope they will be completely removed later, in my Replies to the Objections.[6] One such problem, among others, is how the idea of a supremely perfect being, which is in us, possesses so much objective reality that it can come only from a cause which is supremely perfect. In the Replies this is illustrated by the comparison of a very perfect machine, the idea of which is in the mind of some engineer. Just as the objective intricacy belonging to the idea must have some cause, namely the scientific knowledge of the engineer, or of someone else who passed the idea on to him, so the idea of God which is in us must have God himself as its cause.

In the Fourth Meditation it is proved that everything that we clearly and distinctly perceive is true, and I also explain what the nature of falsity consists in. These results need to be known both in order to confirm what has gone before and also to make intelligible what is to come later. (But here it should be noted in passing that I do not deal at all with sin, i.e., the error which is committed in pursuing good and evil, but only with the error that occurs in distinguishing truth from falsehood. And there is no discussion of matters pertaining to faith or the conduct of life, but

---

4   Bodily, physical.

5   The continuous divine action which many Christians think necessary to maintain things in existence.

6   Descartes' *Meditations* were originally published with an extensive set of objections from other philosophers, scientists, and theologians of the time, and Descartes' responses to those objections. These Objections and Replies are not reprinted here.

simply of speculative truths which are known solely by means of the natural light.)

In the Fifth Meditation, besides an account of corporeal nature taken in general, there is a new argument demonstrating the existence of God. Again, several difficulties may arise here, but these are resolved later in the Replies to the Objections. Finally I explain the sense in which it is true that the certainty even of geometrical demonstrations depends on the knowledge of God.

Lastly, in the Sixth Meditation, the intellect is distinguished from the imagination; the criteria for this distinction are explained; the mind is proved to be really distinct from the body, but is shown, notwithstanding, to be so closely joined to it that the mind and the body make up a kind of unit; there is a survey of all the errors which commonly come from the senses, and an explanation of how they may be avoided; and, lastly, there is a presentation of all the arguments which enable the existence of material things to be inferred. The great benefit of these arguments is not, in my view, that they prove what they establish—namely that there really is a world, and that human beings have bodies and so on—since no sane person has ever seriously doubted these things. The point is that in considering these arguments we come to realize that they are not as solid or as transparent as the arguments which lead us to knowledge of our own minds and of God, so that the latter are the most certain and evident of all possible objects of knowledge for the human intellect. Indeed, this is the one thing that I set myself to prove in these Meditations. And for that reason I will not now go over the various other issues in the book which are dealt with as they come up.

First Meditation:
What can be called into doubt

Some years ago I was struck by the large number of falsehoods that I had accepted as true in my childhood, and by the highly doubtful nature of the whole edifice that I had subsequently based on them. I realized that it was necessary, once in the course of my life, to demolish everything completely and start again right from the foundations if I wanted to establish anything at all in the sciences that was stable and likely to last. But the task looked an enormous one, and I began to wait until I should reach a mature enough age to ensure that no subsequent time of life would be more suitable for tackling such inquiries. This led me to put the project off for so long that I would now be to blame if by pondering over it any further I wasted the time still left for carrying it out. So today I have expressly rid my mind of all worries and arranged for myself a clear stretch of free time. I am here quite alone, and at last I will devote myself sincerely and without reservation to the general demolition of my opinions.

But to accomplish this, it will not be necessary for me to show that all my opinions are false, which is something I could perhaps never manage. Reason now leads me to think that I should hold back my assent from opinions which are not completely certain and indubitable just as carefully as I do from those which are patently false. So, for the purpose of rejecting all my opinions, it will be enough if I find in each of them at least some reason for doubt. And to do this I will not need to run through them all individually, which would be an endless task. Once the foundations of a building are undermined, anything built on them collapses of its own accord; so I will go straight for the basic principles on which all my former beliefs rested.

Whatever I have up till now accepted as most true I have acquired either from the senses or through the senses. But from time to time I have found that the senses deceive, and it is prudent never to trust completely those who have deceived us even once.

Yet although the senses occasionally deceive us with respect to objects which are very small or in the distance, there are many other beliefs about which doubt is quite impossible, even though they are derived from the senses—for example, that I am here, sitting by the fire, wearing a winter dressing-gown, holding this piece of paper in my hands, and so on. Again, how could it be denied that these hands or this whole body are mine? Unless perhaps I were to liken myself to madmen, whose brains are so damaged by the persistent vapours of melancholia that they firmly maintain they are kings when they are paupers, or say they are dressed in purple when they are naked, or that their heads are made of earthenware, or that they are pumpkins, or made of glass. But such people are insane, and I would be thought equally mad if I took anything from them as a model for myself.

A brilliant piece of reasoning! As if I were not a man who sleeps at night, and regularly has all the same experiences while asleep as madmen do when awake—indeed sometimes even more improbable ones. How often, asleep at night, am I convinced of just such familiar events—that I am here in my dressing-gown, sitting by the fire—when in fact I am lying undressed in bed! Yet at the moment my eyes are certainly wide awake when I look at this piece of paper; I shake my head and it is not asleep; as I stretch out and feel my hand I do so deliberately, and I know what I am doing. All this would not happen with such distinctness to someone asleep. Indeed! As if I did not remember other occasions when I have been tricked by exactly similar thoughts while asleep! As I think about this more carefully, I see plainly that there are never any sure signs by means of which being awake can be distinguished from being asleep. The result is that I begin to feel dazed, and this very feeling only reinforces the notion that I may be asleep.

Suppose then that I am dreaming, and that these particulars—that my eyes are open, that I am moving my head and stretching out my hands—are not true. Perhaps, indeed, I do not even have such hands or such a body at all. Nonetheless, it must surely be admitted that the visions which come in sleep are like paintings, which must have been fashioned in the likeness of things that are real, and hence that at least these general kinds of things—eyes, head, hands and the body as a whole—are things which are not imaginary but are real and exist. For even when painters try to create sirens and satyrs with the most extraordinary bodies, they cannot give them natures which are new in all respects; they simply jumble up the limbs of different animals. Or if perhaps they manage to think up something so new that nothing remotely similar has ever been seen before—something which is therefore completely fictitious and unreal—at least the colours used in the composition must be real. By similar reasoning, although these general kinds of things—eyes, head, hands and so on—could be imaginary, it must at least be admitted that certain other even simpler and more universal things are real. These are as it were

the real colours from which we form all the images of things, whether true or false, that occur in our thought.

This class appears to include corporeal nature in general, and its extension; the shape of extended things; the quantity, or size and number of these things; the place in which they may exist, the time through which they may endure, and so on.

So a reasonable conclusion from this might be that physics, astronomy, medicine, and all other disciplines which depend on the study of composite things, are doubtful; while arithmetic, geometry and other subjects of this kind, which deal only with the simplest and most general things, regardless of whether they really exist in nature or not, contain something certain and indubitable. For whether I am awake or asleep, two and three added together are five, and a square has no more than four sides. It seems impossible that such transparent truths should incur any suspicion of being false.

And yet firmly rooted in my mind is the long-standing opinion that there is an omnipotent God who made me the kind of creature that I am. How do I know that he has not brought it about that there is no earth, no sky, no extended thing, no shape, no size, no place, while at the same time ensuring that all these things appear to me to exist just as they do now? What is more, just as I consider that others sometimes go astray in cases where they think they have the most perfect knowledge, how do I know that God has not brought it about that I too go wrong every time I add two and three or count the sides of a square, or in some even simpler matter, if that is imaginable? But perhaps God would not have allowed me to be deceived in this way, since he is said to be supremely good. But if it were inconsistent with his goodness to have created me such that I am deceived all the time, it would seem equally foreign to his goodness to allow me to be deceived even occasionally; yet this last assertion cannot be made.

Perhaps there may be some who would prefer to deny the existence of so powerful a God rather than believe that everything else is uncertain. Let us not argue with them, but grant them that everything said about God is a fiction. According to their supposition, then, I have arrived at my present state by fate or chance or a continuous chain of events, or by some other means; yet since deception and error seem to be imperfections, the less powerful they make my original cause, the more likely it is that I am so imperfect as to be deceived all the time. I have no answer to these arguments, but am finally compelled to admit that there is not one of my former beliefs about which a doubt may not properly be raised; and this is not a flippant or ill-considered conclusion, but is based on powerful and well thought-out reasons. So in future I must withhold my assent from these former beliefs just as carefully as I would from obvious falsehoods, if I want to discover any certainty.

But it is not enough merely to have noticed this; I must make an effort to remember it. My habitual opinions keep coming back, and, despite my wishes, they capture my belief, which is as it were bound over to them as a result of long occupation and the law of custom. I shall never get out of the habit of confidently assenting to these opinions, so long as I suppose them to be what in fact they are, namely highly probable opinions—opinions which, despite the fact that they are in a sense doubtful, as has just been shown, it is still much more reasonable to believe than to deny. In view of this, I think it will be a good plan to turn my will in completely the opposite direction and deceive myself, by pretending for a time that these former opinions are utterly false and imaginary. I shall do this until the weight of preconceived opinion is counter-balanced and the distorting influence of habit no longer prevents my judgement from perceiving things correctly. In the meantime, I know that no danger or error will result from my plan, and that I cannot possibly go too far in my distrustful attitude. This is because the task now in hand does not involve action but merely the acquisition of knowledge.

I will suppose therefore that not God, who is supremely good and the source of truth, but rather some malicious demon of the utmost power and cunning has employed all his energies in order to deceive me. I shall think that the sky, the air, the earth, colours, shapes, sounds and all external things are merely the delusions of dreams which he has devised to ensnare my judgement. I shall consider myself as not having hands or eyes, or flesh, or blood or senses, but as falsely believing that I have all these things. I shall

stubbornly and firmly persist in this meditation; and, even if it is not in my power to know any truth, I shall at least do what is in my power, that is, resolutely guard against assenting to any falsehoods, so that the deceiver, however powerful and cunning he may be, will be unable to impose on me in the slightest degree. But this is an arduous undertaking, and a kind of laziness brings me back to normal life. I am like a prisoner who is enjoying an imaginary freedom while asleep; as he begins to suspect that he is asleep, he dreads being woken up, and goes along with the pleasant illusion as long as he can. In the same way, I happily slide back into my old opinions and dread being shaken out of them, for fear that my peaceful sleep may be followed by hard labour when I wake, and that I shall have to toil not in the light, but amid the inextricable darkness of the problems I have now raised.

Second Meditation: The nature of the human mind, and how it is better known than the body

So serious are the doubts into which I have been thrown as a result of yesterday's meditation that I can neither put them out of my mind nor see any way of resolving them. It feels as if I have fallen unexpectedly into a deep whirlpool which tumbles me around so that I can neither stand on the bottom nor swim up to the top. Nevertheless I will make an effort and once more attempt the same path which I started on yesterday. Anything which admits of the slightest doubt I will set aside just as if I had found it to be wholly false; and I will proceed in this way until I recognize something certain, or, if nothing else, until I at least recognize for certain that there is no certainty. Archimedes[7] used to demand just one firm and immovable point in order to shift the entire earth; so I too can hope for great things if I manage to find just one thing, however slight, that is certain and unshakeable.

I will suppose then, that everything I see is spurious. I will believe that my memory tells me lies, and that none of the things that it reports ever happened. I have no senses. Body, shape, extension, movement

---

7   A Greek mathematician, engineer, and physicist who died in 212 BCE.

and place are chimeras. So what remains true? Perhaps just the one fact that nothing is certain.

Yet apart from everything I have just listed, how do I know that there is not something else which does not allow even the slightest occasion for doubt? Is there not a God, or whatever I may call him, who puts into me the thoughts I am now having? But why do I think this, since I myself may perhaps be the author of these thoughts? In that case am not I, at least, something? But I have just said that I have no senses and no body. This is the sticking point: what follows from this? Am I not so bound up with a body and with senses that I cannot exist without them? But I have convinced myself that there is absolutely nothing in the world, no sky, no earth, no minds, no bodies. Does it now follow that I too do not exist? No: if I convinced myself of something then I certainly existed. But there is a deceiver of supreme power and cunning who is deliberately and constantly deceiving me. In that case I too undoubtedly exist, if he is deceiving me; and let him deceive me as much as he can, he will never bring it about that I am nothing so long as I think that I am something. So after considering everything very thoroughly, I must finally conclude that this proposition, *I am, I exist*, is necessarily true whenever it is put forward by me or conceived in my mind.

But I do not yet have a sufficient understanding of what this 'I' is, that now necessarily exists. So I must be on my guard against carelessly taking something else to be this 'I', and so making a mistake in the very item of knowledge that I maintain is the most certain and evident of all. I will therefore go back and meditate on what I originally believed myself to be, before I embarked on this present train of thought. I will then subtract anything capable of being weakened, even minimally, by the arguments now introduced, so that what is left at the end may be exactly and only what is certain and unshakeable.

What then did I formerly think I was? A man. But what is a man? Shall I say 'a rational animal'? No; for then I should have to inquire what an animal is, what rationality is, and in this way one question would lead me down the slope to other harder ones, and I do not now have the time to waste on subtleties of this kind. Instead I propose to concentrate on what came into my thoughts spontaneously and quite naturally whenever I used to consider what I was. Well, the first thought to come to mind was that I had a face, hands, arms and the whole mechanical structure of limbs which can be seen in a corpse, and which I called the body. The next thought was that I was nourished, that I moved about, and that I engaged in sense-perception and thinking; and these actions I attributed to the soul. But as to the nature of this soul, either I did not think about this or else I imagined it to be something tenuous, like a wind or fire or ether, which permeated my more solid parts. As to the body, however, I had no doubts about it, but thought I knew its nature distinctly. If I had tried to describe the mental conception I had of it, I would have expressed it as follows: by a body I understand whatever has a determinable shape and a definable location and can occupy a space in such a way as to exclude any other body; it can be perceived by touch, sight, hearing, taste or smell, and can be moved in various ways, not by itself but by whatever else comes into contact with it. For, according to my judgement, the power of self-movement, like the power of sensation or of thought, was quite foreign to the nature of a body; indeed, it was a source of wonder to me that certain bodies were found to contain faculties of this kind.

But what shall I now say that I am, when I am supposing that there is some supremely powerful and, if it is permissible to say so, malicious deceiver, who is deliberately trying to trick me in every way he can? Can I now assert that I possess even the most insignificant of all the attributes which I have just said belong to the nature of a body? I scrutinize them, think about them, go over them again, but nothing suggests itself; it is tiresome and pointless to go through the list once more. But what about the attributes I assigned to the soul? Nutrition or movement? Since now I do not have a body, these are mere fabrications. Sense-perception? This surely does not occur without a body, and besides, when asleep I have appeared to perceive through the senses many things which I afterwards realized I did not perceive through the senses at all. Thinking? At last I have discovered it—thought; this alone is inseparable from me. I am, I exist—that is certain. But for how long? For as long as I am thinking. For it could be that were I totally to cease from thinking, I should totally cease to exist. At present I am not admitting anything except what is necessarily true. I am, then, in the strict sense only a thing that thinks; that is, I am a mind, or intelligence, or intellect, or reason—words whose meaning I have been ignorant of until now. But for all that I am a thing which is real and which truly exists. But what kind of a thing? As I have just said—a thinking thing.

What else am I? I will use my imagination. I am not that structure of limbs which is called a human body. I am not even some thin vapour which permeates the limbs—a wind, fire, air, breath, or whatever I depict in my imagination; for these are things which I have supposed to be nothing. Let this supposition stand; for all that I am still something. And yet may it not perhaps be the case that these very things which I am supposing to be nothing, because they are unknown to me, are in reality identical with the 'I' of which I am aware? I do not know, and for the moment I shall not argue the point, since I can make judgements only about things which are known to me. I know that I exist; the question is, what is this 'I' that I know? If the 'I' is understood strictly as we have been taking it, then it is quite certain that knowledge of it does not depend on things of whose existence I am as yet unaware; so it cannot depend on any of the things which I invent in my imagination. And this very word 'invent' shows me my mistake. It would indeed be a case of fictitious invention if I used my imagination to establish that I was something or other; for imagining is simply contemplating the shape or image of a corporeal thing. Yet now I know for certain both that I exist and at the same time that all such images and, in general, everything relating to the nature of body, could be mere dreams <and chimeras>. Once this point has been grasped, to say 'I will use my imagination to get to know more distinctly what I am' would seem to be as silly as saying 'I am now awake, and see some truth; but since my vision is not yet clear enough, I will deliberately fall asleep so that my dreams may provide a truer and clearer representation.' I thus realize that none of the things that the imagination enables me to grasp is at all relevant to this knowledge of myself which I possess, and that the mind must therefore be most carefully diverted from such things if it is to perceive its own nature as distinctly as possible.

But what then am I? A thing that thinks. What is that? A thing that doubts, understands, affirms, denies, is willing, is unwilling, and also imagines and has sensory perceptions.

This is a considerable list, if everything on it belongs to me. But does it? Is it not one and the same 'I' who is now doubting almost everything, who nonetheless understands some things, who affirms that this one thing is true, denies everything else, desires to know more, is unwilling to be deceived, imagines many things even involuntarily, and is aware of many things which apparently come from the senses? Are not all these things just as true as the fact that I exist, even if I am asleep all the time, and even if he who created me is doing all he can to deceive me? Which of all these activities is distinct from my thinking? Which of them can be said to be separate from myself? The fact that it is I who am doubting and understanding and willing is so evident that I see no way of making it any clearer. But it is also the case that the 'I' who imagines is the same 'I'. For even if, as I have supposed, none of the objects of imagination are real, the power of imagination is something which really exists and is part of my thinking. Lastly, it is also the same 'I' who has sensory perceptions, or is aware of bodily things as it were through the senses. For example, I am now seeing light, hearing a noise, feeling heat. But I am asleep, so all this is false. Yet I certainly *seem* to see, to hear, and to be warmed. This cannot be false; what is called 'having a sensory perception' is strictly just this, and in this restricted sense of the term it is simply thinking.

From all this I am beginning to have a rather better understanding of what I am. But it still appears—and I cannot stop thinking this—that the corporeal things of which images are formed in my thought, and which the senses investigate, are known with much more distinctness than this puzzling 'I' which cannot be pictured in the imagination. And yet it is surely surprising that I should have a more distinct grasp of things which I realize are doubtful, unknown and foreign to me, than I have of that which is true and known—my own self. But I see what it is: my mind enjoys wandering off and will not yet submit to being restrained within the bounds of truth. Very well then; just this once let us give it a completely free rein, so that after a while, when it is time to tighten the reins, it may more readily submit to being curbed.

Let us consider the things which people commonly think they understand most distinctly of all; that is, the bodies which we touch and see. I do not mean bodies in general—for general perceptions are apt to be somewhat more confused—but one particular body. Let us take, for example, this piece of wax. It has just been taken from the honeycomb; it has not yet quite lost the taste of the honey; it retains some of the scent of the flowers from which it was gathered; its colour, shape and size are plain to see; it is hard, cold and can be handled without difficulty; if you rap it with your knuckle it makes a sound. In short, it has everything which appears necessary to enable a body to be known as distinctly as possible. But even as I speak, I put the wax by the fire, and look: the residual taste is eliminated, the smell goes away, the colour changes, the shape is lost, the size increases; it becomes liquid and hot; you can hardly touch it, and if you strike it, it no longer makes a sound. But does the same wax remain? It must be admitted that it does; no one denies it, no one thinks otherwise. So what was it in the wax that I understood with such distinctness? Evidently none of the features which I arrived at by means of the senses; for whatever came under taste, smell, sight, touch or hearing has now altered—yet the wax remains.

Perhaps the answer lies in the thought which now comes to my mind; namely, the wax was not after all the sweetness of the honey, or the fragrance of the flowers, or the whiteness, or the shape, or the sound, but was rather a body which presented itself to me in these various forms a little while ago, but which now exhibits different ones. But what exactly is it that I am now imagining? Let us concentrate, take away everything which does not belong to the wax, and see what is left: merely something extended, flexible and changeable. But what is meant here by 'flexible' and 'changeable'? Is it what I picture in my imagination: that this piece of wax is capable of changing from a round shape to a square shape, or from a square shape to a triangular shape? Not at all; for I can grasp that the wax is capable of countless changes of this kind, yet I am unable to run through this immeasurable number of changes in my imagination, from which

it follows that it is not the faculty of imagination that gives me my grasp of the wax as flexible and changeable. And what is meant by 'extended'? Is the extension of the wax also unknown? For it increases if the wax melts, increases again if it boils, and is greater still if the heat is increased. I would not be making a correct judgement about the nature of wax unless I believed it capable of being extended in many more different ways than I will ever encompass in my imagination. I must therefore admit that the nature of this piece of wax is in no way revealed by my imagination, but is perceived by the mind alone. (I am speaking of this particular piece of wax; the point is even clearer with regard to wax in general.) But what is this wax which is perceived by the mind alone? It is of course the same wax which I see, which I touch, which I picture in my imagination, in short the same wax which I thought it to be from the start. And yet, and here is the point, the perception I have of it is a case not of vision or touch or imagination—nor has it ever been, despite previous appearances—but of purely mental scrutiny; and this can be imperfect and confused, as it was before, or clear and distinct as it is now, depending on how carefully I concentrate on what the wax consists in.

But as I reach this conclusion I am amazed at how <weak and> prone to error my mind is. For although I am thinking about these matters within myself, silently and without speaking, nonetheless the actual words bring me up short, and I am almost tricked by ordinary ways of talking. We say that we see the wax itself, if it is there before us, not that we judge it to be there from its colour or shape; and this might lead me to conclude without more ado that knowledge of the wax comes from what the eye sees, and not from the scrutiny of the mind alone. But then if I look out of the window and see men crossing the square, as I just happen to have done, I normally say that I see the men themselves, just as I say that I see the wax. Yet do I see any more than hats and coats which could conceal automatons? I *judge* that they are men. And so something which I thought I was seeing with my eyes is in fact grasped solely by the faculty of judgement which is in my mind.

However, one who wants to achieve knowledge above the ordinary level should feel ashamed at having taken ordinary ways of talking as a basis for doubt. So let us proceed, and consider on which occasion my perception of the nature of the wax was more perfect and evident. Was it when I first looked at it, and believed I knew it by my external senses, or at least by what they call the 'common' sense[8]—that is, the power of imagination? Or is my knowledge more perfect now, after a more careful investigation of the nature of the wax and of the means by which it is known? Any doubt on this issue would clearly be foolish; for what distinctness was there in my earlier perception? Was there anything in it which an animal could not possess? But when I distinguish the wax from its outward forms—take the clothes off, as it were, and consider it naked—then although my judgement may still contain errors, at least my perception now requires a human mind.

But what am I to say about this mind, or about myself? (So far, remember, I am not admitting that there is anything else in me except a mind.) What, I ask, is this 'I' which seems to perceive the wax so distinctly? Surely my awareness of my own self is not merely much truer and more certain than my awareness of the wax, but also much more distinct and evident. For if I judge that the wax exists from the fact that I see it, clearly this same fact entails much more evidently that I myself also exist. It is possible that what I see is not really the wax; it is possible that I do not even have eyes with which to see anything. But when I see, or think I see (I am not here distinguishing the two), it is simply not possible that I who am now thinking am not something. By the same token, if I judge that the wax exists from the fact that I touch it, the same result follows, namely that I exist. If I judge that it exists from the fact that I imagine it, or for any other reason, exactly the same thing follows. And the result that I have grasped in the case of the wax may be applied to everything else located outside me. Moreover, if my perception of the wax seemed more distinct after it was established not just by sight or touch but by many other considerations, it must be admitted that I now know myself even more distinctly. This is because

every consideration whatsoever which contributes to my perception of the wax, or of any other body, cannot but establish even more effectively the nature of my own mind. But besides this, there is so much else in the mind itself which can serve to make my knowledge of it more distinct, that it scarcely seems worth going through the contributions made by considering bodily things.

I see that without any effort I have now finally got back to where I wanted. I now know that even bodies are not strictly perceived by the senses or the faculty of imagination but by the intellect alone, and that this perception derives not from their being touched or seen but from their being understood; and in view of this I know plainly that I can achieve an easier and more evident perception of my own mind than of anything else. But since the habit of holding on to old opinions cannot be set aside so quickly, I should like to stop here and meditate for some time on this new knowledge I have gained, so as to fix it more deeply in my memory.

Third Meditation: The existence of God

I will now shut my eyes, stop my ears, and withdraw all my senses. I will eliminate from my thoughts all images of bodily things, or rather, since this is hardly possible, I will regard all such images as vacuous, false and worthless. I will converse with myself and scrutinize myself more deeply; and in this way I will attempt to achieve, little by little, a more intimate knowledge of myself. I am a thing that thinks: that is, a thing that doubts, affirms, denies, understands a few things, is ignorant of many things, is willing, is unwilling, and also which imagines and has sensory perceptions; for as I have noted before, even though the objects of my sensory experience and imagination may have no existence outside me, nonetheless the modes of thinking which I refer to as cases of sensory perception and imagination, in so far as they are simply modes of thinking, do exist within me—of that I am certain.

In this brief list I have gone through everything I truly know, or at least everything I have so far discovered that I know. Now I will cast around more carefully to see whether there may be other things within me which I have not yet noticed. I am certain that I

---

8   This is the supposed faculty which integrates the data from the five specialized senses into a single experience. The notion goes back to Aristotle.

am a thinking thing. Do I not therefore also know what is required for my being certain about anything? In this first item of knowledge there is simply a clear and distinct perception of what I am asserting; this would not be enough to make me certain of the truth of the matter if it could ever turn out that something which I perceived with such clarity and distinctness was false. So I now seem to be able to lay it down as a general rule that whatever I perceive very clearly and distinctly is true.

Yet I previously accepted as wholly certain and evident many things which I afterwards realized were doubtful. What were these? The earth, sky, stars, and everything else that I apprehended with the senses. But what was it about them that I perceived clearly? Just that the ideas, or thoughts, of such things appeared before my mind. Yet even now I am not denying that these ideas occur within me. But there was something else which I used to assert, and which through habitual belief I thought I perceived clearly, although I did not in fact do so. This was that there were things outside me which were the sources of my ideas and which resembled them in all respects. Here was my mistake; or at any rate, if my judgement was true, it was not thanks to the strength of my perception.

But what about when I was considering something very simple and straightforward in arithmetic or geometry, for example that two and three added together make five, and so on? Did I not see at least these things clearly enough to affirm their truth? Indeed, the only reason for my later judgement that they were open to doubt was that it occurred to me that perhaps some God could have given me a nature such that I was deceived even in matters which seemed most evident. But whenever my preconceived belief in the supreme power of God comes to mind, I cannot but admit that it would be easy for him, if he so desired, to bring it about that I go wrong even in those matters which I think I see utterly clearly with my mind's eye. Yet when I turn to the things themselves which I think I perceive very clearly, I am so convinced by them that I spontaneously declare: let whoever can do so deceive me, he will never bring it about that I am nothing, so long as I continue to think I am something; or make it true at some future time that I have never

existed, since it is now true that I exist; or bring it about that two and three added together are more or less than five, or anything of this kind in which I see a manifest contradiction. And since I have no cause to think that there is a deceiving God, and I do not yet even know for sure whether there is a God at all, any reason for doubt which depends simply on this supposition is a very slight and, so to speak, metaphysical one. But in order to remove even this slight reason for doubt, as soon as the opportunity arises I must examine whether there is a God, and, if there is, whether he can be a deceiver. For if I do not know this, it seems that I can never be quite certain about anything else.

First, however, considerations of order appear to dictate that I now classify my thoughts into definite kinds, and ask which of them can properly be said to be the bearers of truth and falsity. Some of my thoughts are as it were the images of things, and it is only in these cases that the term 'idea' is strictly appropriate—for example, when I think of a man, or a chimera,[9] or the sky, or an angel, or God. Other thoughts have various additional forms: thus when I will, or am afraid, or affirm, or deny, there is always a particular thing which I take as the object of my thought, but my thought includes something more than the likeness of that thing. Some thoughts in this category are called volitions or emotions, while others are called judgements.

Now as far as ideas are concerned, provided they are considered solely in themselves and I do not refer them to anything else, they cannot strictly speaking be false; for whether it is a goat or a chimera that I am imagining, it is just as true that I imagine the former as the latter. As for the will and the emotions, here too one need not worry about falsity; for even if the things which I may desire are wicked or even non-existent, that does not make it any less true that I desire them. Thus the only remaining thoughts where I must be on my guard against making a mistake are judgements. And the chief and most common mistake which is to

---

9   In Greek mythology, a female fire-breathing monster with a lion's head, a goat's body, and a serpent's tail; more generally, an absurd or horrible idea or wild fancy.

be found here consists in my judging that the ideas which are in me resemble, or conform to, things located outside me. Of course, if I considered just the ideas themselves simply as modes of my thought, without referring them to anything else, they could scarcely give me any material for error.

Among my ideas, some appear to be innate,[10] some to be adventitious,[11] and others to have been invented by me. My understanding of what a thing is, what truth is, and what thought is, seems to derive simply from my own nature. But my hearing a noise, as I do now, or seeing the sun, or feeling the fire, comes from things which are located outside me, or so I have hitherto judged. Lastly, sirens, hippogriffs and the like are my own invention. But perhaps all my ideas may be thought of as adventitious, or they may all be innate, or all made up; for as yet I have not clearly perceived their true origin.

But the chief question at this point concerns the ideas which I take to be derived from things existing outside me: what is my reason for thinking that they resemble these things? Nature has apparently taught me to think this. But in addition I know by experience that these ideas do not depend on my will, and hence that they do not depend simply on me. Frequently I notice them even when I do not want to: now, for example, I feel the heat whether I want to or not, and this is why I think that this sensation or idea of heat comes to me from something other than myself, namely the heat of the fire by which I am sitting. And the most obvious judgement for me to make is that the thing in question transmits to me its own likeness rather than something else.

I will now see if these arguments are strong enough. When I say 'Nature taught me to think this,' all I mean is that a spontaneous impulse leads me to believe it, not that its truth has been revealed to me by some natural light. There is a big difference here. Whatever is revealed to me by the natural light—for example that from the fact that I am doubting it follows that I exist, and so on—cannot in any way be open to doubt. This is because there cannot be another faculty both as trustworthy as the natural light and also

capable of showing me that such things are not true. But as for my natural impulses, I have often judged in the past that they were pushing me in the wrong direction when it was a question of choosing the good, and I do not see why I should place any greater confidence in them in other matters.

Then again, although these ideas do not depend on my will, it does not follow that they must come from things located outside me. Just as the impulses which I was speaking of a moment ago seem opposed to my will even though they are within me, so there may be some other faculty not yet fully known to me, which produces these ideas without any assistance from external things; this is, after all, just how I have always thought ideas are produced in me when I am dreaming.

And finally, even if these ideas did come from things other than myself, it would not follow that they must resemble those things. Indeed, I think I have often discovered a great disparity <between an object and its idea> in many cases. For example, there are two different ideas of the sun which I find within me. One of them, which is acquired as it were from the senses and which is a prime example of an idea which I reckon to come from an external source, makes the sun appear very small. The other idea is based on astronomical reasoning, that is, it is derived from certain notions which are innate in me (or else it is constructed by me in some other way), and this idea shows the sun to be several times larger than the earth. Obviously both these ideas cannot resemble the sun which exists outside me; and reason persuades me that the idea which seems to have emanated most directly from the sun itself has in fact no resemblance to it at all.

All these considerations are enough to establish that it is not reliable judgement but merely some blind impulse that has made me believe up till now that there exist things distinct from myself which transmit to me ideas or images of themselves through the sense organs or in some other way.

But it now occurs to me that there is another way of investigating whether some of the things of which I possess ideas exist outside me. In so far as the ideas are <considered> simply <as> modes of thought, there is no recognizable inequality among them: they all

---

10   Inborn—an idea that is already inside me.

11   Coming from outside.

appear to come from within me in the same fashion. But in so far as different ideas <are considered as images which> represent different things, it is clear that they differ widely. Undoubtedly, the ideas which represent substances to me amount to something more and, so to speak, contain within themselves more objective reality than the ideas which merely represent modes or accidents.[12] Again, the idea that gives me my understanding of a supreme God, eternal, infinite, <immutable,> omniscient, omnipotent and the creator of all things that exist apart from him, certainly has in it more objective reality than the ideas that represent finite substances.

Now it is manifest by the natural light that there must be at least as much <reality> in the efficient and total cause as in the effect of that cause. For where, I ask, could the effect get its reality from, if not from the cause? And how could the cause give it to the effect unless it possessed it? It follows from this both that something cannot arise from nothing, and also that what is more perfect—that is, contains in itself more reality—cannot arise from what is less perfect. And this is transparently true not only in the case of effects which possess <what the philosophers call> actual or formal reality, but also in the case of ideas, where one is considering only <what they call> objective reality. A stone, for example, which previously did not exist, cannot begin to exist unless it is produced by something which contains, either formally or eminently everything to be found in the stone;[13] similarly, heat cannot be produced in an object which was not previously hot, except by something of at least the same order <degree or kind> of perfection as heat, and so on. But it is also true that the *idea* of heat, or of a stone, cannot exist in me unless it is put there by some cause which contains at least as much reality as I conceive to be in the heat or in the stone. For although this cause

---

12 See the notes for background information on "substance," "accident," "objective reality," and "formal reality."

13 That is, it has either the same properties as the stone (e.g., a certain hardness) or possesses even more perfect or pronounced versions of those properties (e.g., perfect hardness). An effect is "eminently" in a cause when the cause is more perfect than the effect.

does not transfer any of its actual or formal reality to my idea, it should not on that account be supposed that it must be less real. The nature of an idea is such that of itself it requires no formal reality except what it derives from my thought, of which it is a mode. But in order for a given idea to contain such and such objective reality, it must surely derive it from some cause which contains at least as much formal reality as there is objective reality in the idea. For if we suppose that an idea contains something which was not in its cause, it must have got this from nothing; yet the mode of being by which a thing exists objectively <or representatively> in the intellect by way of an idea, imperfect though it may be, is certainly not nothing, and so it cannot come from nothing.

And although the reality which I am considering in my ideas is merely objective reality, I must not on that account suppose that the same reality need not exist formally in the causes of my ideas, but that it is enough for it to be present in them objectively. For just as the objective mode of being belongs to ideas by their very nature, so the formal mode of being belongs to the causes of ideas—or at least the first and most important ones—by *their* very nature. And although one idea may perhaps originate from another, there cannot be an infinite regress here; eventually one must reach a primary idea, the cause of which will be like an archetype which contains formally <and in fact> all the reality <or perfection> which is present only objectively <or representatively> in the idea. So it is clear to me, by the natural light, that the ideas in me are like <pictures, or> images which can easily fall short of the perfection of the things from which they are taken, but which cannot contain anything greater or more perfect.

The longer and more carefully I examine all these points, the more clearly and distinctly I recognize their truth. But what is my conclusion to be? If the objective reality of any of my ideas turns out to be so great that I am sure the same reality does not reside in me, either formally or eminently, and hence that I myself cannot be its cause, it will necessarily follow that I am not alone in the world, but that some other thing which is the cause of this idea also exists. But if no such idea is to be found in me, I shall have no argument to convince me of the existence of anything apart from myself. For despite a most careful and comprehensive survey, this is the only argument I have so far been able to find.

Among my ideas, apart from the idea which gives me a representation of myself, which cannot present any difficulty in this context, there are ideas which variously represent God, corporeal and inanimate things, angels, animals and finally other men like myself.

As far as concerns the ideas which represent other men, or animals, or angels, I have no difficulty in understanding that they could be put together from the ideas I have of myself, of corporeal things and of God, even if the world contained no men besides me, no animals and no angels.

As to my ideas of corporeal things, I can see nothing in them which is so great <or excellent> as to make it seem impossible that it originated in myself. For if I scrutinize them thoroughly and examine them one by one, in the way in which I examined the idea of the wax yesterday, I notice that the things which I perceive clearly and distinctly in them are very few in number. The list comprises size, or extension in length, breadth and depth; shape, which is a function of the boundaries of this extension; position, which is a relation between various items possessing shape; and motion, or change in position; to these may be added substance, duration and number. But as for all the rest, including light and colours, sounds, smells, tastes, heat and cold and the other tactile qualities, I think of these only in a very confused and obscure way, to the extent that I do not even know whether they are true or false, that is, whether the ideas I have of them are ideas of real things or of non-things. For although, as I have noted before, falsity in the strict sense, or formal falsity, can occur only in judgements, there is another kind of falsity, material falsity, which occurs in ideas, when they represent non-things as things. For example, the ideas which I have of heat and cold contain so little clarity and distinctness that they do not enable me to tell whether cold is merely the absence of heat or vice versa, or whether both of them are real qualities, or neither is. And since there can be no ideas which are not as it were of things, if it is true that cold is nothing but the absence of heat, the idea which represents it to me as something real and positive deserves to be called false; and the same goes for other ideas of this kind.

Such ideas obviously do not require me to posit a source distinct from myself. For on the one hand, if they are false, that is, represent non-things, I know by the natural light that they arise from nothing—that is, they are in me only because of a deficiency and lack of perfection in my nature. If on the other hand they are true, then since the reality which they represent is so extremely slight that I cannot even distinguish it from a non-thing, I do not see why they cannot originate from myself.

With regard to the clear and distinct elements in my ideas of corporeal things, it appears that I could have borrowed some of these from my idea of myself, namely substance, duration, number and anything else of this kind. For example, I think that a stone is a substance, or is a thing capable of existing independently, and I also think that I am a substance. Admittedly I conceive of myself as a thing that thinks and is not extended, whereas I conceive of the stone as a thing that is extended and does not think, so that the two conceptions differ enormously; but they seem to agree with respect to the classification 'substance'. Again, I perceive that I now exist, and remember that I have existed for some time; moreover, I have various thoughts which I can count; it is in these ways that I acquire the ideas of duration and number which I can then transfer to other things. As for all the other elements which make up the ideas of corporeal things, namely extension, shape, position and movement, these are not formally contained in me, since I am nothing but a thinking thing; but since they are merely modes of a substance, and I am a substance, it seems possible that they are contained in me eminently.

So there remains only the idea of God; and I must consider whether there is anything in the idea which could not have originated in myself. By the word 'God' I understand a substance that is infinite, <eternal, immutable,> independent, supremely intelligent, supremely powerful, and which created both myself and everything else (if anything else there be) that exists. All these attributes are such that, the more carefully I concentrate on them, the less possible it seems that they could have originated from me alone.

So from what has been said it must be concluded that God necessarily exists.

It is true that I have the idea of substance in me in virtue of the fact that I am a substance; but this would not account for my having the idea of an infinite substance, when I am finite, unless this idea proceeded from some substance which really was infinite.

And I must not think that, just as my conceptions of rest and darkness are arrived at by negating movement and light, so my perception of the infinite is arrived at not by means of a true idea but merely by negating the finite. On the contrary, I clearly understand that there is more reality in an infinite substance than in a finite one, and hence that my perception of the infinite, that is God, is in some way prior to my perception of the finite, that is myself. For how could I understand that I doubted or desired—that is, lacked something—and that I was not wholly perfect, unless there were in me some idea of a more perfect being which enabled me to recognize my own defects by comparison?

Nor can it be said that this idea of God is perhaps materially false and so could have come from nothing, which is what I observed just a moment ago in the case of the ideas of heat and cold, and so on. On the contrary, it is utterly clear and distinct, and contains in itself more objective reality than any other idea; hence there is no idea which is in itself truer or less liable to be suspected of falsehood. This idea of a supremely perfect and infinite being is, I say, true in the highest degree; for although perhaps one may imagine that such a being does not exist, it cannot be supposed that the idea of such a being represents something unreal, as I said with regard to the idea of cold. The idea is, moreover, utterly clear and distinct; for whatever I clearly and distinctly perceive as being real and true, and implying any perfection, is wholly contained in it. It does not matter that I do not grasp the infinite, or that there are countless additional attributes of God which I cannot in any way grasp, and perhaps cannot even reach in my thought; for it is in the nature of the infinite not to be grasped by a finite being like myself. It is enough that I understand[14] the infinite, and that

I judge that all the attributes which I clearly perceive and know to imply some perfection—and perhaps countless others of which I am ignorant—are present in God either formally or eminently. This is enough to make the idea that I have of God the truest and most clear and distinct of all my ideas.

But perhaps I am something greater than I myself understand, and all the perfections which I attribute to God are somehow in me potentially, though not yet emerging or actualized. For I am now experiencing a gradual increase in my knowledge, and I see nothing to prevent its increasing more and more to infinity. Further, I see no reason why I should not be able to use this increased knowledge to acquire all the other perfections of God. And finally, if the potentiality for these perfections is already within me, why should not this be enough to generate the idea of such perfections?

But all this is impossible. First, though it is true that there is a gradual increase in my knowledge, and that I have many potentialities which are not yet actual, this is all quite irrelevant to the idea of God, which contains absolutely nothing that is potential; indeed, this gradual increase in knowledge is itself the surest sign of imperfection. What is more, even if my knowledge always increases more and more, I recognize that it will never actually be infinite, since it will never reach the point where it is not capable of a further increase; God, on the other hand, I take to be actually infinite, so that nothing can be added to his perfection. And finally, I perceive that the objective being of an idea cannot be produced merely by potential being, which strictly speaking is nothing, but only by actual or formal being.

If one concentrates carefully, all this is quite evident by the natural light. But when I relax my concentration, and my mental vision is blinded by the images of things perceived by the senses, it is not so easy for me to remember why the idea of a being more perfect than myself must necessarily proceed from some being which is in reality more perfect. I

---

14   According to Descartes, one can know or understand something without fully grasping it: "In the same way we can touch a mountain with our hands but we can-

not put our arms around it.... To grasp something is to embrace it in one's thought; to know something, it is sufficient to touch it with one's thought," he wrote in one of his letters.

should therefore like to go further and inquire whether I myself, who have this idea, could exist if no such being existed.

From whom, in that case, would I derive my existence? From myself presumably, or from my parents, or from some other beings less perfect than God; for nothing more perfect than God, or even as perfect, can be thought of or imagined.

Yet if I derived my existence from myself, then I should neither doubt nor want, nor lack anything at all; for I should have given myself all the perfections of which I have any idea, and thus I should myself be God. I must not suppose that the items I lack would be more difficult to acquire than those I now have. On the contrary, it is clear that, since I am a thinking thing or substance, it would have been far more difficult for me to emerge out of nothing than merely to acquire knowledge of the many things of which I am ignorant—such knowledge being merely an accident of that substance. And if I had derived my existence from myself, which is a greater achievement, I should certainly not have denied myself the knowledge in question, which is something much easier to acquire, or indeed any of the attributes which I perceive to be contained in the idea of God; for none of them seem any harder to achieve. And if any of them were harder to achieve, they would certainly appear so to me, if I had indeed got all my other attributes from myself, since I should experience a limitation of my power in this respect.

I do not escape the force of these arguments by supposing that I have always existed as I do now, as if it followed from this that there was no need to look for any author of my existence. For a lifespan can be divided into countless parts, each completely independent of the others, so that it does not follow from the fact that I existed a little while ago that I must exist now, unless there is some cause which as it were creates me afresh at this moment—that is, which preserves me. For it is quite clear to anyone who attentively considers the nature of time that the same power and action are needed to preserve anything at each individual moment of its duration as would be required to create that thing anew if it were not yet in existence. Hence the distinction between preservation and creation is only a con-

ceptual one, and this is one of the things that are evident by the natural light.

I must therefore now ask myself whether I possess some power enabling me to bring it about that I who now exist will still exist a little while from now. For since I am nothing but a thinking thing—or at least since I am now concerned only and precisely with that part of me which is a thinking thing—if there were such a power in me, I should undoubtedly be aware of it. But I experience no such power, and this very fact makes me recognize most clearly that I depend on some being distinct from myself.

But perhaps this being is not God, and perhaps I was produced either by my parents or by other causes less perfect than God. No; for as I have said before, it is quite clear that there must be at least as much in the cause as in the effect. And therefore whatever kind of cause is eventually proposed, since I am a thinking thing and have within me some idea of God, it must be admitted that what caused me is itself a thinking thing and possesses the idea of all the perfections which I attribute to God. In respect of this cause one may again inquire whether it derives its existence from itself or from another cause. If from itself, then it is clear from what has been said that it is itself God, since if it has the power of existing through its own might, then undoubtedly it also has the power of actually possessing all the perfections of which it has an idea—that is, all the perfections which I conceive to be in God. If, on the other hand, it derives its existence from another cause, then the same question may be repeated concerning this further cause, namely whether it derives its existence from itself or from another cause, until eventually the ultimate cause is reached, and this will be God.

It is clear enough that an infinite regress is impossible here, especially since I am dealing not just with the cause that produced me in the past, but also and most importantly with the cause that preserves me at the present moment.

Nor can it be supposed that several partial causes contributed to my creation, or that I received the idea of one of the perfections which I attribute to God from one cause and the idea of another from another—the supposition here being that all the perfections are to be found somewhere in the universe but not joined together in a single being, God. On the contrary, the unity, the simplicity, or the inseparability of all the attributes of God is one of the most important of the perfections which I understand him to have. And surely the idea of the unity of all his perfections could not have been placed in me by any cause which did not also provide me with the ideas of the other perfections; for no cause could have made me understand the interconnection and inseparability of the perfections without at the same time making me recognize what they were.

Lastly, as regards my parents, even if everything I have ever believed about them is true, it is certainly not they who preserve me; and in so far as I am a thinking thing, they did not even make me; they merely placed certain dispositions in the matter which I have always regarded as containing me, or rather my mind, for that is all I now take myself to be. So there can be no difficulty regarding my parents in this context. Altogether then, it must be concluded that the mere fact that I exist and have within me an idea of a most perfect being, that is, God, provides a very clear proof that God indeed exists.

It only remains for me to examine how I received this idea from God. For I did not acquire it from the senses; it has never come to me unexpectedly, as usually happens with the ideas of things that are perceivable by the senses, when these things present themselves to the external sense organs—or seem to do so. And it was not invented by me either; for I am plainly unable either to take away anything from it or to add anything to it. The only remaining alternative is that it is innate in me, just as the idea of myself is innate in me.

And indeed it is no surprise that God, in creating me, should have placed this idea in me to be, as it were, the mark of the craftsman stamped on his work—not that the mark need be anything distinct from the work itself. But the mere fact that God created me is a very strong basis for believing that I am somehow made in his image and likeness, and that I perceive that likeness, which includes the idea of God, by the same faculty which enables me to perceive myself. That is, when I turn my mind's eye upon myself, I understand that I am a thing which is incomplete and dependent on another and which aspires without limit to ever greater and better things; but I also understand at the same time that he on whom I depend has within him all those greater things, not just indefinitely and potentially but actually and infinitely, and hence that he is God. The whole force of the argument lies in this: I recognize that it would be impossible for me to exist with the kind of nature I have—that is, having within me the idea of God—were it not the case that God really existed. By 'God' I mean the very being the idea of whom is within me, that is, the possessor of all the perfections which I cannot grasp, but can somehow reach in my thought, who is subject to no defects whatsoever. It is clear enough from this that he cannot be a deceiver, since it is manifest by the natural light that all fraud and deception depend on some defect.

But before examining this point more carefully and investigating other truths which may be derived from it, I should like to pause here and spend some time in the contemplation of God; to reflect on his attributes, and to gaze with wonder and adoration on the beauty of this immense light, so far as the eye of my darkened intellect can bear it. For just as we believe through faith that the supreme happiness of the next life consists solely in the contemplation of the divine majesty, so experience tells us that this same contemplation, albeit much less perfect, enables us to know the greatest joy of which we are capable in this life.

Fourth Meditation: Truth and falsity

During these past few days I have accustomed myself to leading my mind away from the senses; and I have taken careful note of the fact that there is very little about corporeal things that is truly perceived, whereas much more is known about the human mind, and still more about God. The result is that I now have no difficulty in turning my mind away from imaginable things and towards things which are objects of the intellect alone and are totally separate from matter. And indeed the idea I have of the human mind, in so far as it is a thinking thing, which is not extended in length, breadth or height and has no other bodily characteristics, is much more distinct than the idea of any corporeal thing. And when I consider the fact that I have doubts, or that I am a thing that is incomplete and dependent, then there arises in me a clear and distinct idea of a being who is independent and complete, that is, an idea of God. And from the mere fact that there is such an idea within me, or that I who possess this idea exist, I clearly infer that God also exists, and that every single moment of my entire existence depends on him. So clear is this conclusion that I am confident that the human intellect cannot know anything that is more evident or more certain. And now, from this contemplation of the true God, in whom all the treasures of wisdom and the sciences lie hidden, I think I can see a way forward to the knowledge of other things.

To begin with, I recognize that it is impossible that God should ever deceive me. For in every case of trickery or deception some imperfection is to be found; and although the ability to deceive appears to be an indication of cleverness or power, the will to deceive is undoubtedly evidence of malice or weakness, and so cannot apply to God.

Next, I know by experience that there is in me a faculty of judgement which, like everything else which is in me, I certainly received from God. And since God does not wish to deceive me, he surely did not give me the kind of faculty which would ever enable me to go wrong while using it correctly.

There would be no further doubt on this issue were it not that what I have just said appears to imply that I am incapable of ever going wrong. For if everything that is in me comes from God, and he did not endow me with a faculty for making mistakes, it appears that I can never go wrong. And certainly, so long as I think only of God, and turn my whole attention to him, I can find no cause of error or falsity. But when I turn back to myself, I know by experience that I am prone to countless errors. On looking for the cause of these errors, I find that I possess not only a real and positive idea of God, or a being who is supremely perfect, but also what may be described as a negative idea of nothingness, or of that which is farthest removed from all perfection. I realize that I am, as it were, something intermediate between God and nothingness, or between supreme being and non-being: my nature is such that in so far as I was created by the supreme being, there is nothing in me to enable me to go wrong or lead me astray; but in so far as I participate in nothingness or non-being, that is, in so far as I am not myself the

supreme being and am lacking in countless respects, it is no wonder that I make mistakes. I understand, then, that error as such is not something real which depends on God, but merely a defect. Hence my going wrong does not require me to have a faculty specially bestowed on me by God; it simply happens as a result of the fact that the faculty of true judgement which I have from God is in my case not infinite.

But this is still not entirely satisfactory. For error is not a pure negation, but rather a privation or lack of some knowledge which somehow should be in me. And when I concentrate on the nature of God, it seems impossible that he should have placed in me a faculty which is not perfect of its kind, or which lacks some perfection which it ought to have. The more skilled the craftsman the more perfect the work produced by him; if this is so, how can anything produced by the supreme creator of all things not be complete and perfect in all respects? There is, moreover, no doubt that God could have given me a nature such that I was never mistaken; again, there is no doubt that he always wills what is best. Is it then better that I should make mistakes than that I should not do so?

As I reflect on these matters more attentively, it occurs to me first of all that it is no cause for surprise if I do not understand the reasons for some of God's actions; and there is no call to doubt his existence if I happen to find that there are other instances where I do not grasp why or how certain things were made by him. For since I now know that my own nature is very weak and limited, whereas the nature of God is immense, incomprehensible and infinite, I also know without more ado that he is capable of countless things whose causes are beyond my knowledge. And for this reason alone I consider the customary search for final causes[15] to be totally useless in physics; there is considerable rashness in thinking myself capable of investigating the <impenetrable> purposes of God.

It also occurs to me that whenever we are inquiring whether the works of God are perfect, we

---

15   The final cause of something is (roughly) the purpose or reason for that thing's existence: e.g., the final cause of a statue might be an original idea in the sculptor's head which prompted her to make that particular statue. This terminology goes back to Aristotle.

ought to look at the whole universe, not just at one created thing on its own. For what would perhaps rightly appear very imperfect if it existed on its own is quite perfect when its function as a part of the universe is considered. It is true that, since my decision to doubt everything, it is so far only myself and God whose existence I have been able to know with certainty; but after considering the immense power of God, I cannot deny that many other things have been made by him, or at least could have been made, and hence that I may have a place in the universal scheme of things.

Next, when I look more closely at myself and inquire into the nature of my errors (for these are the only evidence of some imperfection in me), I notice that they depend on two concurrent causes, namely on the faculty of knowledge which is in me, and on the faculty of choice or freedom of the will; that is, they depend on both the intellect and the will simultaneously. Now all that the intellect does is to enable me to perceive the ideas which are subjects for possible judgements; and when regarded strictly in this light, it turns out to contain no error in the proper sense of that term. For although countless things may exist without there being any corresponding ideas in me, it should not, strictly speaking, be said that I am deprived of these ideas, but merely that I lack them, in a negative sense. This is because I cannot produce any reason to prove that God ought to have given me a greater faculty of knowledge than he did; and no matter how skilled I understand a craftsman to be, this does not make me think he ought to have put into every one of his works all the perfections which he is able to put into some of them. Besides, I cannot complain that the will or freedom of choice which I received from God is not sufficiently extensive or perfect, since I know by experience that it is not restricted in any way. Indeed, I think it is very noteworthy that there is nothing else in me which is so perfect and so great that the possibility of a further increase in its perfection or greatness is beyond my understanding. If, for example, I consider the faculty of understanding, I immediately recognize that in my case it is extremely slight and very finite, and I at once form the idea of an understanding which is much greater—indeed supremely great and infinite; and from the very fact that

I can form an idea of it, I perceive that it belongs to the nature of God. Similarly, if I examine the faculties of memory or imagination, or any others, I discover that in my case each one of these faculties is weak and limited, while in the case of God it is immeasurable. It is only the will, or freedom of choice, which I experience within me to be so great that the idea of any greater faculty is beyond my grasp; so much so that it is above all in virtue of the will that I understand myself to bear in some way the image and likeness of God. For although God's will is incomparably greater than mine, both in virtue of the knowledge and power that accompany it and make it more firm and efficacious, and also in virtue of its object, in that it ranges over a greater number of items, nevertheless it does not seem any greater than mine when considered as will in the essential and strict sense. This is because the will simply consists in our ability to do or not do something (that is, to affirm or deny, to pursue or avoid); or rather, it consists simply in the fact that when the intellect puts something forward for affirmation or denial or for pursuit or avoidance, our inclinations are such that we do not feel we are determined by any external force. For in order to be free, there is no need for me to be capable of going in each of two directions; on the contrary, the more I incline in one direction—either because I clearly understand that reasons of truth and goodness point that way, or because of a divinely produced disposition of my inmost thoughts—the freer is my choice. Neither divine grace nor natural knowledge ever diminishes freedom; on the contrary, they increase and strengthen it. But the indifference I feel when there is no reason pushing me in one direction rather than another is the lowest grade of freedom; it is evidence not of any perfection of freedom, but rather of a defect in knowledge or a kind of negation. For if I always saw clearly what was true and good, I should never have to deliberate about the right judgement or choice; in that case, although I should be wholly free, it would be impossible for me ever to be in a state of indifference.

From these considerations I perceive that the power of willing which I received from God is not, when considered in itself, the cause of my mistakes; for it is both extremely ample and also perfect of its kind. Nor is my power of understanding to blame; for since my understanding comes from God, everything that I understand I undoubtedly understand correctly, and any error here is impossible. So what then is the source of my mistakes? It must be simply this: the scope of the will is wider than that of the intellect; but instead of restricting it within the same limits, I extend its use to matters which I do not understand. Since the will is indifferent in such cases, it easily turns aside from what is true and good, and this is the source of my error and sin.

For example, during these past few days I have been asking whether anything in the world exists, and I have realized that from the very fact of my raising this question it follows quite evidently that I exist. I could not but judge that something which I understood so clearly was true; but this was not because I was compelled so to judge by any external force, but because a great light in the intellect was followed by a great inclination in the will, and thus the spontaneity and freedom of my belief was all the greater in proportion to my lack of indifference. But now, besides the knowledge that I exist, in so far as I am a thinking thing, an idea of corporeal nature comes into my mind; and I happen to be in doubt as to whether the thinking nature which is in me, or rather which I am, is distinct from this corporeal nature or identical with it. I am making the further supposition that my intellect has not yet come upon any persuasive reason in favour of one alternative rather than the other. This obviously implies that I am indifferent as to whether I should assert or deny either alternative, or indeed refrain from making any judgement on the matter.

What is more, this indifference does not merely apply to cases where the intellect is wholly ignorant, but extends in general to every case where the intellect does not have sufficiently clear knowledge at the time when the will deliberates. For although probable conjectures may pull me in one direction, the mere knowledge that they are simply conjectures, and not certain and indubitable reasons, is itself quite enough to push my assent the other way. My experience in the last few days confirms this: the mere fact that I found that all my previous beliefs were in some sense open to doubt was enough to turn my absolutely confident belief in their truth into the supposition that they were wholly false.

If, however, I simply refrain from making a judgement in cases where I do not perceive the truth with sufficient clarity and distinctness, then it is clear that I am behaving correctly and avoiding error. But if in such cases I either affirm or deny, then I am not using my free will correctly. If I go for the alternative which is false, then obviously I shall be in error; if I take the other side, then it is by pure chance that I arrive at the truth, and I shall still be at fault since it is clear by the natural light that the perception of the intellect should always precede the determination of the will. In this incorrect use of free will may be found the privation[16] which constitutes the essence of error. The privation, I say, lies in the operation of the will in so far as it proceeds from me, but not in the faculty of will which I received from God, nor even in its operation, in so far as it depends on him.

And I have no cause for complaint on the grounds that the power of understanding or the natural light which God gave me is no greater than it is; for it is in the nature of a finite intellect to lack understanding of many things, and it is in the nature of a created intellect to be finite. Indeed, I have reason to give thanks to him who has never owed me anything for the great bounty that he has shown me, rather than thinking myself deprived or robbed of any gifts he did not bestow.

Nor do I have any cause for complaint on the grounds that God gave me a will which extends more widely than my intellect. For since the will consists simply of one thing which is, as it were, indivisible, it seems that its nature rules out the possibility of anything being taken away from it. And surely, the more widely my will extends, then the greater thanks I owe to him who gave it to me.

Finally, I must not complain that the forming of those acts of will or judgements in which I go wrong happens with God's concurrence. For in so far as these acts depend on God, they are wholly true and good; and my ability to perform them means that there is in a sense more perfection in me than would be the case if I lacked this ability. As for the privation involved—which is all that the essential definition of

---

16   Privation is the state of being deprived of something, or something's being absent.

falsity and wrong consists in—this does not in any way require the concurrence of God, since it is not a thing; indeed, when it is referred to God as its cause, it should be called not a privation but simply a negation. For it is surely no imperfection in God that he has given me the freedom to assent or not to assent in those cases where he did not endow my intellect with a clear and distinct perception; but it is undoubtedly an imperfection in me to misuse that freedom and make judgements about matters which I do not fully understand. I can see, however, that God could easily have brought it about that without losing my freedom, and despite the limitations in my knowledge, I should nonetheless never make a mistake. He could, for example, have endowed my intellect with a clear and distinct perception of everything about which I was ever likely to deliberate; or he could simply have impressed it unforgettably on my memory that I should never make a judgement about anything which I did not clearly and distinctly understand. Had God made me this way, then I can easily understand that, considered as a totality, I would have been more perfect than I am now. But I cannot therefore deny that there may in some way be more perfection in the universe as a whole because some of its parts are not immune from error, while others are immune, than there would be if all the parts were exactly alike. And I have no right to complain that the role God wished me to undertake in the world is not the principal one or the most perfect of all.

What is more, even if I have no power to avoid error in the first way just mentioned, which requires a clear perception of everything I have to deliberate on, I can avoid error in the second way, which depends merely on my remembering to withhold judgement on any occasion when the truth of the matter is not clear. Admittedly, I am aware of a certain weakness in me, in that I am unable to keep my attention fixed on one and the same item of knowledge at all times; but by attentive and repeated meditation I am nevertheless able to make myself remember it as often as the need arises, and thus get into the habit of avoiding error.

It is here that man's greatest and most important perfection is to be found, and I therefore think that today's meditation, involving an investigation into the cause of error and falsity, has been very profit-able. The cause of error must surely be the one I have explained; for if, whenever I have to make a judgement, I restrain my will so that it extends to what the intellect clearly and distinctly reveals, and no further, then it is quite impossible for me to go wrong. This is because every clear and distinct perception is undoubtedly something, and hence cannot come from nothing, but must necessarily have God for its author. Its author, I say, is God, who is supremely perfect, and who cannot be a deceiver on pain of contradiction; hence the perception is undoubtedly true. So today I have learned not only what precautions to take to avoid ever going wrong, but also what to do to arrive at the truth. For I shall unquestionably reach the truth, if only I give sufficient attention to all the things which I perfectly understand, and separate these from all the other cases where my apprehension is more confused and obscure. And this is just what I shall take good care to do from now on.

Fifth Meditation: The essence of material things, and the existence of God considered a second time

There are many matters which remain to be investigated concerning the attributes of God and the nature of myself, or my mind; and perhaps I shall take these up at another time. But now that I have seen what to do and what to avoid in order to reach the truth, the most pressing task seems to be to try to escape from the doubts into which I fell a few days ago, and see whether any certainty can be achieved regarding material objects.

But before I inquire whether any such things exist outside me, I must consider the ideas of these things, in so far as they exist in my thought, and see which of them are distinct, and which confused.

Quantity, for example, or 'continuous' quantity as the philosophers commonly call it, is something I distinctly imagine. That is, I distinctly imagine the extension of the quantity (or rather of the thing which is quantified) in length, breadth and depth. I also enumerate various parts of the thing, and to these parts I assign various sizes, shapes, positions and local motions; and to the motions I assign various durations.

Not only are all these things very well known and transparent to me when regarded in this general way, but in addition there are countless particular features regarding shape, number, motion and so on, which I perceive when I give them my attention. And the truth of these matters is so open and so much in harmony with my nature, that on first discovering them it seems that I am not so much learning something new as remembering what I knew before; or it seems like noticing for the first time things which were long present within me although I had never turned my mental gaze on them before.

But I think the most important consideration at this point is that I find within me countless ideas of things which even though they may not exist anywhere outside me still cannot be called nothing; for although in a sense they can be thought of at will, they are not my invention but have their own true and immutable[17] natures. When, for example, I imagine a triangle, even if perhaps no such figure exists, or has ever existed, anywhere outside my thought, there is still a determinate nature, or essence, or form of the triangle which is immutable and eternal, and not invented by me or dependent on my mind. This is clear from the fact that various properties can be demonstrated of the triangle, for example that its three angles equal two right angles, that its greatest side subtends its greatest angle, and the like; and since these properties are ones which I now clearly recognize whether I want to or not, even if I never thought of them at all when I previously imagined the triangle, it follows that they cannot have been invented by me.

It would be beside the point for me to say that since I have from time to time seen bodies of triangular shape, the idea of the triangle may have come to me from external things by means of the sense organs. For I can think up countless other shapes which there can be no suspicion of my ever having encountered through the senses, and yet I can demonstrate various properties of these shapes, just as I can with the triangle. All these properties are certainly true, since I am clearly aware of them, and therefore they are something, and not merely nothing; for it is obvious that whatever is true is something; and I have already amply demonstrated that everything of which I am clearly aware is true. And even if I had

not demonstrated this, the nature of my mind is such that I cannot but assent to these things, at least so long as I clearly perceive them. I also remember that even before, when I was completely preoccupied with the objects of the senses, I always held that the most certain truths of all were the kind which I recognized clearly in connection with shapes, or numbers or other items relating to arithmetic or geometry, or in general to pure and abstract mathematics.

But if the mere fact that I can produce from my thought the idea of something entails that everything which I clearly and distinctly perceive to belong to that thing really does belong to it, is not this a possible basis for another argument to prove the existence of God? Certainly, the idea of God, or a supremely perfect being, is one which I find within me just as surely as the idea of any shape or number. And my understanding that it belongs to his nature that he always exists is no less clear and distinct than is the case when I prove of any shape or number that some property belongs to its nature. Hence, even if it turned out that not everything on which I have meditated in these past days is true, I ought still to regard the existence of God as having at least the same level of certainty as I have hitherto attributed to the truths of mathematics.

At first sight, however, this is not transparently clear, but has some appearance of being a sophism.[18] Since I have been accustomed to distinguish between existence and essence in everything else, I find it easy to persuade myself that existence can also be separated from the essence of God, and hence that God can be thought of as not existing. But when I concentrate more carefully, it is quite evident that existence can no more be separated from the essence of God than the fact that its three angles equal two right angles can be separated from the essence of a triangle, or than the idea of a mountain can be separated from the idea of a valley. Hence it is just as much of a contradiction to think of God (that is, a supremely perfect being) lacking existence (that is, lacking a perfection), as it is to think of a mountain without a valley.

---

17   Unchangeable.

18   A clever-sounding argument based on unsound reasoning.

However, even granted that I cannot think of God except as existing, just as I cannot think of a mountain without a valley, it certainly does not follow from the fact that I think of a mountain with a valley that there is any mountain in the world; and similarly, it does not seem to follow from the fact that I think of God as existing that he does exist. For my thought does not impose any necessity on things; and just as I may imagine a winged horse even though no horse has wings, so I may be able to attach existence to God even though no God exists.

But there is a sophism concealed here. From the fact that I cannot think of a mountain without a valley, it does not follow that a mountain and valley exist anywhere, but simply that a mountain and a valley, whether they exist or not, are mutually inseparable. But from the fact that I cannot think of God except as existing, it follows that existence is inseparable from God, and hence that he really exists. It is not that my thought makes it so, or imposes any necessity on any thing; on the contrary, it is the necessity of the thing itself, namely the existence of God, which determines my thinking in this respect. For I am not free to think of God without existence (that is, a supremely perfect being without a supreme perfection) as I am free to imagine a horse with or without wings.

And it must not be objected at this point that while it is indeed necessary for me to suppose God exists, once I have made the supposition that he has all perfections (since existence is one of the perfections), nevertheless the original supposition was not necessary. Similarly, the objection would run, it is not necessary for me to think that all quadrilaterals can be inscribed in a circle; but given this supposition, it will be necessary for me to admit that a rhombus can be inscribed in a circle—which is patently false. Now admittedly, it is not necessary that I ever light upon any thought of God; but whenever I do choose to think of the first and supreme being, and bring forth the idea of God from the treasure house of my mind as it were, it is necessary that I attribute all perfections to him, even if I do not at that time enumerate them or attend to them individually. And this necessity plainly guarantees that, when I later realize that existence is a perfection, I am correct in inferring that the first and supreme being exists. In the same way, it is not necessary for me ever to imagine a triangle; but whenever I do wish to consider a rectilinear figure having just three angles, it is necessary that I attribute to it the properties which license the inference that its three angles equal no more than two right angles, even if I do not notice this at the time. By contrast, when I examine what figures can be inscribed in a circle, it is in no way necessary for me to think that this class includes all quadrilaterals. Indeed, I cannot even imagine this, so long as I am willing to admit only what I clearly and distinctly understand. So there is a great difference between this kind of false supposition and the true ideas which are innate in me, of which the first and most important is the idea of God. There are many ways in which I understand that this idea is not something fictitious which is dependent on my thought, but is an image of a true and immutable nature. First of all, there is the fact that, apart from God, there is nothing else of which I am capable of thinking such that existence belongs to its essence. Second, I cannot understand how there could be two or more Gods of this kind; and after supposing that one God exists, I plainly see that it is necessary that he has existed from eternity and will abide for eternity. And finally, I perceive many other attributes of God, none of which I can remove or alter.

But whatever method of proof I use, I am always brought back to the fact that it is only what I clearly and distinctly perceive that completely convinces me. Some of the things I clearly and distinctly perceive are obvious to everyone, while others are discovered only by those who look more closely and investigate more carefully; but once they have been discovered, the latter are judged to be just as certain as the former. In the case of a right-angled triangle, for example, the fact that the square on the hypotenuse is equal to the square on the other two sides is not so readily apparent as the fact that the hypotenuse subtends the largest angle; but once one has seen it, one believes it just as strongly. But as regards God, if I were not overwhelmed by preconceived opinions, and if the images of things perceived by the senses did not besiege my thought on every side, I would certainly acknowledge him sooner and more easily than anything else. For what is more self-evident than the fact that the supreme being exists, or that God, to whose essence alone existence belongs, exists?

Although it needed close attention for me to perceive this, I am now just as certain of it as I am of everything else which appears most certain. And what is more, I see that the certainty of all other things depends on this, so that without it nothing can ever be perfectly known.

Admittedly my nature is such that so long as I perceive something very clearly and distinctly I cannot but believe it to be true. But my nature is also such that I cannot fix my mental vision continually on the same thing, so as to keep perceiving it clearly; and often the memory of a previously made judgement may come back, when I am no longer attending to the arguments which led me to make it. And so other arguments can now occur to me which might easily undermine my opinion, if I were unaware of God: and I should thus never have true and certain knowledge about anything, but only shifting and changeable opinions. For example, when I consider the nature of a triangle, it appears most evident to me, steeped as I am in the principles of geometry, that its three angles are equal to two right angles; and so long as I attend to the proof, I cannot but believe this to be true. But as soon as I turn my mind's eye away from the proof, then in spite of still remembering that I perceived it very clearly, I can easily fall into doubt about its truth, if I am unaware of God. For I can convince myself that I have a natural disposition to go wrong from time to time in matters which I think I perceive as evidently as can be. This will seem even more likely when I remember that there have been frequent cases where I have regarded things as true and certain, but have later been led by other arguments to judge them to be false.

Now, however, I have perceived that God exists, and at the same time I have understood that everything else depends on him, and that he is no deceiver; and I have drawn the conclusion that everything which I clearly and distinctly perceive is of necessity true. Accordingly, even if I am no longer attending to the arguments which led me to judge that this is true, as long as I remember that I clearly and distinctly perceived it, there are no counter-arguments which can

be adduced to make me doubt it, but on the contrary I have true and certain knowledge of it. And I have knowledge not just of this matter, but of all matters which I remember ever having demonstrated, in geometry and so on. For what objections can now be raised? That the way I am made makes me prone to frequent error? But I now know that I am incapable of error in those cases where my understanding is transparently clear. Or can it be objected that I have in the past regarded as true and certain many things which I afterwards recognized to be false? But none of these were things which I clearly and distinctly perceived: I was ignorant of this rule for establishing the truth, and believed these things for other reasons which I later discovered to be less reliable. So what is left to say? Can one raise the objection I put to myself a while ago, that I may be dreaming, or that everything which I am now thinking has as little truth as what comes to the mind of one who is asleep? Yet even this does not change anything. For even though I might be dreaming, if there is anything which is evident to my intellect, then it is wholly true.

Thus I see plainly that the certainty and truth of all knowledge depends uniquely on my awareness of the true God, to such an extent that I was incapable of perfect knowledge about anything else until I became aware of him. And now it is possible for me to achieve full and certain knowledge of countless matters, both concerning God himself and other things whose nature is intellectual, and also concerning the whole of that corporeal nature which is the subject-matter of pure mathematics.

Sixth Meditation: The existence of material things, and the real distinction between mind and body

It remains for me to examine whether material things exist. And at least I now know they are capable of existing, in so far as they are the subject-matter of pure mathematics, since I perceive them clearly and distinctly. For there is no doubt that God is capable of creating everything that I am capable of perceiving in this manner; and I have never judged that something could not be made by him except on the grounds that there would be a contradiction in my perceiving it distinctly. The conclusion that material things exist is also suggested by the faculty of imagination, which I am aware of using when I turn my mind to material things. For when I give more attentive consideration to what imagination is, it seems to be nothing else but an application of the cognitive faculty to a body which is intimately present to it, and which therefore exists.

To make this clear, I will first examine the difference between imagination and pure understanding. When I imagine a triangle, for example, I do not merely understand that it is a figure bounded by three lines, but at the same time I also see the three lines with my mind's eye as if they were present before me; and this is what I call imagining. But if I want to think of a chiliagon, although I understand that it is a figure consisting of a thousand sides just as well as I understand the triangle to be a three-sided figure, I do not in the same way imagine the thousand sides or see them as if they were present before me. It is true that since I am in the habit of imagining something whenever I think of a corporeal thing, I may construct in my mind a confused representation of some figure; but it is clear that this is not a chiliagon. For it differs in no way from the representation I should form if I were thinking of a myriagon, or any figure with very many sides. Moreover, such a representation is useless for recognizing the properties which distinguish a chiliagon from other polygons. But suppose I am dealing with a pentagon: I can of course understand the figure of a pentagon, just as I can the figure of a chiliagon, without the help of the imagination; but I can also imagine a pentagon, by applying my mind's eye to its five sides and the area contained within them. And in doing this I notice quite clearly that imagination requires a peculiar effort of mind which is not required for understanding; this additional effort of mind clearly shows the difference between imagination and pure understanding.

Besides this, I consider that this power of imagining which is in me, differing as it does from the power of understanding, is not a necessary constituent of my own essence, that is, of the essence of my mind. For if I lacked it, I should undoubtedly remain the same individual as I now am; from which it seems to follow that it depends on something distinct from myself. And I can easily understand that, if there does exist some body to which the mind is so joined that it can apply itself to contemplate it, as it were, whenever it pleases, then it may possibly be this very body that enables me to imagine corporeal things. So the difference between this mode of thinking and pure understanding may simply be this: when the mind understands, it in some way turns towards itself and inspects one of the ideas which are within it; but when it imagines, it turns towards the body and looks at something in the body which conforms to an idea understood by the mind or perceived by the senses. I can, as I say, easily understand that this is how imagination comes about, if the body exists; and since there is no other equally suitable way of explaining imagination that comes to mind, I can make a probable conjecture that the body exists. But this is only a probability; and despite a careful and comprehensive investigation, I do not yet see how the distinct idea of corporeal nature which I find in my imagination can provide any basis for a necessary inference that some body exists.

But besides that corporeal nature which is the subject-matter of pure mathematics, there is much else that I habitually imagine, such as colours, sounds, tastes, pain and so on—though not so distinctly. Now I perceive these things much better by means of the senses, which is how, with the assistance of memory, they appear to have reached the imagination. So in order to deal with them more fully, I must pay equal attention to the senses, and see whether the things which are perceived by means of that mode of thinking which I call 'sensory perception' provide me with any sure argument for the existence of corporeal things.

To begin with, I will go back over all the things which I previously took to be perceived by the senses, and reckoned to be true; and I will go over my reasons for thinking this. Next, I will set out my reasons for subsequently calling these things into doubt. And finally I will consider what I should now believe about them.

First of all then, I perceived by my senses that I had a head, hands, feet and other limbs making up the body which I regarded as part of myself, or perhaps even as my whole self. I also perceived by my senses that this body was situated among many other bodies which could affect it in various favourable or unfavourable ways; and I gauged the favourable effects by a sensation of pleasure, and the unfavourable ones by a sensation of pain. In addition to pain and pleasure, I also had sensations within me of hunger, thirst, and other such appetites, and also of physical propensities towards cheerfulness, sadness, anger and similar emotions. And outside me, besides the extension, shapes and movements of bodies, I also had sensations of their hardness and heat, and of the other tactile qualities. In addition, I had sensations of light, colours, smells, tastes and sounds, the variety of which enabled me to distinguish the sky, the earth, the seas, and all other bodies, one from another. Considering the ideas of all these qualities which presented themselves to my thought, although the ideas were, strictly speaking, the only immediate objects of my sensory awareness, it was not unreasonable for me to think that the items which I was perceiving through the senses were things quite distinct from my thought, namely bodies which produced the ideas. For my experience was that these ideas came to me quite without my consent, so that I could not have sensory awareness of any object, even if I wanted to, unless it was present to my sense organs; and I could not avoid having sensory awareness of it when it was present. And since the ideas perceived by the senses were much more lively and vivid and even, in their own way, more distinct than any of those which I deliberately formed through meditating or which I found impressed on my memory, it seemed impossible that they should have come from within me; so the only alternative was that they came from other things. Since the sole source of my knowledge of these things was the ideas themselves, the supposition that the things resembled the ideas was bound to occur to me. In addition, I remembered that the use of my senses had come first, while the use of my reason came only later; and I saw that the ideas which I formed myself were less vivid than those which I perceived with the senses and were, for the most part, made up of elements of sensory ideas. In this way I easily convinced myself that I had nothing at all in the intellect which I had not previously had in sensation. As for the body which by some special right I called 'mine', my belief that this body, more than any other, belonged to me had some justification. For I could never be separated from it, as I could from other bodies; and I felt all my

appetites and emotions in, and on account of, this body; and finally, I was aware of pain and pleasurable ticklings in parts of this body, but not in other bodies external to it. But why should that curious sensation of pain give rise to a particular distress of mind; or why should a certain kind of delight follow on a tickling sensation? Again, why should that curious tugging in the stomach which I call hunger tell me that I should eat, or a dryness of the throat tell me to drink, and so on? I was not able to give any explanation of all this, except that nature taught me so. For there is absolutely no connection (at least that I can understand) between the tugging sensation and the decision to take food, or between the sensation of something causing pain and the mental apprehension of distress that arises from that sensation. These and other judgements that I made concerning sensory objects, I was apparently taught to make by nature; for I had already made up my mind that this was how things were, before working out any arguments to prove it.

Later on, however, I had many experiences which gradually undermined all the faith I had had in the senses. Sometimes towers which had looked round from a distance appeared square from close up; and enormous statues standing on their pediments[19] did not seem large when observed from the ground. In these and countless other such cases, I found that the judgements of the external senses were mistaken. And this applied not just to the external senses but to the internal senses as well. For what can be more internal than pain? And yet I had heard that those who had had a leg or an arm amputated sometimes still seemed to feel pain intermittently in the missing part of the body. So even in my own case it was apparently not quite certain that a particular limb was hurting, even if I felt pain in it. To these reasons for doubting, I recently added two very general ones. The first was that every sensory experience I have ever thought I was having while awake I can also think of myself as sometimes having while asleep; and since I do not

_____

19   In classical architecture, a pediment is a wide, triangular, gable-like area forming the front of a building with a two-pitched roof: pediments would often be situated above a door or portico, and might be decorated with statues.

believe that what I seem to perceive in sleep comes from things located outside me, I did not see why I should be any more inclined to believe this of what I think I perceive while awake. The second reason for doubt was that since I did not know the author of my being (or at least was pretending not to), I saw nothing to rule out the possibility that my natural constitution made me prone to error even in matters which seemed to me most true. As for the reasons for my previous confident belief in the truth of the things perceived by the senses, I had no trouble in refuting them. For since I apparently had natural impulses towards many things which reason told me to avoid, I reckoned that a great deal of confidence should not be placed in what I was taught by nature. And despite the fact that the perceptions of the senses were not dependent on my will, I did not think that I should on that account infer that they proceeded from things distinct from myself, since I might perhaps have a faculty not yet known to me which produced them.

But now, when I am beginning to achieve a better knowledge of myself and the author of my being, although I do not think I should heedlessly accept everything I seem to have acquired from the senses, neither do I think that everything should be called into doubt.

First, I know that everything which I clearly and distinctly understand is capable of being created by God so as to correspond exactly with my understanding of it. Hence the fact that I can clearly and distinctly understand one thing apart from another is enough to make me certain that the two things are distinct, since they are capable of being separated, at least by God. The question of what kind of power is required to bring about such a separation does not affect the judgement that the two things are distinct. Thus, simply by knowing that I exist and seeing at the same time that absolutely nothing else belongs to my nature or essence except that I am a thinking thing, I can infer correctly that my essence consists solely in the fact that I am a thinking thing. It is true that I may have (or, to anticipate, that I certainly have) a body that is very closely joined to me. But nevertheless, on the one hand I have a clear and distinct idea of myself, in so far as I am simply a thinking, non-extended thing; and on the other hand I have a distinct idea of body,

in so far as this is simply an extended, non-thinking thing. And accordingly, it is certain that I am really distinct from my body, and can exist without it.

Besides this, I find in myself faculties for certain special modes of thinking, namely imagination and sensory perception. Now I can clearly and distinctly understand myself as a whole without these faculties; but I cannot, conversely, understand these faculties without me, that is, without an intellectual substance to inhere in. This is because there is an intellectual act included in their essential definition; and hence I perceive that the distinction between them and myself corresponds to the distinction between the modes of a thing and the thing itself. Of course I also recognize that there are other faculties (like those of changing position, of taking on various shapes, and so on) which, like sensory perception and imagination, cannot be understood apart from some substance for them to inhere in, and hence cannot exist without it. But it is clear that these other faculties, if they exist, must be in a corporeal or extended substance and not an intellectual one; for the clear and distinct conception of them includes extension, but does not include any intellectual act whatsoever. Now there is in me a passive faculty of sensory perception, that is, a faculty for receiving and recognizing the ideas of sensible objects; but I could not make use of it unless there was also an active faculty, either in me or in something else, which produced or brought about these ideas. But this faculty cannot be in me, since clearly it presupposes no intellectual act on my part, and the ideas in question are produced without my cooperation and often even against my will. So the only alternative is that it is in another substance distinct from me—a substance which contains either formally or eminently all the reality which exists objectively in the ideas produced by this faculty (as I have just noted). This substance is either a body, that is, a corporeal nature, in which case it will contain formally <and in fact> everything which is to be found objectively <or representatively> in the ideas; or else it is God, or some creature more noble than a body, in which case it will contain eminently whatever is to be found in the ideas. But since God is not a deceiver, it is quite clear that he does not transmit the ideas to me either directly from himself, or indirectly, via some creature which contains the objective reality of the ideas not formally but only eminently. For God has given me no faculty at all for recognizing any such source for these ideas; on the contrary, he has given me a great propensity to believe that they are produced by corporeal things. So I do not see how God could be understood to be anything but a deceiver if the ideas were transmitted from a source other than corporeal things. It follows that corporeal things exist. They may not all exist in a way that exactly corresponds with my sensory grasp of them, for in many cases the grasp of the senses is very obscure and confused. But at least they possess all the properties which I clearly and distinctly understand, that is, all those which, viewed in general terms, are comprised within the subject-matter of pure mathematics.

What of the other aspects of corporeal things which are either particular (for example that the sun is of such and such a size or shape), or less clearly understood, such as light or sound or pain, and so on? Despite the high degree of doubt and uncertainty involved here, the very fact that God is not a deceiver, and the consequent impossibility of there being any falsity in my opinions which cannot be corrected by some other faculty supplied by God, offers me a sure hope that I can attain the truth even in these matters. Indeed, there is no doubt that everything that I am taught by nature contains some truth. For if nature is considered in its general aspect, then I understand by the term nothing other than God himself, or the ordered system of created things established by God. And by my own nature in particular I understand nothing other than the totality of things bestowed on me by God.

There is nothing that my own nature teaches me more vividly than that I have a body, and that when I feel pain there is something wrong with the body, and that when I am hungry or thirsty the body needs food and drink, and so on. So I should not doubt that there is some truth in this.

Nature also teaches me, by these sensations of pain, hunger, thirst and so on, that I am not merely present in my body as a sailor is present in a ship, but that I am very closely joined and, as it were, intermingled with it, so that I and the body form a unit. If this were not so, I, who am nothing but a thinking thing, would not feel pain when the body was hurt, but would perceive the damage purely by the intellect, just as a sailor perceives by sight if anything in his ship is broken. Similarly, when the body needed food or drink, I should have an explicit understanding of the fact, instead of having confused sensations of hunger and thirst. For these sensations of hunger, thirst, pain and so on are nothing but confused modes of thinking which arise from the union and, as it were, intermingling of the mind with the body.

I am also taught by nature that various other bodies exist in the vicinity of my body, and that some of these are to be sought out and others avoided. And from the fact that I perceive by my senses a great variety of colours, sounds, smells and tastes, as well as differences in heat, hardness and the like, I am correct in inferring that the bodies which are the source of these various sensory perceptions possess differences corresponding to them, though perhaps not resembling them. Also, the fact that some of the perceptions are agreeable to me while others are disagreeable makes it quite certain that my body, or rather my whole self, in so far as I am a combination of body and mind, can be affected by the various beneficial or harmful bodies which surround it.

There are, however, many other things which I may appear to have been taught by nature, but which in reality I acquired not from nature but from a habit of making ill-considered judgements; and it is therefore quite possible that these are false. Cases in point are the belief that any space in which nothing is occurring to stimulate my senses must be empty; or that the heat in a body is something exactly resembling the idea of heat which is in me; or that when a body is white or green, the selfsame whiteness or greenness which I perceive through my senses is present in the body; or that in a body which is bitter or sweet there is the selfsame taste which I experience, and so on; or, finally, that stars and towers and other distant bodies have the same size and shape which they present to my senses, and other examples of this kind. But to make sure that my perceptions in this matter are sufficiently distinct, I must more accurately define exactly what I mean when I say that I am taught something by nature. In this context I am taking nature to be something more limited than the totality of things bestowed on me by God. For this includes many things that belong to the mind alone—for example my perception that what is done cannot be undone, and all other things that are known by the natural light; but at this stage I am not speaking of these matters. It also includes much that relates to the body alone, like the tendency to move in a downward direction, and so on; but I am not speaking of these matters either. My sole concern here is with what God has bestowed on me as a combination of mind and body. My nature, then, in this limited sense, does indeed teach me to avoid what induces a feeling of pain and to seek out what induces feelings of pleasure, and so on. But it does not appear to teach us to draw any conclusions from these sensory perceptions about things located outside us without waiting until the intellect has examined the matter. For knowledge of the truth about such things seems to belong to the mind alone, not to the combination of mind and body. Hence, although a star has no greater effect on my eye than the flame of a small light, that does not mean that there is any real or positive inclination in me to believe that the star is no bigger than the light; I have simply made this judgement from childhood onwards without any rational basis. Similarly, although I feel heat when I go near a fire and feel pain when I go too near, there is no convincing argument for supposing that there is something in the fire which resembles the heat, any more than for supposing that there is something which resembles the pain. There is simply reason to suppose that there is something in the fire, whatever it may eventually turn out to be, which produces in us the feelings of heat or pain. And likewise, even though there is nothing in any given space that stimulates the senses, it does not follow that there is no body there. In these cases and many others I see that I have been in the habit of misusing the order of nature. For the proper purpose of the sensory perceptions given me by nature is simply to inform the mind of what is beneficial or harmful for the composite of which the mind is a part; and to this extent they are sufficiently clear and distinct. But I misuse them by treating them as reliable touchstones for immediate judgements about the essential nature of the bodies located outside us; yet this is an area where they provide only very obscure information.

I have already looked in sufficient detail at how, notwithstanding the goodness of God, it may happen that my judgements are false. But a further problem now comes to mind regarding those very things which nature presents to me as objects which I should seek out or avoid, and also regarding the internal sensations, where I seem to have detected errors—e.g., when someone is tricked by the pleasant taste of some food into eating the poison concealed inside it. Yet in this case, what the man's nature urges him to go for is simply what is responsible for the pleasant taste, and not the poison, which his nature knows nothing about. The only inference that can be drawn from this is that his nature is not omniscient. And this is not surprising, since man is a limited thing, and so it is only fitting that his perfection should be limited.

And yet it is not unusual for us to go wrong even in cases where nature does urge us towards something. Those who are ill, for example, may desire food or drink that will shortly afterwards turn out to be bad for them. Perhaps it may be said that they go wrong because their nature is disordered, but this does not remove the difficulty. A sick man is no less one of God's creatures than a healthy one, and it seems no less a contradiction to suppose that he has received from God a nature which deceives him. Yet a clock constructed with wheels and weights observes all the laws of its nature just as closely when it is badly made and tells the wrong time as when it completely fulfils the wishes of the clockmaker. In the same way, I might consider the body of a man as a kind of machine equipped with and made up of bones, nerves, muscles, veins, blood and skin in such a way that, even if there were no mind in it, it would still perform all the same movements as it now does in those cases where movement is not under the control of the will or, consequently, of the mind. I can easily see that if such a body suffers from dropsy,[20] for example, and is affected by the dryness of the throat which normally produces in the mind the sensation of thirst, the resulting condition of the nerves and other parts will dispose the body to take a drink, with the result that the disease will be aggravated. Yet this is just as natural as the body's being stimulated by a similar

---

20   An illness characterized by an abnormal accumulation of watery fluid in certain tissues and cavities of the body.

dryness of the throat to take a drink when there is no such illness and the drink is beneficial. Admittedly, when I consider the purpose of the clock, I may say that it is departing from its nature when it does not tell the right time; and similarly when I consider the mechanism of the human body, I may think that, in relation to the movements which normally occur in it, it too is deviating from its nature if the throat is dry at a time when drinking is not beneficial to its continued health. But I am well aware that 'nature' as I have just used it has a very different significance from 'nature' in the other sense. As I have just used it, 'nature' is simply a label which depends on my thought; it is quite extraneous to the things to which it is applied, and depends simply on my comparison between the idea of a sick man and a badly-made clock, and the idea of a healthy man and a well-made clock. But by 'nature' in the other sense I understand something which is really to be found in the things themselves; in this sense, therefore, the term contains something of the truth.

When we say, then, with respect to the body suffering from dropsy, that it has a disordered nature because it has a dry throat and yet does not need drink, the term 'nature' is here used merely as an extraneous label. However, with respect to the composite, that is, the mind united with this body, what is involved is not a mere label, but a true error of nature, namely that it is thirsty at a time when drink is going to cause it harm. It thus remains to inquire how it is that the goodness of God does not prevent nature, in this sense, from deceiving us.

The first observation I make at this point is that there is a great difference between the mind and the body, inasmuch as the body is by its very nature always divisible, while the mind is utterly indivisible. For when I consider the mind, or myself in so far as I am merely a thinking thing, I am unable to distinguish any parts within myself; I understand myself to be something quite single and complete. Although the whole mind seems to be united to the whole body, I recognize that if a foot or arm or any other part of the body is cut off, nothing has thereby been taken away from the mind. As for the faculties of willing, of understanding, of sensory perception and so on, these cannot be termed parts of the mind, since it is one and the same mind that wills, and understands and has sensory perceptions. By contrast, there is no corporeal or extended thing that I can think of which in my thought I cannot easily divide into parts; and this very fact makes me understand that it is divisible. This one argument would be enough to show me that the mind is completely different from the body, even if I did not already know as much from other considerations.

My next observation is that the mind is not immediately affected by all parts of the body, but only by the brain, or perhaps just by one small part of the brain, namely the part which is said to contain the 'common' sense. Every time this part of the brain is in a given state, it presents the same signals to the mind, even though the other parts of the body may be in a different condition at the time. This is established by countless observations, which there is no need to review here.

I observe, in addition, that the nature of the body is such that whenever any part of it is moved by another part which is some distance away, it can always be moved in the same fashion by any of the parts which lie in between, even if the more distant part does nothing. For example, in a cord ABCD, if one end D is pulled so that the other end A moves, the exact same movement could have been brought about if one of the intermediate points B or C had been pulled, and D had not moved at all. In similar fashion, when I feel a pain in my foot, physiology tells me that this happens by means of nerves distributed throughout the foot, and that these nerves are like cords which go from the foot right up to the brain. When the nerves are pulled in the foot, they in turn pull on inner parts of the brain to which they are attached, and produce a certain motion in them; and nature has laid it down that this motion should produce in the mind a sensation of pain, as occurring in the foot. But since these nerves, in passing from the foot to the brain, must pass through the calf, the thigh, the lumbar region, the back and the neck, it can happen that, even if it is not the part in the foot but one of the intermediate parts which is being pulled, the same motion will occur in the brain as occurs when the foot is hurt, and so it will necessarily come about that the mind feels the same sensation of pain. And we must suppose the same thing happens with regard to any other sensation.

My final observation is that any given movement occurring in the part of the brain that immediately affects the mind produces just one corresponding sensation; and hence the best system that could be devised is that it should produce the one sensation which, of all possible sensations, is most especially and most frequently conducive to the preservation of the healthy man. And experience shows that the sensations which nature has given us are all of this kind; and so there is absolutely nothing to be found in them that does not bear witness to the power and goodness of God. For example, when the nerves in the foot are set in motion in a violent and unusual manner, this motion, by way of the spinal cord, reaches the inner parts of the brain, and there gives the mind its signal for having a certain sensation, namely the sensation of a pain as occurring in the foot. This stimulates the mind to do its best to get rid of the cause of the pain, which it takes to be harmful to the foot. It is true that God could have made the nature of man such that this particular motion in the brain indicated something else to the mind; it might, for example, have made the mind aware of the actual motion occurring in the brain, or in the foot, or in any of the intermediate regions; or it might have indicated something else entirely. But there is nothing else which would have been so conducive to the continued well-being of the body. In the same way, when we need drink, there arises a certain dryness in the throat; this sets in motion the nerves of the throat, which in turn move the inner parts of the brain. This motion produces in the mind a sensation of thirst, because the most useful thing for us to know about the whole business is that we need drink in order to stay healthy. And so it is in the other cases.

It is quite clear from all this that, notwithstanding the immense goodness of God, the nature of man as a combination of mind and body is such that it is bound to mislead him from time to time. For there may be some occurrence, not in the foot but in one of the other areas through which the nerves travel in their route from the foot to the brain, or even in the brain itself; and if this cause produces the same motion which is generally produced by injury to the foot, then pain will be felt as if it were in the foot. This deception of the senses is natural, because a given motion in the brain must always produce the same sensation in the mind; and the origin of the motion in question is much more often going to be something which is hurting the foot, rather than something existing elsewhere. So it is reasonable that this motion should always indicate to the mind a pain in the foot rather than in any other part of the body. Again, dryness of the throat may sometimes arise not, as it normally does, from the fact that a drink is necessary to the health of the body, but from some quite opposite cause, as happens in the case of the man with dropsy. Yet it is much better that it should mislead on this occasion than that it should always mislead when the body is in good health. And the same goes for the other cases.

This consideration is the greatest help to me, not only for noticing all the errors to which my nature is liable, but also for enabling me to correct or avoid them without difficulty. For I know that in matters regarding the well-being of the body, all my senses report the truth much more frequently than not. Also, I can almost always make use of more than one sense to investigate the same thing; and in addition, I can use both my memory, which connects present experiences with preceding ones, and my intellect, which has by now examined all the causes of error. Accordingly, I should not have any further fears about the falsity of what my senses tell me every day; on the contrary, the exaggerated doubts of the last few days should be dismissed as laughable. This applies especially to the principal reason for doubt, namely my inability to distinguish between being asleep and being awake. For I now notice that there is a vast difference between the two, in that dreams are never linked by memory with all the other actions of life as waking experiences are. If, while I am awake, anyone were suddenly to appear to me and then disappear immediately, as happens in sleep, so that I could not see where he had come from or where he had gone to, it would not be unreasonable for me to judge that he was a ghost, or a vision created in my brain, rather than a real man. But when I distinctly see where things come from and where and when they come to me, and when I can connect my perceptions of them with the whole of the rest of my life without a break, then I am quite certain that when I encounter these things I am not asleep but awake. And I ought not to have even the slightest doubt of their reality if, after calling upon

all the senses as well as my memory and my intellect in order to check them, I receive no conflicting
reports from any of these sources. For from the fact
that God is not a deceiver it follows that in cases like
these I am completely free from error. But since the
pressure of things to be done does not always allow
us to stop and make such a meticulous check, it must
be admitted that in this human life we are often liable
to make mistakes about particular things, and we must
acknowledge the weakness of our nature.

JOHN LOCKE

An Essay Concerning Human Understanding

Who Was John Locke?

John Locke was born in the Somerset countryside,
near the town of Bristol, in 1632. His parents were
small landowners—minor gentry—who subjected
the young Locke to a strict Protestant upbringing.
Thanks to the influence of one of his father's friends
Locke was able to gain a place at Westminster School,
at the time the best school in England, where he studied Greek, Latin, and Hebrew. He went on to Christ
Church College, Oxford, and graduated with a BA in
1656. Shortly afterwards he was made a senior student of his college—a kind of teaching position—
which he was to remain until 1684, when the king of
England, Charles II, personally (and illegally) demanded his expulsion.

During the 1650s and early '60s Locke lectured on
Greek and rhetoric at Oxford but he was idle and unhappy, and became increasingly bored by the traditional philosophy of his day. He developed an interest
in medicine and physical science (in 1675 he tried and
failed to gain the degree of Doctor of Medicine), and
in 1665 Locke left the confines of the academic world,
and began to make his way into the world of politics
and science. In the winter of 1665–66 he was ambassador to the German state of Brandenburg, where his
first-hand observation of religious toleration between
Calvinists, Lutherans, Catholics, and Anabaptists made
a big impression on him.

A chance encounter in 1666 was the decisive
turning-point in Locke's life: he met a nobleman
called Lord Ashley, then the Chancellor of the Exche-
quer, and soon went to live at Ashley's London house
as his confidant and medical advisor. In 1668, Locke
was responsible for a life-saving surgical operation
on Ashley, implanting a small silver spigot to drain
off fluid from a cyst on his liver; the lord never forgot
his gratitude (and wore the small tap in his side for
the rest of his life). Under Ashley's patronage, Locke
had both the leisure to spend several years working
on his *Essay Concerning Human Understanding*, and
a sequence of lucrative and interesting government
positions, including one as part of a group drafting
the constitution of the new colony of Carolina in the
Americas.

Ashley's support was also essential in giving
Locke—an introverted and hyper-sensitive soul, who
suffered for most of his life from bad asthma and general poor health—the confidence to do original philosophy. Locke never married, was a life-long celibate,
shied away from drinking parties and a hectic social
life, but enjoyed the attentions of lady admirers, and
throughout his life he had many loyal friends and got
on especially well with some of his friends' children.

Locke spent the years from 1675 until 1679 traveling in France (where he expected to die of tuber-
culosis, but survived—Locke spent a large portion
of his life confidently expecting an early death), and
when he returned to England it was to a very unset-
tled political situation. The heir to the British throne,
Charles II's younger brother James, was a Catholic,
and his succession was feared by many politicians,

including Ashley—who was, by this time, the Earl of Shaftesbury—and his political party, the Whigs. Their greatest worry was that the return of a Catholic monarchy would mean the return of religious oppression to England, as was happening in parts of Europe. Charles, however, stood by his brother and in 1681 Shaftesbury was sent to prison in the Tower of London, charged with high treason. Shaftesbury was acquitted by a grand jury, but he fled to Holland and died a few months later (spending his last few hours, the story goes, discussing a draft of Locke's *Essay* with his friends). Locke, in danger as a known associate of Shaftesbury's, followed his example in 1683 and secretly moved to the Netherlands, where he had to spend a year underground evading arrest by the Dutch government's agents on King Charles's behalf. While in Holland he rewrote material for the *Essay*, molding it towards its final state, and published an abridgement of the book in a French scholarly periodical which immediately attracted international attention.

In 1689 the political tumult in England had subsided enough for Locke to return—James's brief reign (as James II) had been toppled by the Protestant William of Orange and his queen Mary—and he moved as a permanent house-guest to an estate called Oates about twenty five miles from London. He returned to political life (though he refused the post of ambassador to Brandenburg, on grounds of ill health), and played a significant role in loosening restrictions on publishers and authors.

It was in this year, when Locke was 57, that the results of his thirty years of thinking and writing were suddenly published in a flood. First, published anonymously, came the *Letter on Toleration*, then *Two Treatises on Government*. In the *Two Treatises*—which was influential in the liberal movements of the next century that culminated in the French and American revolutions—Locke argued that the authority of monarchs is limited by individuals' rights and the public good. Finally, *An Essay Concerning Human Understanding* was published under his own name, to almost instant acclaim: the publication of this book catapulted Locke overnight to what we would now think of as international superstardom.

These three were his most important works, but Locke—by now one of the most famous men in England—continued to write and publish until his death fifteen years later. He wrote, for example, works on the proper control of the currency for the English government; *Some Thoughts Concerning Education* (which, apparently, was historically important in shaping the toilet-training practices of the English educated classes); a work on the proper care and cultivation of fruit trees; and a careful commentary on the *Epistles* of St. Paul. He died quietly, reading in his study, in October 1704.

What Was Locke's Overall Philosophical Project?

Locke is the leading proponent of a school of philosophy now often called "British empiricism." Some of the central platforms of this doctrine are as follows: First, human beings are born like a blank, white sheet of paper—a *tabula rasa*—without any innate knowledge but with certain natural powers, and we use these powers to adapt ourselves to the social and physical environment into which we are born. Two especially important natural powers are the capacity for conscious sense experience and for feeling pleasure and pain, and it is from the interaction of these capacities with the environment that we acquire all of our ideas, knowledge, and habits of mind. All meaningful language must be connected to the ideas that we thus acquire, and the abuse of language to talk about things of which we have no idea is a serious source of intellectual errors—errors that can have harmful consequences for social and moral life, as well as the growth of the sciences. British empiricism—whose other main exponents were Thomas Hobbes (1588–1679), George Berkeley (1685–1753), and David Hume (1711–1776)—was generally opposed to religious fervor and sectarian strife, and cautious about the human capacity for attaining absolute knowledge about things that go beyond immediate experience.

An Essay Concerning Human Understanding is Locke's attempt to present a systematic and detailed empiricist account of the human mind and human knowledge. It also includes an account of the nature of language, and touches on philosophical issues to do with logic, religion, metaphysics, and ethics. Locke was also consciously interested in defending a certain modern way of thinking against the habits of the past: instead of relatively uncritical and conservative acceptance of Greek and Roman history, literature and philosophy, and of Christian theology, Locke defended independent thought, secular values, and the power of modern ideas and social change to produce useful results.

Locke was optimistic about the power and accuracy of his own theory of human understanding—and thus about the powers of human beings to come to know the world—but he nevertheless thought it was a *limited* power. There are some things human beings just cannot ever come to know with certainty, Locke thought, and we should be humble in our attempts to describe reality. Thus, there are some domains in which, according to Locke, our human capacities are sufficient to produce certain knowledge: mathematics, morality, the existence of God, and the existence of things in the world corresponding to our 'simple ideas' (i.e., roughly, the things we perceive). However, there are other areas where the best we can do is to make skillful guesses: these more difficult questions

have to do with the underlying nature and workings of nature—that is, with scientific theory—and with the details of religious doctrine. God has given us the capacity to effectively get by in the world by making these careful guesses, according to Locke, but he has not given us the capacity to ever know for sure whether our guesses are correct or not. (This is one reason why Locke believed we should be tolerant of other people's religious beliefs.)

What Is the Structure of This Reading?

An Essay Concerning Human Understanding is split into four Books, each of which is further divided into chapters, which in turn are divided into sections. The first Book is primarily an attack on the notion, which Locke found especially in Descartes, that human beings are born with certain "innate ideas"—concepts and knowledge which are not the product of experience but which are, perhaps, implanted in us by God. Book II develops Locke's alternative empiricist theory of ideas: here he describes the different sorts of ideas human beings have (such as our ideas of external objects, space, time, number, cause and effect, and so on), and tries to show how these ideas all derive ultimately from reflection on our own sense-experience. In Book III Locke describes the workings of language, and in particular defends the thesis that all meaningful language derives that meaning from its connections to our ideas. Finally, Book IV is where Locke considers the question of human knowledge and asks how much justification there is for our beliefs about God and nature, concluding that, although limited, the scope of our knowledge is more than enough for practical purposes.

The first two selections collected here come from Book II (and so are about ideas), and the third from Book IV (and so is about knowledge). The first selection asks how much our ideas resemble those things in the world that cause them and, among other things, describes and defends an important distinction between "primary" and "secondary" qualities. The second extract deals with the topic of "substance," the 'stuff' of the material world. The third approaches head-on the issue of the extent and limits of our knowledge of the external world.

Some Useful Background Information

1. Locke writes in a very straightforward and clear style—he deliberately set out to write informally, for a general educated readership—but his language is the English of the seventeenth century and some readers might find this a little distracting. Here is a short glossary of the words which might be either unfamiliar or used in an unfamiliar way.

   Admit of: accept

   Apprehension: understanding, perception

   Bare/barely: mere/merely

   Corpuscles: small particles

   Denominate: apply a name to something

   Doth: does

   Evidences: shows

   Experiment: experience

   Extravagant: odd, peculiar

   Fain: gladly, happily

   Figure: shape

   Hath: has

   Impulse: causal impact

   Manna: the sweet dried juice of the Mediterranean ash tree and other plants, which can be used as a mild laxative (also, a substance miraculously supplied as food to the Israelites in the wilderness, according to the Bible)

   Peculiar: particular, specific

   Sensible/insensible: able to be sensed/invisible to the senses

   Superficies: outside surfaces

   V.g.: for example

   Viz.: in other words, that is

   Without: outside (us)

2. Locke's notion of an *idea* is central to his philosophy—which is even sometimes called "the way of ideas"—and he uses the word in his own special and carefully worked out way. For Locke, ideas are not activities of the mind but instead are the *contents* of the mind—they are the things we think about, the objects of our thought. (In fact, for Locke, thought consists entirely in the succession of ideas through consciousness.) Thus, for example, the things we believe, know, remember, or imagine are what Locke would call ideas.

As the term suggests, Locke probably assumes ideas are mental entities—they are things that exist in our minds rather than in the external world. Certainly, there are no ideas floating around that are not part of someone's consciousness; every idea is necessarily the object of some act of thinking. Furthermore, ideas are the *only* things we directly think about—our thought and our mental experience, for Locke, is internally rather than externally directed: it is an experience of our ideas and the operations of our mind, not directly of the world. When Locke uses the word "perception," for example, he often means the mind's perception (awareness) of its own ideas, not, as we would usually mean, perception of objects outside our own minds.

However, this is not to say that we don't think about or perceive the external world; Locke commonsensically thought that we saw trees, tasted oranges, heard the speech of other human beings, and so on. But it does mean that all our thought and perception is mediated by ideas, which intervene between us and external reality. The ideas we have before our minds are the "immediate objects of perception," and the things those ideas represent are the "indirect objects of perception." Yet it is important to remember that, for Locke, ideas *do* naturally and evidently represent things beyond themselves (although not necessarily the whole, or even the most important aspects, of the nature of those things)—Locke does not believe for a moment that we are locked inside our own heads.

Locke distinguishes between lots of different types of ideas, but one especially important contrast is between simple and complex ideas. A simple idea is "nothing but one uniform appearance, or conception in the mind, and is not distinguishable into different ideas," whereas complex ideas are compounded out of more than one simple idea. For example, redness is a simple idea, while the idea of a London double-decker bus is a complex idea. For Locke, all simple ideas are acquired from experience, either through sense perception or through the perception of our own thoughts (often called "introspection"): we are not free to simply invent or ignore such ideas, as they are physically caused by the things they represent. However, we are free to construct complex ideas out of this raw material as we like, and we can do so in various ways: we can add simple ideas together into a single idea (e.g., the idea of a horse), or we can compare two ideas and perceive the relation that holds between them (e.g., the idea of being taller than), or we can generalize about simple ideas to form abstract ideas (e.g., the idea of time or infinity).

3. Locke held the modern (at the time) "corpuscular" theory of matter, which was developed by Pierre Gassendi (1592–1655) and Robert Boyle (1627–1691) and which, though a "mechanical philosophy," contradicted some important elements of Descartes' physical theory. As a corpuscularian, Locke thought that the physical world was made up of tiny indestructible particles, invisible to the human eye, moving around in empty space, and having only the following properties: solidity, extension in three dimensions, shape (or "figure"), motion or rest, number, location ("situation"), volume ("bulk"), and texture. All the phenomena of the material world are built out of or caused by these particles and their properties and powers. Thus, collections of particles big enough to be visible have certain properties (which Locke called "qualities"), e.g., the shape and size of a gold nugget, its color, malleability, luster, chemical inertness, and so on. Our perception of the world—that is to say, our experience of these qualities—is brought about by invisible streams of tiny particles emanating from the objects in our environment and striking our sense-receptors (our eyes, ears, skin, and so on). Locke and his contemporaries thought this stimulation of our senses causes complex reactions in our "animal spirits," and this is what gives rise to our ideas. Animal spirits were supposed to be a fine fluid (itself made up of tiny particles) flowing through our nervous system and carrying signals from one place to another—ultimately to our brain.

Some Common Misconceptions

1. In reading Locke, it is important not to confuse ideas with qualities. Ideas are mental entities; they constitute our *experience* of the world. Qualities are non-mental attributes of chunks of matter in the world; they are the things ideas are *about*. Thus, in Locke's view, our idea of color should not be confused with the property of color itself. The distinction between primary and secondary qualities, then, is mainly a distinction between types of physical property (though it does have implications for the taxonomy of our ideas).

2. The secondary qualities do not only include colors, tastes, smells, sounds, and feels; they also include properties like solubility, brittleness, flammability, being nutritious, being a painkiller, and so on.

3. It is sometimes thought Locke argued that secondary qualities do not really exist, and that color, smell, taste, and so on are only ideas in our mind. But this is not so. Locke does think that material objects in the world really have secondary qualities, but he argues that we have misunderstood the *nature* of these qualities in a particular way.

4. In thinking about the nature of the secondary qualities it is helpful to consider the nature of their connection with our ideas of them. In this context, two concepts are useful but are sometimes confused with each other. The first notion is that of *perceiver-relativity*: this is the idea that how something *seems* depends on who is perceiving it. To say that "beauty is in the eye of the beholder" is to make a claim about perceiver-relativity; more interestingly, being poisonous is an example of a perceiver-relative property, since substances that are poisonous to one kind of perceiver might not be poisonous to others (e.g., chemicals called avermectins are lethal to many invertebrates but harmless to mammals). The second, different, notion is of *perceiver-dependence*: this is the idea that the very existence of something depends upon be-

ing perceived or thought about. An example of this would be a conscious visual image—there can be no such thing as a conscious image that is not in anybody's consciousness, and so mental images must be mind-dependent.

5. In the third selection below, when Locke is writing about substance, his main topic is the *idea* of substance, not substance itself. That is, he does not ask (directly) whether substance really exists; instead, his question is, do we have an idea of substance? And whatever his conclusions about the idea of substance, Locke denied being skeptical about the actual existence of substance.

How Important and Influential Is This Passage?

"The *Essay* has long been recognized as one of the great works of English literature of the seventeenth century, and one of the epoch-making works in the history of philosophy. It has been one of the most repeatedly reprinted, widely disseminated and read, and profoundly influential books of the past three centuries." So writes Peter Nidditch, an expert on Locke's philosophy. Locke's *Essay* is often credited with being the most thorough and plausible formulation and defense of empiricism ever written, and it has exercised a huge influence on, especially, English-speaking philosophers right up until the present day (though with a period in the philosophical wilderness during the 1800s). In the eighteenth century Locke was widely considered as important for philosophy, and what we would today call psychology, as Newton was for physics.

Although the distinction between primary and secondary qualities was certainly not invented by Locke, his account of it was very influential and was taken as the standard line in subsequent discussions of this important idea. Furthermore, the problem Locke raised about the coherence of our idea of material substance has been an important metaphysical problem since he formulated it, and was an important motivator for Berkeley's idealism (which we consider in the next section).

Suggestions for Critical Reflection

1. It is relatively easy to see roughly how Locke's distinction between primary and secondary qualities is supposed to go, but harder to see what Locke's *argument* for this distinction is. Do you think Locke backs up his claims with arguments? If so, how strong do you think they are? In the end, how plausible is the primary/secondary quality distinction?

2. Similarly, while it is relatively easy to see roughly how Locke's distinction between primary and secondary qualities is supposed to go, it is harder to see *precisely* how the distinction works. For example, what might Locke mean by saying that our ideas of primary qualities resemble their causes while our ideas of secondary qualities do not? Does this really make any sense? If it doesn't, then what other criterion should we use to help us make the distinction?

3. There has recently been some controversy about Locke's position on substance. The traditional view is that Locke defended substance, but was wrong to do so since his own arguments had effectively shown that we could have no such idea. The notion of substance in question here is that of a "bare particular" or "substratum"—that which underlies properties, as opposed to any of the properties themselves. A more recent interpretation holds that Locke did indeed defend some notion of substance, but one which is more defensible. This is the idea of substance as the "real essence" of something: roughly, for Locke, something's real essence is supposed to be the (unknown) set of properties that forms the causal basis for the observable properties of that thing (just as the atomic structure of gold is responsible for its color, softness, shininess, and so on). Which of these two conceptions of substance do you find the more plausible? (Can you see why philosophers have typically found the notion of a substratum difficult to make sense of?) Which of these notions of substance do you think fits better with what Locke actually says? Do you perhaps prefer a third interpretation?

4. What do you make of Locke's response to skepticism about the existence of the external world? Does it convince you? Do you find plausible the way Locke carefully divides up different types of knowledge about the external world and gives different answers for them?

5. What kind of entity might a Lockean idea be? What, if anything, is it made of? How determinate must it be? For example, if I clearly perceive the idea of a speckled hen, must we say that I perceive (have the idea of) a particular number of speckles, say 12,372? If not, does that mean the idea does not *have* a determinate number of speckles (even though it's a perfectly clear idea and not blurry at all)? What kind of object could *that* be? Some recent commentators, such as John Yolton, have tried to defend Locke from these kinds of puzzles by suggesting that Locke never meant ideas to be mental *things* at all: what, then, could they be instead?

6. How could an idea, in Locke's sense, really be *caused* by material objects in the external world? What could the last few steps of this causal chain be like?

7. If ideas are the objects of our thought—the things we "perceive" in thought—then what is it that does the perceiving, do you think? Can we distinguish it from the succession of ideas?

Suggestions for Further Reading

The standard edition of Locke's *An Essay Concerning Human Understanding* is edited by Peter H. Nidditch and was published by Oxford University Press in 1975. Several abridgements are also available, such as one by John Yolton in the Everyman Classics series. The standard biography of Locke is Maurice Cranston's *John Locke: A Biography* (Oxford University Press, 1985), though it is now a little out of date. Two good recent collections of essays about Locke are *Locke* (Oxford University Press, 1998) and *A Cambridge Companion to Locke* (Cambridge University Press, 1994), both edited by Vere Chappell. Finally, here are a few useful books on Locke: Michael Ayers, *Locke: Epistemology and Ontology* (Routledge, 1991); Nicholas Jolley, *Locke: His Philosophical Thought* (Oxford University

Press, 1999); J.L. Mackie, *Problems from Locke*, (Oxford University Press, 1976); and John Yolton, *Locke: An Introduction* (Blackwell, 1985).

from *An Essay Concerning Human Understanding*[1]

Book II, Chapter VIII: Some Farther Considerations Concerning Our Simple Ideas.

§1. Concerning the simple ideas of Sensation, it is to be considered, that whatsoever is so constituted in nature as to be able, by affecting our senses, to cause any perception in the mind, doth thereby produce in the understanding a simple idea, which, whatever be the external cause of it, when it comes to be taken notice of by our discerning faculty, it is by the mind looked on and considered there to be a real positive idea in the understanding, as much as any other whatsoever; though, perhaps, the cause of it be but a privation[2] of the subject.

§2. Thus the ideas of heat and cold, light and darkness, white and black, motion and rest, are equally clear and positive ideas in the mind, though, perhaps, some of the causes which produce them are barely privations in subjects, from whence our senses derive those ideas. These the understanding, in its view of them, considers all as distinct positive ideas, without taking notice of the causes that produce them; which is an inquiry not belonging to the idea, as it is in the understanding, but to the nature of the things existing without us. These are two very different things, and carefully to be distinguished; it being one thing to perceive and know the idea of white or black, and quite another to examine what kind of particles they must be, and how ranged in the superficies, to make any object appear white or black.

---

1   Locke's *An Essay Concerning Human Understanding* was first published in 1690. The excerpts given here are from the sixth edition of 1710, reprinted from Locke's ten-volume *Collected Works* (first published in 1714 and reprinted with corrections in 1823).

2   A privation is a loss or absence of something.

§3. A painter or dyer, who never inquired into their causes, hath the ideas of white and black, and other colours, as clearly, perfectly, and distinctly in his understanding, and perhaps more distinctly, than the philosopher, who hath busied himself in considering their natures, and thinks he knows how far either of them is in its cause positive or privative; and the idea of black is no less positive in his mind than that of white, however the cause of that colour in the external object may be only a privation.

§4. If it were the design of my present undertaking to inquire into the natural causes and manner of perception, I should offer this as a reason why a privative cause might, in some cases at least, produce a positive idea, viz. that all sensation being produced in us only by different degrees and modes of motion in our animal spirits, variously agitated by external objects, the abatement of any former motion must as necessarily produce a new sensation as the variation or increase of it; and so introduce a new idea, which depends only on a different motion of the animal spirits in that organ.

§5. But whether this be so or not I will not here determine, but appeal to every one's own experience, whether the shadow of a man, though it consists of nothing but the absence of light (and the more the absence of light is, the more discernible is the shadow) does not, when a man looks on it, cause as clear and positive idea in his mind as a man himself, though covered over with clear sunshine? And the picture of a shadow is a positive thing. Indeed, we have negative names, which stand not directly for positive ideas, but for their absence, such as insipid, silence, nihil, &c. which words denote positive ideas; *v.g.* taste, sound, being, with a signification of their absence.

§6. And thus one may truly be said to see darkness. For supposing a hole perfectly dark, from whence no light is reflected, it is certain one may see the figure of it, or it may be painted; or whether the ink I write with makes any other idea, is a question. The privative causes I have here assigned of positive ideas are according to the common opinion; but, in truth, it will be hard to determine whether there be really any ideas from a privative cause, till it be determined, whether rest be any more a privation than motion.

§7. To discover the nature of our ideas the better, and to discourse of them intelligibly, it will be convenient to distinguish them as they are ideas or perceptions in our minds; and as they are modifications of matter in the bodies that cause such perceptions in us: that so we may not think (as perhaps usually is done) that they are exactly the images and resemblances of something inherent in the subject; most of those of sensation being in the mind no more the likeness of something existing without us, than the names that stand for them are the likeness of our ideas, which yet upon hearing they are apt to excite in us.

§8. Whatsoever the mind perceives in itself, or is the immediate object of perception, thought, or understanding, that I call idea; and the power to produce any idea in our mind, I call quality of the subject wherein that power is. Thus a snow-ball having the power to produce in us the ideas of white, cold, and round, the powers to produce those ideas in us, as they are in the snow-ball, I call qualities; and as they are sensations or perceptions in our understandings, I call them ideas; which ideas, if I speak of sometimes as in the things themselves, I would be understood to mean those qualities in the objects which produce them in us.

§9. Qualities thus considered in bodies are, first, such as are utterly inseparable from the body, in what state soever it be; such as in all the alterations and changes it suffers, all the force can be used upon it, it constantly keeps; and such as sense constantly finds in every particle of matter which has bulk enough to be perceived; and the mind finds inseparable from every particle of matter, though less than to make itself singly be perceived by our senses: *v.g.* take a grain of wheat, divide it into two parts; each part has still solidity, extension, figure, and mobility; divide it again, and it retains still the same qualities, and so divide it on, till the parts become insensible, they must retain still each of them all those qualities. For division (which is all that a mill, or pestle, or any other body, does upon another, in reducing it to insensible parts) can never take away either solidity, extension, figure, or mobility from any body, but only makes two or more distinct separate masses of matter, of that which was but one before; all which distinct masses, reckoned as so many distinct bodies, after division make a certain number. These I call original or primary qualities of body, which I think we may observe to produce simple ideas in us, viz. solidity, extension, figure, motion or rest, and number.

§10. Secondly, such qualities which in truth are nothing in the objects themselves, but powers to produce various sensations in us by their primary qualities, i.e., by the bulk, figure, texture, and motion of their insensible parts, as colours, sounds, tastes, &c. these I call secondary qualities. To these might be added a third sort, which are allowed to be barely powers; though they are as much real qualities in the subject as those which I, to comply with the common way of speaking, call qualities, but for distinction, secondary qualities. For the power in fire to produce a new colour, or consistency, in wax or clay, by its primary qualities, is as much a quality in fire, as the power it has to produce in me a new idea or sensation of warmth or burning, which I felt not before, by the same primary qualities, viz. the bulk, texture, and motion of its insensible parts.

§11. The next thing to be considered is, how bodies produce ideas in us; and that is manifestly by impulse, the only way which we can conceive bodies to operate in.

§12. If then external objects be not united to our minds, when they produce ideas therein, and yet we perceive these original qualities in such of them as singly fall under our senses, it is evident that some motion must be thence continued by our nerves, or animal spirits, by some parts of our bodies, to the brains or the seat of sensation, there to produce in our minds the particular ideas we have of them. And since the extension, figure, number, and motion of bodies, of an observable bigness, may be perceived at a distance by the sight, it is evident some singly imperceptible bodies must come from them to the eyes, and thereby convey to the brain some motion, which produces these ideas which we have of them in us.

§13. After the same manner, that the ideas of these original qualities are produced in us, we may conceive that the ideas of secondary qualities are also produced, viz. by the operation of insensible particles on our senses. For it being manifest that there are bodies, and good store of bodies, each whereof are so small that we cannot, by any of our senses, discover either their

bulk, figure, or motion, as is evident in the particles of the air and water, and others extremely smaller than those; perhaps as much smaller than the particles of air and water as the particles of air and water are smaller than peas or hail-stones: let us suppose at present, that the different motions and figures, bulk and number of such particles, affecting the several organs of our senses, produce in us those different sensations, which we have from the colours and smells of bodies; *v.g.* that a violet, by the impulse of such insensible particles of matter of peculiar figures and bulks, and in different degrees and modifications of their motions, causes the ideas of the blue colour and sweet scent of that flower to be produced in our minds, it being no more impossible to conceive that God should annex such ideas to such motions, with which they have no similitude, than that he should annex the idea of pain to the motion of a piece of steel dividing our flesh, with which that idea hath no resemblance.

§14. What I have said concerning colours and smells may be understood also of tastes and sounds, and other the like sensible qualities; which, whatever reality we by mistake attribute to them, are in truth nothing in the objects themselves, but powers to produce various sensations in us, and depend on those primary qualities, viz. bulk, figure, texture, and motion of parts as I have said.

§15. From whence I think it easy to draw this observation, that the ideas of primary qualities of bodies are resemblances of them, and their patterns do really exist in the bodies themselves, but the ideas produced in us by these secondary qualities have no resemblance of them at all. There is nothing like our ideas, existing in the bodies themselves. They are, in the bodies we denominate from them, only a power to produce those sensations in us; and what is sweet, blue, or warm in idea, is but the certain bulk, figure, and motion of the insensible parts, in the bodies themselves, which we call so.

§16. Flame is denominated hot and light; snow white and cold; and manna white and sweet, from the ideas they produce in us: which qualities are commonly thought to be the same in those bodies that those ideas are in us, the one the perfect resemblance of the other, as they are in a mirror; and it would by most men be judged very extravagant if one should say otherwise. And yet he that will consider that the same fire, that at one distance produces in us the sensation of warmth, does at a nearer approach produce in us the far different sensation of pain, ought to bethink himself what reason he has to say, that his idea of warmth, which was produced in him by the fire, is actually in the fire; and his idea of pain, which the same fire produced in him the same way, is not in the fire. Why are whiteness and coldness in snow, and pain not, when it produces the one and the other idea in us, and can do neither but by the bulk, figure, number, and motion of its solid parts?

§17. The particular bulk, number, figure, and motion of the parts of fire, or snow, are really in them, whether any one's senses perceive them or no; and therefore they may be called real qualities, because they really exist in those bodies: but light, heat, whiteness, or coldness, are no more really in them than sickness or pain is in manna. Take away the sensation of them; let not the eyes see light or colours, nor the ears hear sounds; let the palate not taste, nor the nose smell; and all colours, tastes, odours, and sounds, as they are such particular ideas, vanish and cease, and are reduced to their causes, i.e., bulk, figure, and motion of parts.

§18. A piece of manna of a sensible bulk is able to produce in us the idea of a round or square figure, and, by being removed from one place to another, the idea of motion. This idea of motion represents it as it really is in manna moving: a circle or square are the same, whether in idea or existence, in the mind or in the manna; and this, both motion and figure, are really in the manna, whether we take notice of them or no: this every body is ready to agree to. Besides, manna, by the bulk, figure, texture, and motion of its parts, has a power to produce the sensations of sickness, and sometimes of acute pains or gripings in us. That these ideas of sickness and pain are not in the manna, but effects of its operations on us, and are nowhere when we feel them not: this also every one readily agrees to. And yet men are hardly to be brought to think, that sweetness and whiteness are not really in manna; which are but the effects of the operations of manna, by the motion, size, and figure of its particles on the eyes and palate; as the pain and sickness caused by manna are confessedly nothing but the effects of its

operations on the stomach and guts, by the size, motion, and figure of its insensible parts, (for by nothing else can a body operate, as has been proved); as if it could not operate on the eyes and palate, and thereby produce in the mind particular distinct ideas, which in itself it has not, as well as we allow it can operate on the guts and stomach, and thereby produce distinct ideas, which in itself it has not. These ideas being all effects of the operations of manna, on several parts of our bodies, by the size, figure, number, and motion of its parts; why those produced by the eyes and palate should rather be thought to be really in the manna than those produced by the stomach and guts; or why the pain and sickness, ideas that are the effect of manna, should be thought to be nowhere when they are not felt: and yet the sweetness and whiteness, effects of the same manna on other parts of the body, by ways equally as unknown, should be thought to exist in the manna, when they are not seen or tasted, would need some reason to explain.

§19. Let us consider the red and white colours in porphyry:[3] hinder light from striking on it, and its colours vanish, it no longer produces any such ideas in us; upon the return of light it produces these appearances on us again. Can any one think any real alterations are made in the porphyry by the presence or absence of light; and that those ideas of whiteness and redness are really in porphyry in the light, when it is plain it has no colour in the dark? It has, indeed, such a configuration of particles, both night and day, as are apt, by the rays of light rebounding from some parts of that hard stone, to produce in us the idea of redness, and from others the idea of whiteness; but whiteness or redness are not in it at any time, but such a texture that hath the power to produce such a sensation in us.

§20. Pound an almond, and the clear white colour will be altered into a dirty one, and the sweet taste into an oily one. What real alteration can the beating of the pestle make in any body, but an alteration of the texture of it?

§21. Ideas being thus distinguished and understood, we may be able to give an account how the same water, at the same time, may produce the idea of

---

3   A hard red rock filled with large red or white crystals.

cold by one hand and of heat by the other; whereas it is impossible that the same water, if those ideas were really in it, should at the same time be both hot and cold: for if we imagine warmth, as it is in our hands, to be nothing but a certain sort and degree of motion in the minute particles of our nerves or animal spirits, we may understand how it is possible that the same water may, at the same time, produce the sensations of heat in one hand, and cold in the other; which yet figure never does, that never producing the idea of a square by one hand, which has produced the idea of a globe by another. But if the sensation of heat and cold be nothing but the increase or diminution of the motion of the minute parts of our bodies, caused by the corpuscles of any other body, it is easy to be understood, that if that motion be greater in one hand than in the other; if a body be applied to the two hands, which has in its minute particles a greater motion, than in those of one of the hands, and a less than in those of the other; it will increase the motion of the one hand and lessen it in the other, and so cause the different sensations of heat and cold that depend thereon.

§22. I have in what just goes before been engaged in physical inquiries a little further than perhaps I intended. But it being necessary to make the nature of sensation a little understood, and to make the difference between the qualities in bodies, and the ideas produced by them in the mind, to be distinctly conceived, without which it were impossible to discourse intelligibly of them, I hope I shall be pardoned this little excursion into natural philosophy, it being necessary in our present inquiry to distinguish the primary and real qualities of bodies, which are always in them (viz. solidity, extension, figure, number, and motion, or rest; and are sometimes perceived by us, viz. when the bodies they are in are big enough singly to be discerned), from those secondary and imputed qualities, which are but the powers of several combinations of those primary ones, when they operate, without being distinctly discerned; whereby we may also come to know what ideas are, and what are not, resemblances of something really existing in the bodies we denominate from them.

§23. The qualities, then, that are in bodies, rightly considered, are of three sorts. First, The bulk, figure, number, situation, and motion, or rest of their solid parts; those are in them, whether we perceive them or no; and when they are of that size that we can discover them, we have by these an idea of the thing, as it is in itself, as is plain in artificial things. These I call primary qualities.

Secondly, The power that is in any body, by reason of its insensible primary qualities, to operate after a peculiar manner on any of our senses, and thereby produce in us the different ideas of several colours, sounds, smells, tastes, &c. These are usually called sensible qualities.

Thirdly, The power that is in any body, by reason of the particular constitution of its primary qualities, to make such a change in the bulk, figure, texture, and motion of another body, as to make it operate on our senses, differently from what it did before. Thus the sun has a power to make wax white, and fire to make lead fluid. These are usually called powers.

The first of these, as has been said, I think may be properly called real, original, or primary qualities; because they are in the things themselves, whether they are perceived or no; and upon their different modifications it is that the secondary qualities depend.

The other two are only powers to act differently upon other things, which powers result from the different modifications of those primary qualities.

§24. But, though the two latter sorts of qualities are powers barely, and nothing but powers, relating to several other bodies, and resulting from the different modifications of the original qualities, yet they are generally otherwise thought of: for the second sort, viz. the powers to produce several ideas in us by our senses, are looked upon as real qualities in the things thus affecting us; but the third sort are called and esteemed barely powers, v.g. the idea of heat, or light, which we receive by our eyes or touch from the sun, are commonly thought real qualities, existing in the sun, and something more than mere powers in it. But when we consider the sun in reference to wax, which it melts or blanches, we look on the whiteness and softness produced in the wax, not as qualities in the sun, but effects produced by powers in it: whereas, if rightly considered, these qualities of light and warmth, which are perceptions in me when I am warmed or enlightened by the sun, are no otherwise in the sun, than the changes made in the wax, when it is blanched or melted, are in the sun. They are all of them equally powers in the sun, depending on its primary qualities; whereby it is able, in the one case, so to alter the bulk, figure, texture, or motion of some of the insensible parts of my eyes or hands, as thereby to produce in me the idea of light or heat; and in the other, it is able so to alter the bulk, figure, texture, or motion of the insensible parts of the wax, as to make them fit to produce in me the distinct ideas of white and fluid.

§25. The reason why the one are ordinarily taken for real qualities, and the other only for bare powers, seems to be, because the ideas we have of distinct colours, sounds, &c., containing nothing at all in them of bulk, figure, or motion, we are not apt to think them the effects of these primary qualities, which appear not, to our senses, to operate in their production, and with which they have not any apparent congruity or conceivable connection. Hence it is that we are so forward to imagine, that those ideas are the resemblances of something really existing in the objects themselves: since sensation discovers nothing of bulk, figure, or motion of parts in their production; nor can reason show how bodies, by their bulk, figure, and motion, should produce in the mind the ideas of blue or yellow, &c. But, in the other case, in the operations of bodies changing the qualities one of another, we plainly discover, that the quality produced hath commonly no resemblance with anything in the thing producing it; wherefore we look on it as a bare effect of power. For, through receiving the idea of heat or light from the sun, we are apt to think it is a perception and resemblance of such a quality in the sun; yet when we see wax, or a fair face, receive change of colour from the sun, we cannot imagine that to be the reception or resemblance of anything in the sun, because we find not those different colours in the sun itself. For our senses being able to observe a likeness or unlikeness of sensible qualities in two different external objects, we forwardly enough conclude the production of any sensible quality in any subject to be an effect of bare power, and not the communication of any quality, which was really in the efficient, when we find no such sensible quality in the thing that produced it. But our senses not being able to discover any unlikeness between the idea produced in us, and the quality of the object producing it, we are apt to imagine, that our ideas are resemblances of something in the objects, and not the effects of certain powers placed in the modification of their primary qualities, with which primary qualities the ideas produced in us have no resemblance.

§26. To conclude, beside those before-mentioned primary qualities in bodies, viz. bulk, figure, extension, number, and motion of their solid parts; all the rest whereby we take notice of bodies, and distinguish them one from another, are nothing else but several powers in them, depending on those primary qualities; whereby they are fitted, either by immediately operating on our bodies to produce several different ideas in us; or else, by operating on other bodies, so to change their primary qualities, as to render them capable of producing ideas in us different from what before they did. The former of these, I think, may be called secondary qualities, immediately perceivable: the latter, secondary qualities, mediately perceivable.

Book II, Chapter XXIII: Of Our Complex Ideas of Substances [§§1–6].

§1. The mind being, as I have declared, furnished with a great number of the simple ideas, conveyed in by the senses, as they are found in exterior things, or by reflection on its own operations, takes notice also, that a certain number of these simple ideas go constantly together; which being presumed to belong to one thing, and words being suited to common apprehensions, and made use of for quick dispatch, are called, so united in one subject, by one name; which, by inadvertency, we are apt afterward to talk of and consider as one simple idea, which indeed is a complication of many ideas together; because, as I have said, not imagining how these simple ideas can subsist by themselves, we accustom ourselves to suppose some substratum wherein they do subsist, and from which they do result; which therefore we call substance.

§2. So that if any one will examine himself concerning his notion of pure substance in general, he will find he has no other idea of it at all, but only a supposition of he knows not what support of such qualities, which are capable of producing simple ideas in us; which qualities are commonly called accidents. If any one should be asked, what is the subject wherein colour or weight inheres, he would have nothing to say, but the solid extended parts: and if he were demanded, what is it that solidity and extension adhere in, he would not be in a much better case than the Indian[4] before mentioned who, saying that the world was supported by a great elephant, was asked what the elephant rested on; to which his answer was a great tortoise. But being again pressed to know what gave support to the broad-backed tortoise, replied, something, he knew not what. And thus here, as in all other cases where we use words without having clear and distinct ideas, we talk like children; who, being questioned what such a thing is, which they know not, readily give this satisfactory answer, that it is something: which in truth signifies no more, when so used, either by children or men, but that they know not what; and that the thing they pretend to know, and talk of, is what they have no distinct idea of at all, and so are perfectly ignorant of it, and in the dark. The idea then we have, to which we give the general name substance, being nothing but the supposed, but unknown support of those qualities we find existing, which we imagine cannot subsist, "*sine re substante*," without something to support them, we call that support *substantia*; which, according to the true import of the word, is, in plain English, standing under or upholding.

§3. An obscure and relative idea of substance in general being thus made, we come to have the ideas of particular sorts of substances, by collecting such combinations of simple ideas as are, by experience and observation of men's senses taken notice of to exist together, and are therefore supposed to flow from the particular internal constitution, or unknown essence of that substance. Thus we come to have the ideas of a man, horse, gold, water, &c. of which substances, whether any one has any other clear idea, farther than of certain simple ideas co-existent together, I appeal to every one's own experience. It is the ordinary qualities observable in iron, or a diamond, put together, that make the true complex idea of those substances, which a smith or a jeweller commonly knows better than a philosopher; who, whatever substantial forms he may talk of, has no other idea of those substances, than what is framed by a collection of those simple ideas which are to be found in them: only we must take notice, that our complex ideas of substances, besides all those simple ideas they are made up of, have always the confused idea of something to which they belong, and in which they subsist. And therefore when we speak of any sort of substance, we say it is a thing having such or such qualities; as body is a thing that is extended, figured, and capable of motion; spirit, a thing capable of thinking; and so hardness, friability,[5] and power to draw iron, we say, are qualities to be found in a loadstone.[6] These, and the like fashions of speaking, intimate, that the substance is supposed always something besides the extension, figure, solidity, motion, thinking, or other observable ideas, though we know not what it is.

§4. Hence, when we talk or think of any particular sort of corporeal substances, as horse, stone, &c., though the idea we have of either of them be but the complication or collection of those several simple ideas of sensible qualities, which we used to find united in the thing called horse or stone; yet, because we cannot conceive how they should subsist alone, nor one in another, we suppose them existing in and supported by some common subject; which support we denote by the name substance, though it be certain we have no clear or distinct idea of that thing we suppose a support.

§5. The same thing happens concerning the operations of the mind, viz. thinking, reasoning, fearing, &c., which we concluding not to subsist of themselves, nor apprehending how they can belong to body, or be produced by it, we are apt to think these the actions of some other substance, which we call spirit: whereby yet it is evident, that having no other idea or notion of matter, but something wherein those many sensible qualities which affect our senses do subsist; by supposing a substance wherein thinking, knowing, doubting, and a power of moving, &c. do subsist, we have as clear a notion of the substance of spirit, as we have of body; the one being supposed

---

4   A person from the subcontinent of India (rather than a native of North America).

5   Brittleness, crumbliness.

6   A piece of magnetite (iron oxide) that has magnetic properties.

to be (without knowing what it is) the substratum to those simple ideas we have from without; and the other supposed (with a like ignorance of what it is) to be the substratum to those operations we experiment in ourselves within. It is plain then, that the idea of corporeal substance in matter is as remote from our conceptions and apprehensions, as that of spiritual substance, or spirit: and therefore, from our not having any notion of the substance of spirit, we can no more conclude its non-existence, than we can for the same reason deny the existence of body; it being as rational to affirm there is no body, because we have no clear and distinct idea of the substance of matter, as to say there is no spirit, because we have no clear and distinct idea of the substance of a spirit.

§6. Whatever therefore be the secret, abstract nature of substance in general, all the ideas we have of particular distinct sorts of substances are nothing but several combinations of simple ideas co-existing in such, though unknown, cause of their union, as make the whole subsist of itself. It is by such combinations of simple ideas, and nothing else, that we represent particular sorts of substances to ourselves; such are the ideas we have of their several species in our minds; and such only do we, by their specific names, signify to others, *v.g.* man, horse, sun, water, iron: upon hearing which words, every one who understands the language, frames in his mind a combination of those several simple ideas, which he has usually observed, or fancied to exist together under that denomination; all which he supposes to rest in, and be as it were, adherent to that unknown common subject, which inheres not in anything else. Though, in the mean time it be manifest, and every one upon inquiry into his own thoughts will find, that he has no other idea of any substance, *v.g.* let it be gold, horse, iron, man, vitriol,[7] bread, but what he has barely of those sensible qualities, which he supposes to inhere, with a supposition of such a substratum, as gives, as it were, a support to those qualities or simple ideas, which he has observed to exist united together. Thus the idea of the sun, what is it but an aggregate of those several simple ideas, bright, hot, roundish, having a constant regular motion, at a certain distance from us, and perhaps some

other? As he who thinks and discourses of the sun has been more or less accurate in observing those sensible qualities, ideas, or properties, which are in that thing which he calls the sun.

Book IV, Chapter XI: Of Our Knowledge of the Existence of Other Things.

§1. The knowledge of our own being we have by intuition. The existence of a God, reason clearly makes known to us, as has been shown.[8]

The knowledge of the existence of any other thing we can have only by sensation: for there being no necessary connection of real existence with any idea a man hath in his memory, nor of any other existence but that of God, with the existence of any particular man; no particular man can know the existence of any other being, but only when, by actual operating upon him, it makes itself perceived by him. For, the having the idea of anything in our mind no more proves the existence of that thing, than the picture of a man evidences his being in the world, or the visions of a dream make thereby a true history.

§2. It is therefore the actual receiving of ideas from without, that gives us notice of the existence of other things, and makes us know that something doth exist at that time without us, which causes that idea in us, though perhaps we neither know nor consider how it does it: for it takes not from the certainty of our senses, and the ideas we receive by them, that we know not the manner wherein they are produced: *v.g.* whilst I write this, I have, by the paper affecting my eyes, that idea produced in my mind, which, whatever object causes, I call white; by which I know that that quality or accident (i.e., whose appearance before my eyes always causes that idea) doth really exist, and hath a being without me. And of this, the greatest assurance I can possibly have, and to which my faculties can attain, is the testimony of my eyes, which are the proper and sole judges of this thing, whose testimony I have reason to rely on as so certain, that I can no

---

7   Sulphuric acid.

8   These two claims were argued for in his previous two chapters (IX and X). Intuition, for Locke, is roughly direct knowledge—something we can directly see to be true—and is to be contrasted with the indirect knowledge we get from sensation, memory, or reason.

more doubt, whilst I write this, that I see white and black, and that something really exists, that causes that sensation in me, than that I write or move my hand; which is a certainty as great as human nature is capable of, concerning the existence of anything but a man's self alone, and of God.

§3. The notice we have by our senses of the existing of things without us, though it be not altogether so certain as our intuitive knowledge, or the deductions of our reason, employed about the clear abstract ideas of our own minds; yet it is an assurance that deserves the name of knowledge. If we persuade ourselves that our faculties act and inform us right, concerning the existence of those objects that affect them, it cannot pass for an ill-grounded confidence: for I think nobody can, in earnest, be so sceptical as to be uncertain of the existence of those things which he sees and feels. At least, he that can doubt so far (whatever he may have with his own thoughts) will never have any controversy with me; since he can never be sure I say anything contrary to his own opinion. As to myself, I think God has given me assurance enough of the existence of things without me; since by their different application I can produce in myself both pleasure and pain, which is one great concernment of my present state. This is certain, the confidence that our faculties do not herein deceive us, is the greatest assurance we are capable of concerning the existence of material beings. For we cannot act anything, but by our faculties; nor talk of knowledge itself, but by the helps of those faculties, which are fitted to apprehend even what knowledge is. But besides the assurance we have from our senses themselves, that they do not err in the information they give us, of the existence of things without us, when they are affected by them, we are further confirmed in this assurance by other concurrent reasons.

§4. First, it is plain those perceptions are produced in us by exterior causes affecting our senses; because those that want the organs of any sense never can have the ideas belonging to that sense produced in their minds. This is too evident to be doubted: and therefore we cannot but be assured that they come in by the organs of that sense, and no other way. The organs themselves, it is plain, do not produce them; for then the eyes of a man in the dark would produce colours, and his nose smell roses in the winter: but we see nobody gets the relish of a pine-apple till he goes to the Indies, where it is, and tastes it.

§5. Secondly, because sometimes I find that I cannot avoid the having those ideas produced in my mind. For though when my eyes are shut, or windows fast, I can at pleasure recall to my mind the ideas of light, or the sun, which former sensations had lodged in my memory; so I can at pleasure lay by that idea, and take into my view that of the smell of a rose, or taste of sugar. But, if I turn my eyes at noon towards the sun, I cannot avoid the ideas, which the light, or sun, then produces in me. So that there is a manifest difference between the ideas laid up in my memory (over which, if they were there only, I should have constantly the same power to dispose of them, and lay them by at pleasure) and those which force themselves upon me, and I cannot avoid having. And therefore it must needs be some exterior cause, and the brisk acting of some objects without me, whose efficacy I cannot resist, that produces those ideas in my mind, whether I will or no. Besides, there is nobody who doth not perceive the difference in himself between contemplating the sun, as he hath the idea of it in his memory, and actually looking upon it; of which two his perception is so distinct, that few of his ideas are more distinguishable one from another. And therefore he hath certain knowledge, that they are not both memory, or the actions of his mind, and fancies only within him; but that actual seeing hath a cause without.

§6. Thirdly, add to this, that many of those ideas are produced in us with pain, which afterwards we remember without the least offence. Thus, the pain of heat or cold, when the idea of it is revived in our minds, gives us no disturbance; which, when felt, was very troublesome, and is again, when actually repeated; which is occasioned by the disorder the external object causes in our bodies when applied to it. And we remember the pains of hunger, thirst, or the head-ache, without any pain at all; which would either never disturb us, or else constantly do it, as often as we thought of it, were there nothing more but ideas floating in our minds, and appearances entertaining our fancies, without the real existence of things affecting us from abroad. The same may be said of pleasure, accompanying several actual sensations: and though mathematical demonstration depends not upon sense, yet the examining them by diagrams gives great credit to the evidence of our sight, and seems to give it a certainty approaching to that of demonstration itself. For it would be very strange that a man should allow it for an undeniable truth, that two angles of a figure, which he measures by lines and angles of a diagram, should be bigger one than the other; and yet doubt of the existence of those lines and angles, which by looking on he makes use of to measure that by.

§7. Fourthly, our senses in many cases bear witness to the truth of each other's report, concerning the existence of sensible things without us. He that sees a fire may, if he doubt whether it be anything more than a bare fancy, feel it too; and be convinced, by putting his hand in it: which certainly could never be put into such exquisite pain by a bare idea or phantom, unless that the pain be a fancy too; which yet he cannot, when the burn is well, by raising the idea of it, bring upon himself again.

Thus I see, whilst I write this, I can change the appearance of the paper: and by designing the letters, tell beforehand what new idea it shall exhibit the very next moment, by barely drawing my pen over it: which will neither appear (let me fancy as much as I will) if my hands stand still; or though I move my pen, if my eyes be shut: nor, when those characters are once made on the paper, can I choose afterwards but see them as they are; that is, have the ideas of such letters as I have made. Whence it is manifest, that they are not barely the sport and play of my own imagination, when I find that the characters, that were made at the pleasure of my own thought, do not obey them; nor yet cease to be, whenever I shall fancy it; but continue to affect my senses constantly and regularly, according to the figures I made them. To which if we will add, that the sight of those shall, from another man, draw such sounds as I beforehand design they shall stand for; there will be little reason left to doubt that those words I write do really exist without me, when they cause a long series of regular sounds to affect my ears, which could not be the effect of my imagination, nor could my memory retain them in that order.

§8. But yet, if after all this any one will be so sceptical as to distrust his senses, and to affirm that all we see and hear, feel and taste, think and do, dur-

ing our whole being, is but the series and deluding appearances of a long dream, whereof there is no reality; and therefore will question the existence of all things, or our knowledge of any thing; I must desire him to consider, that, if all be a dream, then he doth but dream that he makes the question; and so it is not much matter that a waking man should answer him. But yet, if he pleases, he may dream that I make him this answer, that the certainty of things existing *in rerum natura*,[9] when we have the testimony of our senses for it, is not only as great as our frame can attain to, but as our condition needs. For, our faculties being suited not to the full extent of being, nor to a perfect, clear, comprehensive knowledge of things free from all doubt and scruple; but to the preservation of us, in whom they are, and accommodated to the use of life; they serve to our purpose well enough, if they will but give us certain notice of those things which are convenient or inconvenient to us. For he that sees a candle burning, and hath experimented the force of its flame, by putting his finger in it, will little doubt that this is something existing without him, which does him harm, and puts him to great pain: which is assurance enough, when no man requires greater certainty to govern his actions by than what is as certain as his actions themselves. And if our dreamer pleases to try whether the glowing heat of a glass furnace be barely a wandering imagination in a drowsy man's fancy; by putting his hand into it he may perhaps be wakened into a certainty greater than he could wish, that it is something more than bare imagination. So that this evidence is as great as we can desire, being as certain to us as our pleasure or pain, i.e., happiness or misery; beyond which we have no concernment, either of knowing or being. Such an assurance of the existence of things without us is sufficient to direct us in the attaining the good, and avoiding the evil, which is caused by them; which is the important concernment we have of being made acquainted with them.

§9. In fine, then, when our senses do actually convey into our understandings any idea, we cannot but be satisfied that there doth something at that time really exist without us, which doth affect our senses,

---

9   "In the nature of things," or sometimes, more specifically "in physical reality."

and by them give notice of itself to our apprehensive faculties, and actually produce that idea which we then perceive: and we cannot so far distrust their testimony, as to doubt that such collections of simple ideas as we have observed by our senses to be united together, do really exist together. But this knowledge extends as far as the present testimony of our senses, employed about particular objects that do then affect them, and no further. For if I saw such a collection of simple ideas, as is wont to be called man, existing together one minute since, and am now alone, I cannot be certain that the same man exists now, since there is no necessary connection of his existence a minute since with his existence now: by a thousand ways he may cease to be, since I had the testimony of my senses for his existence. And if I cannot be certain that the man I saw last to-day is now in being, I can less be certain that he is so who hath been longer removed from my senses, and I have not seen since yesterday, or since the last year: and much less can I be certain of the existence of men that I never saw. And, therefore, though it be highly probable that millions of men do now exist, yet, whilst I am alone writing this, I have not that certainty of it which we strictly call knowledge; though the great likelihood of it puts me past doubt, and it be reasonable for me to do several things upon the confidence that there are men (and men also of my acquaintance, with whom I have to do) now in the world: but this is but probability, not knowledge.

§10. Whereby yet we may observe how foolish and vain a thing it is for a man of a narrow knowledge, who having reason given him to judge of the different evidence and probability of things, and to be swayed accordingly,—how vain, I say, it is to expect demonstration and certainty in things not capable of it, and refuse assent to very rational propositions, and act contrary to very plain and clear truths, because they cannot be made out so evident, as to surmount every the least (I will not say reason but) pretence of doubting. He that, in the ordinary affairs of life would admit of nothing but direct plain demonstration, would be sure of nothing in this world, but of perishing quickly. The wholesomeness of his meat or drink would not give him reason to venture on it: and I would fain know, what it is he could do upon such grounds as are capable of no doubt, no objection.

§11. As when our senses are actually employed about any object, we do know that it does exist; so by our memory we may be assured, that heretofore things that affected our senses have existed. And thus we have knowledge of the past existence of several things whereof, our senses having informed us, our memories still retain the ideas; and of this we are past all doubt, so long as we remember well. But this knowledge also reaches no further than our senses have formerly assured us. Thus, seeing water at this instant, it is an unquestionable truth to me that water doth exist: and remembering that I saw it yesterday, it will also be always true, and as long as my memory retains it, always an undoubted proposition to me, that water did exist the 10th of July, 1688, as it will also be equally true that a certain number of very fine colours did exist, which at the same time I saw upon a bubble of that water: but, being now quite out of sight both of the water and bubbles too, it is no more certainly known to me that the water doth now exist, than that the bubbles or colours therein do so; it being no more necessary that water should exist to-day, because it existed yesterday, than that the colours or bubbles exist to-day, because they existed yesterday; though it be exceedingly much more probable, because water hath been observed to continue long in existence but bubbles and the colours on them, quickly cease to be.

§12. What ideas we have of spirits,[10] and how we come by them, I have already shown. But though we have those ideas in our minds, and know we have them there, the having the ideas of spirits does not make us know that any such things do exist without us, or that there are any finite spirits, or any other spiritual beings but the eternal God. We have ground from revelation, and several other reasons, to believe with assurance that there are such creatures: but our senses not being able to discover them, we want the means of knowing their particular existences. For we can no more know, that there are finite spirits really existing, by the idea we have of such beings in our minds, than by the ideas any one has of fairies, or centaurs, he can come to know that things answering those ideas do really exist.

_____

10   Spiritual beings such as angels.

And therefore concerning the existence of finite spirits, as well as several other things, we must content ourselves with the evidence of faith; but universal certain propositions concerning this matter are beyond our reach. For however true it may be, *v.g.* that all the intelligent spirits that God ever created do still exist; yet it can never make a part of our certain knowledge. These and the like propositions we may assent to as highly probable, but are not, I fear, in this state capable of knowing. We are not then to put others upon demonstrating, nor ourselves upon search of universal certainty, in all those matters, wherein we are not capable of any other knowledge, but what our senses give us in this or that particular.

§13. By which it appears that there are two sorts of propositions: 1. There is one sort of propositions concerning the existence of any thing answerable to such an idea: as having the idea of an elephant, phoenix, motion, or an angel, in my mind, the first and natural inquiry is, Whether such a thing does anywhere exist? And this knowledge is only of particulars. No existence of anything without us, but only of God, can certainly be known farther than our senses inform us. 2. There is another sort of propositions, wherein is expressed the agreement or disagreement of our abstract ideas, and their dependence on one another. Such propositions may be universal and certain. So having the idea of God and myself, of fear and obedience, I cannot but be sure that God is to be feared and obeyed by me: and this proposition will be certain, concerning man in general, if I have made an abstract idea of such a species, whereof I am one particular. But yet this proposition, how certain soever, that men ought to fear and obey God proves not to me the existence of men in the world, but will be true of all such

creatures, whenever they do exist: which certainty of such general propositions depends on the agreement or disagreement to be discovered in those abstract ideas.

§14. In the former case, our knowledge is the consequence of the existence of things producing ideas in our minds by our senses: in the latter, knowledge is the consequence of the ideas (be they what they will) that are in our minds, producing there general certain propositions. Many of these are called *aeternae veritates*,[11] and all of them indeed are so; not from being written all or any of them in the minds of all men; or that they were any of them propositions in any one's mind till he, having got the abstract ideas, joined or separated them by affirmation or negation. But wheresoever we can suppose such a creature as man is, endowed with such faculties, and thereby furnished with such ideas as we have, we must conclude, he must needs, when he applies his thoughts to the consideration of his ideas, know the truth of certain propositions that will arise from the agreement or disagreement which he will perceive in his own ideas. Such propositions are therefore called eternal truths, not because they are eternal propositions actually formed, and antecedent to the understanding, that at any time makes them; nor because they are imprinted on the mind from any patterns, that are anywhere out of the mind, and existed before: but because being once made about abstract ideas, so as to be true, they will, whenever they can be supposed to be made again at any time past or to come, by a mind having those ideas, always actually be true. For names being supposed to stand perpetually for the same ideas, and the same ideas having immutably the same habitudes one to another; propositions concerning any abstract ideas that are once true, must needs be eternal verities.

---

11 "Eternal verities"—things that are eternally true.

GEORGE BERKELEY

Three Dialogues Between Hylas and Philonous

Who Was George Berkeley?

George Berkeley was born in 1685 near Kilkenny, an attractive medieval town in the southern part of Ireland which, in the 1640s, had briefly been the center of Irish resistance to the British. He was the son of a gentleman farmer and went to one of Ireland's leading schools, Kilkenny College, at the age of 11. At the early age of 15 Berkeley entered Trinity College, Dublin (the pre-eminent Irish university), and in 1707 became a Fellow of the College. Two years later he published *An Essay Towards a New Theory of Vision*, an influential scientific work which remained the standard theory of vision until the mid-nineteenth century, but which Berkeley intended, from the outset, to solve a problem for his developing "immaterialist" theories.[1] In fact, Berkeley probably arrived at his main philosophical views in his early twenties, and never wavered from them thereafter.

---

1   The problem that Berkeley needed to solve was the apparent fact that we seem to just 'see' things as being three-dimensional solids located outside of ourselves; he solved it by arguing that vision itself merely provides us with information about a sequence of color patches in our visual field, and we have to learn to make *inferences* about spatial location on the basis of this data and its correlation with the sensations of touch. In other words, he argued that we don't just 'see' that there is a material world located outside of our heads.

In 1710 Berkeley was ordained a priest in the protestant Church of Ireland and, in the same year, published *A Treatise Concerning the Principles of Human Knowledge,* in which he put forward his theory, today called "subjective idealism." In a nutshell, he claimed matter does not exist. The book met with a cool reception, and Berkeley felt he was merely dismissed as an eccentric: indeed, a London doctor theorized that Berkeley must be insane, and a bishop publicly expressed pity for Berkeley's need to seek notoriety. Gamely, therefore, he set out to re-present his ideas in a more acceptable form; *Three Dialogues Between Hylas and Philonous*, published in London in 1713, was the result. This book was much more successful, and though it persuaded few to agree with his conclusions it made him something of a literary celebrity in London social circles.

Berkeley, who had moved to London in 1713, spent much of the next decade traveling in France and Italy, first as chaplain to the Earl of Peterborough and then as tutor to the son of a bishop. There is a story (probably untrue) that a fit of apoplexy brought on by arguing with Berkeley caused the death of the important Cartesian philosopher Nicolas Malebranche in 1715.

In 1721 Berkeley published *De Motu* ("On Motion"), attacking Newton's philosophy of space on the basis of Berkeley's own philosophical system (despite his great admiration for Newton's work in general). In the same year he published *An Essay Towards Preventing the Ruin of Great Britain,* which diagnosed Britain's economic problems (the result of a huge stock market crash in 1720, known as the collapse of the South

Sea Bubble) as being caused by a general decline in religion, morality, and sense of duty to the public good. Berkeley himself, however, attained economic security just two years later when he was made Dean of Derry, a church position which carried with it a very sizeable income.

In 1724 Berkeley enthusiastically embarked on a project for establishing a college in Bermuda to provide Christian education to both colonial and indigenous North Americans. He raised £6,000 in private donations, managed to convince five Fellows of Trinity to give up their secure academic positions in Dublin and commit themselves to becoming teachers in Bermuda, and with his new wife Anne Forster he set sail for the New World in 1728. He settled in Newport, Rhode Island, and bought a farm to provide extra income for his college. Unfortunately, the £20,000 in funding promised by the British government for the college never materialized and in 1731 Berkeley was forced to abandon the project and return to London, hoping instead for advancement in the church. In 1734 he was duly made Bishop of Cloyne (near Cork, in Ireland), and moved there immediately. He devoted most of his energies for the rest of his life to looking after the spiritual and practical interests of the people of the see of Cloyne. His last publication was the strange *Siris: A Chain of Philosophical Reflections and Inquiries*, in which, among other things, he expounded the medicinal benefits of tar-water (a concoction, served cold, made by boiling pine resin in water). Berkeley died suddenly in Oxford in 1753 whilst visiting his second son, George, who was at university there. He was buried a week later (since, out of fear of being buried alive, he had left instructions that he was not to be buried until his body showed signs of decay) in the nave of Christ Church cathedral.

What Was Berkeley's Overall Philosophical Project?

Berkeley is best known as the inventor of the philosophical theory today called "subjective idealism" (and which he called "immaterialism"). This is the theory that the physical world exists only in the experiences that minds have of it—in other words, that the world consists of nothing more than a set of mental experiences. As it is often put, for Berkeley *esse est percipi*: "to exist is to be perceived."[2]

Berkeley's main philosophical project was to attack the prevailing mechanical philosophy, a general world-outlook given early form by the work of Descartes (1596–1650), embodied in the science of Robert Boyle (1627–1691) and Isaac Newton (1642–1727), and provided with its most influential philosophical defender in Locke (1632–1704). What Berkeley saw in the mechanical philosophy was a complete split between mind and matter as two radically different types of thing, combined with the comfortable assumption that our minds can nevertheless interact with and come to know a great deal about the world of matter. He argued throughout his life that these two claims are mutually inconsistent: that to adopt a mechanical view of the external world inevitably commits us to radical skepticism. Furthermore, the new mechanical philosophy, Berkeley felt, tempts us towards materialism (i.e., the denial of the existence of immaterial spirits) and atheism (since Newton's deterministic physics seems to leave little role in the universe for an active God).

Berkeley's way out of what he saw as a deep conceptual confusion was to deny the reality of any non-mental stuff called "matter." That is, Berkeley tries to save us from skepticism by showing that reality is entirely mental, and pointing out that we have extremely close acquaintance with—and so highly reliable knowledge of—our own ideas and their relations with each other. (For most subsequent philosophers, however, this cure has seemed worse than the disease.)

What Is the Structure of This Reading?

Set in a garden, this reading is a dialogue between Hylas and Philonous. Hylas, whose name is derived from *hyle*, the Greek word for matter, defends the mechanistic, scientific account of the material world as existing independently of the mind. Philonous, whose name means "lover of mind," speaks for Berkeley, and defends idealism.

---

2   Actually, the full version of the maxim is *esse est percipi vel percipere*: "to exist is either to be perceived or to perceive."

The *Three Dialogues* have the following scheme. In the First Dialogue, Berkeley lays out most of his arguments for the non-existence of matter. Then, in the Second Dialogue, he tries to show that his conclusions are neither skeptical nor atheistic, and that they in fact refute skepticism and give God a crucial role in the running of the universe. He goes on to argue that the existence of matter is not only unsupported by argument but actually inconceivable. In the Third Dialogue, Berkeley has Philonous defend subjective idealism against a sequence of over twenty objections from Hylas, and especially against the objection that Berkeley's theory is shocking, strange, skeptical, and generally just as indefensible as materialism has turned out to be.

The First Dialogue, the selection reprinted here, pursues several rather complex lines of argument but can be seen as falling into three parts. After an initial exchange on the dangers of skepticism, Philonous argues against the externality of secondary qualities (see the reading from Locke, above, for the classic account of the primary-secondary qualities distinction). Berkeley presents at least three distinct arguments for this conclusion, which today are often called the argument from illusion, the causal argument, and (what Howard Robinson has called) the "assimilation argument." This last works by trying to show that all sensory states essentially contain an irreducibly subjective component, like pain or pleasure.

In the second part of the argument of the First Dialogue, Philonous argues against the externality of the primary qualities. He starts by using similar arguments to those just applied to the secondary qualities, but then comes a fairly long digression in which Hylas raises two interesting suggestions. First, Hylas tries to defend the mind-independence of reality by distinguishing between the *act* of perception and its *object* (i.e., the thing it is a perception of), and arguing that only the first of these is subjective. After Philonous responds to this argument, Hylas then tries appealing to the notion of a material "substratum" or "substance" underlying the qualities we perceive, and Philonous argues that such a notion is meaningless. Finally, Hylas returns to the question of the mind-independence of the primary qualities and tries to defend a view sometimes called the "representative theory of perception" (which can be found in Locke). This theory treats our ideas or sensations not as

being mind-independent themselves but as *representing* or *resembling* mind-independent qualities in the world. Philonous argues that, if this were the case, we could never know anything about the material causes of our ideas.

In the third and final stage of Berkeley's argument, Philonous continues his critique of the representative theory of perception by making two new points. First, he claims in a small section sometimes called his "Master Argument" (since he says he will let everything rest on this argument alone), it is incoherent even to assert that we can conceive of something existing unconceived. It follows that it is incoherent to talk about objects that are not themselves perceived but that cause our perceptions. Second, Berkeley argues that nothing but an idea can be anything like an idea (this is often called Berkeley's "Likeness Principle"). That is, he criticizes the coherence of the view that some of our ideas resemble their material causes.

Some Useful Background Information

1. Berkeley's use of the term "idea," which is crucial to his philosophical system, is taken from Locke; see the background information notes on Locke for an explanation of this usage.
2. Berkeley's metaphysical system contains the following elements. First, Berkeley claims that the only things that exist are minds, and he restricts the list of minds or "spirits" to something like the usual suspects: humans, animals, angels and so on, and God. So humans and animals do exist, but they have no bodies or brains: they are "pure spirit." These minds are each populated by mental entities which Berkeley calls, following Locke, ideas; so now we have two kinds of thing in the universe (and only two): selves and their ideas.[3]

---

3   Another way of putting this is to say there is just one sort of *substance*—mind—and its *modes* or attributes, which include the ideas. This opposes the dualism of Descartes and Locke, where we have *two* substances, mind and matter. (See the background information section on Descartes for more information about the notion of a substance and its modes.)

In humans, these ideas are related to each other in the ways that are familiar from experience: for example, the visual image of a rose is often shortly followed by the sensation of a certain scent, and the sound of horses on the street outside gives rise to the idea of a carriage passing by. Some of our ideas are within our control, such as when we are using our imagination to invent new mythical animals, but others are not, such as when we feel the pain of frostbite. Those ideas not controlled by us are placed in our minds directly by God: it is God, according to Berkeley, who is constantly bringing about our sensory experiences of sight, taste, touch, etc. In other words, instead of causing our experience by the complicated route of creating a mind-independent world which then causes our sensations, God simply produces sensations directly in our minds. These ideas constitute "the real world"—which we can perfectly well call "the physical world" if we want to—and so there is no barrier between us and physical reality: skepticism and atheism are no longer a temptation.

3. Although Berkeley admitted that his theory makes reality mind-dependent (that is, nothing at all can exist without some mind to perceive or contain it, unless it is itself a mind), he denied that our reality—the physical world—was dependent on our *individual* minds. The difference between reality and illusion and hallucination, for Berkeley, is precisely that hallucinations are experienced privately by only one mind, whereas real objects are publicly available to a range of observers. Reality is mind-dependent, but it is dependent on God's mind, not ours.

Some clear terminology might be helpful here. Berkeley defends the existence of "physical reality," but denies that it has "absolute existence." He calls the sort of physical object supposedly capable of absolute existence a "material" thing or "matter"—hence, he denies that matter exists. The kind of "real existence" for physical objects that he does endorse is one where those objects are independent of their perceivers (us), but are not capable of existing independently of any mind at all. That is, they are ideas in the mind of God.

This problem, of the continued existence of sensible objects even when we are not looking at them, and Berkeley's solution to it, has been summed up in two well-known limericks:

There was a young man who said "God
Must think it exceedingly odd
If he finds that this tree
Continues to be
When there's no one about in the Quad."

(A Quad, short for quadrangle, is the courtyard of an Oxford college.) The reply runs as follows:

Dear Sir:
    Your astonishment's odd;
I am always about in the Quad.
And that's why the tree
Will continue to be,
Since observed by
    Yours faithfully,
    GOD.

4. There is one important aspect of his metaphysical system about which Berkeley seems to be careful to sit on the fence (or unable to give a definite answer). He holds that "sensible things"—that is, things we perceive or sense—are independent of our minds since they can continue to exist even when we cease to perceive them; this is because they continue to be ideas in the mind of God. This raises the following question, which Berkeley never really answers clearly: in perceiving a sensible thing, is what I perceive an idea in my mind which is a *copy* of an 'archetypal' idea in the mind of God, or (alternatively) do I perceive the very idea in *God's* mind?[4]

---

4   Think of it this way. When I dream about clocks, those clocks are ideas in my mind only; if you also dream of clocks, even if your dream clocks are just like mine, your clock images are in your mind and not in mine. Now consider my sensory image of a tree, and ask: is my tree-image actually, somehow, an idea in *another* mind (God's), or is it just a *copy* of a tree-image in

Some Common Misconceptions

1. Berkeley was emphatic that he did not deny the *reality* of the physical world. He believed in the existence of rocks and trees, other people and animals, cities, and paintings just as fervently as everyone else; we can trip over them, look at them, talk to them, live in them, buy and sell them, and so on, just as we always thought we could. In fact, rightly or wrongly, Berkeley would have said he had a much clearer and more commonsensical view of the real existence of trees and stars than philosophers like Locke and Descartes. (When the contemporary essayist Samuel Johnson kicked a pebble and declared, of Berkeley, "I refute him thus," Johnson was simply missing Berkeley's point.) What Berkeley was denying, then, is not the existence of trees but a particular account of the *nature* of so-called physical objects and their existence. One can put it this way: Berkeley denies that 'trees,' as defined by the philosophers, exist; but he does not want to deny that trees, as understood by pre-theoretical common sense, exist and are independent of our minds.

2. Berkeley was not a skeptic, an (intentional) enemy of common sense, nor a purveyor of paradoxes. His main concern was to defend the solidity and truth of the very reality we see, hear, taste, and touch, against a picture that treats this reality as a flimsy and deceptive veil behind which operates a mysterious, mechanical machinery of which we can never have direct knowledge.

3. Berkeley was not anti-science. Berkeley, like Locke, was an empiricist, and believed that all knowledge comes ultimately from experience. He had an intense and genuine admiration for Newton and his scientific achievements, and he believed his immaterialism was not only compatible with most of the data and laws of empirical science, but improved it by removing unnecessary metaphysical baggage.

God's mind? This is analogous to asking: is my dream-clock actually part of your dream, or is it instead a copy of the one in your dream?

How Important and Influential Is This Passage?

Berkeley's subjective idealism won very few converts during his lifetime, and has continued to be a very unpopular philosophical position since then: Berkeley is the only major philosopher to ever seriously adopt it.[5] Ironically, far from saving religion and common sense from the depredations of atheism and skepticism, Berkeley's philosophy is usually seen as an important stepping stone on the way to David Hume's skeptical atheism. The philosophical value of this selection from Berkeley's *Three Dialogues*, then, is not so much the plausibility of Berkeley's conclusions as his brilliant challenge to the apparent consistency of our common-sense assumptions about the external world and its relation with our mind: it is not enough, Berkeley shows, to just vaguely hope that our notions of substance, perception, causation, representation, knowledge, mind, and so on will all fit together satisfactorily, but instead we must give careful thought to what we believe and be prepared to adjust our assumptions, possibly in some quite radical ways.

Suggestions for Critical Reflection

1. Do you think Berkeley proves that "colors, sounds, tastes, in a word all those termed *secondary qualities*, have certainly no existence without the mind"? What exactly would it be to show such a thing? Would, for example, Locke accept this claim about secondary qualities?

2. What do you make of Berkeley's Likeness Principle, that only an idea can be like another idea? Does it seem plausible? If so how, if at all, does it help to show that there can be no such thing as matter?

3. Berkeley denies that matter exists, but he holds that minds do exist, and minds are not themselves ideas (they are conscious spiritual

---

5   Though, to be fair, some philosophical theories that have had periods of popularity owe quite a lot to Berkeley's influence, such as the British neo-Hegelian theories of the late nineteenth century and the scientific phenomenalism of the early twentieth century.

agents which perceive ideas). Is Berkeley being consistent here? Do his arguments against matter work just as well against spirit? In thinking about this question, you should be aware that Berkeley himself considers it in the Third Dialogue so you might want to go and find out what he has to say there.

4. Berkeley wants us to accept that the physical world really exists, independently of us, since it consists of ideas in the mind of God. How satisfactory do you find this notion? What could the relationship be between our sensations of the external world and God's ideas? Is it any clearer than the relation between our sensations and material objects would be?

5. Berkeley recognized the existence of only two sorts of things: minds and ideas. Ideas, for Berkeley, are entirely passive, and the only active agencies in the world are minds. It follows that there can be no causation, as we would normally understand it. One idea cannot cause another, they can only be somehow connected together by a mind. In other words, (an idea of) fire cannot bring about (an idea of) heat, which in turn cannot cause (an idea of) the expansion of metal: all that can happen is that some mind decides the first idea is followed by the second, the second by the third, and so on. Given all this, could we possibly continue to do science if we accepted Berkeley's metaphysics? If so, what might this new science look like?

6. Locke and Berkeley can be seen as presenting two opposed philosophical world-views: which of them is right? If you think that neither is, then what third position is available? Would it help to abandon some of the presuppositions shared by Locke and Berkeley, such as their notion of an *idea*?

Suggestions for Further Reading

The standard edition of Berkeley's works continues to be *Works of George Berkeley, Bishop of Cloyne*, edited by Luce and Jessop and published in nine volumes between 1948 and 1957 by Nelson & Sons. A good student edition of the *Three Dialogues* was published

by Oxford University Press in 1998, with lots of useful supplementary material from Jonathan Dancy. In the same year Oxford published a similar edition of Berkeley's *The Principles of Human Knowledge*. Any serious student of Berkeley's *Three Dialogues* should begin by reading his *Principles*.

The standard biography of Berkeley is by A.A. Luce, *The Life of George Berkeley, Bishop of Cloyne* (Nelson, 1949). There are various useful books about Berkeley's philosophy, including the short *Berkeley*, by J.O. Urmson (Oxford University Press, 1982), the somewhat longer *Berkeley*, by G.J. Warnock (Pelican, 1953), and the even more substantial *Berkeley: An Introduction*, by Jonathan Dancy (Blackwell, 1987). Also available are *Berkeley: The Central Arguments*, by A.C. Grayling (Duckworth, 1986), *Berkeley*, by George Pitcher (Routledge & Kegan Paul, 1977), and *Berkeley: An Interpretation*, by Kenneth Winkler (Oxford University Press, 1989). A collection of essays can be found in *Essays on Berkeley*, ed. Foster and Robinson (Oxford University Press, 1985), and in *Locke and Berkeley*, ed. Martin and Armstrong (Doubleday, 1968). Finally, Jonathan Bennett's *Locke, Berkeley, Hume: Central Themes* (Oxford, 1971) is well worth consulting.

Three Dialogues Between Hylas and Philonous[6]

First Dialogue

Three dialogues between Hylas and Philonous, the design of which is plainly to demonstrate the reality and perfection of human knowledge, the incorporeal nature of the soul, and the immediate providence of a deity: in opposition to sceptics and atheists; also to open a method for rendering the sciences more easy, useful, and compendious.

---

6 Berkeley's *Three Dialogues* was first published in 1713, reissued in 1725, and then revised for a third edition in 1734. The text reprinted here is from the third edition (with mostly modernized spelling, punctuation, and capitalization).

The First Dialogue

PHILONOUS. Good morrow, Hylas: I did not expect to find you abroad so early.

HYLAS. It is indeed something unusual; but my thoughts were so taken up with a subject I was discoursing of last night, that finding I could not sleep, I resolved to rise and take a turn in the garden.

PHILONOUS. It happened well, to let you see what innocent and agreeable pleasures you lose every morning. Can there be a pleasanter time of the day, or a more delightful season of the year? That purple sky, those wild but sweet notes of birds, the fragrant bloom upon the trees and flowers, the gentle influence of the rising sun, these and a thousand nameless beauties of nature inspire the soul with secret transports; its faculties too being at this time fresh and lively, are fit for those meditations, which the solitude of a garden and tranquillity of the morning naturally dispose us to. But I am afraid I interrupt your thoughts: for you seemed very intent on something.

HYLAS. It is true, I was, and shall be obliged to you if you will permit me to go on in the same vein; not that I would by any means deprive myself of your company, for my thoughts always flow more easily in conversation with a friend, than when I am alone: but my request is, that you would suffer me to impart my reflexions to you.

PHILONOUS. With all my heart, it is what I should have requested myself if you had not prevented me.

HYLAS. I was considering the odd fate of those men who have in all ages, through an affectation of being distinguished from the vulgar,[7] or some unaccountable turn of thought, pretended either to believe nothing at all, or to believe the most extravagant things in the world. This however might be borne, if their paradoxes and scepticism did not draw after them some consequences of general disadvantage to mankind. But the mischief lieth here; that when men of less leisure see them who are supposed to have spent their whole time in the pursuits of knowledge professing an entire ignorance of all things, or advancing such notions as are repugnant to plain and commonly received principles, they will be tempted to entertain suspicions concerning

---

7   The common people and their beliefs.

the most important truths, which they had hitherto held sacred and unquestionable.

PHILONOUS. I entirely agree with you, as to the ill tendency of the affected doubts of some philosophers, and fantastical conceits of others. I am even so far gone of late in this way of thinking, that I have quitted several of the sublime notions I had got in their schools for vulgar opinions. And I give it you on my word, since this revolt from metaphysical notions to the plain dictates of nature and common sense, I find my understanding strangely enlightened, so that I can now easily comprehend a great many things which before were all mystery and riddle.

HYLAS. I am glad to find there was nothing in the accounts I heard of you.

PHILONOUS. Pray, what were those?

HYLAS. You were represented, in last night's conversation, as one who maintained the most extravagant opinion that ever entered into the mind of man, to wit, that there is no such thing as *material substance* in the world.

PHILONOUS. That there is no such thing as what *philosophers call material substance*, I am seriously persuaded: but if I were made to see anything absurd or sceptical in this, I should then have the same reason to renounce this that I imagine I have now to reject the contrary opinion.

HYLAS. What! Can anything be more fantastical, more repugnant to common sense, or a more manifest piece of scepticism, than to believe there is no such thing as *matter*?

PHILONOUS. Softly, good Hylas. What if it should prove that you, who hold there is, are by virtue of that opinion a greater sceptic, and maintain more paradoxes and repugnances to common sense, than I who believe no such thing?

HYLAS. You may as soon persuade me the part is greater than the whole, as that, in order to avoid absurdity and scepticism, I should ever be obliged to give up my opinion in this point.

PHILONOUS. Well then, are you content to admit that opinion for true, which upon examination shall appear most agreeable to common sense, and remote from scepticism?

HYLAS. With all my heart. Since you are for raising disputes about the plainest things in nature, I am content for once to hear what you have to say.

PHILONOUS. Pray, Hylas, what do you mean by a *sceptic*?

HYLAS. I mean what all men mean—one that doubts of everything.

PHILONOUS. He then who entertains no doubts concerning some particular point, with regard to that point cannot be thought a sceptic.

HYLAS. I agree with you.

PHILONOUS. Whether doth doubting consist in embracing the affirmative or negative side of a question?

HYLAS. In neither; for whoever understands English cannot but know that *doubting* signifies a suspense between both.

PHILONOUS. He then that denies any point, can no more be said to doubt of it, than he who affirmeth it with the same degree of assurance.

HYLAS. True.

PHILONOUS. And, consequently, for such his denial is no more to be esteemed a sceptic than the other.

HYLAS. I acknowledge it.

PHILONOUS. How cometh it to pass then, Hylas, that you pronounce me *a sceptic*, because I deny what you affirm, to wit, the existence of matter? Since, for aught you can tell, I am as peremptory[8] in my denial, as you in your affirmation.

HYLAS. Hold, Philonous, I have been a little out in my definition; but every false step a man makes in discourse is not to be insisted on. I said indeed that a *sceptic* was one who doubted of everything; but I should have added, or who denies the reality and truth of things.

PHILONOUS. What things? Do you mean the principles and theorems of sciences? But these you know are universal intellectual notions, and consequently independent of matter. The denial therefore of this doth not imply the denying them.

HYLAS. I grant it. But are there no other things? What think you of distrusting the senses, of denying the real existence of sensible things, or pretending to know nothing of them. Is not this sufficient to denominate a man a *sceptic*?

PHILONOUS. Shall we therefore examine which of us it is that denies the reality of sensible things, or pro-

fesses the greatest ignorance of them; since, if I take you rightly, he is to be esteemed the greatest *sceptic*?

HYLAS. That is what I desire.

PHILONOUS. What mean you by sensible things?

HYLAS. Those things which are perceived by the senses. Can you imagine that I mean anything else?

PHILONOUS. Pardon me, Hylas, if I am desirous clearly to apprehend your notions, since this may much shorten our inquiry. Suffer me then to ask you this farther question. Are those things only perceived by the senses which are perceived immediately? Or, may those things properly be said to be *sensible* which are perceived mediately, or not without the intervention of others?

HYLAS. I do not sufficiently understand you.

PHILONOUS. In reading a book, what I immediately perceive are the letters; but mediately, or by means of these, are suggested to my mind the notions of God, virtue, truth, &c. Now, that the letters are truly sensible things, or perceived by sense, there is no doubt: but I would know whether you take the things suggested by them to be so too.

HYLAS. No, certainly: it were absurd to think *God* or *virtue* sensible things; though they may be signified and suggested to the mind by sensible marks, with which they have an arbitrary connexion.

PHILONOUS. It seems then, that by *sensible things* you mean those only which can be perceived *immediately* by sense?

HYLAS. Right.

PHILONOUS. Doth it not follow from this, that though I see one part of the sky red, and another blue, and that my reason doth thence evidently conclude there must be some cause of that diversity of colours, yet that cause cannot be said to be a sensible thing, or perceived by the sense of seeing?

HYLAS. It doth.

PHILONOUS. In like manner, though I hear variety of sounds, yet I cannot be said to hear the causes of those sounds?

HYLAS. You cannot.

PHILONOUS. And when by my touch I perceive a thing to be hot and heavy, I cannot say, with any truth or propriety, that I feel the cause of its heat or weight?

HYLAS. To prevent any more questions of this kind, I tell you once for all, that by *sensible things* I mean

---

8   Decisive, final, confident.

those only which are perceived by sense; and that in truth the senses perceive nothing which they do not perceive *immediately*: for they make no inferences. The deducing therefore of causes or occasions from effects and appearances, which alone are perceived by sense, entirely relates to reason.

PHILONOUS. This point then is agreed between us— That *sensible things are those only which are immediately perceived by sense*. You will farther inform me, whether we immediately perceive by sight anything beside light, and colours, and figures;[9] or by hearing, anything but sounds; by the palate, anything beside tastes; by the smell, beside odours; or by the touch, more than tangible qualities.

HYLAS. We do not.

PHILONOUS. It seems, therefore, that if you take away all sensible qualities, there remains nothing sensible?

HYLAS. I grant it.

PHILONOUS. Sensible things therefore are nothing else but so many sensible qualities, or combinations of sensible qualities?

HYLAS. Nothing else.

PHILONOUS. *Heat* then is a sensible thing?

HYLAS. Certainly.

PHILONOUS. Doth the *reality* of sensible things consist in being perceived? or, is it something distinct from their being perceived, and that bears no relation to the mind?

HYLAS. To *exist* is one thing, and to be *perceived* is another.

PHILONOUS. I speak with regard to sensible things only. And of these I ask, whether by their real existence you mean a subsistence exterior to the mind, and distinct from their being perceived?

HYLAS. I mean a real absolute being, distinct from, and without any relation to, their being perceived.

PHILONOUS. Heat therefore, if it be allowed a real being, must exist without the mind?

HYLAS. It must.

PHILONOUS. Tell me, Hylas, is this real existence equally compatible to all degrees of heat, which we perceive; or is there any reason why we should attribute it to some, and deny it to others? And if there be, pray let me know that reason.

_____

9   Shapes.

HYLAS. Whatever degree of heat we perceive by sense, we may be sure the same exists in the object that occasions it.

PHILONOUS. What! the greatest as well as the least?

HYLAS. I tell you, the reason is plainly the same in respect of both. They are both perceived by sense; nay, the greater degree of heat is more sensibly perceived; and consequently, if there is any difference, we are more certain of its real existence than we can be of the reality of a lesser degree.

PHILONOUS. But is not the most vehement and intense degree of heat a very great pain?

HYLAS. No one can deny it.

PHILONOUS. And is any unperceiving thing capable of pain or pleasure?

HYLAS. No, certainly.

PHILONOUS. Is your material substance a senseless being, or a being endowed with sense and perception?

HYLAS. It is senseless without doubt.

PHILONOUS. It cannot therefore be the subject of pain?

HYLAS. By no means.

PHILONOUS. Nor consequently of the greatest heat perceived by sense, since you acknowledge this to be no small pain?

HYLAS. I grant it.

PHILONOUS. What shall we say then of your external object; is it a material substance, or no?

HYLAS. It is a material substance with the sensible qualities inhering in it.

PHILONOUS. How then can a great heat exist in it, since you own it cannot in a material substance? I desire you would clear this point.

HYLAS. Hold, Philonous, I fear I was out in yielding intense heat to be a pain. It should seem rather, that pain is something distinct from heat, and the consequence or effect of it.

PHILONOUS. Upon putting your hand near the fire, do you perceive one simple uniform sensation, or two distinct sensations?

HYLAS. But one simple sensation.

PHILONOUS. Is not the heat immediately perceived?

HYLAS. It is.

PHILONOUS. And the pain?

HYLAS. True.

PHILONOUS. Seeing therefore they are both immediately perceived at the same time, and the fire affects you only with one simple or uncompounded idea, it follows that this same simple idea is both the intense heat immediately perceived, and the pain; and, consequently, that the intense heat immediately perceived is nothing distinct from a particular sort of pain.

HYLAS. It seems so.

PHILONOUS. Again, try in your thoughts, Hylas, if you can conceive a vehement sensation to be without pain or pleasure.

HYLAS. I cannot.

PHILONOUS. Or can you frame to yourself an idea of sensible pain or pleasure in general, abstracted from every particular idea of heat, cold, tastes, smells? &c.

HYLAS. I do not find that I can.

PHILONOUS. Doth it not therefore follow, that sensible pain is nothing distinct from those sensations or ideas, in an intense degree?

HYLAS. It is undeniable; and, to speak the truth, I begin to suspect a very great heat cannot exist but in a mind perceiving it.

PHILONOUS. What! are you then in that sceptical state of suspense, between affirming and denying?

HYLAS. I think I may be positive in the point. A very violent and painful heat cannot exist without the mind.

PHILONOUS. It hath not therefore according to you, any *real* being?

HYLAS. I own it.

PHILONOUS. Is it therefore certain, that there is no body in nature really hot?

HYLAS. I have not denied there is any real heat in bodies. I only say, there is no such thing as an intense real heat.

PHILONOUS. But, did you not say before that all degrees of heat were equally real; or, if there was any difference, that the greater were more undoubtedly real than the lesser?

HYLAS. True: but it was because I did not then consider the ground there is for distinguishing between them, which I now plainly see. And it is this: because intense heat is nothing else but a particular kind of painful sensation; and pain cannot exist but in a perceiving being; it follows that no intense heat can really exist in an unperceiving corporeal substance. But this is no reason why we should deny heat in an inferior degree to exist in such a substance.

PHILONOUS. But how shall we be able to discern those degrees of heat which exist only in the mind from those which exist without it?

HYLAS. That is no difficult matter. You know the least pain cannot exist unperceived; whatever, therefore, degree of heat is a pain exists only in the mind. But, as for all other degrees of heat, nothing obliges us to think the same of them.

PHILONOUS. I think you granted before that no unperceiving being was capable of pleasure, any more than of pain.

HYLAS. I did.

PHILONOUS. And is not warmth, or a more gentle degree of heat than what causes uneasiness, a pleasure?

HYLAS. What then?

PHILONOUS. Consequently, it cannot exist without[10] the mind in an unperceiving substance, or body.

HYLAS. So it seems.

PHILONOUS. Since, therefore, as well those degrees of heat that are not painful, as those that are, can exist only in a thinking substance; may we not conclude that external bodies are absolutely incapable of any degree of heat whatsoever?

HYLAS. On second thoughts, I do not think it so evident that warmth is a pleasure as that a great degree of heat is a pain.

PHILONOUS. I do not pretend that warmth is as great a pleasure as heat is a pain. But, if you grant it to be even a small pleasure, it serves to make good my conclusion.

HYLAS. I could rather call it an *indolence*. It seems to be nothing more than a privation of both pain and pleasure. And that such a quality or state as this may agree to an unthinking substance, I hope you will not deny.

PHILONOUS. If you are resolved to maintain that warmth, or a gentle degree of heat, is no pleasure, I know not how to convince you otherwise than by appealing to your own sense. But what think you of cold?

HYLAS. The same that I do of heat. An intense degree of cold is a pain; for to feel a very great cold, is to perceive a great uneasiness: it cannot therefore exist

---

10   "Without," here and elsewhere in this selection, means "outside" (rather than "not having").

without the mind; but a lesser degree of cold may, as well as a lesser degree of heat.

PHILONOUS. Those bodies, therefore, upon whose application to our own, we perceive a moderate degree of heat, must be concluded to have a moderate degree of heat or warmth in them; and those, upon whose application we feel a like degree of cold, must be thought to have cold in them.

HYLAS. They must.

PHILONOUS. Can any doctrine be true that necessarily leads a man into an absurdity?

HYLAS. Without doubt it cannot.

PHILONOUS. Is it not an absurdity to think that the same thing should be at the same time both cold and warm?

HYLAS. It is.

PHILONOUS. Suppose now one of your hands hot, and the other cold, and that they are both at once put into the same vessel of water, in an intermediate state; will not the water seem cold to one hand, and warm to the other?

HYLAS. It will.

PHILONOUS. Ought we not therefore, by your principles, to conclude it is really both cold and warm at the same time, that is, according to your own concession, to believe an absurdity?

HYLAS. I confess it seems so.

PHILONOUS. Consequently, the principles themselves are false, since you have granted that no true principle leads to an absurdity.

HYLAS. But, after all, can anything be more absurd than to say, *there is no heat in the fire*?

PHILONOUS. To make the point still clearer; tell me whether, in two cases exactly alike, we ought not to make the same judgment?

HYLAS. We ought.

PHILONOUS. When a pin pricks your finger, doth it not rend and divide the fibres of your flesh?

HYLAS. It doth.

PHILONOUS. And when a coal burns your finger, doth it any more?

HYLAS. It doth not.

PHILONOUS. Since, therefore, you neither judge the sensation itself occasioned by the pin, nor anything like it to be in the pin; you should not, conformably to what you have now granted, judge the sensation occasioned by the fire, or anything like it, to be in the fire.

HYLAS. Well, since it must be so, I am content to yield this point, and acknowledge that heat and cold are only sensations existing in our minds. But there still remain qualities enough to secure the reality of external things.

PHILONOUS. But what will you say, Hylas, if it shall appear that the case is the same with regard to all other sensible qualities, and that they can no more be supposed to exist without the mind, than heat and cold?

HYLAS. Then indeed you will have done something to the purpose; but that is what I despair of seeing proved.

PHILONOUS. Let us examine them in order. What think you of *tastes*, do they exist without the mind, or no?

HYLAS. Can any man in his senses doubt whether sugar is sweet, or wormwood[11] bitter?

PHILONOUS. Inform me, Hylas. Is a sweet taste a particular kind of pleasure or pleasant sensation, or is it not?

HYLAS. It is.

PHILONOUS. And is not bitterness some kind of uneasiness or pain?

HYLAS. I grant it.

PHILONOUS. If therefore sugar and wormwood are unthinking corporeal substances existing without the mind, how can sweetness and bitterness, that is, pleasure and pain, agree to them?

HYLAS. Hold, Philonous, I now see what it was deluded me all this time. You asked whether heat and cold, sweetness and bitterness, were not particular sorts of pleasure and pain; to which I answered simply, that they were. Whereas I should have thus distinguished: those qualities, as perceived by us, are pleasures or pains, but not as existing in the external objects. We must not therefore conclude absolutely, that there is no heat in the fire, or sweetness in the sugar, but only that heat or sweetness, as perceived by us, are not in the fire or sugar. What say you to this?

PHILONOUS. I say it is nothing to the purpose. Our discourse proceeded altogether concerning sensible things, which you defined to be, *the things we immediately perceive by our senses.* Whatever other qualities, therefore, you speak of as distinct from these, I know nothing of them, neither do they at all belong

---

11   A bitter extract of aromatic herbs and shrubs, used for making absinthe and flavoring certain wines.

to the point in dispute. You may, indeed, pretend to have discovered certain qualities which you do not perceive, and assert those insensible qualities exist in fire and sugar. But what use can be made of this to your present purpose, I am at a loss to conceive. Tell me then once more, do you acknowledge that heat and cold, sweetness and bitterness (meaning those qualities which are perceived by the senses), do not exist without the mind?

HYLAS. I see it is to no purpose to hold out, so I give up the cause as to those mentioned qualities. Though I profess it sounds oddly, to say that sugar is not sweet.

PHILONOUS. But, for your farther satisfaction, take this along with you: that which at other times seems sweet, shall, to a distempered palate, appear bitter. And, nothing can be plainer than that divers persons perceive different tastes in the same food; since that which one man delights in, another abhors. And how could this be, if the taste was something really inherent in the food?

HYLAS. I acknowledge I know not how.

PHILONOUS. In the next place, *odours* are to be considered. And, with regard to these, I would fain know whether what hath been said of tastes doth not exactly agree to them? Are they not so many pleasing or displeasing sensations?

HYLAS. They are.

PHILONOUS. Can you then conceive it possible that they should exist in an unperceiving thing?

HYLAS. I cannot.

PHILONOUS. Or, can you imagine that filth and ordure[12] affect those brute animals that feed on them out of choice, with the same smells which we perceive in them?

HYLAS. By no means.

PHILONOUS. May we not therefore conclude of smells, as of the other forementioned qualities, that they cannot exist in any but a perceiving substance or mind?

HYLAS. I think so.

PHILONOUS. Then as to *sounds*, what must we think of them: are they accidents[13] really inherent in external bodies, or not?

HYLAS. That they inhere not in the sonorous bodies is plain from hence: because a bell struck in the exhausted receiver of an air-pump[14] sends forth no sound. The air, therefore, must be thought the subject of sound.

PHILONOUS. What reason is there for that, Hylas?

HYLAS. Because, when any motion is raised in the air, we perceive a sound greater or lesser, according to the air's motion; but without some motion in the air, we never hear any sound at all.

PHILONOUS. And granting that we never hear a sound but when some motion is produced in the air, yet I do not see how you can infer from thence, that the sound itself is in the air.

HYLAS. It is this very motion in the external air that produces in the mind the sensation of *sound*. For, striking on the drum of the ear, it causeth a vibration, which by the auditory nerves being communicated to the brain, the soul is thereupon affected with the sensation called *sound*.

PHILONOUS. What! is sound then a sensation?

HYLAS. I tell you, as perceived by us, it is a particular sensation in the mind.

PHILONOUS. And can any sensation exist without the mind?

HYLAS. No, certainly.

PHILONOUS. How then can sound, being a sensation, exist in the air, if by the *air* you mean a senseless substance existing without the mind?

HYLAS. You must distinguish, Philonous, between sound as it is perceived by us, and as it is in itself; or (which is the same thing) between the sound we immediately perceive, and that which exists without us. The former, indeed, is a particular kind of sensation, but the latter is merely a vibrative or undulatory motion of the air.

PHILONOUS. I thought I had already obviated that distinction, by the answer I gave when you were applying it in a like case before. But, to say no more of that, are you sure then that sound is really nothing but motion?

HYLAS. I am.

PHILONOUS. Whatever therefore agrees to real sound, may with truth be attributed to motion?

HYLAS. It may.

---

12 Excrement, dung.
13 (Non-essential) properties.

14 A near-vacuum. This experiment was first performed by Otto von Guericke in the 1650s.

PHILONOUS. It is then good sense to speak of *motion* as of a thing that is *loud*, *sweet*, *acute*, or *grave*.[15]

HYLAS. I see you are resolved not to understand me. Is it not evident those accidents or modes belong only to sensible sound, or sound in the common acceptation of the word, but not to *sound* in the real and philosophic sense; which, as I just now told you, is nothing but a certain motion of the air?

PHILONOUS. It seems then there are two sorts of sound—the one vulgar, or that which is heard, the other philosophical and real?

HYLAS. Even so.

PHILONOUS. And the latter consists in motion?

HYLAS. I told you so before.

PHILONOUS. Tell me, Hylas, to which of the senses, think you, the idea of motion belongs? to the hearing?

HYLAS. No, certainly; but to the sight and touch.

PHILONOUS. It should follow then, that, according to you, real sounds may possibly be *seen* or *felt*, but never *heard*.

HYLAS. Look you, Philonous, you may, if you please, make a jest of my opinion, but that will not alter the truth of things. I own, indeed, the inferences you draw me into sound something oddly; but common language, you know, is framed by, and for the use of the vulgar: we must not therefore wonder if expressions adapted to exact philosophic notions seem uncouth and out of the way.

PHILONOUS. Is it come to that? I assure you, I imagine myself to have gained no small point, since you make so light of departing from common phrases and opinions; it being a main part of our inquiry, to examine whose notions are widest of the common road, and most repugnant to the general sense of the world. But, can you think it no more than a philosophical paradox, to say that *real sounds are never heard*, and that the idea of them is obtained by some other sense? And is there nothing in this contrary to nature and the truth of things?

HYLAS. To deal ingenuously,[16] I do not like it. And, after the concessions already made, I had as well grant that sounds too have no real being without the mind.

---

15 "Acute" means high-pitched or shrill, and "grave" low-pitched.

16 Openly, honestly.

PHILONOUS. And I hope you will make no difficulty to acknowledge the same of *colours*.

HYLAS. Pardon me: the case of colours is very different. Can anything be plainer than that we see them on the objects?

PHILONOUS. The objects you speak of are, I suppose, corporeal substances existing without the mind?

HYLAS. They are.

PHILONOUS. And have true and real colours inhering in them?

HYLAS. Each visible object hath that colour which we see in it.

PHILONOUS. How! is there anything visible but what we perceive by sight?

HYLAS. There is not.

PHILONOUS. And, do we perceive anything by sense which we do not perceive immediately?

HYLAS. How often must I be obliged to repeat the same thing? I tell you, we do not.

PHILONOUS. Have patience, good Hylas; and tell me once more, whether there is anything immediately perceived by the senses, except sensible qualities. I know you asserted there was not; but I would now be informed, whether you still persist in the same opinion.

HYLAS. I do.

PHILONOUS. Pray, is your corporeal substance either a sensible quality, or made up of sensible qualities?

HYLAS. What a question that is! who ever thought it was?

PHILONOUS. My reason for asking was, because in saying, *each visible object hath that colour which we see in it*, you make visible objects to be corporeal substances; which implies either that corporeal substances are sensible qualities, or else that there is something besides sensible qualities perceived by sight: but, as this point was formerly agreed between us, and is still maintained by you, it is a clear consequence, that your *corporeal substance* is nothing distinct from *sensible qualities*.

HYLAS. You may draw as many absurd consequences as you please, and endeavour to perplex the plainest things; but you shall never persuade me out of my senses. I clearly understand my own meaning.

PHILONOUS. I wish you would make me understand it too. But, since you are unwilling to have your notion of corporeal substance examined, I shall urge that point no farther. Only be pleased to let me know, whether the same colours which we see exist in external bodies, or some other.

HYLAS. The very same.

PHILONOUS. What! are then the beautiful red and purple we see on yonder clouds really in them? Or do you imagine they have in themselves any other form than that of a dark mist or vapour?

HYLAS. I must own, Philonous, those colours are not really in the clouds as they seem to be at this distance. They are only apparent colours.

PHILONOUS. *Apparent* call you them? How shall we distinguish these apparent colours from real?

HYLAS. Very easily. Those are to be thought apparent which, appearing only at a distance, vanish upon a nearer approach.

PHILONOUS. And those, I suppose, are to be thought real which are discovered by the most near and exact survey.

HYLAS. Right.

PHILONOUS. Is the nearest and exactest survey made by the help of a microscope, or by the naked eye?

HYLAS. By a microscope, doubtless.

PHILONOUS. But a microscope often discovers colours in an object different from those perceived by the unassisted sight. And, in case we had microscopes magnifying to any assigned degree, it is certain that no object whatsoever, viewed through them, would appear in the same colour which it exhibits to the naked eye.

HYLAS. And what will you conclude from all this? You cannot argue that there are really and naturally no colours on objects: because by artificial managements they may be altered, or made to vanish.

PHILONOUS. I think it may evidently be concluded from your own concessions, that all the colours we see with our naked eyes are only apparent as those on the clouds, since they vanish upon a more close and accurate inspection which is afforded us by a microscope. Then as to what you say by way of prevention: I ask you whether the real and natural state of an object is better discovered by a very sharp and piercing sight, or by one which is less sharp?

HYLAS. By the former without doubt.

PHILONOUS. Is it not plain from *dioptrics*[17] that microscopes make the sight more penetrating, and represent objects as they would appear to the eye in case it were naturally endowed with a most exquisite sharpness?

HYLAS. It is.

PHILONOUS. Consequently the microscopical representation is to be thought that which best sets forth the real nature of the thing, or what it is in itself. The colours, therefore, by it perceived are more genuine and real than those perceived otherwise.

HYLAS. I confess there is something in what you say.

PHILONOUS. Besides, it is not only possible but manifest, that there actually are animals whose eyes are by nature framed to perceive those things which by reason of their minuteness escape our sight. What think you of those inconceivably small animals perceived by glasses?[18] Must we suppose they are all stark blind? Or, in case they see, can it be imagined their sight hath not the same use in preserving their bodies from injuries, which appears in that of all other animals? And if it hath, is it not evident they must see particles less than their own bodies; which will present them with a far different view in each object from that which strikes our senses? Even our own eyes do not always represent objects to us after the same manner. In the jaundice[19] every one knows that all things seem yellow. Is it not therefore highly probable those animals in whose eyes we discern a very different texture from that of ours, and whose bodies abound with different humours,[20] do not see the same colours in every object that we do? From all which, should it not seem to follow that all colours are equally apparent, and that none of those which we perceive are really inherent in any outward object?

HYLAS. It should.

PHILONOUS. The point will be past all doubt, if you consider that, in case colours were real properties or affections inherent in external bodies, they could admit of no alteration without some change wrought in the very bodies themselves: but, is it not evident from what hath

---

17   The part of optics dealing with the study of refraction.
18   By magnifying lenses (e.g., in a microscope).
19   A yellowing of the skin and the eyes, often caused by liver disease.
20   Bodily fluids.

been said that, upon the use of microscopes, upon a change happening in the humours of the eye, or a variation of distance, without any manner of real alteration in the thing itself, the colours of any object are either changed, or totally disappear? Nay, all other circumstances remaining the same, change but the situation of some objects, and they shall present different colours to the eye. The same thing happens upon viewing an object in various degrees of light. And what is more known than that the same bodies appear differently coloured by candle-light from what they do in the open day? Add to these the experiment of a prism which, separating the heterogeneous rays of light, alters the colour of any object, and will cause the whitest to appear of a deep blue or red to the naked eye. And now tell me whether you are still of opinion that every body hath its true real colour inhering in it; and, if you think it hath, I would fain know farther from you, what certain distance and position of the object, what peculiar texture and formation of the eye, what degree or kind of light is necessary for ascertaining that true colour, and distinguishing it from apparent ones.

HYLAS. I own myself entirely satisfied, that they are all equally apparent, and that there is no such thing as colour really inhering in external bodies, but that it is altogether in the light. And what confirms me in this opinion is, that in proportion to the light colours are still more or less vivid; and if there be no light, then are there no colours perceived. Besides, allowing there are colours on external objects, yet, how is it possible for us to perceive them? For no external body affects the mind, unless it acts first on our organs of sense. But the only action of bodies is motion; and motion cannot be communicated otherwise than by impulse. A distant object therefore cannot act on the eye; nor consequently make itself or its properties perceivable to the soul. Whence it plainly follows that it is immediately some contiguous[21] substance, which, operating on the eye, occasions a perception of colours: and such is light.

PHILONOUS. How! is light then a substance?

HYLAS. I tell you, Philonous, external light is nothing but a thin fluid substance, whose minute particles being agitated with a brisk motion, and in various man-

ners reflected from the different surfaces of outward objects to the eyes, communicate different motions to the optic nerves; which, being propagated to the brain, cause therein various impressions; and these are attended with the sensations of red, blue, yellow, &c.

PHILONOUS. It seems then the light doth no more than shake the optic nerves.

HYLAS. Nothing else.

PHILONOUS. And consequent to each particular motion of the nerves, the mind is affected with a sensation, which is some particular colour.

HYLAS. Right.

PHILONOUS. And these sensations have no existence without the mind.

HYLAS. They have not.

PHILONOUS. How then do you affirm that colours are in the light; since by *light* you understand a corporeal substance external to the mind?

HYLAS. Light and colours, as immediately perceived by us, I grant cannot exist without the mind. But in themselves they are only the motions and configurations of certain insensible particles of matter.

PHILONOUS. Colours then, in the vulgar sense, or taken for the immediate objects of sight, cannot agree to any but a perceiving substance.

HYLAS. That is what I say.

PHILONOUS. Well then, since you give up the point as to those sensible qualities which are alone thought colours by all mankind beside, you may hold what you please with regard to those invisible ones of the philosophers. It is not my business to dispute about *them*; only I would advise you to bethink yourself, whether, considering the inquiry we are upon, it be prudent for you to affirm—*the red and blue which we see are not real colours, but certain unknown motions and figures which no man ever did or can see are truly so.* Are not these shocking notions, and are not they subject to as many ridiculous inferences, as those you were obliged to renounce before in the case of sounds?

HYLAS. I frankly own, Philonous, that it is in vain to stand out any longer. Colours, sounds, tastes, in a word all those termed *secondary qualities*, have certainly no existence without the mind. But by this acknowledgment I must not be supposed to derogate the reality of matter, or external objects; seeing it is no more than several philosophers maintain, who

---

21   Immediately next to, touching.

nevertheless are the farthest imaginable from deny-ing matter. For the clearer understanding of this, you must know sensible qualities are by philosophers divided into *primary* and *secondary*. The former are extension, figure, solidity, gravity, motion, and rest; and these they hold exist really in bodies. The latter are those above enumerated; or, briefly, *all sensible qualities beside the primary*; which they assert are only so many sensations or ideas existing nowhere but in the mind. But all this, I doubt not, you are apprised of. For my part, I have been a long time sensible there was such an opinion current among philosophers, but was never thoroughly convinced of its truth until now.

PHILONOUS. You are still then of opinion that *exten-sion* and *figures* are inherent in external unthinking substances?

HYLAS. I am.

PHILONOUS. But what if the same arguments which are brought against secondary qualities will hold good against these also?

HYLAS. Why then I shall be obliged to think, they too exist only in the mind.

PHILONOUS. Is it your opinion the very figure and extension which you perceive by sense exist in the outward object or material substance?

HYLAS. It is.

PHILONOUS. Have all other animals as good grounds to think the same of the figure and extension which they see and feel?

HYLAS. Without doubt, if they have any thought at all.

PHILONOUS. Answer me, Hylas. Think you the senses were bestowed upon all animals for their preservation and well-being in life? or were they given to men alone for this end?

HYLAS. I make no question but they have the same use in all other animals.

PHILONOUS. If so, is it not necessary they should be enabled by them to perceive their own limbs, and those bodies which are capable of harming them?

·HYLAS. Certainly.

PHILONOUS. A mite[22] therefore must be supposed to see his own foot, and things equal or even less than it, as bodies of some considerable dimension; though at the same time they appear to you scarce discernible, or at best as so many visible points?

HYLAS. I cannot deny it.

PHILONOUS. And to creatures less than the mite they will seem yet larger?

HYLAS. They will.

PHILONOUS. Insomuch that what you can hardly discern will to another extremely minute animal appear as some huge mountain?

HYLAS. All this I grant.

PHILONOUS. Can one and the same thing be at the same time in itself of different dimensions?

HYLAS. That were absurd to imagine.

PHILONOUS. But, from what you have laid down it follows that both the extension by you perceived, and that perceived by the mite itself, as likewise all those perceived by lesser animals, are each of them the true extension of the mite's foot; that is to say, by your own principles you are led into an absurdity.

HYLAS. There seems to be some difficulty in the point.

PHILONOUS. Again, have you not acknowledged that no real inherent property of any object can be changed without some change in the thing itself?

HYLAS. I have.

PHILONOUS. But, as we approach to or recede from an object, the visible extension varies, being at one distance ten or a hundred times greater than another. Doth it not therefore follow from hence likewise that it is not really inherent in the object?

HYLAS. I own I am at a loss what to think.

PHILONOUS. Your judgement will soon be determined, if you will venture to think as freely concerning this quality as you have done concerning the rest. Was it not admitted as a good argument, that neither heat nor cold was in the water, because it seemed warm to one hand and cold to the other?

HYLAS. It was.

PHILONOUS. Is it not the very same reasoning to con-clude, there is no extension or figure in an object, because to one eye it shall seem little, smooth, and round, when at the same time it appears to the other, great, uneven, and regular?

HYLAS. The very same. But does this latter fact ever happen?

---

22 Any of a large number of species of tiny arachnids, often parasites, some of which are so small that they cannot be seen by the naked eye.

PHILONOUS. You may at any time make the experiment, by looking with one eye bare, and with the other through a microscope.

HYLAS. I know not how to maintain it; and yet I am loath to give up *extension*, I see so many odd consequences following upon such a concession.

PHILONOUS. Odd, say you? After the concessions already made, I hope you will stick at nothing for its oddness. But, on the other hand, should it not seem very odd, if the general reasoning which includes all other sensible qualities did not also include extension? If it be allowed that no idea, nor anything like an idea, can exist in an unperceiving substance, then surely it follows that no figure, or mode of extension, which we can either perceive, or imagine, or have any idea of, can be really inherent in matter; not to mention the peculiar difficulty there must be in conceiving a material substance, prior to and distinct from extension, to be the *substratum* of extension. Be the sensible quality what it will—figure, or sound, or colour, it seems alike impossible it should subsist in that which doth not perceive it.

HYLAS. I give up the point for the present, reserving still a right to retract my opinion, in case I shall hereafter discover any false step in my progress to it.

PHILONOUS. That is a right you cannot be denied. Figures and extension being despatched, we proceed next to *motion*. Can a real motion in any external body be at the same time very swift and very slow?

HYLAS. It cannot.

PHILONOUS. Is not the motion of a body swift in a reciprocal proportion to the time it takes up in describing[23] any given space? Thus a body that describes a mile in an hour moves three times faster than it would in case it described only a mile in three hours.

HYLAS. I agree with you.

PHILONOUS. And is not time measured by the succession of ideas in our minds?

HYLAS. It is.

PHILONOUS. And is it not possible ideas should succeed one another twice as fast in your mind as they do in mine, or in that of some spirit of another kind?

HYLAS. I own it.

_____

23 Crossing.

PHILONOUS. Consequently the same body may to another seem to perform its motion over any space in half the time that it doth to you. And the same reasoning will hold as to any other proportion: that is to say, according to your principles (since the motions perceived are both really in the object) it is possible one and the same body shall be really moved the same way at once, both very swift and very slow. How is this consistent either with common sense, or with what you just now granted?

HYLAS. I have nothing to say to it.

PHILONOUS. Then as for *solidity*; either you do not mean any sensible quality by that word, and so it is beside our inquiry: or if you do, it must be either hardness or resistance. But both the one and the other are plainly relative to our senses: it being evident that what seems hard to one animal may appear soft to another, who hath greater force and firmness of limbs. Nor is it less plain that the resistance I feel is not in the body.

HYLAS. I own the very *sensation* of resistance, which is all you immediately perceive, is not in the body; but the *cause* of that sensation is.

PHILONOUS. But the causes of our sensations are not things immediately perceived, and therefore are not sensible. This point I thought had been already determined.

HYLAS. I own it was; but you will pardon me if I seem a little embarrassed: I know not how to quit my old notions.

PHILONOUS. To help you out, do but consider that if *extension* be once acknowledged to have no existence without the mind, the same must necessarily be granted of motion, solidity, and gravity; since they all evidently suppose extension. It is therefore superfluous to inquire particularly concerning each of them. In denying extension, you have denied them all to have any real existence.

HYLAS. I wonder, Philonous, if what you say be true, why those philosophers who deny the secondary qualities any real existence should yet attribute it to the primary. If there is no difference between them, how can this be accounted for?

PHILONOUS. It is not my business to account for every opinion of the philosophers. But, among other reasons which may be assigned for this, it seems probable that pleasure and pain being rather annexed to the former than the latter may be one. Heat and cold, tastes and smells, have something more vividly pleasing or disagreeable than the ideas of extension, figure, and motion affect us with. And, it being too visibly absurd to hold that pain or pleasure can be in an unperceiving substance, men are more easily weaned from believing the external existence of the secondary than the primary qualities. You will be satisfied there is something in this, if you recollect the difference you made between an intense and more moderate degree of heat; allowing the one a real existence, while you denied it to the other. But, after all, there is no rational ground for that distinction; for, surely an indifferent sensation is as truly *a sensation* as one more pleasing or painful; and consequently should not any more than they be supposed to exist in an unthinking subject.

HYLAS. It is just come into my head, Philonous, that I have somewhere heard of a distinction between absolute and sensible extension. Now, though it be acknowledged that *great* and *small*, consisting merely in the relation which other extended beings have to the parts of our own bodies, do not really inhere in the substances themselves; yet nothing obliges us to hold the same with regard to *absolute extension*, which is something abstracted from *great* and *small*, from this or that particular magnitude or figure. So likewise as to motion; *swift* and *slow* are altogether relative to the succession of ideas in our own minds. But, it doth not follow, because those modifications of motion exist not without the mind, that therefore absolute motion abstracted from them doth not.

PHILONOUS. Pray what is it that distinguishes one motion, or one part of extension, from another? Is it not something sensible, as some degree of swiftness or slowness, some certain magnitude or figure peculiar to each?

HYLAS. I think so.

PHILONOUS. These qualities, therefore, stripped of all sensible properties, are without all specific and numerical differences, as the schools call them.

HYLAS. They are.

PHILONOUS. That is to say, they are extension in general, and motion in general.

HYLAS. Let it be so.

PHILONOUS. But it is a universally received maxim that *everything which exists is particular*. How then can motion in general, or extension in general, exist in any corporeal substance?

HYLAS. It will take time to solve your difficulty.

PHILONOUS. But I think the point may be speedily decided. Without doubt you can tell whether you are able to frame this or that idea. Now I am content to put our dispute on this issue. If you can frame in your thoughts a distinct *abstract idea* of motion or extension, divested of all those sensible modes, as swift and slow, great and small, round and square, and the like, which are acknowledged to exist only in the mind, I will then yield the point you contend for. But if you cannot, it will be unreasonable on your side to insist any longer upon what you have no notion of.

HYLAS. To confess ingenuously, I cannot.

PHILONOUS. Can you even separate the ideas of extension and motion from the ideas of all those qualities which they who make the distinction term *secondary*?

HYLAS. What! is it not an easy matter to consider extension and motion by themselves, abstracted from all other sensible qualities? Pray how do the mathematicians treat of them?

PHILONOUS. I acknowledge, Hylas, it is not difficult to form general propositions and reasonings about those qualities, without mentioning any other; and, in this sense, to consider or treat of them abstractedly. But, how doth it follow that, because I can pronounce the word *motion* by itself, I can form the idea of it in my mind exclusive of body? or, because theorems may be made of extension and figures, without any mention of *great* or *small*, or any other sensible mode or quality, that therefore it is possible such an abstract idea of extension, without any particular size or figure, or sensible quality, should be distinctly formed, and apprehended by the mind? Mathematicians treat of quantity, without regarding what other sensible qualities it is attended with, as being altogether indifferent to their demonstrations. But, when laying aside the words, they contemplate the bare ideas, I believe you will find, they are not the pure abstracted ideas of extension.

HYLAS. But what say you to *pure intellect*? May not abstracted ideas be framed by that faculty?

PHILONOUS. Since I cannot frame abstract ideas at all, it is plain I cannot frame them by the help of pure *intellect*, whatsoever faculty you understand by those words. Besides, not to inquire into the nature of pure intellect and its spiritual objects, as *virtue*, *reason*, *God*, or the like, thus much seems manifest—that sensible things are only to be perceived by sense, or represented by the imagination. Figures, therefore, and extension, being originally perceived by sense, do not belong to pure intellect: but, for your farther satisfaction, try if you can frame the idea of any figure, abstracted from all particularities of size, or even from other sensible qualities.

HYLAS. Let me think a little—I do not find that I can.

PHILONOUS. And can you think it possible that should really exist in nature which implies a repugnancy in its conception?

HYLAS. By no means.

PHILONOUS. Since therefore it is impossible even for the mind to disunite the ideas of extension and motion from all other sensible qualities, doth it not follow, that where the one exist there necessarily the other exist likewise?

HYLAS. It should seem so.

PHILONOUS. Consequently, the very same arguments which you admitted as conclusive against the secondary qualities are, without any farther application of force, against the primary too. Besides, if you will trust your senses, is it not plain all sensible qualities coexist, or to them, appear as being in the same place? Do they ever represent a motion, or figure, as being divested of all other visible and tangible qualities?

HYLAS. You need say no more on this head. I am free to own, if there be no secret error or oversight in our proceedings hitherto, that all sensible qualities are alike to be denied existence without the mind. But, my fear is that I have been too liberal in my former concessions, or overlooked some fallacy or other. In short, I did not take time to think.

PHILONOUS. For that matter, Hylas, you may take what time you please in reviewing the progress of our inquiry. You are at liberty to recover any slips you might have made, or offer whatever you have omitted which makes for your first opinion.

HYLAS. One great oversight I take to be this—that I did not sufficiently distinguish the *object* from the *sensation*. Now, though this latter may not exist without the mind, yet it will not thence follow that the former cannot.

PHILONOUS. What object do you mean? the object of the senses?

HYLAS. The same.

PHILONOUS. It is then immediately perceived?

HYLAS. Right.

PHILONOUS. Make me to understand the difference between what is immediately perceived and a sensation.

HYLAS. The sensation I take to be an act of the mind perceiving; besides which, there is something perceived; and this I call the *object*. For example, there is red and yellow on that tulip. But then the act of perceiving those colours is in me only, and not in the tulip.

PHILONOUS. What tulip do you speak of? Is it that which you see?

HYLAS. The same.

PHILONOUS. And what do you see beside colour, figure, and extension?

HYLAS. Nothing.

PHILONOUS. What you would say then is that the red and yellow are coexistent with the extension; is it not?

HYLAS. That is not all; I would say they have a real existence without the mind, in some unthinking substance.

PHILONOUS. That the colours are really in the tulip which I see is manifest. Neither can it be denied that this tulip may exist independent of your mind or mine; but, that any immediate object of the senses—that is, any idea, or combination of ideas—should exist in an unthinking substance, or exterior to *all* minds, is in itself an evident contradiction. Nor can I imagine how this follows from what you said just now, to wit, that the red and yellow were on the tulip *you saw*, since you do not pretend to *see* that unthinking substance.

HYLAS. You have an artful way, Philonous, of diverting our inquiry from the subject.

PHILONOUS. I see you have no mind to be pressed that way. To return then to your distinction between *sensation* and *object*; if I take you right, you distinguish in every perception two things, the one an action of the mind, the other not.

HYLAS. True.

PHILONOUS. And this action cannot exist in, or belong to, any unthinking thing; but whatever beside is implied in a perception may?

HYLAS. That is my meaning.

PHILONOUS. So that if there was a perception without any act of the mind, it were possible such a perception should exist in an unthinking substance?

HYLAS. I grant it. But it is impossible there should be such a perception.

PHILONOUS. When is the mind said to be active?

HYLAS. When it produces, puts an end to, or changes, anything.

PHILONOUS. Can the mind produce, discontinue, or change anything, but by an act of the will?

HYLAS. It cannot.

PHILONOUS. The mind therefore is to be accounted *active* in its perceptions so far forth as *volition* is included in them?

HYLAS. It is.

PHILONOUS. In plucking this flower I am active, because I do it by the motion of my hand, which was consequent upon my volition; so likewise in applying it to my nose. But is either of these smelling?

HYLAS. No.

PHILONOUS. I act too in drawing the air through my nose; because my breathing so rather than otherwise is the effect of my volition. But neither can this be called *smelling*: for, if it were, I should smell every time I breathed in that manner?

HYLAS. True.

PHILONOUS. Smelling then is somewhat consequent to all this?

HYLAS. It is.

PHILONOUS. But I do not find my will concerned any farther. Whatever more there is—as that I perceive such a particular smell, or any smell at all—this is independent of my will, and therein I am altogether passive. Do you find it otherwise with you, Hylas?

HYLAS. No, the very same.

PHILONOUS. Then, as to seeing, is it not in your power to open your eyes, or keep them shut; to turn them this or that way?

HYLAS. Without doubt.

PHILONOUS. But, doth it in like manner depend on *your* will that in looking on this flower you perceive *white* rather than any other colour? Or, directing your open eyes towards yonder part of the heaven, can you avoid seeing the sun? Or is light or darkness the effect of your volition?

HYLAS. No, certainly.

PHILONOUS. You are then in these respects altogether passive?

HYLAS. I am.

PHILONOUS. Tell me now, whether *seeing* consists in perceiving light and colours, or in opening and turning the eyes?

HYLAS. Without doubt, in the former.

PHILONOUS. Since therefore you are in the very perception of light and colours altogether passive, what is become of that action you were speaking of as an ingredient in every sensation? And, doth it not follow from your own concessions, that the perception of light and colours, including no action in it, may exist in an unperceiving substance? And is not this a plain contradiction?

HYLAS. I know not what to think of it.

PHILONOUS. Besides, since you distinguish the *active* and *passive* in every perception, you must do it in that of pain. But how is it possible that pain, be it as little active as you please, should exist in an unperceiving substance? In short, do but consider the point, and then confess ingenuously, whether light and colours, tastes, sounds, &c. are not all equally passions or sensations in the soul. You may indeed call them *external objects*, and give them in words what subsistence you please. But, examine your own thoughts, and then tell me whether it be not as I say?

HYLAS. I acknowledge, Philonous, that, upon a fair observation of what passes in my mind, I can discover nothing else but that I am a thinking being, affected with variety of sensations; neither is it possible to conceive how a sensation should exist in an unperceiving substance. But then, on the other hand, when I look on sensible things in a different view, considering them as so many modes and qualities, I find it necessary to suppose a *material substratum*, without which they cannot be conceived to exist.

PHILONOUS. *Material substratum* call you it? Pray, by which of your senses came you acquainted with that being?

HYLAS. It is not itself sensible; its modes and qualities only being perceived by the senses.

PHILONOUS. I presume then it was by reflexion and reason you obtained the idea of it?

HYLAS. I do not pretend to any proper positive *idea* of it. However, I conclude it exists, because qualities cannot be conceived to exist without a support.

PHILONOUS. It seems then you have only a relative *notion* of it, or that you conceive it not otherwise than by conceiving the relation it bears to sensible qualities?

HYLAS. Right.

PHILONOUS. Be pleased therefore to let me know wherein that relation consists.

HYLAS. Is it not sufficiently expressed in the term *substratum*, or *substance*?

PHILONOUS. If so, the word *substratum* should import that it is spread under the sensible qualities or accidents?

HYLAS. True.

PHILONOUS. And consequently under extension?

HYLAS. I own it.

PHILONOUS. It is therefore somewhat in its own nature entirely distinct from extension?

HYLAS. I tell you, extension is only a mode, and matter is something that supports modes.[24] And is it not evident the thing supported is different from the thing supporting?

PHILONOUS. So that something distinct from, and exclusive of, extension is supposed to be the *substratum* of extension?

HYLAS. Just so.

PHILONOUS. Answer me, Hylas. Can a thing be spread without extension? or is not the idea of extension necessarily included in *spreading*?

HYLAS. It is.

PHILONOUS. Whatsoever therefore you suppose spread under anything must have in itself an extension distinct from the extension of that thing under which it is spread?

HYLAS. It must.

PHILONOUS. Consequently, every corporeal substance, being the *substratum* of extension, must have in itself another extension, by which it is qualified to be a *substratum*: and so on to infinity. And I ask whether this be not absurd in itself, and

repugnant to what you granted just now, to wit, that the *substratum* was something distinct from and exclusive of extension?

HYLAS. Aye but, Philonous, you take me wrong. I do not mean that matter is *spread* in a gross literal sense under extension. The word *substratum* is used only to express in general the same thing with *substance*.

PHILONOUS. Well then, let us examine the relation implied in the term *substance*. Is it not that it stands under accidents?

HYLAS. The very same.

PHILONOUS. But, that one thing may stand under or support another, must it not be extended?

HYLAS. It must.

PHILONOUS. Is not therefore this supposition liable to the same absurdity with the former?

HYLAS. You still take things in a strict literal sense. That is not fair, Philonous.

PHILONOUS. I am not for imposing any sense on your words: you are at liberty to explain them as you please. Only, I beseech you, make me understand something by them. You tell me matter supports or stands under accidents. How! is it as your legs support your body?

HYLAS. No; that is the literal sense.

PHILONOUS. Pray let me know any sense, literal or not literal, that you understand it in.—How long must I wait for an answer, Hylas?

HYLAS. I declare I know not what to say. I once thought I understood well enough what was meant by matter's supporting accidents. But now, the more I think on it the less can I comprehend it: in short I find that I know nothing of it.

PHILONOUS. It seems then you have no idea at all, neither relative nor positive, of matter; you know neither what it is in itself, nor what relation it bears to accidents?

HYLAS. I acknowledge it.

PHILONOUS. And yet you asserted that you could not conceive how qualities or accidents should really exist, without conceiving at the same time a material support of them?

HYLAS. I did.

PHILONOUS. That is to say, when you conceive the real existence of qualities, you do withal conceive something which you cannot conceive?

---

24   For Berkeley (as opposed to Locke) a mode is simply a quality, a kind of property.

HYLAS. It was wrong, I own. But still I fear there is some fallacy or other. Pray what think you of this? It is just come into my head that the ground of all our mistake lies in your treating of each quality by itself. Now, I grant that each quality cannot singly subsist without the mind. Colour cannot without extension, neither can figure without some other sensible quality. But, as the several qualities united or blended together form entire sensible things, nothing hinders why such things may not be supposed to exist without the mind.

PHILONOUS. Either, Hylas, you are jesting, or have a very bad memory. Though indeed we went through all the qualities by name one after another, yet my arguments or rather your concessions, nowhere tended to prove that the secondary qualities did not subsist each alone by itself; but, that they were not *at all* without the mind. Indeed, in treating of figure and motion we concluded they could not exist without the mind, because it was impossible even in thought to separate them from all secondary qualities, so as to conceive them existing by themselves. But then this was not the only argument made use of upon that occasion. But (to pass by all that hath been hitherto said, and reckon it for nothing, if you will have it so) I am content to put the whole upon this issue. If you can conceive it possible for any mixture or combination of qualities, or any sensible object whatever, to exist without the mind, then I will grant it actually to be so.

HYLAS. If it comes to that the point will soon be decided. What more easy than to conceive a tree or house existing by itself, independent of, and unperceived by, any mind whatsoever? I do at this present time conceive them existing after that manner.

PHILONOUS. How say you, Hylas; can you see a thing which is at the same time unseen?

HYLAS. No, that were a contradiction.

PHILONOUS. Is it not as great a contradiction to talk of *conceiving* a thing which is *unconceived*?

HYLAS. It is.

PHILONOUS. The, tree or house therefore which you think of is conceived by you?

HYLAS. How should it be otherwise?

PHILONOUS. And what is conceived is surely in the mind?

HYLAS. Without question, that which is conceived is in the mind.

PHILONOUS. How then came you to say, you conceived a house or tree existing independent and out of all minds whatsoever?

HYLAS. That was I own an oversight; but stay, let me consider what led me into it.—It is a pleasant[25] mistake enough. As I was thinking of a tree in a solitary place, where no one was present to see it, methought that was to conceive a tree as existing unperceived or unthought of; not considering that I myself conceived it all the while. But now I plainly see that all I can do is to frame ideas in my own mind. I may indeed conceive in my own thoughts the idea of a tree, or a house, or a mountain, but that is all. And this is far from proving that I can conceive them *existing out of the minds of all spirits*.

PHILONOUS. You acknowledge then that you cannot possibly conceive how any one corporeal sensible thing should exist otherwise than in the mind?

HYLAS. I do.

PHILONOUS. And yet you will earnestly contend for the truth of that which you cannot so much as conceive?

HYLAS. I profess I know not what to think; but still there are some scruples remain with me. Is it not certain I see things at a distance? Do we not perceive the stars and moon, for example, to be a great way off? Is not this, I say, manifest to the senses?

PHILONOUS. Do you not in a dream too perceive those or the like objects?

HYLAS. I do.

PHILONOUS. And have they not then the same appearance of being distant?

HYLAS. They have.

PHILONOUS. But you do not thence conclude the apparitions in a dream to be without the mind?

HYLAS. By no means.

PHILONOUS. You ought not therefore to conclude that sensible objects are without the mind, from their appearance, or manner wherein they are perceived.

HYLAS. I acknowledge it. But doth not my sense deceive me in those cases?

PHILONOUS. By no means. The idea or thing which you immediately perceive, neither sense nor reason informs you that it actually exists without the mind. By sense you only know that you are affected with

---

25   Amusing.

such certain sensations of light and colours, &c. And these you will not say are without the mind.

HYLAS. True: but, beside all that, do you not think the sight suggests something of *outness* or *distance*?

PHILONOUS. Upon approaching a distant object, do the visible size and figure change perpetually, or do they appear the same at all distances?

HYLAS. They are in a continual change.

PHILONOUS. Sight therefore doth not suggest, or any way inform you, that the visible object you immediately perceive exists at a distance, or will be perceived when you advance farther onward; there being a continued series of visible objects succeeding each other during the whole time of your approach.

HYLAS. It doth not; but still I know, upon seeing an object, what object I shall perceive after having passed over a certain distance: no matter whether it be exactly the same or no: there is still something of distance suggested in the case.

PHILONOUS. Good Hylas, do but reflect a little on the point, and then tell me whether there be any more in it than this: from the ideas you actually perceive by sight, you have by experience learned to collect what other ideas you will (according to the standing order of nature) be affected with, after such a certain succession of time and motion.

HYLAS. Upon the whole, I take it to be nothing else.

PHILONOUS. Now, is it not plain that if we suppose a man born blind was on a sudden made to see, he could at first have no experience of what may be suggested by sight?

HYLAS. It is.

PHILONOUS. He would not then, according to you, have any notion of distance annexed to the things he saw; but would take them for a new set of sensations, existing only in his mind?

HYLAS. It is undeniable.

PHILONOUS. But, to make it still more plain: is not *distance* a line turned endwise to the eye?

HYLAS. It is.

PHILONOUS. And can a line so situated be perceived by sight?

HYLAS. It cannot.

PHILONOUS. Doth it not therefore follow that distance is not properly and immediately perceived by sight?

HYLAS. It should seem so.

PHILONOUS. Again, is it your opinion that colours are at a distance?

HYLAS. It must be acknowledged they are only in the mind.

PHILONOUS. But do not colours appear to the eye as co-existing in the same place with extension and figures?

HYLAS. They do.

PHILONOUS. How can you then conclude from sight that figures exist without, when you acknowledge colours do not; the sensible appearance being the very same with regard to both?

HYLAS. I know not what to answer.

PHILONOUS. But, allowing that distance was truly and immediately perceived by the mind, yet it would not thence follow it existed out of the mind. For, whatever is immediately perceived is an idea: and can any idea exist out of the mind?

HYLAS. To suppose that were absurd: but, inform me, Philonous, can we perceive or know nothing beside our ideas?

PHILONOUS. As for the rational deducing of causes from effects, that is beside our inquiry. And, by the senses you can best tell whether you perceive anything which is not immediately perceived. And I ask you, whether the things immediately perceived are other than your own sensations or ideas? You have indeed more than once, in the course of this conversation, declared yourself on those points; but you seem, by this last question, to have departed from what you then thought.

HYLAS. To speak the truth, Philonous, I think there are two kinds of objects:—the one perceived immediately, which are likewise called *ideas*; the other are real things or external objects, perceived by the mediation of ideas, which are their images and representations. Now, I own ideas do not exist without the mind; but the latter sort of objects do. I am sorry I did not think of this distinction sooner; it would probably have cut short your discourse.

PHILONOUS. Are those external objects perceived by sense or by some other faculty?

HYLAS. They are perceived by sense.

PHILONOUS. How! is there any thing perceived by sense which is not immediately perceived?

HYLAS. Yes, Philonous, in some sort there is. For example, when I look on a picture or statue of Julius

Caesar, I may be said after a manner to perceive him (though not immediately) by my senses.

PHILONOUS. It seems then you will have our ideas, which alone are immediately perceived, to be pictures of external things: and that these also are perceived by sense, inasmuch as they have a conformity or resemblance to our ideas?

HYLAS. That is my meaning.

PHILONOUS. And, in the same way that Julius Caesar, in himself invisible, is nevertheless perceived by sight; real things, in themselves imperceptible, are perceived by sense.

HYLAS. In the very same.

PHILONOUS. Tell me, Hylas, when you behold the picture of Julius Caesar, do you see with your eyes any more than some colours and figures, with a certain symmetry and composition of the whole?

HYLAS. Nothing else.

PHILONOUS. And would not a man who had never known anything of Julius Caesar see as much?

HYLAS. He would.

PHILONOUS. Consequently he hath his sight, and the use of it, in as perfect a degree as you?

HYLAS. I agree with you.

PHILONOUS. Whence comes it then that your thoughts are directed to the Roman emperor, and his are not? This cannot proceed from the sensations or ideas of sense by you then perceived; since you acknowledge you have no advantage over him in that respect. It should seem therefore to proceed from reason and memory: should it not?

HYLAS. It should.

PHILONOUS. Consequently, it will not follow from that instance that anything is perceived by sense which is not immediately perceived. Though I grant we may, in one acceptation,[26] be said to perceive sensible things mediately by sense: that is, when, from a frequently perceived connexion, the immediate perception of ideas by one sense *suggests* to the mind others, perhaps belonging to another sense, which are wont to be connected with them. For instance, when I hear a coach drive along the streets, immediately I perceive only the sound; but, from the experience I have had that such a sound is connected with a coach, I am said to

hear the coach. It is nevertheless evident that, in truth and strictness, nothing can be *heard* but *sound*; and the coach is not then properly perceived by sense, but suggested from experience. So likewise when we are said to see a red-hot bar of iron; the solidity and heat of the iron are not the objects of sight, but suggested to the imagination by the colour and figure which are properly perceived by that sense. In short, those things alone are actually and strictly perceived by any sense, which would have been perceived in case that same sense had then been first conferred on us. As for other things, it is plain they are only suggested to the mind by experience, grounded on former perceptions. But, to return to your comparison of Caesar's picture, it is plain, if you keep to that, you must hold the real things, or archetypes of our ideas, are not perceived by sense, but by some internal faculty of the soul, as reason or memory. I would therefore fain know what arguments you can draw from reason for the existence of what you call *real things* or *material objects*. Or, whether you remember to have seen them formerly as they are in themselves; or, if you have heard or read of any one that did.

HYLAS. I see, Philonous, you are disposed to raillery; but that will never convince me.

PHILONOUS. My aim is only to learn from you the way to come at the knowledge of *material beings*. Whatever we perceive is perceived immediately or mediately: by sense, or by reason and reflexion. But, as you have excluded sense, pray shew me what reason you have to believe their existence; or what *medium* you can possibly make use of to prove it, either to mine or your own understanding.

HYLAS. To deal ingenuously, Philonous, now I consider the point, I do not find I can give you any good reason for it. But, thus much seems pretty plain, that it is at least possible such things may really exist. And, as long as there is no absurdity in supposing them, I am resolved to believe as I did, till you bring good reasons to the contrary.

PHILONOUS. What! Is it come to this, that you only *believe* the existence of material objects, and that your belief is founded barely on the possibility of its being true? Then you will have me bring reasons against it: though another would think it reasonable the proof should lie on him who holds the affirmative. And,

---

26   In one way of using the word.

after all, this very point which you are now resolved to maintain, without any reason, is in effect what you have more than once during this discourse seen good reason to give up. But, to pass over all this; if I understand you rightly, you say our ideas do not exist without the mind, but that they are copies, images, or representations, of certain originals that do?

HYLAS. You take me right.

PHILONOUS. They are then like external things?

HYLAS. They are.

PHILONOUS. Have those things a stable and permanent nature, independent of our senses; or are they in a perpetual change, upon our producing any motions in our bodies—suspending, exerting, or altering, our faculties or organs of sense?

HYLAS. Real things, it is plain, have a fixed and real nature, which remains the same notwithstanding any change in our senses, or in the posture and motion of our bodies; which indeed may affect the ideas in our minds, but it were absurd to think they had the same effect on things existing without the mind.

PHILONOUS. How then is it possible that things perpetually fleeting and variable as our ideas should be copies or images of anything fixed and constant? Or, in other words, since all sensible qualities, as size, figure, colour, &c., that is, our ideas, are continually changing, upon every alteration in the distance, medium, or instruments of sensation; how can any determinate material objects be properly represented or painted forth by several distinct things, each of which is so different from and unlike the rest? Or, if you say it resembles some one only of our ideas, how shall we be able to distinguish the true copy from all the false ones?

HYLAS. I profess, Philonous, I am at a loss. I know not what to say to this.

PHILONOUS. But neither is this all. Which are material objects in themselves—perceptible or imperceptible?

HYLAS. Properly and immediately nothing can be perceived but ideas. All material things, therefore, are in themselves insensible, and to be perceived only by our ideas.

PHILONOUS. Ideas then are sensible, and their archetypes or originals insensible?

HYLAS. Right.

PHILONOUS. But how can that which is sensible be like that which is insensible? Can a real thing, in itself *in-* *visible*, be like a *colour*; or a real thing, which is not *audible*, be like a *sound*? In a word, can anything be like a sensation or idea, but another sensation or idea?

HYLAS. I must own, I think not.

PHILONOUS. Is it possible there should be any doubt on the point? Do you not perfectly know your own ideas?

HYLAS. I know them perfectly; since what I do not perceive or know can be no part of my idea.

PHILONOUS. Consider, therefore, and examine them, and then tell me if there be anything in them which can exist without the mind: or if you can conceive anything like them existing without the mind.

HYLAS. Upon inquiry, I find it is impossible for me to conceive or understand how anything but an idea can be like an idea. And it is most evident that *no idea can exist without the mind*.

PHILONOUS. You are therefore, by your principles, forced to deny the *reality* of sensible things; since you made it to consist in an absolute existence exterior to the mind. That is to say, you are a downright sceptic. So I have gained my point, which was to shew your principles led to scepticism.

HYLAS. For the present I am, if not entirely convinced, at least silenced.

PHILONOUS. I would fain know what more you would require in order to a perfect conviction. Have you not had the liberty of explaining yourself all manner of ways? Were any little slips in discourse laid hold and insisted on? Or were you not allowed to retract or reinforce anything you had offered, as best served your purpose? Hath not everything you could say been heard and examined with all the fairness imaginable? In a word have you not in every point been convinced out of your own mouth? And, if you can at present discover any flaw in any of your former concessions, or think of any remaining subterfuge, any new distinction, colour, or comment whatsoever, why do you not produce it?

HYLAS. A little patience, Philonous. I am at present so amazed to see myself ensnared, and as it were imprisoned in the labyrinths you have drawn me into, that on the sudden it cannot be expected I should find my way out. You must give me time to look about me and recollect myself.

PHILONOUS. Hark; is not this the college bell?

HYLAS. It rings for prayers.

PHILONOUS. We will go in then, if you please, and meet here again tomorrow morning. In the meantime, you may employ your thoughts on this morning's discourse, and try if you can find any fallacy in it, or invent any new means to extricate yourself.

HYLAS. Agreed.

IMMANUEL KANT
Critique of Pure Reason

Who Was Immanuel Kant?

Immanuel Kant—by common consent the most important philosopher of the past 300 years, and arguably the most important of the past 2,300—was born in 1724 on the coast of the Baltic Sea, in Königsberg, a regionally important harbor city in East Prussia.[1] Kant spent his whole life living in this town, and never ventured outside its region. His family were devout members of an evangelical Protestant sect (rather like the Quakers or early Methodists) called the Pietists, and Pietism's strong emphasis on moral responsibility, hard work, and distrust of religious dogma had a deep effect on Kant's character. Kant's father was a craftsman (making harnesses and saddles for horses) and his family was fairly poor; Kant's mother, whom he loved deeply, died when he was 13.

Kant's life is notorious for its outward uneventfulness. He was educated at a strict Lutheran school in Königsberg, and after graduating from the University of Königsberg in 1746 (where he supported himself by some tutoring but also by his skill at billiards and card games) he served as a private tutor to various local families until he became a lecturer at the university in 1755. However his position—that of *Privatdozent*—carried no salary, and Kant was expected to support himself by the income from his lecturing; financial need caused Kant to lecture for thirty or more hours a week on a huge range of subjects (including mathematics, physics, geography, anthropology, ethics, and law). During this period Kant published several scientific works and his reputation as a scholar grew; he turned down opportunities for professorships in other towns (Erlangen and Jena), having his heart set on a professorship in Königsberg. Finally, at the age of 46, Kant became professor of logic and metaphysics at the University of Königsberg, a position he held until his retirement twenty-six years later in 1796. After a tragic period of senility he died in 1804, and was buried with pomp and circumstance in the "professors' vault" at the Königsberg cathedral.[2]

Kant's days were structured by a rigorous and unvarying routine—indeed, it is often said that the housewives of Königsberg were able to set their clocks by the regularity of his afternoon walk. He never married (though twice he nearly did), had very few close friends, and lived by all accounts an austere and outwardly unemotional life. He was something of a hypochondriac, hated noise, and disliked all music

---

1   Prussia is a historical region which included what is today northern Germany, Poland, and the western fringes of Russia. It became a kingdom in 1701, and then a dominant part of the newly unified Germany in 1871. Greatly reduced after World War I, the state of Prussia was formally abolished after World War II, and Königsberg—renamed Kaliningrad during the Soviet era, after one of Stalin's henchmen—now sits on the western rump of Russia (between Poland and Lithuania).

2   His body no longer remains there: in 1950 his sarcophagus was broken open by unknown vandals and his corpse was stolen and never recovered.

except for military marches. Nevertheless, anecdotes by those who knew him give the impression of a warm, impressive, rather noble human being, capable of great kindness and dignity and sparkling conversation. He did not shun society, and in fact his regular daily routine included an extended lunchtime gathering at which he and his guests—drawn from the cosmopolitan stratum of Königsberg society—would discuss politics, science, philosophy, and poetry.

Kant's philosophical life is often divided into three phases: his "pre-Critical" period, his "silent" period, and his "Critical" period. His pre-Critical period began in 1747 when he published his first work (*Thoughts on the True Estimation of Living Forces*) and ended in 1770 when he wrote his Inaugural Dissertation—*Concerning the Form and Principles of the Sensible and Intelligible World*—and became a professor. Between 1770 and 1780, Kant published almost nothing. In 1781, however, at the age of 57, Kant made his first major contribution to philosophy with his monumental *Critique of Pure Reason* (written, Kant said, over the course of a few months "as if in flight"). He spent the next twenty years in unrelenting intellectual labor, trying to develop and answer the new problems laid out in this masterwork. First, in order to clarify and simplify the system of the *Critique* for the educated public, Kant published the much shorter *Prolegomena to Any Future Metaphysics* in 1783. In 1785 came Kant's *Foundations of the Metaphysics of Morals,* and in 1788 he published what is now known as his "second Critique": the *Critique of Practical Reason.* His third and final Critique, the *Critique of Judgement,* was published in 1790—an amazing body of work produced in less than ten years.

By the time he died, Kant had already become known as a great philosopher, with a permanent place in history. Over his grave was inscribed a quote from the *Critique of Practical Reason,* which sums up the impulse for his philosophy: "Two things fill the mind with ever new and increasing admiration and

reverence, the more often and more steadily one reflects on them: the starry heavens above me and the moral law within me."

What Was Kant's Overall Philosophical Project?

Kant began his philosophical career as a follower of rationalism. Rationalism was an important seventeenth- and eighteenth-century intellectual movement begun by Descartes and developed by Leibniz and his follower Christian Wolff, which held that all knowledge was capable of being part of a single, complete "science": that is, all knowledge can be slotted into a total, unified system of *a priori*, and certainly true, claims capable of encompassing everything that exists in the world, whether we have experience of it or not. In other words, for the German rationalists of Kant's day, metaphysical philosophy—which then included theoretical science—was thought of as being very similar to pure mathematics. Rationalism was also, in Kantian terminology, "dogmatic" as opposed to "critical": that is, it sought to construct systems of knowledge without first attempting a careful examination of the scope and limits of possible knowledge. (This is why Kant's rationalist period is usually called his pre-Critical phase.)

In 1781, after ten years of hard thought, Kant rejected this rationalistic view of philosophy: he came to the view that metaphysics, as traditionally understood, is so far from being a rational science that it is not even a body of knowledge at all. Three major stimuli provoked Kant into being "awakened from his dogmatic slumber," as he put it. First, in about 1769, Kant came to the conclusion that he had discovered several "antinomies"—sets of contradictory propositions *each* of which can apparently be *rationally proven* to be true of reality (if we assume that our intellectual concepts apply to reality at all) and yet which can't both be true. For example, Kant argued that rational arguments are available to prove both that reality is finite but also that it is infinite, and that it is composed of indivisible atoms yet also infinitely divisible. Since both halves of these two pairs can't possibly be true at the same time, Kant argued that this casts serious doubt on the power of pure reason to draw metaphysical conclusions.

Second, Kant was worried about the conflict between free will and natural causality (this is a theme that appears throughout Kant's Critical works). He was convinced that genuine morality must be based on *freely* choosing—or "willing"— to do what is right. To be worthy of moral praise, in Kant's view, one must choose to do *X* rather than *Y*, not because some law of nature causes you to do so, but because your rational self is convinced that it is the right thing to do.[3] Yet he also thought that the rational understanding of reality sought by the metaphysicians could only be founded on universally extending the laws we find in the scientific study of nature—and this includes universal causal determination, the principle that nothing (including choosing *X* over *Y*) happens without a cause. This, for Kant, produces an antinomy: some actions are free (i.e., *not* bound by the laws of nature) and yet everything that happens *is* determined by a law of nature.

Kant resolved this paradox by arguing that the scientific view of reality (including that pursued by the rationalists) must in principle be *incomplete*. Roughly, he held that although we can only rationally understand reality by thinking of it as causally deterministic and governed by scientific laws, our intellectual reason can never encompass *all* of reality. According to Kant, there must be a level of ultimate reality which is beyond the scope of pure reason, and which allows for the free activity of what Kant calls "practical reason" (which therefore holds open the possibility of genuine morality).

The third alarm bell to rouse Kant from his pre-Critical dogmatism was his reading of the Scottish philosopher David Hume (see Chapter 3). Hume was not a rationalist but instead represented the culmination of the other main seventeenth- and

eighteenth-century stream of philosophical thought, usually called empiricism. Instead of thinking of knowledge as a unified, systematic, *a priori* whole, as the rationalists did, empiricists like Locke and Hume saw knowledge as being a piecemeal accumulation of claims derived primarily, not from pure logic, but from *sensation*—from our experience of the world. Science, for Hume, is thus not *a priori* but *a posteriori*: for example, we cannot just *deduce* from first principles that heavy objects tend to fall to the ground, as the rationalists supposed we could; we can only learn this by observing it to happen in our experience. The trouble was that Hume appeared to Kant (and to many others) to have shown that experience is simply *inadequate* for establishing the kind of metaphysical principles that philosophers have traditionally defended: no amount of sense-experience could ever either prove or disprove that God exists, that substance is imperishable, that we have an immortal soul, or even that there exist mind-independent "physical" objects which interact with each other according to causal laws of nature. Not just what we now think of as "philosophy" but theoretical science itself seemed to be called into question by Hume's "skeptical" philosophy. Since Kant was quite sure that mathematics and the natural sciences were genuine bodies of knowledge, he needed to show how such knowledge was possible despite Hume's skepticism: that is, as well as combating the excessive claims of rationalism, he needed to show how empiricism went wrong in the other direction.

Prior to Kant, seventeenth- and eighteenth-century philosophers divided knowledge into exactly two camps: "truths of reason" (or "relations of ideas") on the one hand, and "truths of fact" (or "matters of fact") on the other. Rationalism was characterized by the doctrine that all final, complete knowledge was a truth of reason: that is, it was made up entirely of claims that could be proven *a priori* as being necessarily true, as a matter of logic, since it would be self-contradictory for them to be false. Empiricists, on the other hand, believed that all genuinely *informative* claims were truths of fact: if we wanted to find out about the world itself, rather than merely the logical relations between our own concepts, we had to rely upon the (*a posteriori*) data of sensory experience.

---

3   For more on Kant's ethical views, see his *Foundations of the Metaphysics of Morals*.

Kant, however, reshaped this distinction in a new framework which, he argued, cast a vital new light upon the nature of metaphysics. Instead of merely drawing a distinction between truths of reason and truths of fact, Kant replaced this with *two* separate distinctions: that between "*a priori*" and "*a posteriori*" propositions, and that between "analytic" and "synthetic" judgments. On this more complex scheme, the rationalists' truths of reason turn out to be "analytic *a priori*" knowledge, while empirical truths of fact are "synthetic *a posteriori*" propositions. But, Kant pointed out, this leaves open the possibility that there is at least a *third* type of knowledge: *synthetic a priori* judgments. These are judgments which we know *a priori* and thus do not need to learn from experience, but which nevertheless go beyond merely "analytic" claims about our own concepts. Kant's central claim in the *Critique of Pure Reason* is that he is the first philosopher in history to understand that the traditional claims of metaphysics—questions about God, the soul, free will, the underlying nature of space, time and matter—consist entirely of synthetic *a priori* propositions. (He also argues that pure mathematics is synthetic *a priori* as well.)

Kant's question therefore becomes: How is synthetic *a priori* knowledge possible? After all, the source of this knowledge can be neither experience (since it is *a priori*) nor the logical relations of ideas (since it is synthetic), so where could this kind of knowledge possibly come from? Once we have discovered the conditions of synthetic *a priori* knowledge, we can ask what its limits are: in particular, we can ask whether the traditional claims of speculative metaphysics meet those conditions, and thus whether they can be known to be true.

In bald (and massively simplified) summary, Kant's answer to these questions in the *Critique of Pure Reason* is the following. Synthetic *a priori* knowledge is possible insofar as it is knowledge of the *conditions of our experience of the world* (or indeed, of any *possible* experience). For example, for Kant, our judgments about the fundamental nature of space and time are not claims about our experiences themselves, nor are they the results of logic: instead, the forms of space and time are the conditions under which we are capable of having experience *at all*—we *can* only undergo

sensations (either perceived or imaginary) that are arranged in space, and spread out in time; anything else is just impossible for us. So we can know *a priori*, but not analytically, that space and time must have a certain nature, since they are the forms of (the very possibility of) our experience.

Kant, famously, described this insight as constituting a kind of "Copernican revolution" in philosophy: just as Copernicus set cosmology on a totally new path by suggesting (in 1543) that the Earth orbits the Sun and not the other way around, so Kant wanted to breathe new life into philosophy by suggesting that, rather than assuming that "all our knowledge must conform to objects," we might instead "suppose that objects must conform to our knowledge." That is, rather than merely passively representing mind-independent objects in a "real" world, Kant held that the mind actively *constitutes* its objects—by *imposing* the categories of time, space, and causation onto our sensory experience, the subject actually *creates* the only kind of reality to which it has access. (This is why Kant's philosophy is often called "transcendental idealism." However, Kant is not a full-out idealist in the way that, say, Berkeley is. He does not claim that the *existence* of objects is mind-dependent—only God's mind is capable of this kind of creation, according to Kant. Instead, the *a priori properties* of objects are what we constitute, by the structures of our cognition.)

When we turn to speculative metaphysics, however, we try to go beyond experience and its conditions—we attempt to move beyond what Kant called the "phenomena" of experience, and to make judgments about the nature of a reality that lies behind our sensory experience, what Kant called the "noumenal" realm. And here pure reason reaches its limits. If we ask about the nature of "things in themselves," independently of our experience of them, or if we try to show whether a supra-sensible God really exists, then our faculty of reason is powerless to demonstrate that these synthetic *a priori* judgments are either true or false—these metaphysical questions are neither empirical, nor logical, nor about the basic categories of our experience, so there is simply no way to answer them. The questions are meaningful ones (human beings crave answers to them) but they are beyond the scope of our faculty of reason. In short, we can have knowledge only of things that can be objects of possible experience, and cannot know anything that transcends the phenomenal realm.

This result, according to Kant, finally lets philosophy cease its constant oscillation between dogmatism and skepticism. It sets out the area in which human cognition is capable of attaining lasting truth (theoretical science—the metaphysics of experience—and mathematics), and that in which reason leads to self-contradiction and illusion (speculative metaphysics). Importantly, for Kant, this Copernican revolution provides *morality* with all the metaphysical support it needs, by clearing an area for free will.

What Is the Structure of This Reading?

Kant begins by conceding to the empiricists that, as a matter of psychological fact, we acquire a lot of knowledge through our experience of the world. But, he claims, this does not by itself show that all our knowledge is really *empirical*, and in Section I he draws a distinction between "pure" and "empirical" knowledge in order to make this issue clearer. In the next section he lays out two criteria for distinguishing between pure and empirical knowledge and uses these criteria to argue that we do in fact have a quantity of important pure *a priori* knowledge. However, in Section III, Kant claims that a lot of what we think can be known *a priori* is actually mere fabrication: what is needed, therefore, is a way of accurately *telling the difference* between reliable and unreliable *a priori* judgments. The first step in doing this, according to Kant, is to draw a distinction between analytic and synthetic judgments. He proceeds to do this in Section IV. He then argues, in Section V, that all our interesting *a priori* knowledge—mathematics, the principles of natural science, metaphysics—is synthetic. The "general problem of pure reason," therefore (Section VI) is to develop an account of how synthetic *a priori* judgments are possible, which will in turn tell us when they are reliable and when they are not. According to Kant, we must replace dogmatic philosophy with *critical* and *transcendental* philosophy: i.e., we must undertake a critique of pure reason, as Kant explains in Section VII.

Some Useful Background Information

1. *A priori* is Latin for "what is earlier" and *a posteriori* means "what comes after." These terms were used as early as the fourteenth century to mark a distinction (which dates back to Aristotle) between two different directions of *reasoning*: in this usage, now out of date, an *a priori* argument reasons from a ground to its consequence, while to argue *a posteriori* is to argue backwards from a consequence to its ground. For example, Descartes' "Trademark" argument for the existence of God in the Third Meditation is *a posteriori* in this archaic sense since it starts from his idea of God and moves to the 'only' possible cause of that idea, which is God himself. By contrast, St. Anselm of Canterbury's ontological argument is *a priori* in the medieval sense since, while it also begins with the idea of God, it does not argue 'backwards' to the cause of the idea but 'forwards' to the idea's (alleged) logical consequence, which is the necessary existence of God.

The *modern* usage of *a priori* and *a posteriori*, however, was formulated in the late seventeenth and eighteenth century, primarily by Leibniz and Kant, and has now wholly replaced the older meanings. The selection from Kant reprinted here includes the classic statement of the distinction (though the new usage first appeared much earlier—see, for example, section eight of Leibniz's *Discourse on Metaphysics*, published in 1686). One thing to notice is that the distinction is no longer one between two different directions of reasoning but instead distinguishes primarily between two different types of *knowledge*: the standard example of *a priori* knowledge is the truths of mathematics, and of *a posteriori* knowledge, the results of the natural sciences. This distinction between kinds of knowledge then motivates a similar distinction between two kinds of proposition, two kinds of concept, and two kinds of justification.

Kant himself prefers to use the words "pure" and "empirical" for *a priori* and *a posteriori* knowledge themselves, and usually reserves the terms "*a priori*" and "*a posteriori*" to describe the sources of this knowledge—the way in which it is acquired.

2. At the end of the Introduction to the *Critique*, Kant says that there are "two stems of human knowledge": sensibility and understanding. This is an important assumption of Kant's, and is reflected throughout the reading given here (in, for example, Kant's distinction between intuitions and concepts). Furthermore, it structures the way in which Kant proceeds with his critique of pure reason after the introduction: he deals first with what he calls the Transcendental Aesthetic,[4] which has to do with the faculty of sensibility, and secondly with the Transcendental Analytic, which applies to the faculty of understanding. The faculty of sensibility, according to Kant, is our capacity to passively receive objects into our mental world; this is achieved primarily through sensation, but these sensations are possible only if the objects are *intuited*: that is, roughly, represented as concretely existing in space and time. The faculty of understanding, on the other hand, is our capacity to actively produce knowledge through the application of *concepts*. When concepts are compared with each other, we produce logical knowledge; when concepts (such as space, time, and causation) are combined with intuitions we get empirical knowledge. (However, when concepts that arise out of our knowledge of the empirical world are applied to a realm beyond experience we do not get *any* kind of knowledge, according to Kant: he calls these metaphysical concepts *ideas*, the three most important of which are God, freedom, and immortality.)

A Common Misconception

Some people, on reading Kant for the first time, are thrown off by the word "transcendental." For Kant,

transcendental knowledge is knowledge about the necessary conditions for the possibility of experience (for example, "every event has a cause" is a transcendental claim, according to Kant). Thus, transcendental knowledge is *not*, as would be easy to assume, knowledge of *things which are transcendent* (i.e., of things which lie beyond the empirical world, such as God and other spirits). Therefore Kant's "transcendental philosophy" has nothing to do with, say, Transcendental Meditation.

How Important and Influential Is This Passage?

Within just a few years of the publication of the *Critique of Pure Reason*, Kant was recognized by many of his intellectual contemporaries as one of the great philosophers of all time. The first *Critique* is a candidate for being the single most important philosophical book ever written, and can be thought of as decisively changing the path of Western philosophy. In particular, it did away with the assumption that knowledge is a fixed and stable thing which can be more or less passively received into the mind through either experience or reason, and replaced it with a picture that sees human beings as active *participants* in the construction of our representations of the world. That is, the mind is not a passive receptacle of data but is instead an active *filter* and *creator* of our reality. The implications of this view are still being explored by professional philosophers, such as Hilary Putnam and Richard Rorty, today.

The distinction between analytic and synthetic propositions which Kant formulates in the selection reprinted here, as well as being foundational to his new philosophical system, has also had a great impact on philosophy. From the end of the eighteenth century until the 1950s it was generally accepted as marking a fundamental and important difference between kinds of knowledge. Today, however, the distinction has been thrown into question by philosophers who doubt that we can really make good sense of one concept "containing" or being "synonymous" with another.

---

4   When Kant uses the word "aesthetic"—as in "the transcendental aesthetic"—he means generally "having to do with sense-perception" rather than merely "beautiful."

Suggestions for Critical Reflection

1. Kant's two distinctions—between *a priori* and *a posteriori* propositions, and between analytic and synthetic propositions—allow him to distinguish between *four* different types of knowledge. However, he only entertains the possibility of *three* of those classes of proposition: the analytic *a priori*, synthetic *a priori*, and synthetic *a posteriori*. What is it about the notion of *analytic a posteriori* knowledge which causes Kant to dismiss it as incoherent? Is Kant right about this?

2. There is another distinction between types of propositions which Kant was clearly aware of, and which is often listed along with the *a priori/a posteriori* and analytic/synthetic contrasts: this is the distinction between propositions which are *necessarily* true, and those which are only *contingently* true. (A proposition is necessarily true if it is true no matter what—if no change you could possibly make to the world would make it false. A proposition is contingent if it is possibly, but not necessarily, true.) How, if at all, might this necessary/contingent distinction complicate Kant's classification of knowledge? For example, could some synthetic *a posteriori* propositions be necessary and others be contingent?

3. How adequate is Kant's criterion for the distinction between analytic and synthetic propositions? If you try out this distinction on a number of examples, do you find you can easily tell which are analytic and which synthetic? (How about, for example, "nothing is red all over and green all over at the same time," "water is H_2O," "all tigers are mammals," "2 is less than 3," "contradictions are impossible," or "every event has a cause"?)

4. Kant argues that mathematical knowledge is synthetic rather than analytic. Do you think he is right, or do you think it is more plausible to say that mathematics deals entirely with the *analytic* relations between our mathematical *concepts*? If Kant is wrong about mathematics being synthetic, how much harm do you think this causes to his overall philosophical framework—for example, would he then be in danger of turning into just a German Hume?

5. Kant claims that some of the principles of natural science are synthetic *a priori*: that is, they are not learned from experience but are in some sense *prior* to experience. (As he hints at the beginning of the reading, Kant's view is that although all our knowledge *begins* with experience it does not all *arise* out of experience.) How plausible do you find this claim? How radical is it—what implications might it have for the way we think of the relationship between our minds and external reality?

6. Do you share Kant's skepticism about speculative metaphysics? If so, do you agree with his reasons for rejecting it? If not, where does Kant go wrong?

7. Are there really any such things as synthetic *a priori* propositions, or are all *a priori* propositions really analytic and all synthetic propositions really *a posteriori*?

Suggestions for Further Reading

Three translations into English of the *Critique of Pure Reason* are currently available: the old standard by Norman Kemp Smith (Macmillan, 1933), the relatively student-friendly version by Werner Pluhar (Hackett, 1997), and the new scholarly edition by Paul Guyer and Allen Wood (Cambridge University Press, 1998). The *Critique of Pure Reason* is notoriously difficult to read, partly because of its philosophical difficulty but also because of its relatively unattractive prose style and complex structure (the German poet Heinrich Heine accused it of having a "colorless, dry, packing-paper style" with a "stiff, abstract form"). Kant himself was aware of this problem, and his *Prolegomena to Any Future Metaphysics* was intended to be a shorter and more lively summary of the main themes of the *Critique*. Cambridge University Press published a good edition translated by Gary Hatfield in 1997; a well-used older translation is by Lewis White Beck, originally published in 1950 by Bobbs-Merrill.

Kant's Life and Thought, by Ernst Cassirer (translated by James Haden and published by Yale University Press in 1981) is a well-respected intellectual biography of Kant, while perhaps the best single, short introduction to the *Critique* itself is Sebastian Gardner's *Kant and the Critique of Pure Reason* (Routledge, 1999). A.C. Ewing's *Short Commentary on Kant's Critique of Pure Reason* (University of Chicago Press, 1938) is an older but still well-respected brief introduction to this work. Two detailed running commentaries on the *Critique* are by Norman Kemp Smith, *A Commentary to Kant's "Critique of Pure Reason"* (revised and enlarged second edition from Humanities Press, 1992) and H.J. Paton, *A Commentary on the First Half of the "Kritik der reinen Vernunft"* (Allen & Unwin, 1936).

Recent critical commentaries on the *Critique* can be divided into two camps depending, roughly, on whether their authors see Kant as primarily an epistemologist, analyzing the limits of our experience, or primarily a metaphysician, showing how the objects that we experience are *constituted* by the knower; that is, it depends on how seriously the authors take Kant's transcendental idealism. Prominent members of the former group are Peter Strawson, with his *The Bounds of Sense* (Methuen, 1966), and Paul Guyer in *Kant and the Claims of Knowledge* (Cambridge University Press, 1987). The idealists have been particularly active and influential in the past few years, and recent important books on Kant and his first Critique from this side include: Henry Allison, *Kant's Transcendental Idealism* (Yale University Press, 1983); Karl Ameriks, *Kant's Theory of Mind* (Oxford University Press, 1982); Robert Pippin, *Kant's Theory of Form* (Yale University Press, 1982); and Ralph Walker, *Kant* (Routledge, 1978).

A seminal modern article which attacks the viability of the distinction between analytic and synthetic propositions is W.V. Quine's "Two Dogmas of Empiricism," which can be found in *From a Logical Point of View* (Harvard University Press, 1953); H.P. Grice and P.F. Strawson replied to Quine in "In Defense of a Dogma," *Philosophical Review* 65 (1956).

There is an old but still useful anthology of essays about Kant's philosophy called *Kant: A Collection of Critical Essays*, edited by Robert Paul Wolff (Doubleday, 1967). Finally, Paul Guyer has edited a collection of articles on Kant designed to summarize the high points of his philosophy: *The Cambridge Companion to Kant* (Cambridge University Press, 1992).

Critique of Pure Reason

Introduction[5]

I. The Distinction between Pure and Empirical Knowledge

There can be no doubt that all our knowledge begins with experience. For how should our faculty[6] of knowledge be awakened into action did not objects affecting our senses partly of themselves produce representations, partly arouse the activity of our understanding to compare these representations, and, by combining or separating them, work up the raw material of the sensible impressions[7] into that knowledge of objects which is entitled experience? In the order of time, therefore, we have no knowledge antecedent to experience, and with experience all our knowledge begins.

But though all our knowledge begins with experience, it does not follow that it all arises out of experience. For it may well be that even our empirical knowledge is made up of what we receive through impressions and of what our own faculty of knowledge (sensible impressions serving merely as the occasion) supplies from itself. If our faculty of knowledge makes any such addition, it may be that we are not in a position to distinguish it from the raw material,

---

5 Kant's *Critique of Pure Reason*, as first published in German in 1781, is usually called the "A" edition. A significantly different second edition, the "B" edition, was published in 1787. The translation used here, of the Introduction to the "B" edition, was made in 1929 by Norman Kemp Smith (Basingstoke, Hants: Palgrave. Copyright © 1929; revised edition 1933). Reproduced with permission of Palgrave Macmillan.

6 A "faculty," in this sense, is an inherent mental power or capacity, such as the faculty of speech or the faculty of memory.

7 A "sensible impression" is an effect produced on the mind which is received by the faculty of sensory perception. Sensible impressions are, roughly, the data we receive from the world (such as, perhaps, colors, sounds, pains, and so on) out of which our conscious perceptual experience (say the experience of being bitten by a squirrel) is constructed.

until with long practice of attention we have become skilled in separating it.

This, then, is a question which at least calls for closer examination, and does not allow of any off-hand answer:—whether there is any knowledge that is thus independent of experience and even of all impressions of the senses. Such knowledge is entitled *a priori*, and distinguished from the *empirical*, which has its sources *a posteriori*, that is, in experience.

The expression '*a priori*' does not, however, indicate with sufficient precision the full meaning of our question. For it has been customary to say, even of much knowledge that is derived from empirical sources, that we have it or are capable of having it *a priori*, meaning thereby that we do not derive it immediately from experience, but from a universal rule—a rule which is itself, however, borrowed by us from experience. Thus we would say of a man who undermined the foundations of his house, that he might have known *a priori* that it would fall, that is, that he need not have waited for the experience of its actual falling. But still he could not know this completely *a priori*. For he had first to learn through experience that bodies are heavy, and therefore fall when their supports are withdrawn.

In what follows, therefore, we shall understand by *a priori* knowledge, not knowledge independent of this or that experience, but knowledge absolutely independent of all experience. Opposed to it is empirical knowledge, which is knowledge possible only *a posteriori*, that is, through experience. *A priori* modes of knowledge are entitled pure when there is no admixture of anything empirical. Thus, for instance, the proposition, 'every alteration has its cause', while an *a priori* proposition, is not a pure proposition, because alteration is a concept which can be derived only from experience.

II. We Are in Possession of Certain Modes of *a priori* Knowledge, and Even the Common Understanding Is Never Without Them

What we here require is a criterion by which to distinguish with certainty between pure and empirical knowledge. Experience teaches us that a thing is so and so, but not that it cannot be otherwise. First, then, if we have a proposition which in being thought is

thought as *necessary*, it is an *a priori* judgment; and if, besides, it is not derived from any proposition except one which also has the validity of a necessary judgment, it is an absolutely *a priori* judgment. Secondly, experience never confers on its judgments true or strict but only assumed and comparative *universality*, through induction.[8] We can properly only say, therefore, that so far as we have hitherto observed, there is no exception to this or that rule. If, then, a judgment is thought with strict universality, that is, in such manner that no exception is allowed as possible, it is not derived from experience, but is valid absolutely *a priori*. Empirical universality is only an arbitrary extension of a validity holding in most cases to one which holds in all, for instance, in the proposition, 'all bodies are heavy'. When, on the other hand, strict universality is essential to a judgment, this indicates a special source of knowledge, namely, a faculty of *a priori* knowledge. Necessity and strict universality are thus sure criteria of *a priori* knowledge, and are inseparable from one another. But since in the employment of these criteria the contingency of judgments is sometimes more easily shown than their empirical limitation, or, as sometimes also happens, their unlimited universality can be more convincingly proved than their necessity, it is advisable to use the two criteria separately, each by itself being infallible.

Now it is easy to show that there actually are in human knowledge judgments which are necessary and in the strictest sense universal, and which are therefore pure *a priori* judgments. If an example from the sciences be desired, we have only to look to any of the propositions of mathematics; if we seek an example from the understanding in its quite ordinary employment, the proposition, 'every alteration must have a cause', will serve our purpose. In the latter case, indeed, the very concept of a cause so manifestly contains the concept of a necessity of connection with an effect and of the strict universality of the rule, that

---

8 Induction is the inference of a general law from particular instances. For example, if you see that one chickadee is chirpy, and you see that the next chickadee is chirpy, and so on, eventually you might conclude that all chickadees are chirpy. See Chapter 3 for more discussion of induction.

the concept would be altogether lost if we attempted to derive it, as Hume has done,[9] from a repeated association of that which happens with that which precedes, and from a custom of connecting representations, a custom originating in this repeated association, and constituting therefore a merely subjective necessity. Even without appealing to such examples, it is possible to show that pure *a priori* principles are indispensable for the possibility of experience, and so to prove their existence *a priori*. For whence could experience derive its certainty, if all the rules, according to which it proceeds, were always themselves empirical, and therefore contingent? Such rules could hardly be regarded as first principles. At present, however, we may be content to have established the fact that our faculty of knowledge does have a pure employment, and to have shown what are the criteria of such an employment.

Such *a priori* origin is manifest in certain concepts, no less than in judgments. If we remove from our empirical concept of a body, one by one, every feature in it which is [merely] empirical, the colour, the hardness or softness, the weight, even the impenetrability, there still remains the space which the body (now entirely vanished) occupied, and this cannot be removed. Again, if we remove from our empirical concept of any object, corporeal or incorporeal, all properties which experience has taught us, we yet cannot take away that property through which the object is thought as substance or as inhering in a substance (although this concept of substance is more determinate than that of an object in general). Owing, therefore, to the necessity with which this concept of substance forces itself upon us, we have no option save to admit that it has its seat in our faculty of *a priori* knowledge.

---

9   Kant is referring to Hume's *An Enquiry Concerning Human Understanding*, which was published in 1748 and translated into German by 1755. (Hume's earlier book, the *Treatise of Human Nature*, was not translated into German until 1791, and Kant probably had no first-hand acquaintance with most of it.) See the Hume reading in Chapter 3 for more information on this philosopher and his views, and especially for some of his views on causation.

III. Philosophy Stands in Need of a Science Which Shall Determine the Possibility, the Principles, and the Extent of All *a priori* Knowledge

But what is still more extraordinary than all the preceding is this, that certain modes of knowledge leave the field of all possible experiences and have the appearance of extending the scope of our judgments beyond all limits of experience, and this by means of concepts to which no corresponding object can ever be given in experience.

It is precisely by means of the latter modes of knowledge, in a realm beyond the world of the senses, where experience can yield neither guidance nor correction, that our reason carries on those enquiries which owing to their importance we consider to be far more excellent, and in their purpose far more lofty, than all that the understanding can learn in the field of appearances. Indeed we prefer to run every risk of error rather than desist from such urgent enquiries, on the ground of their dubious character, or from disdain and indifference. These unavoidable problems set by pure reason itself are *God*, *freedom*, and *immortality*. The science which, with all its preparations, is in its final intention directed solely to their solution is metaphysics; and its procedure is at first dogmatic, that is, it confidently sets itself to this task without any previous examination of the capacity or incapacity of reason for so great an undertaking.

Now it does indeed seem natural that, as soon as we have left the ground of experience, we should, through careful enquiries, assure ourselves as to the foundations of any building that we propose to erect, not making use of any knowledge that we possess without first determining whence it has come, and not trusting to principles without knowing their origin. It is natural, that is to say, that the question should first be considered, how the understanding can arrive at all this knowledge *a priori*, and what extent, validity, and worth it may have. Nothing, indeed, could be more natural, if by the term 'natural' we signify what fittingly and reasonably ought to happen. But if we mean by 'natural' what ordinarily happens, then on the contrary nothing is more natural and more intelligible than the fact that this enquiry has been so long neglected.

For one part of this knowledge, the mathematical, has long been of established reliability, and so gives rise to a favourable presumption as regards the other part,[10] which may yet be of quite different nature. Besides, once we are outside the circle of experience, we can be sure of not being *contradicted* by experience. The charm of extending our knowledge is so great that nothing short of encountering a direct contradiction can suffice to arrest us in our course; and this can be avoided, if we are careful in our fabrications—which none the less will still remain fabrications. Mathematics gives us a shining example of how far, independently of experience, we can progress in *a priori* knowledge. It does, indeed, occupy itself with objects and with knowledge solely in so far as they allow of being exhibited in intuition.[11] But this circumstance is easily overlooked, since the intuition, in being thought, can itself be given *a priori*, and is therefore hardly to be distinguished from a bare and pure concept. Misled by such a proof of the power of reason, the demand for the extension of knowledge recognises no limits. The light dove, cleaving the air in her free flight, and feeling its resistance, might imagine that its flight would be still easier in empty space. It was thus that Plato left the world of the senses, as setting too narrow limits to the understanding, and ventured out beyond it on the wings of the ideas, in the empty space of the pure understanding. He did not observe that with all his efforts he made no advance—meeting no resistance that might, as it were, serve as a support upon which he could take a stand, to which he could apply his powers, and so set his understanding in motion. It is, indeed, the common fate of human reason to complete its spec-

ulative structures as speedily as may be, and only afterwards to enquire whether the foundations are reliable. All sorts of excuses will then be appealed to, in order to reassure us of their solidity, or rather indeed to enable us to dispense altogether with so late and so dangerous an enquiry. But what keeps us, during the actual building, free from all apprehension and suspicion, and flatters us with a seeming thoroughness, is this other circumstance, namely, that a great, perhaps the greatest, part of the business of our reason consists in analysis of the concepts which we already have of objects. This analysis supplies us with a considerable body of knowledge, which, while nothing but explanation or elucidation of what has already been thought in our concepts, though in a confused manner, is yet prized as being, at least as regards its form, new insight. But so far as the matter or content is concerned, there has been no extension of our previously possessed concepts, but only an analysis of them. Since this procedure yields real knowledge *a priori*, which progresses in an assured and useful fashion, reason is so far misled as surreptitiously to introduce, without itself being aware of so doing, assertions of an entirely different order, in which it attaches to given concepts others completely foreign to them, and moreover attaches them *a priori*. And yet it is not known how reason can be in position to do this. Such a question is never so much as thought of. I shall therefore at once proceed to deal with the difference between these two kinds of knowledge.

IV. The Distinction between Analytic and Synthetic Judgments

In all judgments in which the relation of a subject to the predicate[12] is thought (I take into consideration affirmative judgments only, the subsequent application to negative judgments being easily made), this

---

10   Metaphysics.

11   By "intuition" (*Anschauung*) Kant means the direct perception of an object. An intuition is a mental representation that is *particular* and *concrete*, rather like an image. The main contrast, for Kant, is with *concepts*, which he thinks of as abstract and general representations. For example, the concept of redness is an idea that can apply to many things at once (lots of different things can be red all at the same time); by contrast, an intuition of redness is a sensory impression of some particular instance of red—it is an apprehension of *this* redness.

---

12   A predicate is a describing-phrase, and the subject of a sentence is the thing being described. An affirmative judgment says that some predicate is true of (or "satisfied by") a subject, while a negative judgment says that a subject does not satisfy that predicate. For example, "this nectarine is ripe" is an affirmative judgment (where the nectarine is the subject and '___ is ripe' is the predicate); "this nectarine is not juicy" is a negative judgment.

relation is possible in two different ways. Either the predicate B belongs to the subject A, as something which is (covertly) contained in this concept A; or outside the concept A, although it does indeed stand in connection with it. In the one case I entitle the judgment analytic, in the other synthetic. Analytic judgments (affirmative) are therefore those in which the connection of the predicate with the subject is thought through identity;[13] those in which this connection is thought without identity should be entitled synthetic. The former, as adding nothing through the predicate to the concept of the subject, but merely breaking it up into those constituent concepts that have all along been thought in it, although confusedly, can also be entitled explicative. The latter, on the other hand, add to the concept of the subject a predicate which has not been in any wise thought in it, and which no analysis could possibly extract from it; and they may therefore be entitled ampliative. If I say, for instance, 'All bodies are extended', this is an analytic judgment. For I do not require to go beyond the concept which I connect with 'body' in order to find extension as bound up with it. To meet with this predicate, I have merely to analyse the concept, that is, to become conscious to myself of the manifold which I always think in that concept. The judgment is therefore analytic. But when I say, 'All bodies are heavy', the predicate is something quite different from anything that I think in the mere concept of body in general; and the addition of such a predicate therefore yields a synthetic judgment.

Judgments of experience, as such, are one and all synthetic. For it would be absurd to found an analytic judgment on experience. Since, in framing the judgment, I must not go outside my concept, there is no need to appeal to the testimony of experience in its support. That a body is extended is a proposition that holds *a priori* and is not empirical. For, before appealing to experience, I have already in the concept of body all the conditions required for my judgment. I have only to extract from it, in accordance with the principle of contradiction,[14] the required predicate, and in so doing can at the same time become conscious of the necessity of the judgment—and that is what experience could never have taught me. On the other hand, though I do not include in the concept of a body in general the predicate 'weight', none the less this concept indicates an object of experience through one of its parts, and I can add to that part other parts of this same experience, as in this way belonging together with the concept. From the start I can apprehend the concept of body analytically through the characters of extension, impenetrability, figure, etc., all of which are thought in the concept. Now, however, looking back on the experience from which I have derived this concept of body, and finding weight to be invariably connected with the above characters, I attach it as a predicate to the concept; and in doing so I attach it synthetically, and am therefore extending my knowledge. The possibility of the synthesis of the predicate 'weight' with the concept of 'body' thus rests upon experience. While the one concept is not contained in the other, they yet belong to one another, though only contingently, as parts of a whole, namely, of an experience which is itself a synthetic combination of intuitions.

But in *a priori* synthetic judgments this help is entirely lacking. [I do not here have the advantage of looking around in the field of experience.] Upon what, then, am I to rely, when I seek to go beyond the concept A, and to know that another concept B is connected with it? Through what is the synthesis made possible? Let us take the proposition, 'Everything which happens has its cause'. In the concept

---

13   By "identity" here Kant means self-identity: for example, to say that rapper Eminem *is identical with* Slim Shady (or that Garth Brooks is identical with Chris Gaines, or even that Cicero is identical with Tully) is to say that they are not two different people but are one and the same person being named in different ways. Another example, more relevant to Kant's concerns in this passage, is that being a vixen *is identical with* being a female fox: these are just two different ways of describing one and the same property.

14   The principle of contradiction states that a proposition and its negation cannot both be true. For example it can't *both* be true that it is now Sunday *and* true that it is not now Sunday; if it is true that the spiny anteater lays eggs then it is not true that it is false that the spiny anteater lays eggs. As Aristotle once pithily put it, "nothing can both be and not be at the same time in the same respect."

of 'something which happens', I do indeed think an existence which is preceded by a time, etc., and from this concept analytic judgments may be obtained. But the concept of a 'cause' lies entirely outside the other concept, and signifies something different from 'that which happens', and is not therefore in any way contained in this latter representation. How come I then to predicate of that which happens something quite different, and to apprehend that the concept of cause, though not contained in it, yet belongs, and indeed necessarily belongs to it? What is here the unknown = X which gives support to the understanding when it believes that it can discover outside the concept A a predicate B foreign to this concept, which it yet at the same time considers to be connected with it? It cannot be experience, because the suggested principle has connected the second representation with the first, not only with greater universality, but also with the character of necessity, and therefore completely *a priori* and on the basis of mere concepts. Upon such synthetic, that is, ampliative principles, all our *a priori* speculative knowledge must ultimately rest; analytic judgments are very important, and indeed necessary, but only for obtaining that clearness in the concepts which is requisite for such a sure and wide synthesis as will lead to a genuinely new addition to all previous knowledge.

V. In All Theoretical Sciences of Reason Synthetic *a priori* Judgments Are Contained as Principles

1. *All mathematical judgments, without exception, are synthetic.* This fact, though incontestably certain and in its consequences very important, has hitherto escaped the notice of those who are engaged in the analysis of human reason, and is, indeed, directly opposed to all their conjectures. For as it was found that all mathematical inferences proceed in accordance with the principle of contradiction[15] (which the nature of all apodeictic[16] certainty requires), it was supposed

that the fundamental propositions of the science can themselves be known to be true through that principle. This is an erroneous view. For though a synthetic proposition can indeed be discerned in accordance with the principle of contradiction, this can only be if another synthetic proposition is presupposed, and if it can then be apprehended as following from this other proposition; it can never be so discerned in and by itself. First of all, it has to be noted that mathematical propositions, strictly so called, are always judgments *a priori*, not empirical; because they carry with them necessity, which cannot be derived from experience. If this be demurred to, I am willing to limit my statement to *pure* mathematics, the very concept of which implies that it does not contain empirical, but only pure *a priori* knowledge.

We might, indeed, at first suppose that the proposition $7 + 5 = 12$ is a merely analytic proposition, and follows by the principle of contradiction from the concept of a sum of 7 and 5. But if we look more closely we find that the concept of the sum of 7 and 5 contains nothing save the union of the two numbers into one, and in this no thought is being taken as to what that single number may be which combines both. The concept of 12 is by no means already thought in merely thinking this union of 7 and 5; and I may analyse my concept of such a possible sum as long as I please, still I shall never find the 12 in it. We have to go outside these concepts, and call in the aid of the intuition which corresponds to one of them, our five fingers, for instance, or, as Segner does in his *Arithmetic*,[17] five points, adding to the concept of 7, unit by unit, the five given in intuition. For starting with the number 7, and for the concept of 5 calling in the aid of the fingers of my hand as intuition, I now add one by one to the number 7 the units which I previously took together to form the number 5, and with the aid of that figure [the hand] see the number 12

---

terminology, an "assertoric" proposition says what *is* the case—i.e., what is actual—and a "problematic" proposition asserts what *can* be the case, i.e., what is possible.)

17   The book Kant refers to is *Anfangsgründe der Arithmetik*, translated from the original Latin, the second edition of which was published in 1773.

---

15   By showing that they must be true, since if they were false this would lead to a contradiction.

16   For Kant, an apodeictic proposition states what *must* be the case, i.e., what is necessary. (By contrast, in Kant's

come into being. That 5 should be added to 7, I have indeed already thought in the concept of a sum = 7 + 5, but not that this sum is equivalent to the number 12. Arithmetical propositions are therefore always synthetic. This is still more evident if we take larger numbers. For it is then obvious that, however we might turn and twist our concepts, we could never, by the mere analysis of them, and without the aid of intuition, discover what [the number is that] is the sum.

Just as little is any fundamental proposition of pure geometry analytic. That the straight line between two points is the shortest, is a synthetic proposition. For my concept of *straight* contains nothing of quantity, but only of quality. The concept of the shortest is wholly an addition, and cannot be derived, through any process of analysis, from the concept of the straight line. Intuition, therefore, must here be called in; only by its aid is the synthesis possible. What here causes us commonly to believe that the predicate of such apodeictic judgments is already contained in our concept, and that the judgment is therefore analytic, is merely the ambiguous character of the terms used. We are required to join in thought a certain predicate to a given concept, and this necessity is inherent in the concepts themselves. But the question is not what we *ought* to join in thought to the given concept, but what we *actually* think in it, even if only obscurely; and it is then manifest that, while the predicate is indeed attached necessarily to the concept, it is so in virtue of an intuition which must be added to the concept, not as thought in the concept itself.

Some few fundamental propositions, presupposed by the geometrician, are, indeed, really analytic, and rest on the principle of contradiction. But, as identical propositions,[18] they serve only as links in the chain of method and not as principles; for instance, $a = a$; the whole is equal to itself; or $(a + b) > a$, that is, the whole is greater than its part. And even these propositions, though they are valid according to pure concepts, are only admitted in mathematics because they can be exhibited in intuition.

2. *Natural science (physics) contains* a priori *synthetic judgments as principles*. I need cite only two such judgments: that in all changes of the mate-

rial world the quantity of matter remains unchanged; and that in all communication of motion, action and reaction must always be equal. Both propositions, it is evident, are not only necessary, and therefore in their origin *a priori*, but also synthetic. For in the concept of matter I do not think its permanence, but only its presence in the space which it occupies. I go outside and beyond the concept of matter, joining to it *a priori* in thought something which I have not thought *in* it. The proposition is not, therefore, analytic, but synthetic, and yet is thought *a priori*; and so likewise are the other propositions of the pure part of natural science.

3. *Metaphysics*, even if we look upon it as having hitherto failed in all its endeavours, is yet, owing to the nature of human reason, a quite indispensable science, and *ought to contain* a priori *synthetic knowledge*. For its business is not merely to analyse concepts which we make for ourselves *a priori* of things, and thereby to clarify them analytically, but to extend our *a priori* knowledge. And for this purpose we must employ principles which add to the given concept something that was not contained in it, and through *a priori* synthetic judgments venture out so far that experience is quite unable to follow us, as, for instance, in the proposition, that the world must have a first beginning, and such like. Thus metaphysics consists, at least *in intention*, entirely of *a priori* synthetic propositions.

VI. The General Problem of Pure Reason

Much is already gained if we can bring a number of investigations under the formula of a single problem. For we not only lighten our own task, by defining it accurately, but make it easier for others, who would test our results, to judge whether or not we have succeeded in what we set out to do. Now the proper problem of pure reason is contained in the question: How are *a priori* synthetic judgments possible?

That metaphysics has hitherto remained in so vacillating a state of uncertainty and contradiction, is entirely due to the fact that this problem, and perhaps even the distinction between analytic and synthetic judgments, has never previously been considered. Upon the solution of this problem, or upon a sufficient proof that the possibility which it desires to have

_____

18   As assertions of identities (or non-identities).

explained does in fact not exist at all, depends the success or failure of metaphysics. Among philosophers, David Hume came nearest to envisaging this problem, but still was very far from conceiving it with sufficient definiteness and universality. He occupied himself exclusively with the synthetic proposition regarding the connection of an effect with its cause (*principium causalitatis*[19]), and he believed himself to have shown that such an *a priori* proposition is entirely impossible. If we accept his conclusions, then all that we call metaphysics is a mere delusion whereby we fancy ourselves to have rational insight into what, in actual fact, is borrowed solely from experience, and under the influence of custom has taken the illusory semblance of necessity. If he had envisaged our problem in all its universality, he would never have been guilty of this statement, so destructive of all pure philosophy. For he would then have recognised that, according to his own argument, pure mathematics, as certainly containing *a priori* synthetic propositions, would also not be possible; and from such an assertion his good sense would have saved him.

In the solution of the above problem, we are at the same time deciding as to the possibility of the employment of pure reason in establishing and developing all those sciences which contain a theoretical *a priori* knowledge of objects, and have therefore to answer the questions:

How is pure mathematics possible?

How is pure science of nature possible?

Since these sciences actually exist, it is quite proper to ask *how* they are possible; for that they must be possible is proved by the fact that they exist.[20] But the

---

19   "The origin of causation."

20   [Author's note] Many may still have doubts as regards pure natural science. We have only, however, to consider the various propositions that are to be found at the beginning of (empirical) physics, properly so called, those, for instance, relating to the permanence in the quantity of matter, to inertia, to the equality of action and reaction, etc., in order to be soon convinced that they constitute a *physica pura*, or *rationalis*, which well deserves, as an independent science, to be separately dealt with in its whole extent, be that narrow or wide.

poor progress which has hitherto been made in metaphysics, and the fact that no system yet propounded can, in view of the essential purpose of metaphysics, be said really to exist, leaves everyone sufficient ground for doubting as to its possibility.

Yet, in a certain sense, this *kind of knowledge* is to be looked upon as given; that is to say, metaphysics actually exists, if not as a science, yet still as natural disposition (*metaphysica naturalis*[21]). For human reason, without being moved merely by the idle desire for extent and variety of knowledge, proceeds impetuously, driven on by an inward need, to questions such as cannot be answered by any empirical employment of reason, or by principles thence derived. Thus in all men, as soon as their reason has become ripe for speculation, there has always existed and will always continue to exist some kind of metaphysics. And so we have the question:

How is metaphysics, as natural disposition, possible?

that is, how from the nature of universal human reason do those questions arise which pure reason propounds to itself, and which it is impelled by its own need to answer as best it can?

But since all attempts which have hitherto been made to answer these natural questions—for instance, whether the world has a beginning or is from eternity—have always met with unavoidable contradictions, we cannot rest satisfied with the mere natural disposition to metaphysics, that is, with the pure faculty of reason itself, from which, indeed, some sort of metaphysics (be it what it may) always arises. It must be possible for reason to attain to certainty whether we know or do not know the objects of metaphysics, that is, to come to a decision either in regard to the objects of its enquiries or in regard to the capacity or incapacity of reason to pass any judgment upon them, so that we may either with confidence extend our pure reason or set to it sure and determinate limits. This last question, which arises out of the previous general problem, may, rightly stated, take the form:

How is metaphysics, as science, possible?

Thus the critique of reason, in the end, necessarily leads to scientific knowledge; while its dogmatic em-

---

21   "Natural metaphysics."

ployment, on the other hand, lands us in dogmatic assertions to which other assertions, equally specious,[22] can always be opposed—that is, in *scepticism*.

This science cannot be of any very formidable prolixity,[23] since it has to deal not with the objects of reason, the variety of which is inexhaustible, but only with itself and the problems which arise entirely from within itself, and which are imposed upon it by its own nature, not by the nature of things which are distinct from it. When once reason has learnt completely to understand its own power in respect of objects which can be presented to it in experience, it should easily be able to determine, with completeness and certainty, the extent and the limits of its attempted employment beyond the bounds of all experience.

We may, then, and indeed we must, regard as abortive all attempts, hitherto made, to establish a metaphysic *dogmatically*. For the analytic part in any such attempted system, namely, the mere analysis of the concepts that inhere in our reason *a priori*, is by no means the aim of, but only a preparation for, metaphysics proper, that is, the extension of its *a priori* synthetic knowledge. For such a purpose, the analysis of concepts is useless, since it merely shows what is contained in these concepts, not how we arrive at them *a priori*. A solution of this latter problem is required, that we may be able to determine the valid employment of such concepts in regard to the objects of all knowledge in general. Nor is much self-denial needed to give up these claims, seeing that the undeniable, and in the dogmatic procedure of reason also unavoidable, contradictions of reason with itself have long since undermined the authority of every metaphysical system yet propounded. Greater firmness will be required if we are not to be deterred by inward difficulties and outward opposition from endeavouring, through application of a method entirely different from any hitherto employed, at last to bring to a prosperous and fruitful growth a science indispensable to human reason—a science whose every branch may be cut away but whose root cannot be destroyed.

---

22   Superficially plausible, but actually false.
23   Tedious length.

VII. The Idea and Division of a Special Science, under the Title "Critique of Pure Reason"

In view of all these considerations, we arrive at the idea of a special science which can be entitled the Critique of Pure Reason. For reason is the faculty which supplies the principles of *a priori* knowledge. Pure reason is, therefore, that which contains the principles whereby we know anything absolutely *a priori*. An organon[24] of pure reason would be the sum-total of those principles according to which all modes of pure *a priori* knowledge can be acquired and actually brought into being. The exhaustive application of such an organon would give rise to a system of pure reason. But as this would be asking rather much, and as it is still doubtful whether, and in what cases, any extension of our knowledge be here possible, we can regard a science of the mere examination of pure reason, of its sources and limits, as the *propaedeutic*[25] to the system of pure reason. As such, it should be called a critique, not a doctrine, of pure reason. Its utility, in speculation, ought properly to be only negative, not to extend, but only to clarify our reason, and keep it free from errors—which is already a very great gain. I entitle *transcendental* all knowledge which is occupied not so much with objects as with the mode of our knowledge of objects in so far as this mode of knowledge is to be possible *a priori*. A system of such concepts might be entitled transcendental philosophy. But that is still, at this stage, too large an undertaking. For since such a science must contain, with completeness, both kinds of *a priori* knowledge, the analytic no less than the synthetic, it is, so far as our present purpose is concerned, much too comprehensive. We have to carry the analysis so far only as is indispensably necessary in order to comprehend, in their whole extent, the principles of *a priori* synthesis, with which alone we are called upon to deal. It is upon this enquiry, which should be entitled not a doctrine,

---

24   An instrument of thought, especially a system of logic or a method for reasoning. (Aristotle's logical writings were historically grouped together as the *Organon*, and Francis Bacon's influential 1620 book on the scientific method was called the *Novum* (new) *Organon*.)
25   Preliminary or introductory instruction (from the Greek, meaning "to teach beforehand").

but only a transcendental critique, that we are now engaged. Its purpose is not to extend knowledge, but only to correct it, and to supply a touchstone of the value, or lack of value, of all *a priori* knowledge. Such a critique is therefore a preparation, so far as may be possible, for an organon; and should this turn out not to be possible, then at least for a canon,[26] according to which, in due course, the complete system of the philosophy of pure reason—be it in extension or merely in limitation of its knowledge—may be carried into execution, analytically as well as synthetically. That such a system is possible, and indeed that it may not be of such great extent as to cut us off from the hope of entirely completing it, may already be gathered from the fact that what here constitutes our subject-matter is not the nature of things, which is inexhaustible, but the understanding which passes judgment upon the nature of things; and this understanding, again, only in respect of its *a priori* knowledge. These *a priori* possessions of the understanding, since they have not to be sought for without, cannot remain hidden from us, and in all probability are sufficiently small in extent to allow of our apprehending them in their completeness, of judging as to their value or lack of value, and so of rightly appraising them. Still less may the reader here expect a critique of books and systems of pure reason; we are concerned only with the critique of the faculty of pure reason itself. Only in so far as we build upon this foundation do we have a reliable touchstone for estimating the philosophical value of old and new works in this field. Otherwise the unqualified historian or critic is passing judgments upon the groundless assertions of others by means of his own, which are equally groundless.

Transcendental philosophy is only the idea of a science, for which the critique of pure reason has to lay down the complete architectonic[27] plan. That is to say, it has to guarantee, as following from principles, the completeness and certainty of the structure in all its parts. It is the system of all principles of pure reason. And if this critique is not itself to be entitled a transcendental philosophy, it is solely because, to

be a complete system, it would also have to contain an exhaustive analysis of the whole of *a priori* human knowledge. Our critique must, indeed, supply a complete enumeration of all the fundamental concepts that go to constitute such pure knowledge. But it is not required to give an exhaustive analysis of these concepts, nor a complete review of those that can be derived from them. Such a demand would be unreasonable, partly because this analysis would not be appropriate to our main purpose, inasmuch as there is no such uncertainty in regard to analysis as we encounter in the case of synthesis, for the sake of which alone our whole critique is undertaken; and partly because it would be inconsistent with the unity of our plan to assume responsibility for the completeness of such an analysis and derivation, when in view of our purpose we can be excused from doing so. The analysis of these *a priori* concepts, which later we shall have to enumerate, and the derivation of other concepts from them, can easily, however, be made complete when once they have been established as exhausting the principles of synthesis, and if in this essential respect nothing be lacking in them.

The critique of pure reason therefore will contain all that is essential in transcendental philosophy. While it is the complete idea of transcendental philosophy, it is not equivalent to that latter science; for it carries the analysis only so far as is requisite for the complete examination of knowledge which is *a priori* and synthetic.

What has chiefly to be kept in view in the division of such a science, is that no concepts be allowed to enter which contain in themselves anything empirical, or, in other words, that it consist in knowledge wholly *a priori*. Accordingly, although the highest principles and fundamental concepts of morality are *a priori* knowledge, they have no place in transcendental philosophy, because, although they do not lay at the foundation of their precepts the concepts of pleasure and pain, of the desires and inclinations, etc., all of which are of empirical origin, yet in the construction of a system of pure morality these empirical concepts must necessarily be brought into the concept of duty, as representing either a hindrance, which we have to overcome, or an allurement, which must not be made into a

---

26 A general principle or criterion.

27 Having to do with the scientific systematization of knowledge.

motive. Transcendental philosophy is therefore a philosophy of pure and merely speculative reason. All that is practical, so far as it contains motives, relates to feelings, and these belong to the empirical sources of knowledge.

If we are to make a systematic division of the science which we are engaged in presenting, it must have first a *doctrine of the elements*,[28] and secondly, a *doctrine of the method of pure reason*. Each of these chief divisions will have its subdivisions, but the grounds of these we are not yet in a position to explain. By way of introduction or anticipation we need only say that

there are two stems of human knowledge, namely, *sensibility*[29] and *understanding*, which perhaps spring from a common, but to us unknown, root. Through the former, objects are given to us; through the latter, they are thought. Now in so far as sensibility may be found to contain *a priori* representations constituting the condition under which objects are given to us, it will belong to transcendental philosophy. And since the conditions under which alone the objects of human knowledge are given must precede those under which they are thought, the transcendental doctrine of sensibility will constitute the first part of the science of the elements.

---

28   The "elements" are the constituents of cognition, which for Kant are intuitions and concepts.

29   The power of sensation.

BERTRAND RUSSELL

The Problems of Philosophy

I heard the beat of centaur's hoofs over the hard turf
As his dry and passionate talk devoured the afternoon.
"He is a charming man"—"But after all what did he
*   mean?"—*
"His pointed ears....He must be unbalanced,"—
"There was something he said that I might have
*   challenged."*

(from a poem by T.S. Eliot about Bertrand Russell called "Mr. Apollinax")

Who Was Bertrand Russell?

Bertrand Arthur William, 3rd Earl Russell was, with G.E. Moore, the founder of modern analytic philosophy in Britain, and one of the most important logicians of the twentieth century. He had a long and checkered career as an academic, a pacifist, a political activist and social reformer, an educational theorist, and a moral "free-thinker."

Born in 1872, Russell was orphaned at the age of 4 and brought up by his aristocratic grandmother, who

educated him at home with the help of tutors. Russell's interest in philosophical problems began early. His older brother introduced him at the age of 11 to Euclidian geometry (which shows how a large swathe of mathematics can be derived from a few apparently self-evident assumptions, or "axioms"). "This was one of the great events of my life, as dazzling as first love," Russell later wrote; however, when he demanded of his brother to be told how the axioms themselves were justified, he was informed that the axioms must simply be accepted as given. This Russell found a deeply unsatisfying answer.

In 1890 Russell went to study mathematics at Trinity College, Cambridge, but three years later he switched to philosophy. After a rather unhappy and lonely childhood, Russell wrote that "Cambridge opened up for me a new world of infinite delight." In 1895 he was elected to a six-year Fellowship at Trinity on the basis of a dissertation on the foundations of geometry. The intellectual turning-point in Russell's life occurred five years later, at the International Congress of Philosophy in Paris, where Russell met the Italian logician and mathematician Giuseppe Peano, who appeared to have done for arithmetic what Euclid had done for geometry: that is, shown how it could be derived from a small number of axioms. Russell set out to master Peano's notation and results and to use them for the general project of setting mathematics on solid foundations:

> The time was one of intellectual intoxication. My sensations resembled those one has after climbing a mountain in a mist, when, on reaching the summit, the mist suddenly clears, and the country becomes visible for forty miles in every direction…. Suddenly, in the space of a few weeks, I discovered what appeared to be definitive answers to the problems which had baffled me for years. (Russell's *Autobiography*)

This period of intellectual joy for Russell was quickly followed by one of emotional unhappiness as he "suddenly" realized he no longer loved his first wife Alys Pearsall Smith, whom he had married in 1894, and also began to see the cracks emerging in his meta-mathematical theory, showing that his answers might be less definitive than he had hoped.

In 1907 he stood unsuccessfully for Parliament as the candidate for the National Union of Women's Suffrage Societies, and in 1910 he tried to be adopted as the Liberal candidate for a London borough. He was rejected, however, because of his public atheism; Russell later called this rejection a lucky escape since it enabled him to accept a Lectureship at Trinity College, Cambridge, which he was offered that year. Between 1910 and 1916 he was a university lecturer at Cambridge, but was dismissed because of his pacifist opposition to World War I. In 1918 he was imprisoned for six months for having written that the US Army used intimidation tactics with strikers.

In 1921 Russell married again—to Dora Black—and had his first child. Since he had already given away most of his inherited money and lost his job at Cambridge, he now needed to find some way of making an income. As a result, most of his writings from this point until the mid-1930s were intended for a popular audience, and he went on several well-paid lecture tours of America. Many of his writings were considered scandalous for their liberal attitude towards sex and marriage—the best known of them are *Marriage and Morals* (1929) and *The Conquest of Happiness* (1930)—but they made him a lot of money. On the other hand, the progressive Beacon Hill School he founded with his wife in 1927, which aimed to provide a less authoritarian education than was then generally available, suffered large losses.

In 1936, after another divorce, Russell married his third wife, Patricia ('Peter') Spence, and two years later went to the United States to take up one-year appointments at the University of Chicago and then the University of California at Los Angeles. In 1939 he was offered a professorship at the College of the City of New York; however, there was a public outcry against the appointment on the grounds that Russell's lifestyle was immoral and his writings "lecherous, libidinous, lustful, venerous, erotomaniac, aphrodisiac, irreverent, narrow-minded, untruthful, and bereft of moral fibre." A lawsuit by some outraged taxpayers against the Municipality of New York led to Russell's appointment being revoked. This caused Russell financial problems but he was rescued by a lecturing job at the Barnes Foundation; it was here that he began his monumental book *A History of Western Philosophy*, which was published in 1945 and won him the 1950 Nobel prize for literature.

In 1944 Russell returned to Trinity College, Cambridge, as a Fellow, and in 1952, after the break-up of his third marriage, wed Edith Finch. In 1958 he became president of the Campaign for Nuclear Disarmament and wrote two books on the dangers of nuclear war: *Common Sense and Nuclear Warfare* (1959) and *Has Man a Future?* (1961). He was jailed for a week in 1961, even though he was then 89 years old, for inciting civil disobedience. He was instrumental in founding the Pugwash Conference, at which distinguished scientists from around the world meet to discuss international issues,[1] and in 1963 he became president of the British wing of the Who Killed Kennedy Committee. In 1964 he founded the Bertrand Russell Peace Foundation and in 1967 he set up an International War Crimes Tribunal which, together with his book *War Crimes in Vietnam*, condemned the foreign policy of the United States. Russell died in 1970 at the age of 97.

What Was Russell's Overall Philosophical Project?

Russell's earliest work, and probably his most lasting contribution to philosophy, was in mathematical logic. His project—which today might seem almost unnecessary but which was an extremely important contribution to mathematical thought at the beginning of the twentieth century—was to place all of pure mathematics on a sound footing by showing that it is reducible to a demonstrably sound logical system. This program was called 'logicism,' and its culmination for Russell was the massive *Principia Mathematica*, co-written with Alfred North Whitehead and published between 1910 and 1913. In the process, Russell created essentially the standard formulation of modern classical logic. (The project ran into dif-

ficulties, however, with the discovery of several very deep paradoxes which threaten any sufficiently powerful logical system which makes use of the notion of a class or set;[2] Russell's solution—called the "theory of types"—is generally considered a rather problematic treatment of these paradoxes.) The best introduction to Russell's logicism is his *Introduction to Mathematical Philosophy*, written while he was in prison in 1918.

Lying behind this early work, as well as many of his other philosophical writings, was the dictum that "all sound philosophy should begin with an analysis of propositions": that is, Russell thought, good philosophy starts by examining a particular feature or type of language—such as mathematics—and looking for its underlying logic. This kind of analysis can be seen at work in two of Russell's most seminal papers, "On Denoting" (1905) and "Knowledge by Acquaintance and Knowledge by Description" (1910). The ultimate aim of this philosophical project is to construct an ideal logically correct language to solve or dissolve many, if not all, of our philosophical problems. Such a system, Russell thought, would reveal how mathematical and scientific reality is a "logical construction" of basic data, such as numbers and sense-data.

This philosophical project gave rise to Russell's second important contribution to philosophy: a theory called "logical atomism."[3] This is a metaphysical

---

1   It is named after the village in Nova Scotia where the first meeting was held in 1957. Pugwash conferences still continue, and the organization received the Nobel peace prize in 1995.

2   The most fundamental of these paradoxes is usually called "Russell's paradox," and goes as follows. Some sets are members of themselves and others are not. For example, the set of chimpanzees is not itself a chimp, but the set of sets is itself a set. Now, consider the following (apparently perfectly legitimate) set: the set of all sets that are not members of themselves. Call this set R. The problematic question is: is R a member of itself or not? It can't be true that R *is* a member of itself, since all the members of R are not members of themselves. On the other hand, it can't be true that R is *not* a member of itself, because then it would be a member of itself. Yet it must surely be one or the other. This is a paradox which seems to arise directly out of the notion of a set itself, and it has big implications for logic and mathematics.

3   Ludwig Wittgenstein's book *Tractatus Logico-Philosophicus* (1922) is the other main source for this theory.

doctrine which is simultaneously about the nature of language, knowledge, and the world. Its central claim is that reality is ultimately composed of atomic facts and that these facts are connected together by certain fundamental relations (such as 'and,' 'or,' or 'if … then …') which can be pictured in formal logic. Language, according to this theory, represents the world by sharing its logical structure: that is, *language* (just like reality) is ultimately composed of 'atomic' units which are joined together by logical rules into more complex compounds (i.e., into phrases and sentences). The business of philosophy, according to logical atomism, is to purify our language until it properly reflects the structure of reality, and this goal is achieved through logical analysis. For example, we want the atomic units of our perfect logical language to include the *names* of the atomic individuals and their basic properties, and the grammatical rules for the construction of compound sentences should be the same as the logical relations by which reality is constructed. Finally, human knowledge of the world, according to logical atomism, turns out to have two different components: our acquaintance with the basic elements of reality (which Russell for a long time thought of as sense-data), and our understanding of how these elements can be and are combined (which Russell labeled "knowledge by description").

Three of Russell's works that describe and develop his logical atomism are *Our Knowledge of the External World* (1914), the lectures "The Philosophy of Logical Atomism" (1918), and *The Analysis of Matter* (1927).

After 1938 Russell switched the main focus of his philosophical research to epistemology, the study of the nature of human knowledge. He began by searching for a method that would guarantee the certainty of our beliefs (for example, our scientific beliefs), but he was forced gradually to the conclusion that "all human knowledge is uncertain, inexact, and partial. To this doctrine we have not found any limitation whatever." Part of the reason for Russell's increasing lack of confidence in scientific knowledge was his growing appreciation of "the problem of induction" (see Chapter 3). His work in epistemology can be found in *An Inquiry into Meaning and Truth* (1940) and his last significant philosophical work, *Human Knowledge: Its Scope and Limits* (1948).

Russell's short book *The Problems of Philosophy* (1912), from which our reading is taken, has become one of the most popular introductions to philosophy ever written. In its day it was also important for drawing attention to the previously underrated work of the British empiricists, especially Berkeley and Hume. The book was written while Russell was still developing his logical atomism: in his later work (for a time) he abandoned the notion that matter is *inferred* from our knowledge of sense-data and replaced it with the idea that matter is simply a *logical construction* of actual and possible sense-data. That is, he moved from the theory that matter is the best explanation for what causes our experiences of the world, to the theory that statements about 'matter' are just shorthand statements about past and future experiences themselves.

What Is the Structure of This Reading?

Russell's *Problems of Philosophy* contains fifteen chapters, and the first three are reprinted here. Russell begins his introduction to philosophy by treating it as the search for *certainty*—for knowledge that no "reasonable man" could doubt. In the first chapter he argues that most everyday knowledge about the world we live in fails sadly to live up to this standard and, as the title of the first chapter suggests, he uses simple examples from daily life to draw a distinction between appearance and reality. Russell then distinguishes between two different sorts of questions about the nature of reality: (1) Is there a real table at all? (2) If so, what sort of object can it be? Chapter 2 addresses the first of these questions (and Russell argues that physical tables do exist); Chapter 3 is about the second (where Russell argues that matter cannot resemble our sense-data).

Suggestions for Critical Reflection

1. Do you think philosophy is best thought of as the search for certainty? Does Russell think of it in that way? Judging from the reading, for example, does he require *certainty* in his philosophical arguments?

2. Do you agree that Russell's appearance/reality distinction is a serious blow to our common-sense beliefs about the world? Why, or why not?

3. Do you agree with Russell that "the supposition that the whole of life is a dream … [is] a less simple hypothesis, viewed as a means of accounting for the facts of our own life, than the common-sense hypothesis that there really are objects independent of us"?

4. How adequate do you find Russell's proof that physical tables exist? What does he mean by "physical" (e.g., does he mean something like "made of sub-atomic particles"?) in this context?

5. What kind of knowledge do you think Russell would be willing to grant us of the real nature of matter? That is, as well as knowing what matter is *not*, how much might we be able to find out (on Russell's picture) about what matter *is*?

Suggestions for Further Reading

After reading the rest of *The Problems of Philosophy* (Oxford University Press, 1912), the best places to start with Russell's philosophy are his *Introduction to Mathematical Philosophy* (George Allen & Unwin, 1919) and the collection of essays edited by R.C. Marsh called *Logic and Knowledge* (George Allen & Unwin, 1956). The latter includes his "The Philosophy of Logical Atomism." Every student of philosophy should at some point read Russell's *A History of Western Philosophy* (George Allen & Unwin, 1945). Probably still the best book about Russell's life is his *Autobiography*, published in three volumes between 1967 and 1969 by George Allen & Unwin. Apart from that, the standard biography continues to be Ronald William Clark's *The Life of Bertrand Russell* (Cape, 1972).

Two useful books about Russell's philosophy are *Bertrand Russell*, by John Slater (Thoemmes Press, 1994) and *Russell*, by R.M. Sainsbury (Routledge & Kegan Paul, 1979). Perhaps the most comprehensive book on Russell's thought is by Ronald Jager, *The Development of Bertrand Russell's Philosophy* (Allen & Unwin, 1972). Essays about Russell's philosophy are collected in David Pears (ed.), *Bertrand Russell: A Collection of Critical Essays* (Anchor Books, 1972).

The Problems of Philosophy

Chapters 1–3[4]

Chapter 1: Appearance and Reality

Is there any knowledge in the world which is so certain that no reasonable man could doubt it? This question, which at first sight might not seem difficult, is really one of the most difficult that can be asked. When we have realized the obstacles in the way of a straightforward and confident answer, we shall be well launched on the study of philosophy—for philosophy is merely the attempt to answer such ultimate questions, not carelessly and dogmatically, as we do in ordinary life and even in the sciences, but critically, after exploring all that makes such questions puzzling, and after realizing all the vagueness and confusion that underlie our ordinary ideas.

In daily life, we assume as certain many things which, on a closer scrutiny, are found to be so full of apparent contradictions that only a great amount of thought enables us to know what it is that we really may believe. In the search for certainty, it is natural to begin with our present experiences, and in some sense, no doubt, knowledge is to be derived from them. But any statement as to what it is that our immediate experiences make us know is very likely to be wrong. It seems to me that I am now sitting in a chair, at a table of a certain shape, on which I see sheets of paper with writing or print. By turning my head I see out of the window buildings and clouds and the sun. I believe that the sun is about ninety-three million miles from the earth; that it is a hot globe many times bigger than the earth; that, owing to the earth's rotation, it rises every morning, and will continue to do so for an indefinite time in the future. I believe that, if any other normal person comes into my room, he will see the same chairs and tables and books and papers as I see, and that the table which I see is the same as the table which I feel pressing against my arm. All this seems to

---

4   *The Problems of Philosophy* was first published in 1912 in the Home University Library series by Williams and Norgate. From Chapters 1–3 of *The Problems of Philosophy*. © Bertrand Russell, 1967. By permission of Oxford University Press.

be so evident as to be hardly worth stating, except in answer to a man who doubts whether I know anything. Yet all this may be reasonably doubted, and all of it requires much careful discussion before we can be sure that we have stated it in a form that is wholly true.

To make our difficulties plain, let us concentrate attention on the table. To the eye it is oblong, brown and shiny, to the touch it is smooth and cool and hard; when I tap it, it gives out a wooden sound. Any one else who sees and feels and hears the table will agree with this description, so that it might seem as if no difficulty would arise; but as soon as we try to be more precise our troubles begin. Although I believe that the table is 'really' of the same colour all over, the parts that reflect the light look much brighter than the other parts, and some parts look white because of reflected light. I know that, if I move, the parts that reflect the light will be different, so that the apparent distribution of colours on the table will change. It follows that if several people are looking at the table at the same moment, no two of them will see exactly the same distribution of colours, because no two can see it from exactly the same point of view, and any change in the point of view makes some change in the way the light is reflected.

For most practical purposes these differences are unimportant, but to the painter they are all-important: the painter has to unlearn the habit of thinking that things seem to have the colour which common sense says they 'really' have, and to learn the habit of seeing things as they appear. Here we have already the beginning of one of the distinctions that cause most trouble in philosophy—the distinction between 'appearance' and 'reality', between what things seem to be and what they are. The painter wants to know what things seem to be, the practical man and the philosopher want to know what they are; but the philosopher's wish to know this is stronger than the practical man's, and is more troubled by knowledge as to the difficulties of answering the question.

To return to the table. It is evident from what we have found, that there is no colour which pre-eminently appears to be *the* colour of the table, or even of any one particular part of the table—it appears to be of different colours from different points of view, and there is no reason for regarding some of these as

more really its colour than others. And we know that even from a given point of view the colour will seem different by artificial light, or to a colour-blind man, or to a man wearing blue spectacles, while in the dark there will be no colour at all, though to touch and hearing the table will be unchanged. This colour is not something which is inherent in the table, but something depending upon the table and the spectator and the way the light falls on the table. When, in ordinary life, we speak of *the* colour of the table, we only mean the sort of colour which it will seem to have to a normal spectator from an ordinary point of view under usual conditions of light. But the other colours which appear under other conditions have just as good a right to be considered real; and therefore, to avoid favouritism, we are compelled to deny that, in itself, the table has any one particular colour.

The same thing applies to the texture. With the naked eye one can see the grain, but otherwise the table looks smooth and even. If we looked at it through a microscope, we should see roughnesses and hills and valleys, and all sorts of differences that are imperceptible to the naked eye. Which of these is the 'real' table? We are naturally tempted to say that what we see through the microscope is more real, but that in turn would be changed by a still more powerful microscope. If, then, we cannot trust what we see with the naked eye, why should we trust what we see through a microscope? Thus, again, the confidence in our senses with which we began deserts us.

The *shape* of the table is no better. We are all in the habit of judging as to the 'real' shapes of things, and we do this so unreflectingly that we come to think we actually see the real shapes. But, in fact, as we all have to learn if we try to draw, a given thing looks different in shape from every different point of view. If our table is 'really' rectangular, it will look, from almost all points of view, as if it had two acute angles and two obtuse angles. If opposite sides are parallel, they will look as if they converged to a point away from the spectator; if they are of equal length, they will look as if the nearer side were longer. All these things are not commonly noticed in looking at a table, because experience has taught us to construct the 'real' shape from the apparent shape, and the 'real' shape is what interests us as practical men. But the 'real' shape is not what we see; it is something inferred from what we see. And what we see is constantly changing in shape as we move about the room; so that here again the senses seem not to give us the truth about the table itself, but only about the appearance of the table.

Similar difficulties arise when we consider the sense of touch. It is true that the table always gives us a sensation of hardness, and we feel that it resists pressure. But the sensation we obtain depends upon how hard we press the table and also upon what part of the body we press with; thus the various sensations due to various pressures or various parts of the body cannot be supposed to reveal *directly* any definite property of the table, but at most to be *signs* of some property which perhaps *causes* all the sensations, but is not actually apparent in any of them. And the same applies still more obviously to the sounds which can be elicited by rapping the table.

Thus it becomes evident that the real table, if there is one, is not the same as what we immediately experience by sight or touch or hearing. The real table, if there is one, is not *immediately* known to us at all, but must be an inference from what is immediately known. Hence, two very difficult questions at once arise; namely, (1) Is there a real table at all? (2) If so, what sort of object can it be?

It will help us in considering these questions to have a few simple terms of which the meaning is definite and clear. Let us give the name of 'sense-data' to the things that are immediately known in sensation: such things as colours, sounds, smells, hardnesses, roughnesses, and so on. We shall give the name 'sensation' to the experience of being immediately aware of these things. Thus, whenever we see a colour, we have a sensation *of* the colour, but the colour itself is a sense-datum, not a sensation. The colour is that *of* which we are immediately aware, and the awareness itself is the sensation. It is plain that if we are to know anything about the table, it must be by means of the sense-data—brown colour, oblong shape, smoothness, etc.—which we associate with the table; but, for the reasons which have been given, we cannot say that the table is the sense-data, or even that the sense-data are directly properties of the table. Thus a problem arises as to the relation of the sense-data to the real table, supposing there is such a thing.

The real table, if it exists, we will call a 'physical object'. Thus we have to consider the relation of sense-data to physical objects. The collection of all physical objects is called 'matter'. Thus our two questions may be re-stated as follows: (1) Is there any such thing as matter? (2) If so, what is its nature?

The philosopher who first brought prominently forward the reasons for regarding the immediate objects of our senses as not existing independently of us was Bishop Berkeley (1685–1753). His *Three Dialogues between Hylas and Philonous, in Opposition to Sceptics and Atheists*,[5] undertake to prove that there is no such thing as matter at all, and that the world consists of nothing but minds and their ideas. Hylas has hitherto believed in matter, but he is no match for Philonous, who mercilessly drives him into contradictions and paradoxes, and makes his own denial of matter seem, in the end, as if it were almost common sense. The arguments employed are of very different value: some are important and sound, others are confused or quibbling. But Berkeley retains the merit of having shown that the existence of matter is capable of being denied without absurdity, and that if there are any things that exist independently of us they cannot be the immediate objects of our sensations.

There are two different questions involved when we ask whether matter exists, and it is important to keep them clear. We commonly mean by 'matter' something which is opposed to 'mind', something which we think of as occupying space and as radically incapable of any sort of thought or consciousness. It is chiefly in this sense that Berkeley denies matter; that is to say, he does not deny that the sense-data which we commonly take as signs of the existence of the table are really signs of the existence of *something* independent of us, but he does deny that this something is non-mental, that it is neither mind nor ideas entertained by some mind. He admits that there must be something which continues to exist when we go out of the room or shut our eyes, and that what we call seeing the table does really give us reason for believing in something which persists even when we are not seeing it. But he thinks that this something cannot be radically

---

5   See the Berkeley selection in this chapter.

different in nature from what we see, and cannot be independent of seeing altogether, though it must be independent of *our* seeing. He is thus led to regard the 'real' table as an idea in the mind of God. Such an idea has the required permanence and independence of ourselves, without being—as matter would otherwise be—something quite unknowable, in the sense that we can only infer it, and can never be directly and immediately aware of it.

Other philosophers since Berkeley have also held that, although the table does not depend for its existence upon being seen by me, it does depend upon being seen (or otherwise apprehended in sensation) by *some* mind—not necessarily the mind of God, but more often the whole collective mind of the universe. This they hold, as Berkeley does, chiefly because they think there can be nothing real—or at any rate nothing known to be real—except minds and their thoughts and feelings. We might state the argument by which they support their view in some such way as this: 'Whatever can be thought of is an idea in the mind of the person thinking of it; therefore nothing can be thought of except ideas in minds; therefore anything else is inconceivable, and what is inconceivable cannot exist.'

Such an argument, in my opinion, is fallacious; and of course those who advance it do not put it so shortly or so crudely. But whether valid or not, the argument has been very widely advanced in one form or another; and very many philosophers, perhaps a majority, have held that there is nothing real except minds and their ideas. Such philosophers are called 'idealists'. When they come to explaining matter, they either say, like Berkeley, that matter is really nothing but a collection of ideas, or they say, like Leibniz (1646–1716), that what appears as matter is really a collection of more or less rudimentary minds.

But these philosophers, though they deny matter as opposed to mind, nevertheless, in another sense, admit matter. It will be remembered that we asked two questions; namely, (1) Is there a real table at all? (2) If so, what sort of object can it be? Now both Berkeley and Leibniz admit that there is a real table, but Berkeley says it is certain ideas in the mind of God, and Leibniz says it is a colony of souls. Thus both of them answer our first question in the affirmative, and only diverge from the views of ordinary mortals in their answer to our second question. In fact, almost all philosophers seem to be agreed that there is a real table: they almost all agree that, however much our sense-data—colour, shape, smoothness, etc.—may depend upon us, yet their occurrence is a sign of something existing independently of us, something differing, perhaps, completely from our sense-data whenever we are in a suitable relation to the real table.

Now obviously this point in which the philosophers are agreed—the view that there *is* a real table, whatever its nature may be—is vitally important, and it will be worth while to consider what reasons there are for accepting this view before we go on to the further question as to the nature of the real table. Our next chapter, therefore, will be concerned with the reasons for supposing that there is a real table at all.

Before we go farther it will be well to consider for a moment what it is that we have discovered so far. It has appeared that, if we take any common object of the sort that is supposed to be known by the senses, what the senses *immediately*[6] tell us is not the truth about the object as it is apart from us, but only the truth about certain sense-data which, so far as we can see, depend upon the relations between us and the object. Thus what we directly see and feel is merely 'appearance', which we believe to be a sign of some 'reality' behind. But if the reality is not what appears, have we any means of knowing whether there is any reality at all? And if so, have we any means of finding out what it is like?

Such questions are bewildering, and it is difficult to know that even the strangest hypotheses may not be true. Thus our familiar table, which has roused but the slightest thoughts in us hitherto, has become a problem full of surprising possibilities. The one thing we know about it is that it is not what it seems. Beyond this modest result, so far, we have the most complete liberty of conjecture. Leibniz tells us it is a community of souls: Berkeley tells us it is an idea in the mind of God; sober science, scarcely less wonderful, tells us it is a vast collection of electric charges in violent motion.

---

6   Without an intermediary (as opposed to "straight away").

Among these surprising possibilities, doubt suggests that perhaps there is no table at all. Philosophy, if it cannot *answer* so many questions as we could wish, has at least the power of *asking* questions which increase the interest of the world, and show the strangeness and wonder lying just below the surface even in the commonest things of daily life.

Chapter 2: The Existence of Matter

In this chapter we have to ask ourselves whether, in any sense at all, there is such a thing as matter. Is there a table which has a certain intrinsic nature, and continues to exist when I am not looking, or is the table merely a product of my imagination, a dream-table in a very prolonged dream? This question is of the greatest importance. For if we cannot be sure of the independent existence of objects, we cannot be sure of the independent existence of other people's bodies, and therefore still less of other people's minds, since we have no grounds for believing in their minds except such as are derived from observing their bodies. Thus if we cannot be sure of the independent existence of objects, we shall be left alone in a desert—it may be that the whole outer world is nothing but a dream, and that we alone exist. This is an uncomfortable possibility; but although it cannot be strictly *proved* to be false, there is not the slightest reason to suppose that it is true. In this chapter we have to see why this is the case.

Before we embark upon doubtful matters, let us try to find some more or less fixed point from which to start. Although we are doubting the physical existence of the table, we are not doubting the existence of the sense-data which made us think there was a table; we are not doubting that, while we look, a certain colour and shape appear to us, and while we press, a certain sensation of hardness is experienced by us. All this, which is psychological, we are not calling in question. In fact, whatever else may be doubtful, some at least of our immediate experiences seem absolutely certain.

Descartes (1596–1650), the founder of modern philosophy, invented a method which may still be used with profit—the method of systematic doubt. He determined that he would believe nothing which he did not see quite clearly and distinctly to be true. Whatever he could bring himself to doubt, he would

doubt, until he saw reason for not doubting it. By applying this method he gradually became convinced that the only existence of which he could be *quite* certain was his own. He imagined a deceitful demon, who presented unreal things to his senses in a perpetual phantasmagoria; it might be very improbable that such a demon existed, but still it was possible, and therefore doubt concerning things perceived by the senses was possible.

But doubt concerning his own existence was not possible, for if he did not exist, no demon could deceive him. If he doubted, he must exist; if he had any experiences whatever, he must exist. Thus his own existence was an absolute certainty to him. 'I think, therefore I am,' he said (*Cogito, ergo sum*); and on the basis of this certainty he set to work to build up again the world of knowledge which his doubt had laid in ruins. By inventing the method of doubt, and by showing that subjective things are the most certain, Descartes performed a great service to philosophy, and one which makes him still useful to all students of the subject.

But some care is needed in using Descartes' argument. 'I think, therefore I am' says rather more than is strictly certain. It might seem as though we were quite sure of being the same person to-day as we were yesterday, and this is no doubt true in some sense. But the real Self is as hard to arrive at as the real table and does not seem to have that absolute, convincing certainty that belongs to particular experiences. When I look at my table and see a certain brown colour, what is quite certain at once is not 'I am seeing a brown colour', but rather, 'a brown colour is being seen'. This of course involves something (or somebody) which (or who) sees the brown colour; but it does not of itself involve that more or less permanent person whom we call 'I'. So far as immediate certainty goes, it might be that the something which sees the brown colour is quite momentary, and not the same as the something which has some different experience the next moment.

Thus it is our particular thoughts and feelings that have primitive certainty. And this applies to dreams and hallucinations as well as to normal perceptions: when we dream or see a ghost, we certainly do have the sensations we think we have, but for various reasons it is held that no physical object corresponds to these sensations. Thus the certainty of our knowledge of our own experiences does not have to be limited in any way to allow for exceptional cases. Here, therefore, we have, for what it is worth, a solid basis from which to begin our pursuit of knowledge.

The problem we have to consider is this: Granted that we are certain of our own sense-data, have we any reason for regarding them as signs of the existence of something else, which we can call the physical object? When we have enumerated all the sense-data which we should naturally regard as connected with the table have we said all there is to say about the table, or is there still something else—something not a sense-datum, something which persists when we go out of the room? Common sense unhesitatingly answers that there is. What can be bought and sold and pushed about and have a cloth laid on it, and so on, cannot be a *mere* collection of sense-data. If the cloth completely hides the table, we shall derive no sense-data from the table, and therefore, if the table were merely sense-data, it would have ceased to exist, and the cloth would be suspended in empty air, resting, by a miracle, in the place where the table formerly was. This seems plainly absurd; but whoever wishes to become a philosopher must learn not to be frightened by absurdities.

One great reason why it is felt that we must secure a physical object in addition to the sense-data, is that we want the same object for different people. When ten people are sitting round a dinner-table, it seems preposterous to maintain that they are not seeing the same tablecloth, the same knives and forks and spoons and glasses. But the sense-data are private to each separate person; what is immediately present to the sight of one is not immediately present to the sight of another: they all see things from slightly different points of view, and therefore see them slightly differently. Thus, if there are to be public neutral objects, which can be in some sense known to many different people, there must be something over and above the private and particular sense-data which appear to various people. What reason, then, have we for believing that there are such public neutral objects?

The first answer that naturally occurs to one is that, although different people may see the table slightly differently, still they all see more or less similar things

when they look at the table, and the variations in what they see follow the laws of perspective and reflection of light, so that it is easy to arrive at a permanent object underlying all the different people's sense-data. I bought my table from the former occupant of my room; I could not buy *his* sense-data, which died when he went away, but I could and did buy the confident expectation of more or less similar sense-data. Thus it is the fact that different people have similar sense-data, and that one person in a given place at different times has similar sense-data, which makes us suppose that over and above the sense-data there is a permanent public object which underlies or causes the sense-data of various people at various times.

Now in so far as the above considerations depend upon supposing that there are other people besides ourselves, they beg the very question at issue.[7] Other people are represented to me by certain sense-data, such as the sight of them or the sound of their voices, and if I had no reason to believe that there were physical objects independent of my sense-data, I should have no reason to believe that other people exist except as part of my dream. Thus, when we are trying to show that there must be objects independent of our own sense-data, we cannot appeal to the testimony of other people, since this testimony itself consists of sense-data, and does not reveal other people's experiences unless our own sense-data are signs of things existing independently of us. We must therefore, if possible, find, in our own purely private experiences, characteristics which show, or tend to show, that there are in the world things other than ourselves and our private experiences.

In one sense it must be admitted that we can never *prove* the existence of things other than ourselves and our experiences. No logical absurdity results from the hypothesis that the world consists of myself and my thoughts and feelings and sensations, and that everything else is mere fancy. In dreams a very complicated world may seem to be present, and yet on waking we find it was a delusion; that is to say, we find that the sense-data in the dream do not appear to have corresponded with such physical objects as we should natu-

---

7   Presuppose the truth of the very thing they are trying to prove.

rally infer from our sense-data. (It is true that, when the physical world is assumed, it is possible to find physical causes for the sense-data in dreams: a door banging, for instance, may cause us to dream of a naval engagement. But although, in this case, there is a physical *cause* for the sense-data, there is not a physical object *corresponding* to the sense-data in the way in which an actual naval battle would correspond.) There is no logical impossibility in the supposition that the whole of life is a dream, in which we ourselves create all the objects that come before us. But although this is not logically impossible, there is no reason whatever to suppose that it is true; and it is, in fact, a less simple hypothesis, viewed as a means of accounting for the facts of our own life, than the common-sense hypothesis that there really are objects independent of us, whose action on us causes our sensations.

The way in which simplicity comes in from supposing that there really are physical objects is easily seen. If the cat appears at one moment in one part of the room, and at another in another part, it is natural to suppose that it has moved from the one to the other, passing over a series of intermediate positions. But if it is merely a set of sense-data, it cannot have ever been in any place where I did not see it; thus we shall have to suppose that it did not exist at all while I was not looking, but suddenly sprang into being in a new place. If the cat exists whether I see it or not, we can understand from our own experience how it gets hungry between one meal and the next; but if it does not exist when I am not seeing it, it seems odd that appetite should grow during non-existence as fast as during existence. And if the cat consists only of sense-data, it cannot be *hungry*, since no hunger but my own can be a sense-datum to me. Thus the behaviour of the sense-data which represent the cat to me, though it seems quite natural when regarded as an expression of hunger, becomes utterly inexplicable when regarded as mere movements and changes of patches of colour, which are as incapable of hunger as a triangle is of playing football.

But the difficulty in the case of the cat is nothing compared to the difficulty in the case of human beings. When human beings speak—that is, when we hear certain noises which we associate with ideas, and simultaneously see certain motions of lips and expressions of face—it is very difficult to suppose that what we hear is not the expression of a thought, as we know it would be if we emitted the same sounds. Of course similar things happen in dreams, where we are mistaken as to the existence of other people. But dreams are more or less suggested by what we call waking life, and are capable of being more or less accounted for on scientific principles if we assume that there really is a physical world. Thus every principle of simplicity urges us to adopt the natural view, that there really are objects other than ourselves and our sense-data which have an existence not dependent upon our perceiving them.

Of course it is not by argument that we originally come by our belief in an independent external world. We find this belief ready in ourselves as soon as we begin to reflect: it is what may be called an *instinctive* belief. We should never have been led to question this belief but for the fact that, at any rate in the case of sight, it seems as if the sense-datum itself were instinctively believed to be the independent object, whereas argument shows that the object cannot be identical with the sense-datum. This discovery, however—which is not at all paradoxical in the case of taste and smell and sound, and only slightly so in the case of touch—leaves undiminished our instinctive belief that there *are* objects *corresponding* to our sense-data. Since this belief does not lead to any difficulties, but on the contrary tends to simplify and systematize our account of our experiences, there seems no good reason for rejecting it. We may therefore admit—though with a slight doubt derived from dreams—that the external world does really exist, and is not wholly dependent for its existence upon our continuing to perceive it.

The argument which has led us to this conclusion is doubtless less strong than we could wish, but it is typical of many philosophical arguments, and it is therefore worth while to consider briefly its general character and validity. All knowledge, we find, must be built up upon our instinctive beliefs, and if these are rejected, nothing is left. But among our instinctive beliefs some are much stronger than others, while many have, by habit and association, become entangled with other beliefs, not really instinctive, but falsely supposed to be part of what is believed instinctively.

Philosophy should show us the hierarchy of our instinctive beliefs, beginning with those we hold most strongly, and presenting each as much isolated and as free from irrelevant additions as possible. It should take care to show that, in the form in which they are finally set forth, our instinctive beliefs do not clash, but form a harmonious system. There can never be any reason for rejecting one instinctive belief except that it clashes with others; thus, if they are found to harmonize, the whole system becomes worthy of acceptance.

It is of course *possible* that all or any of our beliefs may be mistaken, and therefore all ought to be held with at least some slight element of doubt. But we cannot have *reason* to reject a belief except on the ground of some other belief. Hence, by organizing our instinctive beliefs and their consequences, by considering which among them is most possible, if necessary, to modify or abandon, we can arrive, on the basis of accepting as our sole data what we instinctively believe, at an orderly systematic organization of our knowledge, in which, though the *possibility* of error remains, its likelihood is diminished by the interrelation of the parts and by the critical scrutiny which has preceded acquiescence.

This function, at least, philosophy can perform. Most philosophers, rightly or wrongly, believe that philosophy can do much more than this—that it can give us knowledge, not otherwise attainable, concerning the universe as a whole, and concerning the nature of ultimate reality. Whether this be the case or not, the more modest function we have spoken of can certainly be performed by philosophy, and certainly suffices, for those who have once begun to doubt the adequacy of common sense, to justify the arduous and difficult labours that philosophical problems involve.

Chapter 3: The Nature of Matter

In the preceding chapter we agreed, though without being able to find demonstrative reasons, that it is rational to believe that our sense-data—for example, those which we regard as associated with my table—are really signs of the existence of something independent of us and our perceptions. That is to say, over and above the sensations of colour, hardness, noise, and so on, which make up the appearance of the

table to me, I assume that there is something else, *of* which these things are appearances. The colour ceases to exist if I shut my eyes, the sensation of hardness ceases to exist if I remove my arm from contact with the table, the sound ceases to exist if I cease to rap the table with my knuckles. But I do not believe that when all these things cease the table ceases. On the contrary, I believe that it is because the table exists continuously that all these sense-data will reappear when I open my eyes, replace my arm, and begin again to rap with my knuckles. The question we have to consider in this chapter is: What is the nature of this real table, which persists independently of my perception of it?

To this question physical science gives an answer, somewhat incomplete it is true, and in part still very hypothetical, but yet deserving of respect so far as it goes. Physical science, more or less unconsciously, has drifted into the view that all natural phenomena ought to be reduced to motions. Light and heat and sound are all due to wave-motions, which travel from the body emitting them to the person who sees light or feels heat or hears sound. That which has the wave-motion is either aether[8] or 'gross matter', but in either case is what the philosopher would call matter. The only properties which science assigns to it are position in space, and the power of motion according to the laws of motion. Science does not deny that it *may* have other properties; but if so, such other properties are not useful to the man of science, and in no way assist him in explaining the phenomena.

It is sometimes said that 'light *is* a form of wave-motion', but this is misleading, for the light which we immediately see, which we know directly by means of

---

8   This is the invisible, all-pervasive substance assumed by classical physics to fill up all the 'empty' space in the universe and to be the medium through which light waves are propagated (just as water is the medium for watery waves). The hypothesis was rendered obsolete by Einstein's theory of special relativity in 1905. (In a foreword to the German edition of 1926, Russell admitted that when *The Problems of Philosophy* was written in 1911 he had not yet sufficiently understood the importance of Einstein's theories. Later Russell became a well-known popularizer of relativity theory, for example, in his *ABC of Relativity* [1925].)

our senses, is *not* a form of wave-motion, but something quite different—something which we all know if we are not blind, though we cannot describe it so as to convey our knowledge to a man who is blind. A wave-motion, on the contrary, could quite well be described to a blind man, since he can acquire a knowledge of space by the sense of touch; and he can experience a wave-motion by a sea voyage almost as well as we can. But this, which a blind man can understand, is not what we mean by *light*: we mean by *light* just that which a blind man can never understand, and which we can never describe to him.

Now this something, which all of us who are not blind know, is not, according to science, really to be found in the outer world: it is something caused by the action of certain waves upon the eyes and nerves and brain of the person who sees the light. When it is said that light *is* waves, what is really meant is that waves are the physical cause of our sensations of light. But light itself, the thing which seeing people experience and blind people do not, is not supposed by science to form any part of the world that is independent of us and our senses. And very similar remarks would apply to other kinds of sensations.

It is not only colours and sounds and so on that are absent from the scientific world of matter, but also *space* as we get it through sight or touch. It is essential to science that its matter should be in *a* space, but the space in which it is cannot be exactly the space we see or feel. To begin with, space as we see it is not the same as space as we get it by the sense of touch; it is only by experience in infancy that we learn how to touch things we see, or how to get a sight of things which we feel touching us. But the space of science is neutral as between touch and sight; thus it cannot be either the space of touch or the space of sight.

Again, different people see the same object as of different shapes, according to their point of view. A circular coin, for example, though we should always *judge* it to be circular, will *look* oval unless we are straight in front of it. When we judge that it *is* circular, we are judging that it has a real shape which is not its apparent shape, but belongs to it intrinsically apart from its appearance. But this real shape, which is what concerns science, must be in a real space, not the same as anybody's apparent space. The real space is public, the *apparent* space is private to the percipient. In different people's *private* spaces the same object seems to have different shapes; thus the real space, in which it has its real shape, must be different from the private spaces. The space of science, therefore, though *connected* with the spaces we see and feel, is not identical with them, and the manner of its connexion requires investigation.

We agreed provisionally that physical objects cannot be quite like our sense-data, but may be regarded as *causing* our sensations. These physical objects are in the space of science, which we may call 'physical' space. It is important to notice that, if our sensations are to be caused by physical objects, there must be a physical space containing these objects and our sense-organs and nerves and brain. We get a sensation of touch from an object when we are in contact with it; that is to say, when some part of our body occupies a place in physical space quite close to the space occupied by the object. We see an object (roughly speaking) when no opaque body is between the object and our eyes in physical space. Similarly, we only hear or smell or taste an object when we are sufficiently near to it, or when it touches the tongue, or has some suitable position in physical space relatively to our body. We cannot begin to state what different sensations we shall derive from a given object under different circumstances unless we regard the object and our body as both in one physical space, for it is mainly the relative positions of the object and our body that determine what sensations we shall derive from the object.

Now our sense-data are situated in our private spaces, either the space of sight or the space of touch or such vaguer spaces as other senses may give us. If, as science and common sense assume, there is one public all-embracing physical space in which physical objects are, the relative positions of physical objects in physical space must more or less correspond to the relative positions of sense-data in our private spaces. There is no difficulty in supposing this to be the case. If we see on a road one house nearer to us than another, our other senses will bear out the view that it is nearer; for example, it will be reached sooner if we walk along the road. Other people will agree that the house which looks nearer to us is nearer; the ordnance map[9] will take the same view; and thus everything points to a spatial relation between the houses corresponding to the relation between the sense-data which we see when we look at the houses. Thus we may assume that there is a physical space in which physical objects have spatial relations corresponding to those which the corresponding sense-data have in our private spaces. It is this physical space which is dealt with in geometry and assumed in physics and astronomy.

Assuming that there is physical space, and that it does thus correspond to private spaces, what can we know about it? We can know *only* what is required in order to secure the correspondence. That is to say, we can know nothing of what it is like in itself, but we can know the sort of arrangement of physical objects which results from their spatial relations. We can know, for example, that the earth and moon and sun are in one straight line during an eclipse, though we cannot know what a physical straight line is in itself, as we know the look of a straight line in our visual space. Thus we come to know much more about the *relations* of distances in physical space than about the distances themselves; we may know that one distance is greater than another, or that it is along the same straight line as the other, but we cannot have that immediate acquaintance with physical distances that we have with distances in our private spaces, or with colours or sounds or other sense-data. We can know all those things about physical space which a man born blind might know through other people about the space of sight; but the kind of things which a man born blind could never know about the space of sight we also cannot know about physical space. We can know the properties of the relations required to preserve the correspondence with sense-data, but we cannot know the nature of the terms between which the relations hold.

With regard to time, our *feeling* of duration or of the lapse of time is notoriously an unsafe guide as to the time that has elapsed by the clock. Times when we are bored or suffering pain pass slowly, times when we are agreeably occupied pass quickly, and times when we are sleeping pass almost as if they did not exist. Thus, in so far as time is constituted by duration, there is the same necessity for distinguishing a public and a private time as there was in the case of space. But in so far as time consists in an *order* of before and after, there is no need to make such a distinction; the time-order which events seem to have is, so far as we can see, the same as the time-order which they do have. At any rate no reason can be given for supposing that the two orders are not the same. The same is usually true of space: if a regiment of men are marching along a road, the *shape* of the regiment will look different from different points of view, but the men will appear arranged in the same *order* from all points of view. Hence we regard the *order* as true also in physical space, whereas the shape is only supposed to correspond to the physical space so far as is required for the preservation of the order.

In saying that the time-order which events *seem to have* is the same as the time-order which they *really have*, it is necessary to guard against a possible misunderstanding. It must not be supposed that the various states of different physical objects have the same time-order as the sense-data which constitute the perceptions of those objects. Considered as physical objects, the thunder and lightning are simultaneous; that is to say, the lightning is simultaneous with the disturbance of the air in the place where the disturbance begins, namely, where the lightning is. But the sense-datum which we call hearing the thunder does not take place until the disturbance of the air has travelled as far as to where we are. Similarly, it takes about eight minutes for the sun's light to reach us; thus, when we see the sun we are seeing the sun of eight minutes ago. So far as our sense-data afford evidence as to the physical sun they afford evidence as to the physical sun of eight minutes ago; if the physical sun had ceased to exist within the last eight minutes, that would make no difference to the sense-data which we call 'seeing the sun'. This affords a fresh illustration of the necessity of distinguishing between sense-data and physical objects.

What we have found as regards space is much the same as what we find in relation to the correspondence of the sense-data with their physical

---

9 A reference to the standard large-scale maps of Britain made by the Ordnance Survey (originally maps made for the military during the Napoleonic wars).

counterparts. If one object looks blue and another red, we may reasonably presume that there is some corresponding difference between the physical objects; if two objects both look blue, we may presume a corresponding similarity. But we cannot hope to be acquainted directly with the quality in the physical object which makes it look blue or red. Science tells us that this quality is a certain sort of wave-motion, and this sounds familiar, because we think of wave-motions in the space we see. But the wave-motions must really be in physical space, with which we have no direct acquaintance; thus the real wave-motions have not that familiarity which we might have supposed them to have. And what holds for colours is closely similar to what holds for other sense-data. Thus we find that, although the *relations* of physical objects have all sorts of knowable properties, derived from their correspondence with the relations of sense-data, the physical objects themselves remain unknown in their intrinsic nature, so far at least as can be discovered by means of the senses. The question remains whether there is any other method of discovering the intrinsic nature of physical objects.

The most natural, though not ultimately the most defensible, hypothesis to adopt in the first instance, at any rate as regards visual sense-data, would be that, though physical objects cannot, for the reasons we have been considering, be *exactly* like sense-data, yet they may be more or less like. According to this view, physical objects will, for example, really have colours, and we might, by good luck, see an object as of the colour it really is. The colour which an object seems to have at any given moment will in general be very similar, though not quite the same, from many different points of view; we might thus suppose the 'real' colour to be a sort of medium colour, intermediate between the various shades which appear from the different points of view.

Such a theory is perhaps not capable of being definitely refuted, but it can be shown to be groundless. To begin with, it is plain that the colour we see depends only upon the nature of the light-waves that strike the eye, and is therefore modified by the medium intervening between us and the object, as well as by the manner in which light is reflected from the object in the direction of the eye. The intervening air alters colours unless it is perfectly clear, and any strong reflection will alter them completely. Thus the colour we see is a result of the ray as it reaches the eye, and not simply a property of the object from which the ray comes. Hence, also, provided certain waves reach the eye, we shall see a certain colour, whether the object from which the waves start has any colour or not. Thus it is quite gratuitous to suppose that physical objects have colours, and therefore there is no justification for making such a supposition. Exactly similar arguments will apply to other sense-data.

It remains to ask whether there are any general philosophical arguments enabling us to say that, if matter is real, it *must* be of such and such a nature. As explained above, very many philosophers, perhaps most, have held that whatever is real must be in some sense mental, or at any rate that whatever we can know anything about must be in some sense mental. Such philosophers are called 'idealists'. Idealists tell us that what appears as matter is really something mental; namely, either (as Leibniz held) more or less rudimentary minds, or (as Berkeley contended) ideas in the minds which, as we should commonly say, 'perceive' the matter. Thus idealists deny the existence of matter as something intrinsically different from mind, though they do not deny that our sense-data are signs of something which exists independently of our private sensations. In the following chapter we shall consider briefly the reasons—in my opinion fallacious—which idealists advance in favour of their theory.

G.E. MOORE
"Proof of an External World"

Who Was G.E. Moore?

George Edward Moore was a leading figure in the generation of philosophers—including Bertrand Russell and the young Ludwig Wittgenstein—which set British philosophy on a new path at the start of the twentieth century by founding the important stream of thought called "analytic philosophy" (which, in somewhat altered form, is still dominant today in the English-speaking philosophical world).

Born to middle-class, devoutly religious parents in a London suburb in 1873, Moore studied Greek and Latin (but, by his own admission, no science at all) at Dulwich College, and then went up to Trinity College, Cambridge, to study classics. Bertrand Russell, who was a student there at the same time, persuaded Moore to switch to the study of philosophy, and after his undergraduate education (on his second attempt) Moore won a six-year prize fellowship at Trinity. It paid £200 a year, plus board and lodging in college, from 1898 until 1904.

During these early years of his philosophical career Moore had two notable triumphs. First, he published papers (in particular "The Refutation of Idealism," in 1903) which, it turned out, signaled the death knell of the then-dominant form of philosophy in Britain—a philosophy called "absolute idealism" which, roughly, held that the universe is constituted, not of matter, but of the thought of an absolute spirit. Second, he wrote a book on ethics called *Principia Ethica* (also

published in 1903) which influentially declared that all previous ethical theories were guilty of a major fallacy, the "naturalistic fallacy" of trying to define moral values in non-ethical terms. By contrast, Moore said, goodness is an intrinsic, unanalyzable quality known to us by intuition. This book, as well as having a major influence on professional philosophers, became the manifesto for a group of artists and writers known as the Bloomsbury Group, which included Virginia and Leonard Woolf, E.M. Forster, John Maynard Keynes, Lytton Strachey, and Clive Bell.

In his later work, Moore became known for his defense of common sense: he believed that whenever a philosophical doctrine contradicts common sense, it was more likely that the philosophical argument had gone awry than that common sense had done so. He disagreed with those philosophers (such as Russell and Wittgenstein) who held that our ordinary language concealed philosophical errors that needed to be eliminated in an artificial, perfect, logical language. Similarly, he did not think that our everyday beliefs were false and in need of replacement by more rigorous philosophical or scientific claims. What, then, is the role of philosophy according to Moore? It is to *analyze* our everyday beliefs and find out what, exactly, they are telling us. What, for example, Moore asks, do we really *mean* when we say, "I think that table over there exists outside of my mind"?

Moore left Cambridge in 1904, lived in Edinburgh and London for a while, but then returned to Cambridge as a university lecturer in 1911. He spent the rest of his life there, except for a lengthy visit to the United States shortly after his retirement in 1939. In 1916 he married one of his students (a "Miss D.M. Ely," who for some reason always called him either "Moore" or "Bill"), and had two sons, one of whom became a poet and the other a musician. Moore quickly became one of the most well-respected philosophers in Britain and, partly under his influence, Cambridge was the most important center for philosophy in the world during these years. Though he had a rather retiring personality, Moore's acute intelligence and his intense concern to lay out problems with total precision and thereby get matters exactly right seems to have exerted a powerful and uplifting influence on those around him. A British philosopher from the generation after Moore's, Gilbert Ryle, said of him:

> For some of us there still lives the Moore whose voice is never quite resuscitated by his printed words. This is the Moore whom we met at Cambridge and at the annual Joint Session of the Mind Association and the Aristotelian Society. Moore was a dynamo of courage. He gave us courage not by making concessions, but by making no concessions to our youth or to our shyness. He treated us as corrigible and therefore as responsible thinkers. He would explode at our mistakes and muddles with just that genial ferocity with which he would explode at the mistakes and muddles of philosophical highups, and with just the genial ferocity with which he would explode at mistakes and muddles of his own. He would listen with minute attention to what we said, and then, without a trace of discourtesy or courtesy, treat our remarks simply on their merits, usually, of course, and justly inveighing against their inadequacy, irrelevance or confusedness, but sometimes, without a trace of politeness or patronage, crediting them with whatever positive utility he thought that they possessed. If, as sometimes happened, he found in someone's interposition the exposure of a confusion or a fallacy of his own, he would announce that this was so, confess to his own unbelievable muddle-headedness or slackness of reasoning, and then with full acknowledgment, adopt and work with the clarification.

What Is the Structure of This Reading?

Moore begins by introducing the problem he will be discussing: the problem of the existence of the external world. He does not proceed immediately to try to answer it, however, but begins by trying to clarify exactly what the question is asking (and thus what would count as a correct answer). He starts with the phrase "things outside of us" and sets out to refine it into a more exact expression, ending up with "things which are to be met with in space." Then he tries to make clearer what precisely this means, contrasting it with "things which are presented in space" in order to do so: this involves showing, first, that some things presented in space are not to be met with in space, and second that some things to be met with in space are not presented in space. Moore now claims (though he admits he has not succeeded in making the notion *absolutely* clear) he has said enough to show that, if only he can prove there exist some things which are to be met with in space (such as tables, stars, and sheets of paper), it would trivially follow that "there are things to be met with in space" is true.

Moore now faces another problem: even if he can prove that there are things to be met with in space, why should we admit that these objects are *external to our minds*? That is, how can Moore prove that tables, even though they are importantly different from after-images, are not nevertheless another kind of mental object? Moore's reasoning needs to be followed carefully here, but his central idea is that statements about things external to our minds are logically independent of claims about experience. That is, for example, its being true that a sheet of paper exists does not logically entail the truth of the claim that someone is perceiving that paper, whereas to say that someone is seeing double at a particular time *commits* one to the claim that someone is having an experience of a double image at that time.

Moore points out that this means that "external to our minds" is not synonymous with "to be met with in space," but suggests that if something *is* to be met with in space then it must also be external to our minds. Moore is now at the point in his argument where, he says, if he can just show that two things are to be met with in space this will prove that some external things exist and so definitively answer his original question. *Can* he show that at least two things are to be met with in space? He can, he says, and demonstrates by proving that his two hands exist.

Philosophers, however, will wonder if it can really be so simple? *Did* Moore actually prove that his hands exist outside of his (and our) mind? Moore completes his paper by attempting to defend his argument against possible objections and showing that it satisfies the three "conditions necessary for a rigorous proof."

Some Common Misconceptions

1. Moore is sometimes caricatured as merely gesticulating with his hands in the air and claiming that he has proved the external world exists. Although there is *some* truth to this, you should be able to see that what Moore is doing is much more complicated and careful than mere hand-waving.

2. "Moore," I said, "have you any apples in that basket?" "No," he replied and smiled seraphically as was his wont. I decided to try a different logical tack. "Moore," I said, "do you then have some apples in that basket?" "No," he said once again. Now I was in a logical cleft-stick, so to speak, and had but one way out. "Moore," I said, "do you then have apples in that basket?" "Yes," he replied, and from that day forth we remained the very best of friends.

This piece of comedy—written by Jonathan Miller for the 1960s show *Beyond the Fringe*—illustrates another common but over-hasty perception of Moore's philosophical method. This is the impression that Moore's work consisted in making, for their own sake, a sequence of trivial and unnecessary logical distinctions and clarifications which perhaps sound clever but which are irrelevant to the "big" concerns of philosophy. You should decide for yourself how fruitful Moore's method of analysis is, but it is certainly untrue that Moore was not at least sincerely *attempting* to deal with real, important philosophical questions by, for example, distinguishing carefully between the logic of the phrases "to be met with in space" and "presented in space."

Suggestions for Critical Reflection

1. Do you think Moore is attempting to refute philosophical skepticism in this paper, or do you think he might be trying to do something slightly different or more focussed? Does his proof of the existence of the external world, if it works, show that skepticism must be false? Do you think Moore even takes the possibility of skepticism *seriously*? (And if not, should he?)

2. Do you think that Moore manages to prove that the things which are "to be met with in space" (such as shrubbery or furniture) *must* be "external to our minds"? And even if he does that, does he also demonstrate that something like Berkeley's idealism is false: that is, does he show that trees and tables must be external to *any* mind at all (even God's)?

3. How, if at all, does Moore *justify* his claim that he knows his hands exist? Is this a good enough justification (at least, good enough for what Moore is trying to do)?

4. Moore's defense of his final proof that objects exist in the external world may depend upon making a distinction between proving something and proving *that one knows* that thing. Do you think this is a viable distinction? Put it this way: could someone know *p* without knowing that they know *p*?

Suggestions for Further Reading

A good entrée into Moore's philosophy is his book *Some Main Problems of Philosophy* (George Allen & Unwin, 1953). Several of his most important papers are collected in *G.E. Moore: Selected Writings*, edited by Thomas Baldwin (Routledge, 1993); Baldwin also wrote what is probably the best book about Moore's philosophy, *G.E. Moore* (Routledge, 1990). Also interesting is E.D. Klemke, *A Defense of Realism: Reflections on the Metaphysics of G.E. Moore* (Humanity Books, 1999). The best collection of essays about Moore, which includes his rather charming autobiography and replies to the essays, is *The Philosophy of G.E. Moore*, edited by P.A. Schilpp (Open Court, 1968).

"Proof of an External World"[1]

In the Preface to the second edition of Kant's *Critique of Pure Reason* some words occur, which, in Professor Kemp Smith's translation, are rendered as follows:[2]

> It still remains a scandal to philosophy … that the existence of things outside of us … must be accepted merely on *faith*, and that, if anyone thinks good to doubt their existence, we are unable to counter his doubts by any satisfactory proof.[3]

It seems clear from these words that Kant thought it a matter of some importance to give a proof of 'the existence of things outside of us' or perhaps rather (for it seems to me possible that the force of the German words is better rendered in this way) of 'the existence of *the* things outside of us'; for had he not thought it important that a proof should be given, he would scarcely have called it a 'scandal' that no proof had been given. And it seems clear also that he thought that the giving of such a proof was a task which fell properly within the province of philosophy; for, if it did not, the fact that no proof had been given could not possibly be a scandal to *philosophy*.

---

1   This paper was first published in 1939 in the *Proceedings of the British Academy* (Volume 25, pp. 273–300). It is reprinted here by kind permission of Dr. Thomas Baldwin, Literary Executor to G.E. Moore.

2   The introduction to the second (or 'B') edition of the *Critique of Pure Reason* appears as a reading in this chapter. More information about Kant appears in the notes to that selection.

3   [Author's note] B xxxix, note: Kemp Smith, p.34. The German words are 'so bleibt es immer ein Skandal der Philosophie …, das Dasein der Dinge ausser uns …, bloss auf *Glauben* annehmen zu müssen, und wenn es jemand einfällt es zu bezweifeln, ihm keinen genugtuenden Beweis entgegenstellen zu können'.

Now, even if Kant was mistaken in both of these two opinions there seems to me to be no doubt whatever that it is of some importance and also a matter which falls properly within the province of philosophy, to discuss the question what sort of proof, if any, can be given of 'the existence of things outside of us'. And to discuss this question was my object when I began to write the present lecture. But I may say at once that, as you will find, I have only, at most, succeeded in saying a very small part of what ought to be said about it.

The words 'it … remains a scandal to philosophy … that we are unable …' would, taken strictly, imply that, at the moment at which he wrote them, Kant himself was unable to produce a satisfactory proof of the point in question. But I think it is unquestionable that Kant himself did not think that he personally was at the time unable to produce such a proof. On the contrary, in the immediately preceding sentence, he has declared that he has, in the second edition of his *Critique*, to which he is now writing the Preface, given a 'rigorous proof' of this very thing; and has added that he believes this proof of his to be 'the only possible proof'. It is true that in this preceding sentence he does not describe the proof which he has given as a proof of 'the existence of things outside of us' or of 'the existence of the things outside of us', but describes it instead as a proof of 'the objective reality of outer intuition'. But the context leaves no doubt that he is using these two phrases, 'the objective reality of outer intuition' and 'the existence of things (*or* 'the things') outside of us', in such a way that whatever is a proof of the first is also necessarily a proof of the second. We must, therefore, suppose that when he speaks as if *we* are unable to give a satisfactory proof, he does not mean to say that he himself, as well as others, is *at the moment* unable; but rather that, until he discovered the proof which he has given, both he himself and everybody else *were* unable. Of course, if he is right in thinking that he has given a satisfactory proof, the state of things which he describes came to an end as soon as his proof was published. As soon as that happened, anyone who read it was able to give a satisfactory proof by simply repeating that which Kant had given, and the 'scandal' to philosophy had been removed once for all.

If, therefore, it were certain that the proof of the point in question given by Kant in the second edition is a satisfactory proof, it would be certain that at least one satisfactory proof can be given; and all that would remain of the question which I said I proposed to discuss would be, firstly, the question as to what *sort* of a proof this of Kant's is, and secondly the question whether (contrary to Kant's own opinion) there may not perhaps be other proofs, of the same or of a different sort, which are also satisfactory. But I think it is by no means certain that Kant's proof is satisfactory. I think it is by no means certain that he did succeed in removing once for all the state of affairs which he considered to be a scandal to philosophy. And I think, therefore, that the question whether it is possible to give *any* satisfactory proof of the point in question still deserves discussion.

But what is the point in question? I think it must be owned that the expression 'things outside of us' is rather an odd expression, and an expression the meaning of which is certainly not perfectly clear. It would have sounded less odd if, instead of 'things outside of us' I had said 'external things', and perhaps also the meaning of this expression would have seemed to be clearer; and I think we make the meaning of 'external things' clearer still if we explain that this phrase has been regularly used by philosophers as short for 'things external to *our minds*'. The fact is that there has been a long philosophical tradition, in accordance with which the three expressions 'external things', 'things external to *us*', and 'things external to *our minds*' have been used as equivalent to one another, and have, each of them, been used as if they needed no explanation. The origin of this usage I do not know. It occurs already in Descartes; and since he uses the expressions as if they needed no explanation, they had presumably been used with the same meaning before. Of the three, it seems to me that the expression 'external to *our minds*' is the clearest, since it at least makes clear that what is meant is not 'external to *our bodies*'; whereas both the other expressions might be taken to mean this: and indeed there has been a good deal of confusion, even among philosophers, as to the relation of the two conceptions 'external things' and 'things external to *our bodies*'. But even the expression 'things external to our minds' seems to me to be far from perfectly clear; and if I am to make really clear what I mean by 'proof of the existence of things outside of us', I cannot do it by merely saying that by 'outside of us' I mean 'external to our minds'.

There is a passage (*Kritik der reinen Vernunft*, A373)[4] in which Kant himself says that the expression 'outside of us' 'carries with it an unavoidable ambiguity'. He says that 'sometimes it means something which exists *as a thing in itself* distinct from us, and sometimes something which merely belongs to external *appearance*'; he calls things which are 'outside of us' in the first of these two senses 'objects which might be called external in the transcendental sense', and things which are so in the second '*empirically external objects*'; and he says finally that, in order to remove all uncertainty as to the latter conception, he will distinguish empirically external objects from objects which might be called 'external' in the transcendental sense, 'by calling them outright things which are *to be met with in space*'.

I think that this last phrase of Kant's, 'things which are to be met with in space', does indicate fairly clearly what sort of things it is with regard to which I wish to inquire what sort of proof, if any, can be given that there are any things of that sort. My body, the bodies of other men, the bodies of animals, plants of all sorts, stones, mountains, the sun, the moon, stars, and planets, houses and other buildings, manufactured articles of all sorts—chairs, tables, pieces of paper, etc., are all of them 'things which are to be met with in space'. In short, all things of the sort that philosophers have been used to call 'physical objects', 'material things', or 'bodies' obviously come under this head. But the phrase 'things that are to be met with in space' can be naturally understood as applying also in cases where the names 'physical object', 'material thing', or 'body' can hardly be applied. For instance, shadows are sometimes to be met with in space, although they could hardly be properly called 'physical objects'; 'material things', or 'bodies'; and although in one usage of the term 'thing' it would not be proper to call a shadow a 'thing', yet the phrase 'things which are to be met with in space' can be naturally understood as synonymous

---

4   *Critique of Pure Reason*, first ("A") edition, page 373 (of the original German).

with 'whatever can be met with in space', and this is an expression which can quite properly be understood to include shadows. I wish the phrase 'things which are to be met with in space' to be understood in this wide sense; so that if a proof can be found that there ever have been as many as two different shadows it will follow at once that there have been at least two 'things which were to be met with in space', and this proof will be as good a proof of the point in question as would be a proof that there have been at least two 'physical objects' of no matter what sort.

The phrase 'things which are to be met with in space' can, therefore, be naturally understood as having a very wide meaning—a meaning even wider than that of 'physical object' or 'body', wide as is the meaning of these latter expressions. But wide as is its meaning, it is not, in one respect, so wide as that of another phrase which Kant uses as if it were equivalent to this one; and a comparison between the two will, I think, serve to make still clearer what sort of things it is with regard to which I wish to ask what proof, if any, can be given that there are such things.

The other phrase which Kant uses as if it were equivalent to 'things which are to be met with in space' is used by him in the sentence immediately preceding that previously quoted in which he declares that the expression 'things outside of us' 'carries with it an unavoidable ambiguity' (A373). In this preceding sentence he says that an 'empirical object' 'is called *external*, if it is presented (*vorgestellt*) in space'. He treats, therefore, the phrase 'presented in space' as if it were equivalent to 'to be met with in space'. But it is easy to find examples of 'things', of which it can hardly be denied that they are 'presented in space', but of which it could, quite naturally, be emphatically denied that they are 'to be met with in space'. Consider, for instance, the following description of one set of circumstances under which what some psychologists have called a 'negative after-image' and others a 'negative after-sensation' can be obtained. 'If, after looking steadfastly at a white patch on a black ground, the eye be turned to a white ground, a grey patch is seen for some little time' (Foster's *Text-book of Physiology*, IV, iii, 3, p.1266; quoted in Stout's *Manual of Psychology*, 3rd edition, p. 280). Upon reading these words recently, I took the trouble to cut

out of a piece of white paper a four-pointed star, to place it on a black ground, to 'look steadfastly' at it, and then to turn my eyes to a white sheet of paper: and I did find that I saw a grey patch for some little time—I not only saw a grey patch, but I saw it on the white ground, and also this grey patch was of roughly the same shape as the white four-pointed star at which I had 'looked steadfastly' just before—it also was a four-pointed star. I repeated this simple experiment successfully several times. Now each of those grey four-pointed stars, one of which I saw in each experiment, was what is called an 'after-image' or 'after-sensation'; and can anybody deny that each of these after-images can be quite properly said to have been 'presented in space'? I saw each of them on a real white background, and, if so, each of them was 'presented' on a real white background. But though they were 'presented in space' everybody, I think, would feel that it was gravely misleading to say that they were 'to be met with in space'. The white star at which I 'looked steadfastly', the black ground on which I saw it, and the white ground on which I saw the after-images, were, of course, 'to be met with in space': they were, in fact, 'physical objects' or surfaces of physical objects. But one important difference between them, on the one hand, and the grey after-images, on the other, can be quite naturally expressed by saying that the latter were *not* 'to be met with in space'. And one reason why this is so is, I think, plain. To say that so and so was at a given time 'to be met with in space' naturally suggests that there are conditions such that *any one* who fulfilled them might, conceivably, have 'perceived' the 'thing' in question—might have seen it, if it was a visible object, have felt it, if it was a tangible one, have heard it, if it was a sound, have smelt it, if it was a smell. When I say that the white four-pointed paper star, at which I looked steadfastly, was a 'physical object' and was 'to be met with in space', I am implying that *anyone*, who had been in the room at the time, and who had normal eyesight and a normal sense of touch, might have seen and felt it. But, in the case of those grey after-images which I saw, it is not conceivable that anyone besides myself should have seen any one of them. It is, of course, quite conceivable that other people, if they had been in the room with me at the time, and had carried out the same experiment which I carried out, would have seen grey after-images *very like* one of those which I saw: there is no absurdity in supposing even that they might have seen after-images *exactly* like one of those which I saw. But there is an absurdity in supposing that any one of the after-images which I saw could also have been seen by anyone else: in supposing that two different people can ever see the very same after-image. One reason, then, why we should say that none of those grey after-images which I saw was 'to be met with in space', although each of them was certainly 'presented in space' to me, is simply that none of them could conceivably have been seen by anyone else. It is natural so to understand the phrase 'to be met with in space', that to say of anything which a man perceived that it was to be met with in space is to say that it might have been perceived by *others* as well as by the man in question.

Negative after-images of the kind described are, therefore, one example of 'things' which, though they must be allowed to be 'presented in space', are nevertheless *not* 'to be met with in space', and are *not* 'external to our minds' in the sense with which we shall be concerned. And two other important examples may be given.

The first is this. It is well known that people sometimes see things double, an occurrence which has also been described by psychologists by saying that they have a 'double image', or two 'images', of some object at which they are looking. In such cases it would certainly be quite natural to say that each of the two 'images' is 'presented in space': they are seen, one in one place, and the other in another, in just the same sense in which each of those grey after-images which I saw was seen at a particular place on the white background at which I was looking. But it would be utterly unnatural to say that, when I have a double image, each of the two images is 'to be met with in space'. On the contrary it is quite certain that *both* of them are not 'to be met with in space'. If both were, it would follow that somebody else might see the *very same* two images which I see; and, though there is no absurdity in supposing that another person might see a pair of images exactly similar to a pair which I see, there is an absurdity in supposing that anyone else might see the *same identical pair*. In every case, then,

in which anyone sees anything double, we have an example of at least one 'thing' which, though 'presented in space' is certainly not 'to be met with in space'.

And the second important example is this. Bodily pains can, in general, be quite properly said to be 'presented in space'. When I have a toothache, I feel it *in* a particular region of my jaw or *in* a particular tooth; when I make a cut on my finger smart by putting iodine on it, I feel the pain in a particular place in my finger; and a man whose leg has been amputated may feel a pain *in* a place where his foot might have been if he had not lost it. It is certainly perfectly natural to understand the phrase 'presented in space' in such a way that if, in the sense illustrated, a pain is felt *in* a particular place, that pain is 'presented in space'. And yet of pains it would be quite unnatural to say that they are 'to be met with in space', for the same reason as in the case of after-images or double images. It is quite conceivable that another person should feel a pain exactly like one which I feel, but there is an absurdity in supposing that he could feel *numerically the same*[5] pain which I feel. And pains are in fact a typical example of the sort of 'things' of which philosophers say that they are *not* 'external' to our minds, but 'within' them. Of any pain which I feel they would say that it is necessarily *not* external to my mind but *in* it.

And finally it is, I think, worth while to mention one other class of 'things', which are certainly not 'external' objects and certainly not 'to be met with in space', in the sense with which I am concerned, but which yet some philosophers would be inclined to say are 'presented in space', though they are not 'presented in space' in quite the same sense in which pains, double images, and negative after-images of the sort I described are so. If you look at an electric light and then close your eyes, it sometimes happens that you see, for some little time, against the dark background which you usually see when your eyes are shut, a bright patch similar in shape to the light at which you have just been looking. Such a bright patch, if you see one, is another example of what some psychologists have called 'after-images' and others 'after-sensations'; but, unlike the negative

---

5   One and the same, self-identical with.

after-images of which I spoke before, it is seen when your eyes are shut. Of such an after-image, seen with closed eyes, some philosophers might be inclined to say that this image too was 'presented in space', although it is certainly not 'to be met with in space'. They would be inclined to say that it is 'presented in space', because it certainly is presented as at some little distance from the person who is seeing it: and how can a thing be presented as at some little distance from me, without being 'presented in space'? Yet there is an important difference between such after-images, seen with closed eyes, and after-images of the sort I previously described—a difference which might lead other philosophers to deny that these after-images, seen with closed eyes, are 'presented in space' at all. It is a difference which can be expressed by saying that when your eyes are shut, you are not seeing any part of *physical* space at all—of the space which is referred to when we talk of 'things which are to be met with in *space*'. An after-image seen with closed eyes certainly is presented in *a* space, but it may be questioned whether it is proper to say that it is presented in *space*.

It is clear, then, I think, that by no means everything which can naturally be said to be 'presented in space' can also be naturally said to be 'a thing which is to be met with in space'. Some of the 'things', which are presented in space, are very emphatically *not* to be met with in space: or, to use another phrase, which may be used to convey the same notion, they are emphatically *not* 'physical realities' at all. The conception 'presented in space' is therefore, in one respect, much wider than the conception 'to be met with in space': many 'things' fall under the first conception which do not fall under the second—many after-images, one at least of the pair of 'images' seen whenever anyone sees double, and most bodily pains, are 'presented in space', though none of them are to be met with in space. From the fact that a 'thing' is presented in space, it by no means follows that it is to be met with in space. But just as the first conception is, in one respect, wider than the second, so, in another, the second is wider than the first. For there are many 'things' to be met with in space, of which it is not true that they are presented in space. From the fact that a 'thing' is to be met with in space, it by

no means follows that it is presented in space. I have taken 'to be met with in space' to imply, as I think it naturally may, that a 'thing' *might be* perceived; but from the fact that a thing *might be* perceived, it does not follow that it is perceived; and if it is not actually perceived, then it will not be presented in space. It is characteristic of the sorts of 'things', including shadows, which I have described as 'to be met with in space', that there is no absurdity in supposing with regard to any one of them which is, at a given time, perceived, both (1) that it might have existed at that very time, without being perceived; (2) that it might have existed at another time, without being perceived at that other time; and (3) that during the whole period of its existence, it need not have been perceived at any time at all. There is, therefore, no absurdity in supposing that many things, which were at one time to be met with in space, never were 'presented' at any time at all, and that many things which *are* to be met with in space now, are not now 'presented' and also never were and never will be. To use a Kantian phrase, the conception of 'things which are to be met with in space', embraces not only objects of actual experience, but also objects *of possible* experience; and from the fact that a thing is or was an object of *possible* experience, it by no means follows that it either was or is or will be 'presented' at all.

I hope that what I have now said may have served to make clear enough what sorts of 'things' I was originally referring to as 'things outside us' or 'things external to our minds'. I said that I thought that Kant's phrase 'things that are to be met with in space' indicated fairly clearly the sorts of 'things' in question; and I have tried to make the range clearer still, by pointing out that this phrase only serves the purpose, if (*a*) you understand it in a sense, in which many 'things', e.g., after-images, double images, bodily pains, which might be said to be 'presented in space', are nevertheless *not* to be reckoned as 'things that are to be met with in space', and (*b*) you realise clearly that there is no contradiction in supposing that there have been and are 'to be met with in space' things which never have been, are not now, and never will be perceived, nor in supposing that among those of them which have at some time been perceived many existed at times at which they were not being perceived. I think it will now be clear to everyone that, since I do not reckon as 'external things' after-images, double images, and bodily pains, I also should not reckon as 'external things', any of the 'images' which we often 'see with the mind's eye' when we are awake, nor any of those which we see when we are asleep and dreaming; and also that I was so using the expression 'external' that from the fact that a man was at a given time having a visual hallucination, it will follow that he was seeing at that time something which was *not* 'external' to his mind, and from the fact that he was at a given time having an auditory hallucination, it will follow that he was at the time hearing a sound which was *not* 'external' to his mind. But I certainly have not made my use of these phrases, 'external to our minds' and 'to be met with in space', so clear that in the case of every kind of 'thing' which might be suggested, you would be able to tell at once whether I should or should not reckon it as 'external to our minds' and 'to be met with in space'. For instance, I have said nothing which makes it quite clear whether a reflection which I see in a looking-glass is or is not to be regarded as 'a thing that is to be met with in space' and 'external to our minds', nor have I said anything which makes it quite clear whether the sky is or is not to be so regarded. In the case of the sky, everyone, I think, would feel that it was quite inappropriate to talk of it as 'a thing that is to be met with in space'; and most people, I think, would feel a strong reluctance to affirm, without qualification, that reflections which people see in looking-glasses are 'to be met with in space'. And yet neither the sky nor reflections seen in mirrors are in the same position as bodily pains or after-images in the respect which I have emphasised as a reason for saying of these latter that they are *not* to be met with in space—namely that there is an absurdity in supposing that *the very same* pain which I feel could be felt by someone else or that *the very same* after-image which I see could be seen by someone else. In the case of reflections in mirrors we should quite naturally, in certain circumstances, use language which implies that another person may see the same reflection which we see. We might quite naturally say to a friend: 'Do you see that reddish reflection in the water there? I can't make out what it's a reflection of', just as we might say, pointing to

a distant hill-side: 'Do you see that white speck on the hill over there? I can't make out what it is'. And in the case of the sky, it is quite obviously *not* absurd to say that other people see it as well as I.

It must, therefore, be admitted that I have not made my use of the phrase 'things to be met with in space', nor therefore that of 'external to our minds', which the former was used to explain, so clear that in the case of every kind of 'thing' which may be mentioned, there will be no doubt whatever as to whether things of that kind are or are not 'to be met with in space' or 'external to our minds'. But this lack of a clear-cut definition of the expression 'things that are to be met with in space', does not, so far as I can see, matter for my present purpose. For my present purpose it is, I think, sufficient if I make clear, in the case of many kinds of things, that I am so using the phrase 'things that are to be met with in space', that, in the case of each of these kinds, from the proposition that there are things of that kind it *follows* that there are things to be met with in space. And I have, in fact, given a list (though by no means an exhaustive one) of kinds of things which are related to my use of the expression 'things that are to be met with in space' in this way. I mentioned among others the bodies of men and of animals, plants, stars, houses, chairs, and shadows; and I want now to emphasise that I am so using 'things to be met with in space' that, in the case of each of these kinds of 'things', from the proposition that there are 'things' of that kind it *follows* that there are things to be met with in space: e.g., from the proposition that there are plants or that plants exist it *follows* that there are things to be met with in space, from the proposition that shadows exist, it *follows* that there are things to be met with in space, and so on, in the case of all the kinds of 'things' which I mentioned in my first list. That this should be clear is sufficient for my purpose, because, if it is clear, then it will also be clear that, as I implied before, if you have proved that two plants exist, or that a plant and a dog exist, or that a dog and a shadow exist, etc., etc., you will *ipso facto*[6] have proved that there are things to be met with in space: you will not require *also* to give a separate proof that

6   "By that very fact," "by the fact itself."

from the proposition that there are plants it *does* follow that there are things to be met with in space.

Now with regard to the expression 'things that are to be met with in space' I think it will readily be believed that I may be using it in a sense such that no proof is required that from 'plants exist' there follows 'there are things to be met with in space'; but with regard to the phrase 'things external to our minds' I think the case is different. People may be inclined to say: 'I can see quite clearly that from the proposition "At least two dogs exist at the present moment" there *follows* the proposition "At least two things are to be met with in space at the present moment", so that if you can prove that there are two dogs in existence at the present moment you will *ipso facto* have proved that two things at least are to be met with in space at the present moment. I can see that you do not also require a separate proof that from "Two dogs exist" "Two things are to be met with in space" *does* follow; it is quite obvious that there couldn't be a dog which wasn't to be met with in space. But it is not by any means so clear to me that if you can prove that there are two dogs or two shadows, you will *ipso facto* have proved that there are two things *external to our minds*. Isn't it possible that a dog, though it certainly must be "to be met with in space", might *not* be an external object—an object external to our minds? Isn't a separate proof required that anything that is to be met with in space must be external to our minds? Of course, if you are using "external" as a mere synonym for "to be met with in space", no proof will be required that dogs are external objects: in that case, if you can prove that two dogs exist, you will *ipso facto* have proved that there are some external things. But I find it difficult to believe that you, or anybody else, do really use "external" as a mere synonym for "to be met with in space"; and if you don't, isn't some proof required that whatever is to be met with in space must be external to our minds?

Now Kant, as we saw, asserts that the phrases 'outside of us' or 'external' are in fact used in two very different senses; and with regard to one of these two senses, that which he calls the 'transcendental' sense, and which he tries to explain by saying that it is a sense in which 'external' means 'existing *as a thing in itself* distinct from us', it is notorious that he himself held that things which are to be met with in space are *not* 'external' in that sense.[7] There is, therefore, according to him, *a* sense of 'external', a sense in which the word has been commonly used by philosophers—such that, if 'external' be used in that sense, then from the proposition 'Two dogs exist' it will *not* follow that there are some external things. What this supposed sense is I do not think that Kant himself ever succeeded in explaining clearly; nor do I know of any reason for supposing that philosophers ever have used 'external' in a sense, such that in *that* sense things that are to be met with in space are *not* external. But how about the other sense, in which, according to Kant, the word 'external' has been commonly used—that which he calls 'empirically external'? How is this conception related to the conception 'to be met with in space'? It may be noticed that, in the passages which I quoted (A373), Kant himself does not tell us at all clearly what he takes to be the proper answer to this question. He only makes the rather odd statement that, in order to remove all uncertainty as to the conception 'empirically external', he will distinguish objects to which it applies from those which might be called 'external' in the transcendental sense, by 'calling them outright things which are *to be met with in space*'. These odd words certainly suggest, as one possible interpretation of them, that in Kant's opinion the conception 'empirically external' is *identical* with the conception 'to be met with in space'—that he does think that 'external', when used in this second sense, is a mere synonym for 'to be met with in space'. But, if this is his meaning, I do find it very difficult to believe that he is right. Have philosophers, in fact, ever used 'external' as a mere synonym for 'to be met with in space'? Does he himself do so?

---

7   Basically, this is because, for Kant, the things we "meet with in space" are always *appearances* of things, rather than "things in themselves" (the hidden nature behind those appearances). That is, we never meet with "things in themselves" in space, so if *those* things are what we mean by "the things external to us" then none of the things which we *do* meet with in space could be external. See the notes on the Kant selection in this chapter for more information.

I do not think they have, nor that he does himself; and, in order to explain how they have used it, and how the two conceptions 'external to our minds' and 'to be met with in space' are related to one another, I think it is important expressly to call attention to a fact which hitherto I have only referred to incidentally: namely the fact that those who talk of certain things as 'external to' our minds, do, in general, as we should naturally expect, talk of other 'things', with which they wish to contrast the first, as 'in' our minds. It has, of course, been often pointed out that when 'in' is thus used, followed by 'my mind', 'your mind', 'his mind', etc., 'in' is being used metaphorically. And there are some metaphorical uses of 'in', followed by such expressions, which occur in common speech, and which we all understand quite well. For instance, we all understand such expressions as 'I had you in mind, when I made that arrangement' or 'I had you in mind, when I said that there are some people who can't bear to touch a spider'. In these cases 'I was thinking of you' can be used to mean the same as 'I had you in mind'. But it is quite certain that this particular metaphorical use of 'in' is not the one in which philosophers are using it when they contrast what is 'in' my mind with what is 'external' to it. On the contrary, in their use of 'external', you will be external to my mind even at a moment when I have you in mind. If we want to discover what this peculiar metaphorical use of '*in* my mind' is, which is such that nothing, which is, in the sense we are now concerned with, 'external' to my mind, can ever be 'in' it, we need, I think, to consider instances of the sort of 'things' which they would say are 'in' my mind in this special sense. I have already mentioned three such instances, which are, I think, sufficient for my present purpose: any bodily pain which I feel, any after-image which I see with my eyes shut, and any image which I 'see' when I am asleep and dreaming, are typical examples of the sort of 'thing' of which philosophers have spoken as '*in* my mind'. And there is no doubt, I think, that when they have spoken of such things as my body, a sheet of paper, a star—in short 'physical objects' generally—as 'external', they have meant to emphasize some important difference which they feel to exist between such things as these and such 'things' as a pain, an after-image seen with

closed eyes, and a dream-image. But *what* difference? What difference do they feel to exist between a bodily pain which I feel or an after-image which I see with closed eyes, on the one hand, and my body itself, on the other—what difference which leads them to say that whereas the bodily pain and the after-image are 'in' my mind, my body itself is *not* 'in' my mind—not even when I am feeling it and seeing it or thinking of it? I have already said that one difference which there is between the two, is that my body is to be met with in space, whereas the bodily pain and the after-image are not. But I think it would be quite wrong to say that this is *the* difference which has led philosophers to speak of the two latter as 'in' my mind, and of my body as *not* 'in' my mind.

The question what the difference is which has led them to speak in this way, is not, I think, at all an easy question to answer; but I am going to try to give, in brief outline, what I *think* is a right answer.

It should, I think, be noted, first of all, that the use of the word 'mind', which is being adopted when it is said that any bodily pains which I feel are 'in my mind', is one which is not quite in accordance with any usage common in ordinary speech, although we are very familiar with it in philosophy. Nobody, I think, would say that bodily pains which I feel are 'in my mind', unless he was also prepared to say that it is *with* my mind that I feel bodily pains; and to say this latter is, I think, not quite in accordance with common non-philosophic usage. It is natural enough to say that it is with my mind that I remember, and think, and imagine, and feel *mental* pains—e.g., disappointment, but not, I think, quite so natural to say that it is with my mind that I feel *bodily* pains, e.g., a severe headache; and perhaps even less natural to say that it is with my mind that I see and hear and smell and taste. There is, however, a well-established philosophical usage according to which seeing, hearing, smelling, tasting, and having a bodily pain are just as much *mental* occurrences or processes as are remembering, or thinking, or imagining. This usage was, I think, adopted by philosophers, because they saw a real resemblance between such statements as 'I saw a cat', 'I heard a clap of thunder', 'I smelt a strong smell of onions', 'My finger smarted horribly', on the one hand, and such statements as 'I remembered having seen him', 'I was thinking out a plan of action', 'I pictured the scene to myself', 'I felt bitterly disappointed', on the other—a resemblance which puts all these statements in one class together, as contrasted with other statements in which 'I' or 'my' is used, such as, e.g., 'I was less than four feet high', 'I was lying on my back', 'My hair was very long'. What is the resemblance in question? It is a resemblance which might be expressed by saying that all the first eight statements are the sort of statements which furnish data for psychology, while the three latter are not. It is also a resemblance which may be expressed, in a way now common among philosophers, by saying that in the case of all the first eight statements, if we make the statement more specific by adding a date, we get a statement such that, if it is true, then it *follows* that I was 'having an experience' at the date in question, whereas this does not hold for the three last statements. For instance, if it is true that I saw a cat between 12 noon and 5 minutes past, today, it *follows* that I was 'having some experience' between 12 noon and 5 minutes past, today; whereas from the proposition that I was less than four feet high in December 1877, it does not *follow* that I had any experiences in December 1877. But this philosophic use of 'having an experience' is one which itself needs explanation, since it is not identical with any use of the expression that is established in common speech. An explanation, however, which is, I think, adequate for the purpose, can be given by saying that a philosopher, who was following this usage, would say that I was at a given time 'having an experience' if and only if either (1) I was conscious at the time or (2) I was dreaming at the time or (3) something else was true of me at the time, which resembled what is true of me when I am conscious and when I am dreaming, in a certain very obvious respect in which what is true of me when I am dreaming resembles what is true of me when I am conscious, and in which what would be true of me, if at any time, for instance, I had a vision, would resemble both. This explanation is, of course, in some degree vague; but I think it is clear enough for our purpose. It amounts to saying that, in this philosophic usage of 'having an experience', it would be said of me that I was, at a given time, having *no* experience, if I was at the time neither conscious nor dreaming nor having a

vision nor *anything else of the sort*; and, of course, this is vague in so far as it has not been specified what else would be *of the sort*: this is left to be gathered from the instances given. But I think this is sufficient: often at night when I am asleep, I am neither conscious nor dreaming nor having a vision nor *anything else of the sort*—that is to say, I am having no experiences. If this explanation of this philosophic usage of 'having an experience' is clear enough, then I think that what has been meant by saying that any pain which I feel or any after-image which I see with my eyes closed is '*in* my mind', can be explained by saying that what is meant is neither more nor less than that there would be a contradiction in supposing *that very same pain* or *that very same after-image* to have existed at a time at which I was having no experience; or, in other words, that from the proposition, with regard to any time, that *that* pain or *that* after-image existed at that time, it *follows* that I was having some experience at the time in question. And if so, then we can say that the felt difference between bodily pains which I feel and after-images which I see, on the one hand, and my body on the other, which has led philosophers to say that any such pain or after-image is '*in* my mind', whereas my body *never* is but is always 'outside of' or 'external to' my mind, is just this, that whereas there is a contradiction in supposing a pain which I feel or an after-image which I see to exist at a time when I am having no experience, there is no contradiction in supposing my body to exist at a time when I am having no experience; and we can even say, I think, that just this and nothing more is what they have meant by these puzzling and misleading phrases 'in my mind' and 'external to my mind'.

But now, if to say of anything, e.g., my body, that it is external to my mind, means merely that from a proposition to the effect that it existed at a specified time, there in no case follows the further proposition that I was having an experience at the time in question, then to say of anything that it is external to *our* minds, will mean similarly that from a proposition to the effect that it existed at a specified time, it in no case follows that any of us were having experiences at the time in question. And if by *our* minds be meant, as is, I think, usually meant, the minds of human beings living on the earth, then it will follow that any pains which animals may feel, any after-images they may see, any experiences they may have, though not external to *their* minds, yet are external to *ours*. And this at once makes plain how different is the conception 'external to our minds' from the conception 'to be met with in space'; for, of course, pains which animals feel or after-images which they see are no more to be met with in space than are pains which *we* feel or after-images which *we* see. From the proposition that there are external objects—objects that are not in any of *our* minds, it does *not* follow that there are things to be met with in space; and hence 'external to our minds' is not a mere synonym for 'to be met with in space': that is to say, 'external to our minds' and 'to be met with in space' are two different conceptions. And the true relation between these conceptions seems to me to be this. We have already seen that there are ever so many kinds of 'things', such that, in the case of each of these kinds, from the proposition that there is at least one thing of that kind there *follows* the proposition that there is at least one thing to be met with in space: e.g., this follows from 'There is at least one star', from 'There is at least one human body', from 'There is at least one shadow', etc. And I think we can say that of every kind of thing of which this is true, it is also true that from the proposition that there is at least one 'thing' of that kind there *follows* the proposition that there is at least one thing external to our minds: e.g., from 'There is at least one star' there follows not only 'There is at least one thing to be met with in space' but also 'There is at least one external thing', and similarly in all other cases. My reason for saying this is as follows. Consider any kind of thing, such that anything of that kind, if there is anything of it, must be 'to be met with in space': e.g., consider the kind 'soap-bubble'. If I say of anything which I am perceiving, 'That is a soap-bubble', I am, it seems to me, certainly implying that there would be no contradiction in asserting that it existed before I perceived it and that it will continue to exist, even if I cease to perceive it. This seems to me to be part of what is meant by saying that it is a real soap-bubble, as distinguished, for instance, from an hallucination of a soap-bubble. Of course, it by no means follows, that if it really is a soap-bubble, it did in fact exist before I perceived it or will continue to exist after I

cease to perceive it: soap-bubbles are an example of a kind of 'physical object' and 'thing to be met with in space', in the case of which it is notorious that particular specimens of the kind often do exist only so long as they are perceived by a particular person. But a thing which I perceive would not be a soap-bubble unless its existence at any given time were logically *independent* of my perception of it at that time; unless that is to say, from the proposition, with regard to a particular time, that it existed at that time, it *never* follows that I perceived it at that time. But, if it is true that it would not be a soap-bubble, unless it *could* have existed at any given time without being perceived by me at that time, it is certainly also true that it would not be a soap-bubble, unless it *could* have existed at any given time, without its being true that I was having any experience of any kind at the time in question: it would not be a soap-bubble, unless, whatever time you take, from the proposition that it existed at that time it does *not* follow that I was having any experience at that time. That is to say, from the proposition with regard to anything which I am perceiving that it is a soap-bubble, there *follows* the proposition that it is external to *my* mind. But if, when I say that anything which I perceive is a soap-bubble, I am implying that it is external to *my* mind, I am, I think, certainly also implying that it is also external to all other minds: I am implying that it is not a thing of a sort such that things of that sort can only exist at a time when somebody is having an experience. I think, therefore, that from any proposition of the form 'There's a soap-bubble!' there does really *follow* the proposition 'There's an external object!' 'There's an object external to all our minds!' And, if this is true of the kind 'soap-bubble', it is certainly also true of any other kind (including the kind 'unicorn') which is such that, if there are any things of that kind, it follows that there are *some* things to be met with in space.

I think, therefore, that in the case of all kinds of 'things', which are such that if there is a pair of things, both of which are of one of these kinds, or a pair of things one of which is of one of them and one of them of another, then it will follow at once that there are some things to be met with in space, it is true also that if I can prove that there are a pair of things, one of which is of one of these kinds and another of another, or a pair both of which are of one of them, then I shall have proved *ipso facto* that there are at least two 'things outside of us'. That is to say, if I can prove that there exist now both a sheet of paper and a human hand, I shall have proved that there are now 'things outside of us'; if I can prove that there exist now both a shoe and sock, I shall have proved that there are now 'things outside of us', etc.; and similarly I shall have proved it, if I can prove that there exist now two sheets of paper, or two human hands, or two shoes, or two socks, etc. Obviously, then, there are thousands of different things such that, if, at any time, I can prove any one of them, I shall have proved the existence of things outside of us. Cannot I prove any of these things?

It seems to me that, so far from its being true, as Kant declares to be his opinion, that there is only one possible proof of the existence of things outside of us, namely the one which he has given, I can now give a large number of different proofs, each of which is a perfectly rigorous proof; and that at many other times I have been in a position to give many others. I can prove now, for instance, that two human hands exist. How? By holding up my two hands, and saying, as I make a certain gesture with the right hand, 'Here is one hand', and adding, as I make a certain gesture with the left, 'and here is another'. And if, by doing this, I have proved *ipso facto* the existence of external things, you will all see that I can also do it now in numbers of other ways: there is no need to multiply examples.

But did I prove just now that two human hands were then in existence? I do want to insist that I did; that the proof which I gave was a perfectly rigorous one; and that it is perhaps impossible to give a better or more rigorous proof of anything whatever. Of course, it would not have been a proof unless three conditions were satisfied; namely (1) unless the premiss which I adduced as proof of the conclusion was different from the conclusion I adduced it to prove; (2) unless the premiss which I adduced was something which I *knew* to be the case, and not merely something which I believed but which was by no means certain, or something which, though in fact true, I did not know to be so; and (3) unless the conclusion did really follow from the premiss. But all these three

conditions were in fact satisfied by my proof. (1) The premiss which I adduced in proof was quite certainly different from the conclusion, for the conclusion was merely 'Two human hands exist at this moment'; but the premiss was something far more specific than this—something which I expressed by showing you my hands, making certain gestures, and saying the words 'Here is one hand, and here is another'. It is quite obvious that the two were different, because it is quite obvious that the conclusion might have been true, even if the premiss had been false. In asserting the premiss I was asserting much more than I was asserting in asserting the conclusion. (2) I certainly did at the moment *know* that which I expressed by the combination of certain gestures with saying the words 'There is one hand and here is another'. I *knew* that there was one hand in the place indicated by combining a certain gesture with my first utterance of 'here' and that there was another in the different place indicated by combining a certain gesture with my second utterance of 'here'. How absurd it would be to suggest that I did not know it, but only believed it, and that perhaps it was not the case! You might as well suggest that I do not know that I am now standing up and talking—that perhaps after all I'm not, and that it's not quite certain that I am! And finally (3) it is quite certain that the conclusion did follow from the premiss. This is as certain as it is that if there is one hand here and another here *now*, then it follows that there are two hands in existence *now*.

My proof, then, of the existence of things outside of us did satisfy three of the conditions necessary for a rigorous proof. Are there any other conditions necessary for a rigorous proof, such that perhaps it did not satisfy one of them? Perhaps there may be; I do not know; but I do want to emphasise that, so far as I can see, we all of us do constantly take proofs of this sort as absolutely conclusive proofs of certain conclusions—as finally settling certain questions, as to which we were previously in doubt. Suppose, for instance, it were a question whether there were as many as three misprints on a certain page in a certain book. A says there are, B is inclined to doubt it. How could A prove that he is right? Surely he *could* prove it by taking the book, turning to the page, and pointing to three separate places on it, saying 'There's one misprint here, another here, and another here': surely that is a method by which it *might* be proved! Of course, A would not have proved, by doing this, that there were at least three misprints on the page in question, unless it was certain that there was a misprint in each of the places to which he pointed. But to say that he *might* prove it in this way, is to say that it *might* be certain that there was. And if such a thing as that could ever be certain, then assuredly it was certain just now that there was one hand in one of the two places I indicated and another in the other.

I did, then, just now, give a proof that there were *then* external objects; and obviously, if I did, I could *then* have given many other proofs of the same sort that there were external objects *then*, and could now give many proofs of the same sort that there are external objects *now*.

But, if what I am asked to do is to prove that external objects have existed in *the past*, then I can give many different proofs of this also, but proofs which are in important respects of a different *sort* from those just given. And I want to emphasise that, when Kant says it is a scandal not to be able to give a proof of the existence of external objects, a proof of their existence in the past would certainly *help* to remove the scandal of which he is speaking. He says that, if it occurs to anyone to question their existence, we ought to be able to confront him with a satisfactory proof. But by a person who questions their existence, he certainly means not merely a person who questions whether any exist at the moment of speaking, but a person who questions whether any have *ever* existed; and a proof that some have existed in the past would certainly therefore be relevant to *part* of what such a person is questioning. How then can I prove that there have been external objects in the past? Here is one proof. I can say: 'I held up two hands above this desk not very long ago; therefore two hands existed not very long ago; therefore at least two external objects have existed at some time in the past, QED'.[8] This is a perfectly good proof, provided I *know* what is asserted in the premiss. But I do know that I held up two hands above this desk not very long ago. As a

matter of fact, in this case you all know it too. There's no doubt whatever that I did. Therefore I have given a perfectly conclusive proof that external objects have existed in the past; and you will all see at once that, if this is a conclusive proof, I could have given many others of the same sort, and could now give many others. But it is also quite obvious that this sort of proof differs in important respects from the sort of proof I gave just now that there were two hands existing *then*.

I have, then, given two conclusive proofs of the existence of external objects. The first was a proof that two human hands existed at the time when I gave the proof; the second was a proof that two human hands had existed at a time previous to that at which I gave the proof. These proofs were of a different sort in important respects. And I pointed out that I could have given, then, many other conclusive proofs of both sorts. It is also obvious that I could give many others of both sorts now. So that, if these are the sort of proof that is wanted, nothing is easier than to prove the existence of external objects.

But now I am perfectly well aware that, in spite of all that I have said, many philosophers will still feel that I have not given any satisfactory proof of the point in question. And I want briefly, in conclusion, to say something as to why this dissatisfaction with my proofs should be felt.

One reason why, is, I think, this. Some people understand 'proof of an external world' as including a proof of things which I haven't attempted to prove and haven't proved. It is not quite easy to say *what* it is that they want proved—*what* it is that is such that unless they got a proof of it, they would not say that they had a proof of the existence of external things; but I can make an approach to explaining what they want by saying that if I had proved the propositions which I used as *premisses* in my two proofs, then they would perhaps admit that I had proved the existence of external things, but, in the absence of such a proof (which, of course, I have neither given nor attempted to give), they will say that I have not given what they mean by a proof of the existence of external things. In other words, they want a proof of what I assert *now* when I hold up my hands and say 'Here's one hand and here's another'; and, in the other case, they want a proof of what I assert *now* when I say 'I

---

8   *Quod erat demonstrandum*—Latin for "which was to be demonstrated."

did hold up two hands above this desk just now'. Of course, what they really want is not merely a proof of these two propositions, but something like a general statement as to how *any* propositions of this sort may be proved. This, of course, I haven't given; and I do not believe it can be given: if this is what is meant by proof of the existence of external things, I do not believe that any proof of the existence of external things is possible. Of course, in some cases what might be called a proof of propositions which seem like these can be got. If one of you suspected that one of my hands was artificial he might be said to get a proof of my proposition 'Here's one hand, and here's another', by coming up and examining the suspected hand close up, perhaps touching and pressing it, and so establishing that it really was a human hand. But I do not believe that any proof is possible in nearly all cases. How am I to prove now that 'Here's one hand, and here's another'? I do not believe I can do it. In order to do it, I should need to prove for one thing, as Descartes pointed out, that I am not now dreaming. But how can I prove that I am not? I have, no doubt, conclusive reasons for asserting that I am not now dreaming; I have conclusive evidence that I am awake: but that is a very different thing from being able to prove it. I could not tell you what all my evidence is; and I should require to do this at least, in order to give you a proof.

But another reason why some people would feel dissatisfied with my proofs is, I think, not merely that they want a proof of something which I haven't proved, but that they think that, if I cannot give such extra proofs, then the proofs that I have given are not conclusive proofs at all. And this, I think, is a definite mistake. They would say: 'If you cannot prove your premiss that here is one hand and here is another, then you do not know it. But you yourself have admitted that, if you did not know it, then your proof was not conclusive. Therefore your proof was not, as you say it was, a conclusive proof'. This view that, if I cannot prove such things as these, I do not know them, is, I think, the view that Kant was expressing in the sentence which I quoted at the beginning of this lecture, when he implies that so long as we have no proof of the existence of external things, their existence must be accepted merely on *faith*. He means to say, I think, that if I cannot prove that there is a hand here, I must accept it merely as a matter of faith—I cannot know it. Such a view, though it has been very common among philosophers, can, I think, be shown to be wrong—though shown only by the use of premisses which are not known to be true, unless we do know of the existence of external things. I can know things, which I cannot prove; and among things which I certainly did know, even if (as I think) I could not prove them, were the premisses of my two proofs. I should say, therefore, that those, if any, who are dissatisfied with these proofs merely on the ground that I did not know their premisses, have no good reason for their dissatisfaction.

EDMUND L. GETTIER
"Is Justified True Belief Knowledge?"

Who Is Edmund Gettier?

Edmund Gettier's career has been one of the most unusual in contemporary academic philosophy. His first teaching job was at Wayne State University, in Detroit, Michigan. During the early sixties, the chair of his department suggested that, as tenure consideration approached, some publication might help. The result was "Is Justified True Belief Knowledge?" This article took up all of three pages of a 1963 issue of *Analysis*, but it's the best-known article ever published in epistemology. All Gettier did there was to present two examples, but these two showed that the most basic assumption of epistemology since Plato was wrong. David Lewis cited Gettier (and Gödel) as maybe the only philosophers ever who conclusively refuted a philosophical theory.[1]

Opinions differ on the extent of the remainder of Gettier's publication dossier. One of his friends thinks there's a second article in print; the other believes there are two others.[2] The Philosopher's Index lists only two others, both translations; the title listed for one of these, clearly translated into Hungarian and back, is "If Knowledge Is a Justified True Belief?"[3]

But Gettier has not been relaxing since his career began in the late 1950s. His friends agree that, coupled with his "massive indifference to the usual trappings of an academic career," Gettier has shown an "abiding, deep commitment to philosophy."[4] Colleagues and students have enjoyed decades of energetic, creative philosophical interchange. In 1967 Gettier moved to the University of Massachusetts, Amherst, where he is now Professor Emeritus.

What Was Gettier's Overall Philosophical Project?

Gettier attacks a widely-accepted analysis of the concept of *knowledge*. The analysis of knowledge Gettier attacks is the claim that the necessary and sufficient conditions for S knows that P are that (a) P is true; (b) S believes P; (c) S has justification for this belief.

What Is the Structure of This Reading?

Gettier begins with two assumptions. The first is that one can have justification for believing something that's false.

---

1   *Philosophical Papers*, Vol I (London: Oxford University Press, 1983), p. x.

2   The first opinion from Robert C. Sleigh, Jr., "Knowing Edmund Gettier," *Philosophical Analysis: A Defense by Example*, ed. by David F. Austin (Dordrecht: Kluwer, 1987), p. xiv; the second from Austin's Preface to that book, p. xii.

3   *Magyar Filozofiai Szemle*, no. 1–2, pp. 231–233 (1995).

4   Sleigh, p. xiii.

A tiny bit of background in logic is necessary for understanding the second. Logicians say that a statement P is *entailed* by another statement Q when it's logically impossible for P to be false given the truth of Q. So, for example, *The picnic is off* is entailed by *It's raining; and if it's raining, the picnic is off.*

Gettier's second assumption is that whenever P is entailed by Q, and a person believes Q, and is justified in this belief, and deduces P from Q, and accepts P on this basis, then that person is justified in believing P. Suppose, for example, you believe, with good justification, that it's raining and if it's raining, the picnic is off. And so you deduce from this, and accordingly believe, that the picnic is off. According to Gettier's second assumption, you're justified in believing that the picnic is off.

The second assumption seems quite reasonable. After all, the fact that one's belief that Q is justified means that you'd count Q as likely to be true; and the fact that Q entails P means that P is likely to be true also; so you'd also be justified in believing P.

Applying these reasonable assumptions to Smith's belief in each of Gettier's two examples, we'd conclude that Smith is justified in his belief in both cases. Since both beliefs are true, they should count as knowledge, under the traditional analysis of knowledge as justified true belief; but in neither case would we agree that Smith's true beliefs are knowledge.

There has been an enormous amount of discussion in print concerning what to do about Gettier's examples (and other similar sorts of examples, known as Gettier-type cases). Some philosophers have tried to propose an account of justification that would account better for our judgments about the beliefs of Smith (and the believers in other Gettier-type cases). Others have argued that what's needed is that an additional condition (beside justified true belief) should be added for the correct analysis of knowledge.

Some Useful Background Information

1. In Gettier's time, but less frequently nowadays, philosophers took it that their job (or one of them) was to provide analyses of concepts; an analysis, in this sense, provides the conditions for the concept's application, and it was generally thought that the ideal analysis of any concept would provide a list of *necessary* and *sufficient* application conditions.

    The *necessary conditions* for application of a concept are those such that if something doesn't meet those conditions, the concept doesn't apply to it. Thus, for example, one of the necessary conditions for being someone's brother is being male. You can't be anyone's brother unless you're male. The sufficient conditions are those such that if something does meet these conditions, the concept does apply to it. Thus, being someone's male sibling is sufficient for the application of the concept *brother*. In this case, being someone's male sibling is also necessary. So it's necessary and sufficient; and the successful analysis of the concept *brother* is given by providing this list of conditions which are each necessary and together sufficient: (a) male; (b) somebody's sibling.

2. It's clear, and hardly needs argument, that believing P is necessary for knowing P. If you don't believe it, you wouldn't be said to know it. And the truth of P is another obvious necessary condition; your beliefs that are in fact false aren't knowledge, even though you think they are. The third necessary condition—that P be justified—needs a bit more explanation. This is added to distinguish between genuine knowledge and just a lucky guess. If S believes some true P merely because of a hunch, S's belief has no firm grounding, no justification, so it doesn't merit being called knowledge. When Fred wins the lottery, and says he *knew* he'd win, what he says is false. He may have been firmly convinced he'd win, but he had no justification for this, so he didn't know it. (Note that one may sometimes have justification for a false belief, when a large preponderance of evidence points toward it. But then it's not knowledge either.)

3. The places in Plato's writing Gettier mentions in a footnote, where Plato appears to suggest that knowledge is justified true belief, are these:

From Plato, *Theaetetus*

SOCRATES: But, my friend, if true opinion and knowledge were the same thing in law courts, the best of judges could never have true opinion without knowledge; in fact, however, it appears that the two are different.

THEAETETUS: Oh yes, I remember now, Socrates, having heard someone make the distinction, but I had forgotten it. He said that knowledge was true opinion accompanied by reason, but that unreasoning true opinion was outside of the sphere of knowledge; and matters of which there is not a rational explanation are unknowable—yes, that is what he called them—and those of which there is are knowable.

From Plato, *Meno*

SOCRATES: Well, and a person who had a right opinion as to which was the way, but had never been there and did not really know, might give right guidance, might he not?

MENO: Certainly.

SOCRATES: And so long, I presume, as he has right opinion about that which the other man really knows, he will be just as good a guide—if he thinks the truth instead of knowing it—as the man who has the knowledge.

MENO: Just as good.

SOCRATES: Hence true opinion is as good a guide to rightness of action as knowledge; and this is a point we omitted just now in our consideration of the nature of virtue, when we stated that knowledge is the only guide of right action; whereas we find there is also true opinion.

MENO: So it seems.

SOCRATES: Then right opinion is just as useful as knowledge.

MENO: With this difference, Socrates, that he who has knowledge will always hit on the right way, whereas he who has right opinion will sometimes do so, but sometimes not.

SOCRATES: How do you mean? Will not he who always has right opinion be always right, so long as he opines rightly?

MENO: It appears to me that he must; and therefore I wonder, Socrates, this being the case, that knowledge should ever be more prized than right opinion, and why they should be two distinct and separate things.

SOCRATES: Well, do you know why it is that you wonder, or shall I tell you?

MENO: Please tell me.

SOCRATES: It is because you have not observed with attention the images of Daedalus.[5] But perhaps there are none in your country.

MENO: What is the point of your remark?

SOCRATES: That if they are not fastened up they play truant and run away; but, if fastened, they stay where they are.

MENO: Well, what of that?

SOCRATES: To possess one of his works which is let loose does not count for much in value; it will not stay with you any more than a runaway slave: but when fastened up it is worth a great deal, for his productions are very fine things. And to what am I referring in all this? To true opinion. For these, so long as they stay with us, are a fine possession, and effect all that is good; but they do not care to stay for long, and run away out of the human soul, and thus are of no great value until one makes them fast with causal reasoning. And this process, friend Meno, is recollection,[6] as in our previous talk we have agreed. But when once they are fastened, in the first place they turn into knowledge, and in the second, are abiding. And this is why knowledge is more prized than right opinion: the one transcends the other by its trammels.

MENO: Upon my word, Socrates, it seems to be very much as you say.

[Both translations by Jowett.]

---

5   Socrates refers here to the legend that the first sculptor, Daedalus, put mechanisms inside his works that made them move.

6   Socrates argues earlier in this dialogue that real knowledge comes from recollection of the general Forms of things encountered before birth.

Suggestions for Critical Reflection

1. Sometimes you say, "I just know that …" when what you're saying is merely that you feel certain. But most philosophers would say that feeling certain that P is not a sufficient condition for knowing that P. Do you agree? Why / why not? Perhaps a more likely claim is that feeling certain that P is a necessary condition for knowing that P. Do you agree? Why / why not?

2. One suggestion to deal with Gettier-type cases is to add an additional necessary condition to the traditional analysis: that S's belief not be the result of S's inference from a false belief. But consider this example: S believes that there are sheep in the field, and this is true; but what S in fact has seen is really a large furry dog. So S doesn't know there are sheep there. It's sometimes thought that there's no inference from a false belief in this case—why might this be, and do you agree? If so, why might this show the inadequacy of the current proposal?

3. Another suggestion is that S's belief has to have been arrived at by a generally reliable method. But consider this example: S's watch has kept perfect time for years, so looking at her watch is a generally reliable way of finding out what time it is. Today, S looks at her watch at exactly 1 pm, and the watch shows 1:00. S believes correctly that it's 1 pm. But the watch stopped the previous night at 1 am. So S doesn't know that it's 1 pm. This is sometimes taken to show the inadequacy of this proposal—does it?

4. Here's a third troublesome Gettier-type case. S knows a barn when she sees one. But today, unbeknownst to her, she's traveling in an area where they're making a movie, and have built a large number of barn-facades that look just like real barns from the road. By fortunate coincidence, S sees, however, what is the only real barn in the area, and believes (correctly) that there's a real barn there. Does S know that there's a (real) barn there? Is this true belief justified, given that S is an excellent barn-detector?

Suggestions for Further Reading

These articles survey the problem and its main responses: "An Introduction to the Analysis of Knowledge" by Jack Crumley, in *Introduction to Epistemology* by Jack Crumley (Broadview Press, 2009); "Gettier problem" by Paul K. Moser, in *A Companion to Epistemology* (Blackwell, 1992); "Conditions and Analyses of Knowing" by Robert Shope, in *The Oxford Handbook of Epistemology*, Paul K. Moser, ed. (Oxford University Press, 2002); "Knowledge" by Jonathan Dancy, Chapter 2 of *An Introduction to Contemporary Epistemology* by Jonathan Dancy (Blackwell, 1985); "Gettier Problems" by Stephen Hetherington and "Epistemology" by David A. Truncellito, Part 2d, both online in the *Internet Encyclopedia of Philosophy*; "Epistemology" by Matthias Steup, Part 1.2, online in the *Stanford Encyclopedia of Philosophy*.

These articles argue for important positions responding to Gettier. "Knowledge: Undefeated Justified True Belief" by Keith Lehrer and Thomas D. Paxson, Jr., *Journal of Philosophy*, 66, pp. 225–237. Reprinted in *Epistemology: Contemporary Readings*, Michael Huemer, ed. (Routledge, 2002), and in *Readings in Contemporary Epistemology*, Sven Bernecker and Fred Dretske, eds. (Oxford University Press, 2000), and in *Justification and Knowledge*, G. Pappas and M. Swain, eds. (Cornell University Press, 1978). "A Causal Theory of Knowing" by Alvin I. Goldman, *Journal of Philosophy* 64, pp. 355–372. Reprinted in *Justification and Knowledge*, G. Pappas and M. Swain, eds. (Cornell University Press, 1978). "Epistemic Defeasibility" by Marshal Swain, *American Philosophical Quarterly*, 11, pp. 15–25. Reprinted in *Justification and Knowledge*, G. Pappas and M. Swain, eds. (Cornell University Press, 1978). "Knowledge and Grounds: A Comment on Mr. Gettier's Paper" by Michael Clark, *Analysis* 24 (2) (December, 1963), pp. 46–48. Reprinted in *Epistemology: Contemporary Readings*, Michael Huemer, ed. (Routledge, 2002). "An Alleged Defect in Gettier Counter-Examples" by Richard Feldman, *Australasian Journal of Philosophy* 52 (1), pp. 68–69. Reprinted in *Knowledge: Readings in Contemporary Epistemology*, Sven Bernecker and Fred Dretske, eds. (Oxford University Press, 2000). "Conclusive Reasons" by Fred Dretske, *Australasian Journal of Philosophy* 49, pp. 1–22. Reprinted in *Justification and Knowledge*, G. Pappas and M. Swain, eds. (Cornell University Press, 1978).

"Is Justified True Belief Knowledge?"[7]

Various attempts have been made in recent years to state necessary and sufficient conditions for someone's knowing a given proposition. The attempts have often been such that they can be stated in a form similar to the following:[8]

(a) S knows that P   *IFF*[9]
    (i)   P is true,
    (ii) S believes that P, and
    (iii) S is justified in believing that P.

For example, Chisholm has held that the following gives the necessary and sufficient conditions for knowledge:[10]

(b) S knows that P   *IFF*
    (i)   S accepts P,
    (ii) S has adequate evidence for P, and
    (iii) P is true.

Ayer has stated the necessary and sufficient conditions for knowledge as follows:[11]

(c) S knows that P   *IFF*
    (i)   P is true,
    (ii) S is sure that P is true, and
    (iii) S has the right to be sure that P is true.

I shall argue that (a) is false in that the conditions stated therein do not constitute a *sufficient* condition for the truth of the proposition that S knows that P. The same argument will show that (b) and (c) fail if 'has adequate evidence for' or 'has the right to be sure that' is substituted for 'is justified in believing that' throughout.

I shall begin by noting two points. First, in that sense of 'justified' in which S's being justified in believing P is a necessary condition of S's knowing that P, it is possible for a person to be justified in believing a proposition that is in fact false. Secondly, for any proposition P, if S is justified in believing P, and P entails Q, and S deduces Q from P and accepts Q as a result of this deduction, then S is justified in believing Q. Keeping these two points in mind, I shall now present two cases in which the conditions stated in (a) are true for some proposition, though it is at the same time false that the person in question knows that proposition.

Case I

Suppose that Smith and Jones have applied for a certain job. And suppose that Smith has strong evidence for the following conjunctive proposition:[12]

(d) Jones is the man who will get the job, and Jones has ten coins in his pocket.

Smith's evidence for (d) might be that the president of the company assured him that Jones would in the end be selected, and that he, Smith, had counted the coins in Jones's pocket ten minutes ago. Proposition (d) entails:

(e) The man who will get the job has ten coins in his pocket.

Let us suppose that Smith sees the entailment from (d) to (e), and accepts (e) on the grounds of (d), for

---

7   "Is Justified True Belief Knowledge?" *Analysis* 23, June 1963, pp. 121–123. By permission of Oxford University Press.

8   [Author's footnote] Plato seems to be considering some such definition at *Theaetetus* 201, and perhaps accepting one at *Meno* 98. [See "Some Useful Background Information" in Introduction to this reading.]

9   'IFF' is an abbreviation for 'If and only if.' 'X if and only if Y' means if X then Y, and if Y then X.

10 [Author's footnote] Roderick M. Chisholm, *Perceiving: a Philosophical Study*, Cornell University Press (Ithaca, New York, 1957), p. 16.

11 [Author's footnote] A.J. Ayer, *The Problem of Knowledge*, Macmillan (London, 1956), p. 34.

12 A conjunctive proposition is a statement composed of two propositions connected by 'and.' 'It's raining and it's Tuesday' is an example. A conjunctive proposition is true when both of its components are true; otherwise, it's false.

which he has strong evidence. In this case, Smith is clearly justified in believing that (e) is true.

But imagine, further, that unknown to Smith, he himself, not Jones, will get the job. And, also, unknown to Smith, he himself has ten coins in his pocket. Proposition (e) is then true, though proposition (d), from which Smith inferred (e), is false. In our example, then, all of the following are true: (*i*) (e) is true, (*ii*) Smith believes that (e) is true, and (*iii*) Smith is justified in believing that (e) is true. But it is equally clear that Smith does not *know* that (e) is true; for (e) is true in virtue of the number of coins in Smith's pocket, while Smith does not know how many coins are in Smith's pocket, and bases his belief in (e) on a count of the coins in Jones's pocket, whom he falsely believes to be the man who will get the job.

Case II

Let us suppose that Smith has strong evidence for the following proposition:

  (f) Jones owns a Ford.

Smith's evidence might be that Jones has at all times in the past within Smith's memory owned a car, and always a Ford, and that Jones has just offered Smith a ride while driving a Ford. Let us imagine, now, that Smith has another friend, Brown, of whose whereabouts he is totally ignorant. Smith selects three place-names quite at random, and constructs the following three propositions:

  (g) Either Jones owns a Ford, or Brown is in Boston;
  (h) Either Jones owns a Ford, or Brown is in Barcelona;
  (i) Either Jones owns a Ford, or Brown is in Brest-Litovsk.

Each of these propositions is entailed by (f).[13] Imagine that Smith realizes the entailment of each of these propositions he has constructed by (f), and proceeds to accept (g), (h), and (i) on the basis of (f). Smith has correctly inferred (g), (h), and (i) from a proposition for which he has strong evidence. Smith is therefore completely justified in believing each of these three propositions. Smith, of course, has no idea where Brown is.

But imagine now that two further conditions hold. First, Jones does *not* own a Ford, but is at present driving a rented car. And secondly, by the sheerest coincidence, and entirely unknown to Smith, the place mentioned in proposition (h) happens really to be the place where Brown is. If these two conditions hold then Smith does *not* know that (h) is true, even though (*i*) (h) *is* true, (*ii*) Smith does believe that (h) is true, and (*iii*) Smith is justified in believing that (h) is true.

These two examples show that definition (a) does not state a *sufficient* condition for someone's knowing a given proposition. The same cases, with appropriate changes, will suffice to show that neither definition (b) nor definition (c) do so either.

---

13 Note that a statement 'P' entails 'P or Q,' where 'Q' is any proposition at all. That's because a disjunctive proposition—one composed by connecting two component propositions with 'or'—is true when (at least) one of its components is true. So assuming that P is true, then it follows that P or anything-at-all must also be true.

LORRAINE CODE

"Is the Sex of the Knower Epistemologically Significant?"

Who Is Lorraine Code?

Lorraine Code (1937–) is Distinguished Research Professor of Philosophy at York University, Toronto, Canada. She received her undergraduate degree from Queen's University and her PhD from the University of Guelph, both in Ontario. Her main areas of interest are epistemology, ethics, feminist philosophy, and the politics of knowledge. She was named the Distinguished Woman Philosopher for 2009 by the US Society for Women in Philosophy.

How Important and Influential Is This Passage?

An idea which has moved from the fringes to the mainstream of philosophical ethics and social/political theory in the past few decades is *feminism*. The notion that women have, throughout history, been systematically subordinated and disparaged by male-dominated society—and that this immoral situation must be changed not only through the reform of social structures but also by adjustments to some of our most basic philosophical concepts and assumptions—was once controversial but is now widely accepted by the philosophical community. Thus, there are today a range of feminist projects to critique traditional ways of doing philosophy, and the present article illustrates one of these.

Feminist epistemology examines the assumptions which lie at the basis of traditional epistemology— such as that the ideal knower is perfectly rational and objective, or that the paradigm model for knowledge-acquisition is the scientific method—and subjects them to critical assessment from a feminist point of view. The central concept of feminist epistemology is that of a *situated knower*—and thus of situated knowl-

edge: knowledge that reflects the particular perspectives of the subject—and a central feminist argument is that gender is a particularly important way of being situated. Code lays out these ideas in a clear and careful way.

Suggestions for Critical Reflection

1. Code contrasts the traditional idea that knowledge claims should be assessed "on their own merits" with the claim that "the circumstances of knowledge acquisition" are relevant to their evaluation. Which of these two stances do you think is the most plausible—or epistemically responsible—on the face of it? After reading Code's article carefully, does she change your views?

2. Exactly *how* do "the circumstances of knowledge acquisition," and especially who the knower is, affect the evaluation of knowledge claims, on Code's view? For example, can some factual claim be true or justified if it is asserted by one knower but not if it is asserted by another? (Does Code in fact think that the circumstances of the knower are relevant to the *justification* of knowledge claims at all?) Are all types of knowledge claims equally relative to their knower, or are there differences between kinds of knowledge (e.g., between ethical knowledge and geographical knowledge)?

3. What is the significance of Code's claim that most pieces of knowledge are not 'all or nothing' but are a matter of *degree*?

4. Do you agree with Code—if this is indeed her view—that "there is no universal, unchanging framework or scheme for rational adjudication among competing knowledge claims"? How

radical do you think this claim is? Is the kind of relativism that Code adopts, as she claims, an 'enabling' rather than a problematic position?

5. Code suggests that the nature and circumstances of the knower have not been ignored or treated neutrally in traditional epistemology. Rather, traditional epistemology—such as that of Descartes—has been shaped by tacit, often concealed, and sexist assumptions about the nature of the knower. What do you make of this claim? What is its significance for Code's project?

6. Why does Code reject essentialism about female nature? Is she pragmatically or theoretically right to do so? What is the significance of this stance for her version of feminist epistemology?

Suggestions for Further Reading

Among Lorraine Code's books are *What Can She Know? Feminist Theory and the Construction of Knowledge* (Cornell University Press, 1991), *Rhetorical Spaces: Essays on (Gendered) Locations* (Routledge, 1995), and *Ecological Thinking: The Politics of Epistemic Location* (Oxford University Press, 2006); she has also edited several collections, including the *Encyclopedia of Feminist Theories* (Routledge, 2000) and, with Sandra Burt, *Changing Methods: Feminists Transforming Practice* (Broadview Press, 1995). Some other central readings in feminist epistemology are: Linda Alcoff and Elizabeth Potter, eds., *Feminist Epistemologies* (Routledge, 1993); Louise Antony and Charlotte Witt, eds., *A Mind of One's Own: Feminist Essays on Reason and Objectivity* (Westview Press, 1993); Ann Garry and Marilyn Pearsall, eds., *Women, Knowledge and Reality* (2nd edition, Routledge, 1996); Carol Gilligan, *In a Different Voice* (Harvard University Press, 1982); Sandra Harding, *Whose Science? Whose Knowledge?* (Cornell University Press, 1991); Evelyn Fox Keller, *Reflections on Gender and Science* (Yale University Press, 1985); Kathleen Lennon and Margaret Whitford, eds., *Knowing the Difference: Feminist Perspectives in Epistemology* (Routledge, 1994); Helen Longino, *Science As Social Knowledge* (Princeton University Press, 1990); Genevieve Lloyd, *The Man of Reason: 'Male' and 'Female' in Western Philosophy* (2nd edition, University of Minnesota Press, 1993); and Alessandra Tanesini, *An Introduction to Feminist Epistemologies* (Blackwell, 1999). There is also *The Cambridge Companion to Feminism in Philosophy*, edited by Miranda Fricker and Jennifer Hornsby (Cambridge University Press, 2000).

"Is the Sex of the Knower Epistemologically Significant?"[1]

The Question

A question that focuses on the knower, as the title of this chapter does, claims that there are good reasons for asking who that knower is.[2] Uncontroversial as

---

1　This is Chapter One of Lorraine Code's *What Can She Know? Feminist Theory and the Construction of Knowledge* (Ithaca: Cornell University Press, 1991), pp. 1–26. Copyright © 1991 by Cornell University. Used by permission of the publisher, Cornell University Press.

2　[Author's note] This question is the title of my paper published in *Metaphilosophy* 12 (July–October 1981): pp. 267–276. In this early essay I endorse an essentialism with respect to masculinity and femininity, and

such a suggestion would be in ordinary conversations about knowledge, academic philosophers commonly treat 'the knower' as a featureless abstraction. Sometimes, indeed, she or he is merely a place holder in the proposition 'S knows that p'. Epistemological analyses of the proposition tend to focus on the 'knowing that', to determine conditions under which a knowledge claim can legitimately be made. Once discerned, it is believed, such conditions will hold across all possible utterances of the proposition. Indeed, throughout the history of modern philosophy the central 'problem of knowledge' has been to determine necessary and sufficient conditions for the possibility and justification of knowledge claims. Philosophers have sought ways of establishing a relation of correspondence between knowledge and 'reality' and/or ways of establishing the coherence of particular knowledge claims within systems of already-established truths. They have proposed methodologies for arriving at truth, and criteria for determining the validity of claims to the effect that 'S knows that p'. Such endeavors are guided by the putatively self-evident principle that truth once discerned, knowledge once established, claim their status as truth and knowledge by virtue of a grounding in or coherence within a permanent, objective, ahistorical, and circumstantially neutral framework or set of standards.

The question 'Who is S?' is regarded neither as legitimate nor as relevant in these endeavors. As inquirers into the nature and conditions of human knowledge, epistemologists commonly work from the assumption that they need concern themselves only with knowledge claims that meet certain standards of *purity*. Questions about the circumstances of knowledge acquisition serve merely to clutter and confuse the issue with contingencies and other impurities. The question 'Who is S?' is undoubtedly such a question. If it matters who S is, then it must follow that something peculiar to S's character or nature could bear on the validity of the knowledge she or he claims: that S's *identity* might count among the conditions that make that knowledge claim possible. For many philosophers, such a suggestion would undermine the cherished assumption that knowledge can—and should—be evaluated on its own merits. More seriously still, a proposal that it matters who the knower is looks suspiciously like a move in the direction of epistemological relativism. For many philosophers, an endorsement of relativism signals the end of knowledge and of epistemology.

Broadly described, epistemological relativists hold that knowledge, truth, or even 'reality' can be understood only in relation to particular sets of cultural or social circumstances, to a theoretical framework, a specifiable range of perspectives, a conceptual scheme, or a form of life. Conditions of justification, criteria of truth and falsity, and standards of rationality are likewise relative: there is no universal, unchanging framework or scheme for rational adjudication among competing knowledge claims.

Critics of relativism often argue that relativism entails incommensurability: that a relativist cannot evaluate knowledge claims comparatively. This argument is based on the contention that epistemological relativism entails conceptual relativism: that it contextualizes language just as it contextualizes knowledge, so that there remains no 'common' or neutral linguistic framework for discussion, agreement, *or* disagreement. Other critics maintain that the very concept 'knowledge' is rendered meaningless by relativism: that the only honest—and logical—move a relativist can make is once and for all to declare her or his skepticism. Where there are no universal standards, the argument goes, there can be no knowledge worthy of the name. Opponents often contend that relativism is simply incoherent because of its inescapable self-referentiality. Relativism, they argue, is subject to the same constraints as every other claim to knowledge and truth. Any claim for the truth of relativism must itself be relative to the circumstances of the claimant; hence relativism itself has no claim to objective or universal truth. In short, relativism is often perceived as a denial of the very possibility of epistemology.[3]

---

convey the impression that 'positive thinking' can bring an end to gender imbalances. I would no longer make these claims.

3   [Author's note] I consider some of these objections to relativism at greater length in "The Importance of Historicism for a Theory of Knowledge," *International Philosophical Quarterly* 22 (June 1982): pp. 157–174.

Now posing the question 'Who is S?'—that is, 'Who is the knowing subject?'—does indeed count as a move in the direction of relativism, and my intention in posing it is to suggest that the answer has epistemological import. But I shall invoke certain caveats[4] to demonstrate that such a move is not the epistemological disaster that many theorists of knowledge believe it to be.

It is true that, on its starkest construal, relativism may threaten to slide into subjectivism, into a position for which knowledge claims are indistinguishable from expressions of personal opinion, taste, or bias. But relativism need not be construed so starkly, nor do its *limitations* warrant exclusive emphasis. There are advantages to endorsing a measure of epistemological relativism that make of it an enabling rather than a constraining position. By no means the least of these advantages is the fact that relativism is one of the more obvious means of avoiding reductive explanations, in terms of drastically simplified paradigms of knowledge, monolithic explanatory modes, or privileged, decontextualized positions. For a relativist, who contends that there can be many valid ways of knowing any phenomenon, there is the possibility of taking several constructions, many perspectives into account. Hence relativism keeps open a range of interpretive possibilities. At the same time, because of the epistemic choices it affirms, it creates stringent accountability requirements of which knowers have to be cognizant. Thus it introduces a moral-political component into the heart of epistemological enquiry.[5]

There probably is no absolute authority, no practice of all practices or scheme of all schemes. Yet it does not follow that conceptual schemes, practices, and paradigms are radically idiosyncratic or purely subjective. Schemes, practices, and paradigms evolve out of communal projects of inquiry. To sustain viability and authority, they must demonstrate their adequacy in enabling people to negotiate the everyday world and to cope with the decisions, problems, and puzzles they encounter daily. From the claim that no single scheme has absolute explanatory power, it does not follow that all schemes are equally valid. Knowledge is qualitatively variable: some knowledge is *better* than other knowledge. Relativists are in a good position to take such qualitative variations into account and to analyze their implications.

Even if these points are granted, though, it would be a mistake to believe that posing the 'Who is S?' question indicates that the circumstances of the knower are *all* that counts in knowledge evaluation. The point is, rather, that understanding the circumstances of the knower makes possible a more *discerning* evaluation. The claim that certain of those circumstances are epistemologically significant—the sex of the knower, in this instance—by no means implies that they are definitive, capable of bearing the entire burden of justification and evaluation. This point requires special emphasis. Claiming epistemological significance for the sex of the knower might seem tantamount to a dismissal, to a contention that S made such a claim only because of his or her sex. Dismissals of this sort, both of women's knowledge *and* of their claims to be knowers in any sense of the word, are only too common throughout the history of western thought. But claiming that the circumstances of the knower are not epistemologically definitive is quite different from claiming that they are of no epistemological consequence. The position I take in this book is that the sex of the knower is one of a cluster of *subjective* factors (i.e., factors that pertain to the circumstances of cognitive agents) constitutive of received conceptions of knowledge and of what it means to be a knower. I maintain that subjectivity and the specificities of cognitive agency can and must be accorded central epistemological significance, yet that so doing does not commit an inquirer to outright subjectivism. Specificities count, and they require a place in epistemological evaluation, but they cannot tell the whole story.

Knowers and the Known

The only thing that is clear about S from the standard proposition 'S knows that p' is that S is a (would-be) knower. Although the question 'Who is S?' rarely arises, certain assumptions about S as knower perme-

---

4 A caveat is a warning or a reservation.

5 [Author's note] I discuss some of these accountability requirements, and the normative realism from which they derive, in my *Epistemic Responsibility* (Hanover, NH: University Press of New England, 1987).

ate epistemological inquiry. Of special importance for my argument is the assumption that knowers are self-sufficient and solitary individuals, at least in their knowledge-seeking activities. This belief derives from a long and venerable heritage, with its roots in Descartes's quest for a basis of perfect certainty on which to establish his knowledge. The central aim of Descartes's endeavors is captured in this claim: "I shall have the right to conceive high hopes if I am happy enough to discover one thing only which is certain and indubitable."[6] That "one thing," Descartes believed, would stand as the fixed, pivotal, Archimedean point on which all the rest of his knowledge would turn. Because of its systematic relation to that point, his knowledge would be certain and indubitable.

Most significant for this discussion is Descartes's conviction that his quest will be conducted in a private, introspective examination of the contents of his own mind. It is true that, in the last section of the *Discourse on the Method*, Descartes acknowledges the benefit "others may receive from the communication of [his] reflection," and he states his belief that combining "the lives and labours of many"[7] is essential to progress in scientific knowledge. It is also true that this individualistically described act of knowing exercises the aspect of the soul that is common to and alike in all knowers: namely, the faculty of reason. Yet his claim that knowledge seeking is an introspective activity of an individual mind accords no relevance either to a knower's embodiment or to his (or her) intersubjective relations. For each knower, the Cartesian route to knowledge is through private, abstract thought, through the efforts of reason unaided either by the senses or by consultation with other knowers. It is this individualistic, self-reliant, private aspect of Descartes's philosophy that has been influential in shaping subsequent epistemological ideals.

---

6 [Author's note] René Descartes, *Meditations*, in *The Philosophical Works of Descartes*, trans. Elizabeth S. Haldane and G.R.T. Ross (Cambridge: Cambridge University Press, 1969), 1:149.

7 [Author's note] René Descartes, *Discourse on the Method of Rightly Conducting the Reason and Seeking for Truth in the Sciences*, in ibid., pp. 124, 120.

Reason is conceived as autonomous in the Cartesian project in two ways, then. Not only is the quest for certain knowledge an independent one, undertaken separately by each rational being, but it is a journey of reason alone, unassisted by the senses. For Descartes believed that sensory experiences had the effect of distracting reason from its proper course.

The custom of formulating knowledge claims in the 'S knows that p' formula is not itself of Cartesian origin. The point of claiming Cartesian inspiration for an assumption implicit in the formulation is that the knower who is commonly presumed to be the subject of that proposition is modeled, in significant respects, on the Cartesian pure inquirer. For epistemological purposes, all knowers are believed to be alike with respect both to their cognitive capacities and to their methods of achieving knowledge. In the empiricist tradition this assumption is apparent in the belief that simple, basic observational data can provide the foundation of knowledge just because perception is invariant from observer to observer, in standard observation conditions. In fact, a common way of filling the places in the 'S knows that p' proposition is with substitutions such as "Peter knows that the door is open" or "John knows that the book is red." It does not matter who John or Peter is.

Such knowledge claims carry implicit beliefs not only about would-be knowers but also about the knowledge that is amenable to philosophical analysis. Although (Cartesian) rationalists and empiricists differ with respect to what kinds of claim count as foundational, they endorse similar assumptions about the relation of foundational claims to the rest of a body of knowledge. With 'S knows that p' propositions, the belief is that such propositions stand as paradigms for knowledge in general. Epistemologists assume that knowledge is analyzable into propositional 'simples' whose truth can be demonstrated by establishing relations of correspondence to reality, or coherence within a system of known truths. These relatively simple knowledge claims (i.e., John knows that the book is red) could indeed be made by most 'normal' people who know the language and are familiar with the objects named. Knowers would seem to be quite self-sufficient in acquiring such knowledge. Moreover, no one would claim to know "a little" that the book is red or to be in the process of acquiring knowledge about the openness of the door. Nor would anyone be likely to maintain that S knows better than W does that the door is open or that the book is red. Granting such examples paradigmatic status creates the mistaken assumption that all knowledge worthy of the name will be like this.

In some recent epistemological discussion, emphasis has shifted away from simple perceptual claims toward processes of evaluating the 'warranted assertability' of more complex knowledge claims. In such contexts it does make sense to analyze the degree or extent of the knowledge claimed. Yet claims of the simple, perceptual sort are still most commonly cited as exemplary. They are assumed to have an all-or-nothing character; hence they seem not to admit of qualitative assessment. Granting them exemplary status implies that, for knowledge in general, it is appropriate to ask about neither the circumstances of the knowing process nor who the knower is. There would be no point to the suggestion that her or his identity might bear on the *quality* of the knowledge under discussion.

Proposing that the sex of the knower is significant casts doubt both on the autonomy of reason and on the (residual) exemplary status of simple observational knowledge claims. The suggestion that reason might function differently according to whose it is and in what circumstances its capacities are exercised implies that the manner of its functioning is dependent, in some way, on those circumstances, not independent from them. Simple perceptual examples are rendered contestable for their tendency to give a misleading impression of how knowledge is constructed and established and to suppress diversities in knowledge acquisition that derive from the varied circumstances—for example, the sex—of different knowers.

Just what am I asking, then, with this question about the epistemological *significance* of the sex of the knower? First, I do not expect that the question will elicit the answer that the sex of the knower is pertinent among conditions for the existence of knowledge, in the sense that taking it into account will make it possible to avoid skepticism. Again, it is unlikely that information about the sex of the knower could count among criteria of evidence or means of justifying knowledge claims. Nor is it prima facie obvious that the sex of the knower will have a legitimate bearing on the qualitative judgments that could be made about certain claims to know. Comparative judgments of the following kind are not what I expect to elicit: that if the knower is female, her knowledge is likely to be better grounded; if the knower is male, his knowledge will likely be more coherent.

In proposing that the sex of the knower is epistemologically significant, I am claiming that the scope of epistemological inquiry has been too narrowly defined. My point is not to denigrate projects of establishing the best foundations possible or of developing workable criteria of coherence. I am proposing that even if it is not possible (or not *yet* possible) to establish an unassailable foundationalist or coherentist position, there are numerous questions to be asked about knowledge whose answers matter to people who are concerned to know well. Among them are questions that bear not just on criteria of evidence, justification, and warrantability, but on the 'nature' of cognitive agents: questions about their character; their material, historical, cultural circumstances; their interests in the inquiry at issue. These are questions about how credibility is established, about connections between knowledge and power, about the place of knowledge in ethical and aesthetic judgments, and about political agendas and the responsibilities of knowers. I am claiming that all of these questions are epistemologically significant.

The Sex of the Knower

What, then, of the sex of the knower? In the rest of this chapter—and this book—I examine some attempts to give content to the claim that the sex of the knower *is* epistemologically significant.[8] Many of these en-

8   [Author's note] In this chapter I discuss the sex of the knower in a way that may seem to conflate biological sex differences with their cultural elaborations and manifestations as gender differences. I retain the older term—albeit inconsistently—for two reasons. The first, personally historical, reason connects this text with my first thoughts on these matters, published in my *Metaphilosophy* paper (see note [2], above). The second, philosophically historical, reason reflects the

deavors have been less than satisfactory. Nonetheless, I argue that the claim itself is accurate.

Although it has rarely been spelled out prior to the development of feminist critiques, it has long been tacitly assumed that S is male. Nor could S be just any man, the apparently infinite substitutability of the 'S' term notwithstanding. The S who could count as a model, paradigmatic knower has most commonly—if always tacitly—been an adult (but not old), white, reasonably affluent (latterly middle-class) educated man of status, property, and publicly acceptable accomplishments. In theory of knowledge he has been allowed to stand for all men.[9] This assumption does not merely derive from habit or coincidence, but is a manifestation of engrained philosophical convictions. Not only has it been taken for granted that knowers properly so-called are male, but when male philosophers have paused to note this fact, as some indeed have done, they have argued that things are as they should be. Reason may be alike in all men, but it would be a mistake to believe that 'man', in this respect, 'embraces woman'. Women have been judged incapable, for many reasons, of achieving knowledge worthy of the name. It is no exaggeration to say that anyone who wanted to *count* as a knower has commonly had to be male.

In the *Politics*, Aristotle observes: "The freeman rules over the slave after another manner from that in which the male rules over the female, or the man over the child; although the parts of the soul are present in all of them, they are present in different degrees. For the slave has no deliberative faculty at all; the woman has, but it is without authority, and the child has, but it is immature."[10] Aristotle's assumption that a woman will naturally be ruled by a man connects directly with his contention that a woman's deliberative faculty is "without authority." Even if a woman could, in her sequestered, domestic position, acquire deliberative skills, she would remain reliant on her husband for her sources of knowledge and information. She must be ruled by a man because, in the social structure of the *polis*, she enjoys neither the autonomy nor the freedom to put into visible practice the results of the deliberations she may engage in, in private. If she can claim no authority for her rational, deliberative endeavors, then her chances of gaining recognition as a knowledgeable citizen are seriously limited, whatever she may do.[11]

Aristotle is just one of a long line of western thinkers to declare the limitations of women's cognitive capacities.[12] Rousseau maintains that young men and women should be educated quite differently

relatively recent appearance of 'gender' as a theoretical term of art. In the history of 'the epistemological project', which I discuss in these early chapters, 'sex' would have been the term used, had these questions been raised.

9   [Author's note] To cite just one example: in *The Theory of Epistemic Rationality* (Cambridge: Harvard University Press, 1987), Richard Foley appeals repeatedly to the epistemic judgments of people who are "like the rest of us" (p. 108). He contrasts their beliefs with beliefs that seem "crazy or bizarre or outlandish ... beliefs to most of the rest of us" (p. 114), and argues that an account of rational belief is plausible only if it can be presented from "some nonweird perspective" (p. 140). Foley contends that "an individual has to be at least minimally like us in order for charges of irrationality even to make sense" (p. 240). Nowhere does he address the question of who 'we' are. (I take this point up again in Chapter 7 [of *What Can She Know?*].)

10   [Author's note] Aristotle, *Politics*, trans. Benjamin Jowett, in *The Basic Works of Aristotle*, ed. Richard McKeon (New York: Random House, 1941), 1260b.

11   [Author's note] I discuss the implications of this lack of authority more fully in Chapters 9 and 6. See Elizabeth V. Spelman, *Inessential Woman: Problems of Exclusion in Feminist Thought* (Boston: Beacon, 1988), for an interesting discussion of some more complex exclusions effected by Aristotle's analysis.

12   [Author's note] It would be inaccurate, however, to argue that this line is unbroken. Londa Schiebinger demonstrates that in the history of science—and, by implication, the history of the achievement of epistemic authority—there were many periods when women's intellectual achievements were not only recognized but respected. The "long line" I refer to is the dominant, historically most visible one. Schiebinger, *The Mind Has No Sex? Women in the Origins of Modern Science* (Cambridge: Harvard University Press, 1989).

because of women's inferiority in reason and their propensity to be dragged down by their sensual natures. For Kierkegaard, women are merely aesthetic beings: men alone can attain the (higher) ethical and religious levels of existence. And for Nietzsche, the Apollonian (intellectual) domain is the male preserve, whereas women are Dionysian (sensuous) creatures. Nineteenth-century philosopher and linguist Wilhelm von Humboldt, who writes at length about women's knowledge, sums up the central features of this line of thought as follows: "A sense of truth exists in [women] quite literally as a sense: ... their nature also contains a lack or a failing of analytic capacity which draws a strict line of demarcation between ego and world; therefore, they will not come as close to the ultimate investigation of truth as man."[13] The implication is that women's knowledge, if ever the products of their projects deserve that label, is inherently and inevitably *subjective*—in the most idiosyncratic sense—by contrast with the best of men's knowledge.

Objectivity, quite precisely construed, is commonly regarded as a defining feature of knowledge per se.[14] So if women's knowledge is declared to be *naturally* subjective, then a clear answer emerges to my question. The answer is that if the would-be knower is female, then her sex is indeed epistemologically significant, for it disqualifies her as a knower in the fullest sense of that term. Such disqualifications will operate differently for women of different classes, races, ages, and allegiances, but in every circumstance they will operate asymmetrically for women and for men. Just what is to be made of these points—how their epistemological significance is to be construed— is the subject of this book.

The presuppositions I have just cited claim more than the rather simple fact that many kinds of knowledge and skill have, historically, been inaccessible to women on a purely practical level. It is true, historically speaking, that even women who were the racial

and social 'equals' of standard male knowers were only rarely able to become learned. The thinkers I have cited (and others like them) claim to find a rationale for this state of affairs through appeals to dubious 'facts' about women's natural incapacity for rational thought. Yet deeper questions still need to be asked: Is there knowledge that is, quite simply, inaccessible to members of the female, or the male, sex? Are there kinds of knowledge that only men, or only women, can acquire? Is the sex of the knower crucially determining in this respect, across all other specificities? The answers to these questions should not address only the *practical* possibilities that have existed for members of either sex. Such practical possibilities are the constructs of complex social arrangements that are themselves constructed out of historically specific choices, and are, as such, open to challenge and change.

Knowledge, as it achieves credence and authoritative status at any point in the history of the male-dominated mainstream, is commonly held to be a product of the individual efforts of human knowers. References to Pythagoras's theorem, Copernicus's revolution, and Newtonian and Einsteinian physics signal an epistemic community's attribution of pathbreaking contributions to certain of its individual members. The implication is that *that* person, single-handedly, has effected a leap of progress in a particular field of inquiry. In less publicly spectacular ways, other cognitive agents are represented as contributors to the growth and stability of public knowledge.

Now any contention that such contributions are the results of independent endeavor is highly contestable. As I argue elsewhere,[15] a complex of historical and other sociocultural factors produces the conditions that make 'individual' achievement possible, and 'individuals' themselves are socially constituted.[16] The claim that individual *men* are the creators of the authoritative (often Kuhn[17]-paradigm-establishing)

---

13   [Author's note] *Humanist without Portfolio: An Anthology of the Writings of Wilhelm von Humboldt*, trans. with intro. by Marianne Cowan (Detroit: Wayne State University Press, 1963), p. 349.

14   [Author's note] I analyze this precise construal of objectivity in Chapter 2.

15   [Author's note] See chap. 7, "Epistemic Community," of my *Epistemic Responsibility*.

16   [Author's note] I discuss the implications of these points for analyses of subjectivity in Chapter 3.

17   Philosopher of science Thomas Kuhn, who is most associated with the notion that paradigms—roughly,

landmarks of western intellectual life is particularly interesting for the fact that the contributions—both practical and substantive—of their lovers, wives, children, servants, neighbors, friends, and colleagues rarely figure in analyses of their work.[18]

The historical attribution of such achievements to specific cognitive agents does, nonetheless, accord a significance to individual efforts which raises questions pertinent to my project. It poses the problem, in another guise, of whether aspects of human specificity could, in fact, constitute conditions for the existence of knowledge or determine the kinds of knowledge that a knower can achieve. It would seem that such incidental physical attributes as height, weight, or hair color would not count among factors that would determine a person's capacities to know (though the arguments that skin color *does* count are too familiar). It is not necessary to consider how much Archimedes weighed when he made his famous discovery,[19] nor is there any doubt that a thinner or a fatter person could have reached the same conclusion. But in cultures in which sex differences figure prominently in virtually every mode of human interaction,[20] being female or male is far more fundamental to the construction of subjectivity than are such attributes as size or hair

color. So the question is whether femaleness or maleness are the kinds of subjective factor (i.e., factors about the circumstances of a knowing subject) that are constitutive of the form and content of knowledge. Attempts to answer this question are complicated by the fact that sex/gender does not function uniformly and universally, even in western societies. Its implications vary across class, race, age, ability, and numerous other interwoven specificities. A separated analysis of sex/gender, then, always risks abstraction and is limited in its scope by the abstracting process. Further, the question seems to imply that sex and gender are themselves constants, thus obscuring the processes of *their* sociocultural construction. Hence the formulation of adequately nuanced answers is problematic and necessarily partial.

Even if it should emerge that gender-related factors play a crucial role in the construction of knowledge, then, the inquiry into the epistemological significance of the sex of the knower would not be complete. The task would remain of considering whether a distinction between 'natural' and socialized capacity can retain any validity. The equally pressing question as to how the hitherto devalued products of *women's* cognitive projects can gain acknowledgment as 'knowledge' would need to be addressed so as to uproot entrenched prejudices about knowledge, epistemology, and women. 'The epistemological project' will look quite different once its tacit underpinnings are revealed.

Reclaiming 'the Feminine'

Whether this project could or should emerge in a *feminist epistemology* is quite another question. Investigations that start from the conviction that the sex of the knower is epistemologically significant will surely question received conceptions of the nature of knowledge and challenge the hegemony[21] of mainstream epistemologies. Some feminist theorists have maintained that there are distinctively female—or feminine—ways of knowing: neglected ways, from which the label 'knowledge', traditionally, is withheld. Many claim that a recognition of these 'ways of knowing' should prompt the development of new, rival, or even separate epistemologies. Others have adopted Mary

---

sets of key experimental concepts and results—govern scientific research.

18 [Author's note] I owe this point—and the list—to Polly Young-Eisendrath, "The Female Person and How We Talk about Her," in Mary M. Gergen, ed., *Feminist Thought and the Structure of Knowledge* (New York: New York University Press, 1988).

19 The principle, which Archimedes is said to have discovered in his bath, that the apparent loss of weight of a body when immersed in a liquid is equal to the weight of the liquid displaced.

20 [Author's note] Marilyn Frye points out: "Sex-identification intrudes into every moment of our lives and discourse, no matter what the supposedly primary focus or topic of the moment is. Elaborate, systematic, ubiquitous and redundant marking of a distinction between two sexes of humans and most animals is customary and obligatory. One *never* can ignore it." Frye, *The Politics of Reality: Essays in Feminist Theory* (Trumansburg, NY: Crossing Press, 1983), p. 19.

---

21 Domination, especially political or social domination.

O'Brien's brilliant characterization of mainstream epistemology as "malestream,"[22] claiming that one of the principal manifestations of its hegemony is its suppression of female—or 'feminine'—knowledge. In this section I sketch some classic and more recent arguments in favor of feminine 'ways of knowing' and offer a preliminary analysis of their strengths and shortcomings.

Claims that there are specifically female or feminine ways of knowing often find support in the contention that women's significantly different experiences (different, that is, from men's experiences) lead them to know 'the world' differently (i.e., from the ways men do). A putatively different female consciousness, in turn, generates different theories of knowledge, politics, metaphysics, morality, and aesthetics. Features of women's experiences commonly cited are a concern with the concrete, everyday world; a connection with objects of experience rather than an objective distance from them; a marked affective tone; a respect for the environment; and a readiness to listen perceptively and responsibly to a variety of 'voices' in the environment, both animate and inanimate, manifested in a tolerance of diversity.

Many of these features are continuous with the attributes with which the dominant discourse of affluent western societies characterizes a good mother. Indeed, one of the best-known advocates of a caring, maternal approach both to knowledge and to a morality based on that knowledge is Sara Ruddick, in her now-classic article "Maternal Thinking." Maternal thinking, Ruddick believes, grows out of the *practice* of caring for and establishing an intimate connection with another being—a growing child. That practice is marked by a "unity of reflection, judgment and emotion ... [which is] ... no more relative to its particular reality (the growing child) than the thinking that arises from scientific, religious, or other practice"[23]

is relevant to scientific or religious matters alone. Just as scientific or religious thought can structure a knower's characteristic approach to experiences and knowledge in general, Ruddick believes that attitudes and skills developed in the attentive and painstaking practices of caring for infants and small children are generalizable across cognitive domains.

Ruddick's celebration of values traditionally associated with mothering and femininity is not the first such in the history of feminist thought. Among nineteenth-century American feminists, both Margaret Fuller and Matilda Gage praised women's intuition as a peculiarly insightful capacity. Fuller, for example, believed that women have an intuitive perception that enables them to "seize and delineate with unerring discrimination" the connections and links among the various life forms that surround them.[24] In this respect, she maintains, women are superior to men. And Gage believed that women have unique intellectual capacities, manifested especially in an intuitive faculty that does not "need a long process of ratiocination" for its operations.[25] Both Fuller and Gage, albeit in quite different contexts, advocate legitimizing this suppressed and undervalued faculty whose deliverances, they believe, are attuned to and hence better able to reveal the secrets of nature and (for Gage) of spirituality, than masculine ratiocinative practices.[26]

This nineteenth-century belief in the powers of female intuition is echoed in the work of two of the best-known twentieth-century radical feminists, Shulamith Firestone and Mary Daly. For Firestone, there are two sharply contrasting modes or styles of response to experience: an "aesthetic response," which she links to femaleness and characterizes as "subjective, intuitive, introverted, wishful, dreamy or fantastic, concerned with the subconscious (the id), emotional, even tem-

---

22   [Author's note] See Mary O'Brien, *The Politics of Reproduction* (London: Routledge & Kegan Paul, 1980).

23   [Author's note] Sara Ruddick, "Maternal Thinking," *Feminist Studies* 6 (1980): p. 348. I develop a critical analysis of Ruddick's position in Chapter 3. It should be noted that in Ruddick's 1989 book, *Maternal Thinking: Toward a Politics of Peace* (Boston: Beacon,

1989), she addresses some of the issues I raise about the essentialism of this earlier article.

24   [Author's note] Margaret Fuller, *Woman in the Nineteenth Century* (1845; New York: Norton, 1971), p. 103.

25   [Author's note] Matilda Jocelyn Gage, *Women, Church, and State* (1893; Watertown, Mass.: Persephone, 1980), p. 238.

26   Practices having to do with reasoning.

peramental (hysterical)"; and a technological response, which she describes as masculine: "objective, logical, extroverted, realistic, concerned with the conscious mind (the ego), rational, mechanical, pragmatic and down-to-earth, stable."[27] Firestone's claim is not that the aesthetic (= the feminine) should dominate, but that there should be a fusion between the two modes. To overcome patriarchal domination, she believes, it is vital for the aesthetic principle to manifest itself in all cultural and cognitive activity and for technology to cease operating to exclude affectivity.

Daly's concern with spirituality and with the celebration of witchcraft places her closer to Gage than to Fuller. Daly invokes the metaphor of spinning to describe the creation of knowledge and to connect the process with women's traditional creative activities. She claims that "Gyn/Ecology Spins around, past, and through the established fields, opening the coffers/coffins in which 'knowledge' has been stored, re-stored, re-covered ... [where] its meaning will be hidden from the Grave Keepers of tradition." These "Grave Keepers" are the arbiters of knowledge in patriarchal culture: the men who determine the legitimacy of knowledge claims. In consequence of their forced adherence to masculine epistemic norms, Daly contends, "women are encouraged, that is, dis-couraged, to adapt to a maintenance level of cognition and behavior by all the myth-masters and enforcers." Gyn/Ecology is a process of breaking the "spell of patriarchal myth"—by which Daly means all 'received' knowledge in patriarchal cultures—"bounding into freedom"; weaving "the tapestries of [one's] own creation."[28] Once freed from patriarchal myth, women will acquire the knowledge they need to validate their pleasures and powers as marks of their own authority and to unmask patriarchy. Daly's is a vision of female empowerment.

Some theorists maintain that research into the lateralization of brain function reveals 'natural' female-male cognitive differences. The findings of this research are frequently interpreted to indicate that in men, "left-brain" functions predominate, whereas "right-brain" functioning is better developed in women. Evidence that women have better verbal skills and fine motor coordination, whereas men are more adept at spatial skills, mathematics, and abstract thinking, is cited as proof of the existence of female and male cognitive differences. Depending on the political orientation of the inquirer, such findings are read either as confirmations of male supremacy and female inferiority or as indications of a need to revalue 'the feminine'. Among the celebratory interpretations are Gina Covina's claim that women, whom she describes as more "rightbrained" than men, deal with experience "in a diffuse non-sequential way, assimilating many different phenomena simultaneously, finding connections between separate bits of information." By contrast, men, whom she labels "leftbrained," engage typically in thinking that is "focused narrowly enough to squeeze out human or emotional considerations ... [and to enable] ... men to kill (people, animals, plants, natural processes) with free consciousnesses."[29] For Covina, there are 'natural' female-male differences. They are marked not just descriptively but evaluatively.

If brain-lateralization studies, or theories like Daly's and Firestone's, can be read as demonstrations of women's and men's necessarily different cognitive capacities, then my title question requires an affirmative answer. But it is not clear that such conclusions follow unequivocally. Consider the fact that allegedly sex-specific differences are not observable in examinations of the structure of the brain itself, and that in small children "both hemispheres appear to be equally proficient."[30] At most, then, it would seem,

27 [Author's note] Shulamith Firestone, *The Dialectic of Sex: The Case for Feminine Revolution* (New York: Bantam, 1971), p. 175.

28 [Author's note] Mary Daly, *Gyn/Ecology: The Metaethics of Radical Feminism* (Boston: Beacon, 1978), pp. xiii, 53, 57, 320.

29 [Author's note] Gina Covina, "Rosy Rightbrain's Exorcism/Invocation," in G. Covina and Laurel Galana, eds., *The Lesbian Reader* (Oakland, Calif.: Amazon, 1975), p. 96.

30 [Author's note] See Gordon Rattray Taylor, *The Natural History of the Mind* (London: Granada, 1979), p. 127. In an earlier article Taylor points out that "if the eyelids of an animal are sewn up at birth, and freed at maturity, it cannot see and will never learn to do so. The brain has failed to develop the necessary connections at

the brain may come to control certain processes in sexually differentiated ways. Evidence suggests that the brain *develops* its powers through training and practice.[31] Brains of creatures presented with a wide variety of tasks and stimuli develop strikingly greater performance capacities than brains of creatures kept in impoverished environments. As Ruth Bleier points out, "the biology of the brain itself is shaped by the individual's environment and experiences."[32]

Bleier notes the difficulty of assessing the implications of lateralization research. She observes that there are just as many studies that find no sex differences as there are studies that do, and that variability within each sex is greater than variability between them.[33] Janet Sayers suggests that it is as plausible to argue that sex differences in the results of tests to measure spatial ability are the results of sex-specific strategies that subjects adopt to deal with the tests themselves as it is to attribute them to differences in brain organization. She points out that there is no conclusive demonstration that differences in brain organization actually "*cause* sex differences in spatial

ability."[34] It is not easy to see, then, how these studies can plausibly support arguments about general differences in male and female cognitive abilities or about women's incapacity to enter such specific domains as engineering and architecture, where spatial abilities figure largely.

These are just some of the considerations that recommend caution in interpreting brain-lateralization studies. Differences in female and male brain functioning are just as plausibly attributable to sociocultural factors such as the sex-stereotyping of children's activities or to differing parental attitudes to children of different sexes, even from earliest infancy. It would be a mistake to rely on the research in developing a position about the epistemological significance of the sex of the knower, especially as its results are often elaborated and interpreted to serve political ends.[35]

Now Fuller, Gage, Ruddick, Firestone, Daly, and Covina evidently believe—albeit variously—in the effectiveness of *evaluative reversals* of alleged differences as a fundamental revolutionary move. Philosophers should acknowledge the superiority of feminine ideals in knowledge acquisition as much as in social life and institutions, and masculine ways of thought should give way, more generally, to feminine ways. These recommendations apply to theoretical content and to methodology, to rules for the conduct of inquiry, and to principles of justification and legitimation.

The general thesis that inspires these recommendations is that women have an edge in the development and exercise of just those attributes that merit celebration as feminine: in care, sensitivity, responsiveness and responsibility, intuition and trust. There is no

---

the period when it was able to do so." Taylor, "A New View of the Brain," *Encounter* 36, 2 (1971): 30.

31   [Author's note] In this connection Oliver Sacks recounts an illuminating story of a fifty-nine-year-old, congenitally blind woman with cerebral palsy, whose manual sensory capacities, he determined, were intact and quite normal. But when he met her, she had no use of her hands, referring to them as "useless lumps of dough." It became apparent that her hands were functionless because she had never used them: "being 'protected', 'looked after', 'babied' since birth [had] prevented her from the normal exploratory use of the hands which all infants learn in the first months of life." This woman first learned to use her hands in her sixtieth year. Oliver Sacks, "Hands," in *The Man Who Mistook His Wife for a Hat and Other Clinical Tales* (New York: Summit, 1985), p. 57.

32   [Author's note] Ruth Bleier, "Lab Coat: Robe of Innocence or Klansman's Sheet?" in Teresa de Lauretis, ed., *Feminist Studies / Critical Studies* (Bloomington: Indiana University Press, 1986), p. 65.

33   [Author's note] Ibid., pp. 58–59.

34   [Author's note] Janet Sayers, *Biological Politics* (London: Tavistock, 1982), p. 103.

35   [Author's note] Sayers notes: "So germane do ... findings about sex differences in brain organization appear to the current political debate about the justice of continuing sexual inequalities in professional life that they are now regularly singled out for coverage in newspaper reports of scientific meetings." Ibid., p. 101. See Lynda Birke's elaboration of this point in her *Women, Feminism, and Biology* (Brighton: Harvester, 1986), p. 29.

doubt that these traits are commonly represented as constitutive of femininity. Nor is there much doubt that a society that valued them might be a better society than one that denigrates and discourages them. But these very traits are as problematic, both theoretically and practically, as they are attractive. It is not easy to separate their appeal from the fact that women—at least women of prosperous classes and privileged races—have been encouraged to cultivate them throughout so long a history of oppression and exploitation that they have become marks of acquiescence in powerlessness. Hence there is a persistent tension in feminist thought between a laudable wish to celebrate 'feminine' values as tools for the creation of a better social order and a fear of endorsing those same values as instruments of women's continued oppression.

My recurring critique, throughout this book, of theoretical appeals to an *essential* femininity is one I engage in from a position sensitive to the pull of both sides in this tension. By 'essentialism' I mean a belief in an essence, an inherent, natural, eternal female nature that manifests itself in such characteristics as gentleness, goodness, nurturance, and sensitivity. These are some of women's more positive attributes. Women are also represented, in essentialist thought, as naturally less intelligent, more dependent, less objective, more irrational, less competent, more scatterbrained than men: indeed, essential femaleness is commonly defined against a masculine standard of putatively *human* essence.

Essentialist attributions work both normatively and descriptively. Not only do they purport to describe how women essentially *are*, they are commonly enlisted in the perpetuation of women's (usually inferior) social status. Yet essentialist claims are highly contestable. Their diverse manifestations across class, race, and ethnicity attest to their having a sociocultural rather than a 'natural' source. Their deployment as instruments for keeping women in their place means that caution is always required in appealing to them— even though they often appear to designate women's *strengths*. Claims about masculine essence need also to be treated with caution, though it is worth noting that they are less commonly used to oppress men. Essential masculine aggressiveness, sexual needs, and ego-enhancing requirements are often added, rather, to reasons why women should remain subservient. Perhaps there are some essential female or male characteristics, but claims that there are always need to be evaluated and analyzed. The burden of proof falls on theorists who appeal to essences, rather than on those who resist them.

As I have noted, some of the thinkers I have cited advocate an evaluative reversal, in a tacit acceptance of stereotypical, essentialist conceptions of masculinity and femininity. To understand the import of the tension in feminist thought, these stereotypes need careful analysis. The issues of power and theoretical hegemony that are inextricably implicated in their maintenance need likewise to be analyzed. As an initial step toward embarking on this task I offer, in the remainder of this section, a critical analysis of three landmark articles that engage with mainstream epistemology with the intention of revealing grounds for feminist opposition to its traditional structures.

(i) In her early piece, "Methodocracy, Misogyny and Bad Faith: Sexism in the Philosophic Establishment," Sheila Ruth characterizes mainstream philosophy in its content, methodology, and practice as male, masculine, and masculinist. Noting, correctly, that most philosophers—even more in the late 1970s than in the 1990s—are men, Ruth maintains that the content of their philosophy reflects masculine interests and that their standard methodologies reflect imperialist masculine values, values whose normative status derives from their association with maleness. Ruth writes that "philosophical sexism, metasexism ... is epistemological, permeating philosophy to its roots—the structure of its methods and the logic of its criticism." She argues that "what should not be is the raising of ... male [intellectual] constructs to the status of universals—the identification of male constructs with allowable constructs so that women cannot 'legitimately' think, perceive, select, argue, etc. from their unique stance."[36] For Ruth, the sex of the knower *is* epistemologically significant at a fundamental level, with all-pervasive implications.

---

36   [Author's note] Sheila Ruth, "Methodocracy, Misogyny, and Bad Faith: Sexism in the Philosophic Establishment," *Metaphilosophy* 10, 1 (1979): pp. 50, 56.

This essay attests to the surprise and anger occasioned by early 'second wave' feminist realizations that theories that had posed, for centuries, as universal, neutral, and impartial were, in fact, deeply invested in furthering the self-interest of a small segment of the human population. Such realizations brought with them a profound shock, which often resulted in an insistence on affirming contrary, feminine interests and values. These early contributions often appear flawed from the present stage of feminist theoretical development, and I shall draw attention to some of those flaws as reasons why I would not, today, wholeheartedly endorse Ruth's claims.[37] They are worthy of rearticulation, though, for this article is one of the classics of feminist philosophy which created space for the development of subsequent critiques.

There is much that is right about Ruth's contentions, but two interconnected problems make it impossible to agree completely with her: the assumptions that "male constructs" exercise a unified, univocal hegemony and that women occupy a single "unique stance." I have argued in the first section of this chapter that epistemological relativism is a strong position because it creates the possibility of raising questions about the *identity* of knowers. It opens the way for analyses of the historical, racial, social, and cultural specificity of knowers and of knowledge. Now its value would be minimal were it possible to demonstrate that cognitive activity and knowledge have been conceived in exactly the same way by all knowers since the dawn of philosophy. Precisely because it allows the interplay of common threads *and* of specific variations, relativism has a significant explanatory capacity. This capacity is tacitly denied in an account such as Ruth's, based, as it apparently is, on implicit claims about essential, eternal conceptions of femininity and masculinity, mirrored in constant interpretations of knowing and knowledge. In the face of historical, ethnographic, political and class-based evidence to the contrary, the onus would fall

on Ruth, should she still wish to defend these claims, to demonstrate the constancy of the concepts.

Their assumed rigidity presents a still more serious problem. The content Ruth gives to masculinity and femininity plays directly into their essentialist, stereotypical construal in late-twentieth-century western societies. Yet there is no better reason to believe that feminine and masculine characteristics are constant across a complex society at any one time than there is to believe in their historical or cross-cultural constancy. Norms of masculinity and femininity vary across race, class, age, and ethnicity (to name only a few of the axes) within any society at any time. An acceptance of the stereotypes results in a rigidity of thinking that limits possibilities of developing nuanced analyses. In this article it creates for Ruth the troubling necessity of defining her project both *against* and *with reference to* a taken-for-granted masculine norm. No single such norm is discernible in western thought, yet when Ruth's positive recommendations in favor of different philosophical styles are sketched out by contrast with that assumed norm, their explanatory power is diminished. Ruth is right to assert that women have had "no part in defining the content of philosophical speculation, but they have had even less influence over the categories of concern and the modes of articulation."[38] The predominance of feminine and masculine stereotypes in her argument points to an unhappy implication of such early arguments for evaluative reversal: namely, that had women had such influence, their contribution would have been as monolithic as the 'masculine' one.

The broadest of Ruth's claims remains her strongest: philosophy has oppressed women in ways that feminists are still learning to understand. My point is that analyses of this oppression need to be wary lest they replicate the very structures they deplore. Much depends, in the development of feminist projects, on how women's oppression is analyzed. It is important to prevent the reactive aspects of critical response from

---

37   [Author's note] My *Metaphilosophy* article is another pertinent example. Allan Soble criticizes the essentialism of my argument in "Feminist Epistemology and Women Scientists," *Metaphilosophy* 14 (1983): pp. 291–307.

38   [Author's note] Ruth, "Methodocracy, Misogyny, and Bad Faith," p. 54. In my thinking about Ruth's article I am indebted to Jean Grimshaw's discussion in her *Philosophy and Feminist Thinking* (Minneapolis: University of Minnesota Press, 1986), pp. 53–55, 81–82.

overwhelming its creative possibilities. Ruth's analysis leans rather too heavily toward the reactive mode.

(ii) In another early, landmark article, "The Social Function of the Empiricist Conception of Mind," Sandra Harding confronts stereotypes of femininity from a different direction. Her thesis is that "the empiricist model of mind supports social hierarchy by implicitly sanctioning 'underclass' stereotypes." Emphasizing the passivity of knowers in Humean[39] empiricism, Harding contends, first, that classical empiricism can allow no place for creativity, for historical self-consciousness, or for the adoption of a critical stance. Second, she discerns a striking similarity between 'the Humean mind' and stereotypical conceptions of women's minds: "formless, passive, and peculiarly receptive to direction from outside."[40] Her intention is to show that an espousal of empiricist theory, combined with an uncritical acceptance of feminine stereotypes, legitimates manipulative and controlling treatment of women in the social world. There are striking echoes, as Harding herself notes, with the Aristotelian view of woman's lack of rational authority: a lack that, for Aristotle, likewise justifies women's inferior social position.

Present-day empiricists would no doubt contend that Harding's equation of empiricism with a 'passive' epistemology and theory of mind has little validity, given the varieties of contemporary empiricism in its transformations under the influence of philosophers such as Quine.[41] Yet even if Harding has drawn only a caricature of 'the Humean mind', her account has a heuristic value in highlighting certain tendencies of orthodox, classical empiricism. Empiricism, and its latter-day positivist offspring, could indeed serve, either as a philosophy of mind or as a theory of knowledge, to legitimate under the guise of objectivity and impartial neutrality just the kinds of social practice feminists are concerned to eradicate. The impartiality of empiricist analysis, the interchangeability of its subjects of study, work to provide rationalizations for treating people as 'cases' or 'types', rather than as active, creative cognitive agents.[42] Such rationalizations are common in positivistic social science.

More intriguing is a 'double standard' Harding discerns in classical empiricist thought. The *explicit* picture of the Humean inquirer, she maintains, is of a person who is primarily passive, receptive, and hence manipulable. Yet the very existence of Hume's own philosophy counts as evidence that he himself escapes that characterization. His intellectual activity is marked by "a critical attitude, firm purposes and a willingness to struggle to achieve them, elaborate principles of inquiry and hypotheses to be investigated, clarity of vision, precision, and facility at rational argument."[43] This description of the *implicit* Humean inquirer, Harding notes, feeds into standard gender stereotypes, in which men come across as "effective historical agents" while women are incapable of historical agency.

Harding accuses the promulgators of the classical empiricist conception of mind of false consciousness. Their own theoretical activity exempts *their* minds from the very model for which they claim universal validity: the contention that no one is a self-directed agent, everyone is a blank tablet, cannot apply to the authors themselves. Hence the empiricists presuppose a we/they structure in which 'they' indeed are as the theory describes them, but 'we', by virtue of our theoretical creativity, escape the description. In consequence, "the empiricist model of mind ... functions as a self-fulfilling *prescription* beneficial to those already in power: treat people as if they are passive and need direction from others, and they will become or remain

---

39   Relating to David Hume: see the notes to the selection from Hume in Chapter 3.

40   [Author's note] Sandra Harding, "The Social Function of the Empiricist Conception of Mind," *Metaphilosophy* 10 (January 1979): pp. 39, 42.

41   [Author's note] See especially Lynn Hankinson Nelson, *Who Knows: From Quine to a Feminist Empiricism* (Philadelphia: Temple University Press, 1990). Because Nelson's book was published after my manuscript was completed, I have not discussed it in this book.

---

42   [Author's note] I discuss this consequence of empiricist thinking more fully in Chapter 2 [of *What Can She Know*].

43   [Author's note] Harding, "Social Function of the Empiricist Conception of Mind," pp. 43, 44.

able to be manipulated and controlled."[44] Harding maintains that the implicit distinction between active empiricist theorist and passive ordinary inquirer maps onto the stereotypical active male/passive female distinction and acts to legitimate the social and political consequences of that stereotype in androcentered[45] power structures.

Now it is not easy to show that Harding is right either to find an implicit 'double standard' in Humean thought or to suggest that demarcations of the two 'kinds' of knower are appropriately drawn along sexual lines. Hume himself may have meant merely to distinguish a philosopher at his most sophisticated from an ordinary 'vulgar' thinker. His elitism may have been intellect- or class-related, rather than sex-related. If Harding is right, however, the Humean 'double standard' would suggest that the sex of the knower is epistemologically significant, in that it designates men alone as capable of active, creative, critical knowing—and of constructing epistemological theories. By contrast, women are capable only of receiving and shuffling information. Even if she is mistaken in her Humean attributions, then, the parallels Harding draws between the intellectual elitism that empiricism can create and sexual elitism find ample confirmation in the social world. The common relegation of women to low-status forms of employment, which differ from high-status employment partly in the kinds of knowledge, expertise, and cognitive authority they require, is just one confirming practice.[46]

What ensures Harding's paper a place in the history of feminist critiques of philosophy is less the detail of its Hume interpretation than its articulation of the political implications of metaphysical theses. In the face of challenges such as these, which have been more subtly posed both in Harding's later work and elsewhere as feminist thought has increased in sophistication, the neutrality of such theses can never be taken for granted. Should it be declared, the onus is on its declarers to demonstrate the valid-ity of their claims. So despite the flaws in Harding's analysis, her article supports my contention that the sex of the knower is epistemologically significant. If metaphysical theories are marked by the maleness of their creators, then theories of knowledge informed by them cannot escape the marking. Whether the case can be made that both theoretical levels are thus marked, without playing into sexual stereotypes, is a difficult question, but the evidence points compellingly toward the conclusion that the sex of a philosopher informs his theory-building.

(iii) The influence of stereotypically sex-specific traits on conceptions of the proper way to do philosophy is instructively detailed in Janice Moulton's analysis of "The Adversary Method," as she perceptively names it. Moulton shows that a subtle conceptual "conflation of aggression and competence"[47] has produced a paradigm for philosophical inquiry that is modeled on adversarial confrontation between opponents. This conflation depends, above all, on an association of aggression with such positive qualities as energy, power, and ambition: qualities that count as prerequisites for success in the white, middle-class, male professional world. Moulton questions the validity of this association in its conferral of normative status on styles of behavior stereotypically described as male. Yet what is most seriously wrong with the paradigm, she argues, is not so much its maleness as its constitutive role in the production of truncated philosophical problems, inquiries, and solutions.

The adversarial method is most effective, Moulton claims, in structuring isolated disagreements about specific theses and arguments. Hence it depends for its success on the artificial isolation of such claims and arguments from the contexts that occasion their articulation. Adversarial argument aims to show that an opponent is wrong, often by attacking conclusions implicit in, or potentially consequent on, his basic or alleged premises.[48] Under the adversarial paradigm,

---

44   [Author's note] Ibid., p. 46.

45   Male-centered.

46   [Author's note] An example of the hierarchy of cognitive relations created by such assumptions is the theme of Chapter 6.

47   [Author's note] Janice Moulton, "A Paradigm of Philosophy: The Adversary Method," in Sandra Harding and Merrill B. Hintikka, eds., *Discovering Reality* (Dordrecht: Reidel, 1983), p. 151.

48   [Author's note] I am agreeing with Moulton's association of the paradigm with maleness in using the mascu-

the point is to confront the most extreme opposing position, with the object of showing that one's own position is defensible even against such stark opposition. Exploration, explanation, and understanding are lesser goals. The irony, Moulton claims, is that the adversarial paradigm produces bad reasoning, because it leads philosophers to adopt the mode of reasoning best suited to defeat an opponent—she uses "counterexample reasoning" to illustrate her point[49]—as the paradigmatic model for reasoning as such. Diverse modes of reasoning which might be more appropriate to different circumstances, tend to be occluded, as does the possibility that a single problem might be amenable to more than one approach.

Moulton's analysis lends support to the contention that the sex of the knower is significant at the 'metaepistemological' level where the legitimacy of epistemological problems is established. The connection between aggressive cognitive styles and stereotypes of masculine behavior is now a commonplace of feminist thought. Moulton's demonstration that such behavior constitutes the dominant mode—the paradigm—in philosophy, which has so long claimed to stand outside 'the commonplace', is compelling. She shows that mainstream philosophy bears the marks of its androcentric derivation out of a stereotypically constructed masculinity, whatever the limitations of that construction are.

Like all paradigms, the adversarial method has a specific location in intellectual history. While it demarcates the kinds of puzzle a philosopher can legitimately consider, a recognition of its historical specificity shows that this is not how philosophy has always been done nor how it must, of necessity, be done. In according the method (interim) paradigm status, Moulton points to the historical contingency of its current hegemony. The fact that many feminist philosophers report a sense of dissonance between the supposed gender neutrality of the method and their own feminine gender[50] puts the paradigm under serious strains.

Such strains create the space and the possibilities for developing alternative methodological approaches. Whether the sex of the knower will be methodologically and/or epistemologically significant in such approaches must, for now, remain an open question.

Knowledge, Methodology, and Power

The adversarial method is but one manifestation of a complex interweaving of power and knowledge which sustains the hegemony of mainstream epistemology. Like the empiricist theory of the mind, it presents a public demeanor of neutral inquiry, engaged in the disinterested pursuit of truth. Despite its evident interest in triumphing over opponents, it would be unreasonable to condemn this disinterest as merely a pose. There is no reason to believe that practitioners whose work is informed by these methodological assumptions have ruthlessly or tyrannically adopted a theoretical stance for the express purpose of engaging in projects that thwart the intellectual pursuits of women or of other marginalized philosophers. Could such a purpose be discerned, the task of revealing the epistemological significance of the sex of the knower would be easy. Critics could simply offer such practitioners a clear demonstration of the errors of their ways and hope that, with a presumption of goodwill on their part, they would abandon the path of error for that of truth and fairness.

Taking these practitioners at their word, acknowledging the sincerity of their convictions about their neutral, objective, impartial engagement in the pursuit of truth, reveals the intricacy of this task. Certain sets of problems, by virtue of their complexity or their intrinsic appeal, often become so engrossing for researchers that they override and occlude other contenders for attention. Reasons for this suppression are often subtle and not always specifically articulable. Nor is it clear that the exclusionary process is wholly conscious. A network of sociopolitical relationships and intellectual assumptions creates an invisible

---

line pronoun to refer to its practitioners—even though many women have learned to play the game well.

49   [Author's note] Moulton, "Paradigm of Philosophy," p. 159.

50   [Author's note] See, for example, Genevieve Lloyd's

---

observation that "the exercise of writing feminist philosophy came out of [her] experience of dissonance between the supposed gender neutrality of philosophy and [her] gender." Lloyd, "Feminist Philosophy and the Idea of the Feminine" (manuscript, 1986), p. 22.

system of acceptance and rejection, discourse and silence, ascendency and subjugation within and around disciplines. Implicit cultural presuppositions work with the personal idiosyncracies of intellectual authorities to keep certain issues from placing high on research agendas. Critics have to learn how to notice their absence.

In "The Discourse on Language," Michel Foucault makes the astute observation that "within its own limits, every discipline recognizes true and false propositions, but it repulses a whole teratology[51] of learning."[52] The observation captures some of the subtleties involved in attempting to understand the often imperceptible workings of hegemonic, usually masculine power in mainstream philosophy. A discipline defines itself both by what it excludes (repulses) and by what it includes. But the self-definition process removes what is excluded (repulsed) from view so that it is not straightforwardly available for assessment, criticism, and analysis. Even in accepting mainstream avowals of neutral objectivity, critics have to learn to see what is repulsed by the disciplinarily imposed limits on methodology and areas of inquiry. The task is not easy. It is much easier to seek the flaws in existing structures and practices and to work at eradicating them than it is to learn to perceive what is not there to be perceived.

Feminist philosophy simply did not exist until philosophers learned to perceive the near-total absence of women in philosophical writings from the very beginning of western philosophy, to stop assuming that 'man' could be read as a generic term. Explicit denigrations of women, which became the focus of philosophical writing in the early years of the contemporary women's movement, were more readily perceptible. The authors of derogatory views about women in classical texts clearly needed power to be able to utter their pronouncements with impunity: a power they claimed from a 'received' discourse that represented women's nature in such a way that women undoubtedly merited the negative judgments that Aristotle or Nietzsche made about them. Women are now in a position to recognize and refuse these overt manifestations of contempt.

The covert manifestations are more intransigent. Philosophers, when they have addressed the issue at all, have tended to group philosophy with science as the most gender-neutral of disciplines. But feminist critiques reveal that this alleged neutrality masks a bias in favor of institutionalizing stereotypical masculine values into the fabric of the discipline—its methods, norms, and contents. In so doing, it suppresses values, styles, problems, and concerns stereotypically associated with femininity. Thus, whether by chance or by design, it creates a hegemonic philosophical practice in which the sex of the knower is, indeed, epistemologically significant.

---

51 [Author's note] A 'teratology' is a collection of tales about marvellous and improbable creatures (such as sea monsters, or people with heads in their chests); Foucault's idea is that disciplines restrict themselves to what is familiar, and rule out or ignore the possibility of things that would be—from the perspective of the discipline—considered strange or unlikely.

52 [Author's note] Michel Foucault, "The Discourse on Language," in *The Archaeology of Knowledge*, trans. Alan Sheridan (New York: Pantheon, 1972), p. 223.

CHAPTER 3

Philosophy of Science—When, if Ever, Are Scientific Inferences Justified?

INTRODUCTION TO THE QUESTION

The philosophy of science can be thought of as being made up of two broad, intersecting streams: the epistemology of science and the metaphysics of science. The epistemology of science concerns itself with the justification, rationality, and objectivity of scientific knowledge and the so-called 'scientific method,' while the metaphysics of science examines philosophical puzzles about the reality uncovered by the various sciences. Furthermore, each of these two types of investigation can be directed at science in general or at one of the particular sciences: there are thus sub-disciplines within the philosophy of science such as 'philosophy of physics,' 'philosophy of mathematics,' 'philosophy of biology,' and 'philosophy of the social sciences.'

Many of the threads of the epistemological strand of philosophy of science can be unraveled from the following question: *What, if anything, is 'the scientific method,' and how rational is it?* Once one attempts to answer this question, a flurry of subsidiary questions arise: What is the methodological difference (if any) between science and other, non-scientific, areas of human endeavor (such as philosophy, history or astrology)? Do all the 'real' sciences share a common methodology? If not, can we discover a single, underlying 'unified science' which is in principle capable of encompassing all the special sciences? How *rational* are the methods of science: how much reason do they give us to accept their conclusions? How *objective* are the methods of science: how much is science influenced by its social context and the personalities of individual scientists? Are the theories produced by science ever in fact true descriptions of reality, and is

that what science should aspire to anyway? What exactly *is* a theory, anyway (for example, is it a set of logical equations, or a kind of model, or a more informal bundle of assumptions and claims)? How adequately does science explain the natural phenomena we want explained, and what counts as a scientific explanation? And so on: these, and other similar questions, are investigated by philosophers of science.

Metaphysical questions about science can be thought of as centered on the following issue: *Are the principles and entities postulated by science actually real?* For example, many scientific theories postulate unobservable entities in order to explain the observed data. Most subatomic particles such as quarks, for instance, have never in any sense been *seen* by a scientist: rather, they are assumed to exist because their existence is the best explanation for a certain set of experimental data. In such situations, are we entitled to infer that such unobservable entities actually do exist, or should we instead treat them as instrumental fictions which are useful in generating observable predictions but which aren't literally real? (After all, plenty of unobserved entities which we now realize do not actually exist have been postulated by science in the past, such as the mythical substance of 'phlogiston' which was invoked to explain many chemical properties, or the massless 'ether' which was thought to fill the gaps between objects and serve as the medium for the transmission of light. Why should our current theories be any luckier in the hypothetical entities they invent?)

One fundamental 'unobservable' principle of science, which has historically been of great interest to philosophers of science, is the principle of *causality*. The sense in which causality is unobservable was pointed out by the philosopher David Hume in the eighteenth century: although we certainly can and do observe that events of type *A* are always followed by events of type *B* (for example, that all objects propelled with force *x* will always accelerate at rate *y*), this necessarily falls short of being able to observe *causation* itself. All we actually see is what Hume called the 'constant conjunction' of *A* things with *B* things, but we do not see the causal law which lies behind and is the reason for this conjunction: that is, we do not *see* laws of nature, but we *infer* them from regularities which we detect in nature. So it is legitimate to ask questions like the following: *Are* there really causal laws lying behind the constant conjunctions we observe—are laws of nature real? If causal laws do exist, how can we reliably tell when we've identified one—how can we tell the difference between a genuine law and a merely accidental constant conjunction? And, if causal laws exist, what is their nature—for example, are they always deterministic, or can they be probabilistic (as quantum mechanics might be taken to suggest)?

The readings in this chapter focus primarily on the epistemological aspects of the philosophy of science: what is the method of science, and how rationally justifiable is it? It is natural to begin with something like the following account of science: scientists first accumulate facts about the world by conducting careful experiments, and then use these observations to support—or 'verify'—one scientific theory rather than another. For example, one might think, by the careful observation of various chemical reactions, scientists are able to formulate and prove true general laws about the underlying chemistry. Furthermore, it is common to suppose that it is this 'experimental' method which is unique to science and the source of its special epistemological power. The first two selections collected here introduce a fundamental problem for this view of scientific method, *the problem of induction*. Induction is, roughly, the process by which we infer general truths from particular observations (for example, inferring that all copper turns green in the rain by noticing that many old copper roofs are now green). The scientific method just described rests

heavily on inductive inferences to move from a finite set of experimental observations to claims about laws of nature. But the question is: is induction rational? Are inductive inferences from the particular to the general justified? David Hume argues compellingly that inductive inferences are *not* rationally justified; and if he is right, then it follows that the scientific method—at least as we have so far understood it—is not rational. In the following reading, Nelson Goodman argues that Hume's problem can be solved … but then promptly introduces what he considers a different and even more difficult version of the problem, which he calls the 'new riddle of induction.'

The next four readings—the authors of all of which are to some degree reacting to the problem of induction—introduce three different accounts of the scientific method, in an effort to improve on the simplistic 'experimental' model described above. Carl Hempel presents a mature version of the influential 'logical positivist' or 'verificationist' account of science; Karl Popper rejects verificationism and argues instead for a 'falsificationist' view of science; and C.S. Peirce describes a view of science which is usually thought of as 'pragmatic.' The other reading in this group, by Wesley Salmon, is critical of all of these attempts to solve the problem of induction, but makes a renewed case for the importance of finding some solution.

The seventh selection in this chapter, from Thomas Kuhn, introduces an important turn in late-twentieth-century philosophy away from the attempt to understand science as a rational enterprise and in favor of seeing it as a sociological phenomenon embedded in a particular historical context. Kuhn has thus been seen as launching an attack on the rationality of science. Finally the article from Helen Longino asks "Can there be a feminist science?" and if so, how different would it look from historical, supposedly 'value-free,' science?

The philosophy of science was a very active area of philosophy for a large part of the twentieth century, and there are many good books which will take you beyond the readings included in this chapter. Among them are: Brody and Grandy, eds., *Readings in the Philosophy of Science* (Prentice Hall, 1989); Alan Chalmers, *What is This Thing Called Science?* (Hackett, 1999); Curd and Cover, eds., *Philosophy of Science: The*

Central Issues (W.W. Norton, 1998); James Franklin, *What Science Knows: And How It Knows It* (Encounter Books, 2009); Donald Gillies, *Philosophy of Science in the Twentieth Century* (Blackwell, 1993); Peter Godfrey-Smith, *Theory and Reality: An Introduction to the Philosophy of Science* (University of Chicago Press, 2003); Ian Hacking, *Representing and Intervening* (Cambridge University Press, 1983); Philip Kitcher, *The Advancement of Science* (Oxford University Press, 1993); Robert Klee, *Introduction to the Philosophy of Science: Cutting Nature at Its Seams* (Oxford University Press, 1996); James Ladyman, *Understanding Philosophy of Science* (Routledge, 2001); W.H. Newton-Smith, *The Rationality of Science* (Routledge, 1981); David Papineau, ed., *The Philosophy of Science* (Oxford University Press, 1996); Alexander Rosenberg, *The Philosophy of Science* (Routledge, 2011); Merrilee Salmon et al., *Introduction to the Philosophy of Science* (Hackett, 1999); and Bas van Fraassen, *The Scientific Image* (Oxford University Press, 1982). Useful references are *A Companion to the Philosophy of Science*, edited by W.H. Newton-Smith (Blackwell, 2001), and Psillos and Curd (eds.), *The Routledge Companion to Philosophy of Science* (Routledge, 2010).

DAVID HUME

An Enquiry Concerning Human Understanding

There is a peculiarly painful chamber inhabited solely by philosophers who have refuted Hume. These philosophers, though in Hell, have not learned wisdom. They continue to be governed by their animal propensity towards induction. But every time that they make an induction, the next instance falsifies it. This, however, happens only during the first hundred years of their damnation. After that, they learn to expect that an induction will be falsified, and therefore it is not falsified until another century of logical torment has altered their expectation. Throughout all eternity surprise continues, but each time at a higher logical level.

(Bertrand Russell)

Who Was David Hume?

David Hume has been called the most important philosopher ever to have written in English. He was born to a strict Calvinist family in Edinburgh, Scotland's capital, in 1711, and spent his youth there and in Ninewells, his family's small land-holding near the border with England. Little is known of Hume's early childhood. His father, Joseph, died when he was two, and he was educated by his mother Katherine—who

never remarried—from an early age. He was a precociously intelligent and well-read child. As his mother put it, in her Scottish dialect: "Our Davie's a fine good-natured crater, but uncommon wake-minded." By the age of 16 he had begun composing his first philosophical master-work, *A Treatise of Human Nature*, on which he was to work, more or less continuously, for the next ten years.

Hume spent the years between 1723 and 1726 (i.e., between the ages of 12 and 15) studying a wide range of subjects at the University of Edinburgh but, like many students of that era, did not take a degree. His father and grandfather had both been lawyers, and his family expected him also to go into law, but, Hume later wrote, he found the law "nauseous" and discovered in himself "an unsurmountable aversion to every thing but the pursuits of philosophy and general learning."

Hume continued to read and write and, as a result of his feverish intellectual activity—motivated by his belief that he had made a major philosophical discovery—he suffered a nervous breakdown in 1734. He was forced to put philosophy aside for several months (during which time he attempted life as a businessman at

Bristol, in the employ of a Portsmouth merchant, but found that it didn't suit him) and then left Britain for France. There, in the following three years, living frugally in the countryside in Anjou (and using up all his savings), he completed most of his book.

Hume's *A Treatise of Human Nature* was published anonymously when he was 27. Hume later wrote, it "fell *dead-born from the press*, without reaching such distinction as even to excite a murmur among the zealots." Hume's career as an intellectual and man of letters seemed to have ended before it had begun, and Hume blamed not the substance of his work but its style. "I was carry'd away by the Heat of Youth & Invention to publish too precipitately. So vast an Undertaking, plan'd before I was one and twenty, & compos'd before twenty-five, must necessarily be very defective. I have repented my Haste a hundred, & a hundred times." Hume returned to Scotland to live with his mother, and began to re-cast the material of the *Treatise* into two new books, which have become philosophical classics in their own right: *An Enquiry Concerning Human Understanding* (1748), and *An Enquiry Concerning the Principles of Morals* (1751). However both these books—though more successful than the *Treatise*—were slow to become influential during Hume's own lifetime.

Needing money, Hume got his first real job at the age of 34 and spent a well-paid year as tutor to a mad nobleman (the Marquess of Annandale). In 1746 Hume accepted a position as secretary to General St. Clair's military expedition to Canada (which never reached Canada and ended, oddly enough, with a brief attack on the French coast), and for two years after that was part of a secret diplomatic and military embassy by St. Clair to the courts of Vienna and Turin. During this period Hume was twice refused academic appointments at Scottish universities—first Edinburgh, then Glasgow— because of his reputation as a religious skeptic. Shortly afterwards, between 1755 and 1757, unsuccessful attempts were made in Edinburgh to have Hume excommunicated from the Church of Scotland.

In 1752 Hume was offered the Keepership of the Advocates' Library at Edinburgh and there, poorly paid but surrounded by books, he wrote the colossal six-volume *History of England*, which (though unpopular at first) eventually became his first major literary success. At this time he also published a controversial *Natural History of Religion*.

In 1763 Hume was made secretary of the English embassy at Paris, where he found himself very much in fashion and seems to have enjoyed the experience. There he fell in love with, but failed to win the hand of, the Comtesse de Boufflers, the mistress of a prominent French noble. (Some unkindly suggest this might have been partly because at the time, when Hume was in his fifties, he had come to resemble "a fat well-fed Bernardine monk.") In 1767, back in Scotland and now a fairly wealthy man, Hume was appointed an Under-Secretary of State, a senior position in the British civil service.

By the time Hume died in 1776, of cancer of the bowel, he had become respected as one of Europe's leading men of letters and a principal architect of the Enlightenment. His death gave him the reputation of something of a secular saint, as he faced his incurable condition with cheerfulness and resignation and refused to abandon his religious skepticism. In a short autobiography, written just before he died, Hume described his own character.

I was … a man of mild dispositions, of command of temper, of an open, social, and cheerful humour, capable of attachment, but little susceptible of enmity, and of great moderation in all my passions. Even my love of literary fame, my ruling passion, never soured my temper, notwithstanding my frequent disappointments. My company was not unacceptable to the young and careless, as well as to the studious and literary; and as I took a particular pleasure in the company of modest women, I had no reason to be displeased with the reception I met from them.... I cannot say there is no vanity in making this funeral oration of myself, but I hope it is not a misplaced one; and this is a matter of fact which is easily cleared and ascertained.

What Was Hume's Overall Philosophical Project?

Hume can be called the first 'post-skeptical' modern philosopher. He was wholly convinced (by, among others, the writings of his predecessors Descartes, Locke, and Berkeley, who appear elsewhere in this volume) that no knowledge that goes beyond the mere data of our own minds has anything like secure and reliable foundations: that is, he believed, we have no certain knowledge of the inner workings of the physical world and its laws, or of God, or of absolute moral 'truth,' or even of our own 'real selves.' All we have secure knowledge of is our own mental states and their relations: our sensory impressions, our ideas, our emotions, and so on.

Despite all this, Hume's philosophical project was a positive one: he wanted to develop a new, constructive science of human nature that would provide a defensible foundation for all the sciences, including ethics, physics, and politics. Where Hume's predecessors tried in vain to argue against philosophical skepticism, Hume assumed that a certain kind of skepticism was actually true and tried to go beyond it, to say something positive about how we are to get on with our lives (including our lives as scientists and philosophers).

Much of Hume's philosophical writing, therefore, begins by showing the unstoppable power of skepticism in some domain—such as skepticism about causation or objective ethical truths—and then goes on to show how we can still talk sensibly about causation or ethics after all. The selection from *An Enquiry Concerning Human Understanding* which appears below follows this pattern.

One of the central aspects of both Hume's skeptical and his constructive philosophy is his strictly empirical methodology—a development of what was called in Hume's day 'the experimental method.' His science of human nature is based firmly on the experimental methods of the natural sciences, which emphasize the data of experience and observation, sometimes combined with mathematical or logical reasoning. Any other method of investigation—such as an appeal to 'innate intuition,' for example—is illegitimate. As Hume put it:

> If we take in our hand any volume; of divinity or school metaphysics, for instance; let us ask, *Does it contain any abstract reasoning concerning quantity or number?* No. *Does it contain any experimental reasoning concerning matter of fact and existence?* No. Commit it then to the flames: for it can contain nothing but sophistry and illusion. [This is the final paragraph of his *An Enquiry Concerning Human Understanding*.]

This assumption that all human knowledge is either a "matter of fact" or a matter of "relations of ideas"—the product of experience or of reason—is often known as 'Hume's Fork.'

What Is the Structure of This Reading?

An Enquiry Concerning Human Understanding first appeared (in 1748) under the title *Philosophical Essays Concerning Human Understanding*, and it does indeed consist of twelve somewhat loosely related philosophical essays. The underlying theme which ties the essays together is the primacy of experience and causal inference in establishing our ideas, especially such philosophically important ideas as necessity and probability, free will, and God.

Hume's argument in this reading has two parts. In the first part he argues there can be no rational justification for our expectations about those parts of the physical world we have not yet observed; in the second he presents his "skeptical solution of these doubts." First, in Section IV Part I, he introduces a distinction between relations of ideas and matters of fact. He then argues that all empirical claims which go beyond "the present testimony of our senses, or the records of our memory" are based on reasonings "founded on the relation of cause and effect." How do we come to discover relations of cause and effect? Not, Hume argues, from "reasonings *a priori*" but from experience. In Part II, Hume addresses the question: "What is the foundation of all conclusions from experience?" and, for the remainder of this part, "contents himself" with a negative answer. He argues that conclusions from experience are not "founded on reasoning, or on any process of the understanding." Part of his argument here has the following structure: Hume tries to show that all experimental arguments rely upon the assumption that nature is generally uniform—the assumption that observed regularities in nature (like the whiteness of swans or day following night) will persist from the present into the future. He then argues—very ingeniously and persuasively—that this assumption is impossible to rationally justify. His conclusion is that inductive inferences are never rationally justifiable.

Hume's constructive project, presented in Section V, has the following pattern. He begins by describing the benefits of a generally skeptical frame of mind. Then he goes on to discuss the principle that *does* cause us to leap to inductive conclusions, since we have no rational reason to do so—this psychological principle, he suggests, is "custom or habit." In Part II, Hume gives us more detail about what he thinks is really going on when we come to have beliefs about the future: he argues that *belief* is a kind of involuntary feeling, "added" to our imagination of some event. That is, we can freely *imagine* almost any future event we like, but we usually cannot make ourselves *believe* that it will happen. This "extra" feeling of belief in a future event, Hume argues, can only be generated automatically in our minds by a certain sequence of past experiences.

Some Useful Background Information

1. Hume, like John Locke (see Chapter 2), began his philosophy with a 'theory of ideas': it is useful to be aware of a few of the basics of this theory when reading this selection. For Hume, the smallest elements of thought are what he called *basic perceptions*. These can usefully be thought of as analogous to atoms, since these basic perceptions are, in Hume's view, bound together in various ways into larger units—*complex perceptions*—according to certain fundamental psychological laws; Hume called these laws "the principle of the association of ideas." Hume thought of this system as being the counterpart of Newtonian physics: on this view, physics is the science of matter, and Humean philosophy is the science of human nature or mind. Hume himself considered this general picture, and the use he made of it, to be his greatest contribution to human thought. It is especially notable that *rationality* plays relatively little part in Hume's naturalistic picture of human nature: instead, our ideas are connected together by deterministic laws based, for example, on their similarity or their history of "constant conjunction" (that is, a history of having always appeared together in the past). Finally, for Hume, these "laws of association" may defy further explanation: we might need to treat them as basic laws—brute regularities—just as the law of gravity was for Newton.

2. Unlike Locke, Hume divides his "perceptions" into two distinct sorts: *impressions* and *ideas*. Impressions are "all our sensations, passions and emotions, as they make their first appearance in the soul," and come in two flavors: *impressions of sensation* and *impressions of reflection*. Impressions of sensation, according to Hume, appear in the mind "from unknown causes," and the reasons for their occurrence are best studied by "anatomists and natural philosophers," rather than by those, like Hume himself, interested in studying human nature. Examples of such sensations might be the visual image of a cat on the mat, or the taste of a grape-flavored Popsicle. Impressions of reflection (such as disgust, pride, or desire) arise, usually, from our perception of and reaction to our own ideas. Finally, our *ideas* are, according to Hume, "the faint images" of impressions: that is, they are copies of earlier impressions (and so, causally dependent on them: you cannot possibly have an idea of something which you haven't previously experienced). Ideas, for Hume, have been

described as "the mental tokens by which we reason," and would include, for example, our concepts of colors and shapes, of types of objects, of mathematical relationships, of historical individuals, of moral values, and so on.

3. Hume's arguments in this passage rely on two important distinctions, which it is helpful to have clear in your mind as you read. The first is the distinction which is often called 'Hume's fork' between *relations of ideas* and *matters of fact*. Relations of ideas are propositions whose truth or falsity can be discovered merely by thinking about the concepts involved, and which if true are necessarily true. For example, "a triangle has three sides" must be true since *by definition* triangles have three sides—it's just part of the concept 'triangle' that it be three-sided. In modern jargon, relations of ideas are 'analytic *a priori*' propositions. The simplest kind of relation of ideas Hume calls "intuitively certain": these propositions are just self-evidently true to anyone who understands them, such as "1 is smaller than 2."[1] Other propositions, which are also relations of ideas, may be more complex and need to be shown by some kind of 'demonstrative argument' (the proposition that 2^{16} is 65,536, for example, might not be immediately obvious, but it can be proven by a sequence of small and obvious steps).

Matters of fact, by contrast, are 'synthetic *a posteriori*' propositions—that is, only observation and experience can tell us whether they are true or false (and thus they cannot be *necessarily* true, but are only contingently true). An example might be, "sticking your finger inside a hot toaster really hurts." One of Hume's key claims is that propositions about relations of ideas never assert the existence of any non-abstract entities (such as physical objects), while claims about matters of fact often do.

4. The second important distinction used in this reading is one between *demonstrative arguments* and *experimental arguments*. Demonstrative arguments, for Hume, are deductively valid arguments where all the premises are relations of ideas. We can know that the conclusion of a demonstrative argument is true (indeed, necessarily true) without knowing anything about the actual world—this is why Hume often calls them "reasonings *a priori*." Experimental arguments are arguments of any other kind: that is, they are either arguments which have matters of fact among their premises, or arguments which are not deductive, or (most commonly) both.

5. Finally, a word about "induction." Although Hume does not actually use the word in this reading, Section IV Part II of the *Enquiry* is usually thought of as presenting, for the first time, "the problem of induction." Induction is the modern term for the process of arriving at justified beliefs about the future on the basis of experience of the past; to put the same idea in another way, induction is the method for finding out what as-yet unobserved things are like on the basis of a sample of things we have observed. For example, we might notice that every swan we have ever seen has been white, and conclude that, very probably, the next swan we see will also be white. Furthermore, we might think, we've seen enough swans to justify concluding that probably *every* swan is white. Thus we use our experience of observing swans to draw inductive conclusions about unseen swans—generalizations about other swans in the world (such as Australian swans), and predictions about future swans as yet unhatched. This method of reasoning is extremely common. It is what (apparently) supports much of our everyday behavior, such as getting up at a certain time in the morning to go to work or school, using a kettle to make tea, relying on the morning weather forecast to help us decide what to wear, expecting the bus to come at a certain time and place, and so on. All of these

---

1 If you have already read Descartes and Locke you might notice that Hume's notion of 'intuition' is significantly different from that used by his philosophical predecessors. For example, Descartes' "I think therefore I am" would not count as 'intuitively certain' for Hume.

activities and beliefs are based on assuming that past experience is reliable evidence for expectations about the future. Science, too, is largely based on induction—physicists have only observed a tiny, infinitesimal fraction of all the electrons in the universe, for example, yet they assume that all electrons everywhere have the same charge.

We speak of "the problem of induction," because Hume has apparently shown us that we have no rational justification for induction. This would be an extremely radical conclusion if in fact it is so!

Some Common Misconceptions

1. Hume's philosophical concerns were not primarily negative or destructive: although he frequently attacks the role of reason in science and human affairs, and points out the limitations of our own experiential knowledge, he does not do so in order to leave us in a skeptical dead end. Instead, these attacks are part of his attempt to place the science of human nature upon a more reliable footing, by actually examining how we come to have the beliefs that we do.

2. Although there are differences of interpretation on this matter, it seems likely that Hume was not merely pointing out that inductive conclusions cannot be known *with certainty* to be true—that induction cannot be 100% rationally justified. For that would simply be to say that induction is not deduction, which is trivial. (It is today part of the *definition* of an inductive, as opposed to deductive, argument that its conclusion may possibly be false even if all its premises are true, and this seems to correspond reasonably well with Hume's own distinction between experimental and demonstrative methods of reasoning.) Instead, Hume is making the much more radical claim that the conclusions of inductive arguments *have no rational support at all*: they are not "founded on reasoning, or on any process of the understanding." Inductive arguments, if Hume is right, completely fail to justify their conclusions—their

premises, if true, do not make their conclusions *any* more likely to be true. (Analogously, the argument "roses are red, violets are blue, therefore Brad Pitt will become President of America" is not rationally compelling since the truth of the premises—the respective colors of roses and violets—does nothing to make it more likely to be true that this particular actor will have successful political ambitions. Chapter 1 contains more information on inductive and deductive arguments.)

3. On the other hand, Hume is not arguing that induction does not actually *work*—he's not arguing that human beings are systematically *wrong* in their predictions about the future. On the contrary, he thinks that human beings are usually very successful in coming to have true beliefs about the future (that the sun will rise tomorrow, or that the next chunk of copper we mine from the earth will conduct electricity). And although it's admittedly a bit tricky to hold both that this is the case and that induction is not at all justified, it's not flat out inconsistent: it's perfectly coherent to say that some of our beliefs are true but unjustified.

How Important and Influential Is This Passage?

An influential British philosopher named C.D. Broad once called inductive reasoning "the glory of Science … [and] … the scandal of Philosophy." The scandal Broad had in mind was the failure of philosophers over the previous two hundred years (he was writing in 1952) to find a convincing answer to Hume's skeptical arguments … and this despite the wholesale (and apparently successful) reliance of the natural sciences on inductive arguments. If induction is not rationally justified, recall, then neither are most of the claims of physics, biology, chemistry, economics, and so on. Thus Hume, in effect, discovered and incisively formulated a serious new philosophical problem—the problem of induction. (H.H. Price once called Hume's discovery of this problem "one of the most important advances in the whole history of thought.") This problem has very far-reaching consequences indeed, but it is so difficult a puzzle to solve that many philosophers feel Hume has not yet been satisfactorily answered. Hume's problem of induction is still a live problem today; various answers have been proposed but no single solution has yet found widespread acceptance.

Hume's own "skeptical solution" has been much less influential than his skeptical problem: even if Hume's account in Part V is successful (which many contemporary philosophers and psychologists doubt), it will still only be a *psychological* explanation for why we believe the things we do about the future, whereas what we seem to need to defend science—and most of our everyday beliefs—is a *rational justification* for induction.

Suggestions for Critical Reflection

1. *Are* "all the objects of human reason or enquiry" divisible into exactly two piles: relations of ideas and matters of fact? What about, for example, the claim that a wall can't be simultaneously red all over and green all over: which of the two categories does this fall into? How about the statement that water is identical with H_2O?

2. Does Hume think we are being unreasonable or irrational if we continue to act as if inductive inferences are justified? Given what Hume has argued, what do you think?

3. What exactly would it mean to claim that the future resembles the past or that nature is "uniform"? Is nature uniform in *every* respect? (For example, is the sky always blue?) So what *kind* of uniformity do you think we need to look for?

4. Does the past reliability *of induction* provide evidence that future instances of induction will also be reliable? For example, on several hundred occasions in the past I inferred on the basis of previous experience that the Big Mac I was about to eat would not be poisonous, and each time I was right; do these several hundred instances of correct induction provide any evidence that induction is *generally* reliable? Why, or why not?

5. What's the difference (if any) between the psychological claim that people believe certain things about the future only out of habit, rather than because they have gone through some process of reasoning, and the claim that there is no rational justification available for our beliefs about the future? Which claim is Hume making?

6. Is it possible to formulate a skeptical problem about *deduction* that is similar to Hume's problem about induction?

7. What is the difference between believing something and merely imagining that it is true? Does Hume think that when we believe some future event will occur, as opposed to merely imagining it will occur, there is some *extra* idea present in our mind—a sort of idea of belief itself, added to the idea of the future event? Are Hume's views on the nature of belief plausible?

Suggestions for Further Reading

The following two sections of the *Enquiry* re-cast portions of Part III, Book I of the *Treatise*, so that is a good place to begin your extra reading. A critical edition of Hume's philosophical writings is currently being prepared by Oxford University Press, but in the meantime the standard editions are: *A Treatise of Human Nature* (Oxford University Press, 1978) and *Enquiries Concerning Human Understanding and Concerning the Principles of Morals* (Oxford University Press, 1975), both edited by L.A. Selby-Bigge and P.H. Nidditch.

Many good books have been written about Hume's philosophy: a handful of the best and most relevant are *Hume's Epistemology and Metaphysics* by Georges Dicker (Routledge, 1998), *Hume's Philosophy of Belief* by Antony Flew (Routledge & Kegan Paul, 1961), *Hume's Skepticism* by Robert J. Fogelin (Routledge & Kegan Paul, 1985), *David Hume* by Terence Penelhum (Purdue University Press, 1992), *Probability and Hume's Inductive Scepticism* by David Stove (Oxford University Press, 1973), and *Hume* by Barry Stroud (Routledge, 1977). Tom Beauchamp and Alexander Rosenberg defend the view that Hume is not in fact a skeptic about induction in *Hume and the Problem of Causation* (Oxford University Press, 1981).

The Cambridge Companion to Hume, edited by David Fate Norton (Cambridge University Press, 1993), is a helpful collection of specially written essays on different aspects of Hume's philosophy, which also includes Hume's short autobiography. An old, but still good, collection of critical essays on Hume is V.C. Chappell's *Hume: A Collection of Critical Essays* (Doubleday, 1966).

Some influential attempts to solve Hume's riddle of induction—apart from those encompassed by the next few readings in this text—include: P.F. Strawson in the final chapter of his book *An Introduction to Logical Theory* (Methuen, 1952); Max Black, "Inductive Support of Inductive Rules," in *Problems of Analysis* (Cornell University Press, 1954); and James Van Cleve, "Reliability, Justification, and the Problem of Induction," in *Midwest Studies in Philosophy* IX (1984). A good review article criticizing many of these attempted solutions (and tentatively suggesting another) is Wesley C. Salmon's "Unfinished Business: The Problem of Induction," *Philosophical Studies* 33 (1978) (reprinted below).

from *An Enquiry Concerning Human Understanding*[2]

Section IV: Sceptical Doubts Concerning the Operations of the Understanding.

PART I.

All the objects of human reason or enquiry may naturally be divided into two kinds, to wit,[3] *relations of ideas*, and *matters of fact*. Of the first kind are the sciences of geometry, algebra, and arithmetic; and in short, every affirmation which is either intuitively or demonstratively certain. *That the square of the hypotenuse*[4] *is equal to the square of the two sides*, is a proposition which expresses a relation between these figures. *That three times five is equal to the half*

of *thirty*, expresses a relation between these numbers. Propositions of this kind are discoverable by the mere operation of thought, without dependence on what is anywhere existent in the universe. Though there never were a circle or triangle in nature, the truths demonstrated by Euclid would for ever retain their certainty and evidence.

Matters of fact, which are the second objects of human reason, are not ascertained in the same manner; nor is our evidence of their truth, however great, of a like nature with the foregoing. The contrary of every matter of fact is still possible; because it can never imply a contradiction, and is conceived by the mind with the same facility and distinctness, as if ever so conformable to reality. *That the sun will not rise to-morrow* is no less intelligible a proposition, and implies no more contradiction than the affirmation, *that it will rise*. We should in vain, therefore, attempt to demonstrate its falsehood. Were it demonstratively false, it would imply a contradiction, and could never be distinctly conceived by the mind.

It may, therefore, be a subject worthy of curiosity, to enquire what is the nature of that evidence which assures us of any real existence and matter of fact, beyond the present testimony of our senses, or the records of our memory. This part of philosophy, it is observable, has been little cultivated, either by the ancients or moderns; and therefore our doubts and errors, in the prosecution of so important an enquiry, may be the more excusable; while we march through such difficult paths without any guide or direction. They may even prove useful, by exciting curiosity, and destroying that implicit faith and security, which is the bane of all reasoning and free enquiry. The discovery of defects in the common philosophy, if any such there be, will not, I presume, be a discouragement, but rather an incitement, as is usual, to attempt something more full and satisfactory than has yet been proposed to the public.

All reasonings concerning matter of fact seem to be founded on the relation of *cause and effect*. By means of that relation alone we can go beyond the evidence of our memory and senses. If you were to ask a man, why he believes any matter of fact, which is absent; for instance, that his friend is in the country, or in France; he would give you a reason; and this

---

2   Hume's *An Enquiry Concerning Human Understanding* was first published in 1748. This selection is taken from the 1777 "new edition," generally considered the final version authorized by Hume. Most of the spelling, capitalization, and punctuation have been modernized.

3   "To wit" is a phrase meaning "that is to say" or "namely."

4   The hypotenuse is the side opposite the right angle of a right-angled triangle.

reason would be some other fact; as a letter received from him, or the knowledge of his former resolutions and promises. A man finding a watch or any other machine in a desert island, would conclude that there had once been men in that island. All our reasonings concerning fact are of the same nature. And here it is constantly supposed that there is a connection between the present fact and that which is inferred from it. Were there nothing to bind them together, the inference would be entirely precarious. The hearing of an articulate voice and rational discourse in the dark assures us of the presence of some person: Why? Because these are the effects of the human make and fabric, and closely connected with it. If we anatomize[5] all the other reasonings of this nature, we shall find that they are founded on the relation of cause and effect, and that this relation is either near or remote, direct or collateral. Heat and light are collateral effects of fire, and the one effect may justly be inferred from the other.

If we would satisfy ourselves, therefore, concerning the nature of that evidence, which assures us of matters of fact, we must enquire how we arrive at the knowledge of cause and effect.

I shall venture to affirm, as a general proposition, which admits of no exception, that the knowledge of this relation is not, in any instance, attained by reasonings *a priori*;[6] but arises entirely from experience, when we find that any particular objects are constantly conjoined with each other. Let an object be presented to a man of ever so strong natural reason and abilities; if that object be entirely new to him, he will not be able, by the most accurate examination of its sensible[7] qualities, to discover any of its causes or effects. Adam,[8] though his rational faculties be supposed, at the very first, entirely perfect, could not have inferred from the fluidity and transparency of water that it would suffocate him, or from the light and warmth of fire that it would consume him. No object ever discovers,[9] by the qualities which appear to the senses, either the causes which produced it, or the effects which will arise from it; nor can our reason, unassisted by experience, ever draw any inference concerning real existence and matter of fact.

This proposition, *that causes and effects are discoverable, not by reason but by experience*, will readily be admitted with regard to such objects as we remember to have once been altogether unknown to us; since we must be conscious of the utter inability, which we then lay under, of foretelling what would arise from them. Present two smooth pieces of marble to a man who has no tincture of natural philosophy;[10] he will never discover that they will adhere together in such a manner as to require great force to separate them in a direct line, while they make so small a resistance to a lateral pressure. Such events, as bear little analogy to the common course of nature, are also readily confessed to be known only by experience; nor does any man imagine that the explosion of gunpowder, or the attraction of a loadstone,[11] could ever be discovered by arguments *a priori*. In like manner, when an effect is supposed to depend upon an intricate machinery or secret structure of parts, we make no difficulty in attributing all our knowledge of it to experience. Who will assert that he can give the ultimate reason, why milk or bread is proper nourishment for a man, not for a lion or a tiger?

But the same truth may not appear, at first sight, to have the same evidence with regard to events, which have become familiar to us from our first appearance in the world, which bear a close analogy to the whole course of nature, and which are supposed to depend on the simple qualities of objects, without any secret structure of parts. We are apt to imagine that we could discover these effects by the mere operation of our reason, without experience. We fancy, that were we brought on a sudden into this world, we could at first have inferred that one billiard-ball would com-

---

5   Closely examine.
6   Prior to experience; purely deductively.
7   "Sensible" means, here and elsewhere, able to be perceived or sensed.
8   According to the Old Testament, the first human being.

9   Here (and sometimes elsewhere) "discovers" means reveals or discloses (rather than finds out).
10 That is: no trace of knowledge of physical science.
11 A magnet (made from naturally occurring magnetic iron oxide).

municate motion to another upon impulse;[12] and that we needed not to have waited for the event, in order to pronounce with certainty concerning it. Such is the influence of custom,[13] that, where it is strongest, it not only covers our natural ignorance, but even conceals itself, and seems not to take place, merely because it is found in the highest degree.

But to convince us that all the laws of nature, and all the operations of bodies without exception, are known only by experience, the following reflections may, perhaps, suffice. Were any object presented to us, and were we required to pronounce concerning the effect, which will result from it, without consulting past observation; after what manner, I beseech you, must the mind proceed in this operation? It must invent or imagine some event, which it ascribes to the object as its effect; and it is plain that this invention must be entirely arbitrary. The mind can never possibly find the effect in the supposed cause, by the most accurate scrutiny and examination. For the effect is totally different from the cause, and consequently can never be discovered in it. Motion in the second billiard-ball is a quite distinct event from motion in the first; nor is there any thing in the one to suggest the smallest hint of the other. A stone or piece of metal raised into the air, and left without any support, immediately falls: but to consider the matter *a priori*, is there any thing we discover in this situation which can beget the idea of a downward, rather than an upward, or any other motion, in the stone or metal?

And as the first imagination or invention of a particular effect, in all natural operations, is arbitrary, where we consult not experience; so must we also esteem the supposed tie or connection between the cause and effect, which binds them together, and renders it impossible that any other effect could result from the operation of that cause. When I see, for instance, a billiard-ball moving in a straight line towards another; even suppose motion in the second ball should by accident be suggested to me, as the result of their contact or impulse; may I not conceive, that a hundred different events might as well follow from that cause? May not both these balls remain at absolute rest? May

not the first ball return in a straight line, or leap off from the second in any line or direction? All these suppositions are consistent and conceivable. Why then should we give the preference to one, which is no more consistent or conceivable than the rest? All our reasonings *a priori* will never be able to show us any foundation for this preference.

In a word, then, every effect is a distinct event from its cause. It could not, therefore, be discovered in the cause, and the first invention or conception of it, *a priori*, must be entirely arbitrary. And even after it is suggested, the conjunction of it with the cause must appear equally arbitrary; since there are always many other effects, which, to reason, must seem fully as consistent and natural. In vain, therefore, should we pretend to determine any single event, or infer any cause or effect, without the assistance of observation and experience.

Hence we may discover the reason why no philosopher,[14] who is rational and modest, has ever pretended to assign the ultimate cause of any natural operation, or to show distinctly the action of that power, which produces any single effect in the universe. It is confessed, that the utmost effort of human reason is to reduce the principles, productive of natural phenomena, to a greater simplicity, and to resolve the many particular effects into a few general causes, by means of reasonings from analogy, experience, and observation. But as to the causes of these general causes, we should in vain attempt their discovery; nor shall we ever be able to satisfy ourselves, by any particular explication of them. These ultimate springs and principles are totally shut up from human curiosity and enquiry. Elasticity, gravity, cohesion of parts, communication of motion by impulse; these are probably the ultimate causes and principles which we shall ever discover in nature; and we may esteem ourselves sufficiently happy, if, by accurate enquiry and reasoning, we can trace up the particular phenomena to, or near to, these general principles. The most perfect philosophy of the natural kind only staves off our ignorance a little longer: as perhaps the most perfect philosophy of the moral or metaphysical kind

---

12 Impact, collision.

13 Habit, repeated similar experience.

14 The word "philosopher" at this time included natural scientists.

serves only to discover larger portions of it. Thus the observation of human blindness and weakness is the result of all philosophy, and meets us at every turn, in spite of our endeavours to elude or avoid it.

Nor is geometry, when taken into the assistance of natural philosophy, ever able to remedy this defect, or lead us into the knowledge of ultimate causes, by all that accuracy of reasoning for which it is so justly celebrated. Every part of mixed mathematics[15] proceeds upon the supposition that certain laws are established by nature in her operations; and abstract reasonings are employed, either to assist experience in the discovery of these laws, or to determine their influence in particular instances, where it depends upon any precise degree of distance and quantity. Thus, it is a law of motion, discovered by experience, that the moment[16] or force of any body in motion is in the compound ratio or proportion of its solid contents[17] and its velocity; and consequently, that a small force may remove the greatest obstacle or raise the greatest weight, if, by any contrivance or machinery, we can increase the velocity of that force, so as to make it an overmatch for its antagonist.[18] Geometry assists us in the application of this law, by giving us the just dimensions of all the parts and figures which can enter into any species of machine; but still the discovery of the law itself is owing merely to experience, and all the abstract reasonings in the world could never lead us one step towards the knowledge of it. When we reason *a priori*, and consider merely any object or cause, as it appears to the mind, independent of all observation,

it never could suggest to us the notion of any distinct object, such as its effect; much less, show us the inseparable and inviolable connection between them. A man must be very sagacious[19] who could discover by reasoning that crystal is the effect of heat, and ice of cold, without being previously acquainted with the operation of these qualities.

PART II.

But we have not yet attained any tolerable satisfaction with regard to the question first proposed. Each solution still gives rise to a new question as difficult as the foregoing, and leads us on to farther enquiries. When it is asked, *What is the nature of all our reasonings concerning matter of fact?* the proper answer seems to be, that they are founded on the relation of cause and effect. When again it is asked, *What is the foundation of all our reasonings and conclusions concerning that relation?* it may be replied in one word, Experience. But if we still carry on our sifting humour,[20] and ask, *What is the foundation of all conclusions from experience?* this implies a new question, which may be of more difficult solution and explication. Philosophers, that give themselves airs of superior wisdom and sufficiency,[21] have a hard task when they encounter persons of inquisitive dispositions, who push them from every corner to which they retreat, and who are sure at last to bring them to some dangerous dilemma. The best expedient to prevent this confusion, is to be modest in our pretensions; and even to discover the difficulty ourselves before it is objected to us. By this means, we may make a kind of merit of our very ignorance.

I shall content myself, in this section, with an easy task, and shall pretend[22] only to give a negative answer to the question here proposed. I say then, that, even after we have experience of the operations of cause and effect, our conclusions from that experience are *not* founded on reasoning, or any process of the

---

15 Mathematical physics (mathematics applied to the physical world).

16 Momentum.

17 Mass.

18 Here is what Hume means by this example (which comes from Newtonian physics). Imagine two bodies A and B: suppose that A has a mass of 2 and a velocity of 4 and that B has a mass of 6 and a velocity of 1. Thus the ratios of their respective masses will be 2:6 and their respective velocities 4:1. Then, A will have a higher momentum or force than B (despite only having one third the mass), since the "compound ratio" of its momentum to that of B will be 2x4 to 6x1, which is 8:6.

---

19 Mentally penetrating, insightful (Hume is being ironic).

20 Searching frame of mind.

21 Here "sufficiency" means ability.

22 Aim, venture.

understanding. This answer we must endeavour both to explain and to defend.

It must certainly be allowed, that nature has kept us at a great distance from all her secrets, and has afforded us only the knowledge of a few superficial qualities of objects; while she conceals from us those powers and principles on which the influence of those objects entirely depends. Our senses inform us of the colour, weight, and consistence[23] of bread; but neither sense nor reason can ever inform us of those qualities which fit it for the nourishment and support of a human body. Sight or feeling conveys an idea of the actual motion of bodies; but as to that wonderful force or power, which would carry on a moving body for ever in a continued change of place, and which bodies never lose but by communicating it to others; of this we cannot form the most distant conception. But notwithstanding this ignorance of natural powers[24] and principles, we always presume, when we see like[25] sensible qualities, that they have like secret powers, and expect that effects, similar to those which we have experienced, will follow from them. If a body of like colour and consistence with that bread, which we have formerly eat,[26] be presented to us, we make no scruple of repeating the experiment,[27] and foresee, with certainty, like nourishment and support. Now this is a process of the mind or thought, of which I would willingly know the foundation. It is allowed on all hands that there is no known connection between the sensible qualities and the secret powers; and consequently, that the mind is not led to form such a conclusion concerning their constant and regular conjunction, by any thing which it knows of their nature. As to past *experience*, it can be allowed to give *direct* and *certain* information of those precise objects only, and that precise period of time, which fell under its cognizance: But why this experience should be extended to future times, and to other objects, which for aught we know, may be only in appearance similar; this is the main question on which I would insist. The bread, which I formerly eat, nourished me; that is, a body of such sensible qualities was, at that time, endued with[28] such secret powers: but does it follow, that other bread must also nourish me at another time, and that like sensible qualities must always be attended with like secret powers? The consequence seems nowise necessary. At least, it must be acknowledged that there is here a consequence drawn by the mind; that there is a certain step taken; a process of thought, and an inference, which wants to be explained. These two propositions are far from being the same, *I have found that such an object has always been attended with such an effect*, and *I foresee, that other objects, which are, in appearance, similar, will be attended with similar effects*. I shall allow, if you please, that the one proposition may justly be inferred from the other: I know, in fact, that it always is inferred. But if you insist that the inference is made by a chain of reasoning, I desire you to produce that reasoning. The connection between these propositions is not intuitive. There is required a medium,[29] which may enable the mind to draw such an inference, if indeed it be drawn by reasoning and argument. What that medium is, I must confess, passes my comprehension; and it is incumbent on those to produce it, who assert that it really exists, and is the origin of all our conclusions concerning matter of fact.

This negative argument must certainly, in process of time, become altogether convincing, if many penetrating and able philosophers shall turn their enquiries this way and no one be ever able to discover any connecting proposition or intermediate step, which supports the understanding in this conclusion. But as the question is yet new, every reader may not trust so far to his own penetration, as to conclude, because an argument escapes his enquiry, that therefore it does not really exist. For this reason it may be requisite to venture upon a more difficult task; and enumerating all the branches of human knowledge, endeavour to show that none of them can afford such an argument.

23   Consistency, texture.

24   [Author's note] The word, Power, is here used in a loose and popular sense. The more accurate explication of it would give additional evidence to this argument. See Sect. 7 [not reprinted here].

25   Similar.

26   Eaten.

27   Experience.

28   Endowed with, possessed of.

29   A ground of inference; a further premise.

All reasonings may be divided into two kinds, namely, demonstrative reasoning, or that concerning relations of ideas, and moral[30] reasoning, or that concerning matter of fact and existence. That there are no demonstrative arguments in the case seems evident; since it implies no contradiction that the course of nature may change, and that an object, seemingly like those which we have experienced, may be attended with different or contrary effects. May I not clearly and distinctly conceive that a body, falling from the clouds, and which, in all other respects, resembles snow, has yet the taste of salt or feeling of fire? Is there any more intelligible proposition than to affirm, that all the trees will flourish in December and January, and decay in May and June? Now whatever is intelligible, and can be distinctly conceived, implies no contradiction, and can never be proved false by any demonstrative argument or abstract reasoning *a priori*.

If we be, therefore, engaged[31] by arguments to put trust in past experience, and make it the standard of our future judgement, these arguments must be probable only, or such as regard matter of fact and real existence according to the division above mentioned. But that there is no argument of this kind, must appear, if our explication of that species of reasoning be admitted as solid and satisfactory. We have said that all arguments concerning existence are founded on the relation of cause and effect; that our knowledge of that relation is derived entirely from experience; and that all our experimental conclusions proceed upon the supposition that the future will be conformable to the past. To endeavour, therefore, the proof of this last supposition by probable arguments, or arguments regarding existence, must be evidently going in a circle, and taking that for granted, which is the very point in question.

In reality, all arguments from experience are founded on the similarity which we discover among natural objects, and by which we are induced to expect effects similar to those which we have found to follow from such objects. And though none but a fool or madman will ever pretend to dispute the authority of experience, or to reject that great guide of human life, it may surely be allowed a philosopher to have so much curiosity at least as to examine the principle of human nature, which gives this mighty authority to experience, and makes us draw advantage from that similarity which nature has placed among different objects. From causes which, appear *similar*, we expect similar effects. This is the sum of all our experimental conclusions. Now it seems evident that, if this conclusion were formed by reason, it would be as perfect at first, and upon one instance, as after ever so long a course of experience. But the case is far otherwise. Nothing so like as eggs; yet no one, on account of this appearing similarity, expects the same taste and relish in all of them. It is only after a long course of uniform experiments in any kind, that we attain a firm reliance and security with regard to a particular event. Now where is that process of reasoning which, from one instance, draws a conclusion, so different from that which it infers from a hundred instances that are nowise different from that single one? This question I propose as much for the sake of information, as with an intention of raising difficulties. I cannot find, I cannot imagine any such reasoning. But I keep my mind still open to instruction, if any one will vouchsafe to bestow it on me.

Should it be said that, from a number of uniform experiments, we *infer* a connection between the sensible qualities and the secret powers; this, I must confess, seems the same difficulty, couched in different terms. The question still recurs, on what process of argument this *inference* is founded? Where is the medium, the interposing ideas, which join propositions so very wide of each other? It is confessed that the colour, consistence, and other sensible qualities of bread appear not, of themselves, to have any connection with the secret powers of nourishment and support. For otherwise we could infer these secret powers from the first appearance of these sensible qualities, without the aid of experience; contrary to the sentiment[32] of all philosophers, and contrary to plain

---

30 Here "moral" means inductive or having at best only a probable conclusion. (Often, however, Hume uses the phrase "moral philosophy" in a somewhat different way, to mean the study of the nature of human beings, contrasted with "natural philosophy," the study of nature.)

31 Induced, persuaded.

32 Opinion.

matter of fact. Here, then, is our natural state of ignorance with regard to the powers and influence of all
objects. How is this remedied by experience? It only
shows us a number of uniform effects, resulting from
certain objects, and teaches us that those particular
objects, at that particular time, were endowed with
such powers and forces. When a new object, endowed
with similar sensible qualities, is produced, we expect
similar powers and forces, and look for a like effect.
From a body of like colour and consistence with bread
we expect like nourishment and support. But this
surely is a step or progress of the mind, which wants
to be explained. When a man says, *I have found, in all
past instances, such sensible qualities conjoined with
such secret powers*: and when he says, *similar sensible
qualities will always be conjoined with similar secret
powers,* he is not guilty of a tautology, nor are these
propositions in any respect the same. You say that the
one proposition is an inference from the other. But
you must confess that the inference is not intuitive;
neither is it demonstrative: Of what nature is it, then?
To say it is experimental, is begging the question.
For all inferences from experience suppose, as their
foundation, that the future will resemble the past, and
that similar powers will be conjoined with similar
sensible qualities. If there be any suspicion that the
course of nature may change, and that the past may
be no rule for the future, all experience becomes useless, and can give rise to no inference or conclusion.
It is impossible, therefore, that any arguments from
experience can prove this resemblance of the past to
the future; since all these arguments are founded on
the supposition of that resemblance. Let the course of
things be allowed hitherto ever so regular; that alone,
without some new argument or inference, proves not
that, for the future, it will continue so. In vain do you
pretend to have learned the nature of bodies from your
past experience. Their secret nature, and consequently
all their effects and influence, may change, without
any change in their sensible qualities. This happens
sometimes, and with regard to some objects: why may
it not happen always, and with regard to all objects?
What logic, what process or argument secures you
against this supposition? My practice, you say, refutes
my doubts. But you mistake the purport of my question. As an agent, I am quite satisfied in the point; but

as a philosopher, who has some share of curiosity, I
will not say scepticism, I want to learn the foundation
of this inference. No reading, no enquiry has yet been
able to remove my difficulty, or give me satisfaction
in a matter of such importance. Can I do better than
propose the difficulty to the public, even though,
perhaps, I have small hopes of obtaining a solution?
We shall at least, by this means, be sensible of our
ignorance, if we do not augment our knowledge.

I must confess that a man is guilty of unpardonable
arrogance who concludes, because an argument has
escaped his own investigation, that therefore it does
not really exist. I must also confess that, though all
the learned, for several ages, should have employed
themselves in fruitless search upon any subject, it
may still, perhaps, be rash to conclude positively that
the subject must, therefore, pass all human comprehension. Even though we examine all the sources of
our knowledge, and conclude them unfit for such a
subject, there may still remain a suspicion, that the
enumeration is not complete, or the examination not
accurate. But with regard to the present subject, there
are some considerations which seem to remove all
this accusation of arrogance or suspicion of mistake.

It is certain that the most ignorant and stupid peas-
ants—nay infants, nay even brute beasts—improve
by experience, and learn the qualities of natural
objects, by observing the effects which result from
them. When a child has felt the sensation of pain
from touching the flame of a candle, he will be
careful not to put his hand near any candle; but will
expect a similar effect from a cause which is similar
in its sensible qualities and appearance. If you assert,
therefore, that the understanding of the child is led
into this conclusion by any process of argument or
ratiocination, I may justly require you to produce
that argument; nor have you any pretence to refuse so
equitable a demand. You cannot say that the argument
is abstruse, and may possibly escape your enquiry;
since you confess that it is obvious to the capacity of a
mere infant. If you hesitate, therefore, a moment, or if,
after reflection, you produce any intricate or profound
argument, you, in a manner, give up the question, and
confess that it is not reasoning which engages us to
suppose the past resembling the future, and to expect
similar effects from causes which are, to appearance,

similar. This is the proposition which I intended to enforce in the present section. If I be right, I pretend not to have made any mighty discovery. And if I be wrong, I must acknowledge myself to be indeed a very backward scholar; since I cannot now discover an argument which, it seems, was perfectly familiar to me long before I was out of my cradle.

Section V: Sceptical Solution of these Doubts.

PART I.

The passion for philosophy, like that for religion, seems liable to this inconvenience, that, though it aims at the correction of our manners, and extirpation of our vices, it may only serve, by imprudent management, to foster a predominant inclination, and push the mind, with more determined resolution, towards that side which already *draws* too much,[33] by the bias and propensity of the natural temper. It is certain that, while we aspire to the magnanimous firmness of the philosophic sage, and endeavour to confine our pleasures altogether within our own minds, we may, at last, render our philosophy like that of Epictetus, and other *Stoics*,[34] only a more refined system of selfishness, and reason ourselves out of all virtue as well as social enjoyment. While we study with attention the vanity of human life, and turn all our thoughts towards the empty and transitory nature of riches and honours, we are, perhaps, all the while flattering our natural indolence, which, hating the bustle of the world, and drudgery of business, seeks a pretence of reason to give itself a full and uncontrolled indulgence. There is, however, one species of philosophy which seems little liable to this inconvenience, and that because it strikes in with no disorderly passion of the human

mind, nor can mingle itself with any natural affection or propensity; and that is the Academic or Sceptical philosophy.[35] The academics always talk of doubt and suspense of judgement, of danger in hasty determinations, of confining to very narrow bounds the enquiries of the understanding, and of renouncing all speculations which lie not within the limits of common life and practice. Nothing, therefore, can be more contrary than such a philosophy to the supine indolence of the mind, its rash arrogance, its lofty pretensions, and its superstitious credulity. Every passion is mortified by it, except the love of truth; and that passion never is, nor can be, carried to too high a degree. It is surprising, therefore, that this philosophy, which, in almost every instance, must be harmless and innocent, should be the subject of so much groundless reproach and obloquy. But, perhaps, the very circumstance which renders it so innocent is what chiefly exposes it to the public hatred and resentment. By flattering no irregular passion, it gains few partisans: by opposing so many vices and follies, it raises to itself abundance of enemies, who stigmatize it as libertine, profane, and irreligious.

Nor need we fear that this philosophy, while it endeavours to limit our enquiries to common life, should ever undermine the reasonings of common life, and carry its doubts so far as to destroy all action, as well as speculation. Nature will always maintain her rights, and prevail in the end over any abstract reasoning whatsoever. Though we should conclude, for instance, as in the foregoing section, that, in all reasonings from experience, there is a step taken by the mind which is not supported by any argument or process of the understanding; there is no danger that these reasonings, on which almost all knowledge depends, will ever be affected by such a discovery. If the mind be not engaged by argument to make this step, it must be induced by some other principle of equal weight and

---

33 Pulls too much—i.e., toward the side we already favor.

34 Epictetus (c. 55–135 CE) was a leading Stoic of the Roman era. Stoicism was a philosophical movement that flourished between roughly 300 BCE and 200 CE, and its main doctrine was that the guiding principle of nature is Reason (*logos*) and the highest virtue is to live in harmony with this rational order.

35 Hume means a kind of moderate scepticism, associated with Plato and the school he founded in Athens around 380 BCE, the Academy. This is to be contrasted with the extreme scepticism sometimes called Pyrrhonism, which seeks to suspend judgment on any question having conflicting evidence—which is to say, on nearly all questions.

authority; and that principle will preserve its influence as long as human nature remains the same. What that principle is may well be worth the pains of enquiry.

Suppose a person, though endowed with the strongest faculties of reason and reflection, to be brought on a sudden into this world; he would, indeed, immediately observe a continual succession of objects, and one event following another; but he would not be able to discover anything farther. He would not, at first, by any reasoning, be able to reach the idea of cause and effect; since the particular powers, by which all natural operations are performed, never appear to the senses; nor is it reasonable to conclude, merely because one event, in one instance, precedes another, that therefore the one is the cause, the other the effect. Their conjunction may be arbitrary and casual. There may be no reason to infer the existence of one from the appearance of the other. And in a word, such a person, without more experience, could never employ his conjecture or reasoning concerning any matter of fact, or be assured of any thing beyond what was immediately present to his memory and senses.

Suppose, again, that he has acquired more experience, and has lived so long in the world as to have observed familiar objects or events to be constantly conjoined together; what is the consequence of this experience? He immediately infers the existence of one object from the appearance of the other. Yet he has not, by all his experience, acquired any idea or knowledge of the secret power by which the one object produces the other; nor is it by any process of reasoning, he is engaged to draw this inference. But still he finds himself determined to draw it: And though he should be convinced that his understanding has no part in the operation, he would nevertheless continue in the same course of thinking. There is some other principle which determines him to form such a conclusion.

This principle is custom or habit. For wherever the repetition of any particular act or operation produces a propensity to renew the same act or operation, without being impelled by any reasoning or process of the understanding, we always say, that this propensity is the effect of *custom*. By employing that word, we pretend not to have given the ultimate reason of such a propensity. We only point out a principle of

human nature, which is universally acknowledged, and which is well known by its effects. Perhaps we can push our enquiries no farther, or pretend to give the cause of this cause; but must rest contented with it as the ultimate principle, which we can assign, of all our conclusions from experience. It is sufficient satisfaction, that we can go so far, without repining at the narrowness of our faculties because they will carry us no farther. And it is certain we here advance a very intelligible proposition at least, if not a true one, when we assert that, after the constant conjunction of two objects—heat and flame, for instance, weight and solidity—we are determined[36] by custom alone to expect the one from the appearance of the other. This hypothesis seems even the only one which explains the difficulty, why we draw, from a thousand instances, an inference which we are not able to draw from one instance, that is, in no respect, different from them. Reason is incapable of any such variation. The conclusions which it draws from considering one circle are the same which it would form upon surveying all the circles in the universe. But no man, having seen only one body move after being impelled by another, could infer that every other body will move after a like impulse. All inferences from experience, therefore, are effects of custom, not of reasoning.[37]

---

36   Caused.

37   [Author's note] Nothing is more usual than for writers, even, on *moral*, *political*, or *physical* subjects to distinguish between *reason* and *experience*, and to suppose, that these species of argumentation are entirely different from each other. The former are taken for the mere result of our intellectual faculties, which, by considering *a priori* the nature of things, and examining the effects, that must follow from their operation, establish particular principles of science and philosophy. The latter are supposed to be derived entirely from sense and observation, by which we learn what has actually resulted from the operation of particular objects, and are thence able to infer, what will, for the future, result from them. Thus, for instance, the limitations and restraints of civil government, and a legal constitution, may be defended, either from *reason*, which reflecting on the great frailty and corruption of human nature, teaches, that no man can safely be

Custom, then, is the great guide of human life. It is

trusted with unlimited authority; or from *experience* and history, which inform us of the enormous abuses, that ambition, in every age and country, has been found to make so imprudent a confidence.

The same distinction between reason and experience is maintained in all our deliberations concerning the conduct of life; while the experienced statesman, general, physician, or merchant is trusted and followed; and the unpractised novice, with whatever natural talents endowed, neglected and despised. Though it be allowed, that reason may form very plausible conjectures with regard to the consequences of such a particular conduct in such particular circumstances; it is still supposed imperfect, without the assistance of experience, which is alone able to give stability and certainty to the maxims, derived from study and reflection.

But notwithstanding that this distinction be thus universally received, both in the active and speculative scenes of life, I shall not scruple to pronounce, that it is, at bottom, erroneous, at least, superficial.

If we examine those arguments, which, in any of the sciences above mentioned, are supposed to be mere effects of reasoning and reflection, they will be found to terminate, at last, in some general principle or, conclusion, for which we can assign no reason but observation and experience. The only difference between them and those maxims, which are vulgarly esteemed the result of pure experience, is, that the former cannot be established without some process of thought, and some reflection on what we have observed, in order to distinguish its circumstances, and trace its consequences: Whereas in the latter, the experienced event is exactly and fully familiar to that which we infer as the result of any particular situation. The history of a Tiberius or a Nero makes us dread a like tyranny, were our monarchs freed from the restraints of laws and senates: but the observation of any fraud or cruelty in private life is sufficient, with the aid of a little thought, to give us the same apprehension; while it serves as an instance of the general corruption of human nature, and shows us the danger which we must incur by reposing an entire confidence in mankind. In both cases, it is experience which is ultimately the foundation of our inference and conclusion.

that principle alone which renders our experience useful to us, and makes us expect, for the future, a similar train of events with those which have appeared in the past. Without the influence of custom, we should be entirely ignorant of every matter of fact beyond what is immediately present to the memory and senses. We should never know how to adjust means to ends, or to employ our natural powers in the production of any effect. There would be an end at once of all action, as well as of the chief part of speculation.

But here it may be proper to remark, that though our conclusions from experience carry us beyond our memory and senses, and assure us of matters of fact which happened in the most distant places and most remote ages, yet some fact must always be present to the senses or memory, from which we may first proceed in drawing these conclusions. A man, who should find in a desert country the remains of pompous[38] buildings, would conclude that the country had, in ancient times, been cultivated by civilized inhabitants; but did nothing of this nature occur to him, he could never form such an inference. We learn the events of former ages from history; but then we must

---

There is no man so young and inexperienced, as not to have formed, from observation, many general and just maxims concerning human affairs and the conduct of life; but it must be confessed, that, when a man comes to put these in practice, he will be extremely liable to error, till time and farther experience both enlarge these maxims, and teach him their proper use and application. In every situation or incident, there are many particular and seemingly minute circumstances, which the man of greatest talent is, at first, apt to overlook, though on them the justness of his conclusions, and consequently the prudence of his conduct, entirely depend. Not to mention, that, to a young beginner, the general observations and maxims occur not always on the proper occasions, nor can be immediately applied with due calmness and distinction. The truth is, an unexperienced reasoner could be no reasoner at all, were he absolutely unexperienced; and when we assign that character to any one, we mean it only in a comparative sense, and suppose him possessed of experience, in a smaller and more imperfect degree.

38 Splendid, full of pomp.

peruse the volumes in which this instruction is contained, and thence carry up our inferences from one testimony to another, till we arrive at the eyewitnesses and spectators of these distant events. In a word, if we proceed not upon some fact, present to the memory or senses, our reasonings would be merely hypothetical; and however the particular links might be connected with each other, the whole chain of inferences would have nothing to support it, nor could we ever, by its means, arrive at the knowledge of any real existence. If I ask why you believe any particular matter of fact, which you relate, you must tell me some reason; and this reason will be some other fact, connected with it. But as you cannot proceed after this manner, *in infinitum*,[39] you must at last terminate in some fact, which is present to your memory or senses; or must allow that your belief is entirely without foundation.

What, then, is the conclusion of the whole matter? A simple one; though, it must be confessed, pretty remote from the common theories of philosophy. All belief of matter of fact or real existence is derived merely from some object, present to the memory or senses, and a customary conjunction between that and some other object. Or in other words; having found, in many instances, that any two kinds of objects—flame and heat, snow and cold—have always been conjoined together; if flame or snow be presented anew to the senses, the mind is carried by custom to expect heat or cold, and to *believe* that such a quality does exist, and will discover itself upon a nearer approach. This belief is the necessary result of placing the mind in such circumstances. It is an operation of the soul, when we are so situated, as unavoidable as to feel the passion of love, when we receive benefits; or hatred, when we meet with injuries. All these operations are a species of natural instincts, which no reasoning or process of the thought and understanding is able either to produce or to prevent.

At this point, it would be very allowable for us to stop our philosophical researches. In most questions we can never make a single step farther; and in all questions we must terminate here at last, after our most restless and curious enquiries. But still our curiosity will be pardonable, perhaps commendable, if

it carry us on to still farther researches, and make us examine more accurately the nature of this *belief*, and of the *customary conjunction*, whence it is derived. By this means we may meet with some explications and analogies that will give satisfaction; at least to such as love the abstract sciences, and can be entertained with speculations, which, however accurate, may still retain a degree of doubt and uncertainty. As to readers of a different taste; the remaining part of this section is not calculated for them, and the following enquiries may well be understood, though it be neglected.

PART II.

Nothing is more free than the imagination of man; and though it cannot exceed that original stock of ideas furnished by the internal and external senses, it has unlimited power of mixing, compounding, separating, and dividing these ideas, in all the varieties of fiction and vision. It can feign[40] a train of events, with all the appearance of reality, ascribe to them a particular time and place, conceive them as existent, and paint them out to itself with every circumstance, that belongs to any historical fact, which it believes with the greatest certainty. Wherein, therefore, consists the difference between such a *fiction* and *belief*? It lies not merely in any peculiar idea, which is annexed to such a conception as commands our assent, and which is wanting[41] to every known fiction. For as the mind has authority over all its ideas, it could voluntarily annex this particular idea to any fiction, and consequently be able to believe whatever it pleases; contrary to what we find by daily experience. We can, in our conception, join the head of a man to the body of a horse; but it is not in our power to believe that such an animal has ever really existed.

It follows, therefore, that the difference between *fiction* and *belief* lies in some sentiment or feeling, which is annexed to the latter, not to the former, and which depends not on the will, nor can be commanded at pleasure. It must be excited by nature, like all other sentiments; and must arise from the particular situation, in which the mind is placed at any particular juncture. Whenever any object is presented to the

39 For ever, to infinity.

40 Simulate, imagine.
41 Lacking.

memory or senses, it immediately, by the force of custom, carries the imagination to conceive that object, which is usually conjoined to it; and this conception is attended with a feeling or sentiment, different from the loose reveries of the fancy. In this consists the whole nature of belief. For as there is no matter of fact which we believe so firmly that we cannot conceive the contrary, there would be no difference between the conception assented to and that which is rejected, were it not for some sentiment which distinguishes the one from the other. If I see a billiard-ball moving toward another, on a smooth table, I can easily conceive it to stop upon contact. This conception implies no contradiction; but still it feels very differently from that conception by which I represent to myself the impulse and the communication of motion from one ball to another.

Were we to attempt a *definition* of this sentiment, we should, perhaps, find it a very difficult, if not an impossible task; in the same manner as if we should endeavour to define the feeling of cold or passion of anger, to a creature who never had any experience of these sentiments. Belief is the true and proper name of this feeling; and no one is ever at a loss to know the meaning of that term; because every man is every moment conscious of the sentiment represented by it. It may not, however, be improper to attempt a *description* of this sentiment; in hopes we may, by that means, arrive at some analogies, which may afford a more perfect explication of it. I say, then, that belief is nothing but a more vivid, lively, forcible, firm, steady conception of an object, than what the imagination alone is ever able to attain. This variety of terms, which may seem so unphilosophical, is intended only to express that act of the mind, which renders realities, or what is taken for such, more present to us than fictions, causes them to weigh more in the thought, and gives them a superior influence on the passions and imagination. Provided we agree about the thing, it is needless to dispute about the terms. The imagination has the command over all its ideas, and can join and mix and vary them, in all the ways possible. It may conceive fictitious objects with all the circumstances of place and time. It may set them, in a manner, before our eyes, in their true colours, just as they might have existed. But as it is impossible that this faculty

of imagination can ever, of itself, reach belief, it is evident that belief consists not in the peculiar nature or order of ideas, but in the *manner* of their conception, and in their *feeling* to the mind. I confess, that it is impossible perfectly to explain this feeling or manner of conception. We may make use of words which express something near it. But its true and proper name, as we observed before, is *belief*; which is a term that every one sufficiently understands in common life. And in philosophy, we can go no farther than assert, that *belief* is something felt by the mind, which distinguishes the ideas of the judgement from the fictions of the imagination. It gives them more weight and influence; makes them appear of greater importance; enforces them in the mind; and renders them the governing principle of our actions. I hear at present, for instance, a person's voice, with whom I am acquainted; and the sound comes as from the next room. This impression of my senses immediately conveys my thought to the person, together with all the surrounding objects. I paint them out to myself as existing at present, with the same qualities and relations, of which I formerly knew them possessed. These ideas take faster hold of my mind than ideas of an enchanted castle. They are very different to the feeling, and have a much greater influence of every kind, either to give pleasure or pain, joy or sorrow.

Let us, then, take in the whole compass of this doctrine, and allow, that the sentiment of belief is nothing but a conception more intense and steady than what attends the mere fictions of the imagination, and that this *manner* of conception arises from a customary conjunction of the object with something present to the memory or senses: I believe that it will not be difficult, upon these suppositions, to find other operations of the mind analogous to it, and to trace up these phenomena to principles still more general.

We have already observed that nature has established connections among particular ideas, and that no sooner one idea occurs to our thoughts than it introduces its correlative,[42] and carries our attention towards it, by a gentle and insensible movement. These principles of connection or association we have reduced to three, namely, *resemblance, contiguity*

---

42   The thing normally related or connected to it.

and *causation*; which are the only bonds that unite our thoughts together, and beget that regular train of reflection or discourse, which, in a greater or less degree, takes place among all mankind. Now here arises a question, on which the solution of the present difficulty will depend. Does it happen, in all these relations, that, when one of the objects is presented to the senses or memory, the mind is not only carried to the conception of the correlative, but reaches a steadier and stronger conception of it than what otherwise it would have been able to attain? This seems to be the case with that belief which arises from the relation of cause and effect. And if the case be the same with the other relations or principles of associations, this may be established as a general law, which takes place in all the operations of the mind.

We may, therefore, observe, as the first experiment to our present purpose, that, upon the appearance of the picture of an absent friend, our idea of him is evidently enlivened by the *resemblance*, and that every passion, which that idea occasions, whether of joy or sorrow, acquires new force and vigour. In producing this effect, there concur both a relation and a present impression. Where the picture bears him no resemblance, at least was not intended for[43] him, it never so much as conveys our thought to him: and where it is absent, as well as the person, though the mind may pass from the thought of the one to that of the other, it feels its idea to be rather weakened than enlivened by that transition. We take a pleasure in viewing the picture of a friend, when it is set before us; but when it is removed, rather choose to consider him directly than by reflection in an image, which is equally distant and obscure.

The ceremonies of the Roman Catholic religion may be considered as instances of the same nature. The devotees of that superstition usually plead in excuse for the mummeries,[44] with which they are upbraided, that they feel the good effect of those external motions, and postures, and actions, in enlivening their devotion and quickening their fervour, which otherwise would decay, if directed entirely to distant and immaterial objects. We shadow out the objects of our faith, say they, in sensible types and images, and render them more present to us by the immediate presence of these types, than it is possible for us to do merely by an intellectual view and contemplation. Sensible objects have always a greater influence on the fancy than any other; and this influence they readily convey to those ideas to which they are related, and which they resemble. I shall only infer from these practices, and this reasoning, that the effect of resemblance in enlivening the ideas is very common; and as in every case a resemblance and a present impression must concur, we are abundantly supplied with experiments to prove the reality of the foregoing principle.

We may add force to these experiments by others of a different kind, in considering the effects of *contiguity* as well as of *resemblance*. It is certain that distance diminishes the force of every idea, and that, upon our approach to any object; though it does not discover itself to our senses; it operates upon the mind with an influence, which imitates an immediate impression. The thinking on any object readily transports the mind to what is contiguous; but it is only the actual presence of an object, that transports it with a superior vivacity. When I am a few miles from home, whatever relates to it touches me more nearly than when I am two hundred leagues[45] distant; though even at that distance the reflecting on any thing in the neighbourhood of my friends or family naturally produces an idea of them. But as in this latter case, both the objects of the mind are ideas; notwithstanding there is an easy transition between them; that transition alone is not able to give a superior vivacity to any of the ideas, for want of some immediate impression.[46]

---

43   Supposed to be.
44   Silly rituals.
45   A league is roughly three miles (4.8 km).
46   [Author's note] '*Naturane nobis, inquit, datum dicam, an errore quodam, ut, cum ea loca videamus, in quibus memoria dignos viros acceperimus multim esse versatos, magis moveamur, quam siquando eorum ipsorum aut facta audiamus aut scriptum aliquod legamus? Velut ego nunc moveor. Venit enim mihi Plato in mentem, quem accepimus primum hic disputare solitum; cuius etiam illi hortuli propinqui non memoriam solum mihi afferunt, sed ipsum videntur in conspectu meo hic ponere. Hic Speusippus, hic Xenocrates, hic eius auditor Polemo; cuius ipsa illa sessio fuit, quam*

No one can doubt but causation has the same influence as the other two relations of resemblance and contiguity. Superstitious people are fond of the reliques of saints and holy men, for the same reason, that they seek after types or images, in order to enliven their devotion, and give them a more intimate and strong conception of those exemplary lives, which they desire to imitate. Now it is evident, that one of the best reliques, which a devotee could procure, would be the handywork of a saint; and if his clothes and furniture are ever to be considered in this light, it is because they were once at his disposal, and were moved and affected by him; in which respect they are to be considered as imperfect effects, and as connected with him by a shorter chain of consequences than any of those, by which we learn the reality of his existence.

Suppose, that the son of a friend, who had been long dead or absent, were presented to us; it is evident, that this object would instantly revive its correlative idea, and recall to our thoughts all past intimacies and familiarities, in more lively colours than they would otherwise have appeared to us. This is another phenomenon, which seems to prove the principle above mentioned.

We may observe, that, in these phenomena, the belief of the correlative object is always presupposed; without which the relation could have no effect. The influence of the picture supposes, that we *believe* our friend to have once existed. Contiguity to home can never excite our ideas of home, unless we *believe* that it really exists. Now I assert, that this belief, where it reaches beyond the memory or senses, is of a similar nature, and arises from similar causes, with the transition of thought and vivacity of conception here explained. When I throw a piece of dry wood into a fire, my mind is immediately carried to conceive, that it augments, not extinguishes the flame. This transition of thought from the cause to the effect proceeds not from reason. It derives its origin altogether from custom and experience. And as it first begins from an object, present to the senses, it renders the idea or conception of flame more strong and lively than any loose, floating reverie of the imagination. That idea arises immediately. The thought moves instantly towards it, and conveys to it all that force of conception, which is derived from the impression present to the senses. When a sword is levelled at my breast, does not the idea of wound and pain strike me more strongly, than when a glass of wine is presented to me, even though by accident this idea should occur after the appearance of the latter object? But what is there in this whole matter to cause such a strong conception, except only a present object and a customary transition of the idea of another object, which we have been accustomed to conjoin with the former? This is the whole operation of the mind, in all our conclusions concerning matter of fact and existence; and it is a satisfaction to find some analogies, by which it may be explained. The transition from a present object does in all cases give strength and solidity to the related idea.

Here, then, is a kind of pre-established harmony between the course of nature and the succession of our ideas; and though the powers and forces, by which the former is governed, be wholly unknown to us; yet our thoughts and conceptions have still, we find, gone

---

videmus. Equidem etiam curiam nostram, Hostiliam dico, non hanc novam, quae mihi minor esse videtur postquam est maior, solebam intuens, Scipionem, Catonem, Laelium, nostrum vero in primis avum cogitare. Tanta vis admonitionis est in locis; ut non sine causa ex his memopriae deducta sit disciplina.'—Cicero de Finibus. Lib. v. ["Should I say," he asked, "that it is natural or just an error that makes us more greatly moved when we see places where, as we have been told, famous men spent a lot of time, than we are if, at some time or another, we hear about the things which they have done, or read something written by them? I, for example, feel moved at present. For Plato comes to my mind who, we know, was the first to hold regular discussions here: that garden nearby not only brings him to memory but seems to make me see him. Here is Speusippus, here is Xenocrates, and here also is his pupil Polemo: it is the place where he used to sit that we see before us. Similarly, when I looked at our senate house (I mean the one Hostilius built and not the new building which seems to me lesser since it has been enlarged) I used to think of Scipio, Cato, and Lælius, and above all of my grandfather. Places can remind us of so much; it is not without good reason that the formal training of memory is based on them." Cicero, *On the Chief Good and Evil*, from Book V]

on in the same train with the other works of nature. Custom is that principle, by which this correspondence has been effected; so necessary to the subsistence of our species, and the regulation of our conduct, in every circumstance and occurrence of human life. Had not the presence of an object, instantly excited the idea of those objects, commonly conjoined with it, all our knowledge must have been limited to the narrow sphere of our memory and senses; and we should never have been able to adjust means to ends, or employ our natural powers, either to the producing of good, or avoiding of evil. Those, who delight in the discovery and contemplation of *final causes*,[47] have here ample subject to employ their wonder and admiration.

I shall add, for a further confirmation of the foregoing theory, that, as this operation of the mind, by which we infer like effects from like causes, and *vice*

---

47   In this context, the purpose for the nature and arrangement of things in the universe.

versa, is so essential to the subsistence of all human creatures, it is not probable, that it could be trusted to the fallacious deductions of our reason, which is slow in its operations; appears not, in any degree, during the first years of infancy; and at best is, in every age and period of human life, extremely liable to error and mistake. It is more conformable to the ordinary wisdom of nature to secure so necessary an act of the mind, by some instinct or mechanical tendency, which may be infallible in its operations, may discover itself at the first appearance of life and thought, and may be independent of all the laboured deductions of the understanding. As nature has taught us the use of our limbs, without giving us the knowledge of the muscles and nerves, by which they are actuated; so has she implanted in us an instinct, which carries forward the thought in a correspondent course to that which she has established among external objects; though we are ignorant of those powers and forces, on which this regular course and succession of objects totally depends.

NELSON GOODMAN

Fact, Fiction, and Forecast

Who Was Nelson Goodman?

Nelson Goodman—who has been called "one of the two or three greatest analytic philosophers of the post-World War II period"—was born in Somerville, Massachusetts in 1906. He graduated in 1928 from Harvard University with a bachelor of science degree and became a successful art dealer and gallery owner in Boston. Still keeping up his art business, he wrote a PhD thesis (according to his colleague Hilary Putnam, "a masterpiece") which he completed in 1941 at Harvard. After serving in the US Army during World War II, Goodman took up a succession of academic positions at Tufts College, the University of Pennsylvania, and

Brandeis University; in 1968 he was appointed Professor of Philosophy at Harvard, where he stayed for the rest of his career.

Goodman published many articles and several books during his lifetime, including *The Structure of Appearance* (1951), *Fact, Fiction, and Forecast* (1954), *Languages of Art* (1968), and *Ways of Worldmaking* (1978). Hilary Putnam has called *Fact, Fiction, and Forecast* "one of the few books that every serious student of philosophy in our time *has* to have read." At the center of Goodman's philosophy is the view that there are no absolute truths or foundations or certainties: according to Goodman there are no propositions, even in logic or mathematics, which are always and everywhere true, and there is no mind-independent, objective world which provides us with a set of 'facts' to which our beliefs should correspond. Instead, in Goodman's view, by creating and using systems of symbols such as mathematics, language, and art we *construct* worlds for ourselves—we *create* facts and standards by choosing to think and talk in one way rather than another.

Goodman's basic argument for this "irrealist" view runs as follows. First, the 'identity conditions' for objects (such as stars) and types (such as purple things) depend entirely upon our system of classification: that is, to ask whether or not something counts as a star is to do no more and no less than to ask whether we would apply the name "star" to it, and *this* fact is not so much a fact about astral bodies as it is a fact about our linguistic categories. For example, we can change a black hole from a non-star into a star (or vice versa) simply by adjusting our usage of the word "star." If this doctrine—a fairly extreme version of  a philosophical theory called "nominalism"—is correct, it follows that in adopting a particular system of symbols, such as a language or a scientific theory, *we are determining what things exist*. By choosing how to use words, we are deciding which things are stars and which are not, or even whether anything counts as a star at all (and the same goes for every other possible type of thing). Furthermore, two irreducibly different category schemes must then be about two entirely different sets of things. Two incompatible symbol systems are not to be thought of as two different descriptions of the same thing (the world), one of which might be correct and the other incorrect: instead, they are simply two different collections of things, and hence two different worlds. To put it another way, there are no facts outside of symbol-systems: everything is either true or false only relative to a particular way of categorizing. There are many worlds if any, and worlds are made rather than found.

None of this, according to Goodman, means that we can do or believe just what we like: to say that there are many possible, equally 'factual' worlds, is not to say that *we* don't live in any world in particular. Propositions are still true or false (within a certain set of community standards) and actions right or wrong (given a set of community practices). It's just that, 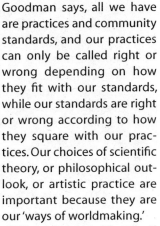 Goodman says, all we have are practices and community standards, and our practices can only be called right or wrong depending on how they fit with our standards, while our standards are right or wrong according to how they square with our practices. Our choices of scientific theory, or philosophical outlook, or artistic practice are important because they are our 'ways of worldmaking.'

Throughout his life, Goodman was interested not only in science and philosophy but also—and perhaps even more so—in art and arts education. In 1947 he married Katharine Sturgess, a talented painter whom he met when she brought her watercolors to his Boston gallery. He founded and directed the Dance Center of the Harvard Summer School, and was also a founder of Project Zero, an interdisciplinary center for the study of thinking and of aesthetic education at the Harvard Graduate School of Education. Goodman was also passionately devoted to animal welfare, and was especially generous in funding efforts to protect animals from the effects of war or natural disaster (for example, he paid for animal rescue efforts in Kuwait during the first Gulf War, in Bosnia, at Montserrat following a volcanic eruption, and after serious forest fires in Borneo).

Goodman died in Massachusetts in 1998. In the foreword of *Ways of Worldmaking*, Goodman sums up his philosophical approach in the following words:

Few familiar philosophical labels fit comfortably a book that is at odds with rationalism and empiricism alike, with materialism and idealism and dualism, with essentialism and existentialism, with mechanism and vitalism, with mysticism and scientism, and with most other ardent doctrines…. Nevertheless I think of this book as belonging in that mainstream of modern philosophy that began when Kant exchanged the structure of the world for the structure of the mind, continued when C.I. Lewis exchanged the structure of the mind for the structure of concepts, and that now proceeds to exchange the structure of concepts for the structure of the several symbol systems of the sciences, philosophy, the arts, perception, and everyday discourse. The movement is from unique truth and a world fixed and found to a diversity of right and even conflicting versions or worlds in the making.

What Is the Structure of This Reading?

Goodman's book *Fact, Fiction, and Forecast* has two parts. The first part "Predicament—1946" describes Goodman's failed, early attempts to provide a theory of potentiality—of how we can describe and know about what physical objects *will* do or *would* do, even though they are not doing it now. (For example, to say that a glass vase is fragile is to say, roughly, that if it were struck with sufficient force it would shatter.) The second part of the book, "Project—1953," consists of three lectures Goodman gave at the University of London, in which he attempted to make a fresh approach to the solution of his earlier difficulties. In the first lecture Goodman describes the pressing need to develop a theory of potentiality in order to solve a cluster of important philosophical problems (such as, for example, the nature of possibility), and suggests that such a theory would be tantamount to a solution for the problem of induction.

In the second lecture—which is the selection reprinted here—Goodman argues, first, that the traditional problem of induction (raised by Hume in the previous reading) has been widely misunderstood, and when properly understood is perfectly soluble by an adequate formulation of the rules of inductive inference. Developing such a theory is what Goodman calls, in section 3, "the constructive task of confirmation theory." Goodman describes some of the advances in confirmation theory, but then argues that a deeper philosophical problem remains: this is his "new riddle of induction," which involves the difficulty in distinguishing between general statements which are "lawlike" and those which are merely accidental. Goodman considers several apparently easy ways of dealing with this problem, and argues that none of them work: the new riddle of induction, it turns out, is a very hard philosophical nut to crack.

In the third and final lecture (which is not included here) Goodman lays out his own preliminary attempt to solve the new riddle of induction. His solution is essentially a pragmatic one: he argues that "green" is to be preferred to "grue" as a classification of the inductive evidence for no reason except that the concept of greenness is "entrenched" in our existing habits of thought, and fits more comfortably within the system of classification and explanation that we happen to have used successfully in the past.

Some Common Misconceptions

1. It's not a good objection to Goodman's argument just to point out that "grue" is a made-up word. I could invent a word for my favorite color—such as "Andrewhue"—and use this instead of "green," but this would not make greenness any less genuine (or "projectible") a property. Furthermore, sometimes science discovers previously unknown properties—such as the "charm" or "color" of certain quarks—and has to invent new names for them, but again, this does not all by itself cast any aspersions on the lawlikeness of these properties.

2. It's not a good objection to Goodman's argument just to say that grue is a complicated— often called a 'gruesome' or a 'bent'—predicate. After all, many perfectly respectable predicates are 'bent' in just this way: for example, *being solid and less than 0°C, or liquid and more than 0°C but less than 100°C, or gaseous and more than 100°C.*

3. It's not a good objection to Goodman's argument just to claim that grue is not an 'observable property,' in the same way as greenness or magnetism are. One could build a perfectly good "grue detector" by making a machine which gave a positive result exactly when it was scanning something green before time t (by the machine's internal clock) or blue after t, and one could then use this grue detector, just like a spectrometer or magnetometer, to observe grue things even without knowing what time it is.

4. It's not a good objection to Goodman's argument just to say that projectible predicates are those that remain after extensive testing—a kind of "survival of the fittest." Even though the claim that an emerald is grue might be ruled out if it continues to be green after time t, the real point is that there will *always* be an infinite number of *other* 'bent predicates' which remain to be ruled out (for example, grue': green before time $t + n$ and blue after).

Suggestions for Critical Reflection

1. Are emeralds really grue? If they were grue, would this mean that they are not green?

2. Hilary Putnam has said, "Goodman totally recasts the problem of induction. For him the problem is not to guarantee that induction will succeed in the future … but to characterize what induction *is* in a way that is neither too permissive nor too vague." Do you agree with Putnam's assessment? Do you think that Goodman has shown that the "old" problem of induction—the one raised by Hume—has been solved, or at least can be left behind?

3. Another way of understanding Goodman's conclusion is the following: Goodman showed that the strength of inductive inferences is independent of either their syntax (their logical form) or their semantics (the meanings of the words involved). There must therefore be some *third* way to distinguish between good and bad inductive arguments, and 'the new riddle of induction' is to find that third way. What do you

think of this interpretation of Goodman? If it is right, then what has Goodman shown about the difference between deductive and inductive logic?

4. Is there an objective fact of the matter about which predicates are 'projectible' and which are not? Do you think Goodman thinks there is? If projectibility is not objective, where does this leave science? If projectibility is objective, how do you think we could find out about it?

5. How serious is the new riddle of induction? Can you outline a plausible solution to the problem that Goodman has not already rejected? Was Goodman right to reject so quickly the attempted solutions that he considers? If the new riddle of induction cannot be solved, where does that leave us? For example, what implications would this have for science?

Suggestions for Further Reading

In addition to the rest of *Fact, Fiction, and Forecast* (Harvard University Press,1983), Goodman explores the problem of induction in several essays in his *Problems and Projects* (Hackett, 1972). The interested reader can pursue the rest of Goodman's philosophy in his books *The Structure of Appearance* (Reidel, 1977), *Languages of Art: An Approach to a Theory of Symbols* (Hackett, 1976), *Ways of Worldmaking* (Hackett, 1978) and *Of Mind and Other Matters* (Harvard University Press, 1984).

There is a collection of essays specifically about Goodman's new riddle of induction edited by Douglas Stalker and called *Grue! The New Riddle of Induction* (Open Court, 1994), and there have been two special issues of *The Journal of Philosophy* on the new riddle of induction: Volume 63, Issue 11 (1966) and Volume 64, Issue 9 (1967). Goodman's friend and collaborator Catherine Elgin has written about his philosophy in *With Reference to Reference* (Hackett, 1983) and edited a collection of essays on his new riddle *Philosophy of Nelson Goodman* (vol. 2, Garland Publishing, 1997). Peter McCormick's *Starmaking: Realism, Anti-Realism, and Irrealism* (MIT Press, 1996)—a three-way debate between Goodman, Hilary Putnam and Israel Scheffler—contains much of interest about irrealism.

"The New Riddle of Induction"[1]

1. The Old Problem of Induction

At the close of the preceding lecture, I said that today I should examine how matters stand with respect to the problem of induction. In a word, I think they stand ill. But the real difficulties that confront us today are not the traditional ones. What is commonly thought of as the Problem of Induction has been solved, or dissolved; and we face new problems that are not as yet very widely understood. To approach them, I shall have to run as quickly as possible over some very familiar ground.

The problem of the validity of judgments about future or unknown cases arises, as Hume pointed out, because such judgments are neither reports of experience nor logical consequences of it. Predictions, of course, pertain to what has not yet been observed. And they cannot be logically inferred from what has been observed; for what *has* happened imposes no logical restrictions on what *will* happen. Although Hume's dictum that there are no necessary connections of matters of fact has been challenged at times, it has withstood all attacks. Indeed, I should be inclined not merely to agree that there are no necessary connections of matters of fact, but to ask whether there are any necessary connections at all[2]—but that is another story.

---

1   *Fact, Fiction, and Forecast* was originally published in 1954, and was based largely on three lectures Goodman gave at the University of London in 1953. This selection is reprinted from the fourth edition (Harvard University Press, 1983). Reprinted by permission of the publisher from "The New Riddle of Induction" in *Fact, Fiction, and Forecast* by Nelson Goodman, pp. 59–83, Cambridge, Mass.: Harvard University Press, Copyright © 1979, 1983 by Nelson Goodman.

2   [Author's note] Although this remark is merely an aside, perhaps I should explain for the sake of some unusually sheltered reader that the notion of a necessary connection of ideas, or of an absolutely analytic statement, is no longer sacrosanct. Some, like Quine and White, have forthrightly attacked the notion; others, like myself, have simply discarded it; and still others have begun to feel acutely uncomfortable about it.

Hume's answer to the question how predictions are related to past experience is refreshingly non-cosmic. When an event of one kind frequently follows upon an event of another kind in experience, a habit is formed that leads the mind, when confronted with a new event of the first kind, to pass to the idea of an event of the second kind. The idea of necessary connection arises from the felt impulse of the mind in making this transition.

Now if we strip this account of all extraneous features, the central point is that to the question "Why one prediction rather than another?", Hume answers that the elect prediction is one that accords with a past regularity, because this regularity has established a habit. Thus among alternative statements about a future moment, one statement is distinguished by its consonance with habit and thus with regularities observed in the past. Prediction according to any other alternative is errant.

How satisfactory is this answer? The heaviest criticism has taken the righteous position that Hume's account at best pertains only to the source of predictions, not their legitimacy; that he sets forth the circumstances under which we make given predictions—and in this sense explains why we make them—but leaves untouched the question of our license for making them. To trace origins, runs the old complaint, is not to establish validity: the real question is not why a prediction is in fact made but how it can be justified. Since this seems to point to the awkward conclusion that the greatest of modern philosophers completely missed the point of his own problem, the idea has developed that he did not really take his solution very seriously, but regarded the main problem as unsolved and perhaps as insoluble. Thus we come to speak of 'Hume's problem' as though he propounded it as a question without answer.

All this seems to me quite wrong. I think Hume grasped the central question and considered his answer to be passably effective. And I think his answer is reasonable and relevant, even if it is not entirely satisfactory. I shall explain presently. At the moment, I merely want to record a protest against the prevalent notion that the problem of justifying induction, when it is so sharply dissociated from the problem of describing how induction takes place, can fairly be called Hume's problem.

I suppose that the problem of justifying induction has called forth as much fruitless discussion as has any halfway respectable problem of modern philosophy. The typical writer begins by insisting that some way of justifying predictions must be found; proceeds to argue that for this purpose we need some resounding universal law of the Uniformity of Nature, and then inquires how this universal principle itself can be justified. At this point, if he is tired, he concludes that the principle must be accepted as an indispensable assumption; or if he is energetic and ingenious, he goes on to devise some subtle justification for it. Such an invention, however, seldom satisfies anyone else; and the easier course of accepting an unsubstantiated and even dubious assumption much more sweeping than any actual predictions we make seems an odd and expensive way of justifying them.

2. Dissolution of the Old Problem

Understandably, then, more critical thinkers have suspected that there might be something awry with the problem we are trying to solve. Come to think of it, what precisely would constitute the justification we seek? If the problem is to explain how we know that certain predictions will turn out to be correct, the sufficient answer is that we don't know any such thing. If the problem is to *find* some way of distinguishing antecedently between true and false predictions, we are asking for prevision rather than for philosophical explanation. Nor does it help matters much to say that we are merely trying to show that or why certain predictions are *probable*. Often it is said that while we cannot tell in advance whether a prediction concerning a given throw of a die is true, we can decide whether the prediction is a probable one. But if this means determining how the prediction is related to actual frequency distributions of future throws of the die, surely there is no way of knowing or proving this in advance. On the other hand, if the judgment that the prediction is probable has nothing to do with subsequent occurrences, then the question remains in what sense a probable prediction is any better justified than an improbable one.

Now obviously the genuine problem cannot be one of attaining unattainable knowledge or of accounting for knowledge that we do not in fact have. A better understanding of our problem can be gained by looking for a moment at what is involved in justifying noninductive inferences. How do we justify a *de*duction? Plainly, by showing that it conforms to the general rules of deductive inference. An argument that so conforms is justified or valid, even if its conclusion happens to be false. An argument that violates a rule is fallacious even if its conclusion happens to be true. To justify a deductive conclusion therefore requires no knowledge of the facts it pertains to. Moreover, when a deductive argument has been shown to conform to the rules of logical inference, we usually consider it justified without going on to ask what justifies the rules. Analogously, the basic task in justifying an inductive inference is to show that it conforms to the general rules of *in*duction. Once we have recognized this, we have gone a long way towards clarifying our problem.

Yet, of course, the rules themselves must eventually be justified. The validity of a deduction depends not upon conformity to any purely arbitrary rules we may contrive, but upon conformity to valid rules. When we speak of *the* rules of inference we mean the valid rules—or better, *some* valid rules, since there may be alternative sets of equally valid rules. But how is the validity of rules to be determined? Here again we encounter philosophers who insist that these rules follow from some self-evident axiom, and others who try to show that the rules are grounded in the very nature of the human mind. I think the answer lies much nearer the surface. Principles of deductive inference are justified by their conformity with accepted deductive practice. Their validity depends upon accordance with the particular deductive inferences we actually make and sanction. If a rule yields inacceptable inferences, we drop it as invalid. Justification of general rules thus derives from judgments rejecting or accepting particular deductive inferences.

This looks flagrantly circular. I have said that deductive inferences are justified by their conformity to valid general rules, and that general rules are justified by their conformity to valid inferences. But this circle is a virtuous one. The point is that rules and particular inferences alike are justified by being brought into agreement with each other. *A rule is amended if it yields an inference we are unwilling to accept; an inference is rejected if it violates a rule we are unwilling to amend.* The process of justification is the delicate one of making mutual adjustments between rules and accepted inferences; and in the agreement achieved lies the only justification needed for either.

All this applies equally well to induction. An inductive inference, too, is justified by conformity to general rules, and a general rule by conformity to accepted inductive inferences. Predictions are justified if they conform to valid canons of induction; and the canons are valid if they accurately codify accepted inductive practice.

A result of such analysis is that we can stop plaguing ourselves with certain spurious questions about induction. We no longer demand an explanation for guarantees that we do not have, or seek keys to knowledge that we cannot obtain. It dawns upon us that the traditional smug insistence upon a hard-and-fast line between justifying induction and describing ordinary inductive practice distorts the problem. And we owe belated apologies to Hume. For in dealing with the question how normally accepted inductive judgments are made, he was in fact dealing with the question of inductive validity.[3] The validity of a prediction consisted for him in its arising from habit, and thus in its exemplifying some past regularity. His answer was incomplete and perhaps not entirely correct; but it was not beside the point. The problem of induction is not a problem of demonstration but a problem of defining the difference between valid and invalid predictions.

This clears the air but leaves a lot to be done. As principles of *de*ductive inference, we have the familiar and highly developed laws of logic; but there are available no such precisely stated and well-recognized principles of inductive inference. Mill's canons[4] hardly rank with Aristotle's rules of the syllogism, let alone with *Principia Mathematica.*[5] Elaborate and valuable treatises on probability usually leave certain fundamental questions untouched. Only in very recent years has there been any explicit and systematic work upon what I call the constructive task of confirmation theory.

3. The Constructive Task of Confirmation Theory

The task of formulating rules that define the difference between valid and invalid inductive inferences is much like the task of defining any term with an established usage. If we set out to define the term "tree", we try to compose out of already understood words an expression that will apply to the familiar objects that standard usage calls trees, and that will not apply to objects that standard usage refuses to call trees. A proposal that plainly violates either condition is rejected; while a definition that meets these tests may be adopted and used to decide cases that are not already settled by actual usage. Thus the interplay we observed between rules of induction and particular inductive inferences is simply

---

3   [Author's note] A hasty reader might suppose that my insistence here upon identifying the problem of justification with a problem of description is out of keeping with my parenthetical insistence in the preceding lecture that the goal of philosophy is something quite different from the mere description of ordinary or scientific procedure. Let me repeat that the point urged there was that the organization of the explanatory account need not reflect the manner or order in which predicates are adopted in practice. It surely must describe practice, however, in the sense that the extensions of predicates as explicated must conform in certain ways to the extensions of the same predicates as applied in practice. Hume's account is a description in just this sense. For it is an attempt to set forth the circumstances under which those inductive judgments are made that are normally accepted as valid; and to do that is to state necessary and sufficient conditions for, and thus to define, valid induction. What I am maintaining above is that the problem of justifying induction is not something over and above the problem of describing or defining valid induction.

---

4   Goodman is referring to John Stuart Mill's *System of Logic,* first published in 1843, which tried to lay down general methods for deriving scientific claims from experience.

5   Aristotle developed the foundations of deductive logic—the theory of syllogisms—in the fourth century BCE, and Bertrand Russell and Alfred North Whitehead encapsulated modern logic in their massive *Principia Mathematica,* published in three volumes between 1910 and 1913.

an instance of this characteristic dual adjustment between definition and usage, whereby the usage informs the definition, which in turn guides extension of the usage.

Of course this adjustment is a more complex matter than I have indicated. Sometimes, in the interest of convenience or theoretical utility, we deliberately permit a definition to run counter to clear mandates of common usage. We accept a definition of "fish" that excludes whales. Similarly we may decide to deny the term "valid induction" to some inductive inferences that are commonly considered valid, or apply the term to others not usually so considered. A definition may modify as well as extend ordinary usage.[6]

Some pioneer work on the problem of defining confirmation or valid induction has been done by Professor Hempel.[7] Let me remind you briefly of a few of his results. Just as deductive logic is concerned primarily with a relation between statements—namely the consequence relation—that is independent of their truth or falsity, so inductive logic as Hempel conceives it is concerned primarily with a comparable relation of confirmation between statements. Thus the problem is to define the relation that obtains between any statement S_1 and another S_2 if and only if S_1 may properly be said to confirm S_2 in any degree.

With the question so stated, the first step seems obvious. Does not induction proceed in just the opposite direction from deduction? Surely some of the evidence-statements that inductively support a general hypothesis are consequences of it. Since the consequence relation is already well defined by deductive logic, will we not be on firm ground in saying that confirmation embraces the converse relation? The laws of deduction in reverse will then be among the laws of induction.

Let's see where this leads us. We naturally assume further that whatever confirms a given statement confirms also whatever follows from that statement.[8] But if we combine this assumption with our proposed principle, we get the embarrassing result that every statement confirms every other. Surprising as it may be that such innocent beginnings lead to such an intolerable conclusion, the proof is very easy. Start with any statement S_1. It is a consequence of, and so by our present criterion confirms, the conjunction of S_1 and any statement whatsoever—call it S_2. But the confirmed conjunction,[9] $S_1 \cdot S_2$, of course has S_2 as a consequence. Thus every statement confirms all statements.

The fault lies in careless formulation of our first proposal. While some statements that confirm a general hypothesis are consequences of it, not all its consequences confirm it. This may not be immediately evident; for indeed we do in some sense furnish support for a statement when we establish one of its consequences. We settle one of the questions about it. Consider the heterogeneous conjunction:

---

6   [Author's note] For a fuller discussion of definition in general see Chapter I of *The Structure of Appearance* [by Nelson Goodman (Kluwer, 1977)].

7   [Author's note] The basic article is 'A Purely Syntactical Definition of Confirmation', *Journal of Symbolic Logic*, vol. 8 (1943), pp. 122–43. A much less technical account is given in 'Studies in the Logic of Confirmation', *Mind*, n.s., vol. 54 (1945), pp. 1–26 and 97–121. Later work by Hempel and others on defining degree of confirmation does not concern us here.

8   [Author's note] I am not here asserting that this is an indispensable requirement upon a definition of confirmation. Since our commonsense assumptions taken in combination quickly lead us to absurd conclusions, some of these assumptions have to be dropped; and different theorists may make different decisions about which to drop and which to preserve. Hempel gives up the converse consequence condition, while Carnap (*Logical Foundations of Probability*, Chicago and London, 1950, pp. 474–76) drops both the consequence condition and the converse consequence condition. Such differences of detail between different treatments of confirmation do not affect the central points I am making in this lecture.

9   A conjunction is an 'and' statement: "A and B." It is a simple law of logic that if "A and B" is true, then "A" must be as well, and so must "B." For example, if "Sharks are fish and whales are mammals" is true, then it follows that the following two sentences must also be true: "Sharks are fish" and "Whales are mammals."

8497 is a prime number and the other side of the moon is flat and Elizabeth the First was crowned on a Tuesday.

To show that any one of the three component statements is true is to support the conjunction by reducing the net undetermined claim. But support[10] of this kind is not confirmation; for establishment of one component endows the whole statement with no credibility that is transmitted to other component statements. Confirmation of a hypothesis occurs only when an instance imparts to the hypothesis some credibility that is conveyed to other instances. Appraisal of hypotheses, indeed, is incidental to prediction, to the judgment of new cases on the basis of old ones.

Our formula thus needs tightening. This is readily accomplished, as Hempel points out, if we observe that a hypothesis is genuinely confirmed only by a statement that is an instance of it in the special sense of entailing not the hypothesis itself but its relativization or restriction to the class of entities mentioned by that statement. The relativization of a general hypothesis to a class results from restricting the range of its universal and existential quantifiers to the members of that class.[11] Less technically, what the hypothesis says of all things the evidence statement says of one thing (or of one pair or other n-ad[12] of things). This obviously covers the confirmation of the conductivity of all copper by the conductivity of a given piece; and it excludes confirmation of our heterogeneous conjunction by any of its components. And, when taken together with the principle that what confirms a statement confirms all its consequences, this criterion does not yield the untoward conclusion that every statement confirms every other.

New difficulties promptly appear from other directions, however. One is the infamous paradox of the ravens. The statement that a given object, say this piece of paper, is neither black nor a raven confirms the hypothesis that all non-black things are non-ravens. But this hypothesis is logically equivalent to the hypothesis that all ravens are black. Hence we arrive at the unexpected conclusion that the statement that a given object is neither black nor a raven confirms the hypothesis that all ravens are black. The prospect of being able to investigate ornithological theories without going out in the rain is so attractive that we know there must be a catch in it. The trouble this time, however, lies not in faulty definition, but in tacit and illicit reference to evidence not stated in our example. Taken by itself, the statement that the given object is neither black nor a raven confirms the hypothesis that everything that is not a raven is not black as well as the hypothesis that everything that is not black is not a raven. We tend to ignore the former hypothesis because we know it to be false from abundant other evidence— from all the familiar things that are not ravens but are black. But we are required to assume that no such evidence is available. Under this circumstance, even a much stronger hypothesis is also obviously confirmed: that nothing is either black or a raven. In the light of this confirmation of the hypothesis that there are no ravens, it is no longer surprising that under the artificial restrictions of the example, the hypothesis that all ravens are black is also confirmed. And the prospects for indoor ornithology vanish when we notice that under these same con-

---

10   [Author's note] Any hypothesis is 'supported' by its own positive instances; but support—or better, direct factual support—is only one factor in confirmation. This factor has been separately studied by John G. Kemeny and Paul Oppenheim in 'Degree of Factual Support', *Philosophy of Science*, vol. 19 (1952), pp. 307–24. As will appear presently, my concern in these lectures is primarily with certain other important factors in confirmation, some of them quite generally neglected.

11   For example, a general hypothesis might be that all plants of the genus *Helleborus* are poisonous to humans; one relativization of this hypothesis would be the claim that this sprig of Christmas Rose which I have in my hand is poisonous to humans. (In this case, we have moved from a claim about *all* the members of the genus *Helleborus* to a claim about *one* member of that genus: that is we have restricted the range of the universal quantifier word "all" in the original hypothesis.)

---

12   For example, a triad (three things), tetrad (four things), etc.

ditions, the contrary hypothesis that no ravens are black is equally well confirmed.[13]

On the other hand, our definition does err in not forcing us to take into account all the stated evidence. The unhappy results are readily illustrated. If two compatible evidence statements confirm two hypotheses, then naturally the conjunction of the evidence statements should confirm the conjunction of the hypotheses.[14] Suppose our evidence consists of the statements E_1 saying that a given thing b is black, and E_2 saying that a second thing c is not black. By our present definition, E_1 confirms the hypothesis that everything is black, and E_2 the hypothesis that everything is non-black. The conjunction of these perfectly compatible evidence statements will then confirm the self-contradictory hypothesis that everything is both black and non-black. Simple as this anomaly is, it requires drastic modification of our definition. What given evidence confirms is not what we arrive at by generalizing from separate items of it, but—roughly speaking—what we arrive at by generalizing from the total stated evidence. The central idea for an improved definition is that, within certain limitations, what is asserted to be true for the narrow universe of the evidence statements is confirmed for the whole universe of discourse.[15] Thus if our evidence is E_1

and E_2, neither the hypothesis that all things are black nor the hypothesis that all things are non-black is confirmed; for neither is true for the evidence-universe consisting of b and c. Of course, much more careful formulation is needed, since some statements that are true of the evidence-universe—such as that there is only one black thing—are obviously not confirmed for the whole universe. These matters are taken care of by the studied formal definition that Hempel develops on this basis; but we cannot and need not go into further detail here.

No one supposes that the task of confirmation-theory has been completed. But the few steps I have reviewed—chosen partly for their bearing on what is to follow—show how things move along once the problem of definition displaces the problem of justification. Important and long-unnoticed questions are brought to light and answered; and we are encouraged to expect that the many remaining questions will in time yield to similar treatment.

But our satisfaction is shortlived. New and serious trouble begins to appear.

4. The New Riddle of Induction

Confirmation of a hypothesis by an instance depends rather heavily upon features of the hypothesis other than its syntactical form. That a given piece of copper conducts electricity increases the credibility of statements asserting that other pieces of copper conduct electricity, and thus confirms the hypothesis that all copper conducts electricity. But the fact that a given man now in this room is a third son does not increase the credibility of statements asserting that other men now in this room are third sons, and so does not confirm the hypothesis that all men now in this room are third sons. Yet in both cases our hypothesis is a generalization of the evidence statement. The difference is that in the former case the hypothesis is a *lawlike* statement; while in the latter case, the hypothesis is a merely contingent or accidental generality. Only a statement that is *lawlike*—regardless of its truth or falsity or its scientific importance—is capable of receiving confirmation from an instance of it; accidental statements are not. Plainly, then, we must look for a way of distinguishing lawlike from accidental statements.

13   [Author's note] An able and thorough exposition of this paragraph is given by Israel Scheffler in his *Anatomy of Inquiry*, New York, 1963, pp. 286–91.

14   [Author's note] The status of the conjunction condition is much like that of the consequence condition—see Note 5 [8 in this text]. Although Carnap drops the conjunction condition also (p. 394), he adopts for different reasons the requirement we find needed above: that the total available evidence must always be taken into account (pp. 211–13).

15   The "universe of discourse" is the collection of things under discussion, whose existence is presupposed by the participants in the discussion. For example, if I say "everyone got ridiculously drunk" then the universe of discourse for our conversation is probably not the whole human race—since not *everybody* in the world got drunk—but, perhaps, the attendees at a particular New Year's Eve party. In science, the universe of discourse is typically the entire physical universe (but not, for example, angels and immaterial souls).

So long as what seems to be needed is merely a way of excluding a few odd and unwanted cases that are inadvertently admitted by our definition of confirmation, the problem may not seem very hard or very pressing. We fully expect that minor defects will be found in our definition and that the necessary refinements will have to be worked out patiently one after another. But some further examples will show that our present difficulty is of a much graver kind.

Suppose that all emeralds examined before a certain time t are green.[16] At time t, then, our observations support the hypothesis that all emeralds are green; and this is in accord with our definition of confirmation. Our evidence statements assert that emerald a is green, that emerald b is green, and so on; and each confirms the general hypothesis that all emeralds are green. So far, so good.

Now let me introduce another predicate less familiar than "green". It is the predicate "grue" and it applies to all things examined before t just in case they are green but to other things just in case they are blue. Then at time t we have, for each evidence statement asserting that a given emerald is green, a parallel evidence statement asserting that that emerald is grue. And the statements that emerald a is grue, that emerald b is grue, and so on, will each confirm the general hypothesis that all emeralds are grue. Thus according to our definition, the prediction that all emeralds subsequently examined will be green and the prediction that all will be grue are alike confirmed by evidence statements describing the same observations. But if an emerald subsequently examined is grue, it is blue and hence not green. Thus although we are well aware which of the two incompatible predictions is genuinely confirmed, they are equally well confirmed according to our present definition. Moreover, it is clear that if we simply choose an appropriate predicate, then on the basis of these same observations we shall have equal confirmation, by our definition, for any prediction whatever about other emeralds—or

indeed about anything else.[17] As in our earlier example, only the predictions subsumed under lawlike hypotheses are genuinely confirmed; but we have no criterion as yet for determining lawlikeness. And now we see that without some such criterion, our definition not merely includes a few unwanted cases, but is so completely ineffectual that it virtually excludes nothing. We are left once again with the intolerable result that anything confirms anything. This difficulty cannot be set aside as an annoying detail to be taken care of in due course. It has to be met before our definition will work at all.

Nevertheless, the difficulty is often slighted because on the surface there seem to be easy ways of dealing with it. Sometimes, for example, the problem is thought to be much like the paradox of the ravens. We are here again, it is pointed out, making tacit and illegitimate use of information outside the stated evidence: the information, for example, that different samples of one material are usually alike in conductivity, and, the information that different men in a lecture audience are usually not alike in the number of their older brothers. But while it is true that such information is being smuggled in, this does not by itself settle the matter as it settles the matter of the ravens. There the point was that when the smuggled information is forthrightly declared, its effect upon the confirmation of the hypothesis in question is immediately and properly registered by the definition we are using. On the other hand, if to our initial evidence we add statements concerning the conductivity of pieces of other materials or concerning the number of older brothers of members of other lecture audiences, this will not in the least

---

16   [Author's note] Although the example used is different, the argument to follow is substantially the same as that set forth in my note 'A Query on Confirmation', *Journal of Philosophy*, vol. xliii (1946), pp. 383–85.

17   [Author's note] For instance, we shall have equal confirmation, by our present definition, for the prediction that roses subsequently examined will be blue. Let "emerose" apply just to emeralds examined before time t, and to roses examined later. Then all emeroses so far examined are grue, and this confirms the hypothesis that all emeroses are grue and hence the prediction that roses subsequently examined will be blue. The problem raised by such antecedents has been little noticed, but is no easier to meet than that raised by similarly perverse consequents.

affect the confirmation, according to our definition, of the hypothesis concerning copper or of that concerning this lecture audience. Since our definition is insensitive to the bearing upon hypotheses of evidence so related to them, even when the evidence is fully declared, the difficulty about accidental hypotheses cannot be explained away on the ground that such evidence is being surreptitiously taken into account.

A more promising suggestion is to explain the matter in terms of the effect of this other evidence not directly upon the hypothesis in question but *in*directly through other hypotheses that *are* confirmed, according to our definition, by such evidence. Our information about other materials does by our definition confirm such hypotheses as that all pieces of iron conduct electricity, that no pieces of rubber do, and so on; and these hypotheses, the explanation runs, impart to the hypothesis that all pieces of copper conduct electricity (and also to the hypothesis that none do) the character of lawlikeness—that is, amenability to confirmation by direct positive instances when found. On the other hand, our information about other lecture audiences *dis*confirms many hypotheses to the effect that all the men in one audience are third sons, or that none are; and this strips any character of lawlikeness from the hypothesis that all (or the hypothesis that none) of the men in *this* audience are third sons. But clearly if this course is to be followed, the circumstances under which hypotheses are thus related to one another will have to be precisely articulated.

The problem, then, is to define the relevant way in which such hypotheses must be alike. Evidence for the hypothesis that all iron conducts electricity enhances the lawlikeness of the hypothesis that all zirconium conducts electricity, but does not similarly affect the hypothesis that all the objects on my desk conduct electricity. Wherein lies the difference? The first two hypotheses fall under the broader hypothesis—call it "*H*"—that every class of things of the same material is uniform in conductivity; the first and third fall only under some such hypothesis as—call it "*K*"—that every class of things that are either all of the same material or all on a desk is uniform in conductivity. Clearly the important difference here is that evidence

for a statement affirming that one of the classes covered by *H* has the property in question increases the credibility of any statement affirming that another such class has this property; while nothing of the sort holds true with respect to *K*. But this is only to say that *H* is lawlike and *K* is not. We are faced anew with the very problem we are trying to solve: the problem of distinguishing between lawlike and accidental hypotheses.

The most popular way of attacking the problem takes its cue from the fact that accidental hypotheses seem typically to involve some spatial or temporal restriction, or reference to some particular individual. They seem to concern the people in some particular room, or the objects on some particular person's desk; while lawlike hypotheses characteristically concern all ravens or all pieces of copper whatsoever. Complete generality is thus very often supposed to be a sufficient condition of lawlikeness; but to define this complete generality is by no means easy. Merely to require that the hypothesis contain no term naming, describing, or indicating a particular thing or location will obviously not be enough. The troublesome hypothesis that all emeralds are grue contains no such term; and where such a term does occur, as in hypotheses about men in *this room*, it can be suppressed in favor of some predicate (short or long, new or old) that contains no such term but applies only to exactly the same things. One might think, then, of excluding not only hypotheses that actually contain terms for specific individuals but also all hypotheses that are equivalent to others that do contain such terms. But, as we have just seen, to exclude only hypotheses of which *all* equivalents contain such terms is to exclude nothing. On the other hand, to exclude all hypotheses that have *some* equivalent containing such a term is to exclude everything; for even the hypothesis

All grass is green

has as an equivalent

All grass in London or elsewhere is green.

The next step, therefore, has been to consider ruling out predicates of certain kinds. A syntactically universal hypothesis is lawlike, the proposal runs, if its predicates are 'purely qualitative' or 'non-positional'.[18] This will obviously accomplish nothing if a purely qualitative predicate is then conceived either as one that is equivalent to some expression free of terms for specific individuals, or as one that is equivalent to no expression that contains such a term; for this only raises again the difficulties just pointed out. The claim appears to be rather that at least in the case of a simple enough predicate we can readily determine by direct inspection of its meaning whether or not it is purely qualitative. But even aside from obscurities in the notion of 'the meaning' of a predicate, this claim seems to me wrong. I simply do not know how to tell whether a predicate is qualitative or positional, except perhaps by completely begging the question at issue and asking whether the predicate is 'well-behaved'—that is, whether simple syntactically universal hypotheses applying it are lawlike.

This statement will not go unprotested. "Consider", it will be argued, "the predicates 'blue' and 'green' and the predicate 'grue' introduced earlier, and also the predicate 'bleen' that applies to emeralds examined before time *t* just in case they are blue and to other emeralds just in case they are green. Surely it is clear", the argument runs, "that the first two are purely qualitative and the second two are not; for the meaning of each of the latter two plainly involves reference to a specific temporal position." To this I reply that indeed I do recognize the first two as well-behaved predicates admissible in lawlike hypotheses, and the second two as ill-behaved predicates. But the argument that the former but not the latter are purely qualitative seems to me quite unsound. True enough, if we start with "blue" and "green", then "grue" and "bleen" will be explained in terms of "blue" and "green" and a temporal term. But equally truly, if we

start with "grue" and "bleen", then "blue" and "green" will be explained in terms of "grue" and "bleen" and a temporal term; "green", for example, applies to emeralds examined before time *t* just in case they are grue, and to other emeralds just in case they are bleen. Thus qualitativeness is an entirely relative matter and does not by itself establish any dichotomy of predicates. This relativity seems to be completely overlooked by those who contend that the qualitative character of a predicate is a criterion for its good behavior.

Of course, one may ask why we need worry about such unfamiliar predicates as "grue" or about accidental hypotheses in general, since we are unlikely to use them in making predictions. If our definition works for such hypotheses as are normally employed, isn't that all we need? In a sense, yes; but only in the sense that we need no definition, no theory of induction, and no philosophy of knowledge at all. We get along well enough without them in daily life and in scientific research. But if we seek a theory at all, we cannot excuse gross anomalies resulting from a proposed theory by pleading that we can avoid them in practice. The odd cases we have been considering are clinically pure cases that, though seldom encountered in practice, nevertheless display to best advantage the symptoms of a widespread and destructive malady.

We have so far neither any answer nor any promising clue to an answer to the question what distinguishes lawlike or confirmable hypotheses from accidental or non-confirmable ones; and what may at first have seemed a minor technical difficulty has taken on the stature of a major obstacle to the development of a satisfactory theory of confirmation. It is this problem that I call the new riddle of induction.

5. The Pervasive Problem of Projection

At the beginning of this lecture, I expressed the opinion that the problem of induction is still unsolved, but that the difficulties that face us today are not the old ones; and I have tried to outline the changes that have taken place. The problem of justifying induction has been displaced by the problem of defining confirmation, and our work upon this has left us with the residual problem of distinguishing between confirmable and non-confirmable hypotheses. One might say roughly that the first question was "Why does a

18   [Author's note] Carnap took this course in his paper 'On the Application of Inductive Logic', *Philosophy and Phenomenological Research*, vol. 8 (1947), pp. 133–47, which is in part a reply to my 'A Query on Confirmation', cited in Note 9 [16 in this text]. The discussion was continued in my note 'On Infirmities of Confirmation Theory', *Philosophy and Phenomenological Research*, vol. 8 (1947), pp. 149–51; and in Carnap's 'Reply to Nelson Goodman', same journal, same volume, pp. 461–62.

positive instance of a hypothesis give any grounds for predicting further instances?"; that the newer question was "What is a positive instance of a hypothesis?"; and that the crucial remaining question is "What hypotheses are confirmed by their positive instances?"

The vast amount of effort expended on the problem of induction in modern times has thus altered our afflictions but hardly relieved them. The original difficulty about induction arose from the recognition that anything may follow upon anything. Then, in attempting to define confirmation in terms of the converse of the consequence relation, we found ourselves with the distressingly similar difficulty that our definition would make any statement confirm any other. And now, after modifying our definition drastically, we still get the old devastating result that any statement will confirm any statement. Until we find a way of exercising some control over the hypotheses to be admitted, our definition makes no distinction whatsoever between valid and invalid inductive inferences.

The real inadequacy of Hume's account lay not in his descriptive approach but in the imprecision of his description. Regularities in experience, according to him, give rise to habits of expectation; and thus it is predictions conforming to past regularities that are normal or valid. But Hume overlooks the fact that some regularities do and some do not establish such habits; that predictions based on some regularities are valid while predictions based on other regularities are not. Every word you have heard me say has occurred prior to the final sentence of this lecture; but that does not, I hope, create any expectation that every word you will hear me say will be prior to that sentence. Again, consider our case of emeralds. All those examined before time *t* are green; and this leads us to expect, and confirms the prediction, that the next one will be green. But also, all those examined are grue; and this does not lead us to expect, and does not confirm the prediction, that the next one will be grue. Regularity in greenness confirms the prediction of

further cases; regularity in grueness does not. To say that valid predictions are those based on past regularities, without being able to say *which* regularities, is thus quite pointless. Regularities are where you find them, and you can find them anywhere. As we have seen, Hume's failure to recognize and deal with this problem has been shared even by his most recent successors.

As a result, what we have in current confirmation theory is a definition that is adequate for certain cases that so far can be described only as those for which it is adequate. The theory works where it works. A hypothesis is confirmed by statements related to it in the prescribed way provided it is so confirmed. This is a good deal like having a theory that tells us that the area of a plane figure is one-half the base times the altitude, without telling us for what figures this holds. We must somehow find a way of distinguishing lawlike hypotheses, to which our definition of confirmation applies, from accidental hypotheses, to which it does not.

Today I have been speaking solely of the problem of induction, but what has been said applies equally to the more general problem of projection. As pointed out earlier, the problem of prediction from past to future cases is but a narrower version of the problem of projecting from any set of cases to others. We saw that a whole cluster of troublesome problems concerning dispositions and possibility can be reduced to this problem of projection. That is why the new riddle of induction, which is more broadly the problem of distinguishing between projectible and non-projectible hypotheses, is as important as it is exasperating.

Our failures teach us, I think, that lawlike or projectible hypotheses cannot be distinguished on any merely syntactical grounds or even on the ground that these hypotheses are somehow purely general in meaning. Our only hope lies in re-examining the problem once more and looking for some new approach. This will be my course in the final lecture.

CARL HEMPEL
"Scientific Inquiry: Invention and Test"

Who Was Carl Hempel?

Carl Gustav ('Peter') Hempel—probably, with Popper and Kuhn, one of the three most influential philosophers of science of the twentieth century—was born in 1905 in Orianenberg, near Berlin, Germany. After attending high school in Berlin, at eighteen he went to study mathematics and logic at the University of Göttingen with the famous mathematician David Hilbert. Although Hempel quickly fell in love with mathematical logic, he left Göttingen within the year to study at the University of Heidelberg, and then in 1924 moved back to Berlin where he studied physics with Hans Reichenbach and Max Planck, and logic with John von Neumann (all destined to become towering figures in their fields). Reichenbach introduced him to the members of a group of intellectuals called the Berlin Circle, and in 1929 Hempel took part in the historic first congress on scientific philosophy in Prague, organized by the founders of an important twentieth-century philosophical movement called 'logical positivism.' At that conference Hempel met the philosopher of science Rudolf Carnap, and was so impressed by him that he moved to Carnap's home town of Vienna, Austria; there, he attended classes by the logical positivists Carnap, Moritz Schlick, and Friedrich Waismann and took part in meetings of the 'Vienna Circle.'

The Vienna and Berlin Circles of the 1920s and early 1930s were fairly informal, diverse, collaborative groups of "scientifically interested philosophers and philosophically interested scientists," as Hempel once put it. The members of these groups, especially the Vienna Circle, thought of themselves as decisively breaking with the past and founding a new, more effective kind of philosophical enterprise—a 'modern scientific philosophy' built on the new techniques of logical analysis and modeled on the successful empirical methods of the exact sciences. The past history of philosophy, the new 'logical empiricists' or 'logical positivists' declared, was one of fruitless strife; by contrast, in Hempel's words, "the Vienna Circle held that the purported problems of metaphysics constitute no genuine problems at all and that in an inquiry making use of an appropriately precise conceptual and linguistic apparatus, metaphysical questions could not even be formulated. They were pseudoproblems, devoid of any clear meaning."

In 1934—just a week before Adolf Hitler anointed himself *Führer* of the German Third Reich—Hempel completed his PhD from the University of Berlin, with a dissertation on probability theory. In the previous year, shortly after Hitler was elected Chancellor of Germany, Hempel's supervisor Hans Reichenbach had been summarily dismissed from his Berlin chair because his father had been Jewish; Hempel himself was of pure 'Aryan' stock, but his wife Eva Ahrends had partly 'Jewish blood' and Hempel was frequently accused of the offense of "philosemitism," sympathy with the Jews. As a consequence, in 1934, Hempel fled Germany to Belgium, where he and Eva were supported by his friend and colleague Paul Oppenheim.

In 1937, because of Carnap's influence, Hempel was invited to become a Rockefeller research associate in philosophy at the University of Chicago, and Hempel officially emigrated to the United States in 1939. Between 1939 and 1948 Hempel taught at City College and Queens College in New York; during these years, Hempel's wife Eva died shortly after giving birth to a son, and Hempel married his second wife, Diane Perlow. In 1948 he moved to Yale University, and in 1955 he was made Stuart Professor of Philosophy at Princeton, a post he held until his mandatory 'retirement' at age 68 in 1973. Even after his retirement, Hempel continued to lecture at Princeton and then, as a visiting professor, at Jerusalem, Berkeley, Carleton College, and Pittsburgh; in 1977 (at the age of 72) he was made University Professor of Philosophy at the University of Pittsburgh, a post he held until 1985. Hempel died at Princeton, New Jersey, in 1997.

In a tribute to him after his death, the well-known Princeton logician Richard Jeffrey wrote of Hempel:

> There was no arrogance in him; he got no thrill of pleasure from proving people wrong. His criticisms were always courteous, never triumphant. This quality was deeply rooted in his character. He was made so as to welcome opportunities for kindness, generosity, courtesy; and he gave his whole mind to such projects spontaneously, for pleasure, so that effort disappeared into zest. [His wife] Diane was another such player. (Once, in a restaurant, someone remarked on their politeness to each other, and she said, "Ah, but you should see us when we are alone together. [Pause] Then we are *really* polite.") And play it was, too. He was notably playful and incapable of stuffiness.

Hempel is commonly credited with a leading role in developing the account of scientific explanation and prediction which came to be labeled the 'Received View' by its critics in the last few decades of the twentieth century. (A more technical name for a central plank of this view is the *deductive-nomological* [D-N] or *covering law* model of scientific explanation.) According to this theory, the scientific explanation of a fact consists in the logical *deduction* of a statement that describes the fact (often called the 'explanan-

dum'), from premises (the 'explanans') which include true scientific laws and statements of initial conditions. For example, a simple scientific explanation for why this piece of copper conducts electricity is that my bit of copper is 'covered' by a general law which says that *all* copper conducts electricity under certain circumstances. In this case, the sentence (1) "This copper conducts electricity" is a *logical consequence* of the statements (2) "All copper conducts electricity under conditions C (e.g., the copper is pure, the metal is within a certain temperature range, etc.)" and (3) "Conditions C presently hold for this bit of copper"; according to Hempel, this logical relationship is why (2) and (3) count as *explaining* (1).

Furthermore, according to Hempel, scientific *prediction* turns out to be just the flip-side of explanation. One can start from an observation, and show that a certain theory *explains* that observation because the observation is deducible from the theory; or one can start with a theory, and show that the theory *predicts* some set of observations because they are logical consequences of the theory being true. Either way, in Hempel's view, the essential logical relationship between statements of laws and statements of observations is the same.

When it comes to the issue of *confirming* which scientific laws are true and which are not (i.e., which can feature in good explanations), one of the things Hempel is best known for is formulating, in 1945, 'Hempel's paradox' (also known as the paradox of the ravens, or the paradox of confirmation). This puzzle calls into question the intuitive assumption that a general law is confirmed only by instances of that law—for example, the idea that the claim that "All ravens are black" is supported by observations of black ravens but not at all by the sighting of a blue jay. Here is the paradox. Suppose I see a white running shoe; this is an instance of the general claim that all non-black things are non-ravens (since a white shoe is neither black nor a raven). Therefore, it appears that my shoe sighting is some evidence for the claim that all non-black things are non-ravens. But "all non-black things are non-ravens" is logically equivalent to "all ravens are black." Thus it turns out that—if our intuitive understanding of induction is correct—observations of white shoes (and blue jays, etc.) do in fact partially confirm the hypothesis that all ravens are black. But this seems absurd—it seems ridiculous to think that we could find out about birds by examining footwear; hence the paradox.

Various attempts have been made to deal with this puzzle. Hempel himself proposed that we resolve the paradox by accepting its apparently absurd conclusion: he held that *all* observations are relevant to any hypothesis, though some of them (such as sightings of white shoes) confirm it only much more weakly than others (sightings of black ravens).

What Is the Structure of This Reading?

In this reading Hempel argues that the traditional, or 'narrow inductivist,' view is incorrect, and argues that it should be replaced in our understanding of science by what he calls the 'method of hypothesis.'

Questions for Further Thought

1. "What particular sorts of data it is reasonable to collect is not determined by the problem under study, but by a tentative answer to it that the investigator entertains in the form of a conjecture or hypothesis." Do you agree? What implications would this have for the working practice of scientists?

2. According to Hempel, there can be no possible mechanical rules for generating inductive generalizations from sets of data; that is, as it is sometimes put, there is no 'logic of discovery.' What are Hempel's reasons for claiming this, and are they persuasive? Even if there are no mechanical methods for scientific discovery, might there nevertheless be some useful non-mechanical methods—and if so, what might these look like?

3. Hempel suggests that, although induction is not a useful method for generating hypotheses, it is important for assessing how well supported a theory is by the evidence. How vulnerable does this make Hempel to the kind of skepticism about induction argued for by David Hume (see the Hume reading in this chapter)?

Suggestions for Further Reading

Philosophy of Natural Science (Prentice-Hall, 1966), from which this selection is taken, is still in print and, though a short book, is considered a useful encapsulation of Hempel's philosophy of science and of the 'received view' in general; it is well worth reading. Several of Hempel's most important and influential papers are contained in *Aspects of Scientific Explanation, and Other Essays in the Philosophy of Science* (Free Press, 1965) and in the more recent anthology *The Philosophy of Carl G. Hempel: Studies in Science, Explanation, and Rationality*, edited by James Fetzer (Oxford University Press, 2000). *Selected Philosophical Essays*, edited by Richard Jeffrey (Cambridge University Press, 2000), fills this out with papers from Hempel's earlier and later philosophical phases.

Science, Explanation, and Rationality: The Philosophy of Carl G. Hempel, edited by James Fetzer (Oxford University Press, 2000), is a collection of essays about Hempel's work. Three good works of philosophy of science which address Hempel's work on explanation and confirmation are Wesley C. Salmon's *Four Decades of Scientific Explanation* (University of Minnesota Press, 1990), Israel Scheffler's *The Anatomy of Inquiry* (Hackett, 1982), and Frederick Suppe's *The Structure of Scientific Theories* (University of Illinois Press, 1979).

from "Scientific Inquiry: Invention and Test"[1]

The Role of Induction in Scientific Inquiry

We have considered some scientific investigations in which a problem was tackled by proposing tentative answers in the form of hypotheses that were then tested by deriving from them suitable test implications and checking these by observation or experiment.

But how are suitable hypotheses arrived at in the first place? It is sometimes held that they are inferred from antecedently collected data by means of a procedure called *inductive inference*, as contradistinguished

---

1   From *Philosophy of Natural Science*, 1st Edition, © 1967; pp. 10–15. Reprinted by permission of Pearson Education, Inc., Upper Saddle River, NJ.

from deductive inference, from which it differs in important respects.

In a deductively valid argument, the conclusion is related to the premisses in such a way that if the premisses are true then the conclusion cannot fail to be true as well. This requirement is satisfied, for example, by any argument of the following general form:

> If p, then q.
> It is not the case that q.
> It is not the case that p.

Brief reflection shows that no matter what particular statements may stand at the places marked by the letters 'p' and 'q', the conclusion will certainly be true if the premisses are. In fact, our schema represents the argument form called *modus tollens*....

Another type of deductively valid inference is illustrated by this example:

> Any sodium salt, when put into the flame of a Bunsen burner,[2] turns the flame yellow.
> This piece of rock salt is a sodium salt.
> This piece of rock salt, when put into the flame of a Bunsen burner, will turn the flame yellow.

Arguments of the latter kind are often said to lead from the general (here, the premiss about all sodium salts) to the particular (a conclusion about the particular piece of rock salt). Inductive inferences, by contrast, are sometimes described as leading from premisses about particular cases to a conclusion that has the character of a general law or principle. For example, from premisses to the effect that each of the particular samples of various sodium salts that have so far been subjected to the Bunsen flame test did turn the flame yellow, inductive inference supposedly leads to the general conclusion that all sodium salts, when put into the flame of a Bunsen burner, turn the flame yellow. But in this case, the truth of the premisses obviously does *not* guarantee the truth of the conclusion; for even if it is the case that all samples

of sodium salts examined so far did turn the Bunsen flame yellow, it remains quite possible that new kinds of sodium salt might yet be found that do not conform to this generalization. Indeed, even some kinds of sodium salt that have already been tested with positive result might conceivably fail to satisfy the generalization under special physical conditions (such as very strong magnetic fields or the like) in which they have not yet been examined. For this reason, the premisses of an inductive inference are often said to imply the conclusion only with more or less high probability, whereas the premisses of a deductive inference imply the conclusion with certainty.

The idea that in scientific inquiry, inductive inference from antecedently collected data leads to appropriate general principles is clearly embodied in the following account of how a scientist would ideally proceed:

> If we try to imagine how a mind of superhuman power and reach, but normal so far as the logical processes of its thought are concerned, ... would use the scientific method, the process would be as follows: First, all facts would be observed and recorded, *without selection or a priori* guess as to their relative importance. Secondly, the observed and recorded facts would be analyzed, compared, and classified, *without hypothesis or postulates* other than those necessarily involved in the logic of thought. Third, from this analysis of the facts generalizations would be inductively drawn as to the relations, classificatory or causal, between them. Fourth, further research would be deductive as well as inductive, employing inferences from previously established generalizations.[3]

This passage distinguishes four stages in an ideal scientific inquiry: (1) observation and recording of all facts, (2) analysis and classification of these facts,

---

2   A common piece of laboratory equipment that produces an adjustable gas flame.

3   [Author's note] A.B. Wolfe, "Functional Economics," in *The Trend of Economics*, ed. R.G. Tugwell (New York: Alfred A. Knopf, Inc., 1924), p. 450 (italics are quoted).

(3) inductive derivation of generalizations from them, and (4) further testing of the generalizations. The first two of these stages are specifically assumed not to make use of any guesses or hypotheses as to how the observed facts might be interconnected; this restriction seems to have been imposed in the belief that such preconceived ideas would introduce a bias and would jeopardize the scientific objectivity of the investigation.

But the view expressed in the quoted passage—I will call it *the narrow inductivist conception of scientific inquiry*—is untenable, for several reasons....

First, our scientific investigation as here envisaged could never get off the ground. Even its first phase could never be carried out, for a collection of *all* the facts would have to await the end of the world, so to speak; and even all the facts *up to now* cannot be collected, since there are an infinite number and variety of them. Are we to examine, for example, all the grains of sand in all the deserts and on all the beaches, and are we to record their shapes, their weights, their chemical composition, their distances from each other, their constantly changing temperature, and their equally changing distance from the center of the moon? Are we to record the floating thoughts that cross our minds in the tedious process? The shapes of the clouds overhead, the changing color of the sky? The construction and the trade name of our writing equipment? Our own life histories and those of our fellow investigators? All these, and untold other things, are, after all, among "all the facts up to now".

Perhaps, then, all that should be required in the first phase is that all the *relevant* facts be collected. But relevant to what? Though the author does not mention this, let us suppose that the inquiry is concerned with a specified *problem*. Should we not then begin by collecting all the facts—or better, all available data—relevant to that problem? This notion still makes no clear sense. Semmelweis sought to solve one specific problem, yet he collected quite different kinds of data at different stages of his inquiry.[4] And rightly so; for

what particular sorts of data it is reasonable to collect is not determined by the problem under study, but by a tentative answer to it that the investigator entertains in the form of a conjecture or hypothesis. Given the conjecture that mortality from childbed fever was increased by the terrifying appearance of the priest and his attendant with the death bell, it was relevant to collect data on the consequences of having the priest change his routine; but it would have been totally irrelevant to check what would happen if doctors and students disinfected their hands before examining their patients. With respect to Semmelweis' eventual contamination hypothesis, data of the latter kind were clearly relevant, and those of the former kind totally irrelevant.

Empirical "facts" or findings, therefore, can be qualified as logically relevant or irrelevant only in reference to a given hypothesis, but not in reference to a given problem.

Suppose now that a hypothesis H has been advanced as a tentative answer to a research problem: what kinds of data would be relevant to H? Our earlier examples suggest an answer: A finding is relevant to H if either its occurrence or its nonoccurrence can be inferred from H. Take Torricelli's hypothesis, for example.[5] As we saw, Pascal[6] inferred from it that the mercury column in a barometer should grow shorter if the barometer were carried up a mountain. Therefore, any finding to the effect that this did indeed happen in a particular case is relevant to the hypotheses; but so would be the finding that the length of the mercury column had remained unchanged or that it had decreased

4   Hempel is referring here to a case study he described earlier: that of the Viennese doctor Ignaz Semmelweis who in the mid-nineteenth century discovered that incidences of childbed fever—a major cause of death

in young mothers at that time—could be drastically reduced by disinfecting the hands of the attending doctors.

5   This is also a reference to an earlier case study. Evangelista Torricelli (1608–1647) hypothesized that the earth is surrounded by a sea of air which exerts pressure on the surface below because of its weight; thus, the higher that one is off the ground the less downward pressure the atmosphere would exert (because the less air there is above one pushing down).

6   Blaise Pascal (1623–1662) was a French mathematician and physicist.

and then increased during the ascent, for such findings would refute Pascal's test implication and would thus disconfirm Torricelli's hypothesis. Data of the former kind may be called positively, or favorably, relevant to the hypothesis; those of the latter kind negatively, or unfavorably, relevant.

In sum, the maxim that data should be gathered without guidance by antecedent hypotheses about the connections among the facts under study is self-defeating, and it is certainly not followed in scientific inquiry. On the contrary, tentative hypotheses are needed to give direction to a scientific investigation. Such hypotheses determine, among other things, what data should be collected at a given point in a scientific investigation.

...

The second stage envisaged in our quoted passage is open to similar criticism. A set of empirical "facts" can be analyzed and classified in many different ways, most of which will be unilluminating for the purposes of a given inquiry. Semmelweis could have classified the women in the maternity wards according to criteria such as age, place of residence, marital status, dietary habits, and so forth; but information on these would have provided no clue to a patient's prospects of becoming a victim of childbed fever. What Semmelweis sought were criteria that would be significantly connected with those prospects; and for this purpose, as he eventually found, it was illuminating to single out those women who were attended by medical personnel with contaminated hands; for it was with this characteristic, or with the corresponding class of patients, that high mortality from childbed fever was associated.

Thus, if a particular way of analyzing and classifying empirical findings is to lead to an explanation of the phenomena concerned, then it must be based on hypotheses about how those phenomena are connected; without such hypotheses, analysis and classification are blind.

Our critical reflections on the first two stages of inquiry as envisaged in the quoted passage also undercut the notion that hypotheses are introduced only in the third stage, by inductive inference from antecedently collected data. But some further remarks on the subject should be added here.

Induction is sometimes conceived as a method that leads, by means of mechanically applicable rules, from observed facts to corresponding general principles. In this case, the rules of inductive inference would provide effective canons of scientific discovery; induction would be a mechanical procedure analogous to the familiar routine for the multiplication of integers, which leads, in a finite number of predetermined and mechanically performable steps, to the corresponding product. Actually, however, no such general and mechanical induction procedure is available at present; otherwise, the much studied problem of the causation of cancer, for example, would hardly have remained unsolved to this day. Nor can the discovery of such a procedure ever be expected. For—to mention one reason—scientific hypotheses and theories are usually couched in terms that do not occur at all in the description of the empirical findings on which they rest, and which they serve to explain. For example, theories about the atomic and subatomic structure of matter contain terms such as 'atom', 'electron', 'proton', 'neutron', 'psi-function', etc.; yet they are based on laboratory findings about the spectra of various gases, tracks in cloud and bubble chambers, quantitative aspects of chemical reactions, and so forth—all of which can be described without the use of those "theoretical terms". Induction rules of the kind here envisaged would therefore have to provide a mechanical routine for constructing, on the basis of the given data, a hypothesis or theory stated in terms of some quite novel concepts, which are nowhere used in the description of the data themselves. Surely, no general mechanical rule of procedure can be expected to achieve this. Could there be a general rule, for example, which, when applied to the data available to Galileo concerning the limited effectiveness of suction pumps, would, by a mechanical routine, produce a hypothesis based on the concept of a sea of air?

To be sure, mechanical procedures for inductively "inferring" a hypothesis on the basis of given data may be specifiable for situations of special, and relatively simple, kinds. For example, if the length of a copper rod has been measured at several different temperatures, the resulting pairs of associated values for temperature and length may be represented by points in a plane coordinate system, and a curve may be drawn through them in accordance with some particular rule of curve fitting. The curve then graphically represents a general quantitative hypothesis that expresses the length of the rod as a specific function of its temperature. But note that this hypothesis contains no novel terms; it is expressible in terms of the concepts of temperature and length, which are used also in describing the data. Moreover, the choice of "associated" values of temperature and length as data already presupposes a guiding hypothesis; namely, that with each value of the temperature, exactly one value of the length of the copper rod is associated, so that its length is indeed a function of its temperature alone. The mechanical curve-fitting routine then serves only to select a particular function as the appropriate one. This point is important; for suppose that instead of a copper rod, we examine a body of nitrogen gas enclosed in a cylindrical container with a movable piston as a lid, and that we measure its volume at several different temperatures. If we were to use this procedure in an effort to obtain from our data a *general* hypothesis representing the volume of the gas as a function of its temperature, we would fail, because the volume of a gas is a function both of its temperature and of the pressure exerted upon it, so that at the same temperature, the given gas may assume different volumes.

Thus, even in these simple cases, the mechanical procedures for the construction of a hypothesis do only part of the job, for they presuppose an antecedent, less specific hypothesis (i.e., that a certain physical variable is a function of one single other variable), which is not obtainable by the same procedure.

There are, then, no generally applicable "rules of induction", by which hypotheses or theories can be mechanically derived or inferred from empirical data. The transition from data to theory requires creative imagination. Scientific hypotheses and theories are not *derived* from observed facts, but *invented* in order to account for them. They constitute guesses at the connections that might obtain between the phenomena under study, at uniformities and patterns that might underlie their occurrence. "Happy guesses"[7] of this kind require great ingenuity, especially if they involve a radical departure from current modes of scientific thinking, as did, for example, the theory of relativity and quantum theory. The inventive effort required in scientific research will benefit from a thorough familiarity with current knowledge in the field. A complete novice will hardly make an important scientific discovery, for the ideas that may occur to him are likely to duplicate what has been tried before or to run afoul of well-established facts or theories of which he is not aware.

---

7   [Author's note] This characterization was given already by William Whewell in his work *The Philosophy of the Inductive Sciences*, 2nd ed. (London: John W. Parker, 1847); II, 41. Whewell also speaks of "invention" as "part of induction" (p. 46). In the same vein, K. Popper refers to scientific hypotheses and theories as "conjectures"; see, for example, the essay "Science: Conjectures and Refutations" in his book, *Conjectures and Refutations* (New York and London: Basic Books, 1962). Indeed, A.B. Wolfe, whose narrowly inductivist conception of ideal scientific procedure was quoted earlier, stresses that "the limited human mind" has to use "a greatly modified procedure", requiring scientific imagination and the selection of data on the basis of some "working hypothesis" (p. 450 of the essay cited [above]).

KARL POPPER

"Science: Conjectures and Refutations"

Who Was Karl Popper?

Though Popper's reputation has perhaps waned somewhat since its peak in the 1970s, he is still generally considered one among a small handful of the greatest philosophers of science of the twentieth century. In his day he found a fervent following among prominent scientists such as Peter Medawar (a Nobel Prize winner for medicine, who in 1972 called him "incomparably the greatest philosopher of science that has ever been"), neuroscientist John Eccles (another Nobel laureate, who urged his fellow scientists "to read and meditate upon Popper's writings on the philosophy of science and to adopt them as the basis of one's scientific life"), and mathematician and astronomer Hermann Bondi

(who once stated, "There is no more to science than its method, and there is no more to its method that Popper has said").

Karl Raimund Popper was born in 1902 in Vienna, Austria, to Jewish parents who had converted to Protestantism. His parents were intellectual (his father's library is said to have contained 15,000 volumes) and financially comfortable until rampant inflation in Austria after World War I reduced his family to near-poverty. In his early and middle teens Popper was a Marxist, and then—after witnessing the appalling bloodshed of a brief Communist coup in neighboring Hungary—he became an enthusiastic and active Social Democrat. Vienna after the First World War was a city bubbling over with revolutionary new move-

ments and ideas, and, for Popper, it was a thrilling time and place to be young. As well as studying science and philosophy, Popper was involved with left-wing politics, social work with children, and also the Society for Private Concerts founded by the revolutionary atonal composer Arnold Schönberg (throughout his life, Popper had a great love of music).

During and after his education (he received his PhD in 1928), Popper worked as a schoolteacher in mathematics and physics, and occasionally as a cabinet-maker, but continued to pursue his interest in philosophy. However his ideas were then, as for most of his career, out of tune with contemporary philosophical fashions: Otto Neurath, a member of the "Vienna Circle" of philosophers active during the 1920s and 1930s, nicknamed him "the Official Opposition" for his arguments against the then-dominant philosophy of logical positivism. In 1934 Popper published his first book, *Logik der Forschung*—a heavily edited version of a book originally twice as long—which attacked the main ideas of the logical positivists. This book was later translated into English and published as *The Logic of Scientific Discovery* (1959).

In the 1930s, the Communists and other left wing parties in Austria, Germany, and Italy failed to effectively oppose the rise to power of fascism (believing it to be the last gasp of capitalism before the inevitable Communist revolution, and so offering only a half-hearted resistance) and Popper—accurately foretelling the annexation of Austria by Nazi Germany and the onset of a second European war—fled with his wife to New Zealand. There, from 1937 until 1945, he taught philosophy at the University of Canterbury, at Christchurch. He spent this period teaching himself Greek so he could study the Greek philosophers, and writing *The Open Society and its Enemies* (published in 1943) which, through a critique of the political theories of Plato and Marx, defends the idea of liberty and democracy against that of totalitarianism. Popper considered this to be his contribution to the war against fascism.

According to Popper, no political ideology (either on the political right or the left) can justify large-scale social engineering—it is simply impossible to formulate a demonstrably true, predictive theory of society, and so we should never act as if we alone have the key to the truth about human nature. The proper function of social institutions in an "open society"—one in which any regime can be ousted without violence—is not large-scale utopian planning but, according to Popper, piecemeal reform with the object of minimizing, as much as possible, avoidable suffering. This way, the effectiveness of each small piece of legislation can be publicly assessed, and the society can move forward collectively after learning from its mistakes.

In 1946 Popper moved to England, where he was to live until his death in 1994. Despite his growing reputation (he was knighted in 1965), Popper was never offered a position at either Oxford or Cambridge[1] and he spent the rest of his career as a professor at the London School of Economics, still out of sync with the philosophical tendencies of the day which, during those years in England, were predominantly towards "linguistic" philosophy. Popper was impatient with endless discussion about the meanings of words, and denied that exact precision of terminology was either possible or desirable in science. Popper argued that a

language is an instrument and what matters is what you *do* with that instrument; philosophers who devote their lives exclusively to the analysis of language are, as Bryan Magee has put it, like carpenters who devote all their time to sharpening their tools, but never use them except on each other. Popper wrote in the preface to *The Logic of Scientific Discovery*:

> Language analysts believe that there are no genuine philosophical problems, or that the problems of philosophy, if any, are problems of linguistic usage, or of the meaning of words. I, however, believe that there is at least one problem in which all thinking men are interested. It is the problem of cosmology: *the problem of understanding the world—including ourselves, and our knowledge, as part of the world*. All science is cosmology, I believe, and for me the interest of philosophy, no less than of science, lies solely in the contributions which it has made to it.

Popper's main contribution to the philosophy of science is his proposal of a solution to the 'problem of induction,' which involves the rejection of the previously orthodox view of the scientific method and its replacement with another. The essay reprinted here, "Science: Conjectures and Refutations," is an excellent (and in itself quite influential) summary of these arguments.

What Is the Structure of This Reading?

This article is Popper's own summary of his most important work in the philosophy of science. He begins by laying out the problem which he first became interested in: the problem of the *demarcation* between science and pseudo-science (i.e., of finding a criterion for what makes something a properly scientific theory). By comparing Einstein's relativity theory (an example of science) with the psychoanalytic theories of Freud and Adler (examples of pseudo-science), Popper argues that the proper mark of a scientific theory is its *falsifiability*. In section II Popper goes on to criticize the *ad hoc* modifications of Marxism by Marx's followers that rendered the theory unfalsifiable. However, Popper then takes pains to point out that he does not consider pseudo-scientific theories—or "myths" as he calls them—to be either useless or meaningless. In

---

1   This may have been partly to do with his combative personality. Despite advocating risky conjectures and public refutations, by all accounts Popper was a touchy character, quick to express scorn for those who doubted his ideas. On one famous occasion, at the Moral Sciences Club in Cambridge, he almost came to blows with Ludwig Wittgenstein and—legend has it—had to be restrained by Bertrand Russell (upon which, Wittgenstein stormed out of the room).

section III he contrasts his falsificationism (which is a theory of demarcation and not of meaning) with the logical positivist's "verificationist" account of *meaning*, which did famously entail that all non-science is literally meaningless.

In section IV Popper begins his discussion of the problem of induction. After laying out Hume's description of the problem (see the Hume reading in this chapter), he critiques Hume's psychologistic solution to the problem and uses this critique to motivate his own alternative account: the method of trial and error, or *conjectures and refutations*. In section V Popper suggests that this method of "trial and error" is ultimately rooted in the evolution of the human mind, and he contrasts his views with Kant's doctrine of the *synthetic a priori* (see the Kant reading in Chapter 2). Like Kant, Popper introduces a distinction between *dogmatic* and *critical* thinking, and in section VII he suggests that the scientific, critical attitude has evolved through human history from a pre-scientific dogmatism.

In section VIII Popper turns his attention to the "logic of science," and argues that it is simply a mistake to think that the scientific method is inductive: in fact, Popper asserts, real science proceeds by the method of conjecture and refutation, and scientists have in the past just misdescribed or misunderstood their own practices when they spoke of induction. Popper lays out his final solution to the problem of induction in section IX, and in the last section of the paper he responds to various reformulations of the problem. Particularly important here is his distinction between the claim that science is a *reasonable practice* for human beings to engage in, and the claim that our belief that science will eventually succeed in getting to the truth is a *rational* one: Popper supports the first claim, but unconditionally denies the second one.

Some Useful Background Information

1. Popper sought to replace the traditional inductivist view of science with a quite different account that denies induction plays any role in science at all. In order to see what Popper is reacting against, it is helpful to briefly review the traditional understanding of the scientific method. On this view (sometimes called the "Baconian" view, after Francis Bacon (1561–1626), the first philosopher to systematically lay out rules for good science) the scientist begins by making observations—by carrying out carefully controlled experiments at some outpost on the frontier between our knowledge and our ignorance. The results of these experiments are systematically recorded and shared with other workers in the field. As the body of data grows, certain regularities appear. Individual scientists formulate hypotheses which, if true, would explain all the known facts and reveal an underlying structure explaining the regularities in the data. They then attempt to confirm their hypotheses by performing experiments which will produce supporting evidence. Eventually, after enough experiments are done, some hypothesis is verified and is added to the body of confirmed scientific theory. Science moves on to the next point on the frontier.

    This process, known as the method of induction, was standardly thought to be what marked off scientific investigation from other kinds of intellectual pursuit: science, it might be said, is based on experimental *facts* (rather than, say, on claims rooted in tradition, authority, prejudice, habit, emotion, or whatever). It is this picture of science that Popper attempts to overturn, and replace with his own account of what scientists are actually up to.

2. Popper does not think that good scientific theories are good because they are true. As he once put it, "We cannot identify science with truth, for we think that both Newton's and Einstein's theories belong to science, but they cannot both be true, and they may well both be false." A formative experience for Popper as a young philosopher was the replacement of Newtonian physics—previously the crown jewel of modern science—by Einstein's theories in the early decades of the twentieth century. Newtonian physics was, in 1900, the most successful, well-confirmed, and important scientific theory ever developed, and for more than two hundred years its laws had been unfailingly corroborated by literally billions of scientific ob-

servations and, furthermore, by underpinning the most impressive advances in technology in human history. Yet, despite the huge quantity of inductive evidence apparently confirming the truth of Newtonian physics, it turned out to be false. If this quantity of evidence could not verify a theory, Popper thought, then nothing could. Nothing in science is secure; every scientific theory is open to rejection or revision; all scientific 'knowledge' is probably false, though it aspires eventually to the truth. One of Popper's favorite quotations was from the early Greek philosopher Xenophanes (who lived at about 400 BCE):

The gods did not reveal, from the beginning,
All things to us, but in the course of time
Through seeking we may learn and know
    things better.
But as for certain truth, no man has known it,
Nor shall he know it, neither of the gods
Nor yet of all the things of which I speak.
For even if by chance he were to utter
The final truth, he would himself not know it:
For all is but a woven web of guesses.

3. Popper's approach to knowledge is self-consciously biological in orientation. Human beings, according to Popper, are problem-solving animals, and there is continuity between simple examples of learning by trial and error in the lower animals and the method of conjecture and refutation in human science. The human search for knowledge is ultimately rooted, for Popper, in facts about our evolutionary history.

Some Common Misconceptions

1. Though Popper claims to have "solved the problem of induction," he did not do so by showing that induction *works*. Instead, he 'solves' the problem by issuing a complete ban on induction. The conclusions of science are never positively justified: they are never established as certainly true, or even as probable. In other words, Popper's "corroboration" is not the same

thing as confirmation. Conjectures are not inferences and refutations are not inductive; the failure to refute a hypothesis is *not* evidence in its favor, according to Popper.

2. Unlike the logical positivists, Popper does not dismiss pseudo-science as valueless or meaningless. Falsifiability is not, for him, a demarcation between sense and nonsense, but only between science and non-science. (For the logical positivists, verifiability was a demarcation of both kinds.) Thus, for Popper, although the methods of science have a privileged place in the rational human pursuit of the truth, domains other than science (such as art and religion) can still have substantial value, and can even prove to be valuable starting points—though never finishing posts—in the quest for knowledge.

Suggestions for Critical Reflection

1. Popper claimed to have solved the problem of induction. Did he? If not, did he at least solve the problem of showing how the methods of science could be rational despite Hume's arguments against the rationality of induction?

2. Popper stresses the importance of ruling out *ad hoc* modifications to theories. How helpful is this advice? How easy is to tell when an adjustment to a theory is *ad hoc*, as opposed to when it is a legitimate improvement to a theory under the impact of new data? If it is not so easy, what implications (if any) does this have for Popper's account of science?

3. How plausible is Popper's suggestion that working scientists in fact adopt the method of conjecture and refutation (even though they may not realize they are doing so)? For example, do scientists deliberately pursue highly improbable claims (rather than less contentful, but more probable, hypotheses)? Do they then set out to falsify, rather than to verify, these theories? Do they abandon their theories when faced with single pieces of counter-evidence, rather than modifying their theories to accommodate this new data? If scientists do *not* in fact use the methods Popper prescribes, how much of a problem is this for Popper's philosophy of science?

4. The attempted refutation of our conjectures, according to Popper, can never positively justify those conjectures, or justify us in thinking that they are probably true. On the other hand, according to Popper, the refutation of a conjecture is a step that takes us closer to the truth. Are these two claims compatible?

5. Popper says we ought to act on—provisionally, to believe—those theories that have survived extensive testing. How is this to be distinguished from induction?

6. Popper issues a ban on induction as an irrational method of doing science; but is his own method any more rational? That is, does it give us rational reasons for preferring one theory over another? Does it give us any reason to think scientific theories are getting better and better (i.e., closer to the truth)? Can Popper consistently assert that there is growth in scientific knowledge and that science is a rational activity?

Suggestions for Further Reading

Popper published many books during his lifetime, and since his death a score more have been published based on the papers he left behind. The following six books are among his most important, and together give a fairly complete overview of his thought: *The Logic of Scientific Discovery* (Routledge, 1992), *Conjectures and Refutations: The Growth of Scientific Knowledge* (Routledge 1989), *The Open Society and its Enemies* (Volumes I and II, Princeton University Press, 1972/1976), *Objective Knowledge: An Evolutionary Approach* (Oxford University Press, 1972) and, co-written with John Eccles, *The Self and Its Brain* (Routledge, 1993). A two volume collection of critical essays about Popper's work, with replies from Popper, was published in 1974 by Open Court, edited by Paul A. Schilpp and called *The Philosophy of Karl Popper*. That collection also contains an extended autobiographical essay by Popper, an amended version of which was published under separate cover as *Unended Quest* (Open Court, 1982).

Bryan Magee's *Popper* (Fontana Press, 1973) is short, clear, and stimulating, if sometimes rather breathless in its adoration of Popper's work. A later, somewhat longer, introduction by Magee is his *Philosophy and the Real World: An Introduction to Karl Popper* (Open Court, 1985). Two other reliable summaries of Popper's philosophical work are Anthony O'Hear, *Popper* (Routledge & Kegan Paul, 1980) and Geoff Stokes, *Popper: Philosophy, Politics and Scientific Method* (Polity Press, 1999). Roberta Corvi's *An Introduction to the Thought of Karl Popper* (Routledge, 1996) was approved by Popper just before his death and constitutes a scholarly account of Popper's final philosophical system; however, it is written rather less accessibly than many of Popper's own writings. Finally, there is a fairly recent collection of essays about Popper's work written by prominent philosophers, edited by Anthony O'Hear: *Karl Popper: Philosophy and Problems* (Cambridge University Press, 1996).

"Science: Conjectures and Refutations"[2]

> Mr. Turnbull had predicted evil consequences, … and was now doing the best in his power to bring about the verification of his own prophecies.
>
> (Anthony Trollope)[3]

I.

When I received the list of participants in this course and realized that I had been asked to speak to philosophical colleagues I thought, after some hesitation and consultation, that you would probably prefer me

---

2   This was originally a lecture given at Peterhouse College, Cambridge, in 1953. It was first published under the title "Philosophy of Science: A Personal Report" in 1957 in *British Philosophy in Mid-Century*, edited by C.A. Mace. The copy reprinted here is taken, with permission, from Chapter 1 of *Conjectures and Refutations: The Growth of Scientific Knowledge*, fifth revised edition, London: Routledge, 1989. Copyright © University of Klagenfurt/Karl Popper Library.

3   *Phineas Finn*, Chapter XXV.

to speak about those problems which interest me most, and about those developments with which I am most intimately acquainted. I therefore decided to do what I have never done before: to give you a report on my own work in the philosophy of science, since the autumn of 1919 when I first began to grapple with the problem, "*When should a theory be ranked as scientific?*" or "*Is there a criterion for the scientific character or status of a theory?*"

The problem which troubled me at the time was neither, 'When is a theory true?' nor, 'When is a theory acceptable?' My problem was different. I *wished to distinguish between science and pseudo-science*; knowing very well that science often errs, and that pseudo-science may happen to stumble on the truth.

I knew, of course, the most widely accepted answer to my problem: that science is distinguished from pseudo-science—or from 'metaphysics'—by its *empirical method*, which is essentially *inductive*, proceeding from observation or experiment. But this did not satisfy me. On the contrary, I often formulated my problem as one of distinguishing between a genuinely empirical method and a non-empirical or even a pseudo-empirical method—that is to say, a method which, although it appeals to observation and experiment, nevertheless does not come up to scientific standards. The latter method may be exemplified by astrology, with its stupendous mass of empirical evidence based on observation—on horoscopes and on biographies.

But as it was not the example of astrology which led me to my problem I should perhaps briefly describe the atmosphere in which my problem arose and the examples by which it was stimulated. After the collapse of the Austrian Empire[4] there had been a revolution in Austria: the air was full of revolutionary slogans and ideas, and new and often wild theories. Among the theories which interested me Einstein's theory of relativity was no doubt by far the most important. Three others were Marx's theory of history, Freud's psycho-analysis, and Alfred Adler's so-called 'individual psychology'.

There was a lot of popular nonsense talked about these theories, and especially about relativity (as still happens even today), but I was fortunate in those who introduced me to the study of this theory. We all—the small circle of students to which I belonged—were thrilled with the result of Eddington's eclipse observations[5] which in 1919 brought the first important confirmation of Einstein's theory of gravitation. It was a great experience for us, and one which had a lasting influence on my intellectual development.

The three other theories I have mentioned were also widely discussed among students at that time. I myself happened to come into personal contact with Alfred Adler, and even to co-operate with him in his social work among the children and young people in the working-class districts of Vienna where he had established social guidance clinics.

It was during the summer of 1919 that I began to feel more and more dissatisfied with these three theories—the Marxist theory of history, psychoanalysis, and individual psychology; and I began to feel dubious about their claims to scientific status. My problem perhaps first took the simple form, 'What is wrong with Marxism, psycho-analysis, and individual psychology? Why are they so different from physical theories, from Newton's theory, and especially from the theory of relativity?'

To make this contrast clear I should explain that few of us at the time would have said that we believed in the *truth* of Einstein's theory of gravitation. This shows that it was not my doubting the *truth* of those other three theories which bothered me, but something else. Yet neither was it that I merely felt mathematical physics to be more *exact* than the sociological or psychological type of theory. Thus what worried me was neither the problem of truth, at that stage at least, nor the problem of exactness or measurability. It was rather that I felt that these other three theories, though posing as sciences, had in fact more in common with

---

4   In 1918, with Austria-Hungary's defeat in the First World War.

5   Sir Arthur Stanley Eddington (1882–1944), during an expedition to Africa, observed the positions of stars visible around the sun during an eclipse, compared them to the positions of those same stars seen at night (when, of course, the sun is not in the same region of the sky), and deduced from the shift in their positions that the light from those stars must be bent by its passage through the sun's gravitational field.

primitive myths than with science; that they resembled astrology rather than astronomy.

I found that those of my friends who were admirers of Marx, Freud, and Adler, were impressed by a number of points common to these theories, and especially by their apparent *explanatory power*. These theories appeared to be able to explain practically everything that happened within the fields to which they referred. The study of any of them seemed to have the effect of an intellectual conversion or revelation, opening your eyes to a new truth hidden from those not yet initiated. Once your eyes were thus opened you saw confirming instances everywhere: the world was full of *verifications* of the theory. Whatever happened always confirmed it. Thus its truth appeared manifest; and unbelievers were clearly people who did not want to see the manifest truth; who refused to see it, either because it was against their class interest, or because of their repressions which were still 'un-analysed' and crying out for treatment.

The most characteristic element in this situation seemed to me the incessant stream of confirmations, of observations which 'verified' the theories in question; and this point was constantly emphasized by their adherents. A Marxist could not open a newspaper without finding on every page confirming evidence for his interpretation of history; not only in the news, but also in its presentation—which revealed the class bias of the paper—and especially of course in what the paper did *not* say. The Freudian analysts emphasized that their theories were constantly verified by their 'clinical observations'. As for Adler, I was much impressed by a personal experience. Once, in 1919, I reported to him a case which to me did not seem particularly Adlerian, but which he found no difficulty in analysing in terms of his theory of inferiority feelings, although he had not even seen the child. Slightly shocked, I asked him how he could be so sure. 'Because of my thousandfold experience', he replied; whereupon I could not help saying: 'And with this new case, I suppose, your experience has become thousand-and-one-fold.'

What I had in mind was that his previous observations may not have been much sounder than this new one; that each in its turn had been interpreted in the light of 'previous experience', and at the same time counted as additional confirmation. What, I asked myself, did it confirm? No more than that a case could be interpreted in the light of the theory. But this meant very little, I reflected, since every conceivable case could be interpreted in the light of Adler's theory, or equally of Freud's. I may illustrate this by two very different examples of human behaviour: that of a man who pushes a child into the water with the intention of drowning it; and that of a man who sacrifices his life in an attempt to save the child. Each of these two cases can be explained with equal ease in Freudian and in Adlerian terms. According to Freud the first man suffered from repression (say, of some component of his Oedipus complex[6]), while the second man had achieved sublimation. According to Adler the first man suffered from feelings of inferiority (producing perhaps the need to prove to himself that he dared to commit some crime), and so did the second man (whose need was to prove to himself that he dared to rescue the child). I could not think of any human behaviour which could not be interpreted in terms of either theory. It was precisely this fact—that they always fitted, that they were always confirmed—which in the eyes of their admirers constituted the strongest argument in favour of these theories. It began to dawn on me that this apparent strength was in fact their weakness.

With Einstein's theory the situation was strikingly different. Take one typical instance—Einstein's prediction, just then confirmed by the findings of Eddington's expedition. Einstein's gravitational theory had led to the result that light must be attracted by heavy bodies (such as the sun), precisely as material bodies were attracted. As a consequence it could be calculated that light from a distant fixed star whose apparent position was close to the sun would reach the earth from such a direction that the star would seem to be slightly shifted away from the sun; or, in other words, that stars close to the sun would look as if they had moved a little away from the sun, and from one another. This is a thing which cannot normally be observed since such stars are rendered invisible in daytime by the sun's overwhelming brightness; but during an eclipse it is possible to take photographs

6   According to Freud, the Oedipus complex consists in subconscious sexual desire in a child (especially a boy) for the parent of the opposite sex, usually combined with repressed hostility towards the parent of the same sex.

of them. If the same constellation is photographed at night one can measure the distances on the two photographs, and check the predicted effect.

Now the impressive thing about this case is the *risk* involved in a prediction of this kind. If observation shows that the predicted effect is definitely absent, then the theory is simply refuted. The theory is *incompatible with certain possible results of observation*—in fact with results which everybody before Einstein would have expected.[7] This is quite different from the situation I have previously described, when it turned out that the theories in question were compatible with the most divergent human behaviour, so that it was practically impossible to describe any human behaviour that might not be claimed to be a verification of these theories.

These considerations led me in the winter of 1919–20 to conclusions which I may now reformulate as follows.

(1) It is easy to obtain confirmations, or verifications, for nearly every theory—if we look for confirmations.

(2) Confirmations should count only if they are the result of *risky predictions*; that is to say, if, unenlightened by the theory in question, we should have expected an event which was incompatible with the theory—an event which would have refuted the theory.

(3) Every 'good' scientific theory is a prohibition: it forbids certain things to happen. The more a theory forbids, the better it is.

(4) A theory which is not refutable by any conceivable event is non-scientific. Irrefutability is not a virtue of a theory (as people often think) but a vice.

(5) Every genuine *test* of a theory is an attempt to falsify it, or to refute it. Testability is falsifiability; but there are degrees of testability: some theories are more testable, more exposed to refutation, than others; they take, as it were, greater risks.

(6) Confirming evidence should not count *except when it is the result of a genuine test of the theory*; and this means that it can be presented as a serious

but unsuccessful attempt to falsify the theory. (I now speak in such cases of 'corroborating evidence'.)

(7) Some genuinely testable theories, when found to be false, are still upheld by their admirers—for example by introducing *ad hoc*[8] some auxiliary assumption, or by re-interpreting the theory *ad hoc* in such a way that it escapes refutation. Such a procedure is always possible, but it rescues the theory from refutation only at the price of destroying, or at least lowering, its scientific status. (I later described such a rescuing operation as a '*conventionalist twist*' or a '*conventionalist stratagem*'.)

One can sum up all this by saying that *the criterion of the scientific status of a theory is its falsifiability, or refutability, or testability.*

II.

I may perhaps exemplify this with the help of the various theories so far mentioned. Einstein's theory of gravitation clearly satisfied the criterion of falsifiability. Even if our measuring instruments at the time did not allow us to pronounce on the results of the tests with complete assurance, there was clearly a possibility of refuting the theory.

Astrology did not pass the test. Astrologers were greatly impressed, and misled, by what they believed to be confirming evidence—so much so that they were quite unimpressed by any unfavourable evidence. Moreover, by making their interpretations and prophecies sufficiently vague they were able to explain away anything that might have been a refutation of the theory had the theory and the prophecies been more precise. In order to escape falsification they destroyed the testability of their theory. It is a typical soothsayer's trick to predict things so vaguely that the predictions can hardly fail: that they become irrefutable.

The Marxist theory of history, in spite of the serious efforts of some of its founders and followers, ultimately adopted this soothsaying practice. In some of its earlier formulations (for example in Marx's analysis of the character of the 'coming social revolution') their predictions were testable, and in fact

---

7　[Author's note] This is a slight oversimplification, for about half of the Einstein effect may be derived from the classical theory, provided we assume a ballistic theory of light.

8　*Ad hoc* means "for the particular situation or case at hand and for no other" (from the Latin "to this").

falsified.[9] Yet instead of accepting the refutations the followers of Marx re-interpreted both the theory and the evidence in order to make them agree. In this way they rescued the theory from refutation; but they did so at the price of adopting a device which made it irrefutable. They thus gave a 'conventionalist twist' to the theory; and by this stratagem they destroyed its much advertised claim to scientific status.

The two psycho-analytic theories were in a different class. They were simply non-testable, irrefutable. There was no conceivable human behaviour which could contradict them. This does not mean that Freud and Adler were not seeing certain things correctly: I personally do not doubt that much of what they say is of considerable importance, and may well play its part one day in a psychological science which is testable. But it does mean that those 'clinical observations' which analysts naïvely believe confirm their theory cannot do this any more than the daily confirmations which astrologers find in their practice.[10] And as for Freud's epic of the Ego, the Super-ego, and the Id, no substantially stronger claim to scientific status can be made for it than for Homer's collected stories from Olympus.[11] These theories describe some facts, but in the manner of myths. They contain most interesting psychological suggestions, but not in a testable form.

At the same time I realized that such myths may be developed, and become testable; that historically speaking all—or very nearly all—scientific theories originate from myths, and that a myth may contain important anticipations of scientific theories. Examples are Empedocles' theory of evolution by trial and error, or Parmenides' myth of the unchanging block universe[12] in which nothing ever happens and which,

---

9 [Author's note] See, for example, my *Open Society and Its Enemies*, ch. 15, section iii, and notes 13–14.

10 [Author's note] 'Clinical observations', like all other observations, are *interpretations in the light of theories* (see below, sections iv ff.); and for this reason alone they are apt to seem to support those theories in the light of which they were interpreted. But real support can be obtained only from observations undertaken as tests (by 'attempted refutations'); and for this purpose *criteria of refutation* have to be laid down beforehand: it must be agreed which observable situations, if actually observed, mean that the theory is refuted. But what kind of clinical responses would refute to the satisfaction of the analyst not merely a particular analytic diagnosis but psycho-analysis itself? And have such criteria ever been discussed or agreed upon by analysts? Is there not, on the contrary, a whole family of analytic concepts, such as 'ambivalence' (I do not suggest that there is no such thing as ambivalence), which would make it difficult, if not impossible, to agree upon such criteria? Moreover, how much headway has been made in investigating the question of the extent to which the (conscious or unconscious) expectations and theories held by the analyst influence the 'clinical responses' of the patient? (To say nothing about the conscious attempts to influence the patient by proposing interpretations to him, etc.) Years ago I introduced the term '*Oedipus effect*' to describe the influence of a theory or expectation or prediction *upon the event which it predicts* or describes: it will be remembered that the causal chain leading to Oedipus' parricide was started by the oracle's prediction of this event. This is a characteristic and recurrent theme of such myths, but one which seems to have failed to attract the interest of the analysts, perhaps not accidentally. (The problem of confirmatory dreams suggested by the analyst is discussed by Freud, for example in *Gesammelte Schriften*, III, 1925, where he says on p. 314: 'If anybody asserts that most of the dreams which can be utilized in an analysis … owe their origin to [the analyst's] suggestion, then no objection can be made from the point of view of analytic theory. Yet there is nothing in this fact', he surprisingly adds, 'which would detract from the reliability of our results.')

11 In Freudian theory, the *ego* is the part of the human psyche which is conscious and most directly in control of our thought and behavior, the *id* is the unconscious reservoir of primitive impulses and instincts, and the *superego* is the mostly unconscious part of our psyche which has internalized our community's moral standards and acts as a restraint on the ego. Olympus is the mythical home of many of the gods of classical Greek mythology, and Homer was a Greek epic poet whose verses often deal with the activities of the gods.

12 Empedocles of Acragas (c. 493–c. 433 BCE), a native of Sicily, was a philosopher, poet, politician, scientist

if we add another dimension,[13] becomes Einstein's block universe (in which, too, nothing ever happens, since everything is, four-dimensionally speaking, determined and laid down from the beginning). I thus felt that if a theory is found to be non-scientific, or 'metaphysical' (as we might say), it is not thereby found to be unimportant, or insignificant, or 'meaningless', or 'nonsensical'.[14] But it cannot claim to be backed by empirical evidence in the scientific sense—although it may easily be, in some genetic[15] sense, the 'result of observation'.

(There were a great many other theories of this pre-scientific or pseudo-scientific character, some of them, unfortunately, as influential as the Marxist interpretation of history; for example, the racialist interpretation of history—another of those impressive

---

and—in his own eyes—a miracle worker and a god. He believed in the immortality of the soul and is said to have committed suicide by flinging himself into the volcano Mount Etna. Parmenides of Elea, who was born about twenty years before Empedocles, was perhaps the most important Greek philosopher before Socrates. In his poem "On Nature" he wrote that a goddess had instructed him that, since nature cannot both be and not be, it must necessarily be, and he concluded from this that reality must be perfect, unchanging, motionless, and eternal.

13 The dimension of time.

14 [Author's note] The case of astrology, nowadays a typical pseudo-science, may illustrate this point. It was attacked, by Aristotelians and other rationalists, down to Newton's day, for the wrong reason—for its now accepted assertion that the planets had an 'influence' upon terrestrial ('sublunar') events. In fact Newton's theory of gravity, and especially the lunar theory of the tides, was historically speaking an offspring of astrological lore. Newton, it seems, was most reluctant to adopt a theory which came from the same stable as for example the theory that 'influenza' epidemics are due to an astral 'influence'. And Galileo, no doubt for the same reason, actually rejected the lunar theory of the tides; and his misgivings about Kepler may easily be explained by his misgivings about astrology.

15 Here "genetic" means "having to do with the origins or cause of something."

and all-explanatory theories which act upon weak minds like revelations.)

Thus the problem which I tried to solve by proposing the criterion of falsifiability was neither a problem of meaningfulness or significance, nor a problem of truth or acceptability. It was the problem of drawing a line (as well as this can be done) between the statements, or systems of statements, of the empirical sciences, and all other statements—whether they are of a religious or of a metaphysical character, or simply pseudo-scientific. Years later—it must have been in 1928 or 1929—I called this first problem of mine the 'problem of demarcation'. The criterion of falsifiability is a solution to this problem of demarcation, for it says that statements or systems of statements, in order to be ranked as scientific, must be capable of conflicting with possible, or conceivable, observations.

III.

Today I know, of course, that this *criterion of demarcation*—the criterion of testability, or falsifiability, or refutability—is far from obvious; for even now its significance is seldom realized. At that time, in 1920, it seemed to me almost trivial, although it solved for me an intellectual problem which had worried me deeply, and one which also had obvious practical consequences (for example, political ones). But I did not yet realize its full implications, or its philosophical significance. When I explained it to a fellow student of the Mathematics Department (now a distinguished mathematician in Great Britain), he suggested that I should publish it. At the time I thought this absurd; for I was convinced that my problem, since it was so important for me, must have agitated many scientists and philosophers who would surely have reached my rather obvious solution. That this was not the case I learnt from Wittgenstein's work, and from its reception; and so I published my results thirteen years later in the form of a criticism of Wittgenstein's *criterion of meaningfulness*.

Wittgenstein, as you all know, tried to show in the *Tractatus*[16] (see for example his propositions

---

16 Ludwig Wittgenstein (1889–1951) was one of the twentieth century's most charismatic and influential philosophers. Popper is referring to the *Tractatus*

6.53; 6.54; and 5) that all so-called philosophical or metaphysical propositions were actually non-propositions or pseudo-propositions: that they were senseless or meaningless. All genuine (or meaningful) propositions were truth functions[17] of the elementary or atomic propositions which described 'atomic facts'—i.e., facts which can in principle be ascertained by observation. In other words, meaningful propositions were fully reducible to elementary or atomic propositions which were simple statements describing possible states of affairs, and which could in principle be established or rejected by observation. If we call a statement an 'observation statement' not only if it states an actual observation but also if it states anything that *may* be observed, we shall have to say (according to the *Tractatus*, 5 and 4.52) that every genuine proposition must be a truth-function of, and therefore deducible from, observation statements. All other apparent propositions will be meaningless pseudo-propositions; in fact they will be nothing but nonsensical gibberish.

This idea was used by Wittgenstein for a characterization of science, as opposed to philosophy: We read (for example in 4.11, where natural science is taken to stand in opposition to philosophy): 'The totality of true propositions is the total natural science (or the totality of the natural sciences).' This means that the propositions which belong to science are those deducible from *true* observation statements; they are those propositions which can be *verified* by true observation statements. Could we know all true observation statements, we should also know all that may be asserted by natural science.

This amounts to a crude verifiability criterion of demarcation. To make it slightly less crude, it could be amended thus: 'The statements which may possibly fall within the province of science are those which may possibly be verified by observation statements; and these statements, again, coincide with the class of *all* genuine or meaningful statements.' For this approach, then, *verifiability, meaningfulness, and scientific character all coincide.*

I personally was never interested in the so-called problem of meaning; on the contrary, it appeared to me a verbal problem, a typical pseudo-problem. I was interested only in the problem of demarcation, i.e., in finding a criterion of the scientific character of theories. It was just this interest which made me see at once that Wittgenstein's verifiability criterion of meaning was intended to play the part of a criterion of demarcation as well; and which made me see that, as such, it was totally inadequate, even if all misgivings about the dubious concept of meaning were set aside. For Wittgenstein's criterion of demarcation—to use my own terminology in this context—is verifiability, or deducibility from observation statements. But this criterion is too narrow (*and* too wide): it excludes from science practically everything that is, in fact, characteristic of it (while failing in effect to exclude astrology). No scientific theory can ever be deduced from observation statements, or be described as a truth-function of observation statements.

All this I pointed out on various occasions to Wittgensteinians and members of the Vienna Circle.[18] In 1931–32 I summarized my ideas in a largish book

---

Logico-Philosophicus, published in 1921 and the only book Wittgenstein completed during his lifetime.

17 A 'truth function' is a function from the truth values of input sentences to the truth value of an output sentence. (The two possible 'truth values' are, normally, either True or False.) Thus, a compound sentence is 'truth functional' if its truth value is entirely determined by the truth values of its component sentences: for example, the sentence "*A* and *B*" is true just in case *A* and *B* both have the value 'True,' and is false otherwise. (On the other hand, many other sentences are not, at least on the face of it, truth functional in this way: for example, "*A* because of *B*" does not have its truth value determined entirely by the truth values of *A* and *B*.)

---

18 The Vienna Circle was a group of like-minded philosophers and scientists who met for Saturday morning seminars in Vienna from 1923 until the late 1930s. Strongly influenced by Wittgenstein's *Tractatus*, they held that the task of philosophy was not the production of new knowledge but the clarification of the basic concepts of science and ordinary language, and one of their most important goals was the unification of science under a single logical language. They spread their ideas through a series of congresses and in a journal, started in 1930, called *Erkenntnis*.

(read by several members of the Circle but never published; although part of it was incorporated in my *Logic of Scientific Discovery*); and in 1933 I published a letter to the Editor of *Erkenntnis* in which I tried to compress into two pages my ideas on the problems of demarcation and induction.[19] In this letter and elsewhere I described the problem of meaning as a pseudo-problem, in contrast to the problem of demarcation. But my contribution was classified by members of the Circle as a proposal to replace the verifiability criterion of *meaning* by a falsifiability criterion of *meaning*—which effectively made nonsense of my views.[20] My protests that I was trying to solve, not their pseudo-problem of meaning, but the problem of demarcation, were of no avail.

My attacks upon verification had some effect, however. They soon led to complete confusion in the camp of the verificationist philosophers of sense and nonsense. The original proposal of verifiability as the criterion of meaning was at least clear, simple, and forceful. The modifications and shifts which were now introduced were the very opposite.[21] This, I should say, is now seen even by the participants. But since I am usually quoted as one of them I wish to repeat that although I created this confusion I never participated in it. Neither falsifiability nor testability were proposed by me as criteria of meaning; and although I may plead guilty to having introduced both terms into the discussion, it was not I who introduced them into the theory of meaning.

Criticism of my alleged views was widespread and highly successful. I have yet to meet a criticism of my views.[22] Meanwhile, testability is being widely accepted as a criterion of demarcation.

---

19 [Author's note] My *Logic of Scientific Discovery* (1959, 1960, 1961), here usually referred to as *L.Sc.D.*, is the translation of *Logik der Forschung* (1934), with a number of additional notes and appendices, including (on pp. 312–14) the letter to the Editor of *Erkenntnis* mentioned here in the text which was first published in *Erkenntnis*, 3, 1933, pp. 426 f. Concerning my never published book mentioned here in the text, see R. Carnap's paper 'Ueber Protokollsätze' (On Protocol-Sentences), *Erkenntnis*, 3, 1932, pp. 215–28 where he gives an outline of my theory on pp. 223–28, and accepts it. He calls my theory 'procedure B', and says (p. 224, top): 'Starting from a point of view different from Neurath's' (who developed what Carnap calls on p. 223 'procedure A'), 'Popper developed procedure B as part of his system.' And after describing in detail my theory of tests, Carnap sums up his views as follows (p. 228): 'After weighing the various arguments here discussed, it appears to me that the second language form with procedure B—that is in the form here described—is the most adequate among the forms of scientific language at present advocated … in the … theory of knowledge.' This paper of Carnap's contained the first published report of my theory of critical testing. (See also my critical remarks in *L.Sc.D.*, note 1 to section 29, p. 104, where the date '1933' should read '1932'; and ch. 11, below, text to note 39.)

20 [Author's note] Wittgenstein's example of a nonsensical pseudo-proposition is: 'Socrates is identical'. Obviously, 'Socrates is not identical' must also be nonsense. Thus the negation of any nonsense will be nonsense, and that of a meaningful statement will be meaningful. *But the negation of a testable (or falsifiable) statement need not be testable*, as was pointed out, first in my *L.Sc.D.*, (e.g., pp. 38 f.) and later by my critics. The confusion caused by taking testability as a criterion of *meaning* rather than of *demarcation* can easily be imagined.

21 [Author's note] The most recent example of the way in which the history of this problem is misunderstood is A.R. White's 'Note on Meaning and Verification', *Mind*, 63, 1954, pp. 66 ff. J.L. Evans's article, *Mind*, 62, 1953, pp. I ff., which Mr. White criticizes, is excellent in my opinion, and unusually perceptive. Understandably enough, neither of the authors can quite reconstruct the story. (Some hints may be found in my *Open Society*, notes 46, 51 and 52 to ch. 11; and a fuller analysis in ch. 11 of the present volume.)

22 [Author's note] In *L.Sc.D.* I discussed, and replied to, some likely objections which afterwards were indeed raised, without reference to my replies. One of them is the contention that the falsification of a natural law is just as impossible as its verification. The answer is that this objection mixes two entirely different levels of analysis (like the objection that mathematical demonstrations are impossible since checking, no matter

IV.

I have discussed the problem of demarcation in some detail because I believe that its solution is the key to most of the fundamental problems of the philosophy of science. I am going to give you later a list of some of these other problems, but only one of them—the *problem of induction*—can be discussed here at any length.

I had become interested in the problem of induction in 1923. Although this problem is very closely connected with the problem of demarcation, I did not fully appreciate the connection for about five years.

I approached the problem of induction through Hume. Hume, I felt, was perfectly right in pointing out that induction cannot be logically justified. He held that there can be no valid logical[23] arguments allow-

ing us to establish '*that those instances, of which we have had no experience, resemble those, of which we have had experience*'. Consequently '*even after the observation of the frequent or constant conjunction of objects, we have no reason to draw any inference concerning any object beyond those of which we have had experience*'. For 'shou'd it be said that we have experience'[24]—experience teaching us that objects constantly conjoined with certain other objects continue to be so conjoined—then, Hume says, 'I wou'd renew my question, *why from this experience we form any conclusion beyond those past instances, of which we have had experience*'. This 'renew'd question' indicates that an attempt to justify the practice of induction by an appeal to experience must lead to an *infinite regress*. As a result we can say that theories can never be inferred from observation statements, or rationally justified by them.

I found Hume's refutation of inductive inference clear and conclusive. But I felt completely dissatisfied with his psychological explanation of induction in terms of custom or habit.

It has often been noticed that this explanation of Hume's is philosophically not very satisfactory. Hume, however, without doubt intended it as a *psychological* rather than a philosophical theory; for it tries to give a causal explanation of a psychological fact—*the fact that we believe in laws*, in statements asserting regularities or constantly conjoined kinds of events. Hume explains this fact by asserting that it is due to (i.e., constantly conjoined with) custom or habit. But even this reformulation of Hume's theory is unacceptable; for what I have just called a 'psychological fact' may itself be described as a custom or habit—our custom or our habit of believing in laws or regularities. It is neither surprising nor enlightening to hear that such a custom or habit can be explained as due to custom or habit, or conjoined with a custom or habit (even though a different one). Only when we

---

how often repeated, can never make it quite certain that we have not overlooked a mistake). On the first level, there is a logical asymmetry: one singular statement— say about the perihelion of Mercury—can formally falsify Kepler's laws; but these cannot be formally verified by any number of singular statements. The attempt to minimize this asymmetry can only lead to confusion. On another level, we may hesitate to accept any statement, even the simplest observation statement; and we may point out that every statement involves *interpretation in the light of theories*, and that it is therefore uncertain. This does not affect the fundamental asymmetry, but it is important: most dissectors of the heart before Harvey observed the wrong things—those, which they expected to see. There can never be anything like a completely safe observation, free from the dangers of misinterpretation. (This is one of the reasons why the theory of induction does not work.) The 'empirical basis' consists largely of a mixture of *theories* of lower degree of universality (of 'reproducible effects'). But the fact remains that, relative to whatever basis the investigator may accept (at his peril), he can test his theory only by trying to refute it.

23 [Author's note] Hume does not say 'logical' but 'demonstrative', a terminology which, I think, is a little misleading. The following two quotations are from the *Treatise of Human Nature*, Book I, Part III, sections vi and xii. (The italics are all Hume's.)

24 [Author's note] This and the next quotation are from *loc. cit.*, section vi. See also Hume's *Enquiry Concerning Human Understanding*, section IV, Part II, and his *Abstract*, edited 1938 by J.M. Keynes and P. Sraffa, p. 15, and quoted in *L.Sc.D.*, new appendix *vii, text to note 6.

remember that the words 'custom' and 'habit' are used by Hume, as they are in ordinary language, not merely to *describe* regular behaviour, but rather to *theorize about its origin* (ascribed to frequent repetition), can we reformulate his psychological theory in a more satisfactory way. Hume's theory becomes then the thesis that, like other habits, *our habit of believing in laws is the product of frequent repetition*—of the repeated observation that things of a certain kind are constantly conjoined with things of another kind.

This genetic-psychological theory is, as indicated, incorporated in ordinary language, and it is therefore hardly as revolutionary as Hume thought. It is no doubt an extremely popular psychological theory—part of 'common sense', one might say. But in spite of my love of both common sense and Hume, I felt convinced that this psychological theory was mistaken; and that it was in fact refutable on purely logical grounds.

Hume's psychology, which is the popular psychology, was mistaken, I felt, about at least three different things: (*a*) the typical result of repetition; (*b*) the genesis of habits; and especially (*c*) the character of those experiences or modes of behaviour which may be described as 'believing in a law' or 'expecting a law-like succession of events'.

(*a*) The typical result of repetition—say, of repeating a difficult passage on the piano—is that movements which at first needed attention are in the end executed without attention. We might say that the process becomes radically abbreviated, and ceases to be conscious: it becomes automatized, 'physiological'. Such a development, far from creating a conscious expectation of law-like succession, or a belief in a law, may on the contrary begin with a conscious belief and destroy it by making it superfluous. In learning to ride a bicycle we may start with the belief that we can avoid falling if we steer in the direction in which we threaten to fall, and this belief may be useful for guiding our movements. After sufficient practice we may forget the rule; in any case, we do not need it any longer. On the other hand, even if it is true that repetition may create unconscious expectations, these become conscious only if something goes wrong (we may not have heard the clock tick, but we may hear that it has stopped).

(*b*) Habits or customs do not, as a rule, *originate* in repetition. Even the habit of walking, or of speaking, or of feeding at certain hours, *begins* before repetition can play any part whatever. We may say, if we like, that they deserve to be called 'habits' or 'customs' only after repetition has played its typical part described under (*a*); but we must not say that the practices in question *originated* as the result of many repetitions.

(*c*) Belief in a law is not quite the same thing as behaviour which betrays an expectation of a law-like succession of events; but these two are sufficiently closely connected to be treated together. They may, perhaps, in exceptional cases, result from a mere repetition of sense impressions (as in the case of the stopping clock). I was prepared to concede this, but I contended that normally, and in most cases of any interest, they cannot be so explained. As Hume admits, even a single striking observation may be sufficient to create a belief or an expectation—a fact which he tries to explain as due to an inductive habit, formed as the result of a vast number of long repetitive sequences which had been experienced at an earlier period of life.[25] But this, I contended, was merely his attempt to explain away unfavourable facts which threatened his theory; an unsuccessful attempt, since these unfavourable facts could be observed in very young animals and babies—as early, indeed, as we like. 'A lighted cigarette was held near the noses of the young puppies', reports F. Bäge. 'They sniffed at it once, turned tail, and nothing would induce them to come back to the source of the smell and to sniff again. A few days later, they reacted to the mere sight of a cigarette or even of a rolled piece of white paper, by bounding away, and sneezing.'[26] If we try to explain cases like this by postulating a vast number of long repetitive sequences at a still earlier age we are not only romancing, but forgetting that in the clever puppies' short lives there must be room not only for repetition but also for a great deal of novelty, and consequently of non-repetition.

---

25   [Author's note] *Treatise*, section xiii; section xv, rule 4.

26   [Author's note] F. Bäge, 'Zur Entwicklung, etc.', *Zeitschrift f. Hundeforschung*, 1933; cp. D. Katz, *Animals and Men*, ch. VI, footnote.

But it is not only that certain empirical facts do not support Hume; there are decisive arguments of a *purely logical* nature against his psychological theory.

The central idea of Hume's psychological theory is that of *repetition, based upon similarity* (or 'resemblance'). This idea is used in a very uncritical way. We are led to think of the water-drop that hollows the stone: of sequences of unquestionably like events slowly forcing themselves upon us, as does the tick of the clock. But we ought to realize that in a psychological theory such as Hume's, only repetition-for-us, based upon similarity-for-us, can be allowed to have any effect upon us. We must respond to situations as if they were equivalent; *take* them as similar; *interpret* them as repetitions. In this way they become for us *functionally equal*. The clever puppies, we may assume, showed by their response, their way of acting or of reacting, that they recognized or interpreted the second situation as a repetition of the first: that they expected its main element, the objectionable smell, to be present. The situation was a repetition-for-them because they responded to it by *anticipating* its similarity to the previous one.

This apparently psychological criticism has a purely logical basis which may be summed up in the following simple argument. (It happens to be the one from which I originally started my criticism.) The kind of repetition envisaged by Hume can never be perfect; the cases he has in mind cannot be cases of perfect sameness; they can only be cases of similarity. Thus *they are repetitions only from a certain point of view*. (What has the effect upon me of a repetition may not have this effect upon a spider.) But this means that, for logical reasons, there must always be a point of view—such as a system of expectations, anticipations, assumptions, or interests—*before* there can be any repetition; which point of view, consequently, cannot be merely the result of repetition. (See now also appendix *x, (1), to my *L.Sc.D.*)

We must thus replace, for the purposes of a psychological theory of the origin of our beliefs, the naïve idea of events which *are* similar by the idea of events to which we react by *interpreting* them as being similar. But if this is so (and I can see no escape from it) then Hume's psychological theory of induction leads to an infinite regress, precisely analogous to that other infinite regress which was discovered by Hume himself, and used by him to explode the logical theory of induction. For what do we wish to explain? In the example of the puppies we wish to explain behaviour which may be described as *recognizing or interpreting* a situation as a repetition of another. Clearly, we cannot hope to explain this by an appeal to earlier repetitions, once we realize that the earlier repetitions must also have been repetitions-for-them, so that precisely the same problem arises again: that of *recognizing or interpreting* a situation as a repetition of another.

To put it more concisely, similarity-for-us is the product of a response involving interpretations (which may be inadequate) and anticipations or expectations (which may never be fulfilled). It is therefore impossible to explain anticipations, or expectations, as resulting from many repetitions, as suggested by Hume. For even the first repetition-for-us must be based upon similarity-for-us, and therefore upon expectations—precisely the kind of thing we wished to explain. (Expectations must come first, *before* repetitions.)

We see that there is an infinite regress involved in Hume's psychological theory.

Hume, I felt, had never accepted the full force of his own logical analysis. Having refuted the logical idea of induction he was faced with the following problem: how do we actually obtain our knowledge, as a matter of psychological fact, if induction is a procedure which is logically invalid and rationally unjustifiable? There are two possible answers: (1) We obtain our knowledge by a non-inductive procedure. This answer would have allowed Hume to retain a form of rationalism. (2) We obtain our knowledge by repetition and induction, and therefore by a logically invalid and rationally unjustifiable procedure, so that all apparent knowledge is merely a kind of belief—belief based on habit. This answer would imply that even scientific knowledge is irrational, so that rationalism is absurd, and must be given up. (I shall not discuss here the age-old attempts, now again fashionable, to get out of the difficulty by asserting that though induction is of course logically invalid if we mean by 'logic' the same as 'deductive logic', it is not irrational by its own standards, and as inductive logic admits; as may be seen from the fact that every reasonable man applies it *as a matter of fact*. As against this, it was Hume's great achievement to break this uncritical identification of the question of fact—*quid facti?*[27]—and the question of justification or validity—*quid juris?*[28] [See below, point (13) of the appendix to the present chapter (not reprinted here).])

It seems that Hume never seriously considered the first alternative. Having cast out the logical theory of induction by repetition he struck a bargain with common sense, meekly allowing the re-entry of induction by repetition, in the guise of a psychological fact. I proposed to turn the tables upon this theory of Hume's. Instead of explaining our propensity to expect regularities as the result of repetition, I proposed to explain repetition-for-us as the result of our propensity to expect regularities and to search for them.

Thus I was led by purely logical considerations to replace the psychological theory of induction by the following view. Without waiting, passively, for repetitions to impress or impose regularities upon us, we actively try to impose regularities upon the world. We try to discover similarities in it, and to interpret it in terms of laws invented by us. Without waiting for premises we jump to conclusions. These may have to be discarded later, should observation show that they are wrong.

This was a theory of trial and error—of *conjectures and refutations*. It made it possible to understand why our attempts to force interpretations upon the world were logically prior to the observation of similarities. Since there were logical reasons behind this procedure, I thought that it would apply in the field of science also; that scientific theories were not the digest of observations, but that they were inventions—conjectures boldly put forward for trial, to be eliminated if they clashed with observations; with observations which were rarely accidental but as a rule undertaken with the definite intention of testing a theory by obtaining, if possible, a decisive refutation.

V.

The belief that science proceeds from observation to theory is still so widely and so firmly held that my denial of it is often met with incredulity. I have even been suspected of being insincere—of denying what nobody in his senses can doubt.

But in fact the belief that we can start with pure observations alone, without anything in the nature of a theory, is absurd; as may be illustrated by the story of the man who dedicated his life to natural science, wrote down everything he could observe, and bequeathed his priceless collection of observations to the Royal Society to be used as inductive evidence. This story should show us that though beetles may profitably be collected, observations may not.

Twenty-five years ago I tried to bring home the same point to a group of physics students in Vienna by beginning a lecture with the following instructions: 'Take pencil and paper; carefully observe, and write down what you have observed!' They asked, of course, *what* I wanted them to observe. Clearly the instruction, 'Observe!' is absurd.[29] (It is not even idiomatic, unless the object of the transitive verb can be taken as understood.) Observation is always selective. It needs a chosen object, a definite task, an interest, a point of view, a problem. And its description presupposes a descriptive language, with property words; it presupposes similarity and classification, which in their turn presuppose interests, points of view, and problems. 'A hungry animal', writes Katz,[30] 'divides the environment into edible and inedible things. An animal in flight sees roads to escape and hiding places.... Generally speaking, objects change ... according to the needs of the animal.' We may add that objects can be classified, and can become similar or dissimilar, *only* in this way—by being related to needs and interests. This rule applies not only to animals but also to scientists: For the animal a point of view is provided by its needs, the task of the moment, and its expectations; for the scientist by his theoretical interests, the special problem under investigation, his conjectures and anticipations, and the theories which he accepts as a kind of background: his frame of reference, his 'horizon of expectations'.

The problem 'Which comes first, the hypothesis (H) or the observation (O)?' is soluble; as is the problem, 'Which comes first, the hen (H) or the egg (O)?'.

---

27   What is done?

28   What ought to be done?

29   [Author's note] See section 30 of *L.Sc.D.*

30   [Author's note] Katz, *loc. cit.*

The reply to the latter is, 'An earlier kind of egg'; to the former, 'An earlier kind of hypothesis'. It is quite true that any particular hypothesis we choose will have been preceded by observations—the observations, for example, which it is designed to explain. But these observations, in their turn, presupposed the adoption of a frame of reference: a frame of expectations: a frame of theories. If they were significant, if they created a need for explanation and thus gave rise to the invention of a hypothesis, it was because they could not be explained within the old theoretical framework, the old horizon of expectations. There is no danger here of an infinite regress. Going back to more and more primitive theories and myths we shall in the end find unconscious, *inborn* expectations.

The theory of inborn *ideas* is absurd, I think; but every organism has inborn *reactions* or *responses*; and among them, responses adapted to impending events. These responses we may describe as 'expectations' without implying that these 'expectations' are conscious. The new-born baby 'expects', in this sense, to be fed (and, one could even argue, to be protected and loved). In view of the close relation between expectation and knowledge we may even speak in quite a reasonable sense of 'inborn knowledge'. This 'knowledge', however, is not *valid a priori*;[31] an inborn expectation, no matter how strong and specific, may be mistaken. (The newborn child may be abandoned, and starve.)

Thus we are born with expectations; with 'knowledge' which, although not *valid a priori*, is *psychologically or genetically a priori*, i.e., prior to all observational experience. One of the most important of these expectations is the expectation of finding a regularity. It is connected with an inborn propensity to look out for regularities, or with a *need* to *find* regularities, as we may see from the pleasure of the child who satisfies this need.

This 'instinctive' expectation of finding regularities, which is psychologically *a priori*, corresponds very closely to the 'law of causality' which Kant believed to be part of our mental outfit and to be *a priori* valid. One might thus be inclined to say that Kant failed to distinguish between psychologically *a priori* ways of thinking or responding and *a priori* valid beliefs. But I do not think that his mistake was quite as crude as that. For the expectation of finding regularities is not only psychologically *a priori*, but also logically *a priori*: it is logically prior to all observational experience, for it is prior to any recognition of similarities, as we have seen; and all observation involves the recognition of similarities (or dissimilarities). But in spite of being logically *a priori* in this sense the expectation is not valid *a priori*. For it may fail: we can easily construct an environment (it would be a lethal one) which, compared with our ordinary environment, is so chaotic that we completely fail to find regularities. (All natural laws could remain valid: environments of this kind have been used in the animal experiments mentioned in the next section.)

Thus Kant's reply to Hume came near to being right; for the distinction between an *a priori* valid expectation and one which is both genetically *and* logically prior to observation, but not *a priori* valid, is really somewhat subtle. But Kant proved too much. In trying to show how knowledge is possible, he proposed a theory which had the unavoidable consequence that our quest for knowledge must necessarily succeed, which is clearly mistaken. When Kant said, 'Our intellect does not draw its laws from nature but imposes its laws upon nature', he was right. But in thinking that these laws are necessarily true, or that we necessarily succeed in imposing them upon nature, he was wrong.[32] Nature very often resists quite success-

---

31   It is not something that can be known with certainty, even independently of any experience of the world, to be true.

32   [Author's note] Kant believed that Newton's dynamics was *a priori* valid. (See his *Metaphysical Foundations of Natural Science*, published between the first and the second editions of the *Critique of Pure Reason*.) But if, as he thought, we can explain the validity of Newton's theory by the fact that our intellect imposes its laws upon nature, it follows, I think, that our intellect must succeed in this; which makes it hard to understand why *a priori* knowledge such as Newton's should be so hard to come by. A somewhat fuller statement of this criticism can be found in ch. 2, especially section x, and chs. 7 and 8 of the present volume [*Conjectures and Refutations*].

fully, forcing us to discard our laws as refuted; but if we live we may try again.

To sum up this logical criticism of Hume's psychology of induction we may consider the idea of building an induction machine. Placed in a simplified 'world' (for example, one of sequences of coloured counters) such a machine may through repetition 'learn', or even 'formulate', laws of succession which hold in its 'world'. If such a machine can be constructed (and I have no doubt that it can) then, it might be argued, my theory must be wrong; for if a machine is capable of performing inductions on the basis of repetition, there can be no logical reasons preventing us from doing the same.

The argument sounds convincing, but it is mistaken. In constructing an induction machine we, the architects of the machine, must decide *a priori* what constitutes its 'world'; what things are to be taken as similar or equal; and what *kind* of 'laws' we wish the machine to be able to 'discover' in its 'world'. In other words we must build into the machine a framework determining what is relevant or interesting in its world: the machine will have its 'inborn' selection principles. The problems of similarity will have been solved for it by its makers who thus have interpreted the 'world' for the machine.

VI.

Our propensity to look out for regularities, and to impose laws upon nature, leads to the psychological phenomenon of *dogmatic thinking* or, more generally, dogmatic behaviour: we expect regularities everywhere and attempt to find them even where there are none; events which do not yield to these attempts we are inclined to treat as a kind of 'background noise'; and we stick to our expectations even when they are inadequate and we ought to accept defeat. This dogmatism is to some extent necessary. It is demanded by a situation which can only be dealt with by forcing our conjectures upon the world. Moreover, this dogmatism allows us to approach a good theory in stages, by way of approximations: if we accept defeat too easily, we may prevent ourselves from finding that we were very nearly right.

It is clear that this *dogmatic attitude*, which makes us stick to our first impressions, is indicative of a strong belief; while a *critical attitude*, which is ready to modify its tenets, which admits doubt and demands tests, is indicative of a weaker belief. Now according to Hume's theory, and to the popular theory, the strength of a belief should be a product of repetition; thus it should always grow with experience, and always be greater in less primitive persons. But dogmatic thinking, an uncontrolled wish to impose regularities, a manifest pleasure in rites and in repetition as such, are characteristic of primitives and children; and increasing experience and maturity sometimes create an attitude of caution and criticism rather than of dogmatism.

I may perhaps mention here a point of agreement with psycho-analysis. Psycho-analysts assert that neurotics and others interpret the world in accordance with a personal set pattern which is not easily given up, and which can often be traced back to early childhood. A pattern or scheme which was adopted very early in life is maintained throughout, and every new experience is interpreted in terms of it; verifying it, as it were, and contributing to its rigidity. This is a description of what I have called the dogmatic attitude, as distinct from the critical attitude, which shares with the dogmatic attitude the quick adoption of a schema of expectations—a myth, perhaps, or a conjecture or hypothesis—but which is ready to modify it, to correct it, and even to give it up. I am inclined to suggest that most neuroses may be due to a partially arrested development of the critical attitude; to an arrested rather than a natural dogmatism; to resistance to demands for the modification and adjustment of certain schematic interpretations and responses. This resistance in its turn may perhaps be explained, in some cases, as due to an injury or shock, resulting in fear and in an increased need for assurance or certainty, analogous to the way in which an injury to a limb makes us afraid to move it, so that it becomes stiff. (It might even be argued that the case of the limb is not merely analogous to the dogmatic response, but an instance of it.) The explanation of any concrete case will have to take into account the weight of the difficulties involved in making the necessary adjustments—difficulties which may be considerable, especially in a complex and changing world: we know from experiments on animals that varying degrees of neurotic behaviour may be produced at will by correspondingly varying difficulties.

I found many other links between the psychology of knowledge and psychological fields which are often considered remote from it—for example the psychology of art and music; in fact, my ideas about induction originated in a conjecture about the evolution of Western polyphony.[33] But you will be spared this story.

VII.

My logical criticism of Hume's psychological theory, and the considerations connected with it (most of which I elaborated in 1926–27, in a thesis entitled 'On Habit and Belief in Laws'[34]) may seem a little removed from the field of the philosophy of science. But the distinction between dogmatic and critical thinking, or the dogmatic and the critical attitude, brings us right back to our central problem. For the dogmatic attitude is clearly related to the tendency to *verify* our laws and schemata by seeking to apply them and to confirm them, even to the point of neglecting refutations, whereas the critical attitude is one of readiness to change them—to test them; to refute them; to *falsify* them, if possible. This suggests that we may identify the critical attitude with the scientific attitude, and the dogmatic attitude with the one which we have described as pseudo-scientific.

It further suggests that genetically speaking the pseudo-scientific attitude is more primitive than, and prior to, the scientific attitude: that it is a pre-scientific attitude. And this primitivity or priority also has its logical aspect. For the critical attitude is not so much opposed to the dogmatic attitude as super-imposed upon it: criticism must be directed against existing and influential beliefs in need of critical revision—in other words, dogmatic beliefs. A critical attitude needs for its raw material, as it were, theories or beliefs which are held more or less dogmatically.

Thus science must begin with myths, and with the criticism of myths; neither with the collection of observations, nor with the invention of experiments, but with the critical discussion of myths, and of magical techniques and practices. The scientific tradition is distinguished from the pre-scientific tradition in having two layers. Like the latter, it passes on its theories; but it also passes on a critical attitude towards them. The theories are passed on, not as dogmas, but rather with the challenge to discuss them and improve upon them. This tradition is Hellenic:[35] it may be traced back to Thales,[36] founder of the first *school* (I do not mean 'of the first *philosophical* school', but simply 'of the first school') which was not mainly concerned with the preservation of a dogma.[37]

The critical attitude, the tradition of free discussion of theories with the aim of discovering their weak spots so that they may be improved upon, is the attitude of reasonableness, of rationality. It makes far-reaching use of both verbal argument and observation—of observation in the interest of argument, however. The Greeks' discovery of the critical method gave rise at first to the mistaken hope that it would lead to the solution of all the great old problems; that it would establish certainty; that it would help to *prove* our theories, to *justify* them. But this hope was a residue of the dogmatic way of thinking; in fact nothing can be justified or proved (outside of mathematics and logic). The demand for rational proofs in science indicates a failure to keep distinct the broad realm of rationality and the narrow realm of rational certainty: it is an untenable, an unreasonable demand.

Nevertheless, the role of logical argument, of deductive logical reasoning, remains all-important for the critical approach; not because it allows us to prove our theories, or to infer them from observation

---

33   Music with two or more independent melodic parts sounded together.

34   [Author's note] A thesis submitted under the title '*Gewohnheit und Gesetzerlebnis*' to the Institute of Education of the City of Vienna in 1927. (Unpublished.)

35   Ancient Greek (from *Hellen*, a Greek).

36   Often described as the first philosopher of the Western tradition, Thales of Miletus flourished around 585 BCE. He is thought to be the first Western thinker in recorded history to attempt to give naturalistic, rather than religious, explanations for natural phenomena (such as magnetism).

37   [Author's note] Further comments on these developments may be found in chs. 4 and 5, below.

statements, but because only by purely deductive reasoning is it possible for us to discover what our theories imply, and thus to criticize them effectively. Criticism, I said, is an attempt to find the weak spots in a theory, and these, as a rule, can be found only in the more remote logical consequences which can be derived from it. It is here that purely logical reasoning plays an important part in science.

Hume was right in stressing that our theories cannot be validly inferred from what we can know to be true—neither from observations nor from anything else. He concluded from this that our belief in them was irrational. If 'belief' means here our inability to doubt our natural laws, and the constancy of natural regularities, then Hume is again right: this kind of dogmatic belief has, one might say, a physiological rather than a rational basis. If, however, the term 'belief' is taken to cover our critical acceptance of scientific theories—a *tentative* acceptance combined with an eagerness to revise the theory if we succeed in designing a test which it cannot pass—then Hume was wrong. In such an acceptance of theories there is nothing irrational. There is not even anything irrational in relying for practical purposes upon well-tested theories, for no more rational course of action is open to us.

Assume that we have deliberately made it our task to live in this unknown world of ours; to adjust ourselves to it as well as we can; to take advantage of the opportunities we can find in it; and to explain it, if possible (we need not assume that it is), and as far as possible, with the help of laws and explanatory theories. *If we have made this our task, then there is no more rational procedure than the method of trial and error—of conjecture and refutation*: of boldly proposing theories; of trying our best to show that these are erroneous; and of accepting them tentatively if our critical efforts are unsuccessful.

From the point of view here developed all laws, all theories, remain essentially tentative, or conjectural, or hypothetical, even when we feel unable to doubt them any longer. Before a theory has been refuted we can never know in what way it may have to be modified. That the sun will always rise and set within twenty-four hours is still proverbial as a law 'established by induction beyond reasonable

doubt'. It is odd that this example is still in use, though it may have served well enough in the days of Aristotle and Pytheas of Massalia[38]—the great traveller who for centuries was called a liar because of his tales of Thule, the land of the frozen sea and the *midnight sun*.

The method of trial and error is not, of course, simply identical with the scientific or critical approach—with the method of conjecture and refutation. The method of trial and error is applied not only by Einstein but, in a more dogmatic fashion, by the amoeba also. The difference lies not so much in the trials as in a critical and constructive attitude towards errors; errors which the scientist consciously and cautiously tries to uncover in order to refute his theories with searching arguments, including appeals to the most severe experimental tests which his theories and his ingenuity permit him to design.

The critical attitude might be described as the result of a conscious attempt to make our theories, our conjectures, suffer in our stead in the struggle for the survival of the fittest. It gives us a chance to survive the elimination of an inadequate hypothesis—when a more dogmatic attitude would eliminate it by eliminating us. (There is a touching story of an Indian community which disappeared because of its belief in the holiness of life, including that of tigers.) We thus obtain the fittest theory within our reach by the elimination of those which are less fit. (By 'fitness' I do not mean merely 'usefulness' but truth; see chapters 3 and 10, below.) I do not think that this procedure is irrational or in need of any further rational justification.

VIII.

Let us now turn from our logical criticism of the *psychology of experience* to our real problem—the problem of the *logic of science*. Although some of the things I have said may help us here, in so far as they may have eliminated certain psychological prejudices

---

38   Aristotle lived from 384 to 322 BCE, and Pytheas flourished around 310 BCE. Pytheas described Thule as being six days sail north of Britain, and the ancients thought of it as being at the northernmost tip of the world; the land he visited was most probably Norway.

that favour induction, my treatment of the *logical problem of induction* is completely independent of this criticism, and of all psychological considerations. Provided you do not dogmatically believe in the alleged psychological fact that we make inductions, you may now forget my whole story with the exception of two logical points: my logical remarks on testability or falsifiability as the criterion of demarcation; and Hume's logical criticism of induction.

From what I have said it is obvious that there was a close link between the two problems which interested me at that time: demarcation, and induction or scientific method. It was easy to see that the method of science is criticism, i.e., attempted falsifications. Yet it took me a few years to notice that the two problems—of demarcation and of induction—were in a sense one.

Why, I asked, do so many scientists believe in induction? I found they did so because they believed natural science to be characterized by the inductive method—by a method starting from, and relying upon, long sequences of observations and experiments. They believed that the difference between genuine science and metaphysical or pseudo-scientific speculation depended solely upon whether or not the inductive method was employed. They believed (to put it in my own terminology) that only the inductive method could provide a satisfactory *criterion of demarcation*.

I recently came across an interesting formulation of this belief in a remarkable philosophical book by a great physicist—Max Born's *Natural Philosophy of Cause and Chance*.[39] He writes: 'Induction allows us to generalize a number of observations into a general rule: that night follows day and day follows night ... But while everyday life has no definite criterion for the validity of an induction, ... science has worked out a code, or rule of craft, for its application.' Born nowhere reveals the contents of this inductive code (which, as his wording shows, contains a 'definite criterion for the validity of an induction'); but he stresses that 'there is no logical argument' for its acceptance: 'it is a question of faith'; and he is therefore 'willing to

call induction a metaphysical principle'. But why does he believe that such a code of valid inductive rules must exist? This becomes clear when he speaks of the 'vast communities of people ignorant of, or rejecting, the rule of science, among them the members of anti-vaccination societies and believers in astrology. It is useless to argue with them; I cannot compel them to accept the same criteria of valid induction in which I believe: the code of scientific rules.' This makes it quite clear that *'valid induction' was here meant to serve as a criterion of demarcation between science and pseudo-science.*

But it is obvious that this rule or craft of 'valid induction' is not even metaphysical: it simply does not exist. No rule can ever guarantee that a generalization inferred from true observations, however often repeated, is true. (Born himself does not believe in the truth of Newtonian physics, in spite of its success, although he believes that it is based on induction.) And the success of science is not based upon rules of induction, but depends upon luck, ingenuity, and the purely deductive rules of critical argument.

I may summarize some of my conclusions as follows:

(1) Induction, i.e., inference based on many observations, is a myth. It is neither a psychological fact, nor a fact of ordinary life, nor one of scientific procedure.

(2) The actual procedure of science is to operate with conjectures: to jump to conclusions—often after one single observation (as noticed for example by Hume and Born).

(3) Repeated observations and experiments function in science as *tests* of our conjectures or hypotheses, i.e., as attempted refutations.

(4) The mistaken belief in induction is fortified by the need for a criterion of demarcation which, it is traditionally but wrongly believed, only the inductive method can provide.

(5) The conception of such an inductive method, like the criterion of verifiability, implies a faulty demarcation.

(6) None of this is altered in the least if we say that induction makes theories only probable rather than certain. (See especially chapter 10, below.)

---

39   [Author's note] Max Born, *Natural Philosophy of Cause and Chance*, Oxford, 1949, p. 7.

IX.

If, as I have suggested, the problem of induction is only an instance or facet of the problem of demarcation, then the solution to the problem of demarcation must provide us with a solution to the problem of induction. This is indeed the case, I believe, although it is perhaps not immediately obvious.

For a brief formulation of the problem of induction we can turn again to Born, who writes: '…no observation or experiment, however extended, can give more than a finite number of repetitions'; therefore, 'the statement of a law—B depends on A—always transcends experience. Yet this kind of statement is made everywhere and all the time, and sometimes from scanty material.'[40]

In other words, the logical problem of induction arises from (*a*) Hume's discovery (so well expressed by Born) that it is impossible to justify a law by observation or experiment, since it 'transcends experience'; (*b*) the fact that science proposes and uses laws 'everywhere and all the time'. (Like Hume, Born is struck by the 'scanty material', i.e., the few observed instances upon which the law may be based.) To this we have to add (*c*) *the principle of empiricism* which asserts that in science, only observation and experiment may decide upon the *acceptance or rejection* of scientific statements, including laws and theories.

These three principles, (*a*), (*b*), and (*c*), appear at first sight to clash; and this apparent clash constitutes the *logical problem of induction*.

Faced with this clash, Born gives up (*c*), the principle of empiricism (as Kant and many others, including Bertrand Russell, have done before him), in favour of what he calls a 'metaphysical principle'; a metaphysical principle which he does not even attempt to formulate; which he vaguely describes as a 'code or rule of craft'; and of which I have never seen any formulation which even looked promising and was not clearly untenable.

But in fact the principles (*a*) to (*c*) do not clash. We can see this the moment we realize that the acceptance by science of a law or of a theory is *tentative only*; which is to say that all laws and theories are conjec-

tures, or tentative *hypotheses* (a position which I have sometimes called 'hypotheticism'); and that we may reject a law or theory on the basis of new evidence, without necessarily discarding the old evidence which originally led us to accept it.[41]

The principle of empiricism (*c*) can be fully preserved, since the fate of a theory, its acceptance or rejection, is decided by observation and experiment— by the result of tests. So long as a theory stands up to the severest tests we can design, it is accepted; if it does not, it is rejected. But it is never inferred, in any sense, from the empirical evidence. There is neither a psychological nor a logical induction. *Only the falsity of the theory can be inferred from empirical evidence, and this inference is a purely deductive one.*

Hume showed that it is not possible to infer a theory from observation statements; but this does not affect the possibility of refuting a theory by observation statements. The full appreciation of this possibility makes the relation between theories and observations perfectly clear.

This solves the problem of the alleged clash between the principles (*a*), (*b*), and (*c*), and with it Hume's problem of induction.

X.

Thus the problem of induction is solved. But nothing seems less wanted than a simple solution to an age-old philosophical problem. Wittgenstein and his school hold that genuine philosophical problems do not exist;[42] from which it clearly follows that they cannot be solved. Others among my contemporaries do believe that there are philosophical problems, and respect them; but they seem to respect them too much; they seem to believe that they are insoluble, if not taboo; and they are shocked and horrified by the claim that there is a simple, neat, and lucid, solution

---

40   [Author's note] *Natural Philosophy of Cause and Chance*, p. 6.

41   [Author's note] I do not doubt that Born and many others would agree that theories are accepted only tentatively. But the widespread belief in induction shows that the far-reaching implications of this view are rarely seen.

42   [Author's note] Wittgenstein still held this belief in 1946; see note 8 to ch. 2, below.

to any of them. If there is a solution it must be deep, they feel, or at least complicated.

However this may be, I am still waiting for a simple, neat and lucid criticism of the solution which I published first in 1933 in my letter to the Editor of *Erkenntnis*,[43] and later in *The Logic of Scientific Discovery*.

Of course, one can invent new problems of induction, different from the one I have formulated and solved. (Its formulation was half its solution.) But I have yet to see any reformulation of the problem whose solution cannot be easily obtained from my old solution. I am now going to discuss some of these re-formulations.

One question which may be asked is this: how do we really jump from an observation statement to a theory?

Although this question appears to be psychological rather than philosophical, one can say something positive about it without invoking psychology. One can say first that the jump is not from an observation statement, but from a problem-situation, and that the theory must allow us *to explain* the observations which created the problem (that is, *to deduce* them from the theory strengthened by other accepted theories and by other observation statements, the so-called initial conditions). This leaves, of course, an immense number of possible theories, good and bad; and it thus appears that our question has not been answered.

But this makes it fairly clear that when we asked our question we had more in mind than, 'How do we jump from an observation statement to a theory?' The question we had in mind was, it now appears, 'How do we jump from an observation statement to a *good* theory?' But to this the answer is: by jumping first to *any* theory and then testing it, to find whether it is good or not; i.e., by repeatedly applying the critical method, eliminating many bad theories, and inventing many new ones. Not everybody is able to do this; but there is no other way.

Other questions have sometimes been asked. The original problem of induction, it was said, is the problem of *justifying* induction, i.e., of justifying inductive inference. If you answer this problem by

saying that what is called an 'inductive inference' is always invalid and therefore clearly not justifiable, the following new problem must arise: how do you justify your method of trial and error? Reply: the method of trial and error is a *method of eliminating false theories* by observation statements; and the justification for this is the purely logical relationship of deducibility which allows us to assert the falsity of universal statements if we accept the truth of singular ones.

Another question sometimes asked is this: why is it reasonable to prefer non-falsified statements to falsified ones? To this question some involved answers have been produced, for example pragmatic answers. But from a pragmatic point of view the question does not arise, since false theories often serve well enough: most formulae used in engineering or navigation are known to be false, although they may be excellent approximations and easy to handle; and they are used with confidence by people who know them to be false.

The only correct answer is the straightforward one: because we search for truth (even though we can never be sure we have found it), and because the falsified theories are known or believed to be false, while the non-falsified theories may still be true. Besides, we do not prefer *every* non-falsified theory—only one which, in the light of criticism, appears to be better than its competitors: which solves our problems, which is well tested, and of which we think, or rather conjecture or hope (considering other provisionally accepted theories), that it will stand up to further tests.

It has also been said that the problem of induction is, 'Why is it *reasonable* to believe that the future will be like the past?', and that a satisfactory answer to this question should make it plain that such a belief is, in fact, reasonable. My reply is that it is reasonable to believe that the future will be very different from the past in many vitally important respects. Admittedly it is perfectly reasonable to act on the assumption that it will, in many respects, be like the past, and that well-tested laws will continue to hold (since we can have no better assumption to act upon); but it is also reasonable to believe that such a course of action will lead us at times into severe trouble, since some of the laws upon which we now heavily rely may easily prove unreliable. (Remember the midnight sun!) One might even say that to judge from past experience,

---

43   [Author's note] See note 5 [19 in this text] above.

and from our general scientific knowledge, the future will *not* be like the past, in perhaps most of the ways which those have in mind who say that it will. Water will sometimes not quench thirst, and air will choke those who breathe it. An apparent way out is to say that the future will be like the past *in the sense that the laws of nature will not change*, but this is begging the question. We speak of a 'law of nature' only if we think that we have before us a regularity which does not change; and if we find that it changes then we shall not continue to call it a 'law of nature'. Of course our search for natural laws indicates that we hope to find them, and that we believe that there are natural laws; but our belief in any particular natural law cannot have a safer basis than our unsuccessful critical attempts to refute it.

I think that those who put the problem of induction in terms of the *reasonableness* of our beliefs are perfectly right if they are dissatisfied with a Humean, or post-Humean, sceptical despair of reason. We must indeed reject the view that a belief in science is as irrational as a belief in primitive magical practices—that both are a matter of accepting a 'total ideology', a convention or a tradition based on faith. But we must be cautious if we formulate our problem, with Hume, as one of the reasonableness of our *beliefs*. We should split this problem into three—our old problem of demarcation, or of how to *distinguish* between science and primitive magic; the problem of the rationality of the scientific or critical *procedure*, and of the role of observation within it; and lastly the problem of the rationality of our *acceptance* of theories for scientific and for practical purposes. To all these three problems solutions have been offered here.

One should also be careful not to confuse the problem of the reasonableness of the scientific procedure and the (tentative) acceptance of the results of this procedure—i.e., the scientific theories—with the problem of the rationality or otherwise *of the belief that this procedure will succeed*. In practice, in practical scientific research, this belief is no doubt unavoidable and reasonable, there being no better alternative. But the belief is certainly unjustifiable in a theoretical sense, as I have argued (in section V). Moreover, if we could show, on general logical grounds, that the

scientific quest is likely to succeed, one could not understand why anything like success has been so rare in the long history of human endeavours to know more about our world.

Yet another way of putting the problem of induction is in terms of probability. Let *t* be the theory and *e* the evidence: we can ask for $P(t,e)$, that is to say, the probability of *t*, given *e*. The problem of induction, it is often believed, can then be put thus: construct a calculus of probability which allows us to work out for any theory *t* what its probability is, relative to any given empirical evidence *e*; and show that $P(t,e)$ increases with the accumulation of supporting evidence, and reaches high values—at any rate values greater than ½.

In *The Logic of Scientific Discovery* I explained why I think that this approach to the problem is fundamentally mistaken.[44] To make this clear, I introduced there the distinction between *probability* and *degree of corroboration or confirmation*. (The term 'confirmation' has lately been so much used and misused that I have decided to surrender it to the verificationists and to use for my own purposes 'corroboration' only. The term 'probability' is best used in some of the many senses which satisfy the well-known calculus of probability, axiomatized, for example, by Keynes, Jeffreys,[45] and myself; but nothing of course depends on the choice of words, as long as we do not *assume*, uncritically, that degree of corroboration must also be

---

44   [Author's note] *L.Sc.D.* (see note 5 [19 in this text] above), ch. X, especially sections 80 to 83, also section 34 ff. See also my note 'A Set of Independent Axioms for Probability', *Mind*, N.S. 47, 1938, p. 275. (This note has since been reprinted, with corrections, in the new appendix *ii of *L.Sc.D.* See also the next note but one to the present chapter.)

45   John Maynard Keynes (1883–1946) is known primarily as an economist, but he also produced an influential *Treatise on Probability* in 1921. Harold Jeffreys (1891–1989) was a professor of astronomy at Cambridge (and originated the theory that the core of the earth is liquid). His *The Theory of Probability* (1939) was the first attempt to develop a theory of scientific inference based on the ideas of Bayesian statistics.

a probability—that is to say, that it must satisfy the calculus of probability.)[46]

I explained in my book why we are interested in theories with a *high degree of corroboration*. And I explained why it is a mistake to conclude from this that we are interested in *highly probable* theories. I pointed out that the probability of a statement (or set of statements) is always the greater the less the statement says: it is inverse to the content or the deductive power of the statement, and thus to its explanatory power. Accordingly every interesting and powerful statement must have a low probability; and *vice versa*: a statement with a high probability will be scientifically uninteresting, because it says little and has no explanatory power. Although we seek theories with a high degree of corroboration, *as scientists we do not seek highly probable theories but explanations; that is to say, powerful and improbable theories*. The opposite view—that science aims at high probability—is

a characteristic development of verificationism: if you find that you cannot verify a theory, or make it certain by induction, you may turn to probability as a kind of '*Ersatz*'[47] for certainty, in the hope that induction may yield at least that much.

I have discussed the two problems of demarcation and induction at some length. Yet since I set out to give you in this lecture a kind of report on the work I have done in this field I shall have to add, in the form of an *Appendix*,[48] a few words about some other problems on which I have been working, between 1934 and 1953. I was led to most of these problems by trying to think out the consequences of the solutions to the two problems of demarcation and induction. But time does not allow me to continue my narrative, and to tell you how my new problems arose out of my old ones. Since I cannot even start a discussion of these further problems now, I shall have to confine myself to giving you a bare list of them, with a few explanatory words here and there. But even a bare list may be useful, I think. It may serve to give an idea of the fertility of the approach. It may help to illustrate what our problems look like; and it may show how many there are, and so convince you that there is no need whatever to worry over the question whether philosophical problems exist, or what philosophy is really about. So this list contains, by implication, an apology for my unwillingness to break with the old tradition of trying to solve problems with the help of rational argument, and thus for my unwillingness to participate wholeheartedly in the developments, trends, and drifts, of contemporary philosophy.

---

46   [Author's note] A definition, in terms of probabilities, of $C(t,e)$, i.e., of the degree of corroboration (of a theory t relative to the evidence e) satisfying the demands indicated in my *L.Sc.D.*, sections 82 to 83, is the following:

$$C(t,e) = E(t,e) \, (1 + P(t)P(t,e)),$$

where $E(t,e) = (P(e,t) - P(e))/(P(e,t) + P(e))$ is a (non-additive) measure of the explanatory power of t with respect to e. Note that $C(t,e)$ is not a probability: it may have values between -1 (refutation of t by e) and $C(t,t) \leq +1$. Statements t which are lawlike and thus non-verifiable cannot even reach $C(t,e) = C(t,t)$ upon empirical evidence e. $C(t,t)$ is the *degree of corroborability* of t, and is equal to the *degree of testability* of t, or to the *content* of t. Because of the demands implied in point (6) at the end of section I above, I do not think, however, that it is possible to give a complete formalization of the idea of corroboration (or, as I previously used to say, of confirmation).

(Added 1955 to the first proofs of this paper:)

See also my note 'Degree of Confirmation', *British Journal for the Philosophy of Science*, 5, 1954, pp. 143 fl. (See also 5, pp. 334.) I have since simplified this definition as follows (*B.J.P.S.*, 1955, 5, p. 359):

$$C(t,e) = (P(e,t) - P(e))/(P(e,t) - P(e,t) + P(e))$$

For a further improvement, see *B.J.P.S.* 6, 1955, p. 56.

47   Inferior substitute (from German "replacement").

48   This Appendix is not reprinted here; it can be found in Popper's book *Conjectures and Refutations* (pages 59 to 65).

WESLEY SALMON

"Unfinished Business: The Problem of Induction"

Who Was Wesley Salmon?

Wesley C. Salmon (1925–2001) was an influential philosopher of science, known especially for his work on the attempt to find a sound basis for scientific explanation. He rejected Carl Hempel's then-dominant deductive-nomological view of scientific explanation (see the Hempel reading in this section for more on the D-N model). Instead, Salmon developed and defended an alternative, causal-mechanical, model of explanation where events are to be explained by the way in which they fit into real, underlying causal processes. In order to provide a proper foundation for this account Salmon also devoted a lot of attention to the nature of causation, and formulated a view of causal processes as those which continuously transmit structure or information from one location, or time, to another. One significant difference between Salmon's causal-mechanical model of explanation and Hempel-style covering-law explanation is that Salmon's model is able to treat unlikely or one-off events as nevertheless explicable.

He authored four books on explanation and causation: *The Foundations of Scientific Inference* (University of Pittsburgh Press, 1967), *Scientific Explanation and the Causal Structure of the World* (Princeton University Press, 1984), *Four Decades of Scientific Explanation* (University of Pittsburgh Press, 1990), and *Causality and Explanation* (Oxford University Press, 1998).

Salmon studied for his PhD at the University of California, Los Angeles, where he worked with the eminent philosopher of science Hans Reichenbach. He taught at Brown University, then for a decade (1963–1973) at Indiana University, Bloomington, where he was one of the founding members of the History and Philosophy of Science program. After a stint at the University of Arizona he moved to the University of Pittsburgh in 1981. He spent the rest of his career at Pittsburgh, during a period in which the department of the history and philosophy of science at Pittsburgh consolidated its status as the top HPS program in the US. From 1983 until his retirement in 1999 he held the post of university professor of philosophy, which Hempel had filled before him.

He died with tragic suddenness in a car crash. "His death was brought about by a causal chain that began with a minor two-car incident and eventuated in an outcome that no one could have predicted would have occurred. Ironically, it was a tragic event of a kind that he himself had frequently discussed in his philosophical work: an improbable occurrence, but not therefore an explicable event!"[1]

What Is the Structure of This Reading?

Salmon begins by reminding us of Hume's formulation of the problem of induction, and asserting that we should take seriously the quest for a satisfactory solution to this problem. He rejects Hume's own solu-

---

1   James H. Fetzer, "In Memoriam: Wesley C. Salmon (1925–2001)," *Synthèse* 132 (2002), 1–3, p. 1.

tion, and also canvasses four popular responses each of which, according to Salmon, fails. Indeed, he says, "Hume had already considered and answered each of them." He then goes on to deal in more detail with a succession of more 'serious' responses to the problem of induction. The first sees it as a pseudo-problem, and attempts to dissolve it by marshaling our existing intuitions about when predictions are confirmed (Nowell-Smith, Goodman, Carnap), or by taking a 'Wittgensteinian' or 'ordinary language philosophy' approach (Strawson, Barker, Pollock). Salmon rejects this family of responses to the problem of induction, and also argues fiercely against the second kind of response he considers: Popper's 'method of conjectures and refutations.'

Salmon shows more sympathy for what he calls the 'pragmatic approach' to induction (Feigl, Reichenbach, and himself) but notes the as-yet unsolved problem of justifying the condition that a proper inference rule must be 'symmetrical.' He concludes by asking whether the methods or practices of statistics will be any help in solving the problem of induction—and arguing that they will not—but then making a renewed plea for the importance of finding an answer to Hume's quandary.

Suggestions for Critical Reflection

1. "I must confess, I am not as sanguine as Hume about nature's dependability in keeping us appropriately on course as we plan for the future and make our practical decisions." What does Salmon mean by this? Is he right?

2. Salmon rather cheekily rejects the view that "the fallacy of affirming the consequent—known more politely as the 'hypothetico-deductive method'—is the legitimate method of science." The hypothetico-deductive method is described in a note to this reading, and alluded to elsewhere in this chapter. Why does Salmon call it "the fallacy of affirming the consequent"? Is he right that Goodman makes this mistake? How does Popper seek to avoid it? Does this approach amount to merely aiming to "codify and systematize our feelings about what is or is not legitimate," as Salmon seems to suggest?

3. Salmon argues that, although the principles of induction may not be the kinds of principles that can be *validated*, it is nevertheless reasonable to expect that they should be *vindicated*. What distinction is Salmon making here? What would it be to vindicate induction? Is Hume's problem of induction the problem of vindicating induction?

4. Can the ordinary language approach to induction distinguish in a principled way between induction and other, less rational, principles of inference?

5. How does Salmon argue that, if we adopt Popper's method of conjectures and refutations, "the content of scientific knowledge cannot extend beyond the content of our observation reports"? He suggests that this means that science is no more rational a guide to the future than any other practice (such as astrology): why does he say this? How might Popper reply to Salmon's attack?

6. What do you think Salmon means by the "condition of symmetry" that must be met by any justified basic rule of inference? How difficult a problem do you think it is to justify such a condition? Is this just the problem of induction all over again?

7. "It is manifestly untenable to deny that there is any such thing as rationally grounded prediction," says Salmon. Is it? Is it equally untenable to insist that science is a more rational ground for prediction than, say, reading tea leaves but that we don't know *why* it is (and can't even prove *that* it is)? Is this where the problem of induction leaves us?

Suggestions for Further Reading

Three other articles by Salmon on induction, one earlier and two later than the one reprinted here, are "On Vindicating Induction," *Philosophy of Science* 30 (1963), 252–261; "Rational Prediction," *The British Journal for the Philosophy of Science* 32 (1981), 115–125; and "Hans Reichenbach's Vindication of Induction," *Erkenntnis* 35 (1991), 99–122. Some discussions of Salmon's view of induction are: Brian Skyrms, "On Failing to Vindicate Induction," *Philosophy of Science* 32 (1965), 253–268; Ian Hacking, "Salmon's Vindication of Induction," *The Journal of Philosophy* 62 (1965), 260–266; and Samir Okasha, "What Did Hume Really Show About Induction?", *Philosophical Quarterly* 51 (2001), 307–327.

"Unfinished Business: The Problem of Induction"[2]

Hume's *Enquiry concerning Human Understanding* is widely recognized as a work admirably suited to stimulate genuine epistemological interest and perplexity on the part of beginning students.[3] Composed by a philosophical stylist of consummate skill, it presents, in simple and comprehensible terms, a problem of enormous intellectual and practical import—the problem of the justification of induction. Like most good philosophical problems, this one has proved amazingly refractory against some of the best efforts of first-rate philosophers, past and present. To be sure, many contemporary philosophers believe they possess a definitive answer to this puzzle, but expert opinion differs markedly regarding the nature of the correct answer. Under these circumstances, it seems extraordinary that no mention whatever was made of this problem at the Hume bicentennial conference.[4] Such a lacuna should not, I feel, go unnoticed.

In view of the popularity of the *Enquiry* as an introductory reading, let me continue to pursue the

2   *Philosophical Studies*, Vol. 33, No. 1 (Jan 1978), pp. 1–19. With kind permission from Springer Science+ Business Media.

3   [Author's note] This point was brought home forcefully to me when, recently, trying to free my mind of all philosophical preconceptions, I reread Sections IV– VII of the *Enquiry*. As a result of this effort, I wrote a dialogue, 'An Encounter with David Hume' (published in Joel Feinberg (ed.), *Reason and Responsibility*, 3rd ed., Dickenson Publ. Co., 1975) in which I try to show how this work can speak effectively to contemporary students.

4   The bicentennial of Hume's death was 1976; an international memorial conference was held at the University of Edinburgh in August of that year.

issue from a pedagogic standpoint. How do we go about presenting this material to young minds? We try to challenge them to think about the question of what basis we have for making any inference from the observed to the unobserved. We try to make them grapple with a logical problem: How do we know what's going to happen in the future—in the next few years, the next few hours, the next few minutes? They think they know (partially at least) what's going to happen, and so do we, but how? Not by direct observation, for we do not have the gift of precognition. If we know at all, we know by some sort of inference. And once that is clear, we have them in Hume's grasp. "... [A]s a philosopher, who has some share of curiosity", he said, "I want to learn the foundation of this inference."

As we follow out Hume's analysis for our students, we reveal his inability to find any rational foundation for such inferences. "If there be any suspicion that the course of nature may change, and that the past may be no rule for the future, all experience becomes useless, and can give rise to NO INFERENCE OR CONCLUSION." "... [I]t is not REASONING which engages us to suppose the past resembling the future, and to expect similar effects from causes which are, to appearance, similar." "I am ready to reject ALL BELIEF AND REASONING and look upon *no opinion* as MORE PROBABLE OR LIKELY than another."[5]

Nature, of course, compels us—or exercises friendly persuasion at least—to expect the future to be like the past in significant respects. But psychological expectation is not the same thing as logical inference. Logic—reason—has nothing whatever to do with it. That's what David Hume said, we tell our introductory classes; if Hume is right, any belief about unobserved matters of fact is just as *reasonable* as any other. Not as vivid, or compelling, or natural perhaps—but just as *reasonable* or *probable* or *likely*.

Forgive me for rehearsing this familiar story. My purpose is to ask what response we are to offer. I realize that—if the past be any guide to the future—no vast numbers of students are going to be 'turned on'

5   [Author's note] The foregoing famous quotations are from the *Enquiry*, Part IV, and the *Treatise*, conclusion of Book I. I have added emphasis.

to any such abstract intellectual problem. But what about the small minority who read the assignment, pay attention to the lecture, and try to understand what is going on? What shall we say to them? Was Hume right? Shall we admit that reason has nothing to do with predicting the future? *I do not think we are quite ready for that concession—at least I fervently hope not.* We believe that there are rational methods of prediction, and that there are irrational ones. Moreover, I must confess, I am not as sanguine as Hume about nature's dependability in keeping us appropriately on course as we plan for the future and make our practical decisions. When I observe human behavior—including my own—I'm not encouraged.

Having been presented with a problem, our students would like to be told 'the answer.' It is, of course, contrary to all accepted principles of philosophic pedagogy to satisfy that desire without further ado, so we tell them that the solution (as if we had one to give them) cannot really be appreciated without going through the salient arguments. We therefore consider various alternative approaches; several immediately suggest themselves either for historical reasons or because of their strong psychological appeal.

(1) Many of the brightest students, when asked why they have confidence in the inductive method, will answer, "because it works." This formula has such compelling psychological appeal that it is easy to overlook the temporal ambiguity of the verb 'works.' What the argument amounts to, as Hume so masterfully explained, is the inference that induction *will work* because it *has worked.* This inference is itself inductive, and thus begs the question. Philosophers have, nevertheless, attempted to show how induction could be supported inductively. It has sometimes been suggested that circles can be 'virtuous' rather than 'vicious,' or that an argument can be circular without committing the fallacy of *petitio principii.*[6] But after all of the philosophical squirming—whether they are circular, the type of circularity, and whether it is bad for an argument to be circular—it remains

possible to 'justify' the counter-inductive method[7] by precisely the same type of argument as was used to justify induction.[8] Whatever 'justifies' everything justifies nothing.

(2) Kant's appeal to the synthetic a priori must be mentioned, and not just for reasons of historical completeness. Hume had severely challenged the status of the principle of uniformity of nature. Awakened from his dogmatic slumbers, Kant argued that this principle (in the form of a principle of universal causation) is secured as a synthetic a priori truth of pure reason.[9] Kant had no doubts about the existence of synthetic a priori truths; he was merely formulating in rather clear and precise terms what philosophers had maintained about the status of geometry for more than two millennia. The subsequent discovery of non-Euclidean geometries,[10] and the searching philosophical investigations of their applicability to the physical world, have thoroughly undercut any such view of the nature of geometry. With that (and other) developments, the basis for the synthetic a priori became tenuous indeed. Nevertheless, the last ditch resort to the synthetic a priori in order to get around the problem of induction is not a thing of the remote past. Two of the greatest scientific philosophers of the twentieth century have taken that refuge—how else can we regard Carnap's

---

6   *Petitio principii* (Latin for 'the taking for granted of the principle or starting point') is the fallacy of begging the question.

7   The counter-inductive method is a method of 'justifying' beliefs that is contrary to induction: for example, the so-called 'gambler's fallacy'—the mistake of believing that if the same thing has happened repeatedly (e.g., a coin landing heads) this makes it more likely that something different will happen soon (e.g., the coin will land tails).

8   [Author's note] My critical discussion of this approach can be found in *The Foundations of Scientific Inference* (University of Pittsburgh Press, Pittsburgh, 1967), pp. 12–17.

9   A synthetic a priori judgment is one which is, of course, both synthetic—i.e., not merely a logical truth (or falsehood)—and a priori, i.e., known prior to, or independently of, sense-experience.

10   Non-Euclidean geometries describe a space that is 'curved' so that lines on a two-dimensional plane that would be parallel in Euclidian geometry will either meet or 'curve away' from each other.

a priori measure functions in confirmation theory[11] or Russell's postulates of scientific inference?[12] Although Russell's theory of non-demonstrative inference does not enjoy a great deal of popularity at present, Carnap's inductive logic does stand as the most highly developed and clearly articulated system we have seen to date.

(3) The tradition of British Empiricism—of which Hume was both the ablest champion and the most devastating challenger—lived on into the nineteenth century with John Stuart Mill. Mill was no friend of global synthetic a priori principles, or a priori principles of any sort. His idea was to assume just as much uniformity of nature (causality) as you need for the job at hand—no more. He seems to have adopted a sort of postulational approach. Russell later provided a critique of postulational method which was both brief and apt: "The method of 'postulating' what we want has many advantages; they are the same as the advantages of theft over honest toil."[13] Mill, in anticipation, seems to have felt that many petty larcenies are more excusable than one big heist. Like all others who have resorted to postulates, Mill never really came to grips with Hume's problem.

(4) It has sometimes been maintained that Hume's critique of induction should be no cause for distress to any but those philosophers engaged in a 'quest for certainty.' Hume showed conclusively, they claim, that the inductive method is not infallible. That is a fact of life we must simply learn to live with.[14] This response, however, seriously fails to appreciate the import of Hume's conclusions and the arguments he adduces in their support. He argues, not that induction may upon occasion yield a false conclusion, but rather, that for all we can know, *it may never again yield a true one*. It is not that inductive conclusions fall short of certainty; rather, we have no reason to place *any confidence whatever in any inductive conclusion*. The ancient philosophers were fully aware that neither perception nor a posteriori reasoning yields absolute certainty. Hume did far more than merely to remind us of that banality.

These four approaches come readily to mind; no doubt there are others that could be placed in the same category. They all have one thing in common. Hume had already considered and answered each of them. If we had read carefully and understood, we could have saved ourselves the trouble of going through them. We should be telling our students, at this point, that Hume's arguments stand up remarkably well against all traditional efforts to refute or circumvent them.

The foregoing attempts to deal with the problem of induction are admittedly not among those which enjoy the greatest current popularity. Let us therefore consider the more serious contenders. Many twentieth century philosophers have tried to dismiss the difficulty as a pseudo-problem; this seems to qualify as the most popular way to get around Hume's embarrassing problem.

The basic idea is that Hume did not formulate a real problem, but became enmeshed in a series of conceptual confusions. Once we straighten out those confusions—which may involve considerable subtlety—the problem will vanish. Here are some of the allegations:

- He confused induction with deduction.
- He tried, unsuccessfully of course, to transform induction into deduction.
- He inappropriately applied deductive standards to induction.
- He failed to recognize that induction has its own standards and criteria—that it is an autonomous type of logic, distinct from deduction.

---

11   Rudolf Carnap (1891–1970) was a German-born American philosopher of science and logician. A priori measure functions are, roughly, functions that assign prior probabilities to states described by scientific theories.

12   [Author's note] See *The Foundations of Scientific Inference*, pp. 27–48, 68–79. Russell's introduction of his postulates in *Human Knowledge, Its Scope and Limits* is strikingly similar to a Kantian 'transcendental deduction.'

13   [Author's note] Bertrand Russell, *Introduction to Mathematical Philosophy* (George Allen and Unwin, London, 1919), p. 71.

14   [Author's note] Such an answer has been suggested by Jerrold Katz, *The Problem of Induction and Its Solution* (University of Chicago Press, Chicago, 1962), p. 115.

The whole attempt to find a justification for induction was, according to this charge, a search for something that would be appropriate only in a deductive context.

There is no doubt that we should make every effort to avoid confusing induction with deduction. But will avoidance of such confusion make Hume's problem of induction vanish? The key notion in this approach is *autonomy*; let us see what it amounts to. The general idea seems to be that there are certain forms of argument which are not valid, but which we are not prepared to give up. When we find that our favorite argument turns out to be fallacious, but we want to cling to it, one way to save it is to call it 'inductive.' Recall Morris R. Cohen's famous quip to the effect that a logic text is a book divided into two parts; in the first part (on deduction) the fallacies are explained, while in the second part (on induction) they are committed.

Similar ploys have been adopted in other areas of philosophy. In a famous passage in the *Treatise*, Hume remarked pointedly upon the logical gap in arguments which purport to derive ought-statements from is-statements. Some moral philosophers who hanker after such inferences have sought ways of circumventing this difficulty. One device, suggested by Patrick Nowell-Smith, is the concept of 'contextual implication': "... a statement *p* contextually implies a statement *q* if anyone who knew the normal conventions of the language would be entitled to infer *q* from *p in the context in which they occur*."[15] Contextual implication, Nowell-Smith notes, does not share with standard logical implication (deductive entailment) the severe drawback of being bound by rigid rules. This very feature of contextual implication suits it for use in the 'anything-goes-if-you-want-it-badly-enough' approach to logic.

Unbridled use of contextual implication may, of course, give rise to some disquieting results. For example, in some places at the present time it seems that the statement, 'the victim of the homicide was homosexual,' contextually implies the statement, 'the homicide was not a serious crime.' But what's wrong

with that kind of logic? If moral philosophers want to derive ought-statements from is-statements, why should they deny themselves? If politicians fancy syllogisms with undistributed middle terms,[16] why should they be subject to logical censure? If a particular sort of argument appeals to you—according to this way of thinking—the fact that it is unjustified should present no obstacle.

I am *not* saying that valid deductive arguments are the only admissible types. Valid deduction has a valuable property. The arguments in this category are truth-preserving; from true premises you cannot validly deduce a false conclusion. But other types of arguments are needed as well; that is precisely the reason we have a problem of justification of induction. I *am* saying that the characteristic of *being an invalid argument we prize* does not constitute a sufficient ground for considering an argument rationally admissible. Better grounds must be found.

Lest there be some feeling that, with the discussion of contextual implication, the is-ought fallacy, and undistributed middle, I have strayed too far from the main issue—induction—let me return forthwith. What reason is there to refuse to grant that the fallacy of affirming the consequent[17]—known more politely as the 'hypothetico-deductive method'[18]—is the legitimate method of science? We

---

15 [Author's note] Patrick Nowell-Smith, *Ethics* (Penguin, 1954), p. 80.

16 This is a (fallacious) argument of the following form:
1. A's are B's
2. C's are B's
3. Therefore C's are A's.

For example: beetles are insects; bees are insects; therefore bees are beetles.

17 This is a (deductively invalid) argument of the following form:
1. If P then Q
2. Q
3. Therefore P.

For example: if all swans are white then the next swan I see will be white; the next swan I see is white; so all swans are white. (In this case, the first premise must be true; the second premise was—as it were—repeatedly true for Europeans before the discovery of Australia; but the conclusion is in fact false.)

18 The hypothetico-deductive method is a proposed ac-

all know, of course, that it is not deductively valid, and no one is claiming otherwise. We can, nevertheless, signify our psychological attachment to this type of argument by calling it 'inductive' and saying that it 'confirms' conclusions rather than entailing them. Am I misrepresenting this attitude of logical tolerence? I do not think so, for I find it stated candidly by some of the most significant modern contributors to the philosophy of induction. Consider a famous statement by Nelson Goodman:

> ... rules and particular inferences alike are justified by being brought into agreement with each other. *A rule is amended if it yields an inference we are unwilling to accept; an inference is rejected if it violates a rule we are unwilling to amend.* The process of justification is the delicate one of making mutual adjustments between rules and accepted inferences; and in the agreement achieved lies the only justification needed for either.
>
> All this applies equally well to induction. An inductive inference, too, is justified by conformity to general rules, and a general rule by conformity to accepted inductive inferences. Predictions are justified if they conform to valid canons of induction; and the canons of induction are valid if they accurately codify accepted inductive practice.[19]

Thus, did Goodman dispatch Hume's problem—'the old riddle of induction.'

Rudolf Carnap used somewhat different terms, but espoused essentially the same view; "The reasons [for accepting any axiom of inductive logic] are based upon our intuitive judgments concerning inductive validity, i.e., concerning inductive rationality of practical decisions (e.g., about bets)."[20]

Two of the most influential philosophers to deal with the problem thus agree that there is nothing more that can be done in inductive logic than to codify and systematize our feelings about what is or is not legitimate. To show that the results of these efforts have any rational justification seems to be regarded as beyond the realm of possibility. Hume's problem is, according to them, utterly recalcitrant. They are extremely reluctant to come right out and say so, but as far as I can see, that's what it boils down to.

In an oft-quoted remark, C.D. Broad[21] said that induction is the glory of science and the scandal of philosophy.[22] If, as Carnap and Goodman seem to admit, the problem is so intractable, why aren't contemporary philosophers more scandalized? How can Carnap, Goodman, and countless others accept the situation with such equanimity? For the answer to this query, let us turn to P.F. Strawson,[23] who seems to have become the most prominent spokesman for a 'Wittgensteinian' approach."[24]

The 'ordinary language dissolution' of the problem of induction rests primarily upon the claim that the principles of induction are ultimate principles; they are not amenable to justification because there are no other principles which are more fundamental that

---

count of the proper methodology of science (dating back at least to the early nineteenth century, when William Whewell introduced the term). On this view, scientific investigation proceeds by formulating empirical hypotheses to explain the observed data, and then performing experiments to test these hypotheses. If an experiment gives a result that is consistent with what we would expect if the hypothesis were true, then the hypothesis is (partially) confirmed; if the experiment gives a result that is inconsistent with the hypothesis, then the hypothesis is falsified (or must be modified).

19　[Author's note] Nelson Goodman, *Fact, Fiction, and Forecast,* 2nd ed. (Bobbs-Merrill, 1965), p. 64.

20　[Author's note] P.A. Schilpp (ed.), *The Philosophy of Rudolf Carnap* (Open Court, 1963), p. 978.

21　Charlie Dunbar Broad (1887–1971) was a prominent philosopher of science and epistemologist who held the Knightbridge Professorship of Moral Philosophy at Cambridge University.

22　[Author's note] *The Philosophy of Francis Bacon,* Cambridge, 1926.

23　Sir Peter Frederick Strawson (1919–2006) was the Waynflete Professor of Metaphysical Philosophy at the University of Oxford, and an influential analytic metaphysician.

24　[Author's note] P.F. Strawson, *Introduction to Logical Theory* (Methuen & Co., 1952), Chap. 9.

could be invoked for the purpose of carrying out a justification of induction. The above-mentioned *autonomy* of inductive logic is a result of the *ultimacy* of its principles. To ask whether induction is justified is to ask whether it is reasonable to employ inductive canons. The demand for such a justification must, so the argument goes, be confused or misplaced, because the canons of induction are themselves constitutive of what it *means* to characterize something as reasonable.

This seductive approach has not gone unchallenged. Employing Herbert Feigl's[25] important distinction between two types of justification—validation and vindication—I pointed out that a straightforward significance could be attached to the request for a justification of induction. While *validation* cannot be carried out without appeal to principles more fundamental than those whose justification is at issue, *vindication* is not subject to any such limitation. To vindicate a rule or principle is to show that its adoption will serve some specified end; this type of justification does not require an appeal to more fundamental inductive principles. Strawson's argument correctly shows that the demand for a justification of the basic canons of induction does take us beyond the limits of possible validation. His argument does *not*, however, show that such a demand takes us beyond the limits of possible *justification*, for vindication is a form of justification, and that type of justification is not touched by the appeal to ultimacy. Strawson suggests that the request for a justification of induction is like asking whether it is reasonable to be reasonable; this, he suggests, is a pointless question. I argued that such a question is not vacuous at all if we recognize two senses of 'reasonable' corresponding to Feigl's two senses of 'justification.'[26]

In a reply of somewhat less than a single page—totally ignoring the crucial distinction between validation and vindication—Strawson dismissed the objections with the remark, "If it is said that there is a problem of induction, and that Hume posed it, it must be added that he solved it."[27] One gets a distinct impression of Strawson's impatience with those who insist on dragging out the old philosophical chestnut.

Hume had, of course, maintained that induction is a matter of 'custom and habit.' This is what Strawson sees as Hume's solution to the problem. It might be reformulated in somewhat more modern terminology by saying that inductive behavior is a matter of psychological conditioning. Knowing what we do of Pavlov's dogs we would rephrase once again: "Verily I say unto you that induction is but a certain watering at the mouth!"[28]

What we know about conditioning, and about various other biological and physiological processes, is known scientifically—inductively. It is not at all clear to me how the proponent of this Strawsonian line would argue against those who, on flagrantly unscientific and non-inductive grounds, simply reject that very scientific claim—namely that inductive behavior, in contrast to various other approaches to finding out about unobserved matters of fact, is enforced upon us by nature. As nearly as I can understand the ordinary language approach, one simply resorts to namecalling. The non-inductionist is smeared with such epithets as 'unscientific' and 'irrational.' On the other hand, "If you use inductive procedures you can call yourself 'reasonable'—*and isn't that nice!*"[29] This, it still seems to me, captures the kernel of the 'ordinary language dissolution' of the problem of induction.

Being reasonable, according to ordinary language theorists, involves fashioning one's beliefs in terms of the evidence—and inductive evidence is normally at least part of the evidence. Once more, we are told, the adoption of inductive procedures determines the

---

25   Herbert Feigl (1902–1988) was an Austrian-born philosopher of science who spent much of his career in the United States.

26   [Author's note] I offered these arguments in 'Should We Attempt to Justify Induction?,' *Philosophical Studies* 8 (1957), 38–42.

27   [Author's note] P.F. Strawson, 'On Justifying Induction,' *Philosophical Studies* 9 (1958), 20–21.

28   [Author's note] This is a paraphrase of a famous remark allegedly made by A.N. Whitehead in response to a lecture by Bertrand Russell (with much reference to Pavlov's experiments) on ethics: "Verily, I say unto you that the good is but a certain watering at the mouth."

29   [Author's note] Salmon, 'Should We Attempt to Justify Induction?,' p. 42.

very meaning of the concept of evidence, and hence, what it is to be reasonable. This argument, I believe, is vulnerable to the objection that there are many conceivable rules of inference in terms of which one might fashion one's beliefs. To be concrete, one could cite (1) induction by enumeration, (2) an a priori rule, and (3) a counter-inductive rule.[30] Depending upon which rule is adopted, a radically different concept of evidence emerges. A fact which constitutes positive evidence *for* a given hypothesis on the basis of rule (1) is *irrelevant* to that hypothesis on the basis of rule (2), while precisely the same fact is evidence *against* the very same hypothesis on rule (3). If the standard inductive rule, rather than one of the infinitely many pathological alternatives, is constitutive of rationality, it seems to me that we ought to be able to say on what grounds its superiority rests.

In response to these considerations, Stephen Barker rose to the defense of the dissolutionists. He made no secret of his feeling of fatigue:

> Wittgenstein, Strawson, and others have held that the traditional problem of induction is a pseudo-problem, resulting from conceptual confusion; a puzzle to be dissolved, not a problem to be solved in its own terms. Professor Salmon disagrees and tries to rescue the grand old problem from dissolution; or perhaps I ought rather to say that he tries to resurrect that grand old corpse of a problem which many of us had hoped would now be allowed to molder in peace.[31]

Well, I do apologize for being so tiresome, but I fail to see that Hume's problem of justification of induction is a pseudo-problem. Barker elaborates his claim:

Salmon would like us radically to question the practice of induction which shapes our whole form of life, but words fail. We cannot express such a question. We reach one of those points at which, as Wittgenstein says, one feels like uttering an inarticulate cry.[32]

I find Barker's remark incomprehensible. The claim that the problem of induction cannot be formulated seems manifestly false. Hume had formulated it (whether he had also solved it or not). Russell had formulated it. Reichenbach[33] had formulated it. I had just formulated it in the very paper on which Barker was commenting. None of us, as far as I was aware, had been reduced to inarticulate cries. Still, this response by Barker is the most serious and coherent effort to answer these objections of which I am aware.

In spite of damaging attacks—at least they strike me as utterly devastating—and in the absence of any serious defense against them, the 'ordinary language dissolution' continues to be regarded by many as *the definitive answer* to the problem of the justification of induction. As recently as 1974, in a book whose title declares that it is devoted to *Justification and Knowledge*, John Pollock begins his chapter on induction with these remarks:

> The traditional problem of induction was that of justifying induction ... it is almost obvious that nothing could possibly count as a justification. We cannot justify induction inductively, and, as Strawson remarked, to attempt to give a deductive justification of induction is to attempt to turn induction into deduction, which it is not. This, of course, is just what has always made the traditional problem of induction so puzzling. But the lesson to be learned from all this is that the attempt to justify induction is wrongheaded and must be forsaken. This is because the principles of induction are instrumental in our making justified judgments

---

30   [Author's note] I stated these rules in 'The Concept of Inductive Evidence,' *American Philosophical Quarterly* 2 (1965), 1–6, where I also presented the ensuing argument. The same argument was spelled out more fully and precisely in 'The Justification of Inductive Rules of Inference,' in I. Lakatos (ed.), *The Problem of Inductive Logic* (North-Holland, 1968), pp. 29–33.

31   [Author's note] Stephen F. Barker, 'Discussion: Is There a Problem of Induction?,' *American Philosophical Quarterly* 2 (1965), 7.

32   [Author's note] *Ibid.*, p. 9.

33   Hans Reichenbach (1891–1953) was a German philosopher of science who immigrated to America in 1938. He taught at UCLA, and was Salmon's doctoral advisor.

about the world, and as such are involved in the justification conditions of our concepts. Insofar as the principles of induction are involved in the justification conditions of our concepts, they are partially constitutive of the meanings of these concepts. It is simply part of the meaning of these concepts that one can inductively generalize in connection with them. To *justify* induction would be to somehow derive the justification conditions of these concepts from something deeper, but there is nothing deeper. It is in principle impossible to justify induction, and there is no reason why things should be otherwise. The traditional problem of induction is best regarded as a pseudo-problem.[34]

This is Pollock's *total* comment on Hume's problem of induction; the remainder of the chapter is devoted to Goodman's 'new riddle of induction.'

Appalled at the continued popularity of this attempt to evade an unwanted philosophical problem, I once remarked (of P.F. Strawson and A.J. Ayer), "They seem to argue, by a kind of logic that frankly escapes me, that induction needs no defense because it is indefensible."[35] The logic still escapes me, but I now believe I may have a clue to the willingness of so many philosophers to adopt the dissolutionist approach even in the face of the most damaging arguments (which go largely unacknowledged). The fundamental principle distilled from their approach is one which must be admitted, even by those who do not quite comprehend its derivation, to exhibit great philosophic ingenuity. Once formulated, it can easily be applied again: *The ordinary language 'dissolution' of the problem of induction needs no defense precisely because it is indefensible.*

The straightforward candor of Karl Popper's treatment of Hume's problem of induction makes a refreshing contrast to the ordinary language approach. In the opening paragraph of his 1972 book, *Objective Knowledge*, Popper says,

I think that I have solved a major philosophical problem: the problem of induction. (I must have reached the solution in 1927 or thereabouts.) This solution has been extremely fruitful, and it has enabled me to solve a good number of other philosophical problems.[36]

The solution, very simply, is that Hume proved induction to be an untenable mode of inference, and it must therefore be abandoned. It is not the business of science to attempt to establish hypotheses as true or as probable. The hypothetico-deductive form of *confirmation* is illegitimate and has no place in science. Hypotheses can, however, be refuted by the deductively valid *modus tollens*,[37] and this is the most that science can aspire to. Popper's approach has been characterized as 'deductivism' and as 'the method of conjectures and refutations.'

This way of dealing with Hume's problem of induction would seem to give rise to an immediate difficulty. Deduction, as Popper is fully aware, is nonampliative—that is, the conclusion of a valid deduction has no content which was not already present in the premises. If we grant the plausible assumption that all of our observations are confined to happenings in the past and present, then it follows immediately that observation *plus deduction* can yield no information whatever about the future. Indeed, the total information content of science cannot exceed the content of our observations themselves.

According to Popper's characterization, the method of science is to put forth generalizations as conjectures, and to attempt to falsify them. Let us see how this works. I could use fancier examples of scientific hypotheses, but the principle would be precisely the same. Suppose, on the one hand, that we entertain the

---

34   [Author's note] John Pollock, *Justification and Knowledge* (Princeton University Press, 1974) p. 204.

35   [Author's note] Salmon, 'The Justification of Inductive Rules of Inference,' p. 24.

36   [Author's note] Karl R. Popper, *Objective Knowledge* (Oxford University Press, 1972), p. 1.

37   *Modus tollens* is the name for arguments of the following form:

1.   If P then Q
2.   Not-Q
3.   Therefore Not-P.

For example: if this is an insect then it will have six legs; this does not have six legs; so it's not an insect.

generalization, 'All ravens are black,' and we find that it is impervious to all efforts at falsification. The entire information thereby conveyed is that we have not observed a non-black raven. This says less than a simple report of our observations of birds. Suppose, on the other hand, that we advance the generalization. 'All swans are white,' and find that it is falsified. In this case, the total information conveyed is that we have observed a non-white swan. Again, more would have conveyed by a report of our observations of birds.[38]

According to Popper, bold conjectures and powerful theories are the pride of modern science, but according to the principles of his clearly articulated methodology, the content of scientific knowledge cannot extend beyond the content of our observation reports. Popper has sometimes chided the 'inductivists' for holding the view that science consists merely of observation reports and simple empirical generalizations upon them. He protests that science is not that poverty-stricken—a view with which inductivists heartily agree. But on his theory, the content of scientific knowledge does not even include the generalizations. It is ironic that in recent years Popper and his associates have placed great emphasis upon 'the problem of the growth of knowledge.' According to his own principles, scientific knowledge grows at a rate not exceeding the rate of accumulation of observations. In fairness, I should add, the observations we make are significantly influenced by the hypotheses we are entertaining. But that doesn't change the fact that there is no ampliative form of scientific argument, and consequently, science provides no information whatever about the future. In answer to Hume's question, 'How are we to make reasonable inference from the observed to the unobserved,' Popper's clear and unequivocal answer is, 'No way!'

It may be objected that I am distorting Popper's views by a failure to mention his concept of *corroboration*. Among hypotheses which have not been falsified, some—by reason of greater simplicity, more severe testing, or larger content—receive a higher corroboration rating than others. Popper clearly stresses that 'corroboration' is no synonym for 'confirmation.' If, however, degree of corroboration were some sort of index to the reliance we should place upon a hypothesis for predicting the future, or to the confidence we should have in the truth of the hypothesis, then Popper's deductivism would be polluted with *some* ampliative mode of inference. In that case, Popper would turn out to be an inductivist after all. But Popper adamantly denies that corroboration has any predictive import whatever; the degree of corroboration is an indication of the performance of the generalization *with respect to past occurrences alone*. Popper's deductivism remains pure; science has no predictive import.[39]

When we recover our composure after this shocking news, we may naturally feel impelled to ask on what basis we would make the kind of predictions upon which all of our practical decisions must be grounded. Popper reassures us that for such purposes "a *pragmatic belief in the results of science* is not irrational, because there is nothing more 'rational' than the method of critical discussion [conjectures and refutations], which is the method of science."[40] But recalling what Popper has explicitly stated about the predictive content of science, we must hasten to add that nothing could be *less* 'rational' either. When all methods are on an equal footing with respect to predictive content, Popper seems to draw the astonishing conclusion that belief in the results of none of them is 'irrational.' Predictions based upon the results of science are not irrational, but predictions based upon astrology would likewise not be irrational, since neither science nor astrology has any credentials at all when it comes to predictive value. Popper goes on to say that "it would be irrational to accept any of its [science's] results as certain," but we have recognized from the outset the truism that science is not infallible. Having offered that (unneeded) word of caution (which seems to suggest that those who do not agree with him are

---

38 [Author's note] I have discussed Popper's approach in *The Foundations of Scientific Inference*, pp. 21–27, and again in 'The Justification of Inductive Rules of Inference,' pp. 25–29.

39 [Author's note] See J.W.N. Watkins, 'Non-inductive corroboration,' in I. Lakatos (ed.), *The Problem of Inductive Logic* (North-Holland, 1968), pp. 61–66, and Popper, *Objective Knowledge*, pp. 18–19.

40 [Author's note] Popper, *Objective Knowledge*, p. 27.

committed to an infallibility doctrine), he adds, "there is nothing 'better' [than science] when it comes to practical action: there is no alternative method which might be said to be more rational."[41]

If all methods of making inferences to the future are equally and totally incapable of being justified, then none is any *more* rational than any other, and none is any *less* rational than any other. All are on a par. The correct conclusion to draw, I should think, is that *all* methods, including the scientific method, are irrational bases for prediction. Thus, when the atomic scientists were contemplating the assembly of the first atomic pile in Chicago, it would, according to Popper's principles, have been just as rational to consult a crystal-gazing seer as to consult a scientist for a prediction as to whether a self-sustaining chain reaction would occur, and whether it would engulf the entire city of Chicago and possibly the whole earth in an uncontrolled nuclear blast.

Either science has predictive import or it does not. If it has none, it provides no rational basis for prediction. If it has predictive import, it must incorporate some form of ampliative inference. You can't have it both ways, it has to be one or the other. It is incredible to maintain that the *solution* to the problem of induction lies in the claim that science has no predictive content. *That* sounds a good deal more like a *statement* of the problem.

My own sympathies have lain with an approach by way of a pragmatic vindication of induction, along lines suggested by Herbert Feigl and Hans Reichenbach. Enormous difficulties, however, are encountered along this path. Reichenbach constructed a well-known pragmatic argument based upon the convergence properties of his 'rule of induction.' As he realized, the same argument provided the same sort of justification for an infinite class of 'asymptotic rules'[42] which share the same convergence properties.

On what basis, then, is the 'rule of induction'—the straight rule—to be singled out as the uniquely acceptable member of the class? With a patent misapplication of his principle of descriptive simplicity, Reichenbach claimed to have provided a suitable rationale for the choice. But this answer would not do.

For some time I sought other, more satisfactory, principles on which to narrow down the class of candidates for basic inductive rules. Without boring you with tedious details, let me merely mention two suggestions: (1) a set of *normalizing conditions* and (2) a *criterion of linguistic invariance*. These did seem quite potent in disqualifying large classes of unacceptable asymptotic rules. Moreover, in countering the objection that even Reichenbach's rule of induction would fall victim to the criterion of linguistic invariance, I also offered a proposal for the resolution of Goodman's famous 'grue-bleen paradox'—his 'new riddle of induction'—which still seems fundamentally satisfactory. All of this was enormously pleasing; indeed, in a fit of over-optimism, I thought I had succeeded in providing satisfactory grounds for uniquely justifying the one rule.[43] This happy state of mind was shattered when I. Richard Savage and Ian Hacking independently constructed counter-examples to the general claim.[44]

I do not think either the normalizing conditions or the criterion of linguistic invariance are unsound; the difficulty is that they are not strong enough to do the job I had hoped they would do. Hacking has, however, proved that three principles would be necessary and sufficient to single out Reichenbach's rule of induction: consistency, invariance, and symmetry.[45] If, and only if, it could be shown that a satisfactory basic inductive rule must satisfy these conditions would the desired justification be forthcoming. The question then becomes, what grounds, if any, can be found for imposing just these requirements upon inductive rules.

41   [Author's note] *Ibid.*

42   These are rules that are 'asymptotes' with the 'straight rule' of induction by enumeration (i.e., inference to a general rule—"All a's are F"—from a sequence of instances of that rule: Fa_1, Fa_2, Fa_3, and so on). Two rules are asymptotes if their results get closer and closer together, for ever, as the number of instances is multiplied.

43   [Author's note] The details are given in my article 'On Vindicating Induction,' *Philosophy of Science* 30 (1963), 252–261.

44   [Author's note] See I. Lakatos, *The Problem of Inductive Logic*, pp. 50–51 and pp. 86–87.

45   [Author's note] I. Hacking, 'One Problem About Induction,' in I. Lakatos, *The Problem of Inductive Logic*, pp. 57–59.

Skipping over some technical details, I would remark that the consistency requirement is analogous to my normalizing conditions, while my criterion of linguistic invariance can, I think, be legitimately extended to coincide with the invariance condition formulated by Hacking. These two requirements do not seem to me to pose insuperable difficulties. The remaining condition, symmetry, is something else again.[46]

The crucial problem arising out of the symmetry condition can be illustrated by a simple puzzle. Consider the following initial section of a sequence of heads and tails:

H T T H T H T H H H T H T H H H T H T H

The relative frequency of heads in this observed sequence is 6/10; on the basis of the rule of induction we might infer—or *posit*, to use Reichenbach's term—that the long run frequency of heads, if the sequence is continued, will be somewhere near that value. If, however, we examine the initial section carefully, we note that each toss corresponding to a prime number—the second, third, fifth, seventh, etc.—is a tail, while every other toss yields heads. If we use the rule of induction on the subsequences, we posit that each prime toss will be a tail and all others will be heads. Since it is known that the limiting frequency of primes among the natural numbers is zero,[47] the induction on the subsequences entails that the limiting frequency of heads in the entire sequence is 1. Unless it can be shown how, and why, one of these inductions must supersede the other,[48] adoption of Reichenbach's rule of induction will lead us into genuine paradox. At

present, I do not know how to resolve this paradox— or whether it is, in principle, capable of resolution.

Inasmuch as philosophers have not done an outstanding job of providing answers to Hume's problem of induction, perhaps we might look elsewhere. It would surely make good sense to ask whether statisticians, whose business is to deal with certain kinds of inductive or probabilistic inferences in scientific contexts, can offer any help. The answer, it turns out, is unequivocally negative. There are two major schools of thought regarding foundations of statistics, the bayesian and the orthodox. According to the bayesian school, probabilities are merely subjective degrees of belief; they have no direct bearing upon objective facts in the world. To say that a particular future outcome is highly probable does not mean that it will usually turn out that way in similar circumstances, nor does it mean that we have good reason to believe in any such outcome. The probability, for each individual, is simply the amount of psychological confidence he happens to have—for whatever reason, rational or irrational—in that outcome. The most that statistics can do is to help us avoid a certain type of inconsistency—called *incoherence*—in combinations of beliefs; it cannot tell us whether a given degree of belief is a reasonable basis for predicting the future. L.J. Savage, the most prominent exponent of this viewpoint, explicitly acknowledged that he was a Humean skeptic where prediction is concerned.[49]

Orthodox statisticians regard probabilities as objective entities; if one knows the probabilities that govern certain types of events, one would have a rational basis for prediction and action. The problem, of course, is to establish the values of such objective probabilities. Orthodox statisticians have methods which are used for just such purposes. When these methods are examined carefully, however, it turns out that their application invariably requires synthetic general assumptions about matters of fact. Orthodox statisticians do not, in other words, have methods for making inductive inferences which do not depend upon the results of other,

---

46 A function is symmetrical if it is invariant for any permutations of the constants to which the function is applied. For example, addition is a symmetrical function: $(1 + 7 + 81) = (7 + 81 + 1)$.

47 That is, when you get far enough along the number line—i.e., the natural numbers get big enough—none of them are prime numbers.

48 That is, the basic rule of induction seems to give different results—different predictions about unobserved instances—when applied to subsequences of the series than it does when applied to the series as a whole. The latter application is a symmetrical function—it does not matter in what order the Hs and Ts come in, just how many there are of each—while the former is not.

49 [Author's note] L.J. Savage, 'Implications of Personal Probability for Induction,' *Journal of Philosophy* LXIV (1967), 593–607. In *Foundations of Scientific Inference*, pp. 79–83, I discuss this approach in greater detail.

previous, inductions.[50] Their position is very close, I believe, to that of John Stuart Mill. If we assume some general statistical regularities, we can make inductive inferences. But on what basis are these assumptions—even fairly modest ones—to be justified?

Where can we go from here? Every path we have tried to follow has turned into a blind alley. One feels an almost irresistible tendency to resonate to Hume's own reaction to such frustrations:

> The *intense* view of these manifold contradictions and imperfections in human reason has so wrought upon me, and heated my brain, that I am ready to reject all belief and reasoning, and can look upon no opinion even as more probable or likely than another. Where am I, or what? From what causes do I derive my existence, and to what condition shall I return: Whose favor shall I court, and whose anger must I dread? What beings surround me? and on whom have I any influence, or who have any influence on me? I am confounded with all these questions, and begin to fancy myself in the most deplorable condition imaginable, inviron'd with the deepest darkness, and utterly depriv'd of the use of every member and faculty.
>
> Most fortunately it happens, that since reason is incapable of dispelling these clouds, nature herself suffices to that purpose, and cures me of this philosophical melancholy and delirium, either by relaxing this bent of mind, or by some avocation,[51] and lively impression of my senses, which obliterates all these chimeras.[52] I dine, I play a game of backgammon, I converse, and am merry with my friends; and when after three or four hours' amusement, I wou'd return to these speculations, they appear so cold, and strain'd, and ridiculous, that I cannot find in my heart to enter into them any farther.[53]

Well, perhaps we should just let it rest there. Perhaps these philosophical doubts are empty and sterile. Perhaps, as Robert Ackermann suggests in the Preface of his 1970 introductory text, you have to be crazy to be bothered about such problems:

> I once knew a man who always worried that the roof of any room which he occupied was likely to fall in and injure or kill him. This worry was, in a sense, philosophical; no one could *prove* that the worry was without foundation in fact. But instead of being regarded as a philosopher, this worrier was thought of as a harmless lunatic, known among intimates as 'Crazy Phil.' There is an uncomfortable resemblance between Crazy Phil and many philosophers of science. Like Phil, these philosophers are motivated by private fears.[54]

If this is intended to apply to philosophers who, like Hume, Russell, Reichenbach, and many others, have grappled with the problem of justification of induction, it is a grotesque caricature. Hume was not the victim of neurotic dread.

> Let the course of things be allowed hitherto ever so regular; that alone, without some new argument or inference, proves not that, for the future, it will continue so ... My practice, you say, refutes my doubts. But you mistake the purport of my question. As an agent, I am quite satisfied in the point....[55]

These philosophers were confident that the roof would not fall in, if it was constructed in accord with suitable engineering principles, for they all had full confidence in the laws of physics. Phaedrus, the protagonist of *Zen and the Art of Motorcycle Maintenance*,[56] in

---

50 [Author's note] This matter was surveyed thoroughly by Ben Rogers in 'Foundational Studies in Statistical Inference,' Ph.D. dissertation, Indiana University, 1970.

51 Hobby.

52 Unreal, unpleasant creatures of the imagination.

53 [Author's note] Hume, *Treatise*, Conclusion of Book I.

54 [Author's note] Robert Ackermann, *The Philosophy of Science* (Pegasus, 1970), p. ix.

55 [Author's note] Hume, *Enquiry*, Sec. IV.

56 A 1974 book by Robert M. Pirsig which is a first-person description of a 17-day motorcycle journey across the US, punctuated with philosophical discussions. It has sold more than 4 million copies, making it probably the most widely read work of contemporary philosophy (although Pirsig is not an academic philosopher).

contrast, did end up in an institution on account of his worries about the problem of induction; however he hardly qualifies as a prominent contributor to the philosophical foundations of inductive logic. Concern about the philosophical problem of justification of induction may be pointless; it is not, however, crazy.

But can we really be *that* complacent? Can the problem of induction simply be dismissed as otiose? Much as I'd like to give an affirmative answer, I find I really cannot. Science *is* more reasonable than astrology, superstition, random guessing, divine revelation, and visions in LSD-induced psychedelic states. With scientific techniques we can predict an eclipse. It is reasonable to believe in this prediction. It is not reasonable to accept the prognostication, made by a religious fanatic, that the world will end tomorrow. It is silly to place confidence in forecasts found in fortune cookies in Chinese restaurants.

I am firmly convinced of this—we are all firmly convinced. But how can we show it? With Hume, "I want to know the foundation of this inference."

Without an answer, we open the door to *any mental aberration whatever*—to every form of irrationalism—allowing them all to be just as sound as science. *That simply won't do.* It is unacceptable on philosophical grounds, and it is intolerable on practical grounds. I was not indulging in whimsy when I remarked at the outset that this problem has significant practical ramifications. In a recent case, medical experts agreed that a child with diabetes would die if insulin were not administered. The fundamentalist parents had some sort of divine revelation that the child would not die if medication were halted. No insulin was administered and the child died. In another recent instance, at a commune in Arizona, a 'geomancer'—a person who walks around with hands outstretched sensing the vibrations from the earth—predicted that crops would grow there in arid soil without cultivation or irrigation. The seed was scattered; nothing grew. In this case, the birds and small rodents, at least, benefitted.

It is not intellectually adequate simply to *call* those who practice non-inductive—non-scientific—methods of prediction 'irrational.' It does not solve the

philosophical problem to lock them up, or even to perform lobotomies upon them. Nor is it acceptable to say—as one often hears—that science is, at bottom, a matter of faith; there are many faiths which are all on a par. You just choose the one you like best. It is equally unsatisfactory to give that approach a slight terminological twist and characterize the inductive method as part of 'a form of life'—one among many such 'forms,' I suppose. And it is manifestly untenable to deny that there is any such thing as rationally grounded prediction.

What, then, should we say finally to our students who want to know 'the answer' to Hume's problem of induction? In my opinion we should frankly admit that, as yet, we have no completely satisfactory answer. None of the various attempts—many of them quite ingenious—to solve, resolve, or dissolve the problem is altogether successful. Does that mean that we have been dealing with a pointless question—a pseudo-problem? I do not believe so. The moral seems rather that we have an exceedingly difficult problem on our hands. In his attempts to provide logically adequate foundations of mathematics, Russell turned up a set-theoretical paradox which, he reports, it took him five agonizing years to resolve. We now have every reason to believe that the problems raised by Hume when he said, "I want to learn the foundation of this [inductive] inference," are, if anything, even more difficult. The work of Russell and others on the foundations of mathematics has considerably deepened our understanding of mathematical reasoning. A solution of Hume's problem of induction could plausibly be expected to deepen our understanding of scientific reasoning.

I have been taking an unpopular line—some might even consider it a breach of etiquette on the occasion, when everyone else politely refrained from mentioning this subject. It seems to me, however, that the least we can do on the bicentennial is to acknowledge candidly that part of Hume's legacy is work still to be done. The problem he left us is a tough one, but we have no excuse for pretending that it does not exist. And, I think, we had better not stop trying to solve it.

C.S. PEIRCE
"The Fixation of Belief"

Who Was C.S. Peirce?

Charles Sanders Peirce was born in 1839 in Cambridge, Massachusetts, the second son of Benjamin and Sarah Peirce. Benjamin Peirce was, at the time, the most respected mathematician in America and a distinguished professor at Harvard College; young Charles was a prodigy in both science and philosophy, and widely viewed as likely to become a more talented mathematician than even his father. Growing up well-connected with America's academic and scientific circles, Charles knew personally most of the leading intellectual figures of his time. However, his undoubted genius, originality, and firm independence of mind—as well as his prickly character—did not make his life an easy one. In an increasingly insular and conservative late nineteenth-century New England, Peirce found his ambitions thwarted at almost every turn, and for the last third of his life he was unable to obtain regular employment. He ended his life living in poverty and relative isolation in rural Pennsylvania.

Peirce was educated at Harvard College (where he got a BA) and the Lawrence Scientific School at Harvard (where he received a BSc in chemistry). In 1861, he joined the US Coast and Geodetic Survey[1] where,

frustrated in his attempts to obtain an academic position, he was to spend the next thirty years of his career. He rose through the ranks of the Survey—partly aided by patronage from his influential father—until he was put in charge of gravity experiments and pendulum research. As part of his duties with the Survey, Peirce took several trips to Europe to attend conferences and compare data with British and European scientists, and he became an internationally respected mathematician and scientist. Between 1869 and 1872 he was also an assistant at the Harvard Observatory, and his first published book, *Photometric Researches*, was the result of his astronomical observations there. In 1879 he was appointed a lecturer in logic at Johns Hopkins University, the first true graduate school in America.

This was the high-point of Peirce's career. In 1876 he had become estranged from his first wife, Harriet Melusina Fay, and in 1883 he divorced her in order to marry Juliette Froissy Pourtalès. In 1884, just as Peirce was confidently expecting to be granted tenure at Johns Hopkins, the university—shocked by Peirce's scandalously "consorting" with a French woman while still legally married to his first wife—declined to renew his lecturing contract. After this, Peirce had no hope of regular academic employment anywhere in America.

Seven years later, in 1891, Peirce was forced to resign from the US Coastal Survey. A new cost-cutting administration in Washington decided to sharply reduce the budget for the Survey's geodetic work, but Peirce refused to submit to the lower standards of accuracy and scientific rigor this imposed and ignored the new regulations. The government then apparently applied behind-the-scenes pressure which meant

---

1   Geodesy is the science of the size and shape of the earth, and a geodetic survey involves the mapping of a large region of the Earth's surface in which adjustments need to be made for the curvature of the planet; the precise measurement of very small variations in gravity at different points on the Earth's surface was an important tool for measuring exactly the planet's shape, and hence for geodetic surveys.

that his major report (on which he had worked for several years) of the results of his gravitational experiments was refused publication—this led to his expulsion from the Survey.

Although Peirce was only 52, and still had a quarter-century of life ahead of him, he was never again able to obtain regular employment. It did not help that Peirce was a notoriously difficult man to get along with, prone to extreme mood swings and sudden onsets of paranoia, combining a very high opinion of his own abilities with a sometimes contemptuous view of others' intelligence. Peirce was reduced to writing huge numbers of book reviews and popular articles to make ends meet, and his life came to be sporadically dominated by a succession of "get rich schemes" that never panned out.

He and Juliette moved to a small farmhouse near Milford, Pennsylvania, and Peirce renamed the house "Arisbe," for the Greek town where some of the earliest philosophers had lived. He embarked on ambitious plans to renovate and expand it, and as he was dealing with the physical architecture of his house Peirce also began thinking about the architecture of his philosophical theories and self-consciously trying to bring his various doctrines together into a single, carefully-assembled structure. He was quite convinced that he was poised to make important and original contributions to human knowledge. However, in the end, both architectural projects remained incomplete: Arisbe never became the rambling manor Peirce hoped it would be, and Peirce felt frustrated in his attempts to summarize his system, describing his writings as "a mere table of contents, so abstract, a very snarl of twine."

Increasingly (and accurately) worried that his public academic career had irreversibly failed and that he would never be able to get his mature philosophical system, and his discoveries in mathematics and logic, into print, Peirce made several book proposals to publishing companies and applied for a number of grants. Most of these were rejected, perhaps partly because of the influence of various enemies he had made during his lifetime. After a long period of ill health, Peirce died at Arisbe in the spring of 1914, a nearly forgotten man, two months before the outbreak of the First World War.

Only twenty years after his death, when the Harvard Philosophy Department published a collection of his papers, did Peirce's philosophical importance come to be glimpsed by the wider world. In recent years—since about the late 1970s—there has been an enormously increased interest in Peirce's work. He is now thought of as important in the development of modern formal logic, as the founder of the science of semiotics, and as one of the main figures in American pragmatism. Indeed for some philosophers, such as Karl Popper, he is "one of the greatest philosophers of all time," and his work inspires intense—sometimes almost uncritical—devotion among many of those who study it today.

What Was Peirce's Overall Philosophical Project?

Peirce wrote voluminously: his extant writings on science, mathematics, philosophy, logic, history, and psychology (not including those lost during his travels to Europe and due to poor storage after his death) would fill over a hundred 500-page volumes. Furthermore, his philosophical beliefs were not static during his lifetime but evolved towards a unified, but complex, diverse, and deeply original, system of doctrines. This makes Peirce's philosophical views difficult to summarize. Some of the most important strands in his mature thought, however, were his pragmatism, his theory of "semiotic," and his metaphysics of objective idealism and evolutionary cosmology.

Pragmatism, in Peirce's view, is a method for resolving conceptual confusions or contradictions by getting clear about the meanings of the claims involved. The central idea is that the meaning of a proposition is not to be found somehow contained *within* it, but consists entirely in a set of *relations* between the claim and its consequences. Perhaps his most famous statement of this view comes in "How to Make Our Ideas Clear," a paper written to be read directly after "The Fixation of Belief":

> Consider what effects, which might conceivably have practical bearings, we conceive the object of our conception to have. Then, our conception of these effects is the whole of our conception of the object.

For example, suppose I want to find out whether a sample of soft, white metal is sodium: I can predict that if it is sodium, then if I drop it into hot water it will explosively catch fire; if I heat it up it will melt at 97.8°C; if I combine it with a wide variety of other substances (such as calcium, fluoride, carbon dioxide, or cyanide) it will react with them and form compounds; and so on. The *complete* set of predications that I could make about the consequences of my actions if the substance were sodium is also, according to Peirce, a complete clarification of the *meaning* of the claim that the sample is sodium.

The method of pragmatism was, for Peirce, inspired by scientific practices, but it is not to be restricted to the laboratory, being a general account of meaning. For example, Peirce argued that the method of pragmatism[2] can be used to clarify, or define, the notions of *truth* and *reality*: "the opinion which is fated to be ultimately agreed to by all who investigate is what we mean by the truth, and the object represented in this opinion is the real."

"Semiotic" was the name that Peirce gave[3] to his theory of information, representation, and communication, a theory which came to have great importance for his system as a whole. For Peirce, the study of *signs* was to replace the theory of knowledge, as traditionally understood. A sign is anything that stands *for* something (its object) *to* something (its interpreter): on Peirce's view, all three parts of this relation (the sign, the object, and the interpreter) are necessary for representation to take place. In particular, nothing can stand for (e.g., be a picture of, be an indication of) something else all by itself; in order to be a sign, it must first be interpreted as such by some observer. Peirce went on to develop an elaborate taxonomy of types of signs, but one three-way distinction is especially important: that between *icons, indices,* and *symbols*. An icon is a sign which resembles its object (such as a photograph or a color swatch); an index is a sign which is naturally correlated with its object (such as clouds indicating rain or returning swallows being a sign of spring); and a symbol is a sign which is conventionally used to refer to objects that it does not physically correspond with or resemble (for example, a "Yield" sign or the English word "cow").

"Objective idealism" was the name that Peirce sometimes gave to his metaphysical beliefs. He was a *monistic realist*, which is to say that he believed that there is a real world whose existence does not depend on our thinking about it, which lies behind and causes our perceptions and about which our beliefs can be true or false, and which is entirely made up of just one kind of stuff. However, Peirce had a rather unusual view of what that 'stuff' is: he held that matter is what he called "effete mind." This is perhaps best explained in terms of Peirce's "evolutionary cosmology." Roughly, this is the view that there are exactly three primary moving forces in the universe: chance, love, and habit. The universe began, according to Peirce, in a state of total chance—pure, random possibility. As it evolved over time, the other two forces (love and habit) emerged out of the chaos, and under their influence the universe became a more ordered place. It began to follow certain laws, though these laws should be thought of, in the first instance, as being primarily *psychological* laws. Over time, in the universe at large as in an individual human being, *habit* has gained more and more of a grip over things' behavior, until much of the universe has become so entrenched in certain regular habits that it has become what we call "matter," blindly obeying (what we call) the laws of physics. One upshot of this is that physical laws should not be thought of as different in kind from psychological laws, and so the habitual aspect of human behavior is just as susceptible to mechanical explanation as is the orbiting of the planets and the erosion of a river bed. On the other hand, love, sympathy, and pure chance are still operative principles in the universe, according to Peirce, so our explanations (of either human beings or the natural world) can never be *purely* mechanical.

Peirce was very much a system-builder, and he intended to fit all of these disparate elements of his philosophy together into an overall unifying structure.

---

2   Peirce re-named his version of the doctrine "pragmaticism" after William James—with due acknowledgements to Peirce—had made the pragmatic theory widely known through lectures and writings; Peirce considered this new label "ugly enough to keep it safe from kidnappers."

3   Though the term was first introduced by John Locke in the seventeenth century.

He believed that all human knowledge can be systematically arrayed within a framework founded on the most basic science, abstract mathematics. Peirce thought of this as the study of the most fundamental and universal *categories*. According to Peirce there are exactly three basic categories, which he called Firstness (that which is as it is in itself, independently of anything else), Secondness (that which is as it is relative to something else), and Thirdness (that which is as it is as mediate between two others).[4] In other words, any language adequate for the description of reality must contain at least three sorts of properties and relations: one-place, two-place, and three-place. In particular, in Peirce's view, Thirdness is ineliminable: the universe cannot be fully captured without a proper understanding of the relation of mediation, and this three-way relation is basic—it cannot be analyzed into any set of two-place relations.

The rest of philosophy then falls into three parts, which Peirce called "phenomenology," "normative science," and "metaphysics." Phenomenology takes phenomena as Firsts, and explores their intrinsic nature. Normative science—which includes both physics and ethics, for example—treats phenomena as Seconds, and examines their relations to various goals such as truth, rightness, or beauty. Thus, normative science asks which physical theories are true or which actions are morally right. Finally, metaphysics treats phenomena as Thirds—as intermediate between us and some underlying reality. The most important examples of Thirds, according to Peirce, are signs.

"The Fixation of Belief" was written fairly early in the development of Peirce's philosophical system, but falls within the domain of "normative science" and is closely connected to his views on pragmatism. It is concerned with how we can best bring our beliefs into line with truth.

What Is the Structure of This Reading?

"The Fixation of Belief" is the first of a sequence of six articles by Peirce published in *Popular Science Monthly*, which together were called "Illustrations of the

---

4   Peirce also called these categories "quality," "reaction," and "mediation."

Logic of Science." In them, Peirce laid out his view of the nature and importance of the scientific method, which he equates generally with good habits of reasoning. He begins "The Fixation of Belief" by stressing the importance of logic, or good reasoning, to science, and then in section II goes on to sketch his view of the nature of logic. In section III Peirce draws a distinction between doubt and belief, which he uses in section IV to define *inquiry* as the process of replacing doubt with belief. The rest of the article is a consideration of the best and most reliable method of fixing belief in place of doubt: Peirce considers four methods—the method of tenacity, the method of authority, the *a priori* method, and the scientific method—and argues that the scientific method is to be preferred above the others.

Some Useful Background Information

1. Peirce's philosophy was often informed by his wide reading in the history of philosophy, and in "The Fixation of Belief," although he does not mention this explicitly, Peirce can be seen to be reacting against and rejecting Descartes' view of the scientific method. Peirce takes Descartes to recommend the practice of science as a basically solitary pursuit, which begins by calling almost all existing knowledge into doubt and which aspires to prove once and for all the truth of some settled body of scientific knowledge. (See the Descartes reading in Chapter 2 for more information on his views, and to make up your own mind whether Peirce was right about them or not.) By contrast, Peirce thought of science as a collaborative investigation which takes for granted all the propositions of which we have no doubt as the inquiry begins, and seeks only to replace some (more focussed) doubt with belief. Furthermore, in his view, there is no question of jumping suddenly and as individuals to 'the truth': instead, science consists in fallible investigators continually progressing toward the truth by replacing real doubts with settled beliefs, which may in turn be later called into doubt and revised. The real power of the scien-

tific method, according to Peirce, is that it is *self-correcting*, rather than infallible.

2. "The Fixation of Belief" introduces Peirce's view of the benefits of the scientific method, but does not go into detail about what exactly he thought that method was. Peirce called it the "inductive method," and he identified three stages of scientific inquiry corresponding to three different patterns of inference: abduction, deduction, and induction. First comes *abduction*, the tentative adoption of an explanatory hypothesis that, if true, would explain the phenomena under investigation. For example, it might occur to a group of scientists that the otherwise mysterious behavior of different materials would be explicable if matter were made up of different types of tiny particles—atoms—which combine with each other in fixed proportions to form compounds. Then *deduction* is the use of logic to derive testable consequences from this tentative theory: for example, it follows from this "atomic theory of matter" that some materials are elements and some are compounds, and that different elements will combine together into compounds only according to particular measurable ratios. Finally *induction* is the testing of these predictions through experimentation—testing to see whether there are indeed identifiable ratios in the combination of elements—and the evaluation of the theory in the light of this experimental data.

A Common Misconception

Peirce is perhaps most commonly thought of as a pragmatist, and indeed "The Fixation of Belief" is the first of a sequence of articles which present a largely pragmatic view of science. This does not mean, as is sometimes assumed, that Peirce placed no value on truth, or the correspondence of our beliefs with reality, and was only concerned about the practical *usefulness* of our beliefs. On the contrary, even at this fairly early stage of his philosophical development Peirce was a realist, and indeed he believed that pragmatism would only be held by someone who was convinced of the

existence of a mind-independent world that would, through the consequences of our actions, check our false beliefs and push us in the direction of truth.

How Important and Influential Is This Passage?

Max Fisch has called Peirce's "Illustrations of the Logic of Science," (of which the article reprinted here is the first of six parts) the nineteenth-century equivalent of Descartes' *Discourse on the Method*. At least in Fisch's view, Peirce definitively captured the essence of the modern scientific method which had replaced the now-outmoded Cartesian understanding of science. In particular, Peirce stresses the importance of collaborative, incremental *experimentation* as part of good scientific reasoning, and places less weight on the power of "pure reason." Peirce also has particular importance for laying the foundations for a *pragmatic* account of science, which elucidates and evaluates scientific claims in terms of their experimental consequences. This idea has been very important in twentieth-century philosophy of science, and is arguably a forerunner of (though not the same doctrine as) the influential theory of "logical positivism," which had as one of its central tenets the claim that the meaning of a statement is its method of verification.

Suggestions for Critical Reflection

1. Why do you think Peirce mocks the medieval assumption that logic consists of nothing more than "syllogistic procedures" (i.e., roughly, deductive logic), suggesting that this component of logic by itself is "very easy"? What do you think is the hard and important part of logic, on Peirce's view? Do you agree? What do you think that Peirce means when he talks of reasoning as something "to be done with one's eyes open, by manipulating real things instead of words and fancies"?

2. Peirce defines the mental states of belief and doubt in terms of their relationships to *action* (a belief is a habit of action, and a doubt is a stimulus to action). Does this seem like a good way to explain them? Does this approach work

for mental states generally? Is there more to believing something than just being disposed to act in certain ways under certain conditions?

3. Peirce defines inquiry as the struggle to eliminate doubt and to fix belief; as a consequence, he claims that "the sole object of inquiry is the settlement of opinion." Is this what we normally believe about inquiry, especially scientific inquiry? Do you think Peirce is right about the goals of science?

4. How persuasive do you find Peirce's discussion of the four different methods of fixing belief? How sincere do you think Peirce is being when he praises the first three methods? What do you think Peirce's attitude was toward religion and its relation with science? Do you agree with him?

5. What exactly are Peirce's *reasons* for preferring the scientific method? How pragmatic are these reasons? How good are they?

6. Why does Peirce think it is an *advantage* of the scientific method that it can sometimes be performed badly or incorrectly, while that is not (he claims) true of the other three methods? Is he right that only science can be done badly? Is he right that this is a good sign for science?

Suggestions for Further Reading

The Essential Peirce: Selected Writings (in two volumes edited by Nathan Houser, Christian Kloesel, and members of the Peirce Edition Project, and published by Indiana University Press in 1992 (Vol. 1) and 1998 (Vol. 2) is a good, representative selection of his writings. The six papers which make up Peirce's "Illustrations of the Logic of Science" appear in the first volume; many of his most important later writings on pragmatism feature in the second. A fairly good account of Peirce's rather tragic and eccentric life is Joseph Brent's *Charles Sanders Peirce: A Life* (Indiana University Press, 1998); also quite interesting is Kenneth Laine Ketner's *His Glassy Essence: An Autobiography of Charles Sanders Peirce* (Vanderbilt University Press, 1998).

Four good books about Peirce's philosophy are Max Fisch, *Peirce, Semiotic, and Pragmatism* (Indiana University Press, 1986); Christopher Hookway, *Peirce* (Routledge & Kegan Paul, 1985) and *Truth, Rationality,* *and Pragmatism: Themes from Peirce* (Oxford University Press, 2000); and Murray Murphey, *The Development of Peirce's Philosophy* (Hackett, 1993).

"The Fixation of Belief"[5]

I.

Few persons care to study logic, because everybody conceives himself to be proficient enough in the art of reasoning already. But I observe that this satisfaction is limited to one's own ratiocination,[6] and does not extend to that of other men.

We come to the full possession of our power of drawing inferences the last of all our faculties, for it is not so much a natural gift as a long and difficult art. The history of its practice would make a grand subject for a book. The mediaeval schoolmen, following the Romans, made logic the earliest of a boy's studies after grammar, as being very easy. So it was, as they understood it. Its fundamental principle, according to them, was, that all knowledge rests on either authority or reason; but that whatever is deduced by reason depends ultimately on a premise derived from authority. Accordingly, as soon as a boy was perfect in the syllogistic procedure,[7] his intellectual kit of tools was held to be complete.

To Roger Bacon,[8] that remarkable mind who in the middle of the thirteenth century was almost a scientific man, the schoolmen's conception of reasoning appeared only an obstacle to truth. He saw that experience alone teaches anything—a proposition which to us seems easy to understand, because a dis-

---

5   This article was first printed in *Popular Science Monthly* 12 (November 1877), pp. 1–15. It is the first of six papers, all published in the same magazine, collectively titled "Illustrations of the Logic of Science."

6   Methodical or logical reasoning.

7   The rules for argument first laid down by Aristotle in the fourth century BCE.

8   Roger Bacon (c. 1214–1292), an English scientist and philosopher often credited with foreshadowing the empiricist methodology of modern science (and with inventing spectacles). To later ages he had the nickname *Doctor Mirabilis*, or marvelous doctor.

tinct conception of experience has been handed down to us from former generations; which to him also seemed perfectly clear, because its difficulties had not yet unfolded themselves. Of all kinds of experience, the best, he thought, was interior illumination, which teaches many things about Nature which the external senses could never discover, such as the transubstantiation of bread.[9]

Four centuries later, the more celebrated Bacon,[10] in the first book of his *Novum Organum*, gave his clear account of experience as something which must be open to verification and reëxamination. But, superior as Lord Bacon's conception is to earlier notions, a modern reader who is not in awe of his grandiloquence is chiefly struck by the inadequacy of his view of scientific procedure. That we have only to make some crude experiments, to draw up briefs of the results in certain blank forms, to go through these by rule, checking off everything disproved and setting down the alternatives, and that thus in a few years physical science would be finished up—what an idea! "He wrote on science like a Lord Chancellor," indeed.[11]

The early scientists, Copernicus, Tycho Brahe, Kepler, Galileo, and Gilbert,[12] had methods more like those of their modern brethren. Kepler undertook to draw a curve through the places of Mars;[13] and his greatest service to science was in impressing on men's minds that this was the thing to be done if they wished to improve astronomy; that they were not to content themselves with inquiring whether one system of epicycles[14] was better than another, but that they were to sit down to the figures and find out what the curve, in truth, was. He accomplished this by his incomparable energy and courage, blundering along in the most inconceivable way (to us), from one irrational hypothesis to another, until, after trying twenty-two of these, he fell, by the mere exhaustion of his invention, upon the orbit which a mind well furnished with the weapons of modern logic would have tried almost at the outset.

In the same way, every work of science great enough to be well remembered for a few generations affords some exemplification of the defective state of the art of reasoning of the time when it was written; and each chief step in science has been a lesson in logic. It was so when Lavoisier[15] and his contemporaries took up the study of chemistry. The old chemist's maxim had been, "*Lege, lege, lege, labora, ora, et relege.*"[16] Lavoisier's method was not to read and pray, not to dream that some long and complicated

---

9   According to Catholic belief, the changing of the communion wafer into the body of Christ during the sacrament of Eucharist or Mass.

10   Sir Francis Bacon (1561–1626), another English philosopher and scientist, was Lord Chancellor under James I and was arguably the first writer to try to delineate the proper methods of successful science, in the process providing a fairly sophisticated account of the empirical method. The *Novum Organum*, which lays out these methodological principles, was published in 1620.

11   This was a comment on Francis Bacon by William Harvey. Harvey (1578–1657) was the English physician who discovered the circulation of the blood.

12   Nicolaus Copernicus (or Mikoláj Kopernik, 1473–1543) proposed that the planets orbit the sun rather than the earth. Tycho Brahe (1546–1601) made some of the most accurate astronomical observations ever achieved with the naked eye, and Johannes Kepler (1571–1630) used them to formulate three laws governing planetary motion. Galileo Galilei (1564–1642) formulated the law of the uniform acceleration of

falling bodies and was among the first to apply the telescope to astronomy, discovering craters on the moon, sunspots, and Jupiter's satellites. William Gilbert (1544–1603) was an English court physician who discovered how to make magnets and investigated the Earth's magnetic field.

13   [Author's note] Not quite so, but as nearly as can be told in a few words.

14   Epicycles are small circles which move around the circumference of a larger one: epicycles (and epicycles of epicycles) were used in Ptolemaic (i.e., pre-Copernican) astronomy to geometrically describe the movements of the planets.

15   Antoine Lavoisier (1743–1794), often regarded as the father of modern chemistry, was the discoverer of oxygen.

16   "Read, read, read, work, pray, and read again" (in Latin). By the "old chemist," Peirce means the alchemists of the Middle Ages.

chemical process would have a certain effect, to put it into practice with dull patience, after its inevitable failure to dream that with some modification it would have another result, and to end by publishing the last dream as a fact: his way was to carry his mind into his laboratory, and to make of his alembics and cucurbits[17] instruments of thought, giving a new conception of reasoning as something which was to be done with one's eyes open, by manipulating real things instead of words and fancies.

The Darwinian controversy is, in large part, a question of logic. Mr. Darwin proposed to apply the statistical method to biology. The same thing had been done in a widely different branch of science, the theory of gases. Though unable to say what the movements of any particular molecule of gas would be on a certain hypothesis regarding the constitution of this class of bodies, Clausius and Maxwell[18] were yet able, by the application of the doctrine of probabilities, to predict that in the long run such and such a proportion of the molecules would, under given circumstances, acquire such and such velocities; that there would take place, every second, such and such a number of collisions, etc.; and from these propositions were able to deduce certain properties of gases, especially in regard to their heat-relations. In like manner, Darwin, while unable to say what the operation of variation and natural selection in any individual case will be, demonstrates that in the long run they will adapt animals to their circumstances. Whether or not existing animal forms are due to such action, or what position the theory ought to take, forms the subject of a discussion in which questions of fact and questions of logic are curiously interlaced.

_____

17   A cucurbit is the gourd-shaped flask of an alembic, which was a device used by medieval alchemists for distilling liquids.

18   Rudolf Clausius (1822–1888) developed the concept of entropy and formulated the second law of thermodynamics, as well as carrying out pioneering work on the kinetic theory of gases. James Clerk Maxwell (1831–1879) is best known for unifying the phenomena of electricity and magnetism into a single set of field equations, but he was also important in the development of the kinetic theory of gases.

II.

The object of reasoning is to find out, from the consideration of what we already know, something else which we do not know. Consequently, reasoning is good if it be such as to give a true conclusion from true premises, and not otherwise. Thus, the question of its validity is purely one of fact and not of thinking. A being the premises and B the conclusion, the question is, whether these facts are really so related that if A is B is. If so, the inference is valid; if not, not. It is not in the least the question whether, when the premises are accepted by the mind, we feel an impulse to accept the conclusion also. It is true that we do generally reason correctly by nature. But that is an accident; the true conclusion would remain true if we had no impulse to accept it; and the false one would remain false, though we could not resist the tendency to believe in it.

We are, doubtless, in the main logical animals, but we are not perfectly so. Most of us, for example, are naturally more sanguine[19] and hopeful than logic would justify. We seem to be so constituted that in the absence of any facts to go upon we are happy and self-satisfied; so that the effect of experience is continually to contract our hopes and aspirations. Yet a lifetime of the application of this corrective does not usually eradicate our sanguine disposition. Where hope is unchecked by any experience, it is likely that our optimism is extravagant. Logicality in regard to practical matters is the most useful quality an animal can possess, and might, therefore, result from the action of natural selection; but outside of these it is probably of more advantage to the animal to have his mind filled with pleasing and encouraging visions, independently of their truth; and thus, upon unpractical subjects, natural selection might occasion a fallacious tendency of thought.

That which determines us, from given premises, to draw one inference rather than another, is some habit of mind, whether it be constitutional or acquired. The habit is good or otherwise, according as it produces true conclusions from true premises or not; and an inference is regarded as valid or not, without reference to the truth or falsity of its conclusion specially,

_____

19   Optimistic or cheerfully confident.

but according as the habit which determines it is such as to produce true conclusions in general or not. The particular habit of mind which governs this or that inference may be formulated in a proposition whose truth depends on the validity of the inferences which the habit determines; and such a formula is called a *guiding principle* of inference. Suppose, for example, that we observe that a rotating disk of copper quickly comes to rest when placed between the poles of a magnet, and we infer that this will happen with every disk of copper. The guiding principle is, that what is true of one piece of copper is true of another. Such a guiding principle with regard to copper would be much safer than with regard to many other substances—brass, for example.

A book might be written to signalize all the most important of these guiding principles of reasoning. It would probably be, we must confess, of no service to a person whose thought is directed wholly to practical subjects, and whose activity moves along thoroughly-beaten paths. The problems which present themselves to such a mind are matters of routine which he has learned once for all to handle in learning his business. But let a man venture into an unfamiliar field, or where his results are not continually checked by experience, and all history shows that the most masculine intellect will ofttimes lose his orientation and waste his efforts in directions which bring him no nearer to his goal, or even carry him entirely astray. He is like a ship in the open sea, with no one on board who understands the rules of navigation. And in such a case some general study of the guiding principles of reasoning would be sure to be found useful.

The subject could hardly be treated, however, without being first limited; since almost any fact may serve as a guiding principle. But it so happens that there exists a division among facts, such that in one class are all those which are absolutely essential as guiding principles, while in the others are all which have any other interest as objects of research. This division is between those which are necessarily taken for granted in asking whether a certain conclusion follows from certain premises, and those which are not implied in that question. A moment's thought will show that a variety of facts are already assumed when the logical

question is first asked. It is implied, for instance, that there are such states of mind as doubt and belief—that a passage from one to the other is possible, the object of thought remaining the same, and that this transition is subject to some rules which all minds are alike bound by. As these are facts which we must already know before we can have any clear conception of reasoning at all, it cannot be supposed to be any longer of much interest to inquire into their truth or falsity. On the other hand, it is easy to believe that those rules of reasoning which are deduced from the very idea of the process are the ones which are the most essential; and, indeed, that so long as it conforms to these it will, at least, not lead to false conclusions from true premises. In point of fact, the importance of what may be deduced from the assumptions involved in the logical question turns out to be greater than might be supposed, and this for reasons which it is difficult to exhibit at the outset. The only one which I shall here mention is, that conceptions which are really products of logical reflection, without being readily seen to be so, mingle with our ordinary thoughts, and are frequently the causes of great confusion. This is the case, for example, with the conception of quality. A quality, as such, is never an object of observation. We can see that a thing is blue or green, but the quality of being blue and the quality of being green are not things which we see; they are products of logical reflections. The truth is, that common-sense, or thought as it first emerges above the level of the narrowly practical, is deeply imbued with that bad logical quality to which the epithet *metaphysical* is commonly applied; and nothing can clear it up but a severe course of logic.

III.

We generally know when we wish to ask a question and when we wish to pronounce a judgment, for there is a dissimilarity between the sensation of doubting and that of believing.

But this is not all which distinguishes doubt from belief. There is a practical difference. Our beliefs guide our desires and shape our actions. The Assassins, or followers of the Old Man of the Mountain,[20]

---

20 The Assassins were a militant Muslim religious order founded in Persia in 1090 and, during the time of the

used to rush into death at his least command, because they believed that obedience to him would insure everlasting felicity. Had they doubted this, they would not have acted as they did. So it is with every belief, according to its degree. The feeling of believing is a more or less sure indication of there being established in our nature some habit which will determine our actions. Doubt never has such an effect.

Nor must we overlook a third point of difference. Doubt is an uneasy and dissatisfied state from which we struggle to free ourselves and pass into the state of belief; while the latter is a calm and satisfactory state which we do not wish to avoid, or to change to a belief in anything else.[21] On the contrary, we cling tenaciously, not merely to believing, but to believing just what we do believe.

Thus, both doubt and belief have positive effects upon us, though very different ones. Belief does not make us act at once, but puts us into such a condition that we shall behave in some certain way, when the occasion arises. Doubt has not the least effect of this sort, but stimulates us to action until it is destroyed. This reminds us of the irritation of a nerve and the reflex action produced thereby; while for the analogue of belief, in the nervous system, we must look to what are called nervous associations—for example, to that habit of the nerves in consequence of which the smell of a peach will make the mouth water.

IV.

The irritation of doubt causes a struggle to attain a state of belief. I shall term this struggle *inquiry,* though it must be admitted that this is sometimes not a very apt designation.

Crusades, notorious for their widespread acts of terror. Their leader was called Sheik al-Jebal ('Old Man of the Mountain') and he was said to possess the Holy Spirit and to be obeyed with blind obedience. Numbering 50,000 followers at their height, the Assassins—the word comes from the Arabic *haššaš*, hashish-eater—were finally destroyed in 1272.

21   [Author's note] I am not speaking of secondary effects occasionally produced by the interference of other impulses.

The irritation of doubt is the only immediate motive for the struggle to attain belief. It is certainly best for us that our beliefs should be such as may truly guide our actions so as to satisfy our desires; and this reflection will make us reject any belief which does not seem to have been so formed as to insure this result. But it will only do so by creating a doubt in the place of that belief. With the doubt, therefore, the struggle begins, and with the cessation of doubt it ends. Hence, the sole object of inquiry is the settlement of opinion. We may fancy that this is not enough for us, and that we seek, not merely an opinion, but a true opinion. But put this fancy to the test, and it proves groundless; for as soon as a firm belief is reached we are entirely satisfied, whether the belief be true or false. And it is clear that nothing out of the sphere of our knowledge can be our object, for nothing which does not affect the mind can be the motive for mental effort. The most that can be maintained is, that we seek for a belief that we shall *think* to be true. But we think each one of our beliefs to be true, and, indeed, it is mere tautology to say so.

That the settlement of opinion is the sole end of inquiry is a very important proposition. It sweeps away, at once, various vague and erroneous conceptions of proof. A few of these may be noticed here.

1. Some philosophers have imagined that to start an inquiry it was only necessary to utter a question or set it down upon paper, and have even recommended us to begin our studies with questioning everything! But the mere putting of a proposition into the interrogative form does not stimulate the mind to any struggle after belief. There must be a real and living doubt, and without this all discussion is idle.

2. It is a very common idea that a demonstration must rest on some ultimate and absolutely indubitable propositions. These, according to one school, are first principles of a general nature; according to another, are first sensations. But, in point of fact, an inquiry, to have that completely satisfactory result called demonstration, has only to start with propositions perfectly free from all actual doubt. If the premises are not in fact doubted at all, they cannot be more satisfactory than they are.

3. Some people seem to love to argue a point after all the world is fully convinced of it. But no further

advance can be made. When doubt ceases, mental action on the subject comes to an end; and, if it did go on, it would be without a purpose.

V.

If the settlement of opinion is the sole object of inquiry, and if belief is of the nature of a habit, why should we not attain the desired end, by taking any answer to a question which we may fancy, and constantly reiterating it to ourselves, dwelling on all which may conduce to that belief, and learning to turn with contempt and hatred from anything that might disturb it? This simple and direct method is really pursued by many men. I remember once being entreated not to read a certain newspaper lest it might change my opinion upon free-trade. "Lest I might be entrapped by its fallacies and misstatements," was the form of expression. "You are not," my friend said, "a special student of political economy. You might, therefore, easily be deceived by fallacious arguments upon the subject. You might, then, if you read this paper, be led to believe in protection. But you admit that free-trade is the true doctrine; and you do not wish to believe what is not true." I have often known this system to be deliberately adopted. Still oftener, the instinctive dislike of an undecided state of mind, exaggerated into a vague dread of doubt, makes men cling spasmodically to the views they already take. The man feels that, if he only holds to his belief without wavering, it will be entirely satisfactory. Nor can it be denied that a steady and immovable faith yields great peace of mind. It may, indeed, give rise to inconveniences, as if a man should resolutely continue to believe that fire would not burn him, or that he would be eternally damned if he received his *ingesta*[22] otherwise than through a stomach-pump. But then the man who adopts this method will not allow that its inconveniences are greater than its advantages. He will say, "I hold steadfastly to the truth, and the truth is always wholesome." And in many cases it may very well be that the pleasure he derives from his calm faith overbalances any inconveniences resulting from its deceptive character. Thus, if it be true that death is annihilation, then the man who believes that he will

certainly go straight to heaven when he dies, provided he have fulfilled certain simple observances in this life, has a cheap pleasure which will not be followed by the least disappointment. A similar consideration seems to have weight with many persons in religious topics, for we frequently hear it said, "Oh, I could not believe so-and-so, because I should be wretched if I did." When an ostrich buries its head in the sand as danger approaches, it very likely takes the happiest course. It hides the danger, and then calmly says there is no danger; and, if it feels perfectly sure there is none, why should it raise its head to see? A man may go through life, systematically keeping out of view all that might cause a change in his opinions, and if he only succeeds—basing his method, as he does, on two fundamental psychological laws—I do not see what can be said against his doing so. It would be an egotistical impertinence to object that his procedure is irrational, for that only amounts to saying that his method of settling belief is not ours. He does not propose to himself to be rational, and, indeed, will often talk with scorn of man's weak and illusive reason. So let him think as he pleases.

But this method of fixing belief, which may be called the method of tenacity, will be unable to hold its ground in practice. The social impulse is against it. The man who adopts it will find that other men think differently from him, and it will be apt to occur to him, in some saner moment, that their opinions are quite as good as his own, and this will shake his confidence in his belief. This conception, that another man's thought or sentiment may be equivalent to one's own, is a distinctly new step, and a highly important one. It arises from an impulse too strong in man to be suppressed, without danger of destroying the human species. Unless we make ourselves hermits, we shall necessarily influence each other's opinions; so that the problem becomes how to fix belief, not in the individual merely, but in the community.

Let the will of the state act, then, instead of that of the individual. Let an institution be created which shall have for its object to keep correct doctrines before the attention of the people, to reiterate them perpetually, and to teach them to the young; having at the same time power to prevent contrary doctrines

---

22   Food.

from being taught, advocated, or expressed. Let all possible causes of a change of mind be removed from men's apprehensions. Let them be kept ignorant, lest they should learn of some reason to think otherwise than they do. Let their passions be enlisted, so that they may regard private and unusual opinions with hatred and horror. Then, let all men who reject the established belief be terrified into silence. Let the people turn out and tar-and-feather such men, or let inquisitions be made into the manner of thinking of suspected persons, and when they are found guilty of forbidden beliefs, let them be subjected to some signal punishment. When complete agreement could not otherwise be reached, a general massacre of all who have not thought in a certain way has proved a very effective means of settling opinion in a country. If the power to do this be wanting, let a list of opinions be drawn up, to which no man of the least independence of thought can assent, and let the faithful be required to accept all these propositions, in order to segregate them as radically as possible from the influence of the rest of the world.

This method has, from the earliest times, been one of the chief means of upholding correct theological and political doctrines, and of preserving their universal or catholic[23] character. In Rome, especially, it has been practised from the days of Numa Pompilius to those of Pius Nonus.[24] This is the most perfect example in history; but wherever there is a priesthood—and no religion has been without one—this method has been more or less made use of. Wherever there is an aristocracy, or a guild, or any association of a class of men whose interests depend, or are supposed to depend, on certain propositions, there will be inevitably found some traces of this natural product of social feeling. Cruelties always accompany this

system; and when it is consistently carried out, they become atrocities of the most horrible kind in the eyes of any rational man. Nor should this occasion surprise, for the officer of a society does not feel justified in surrendering the interests of that society for the sake of mercy, as he might his own private interests. It is natural, therefore, that sympathy and fellowship should thus produce a most ruthless power.

In judging this method of fixing belief, which may be called the method of authority, we must, in the first place, allow its immeasurable mental and moral superiority to the method of tenacity. Its success is proportionately greater; and, in fact, it has over and over again worked the most majestic results. The mere structures of stone which it has caused to be put together—in Siam,[25] for example, in Egypt, and in Europe—have many of them a sublimity hardly more than rivaled by the greatest works of Nature. And, except the geological epochs, there are no periods of time so vast as those which are measured by some of these organized faiths. If we scrutinize the matter closely, we shall find that there has not been one of their creeds which has remained always the same; yet the change is so slow as to be imperceptible during one person's life, so that individual belief remains sensibly fixed. For the mass of mankind, then, there is perhaps no better method than this. If it is their highest impulse to be intellectual slaves, then slaves they ought to remain.

But no institution can undertake to regulate opinions upon every subject. Only the most important ones can be attended to, and on the rest men's minds must be left to the action of natural causes. This imperfection will be no source of weakness so long as men are in such a state of culture that one opinion does not influence another—that is, so long as they cannot put two and two together. But in the most priest-ridden states some individuals will be found who are raised above that condition. These men possess a wider sort of social feeling; they see that men in other countries and in other ages have held to very different doctrines from those which they themselves have been brought up to believe; and they cannot help seeing that it is the mere accident of their having been taught as they

---

23　Of broad scope, comprehensive, all-embracing (from a Greek word, *katholikos*, meaning "universal").

24　That is, from the earliest days of Rome to the time in which Peirce was writing. Numa Pompilius was, according to legend, the second king of Rome (715–672 BCE) and Pius IX was pope from 1846 until 1878. Pius IX was the pope who first institutionalized the doctrine of papal infallibility (on July 18, 1870), an event which made a deep impression on Peirce.

25　Thailand.

have, and of their having been surrounded with the manners and associations they have, that has caused them to believe as they do and not far differently. And their candor cannot resist the reflection that there is no reason to rate their own views at a higher value than those of other nations and other centuries; and this gives rise to doubts in their minds.

They will further perceive that such doubts as these must exist in their minds with reference to every belief which seems to be determined by the caprice either of themselves or of those who originated the popular opinions. The willful adherence to a belief, and the arbitrary forcing of it upon others, must, therefore, both be given up, and a new method of settling opinions must be adopted, which shall not only produce an impulse to believe, but shall also decide what proposition it is which is to be believed. Let the action of natural preferences be unimpeded, then, and under their influence let men, conversing together and regarding matters in different lights, gradually develop beliefs in harmony with natural causes. This method resembles that by which conceptions of art have been brought to maturity. The most perfect example of it is to be found in the history of metaphysical philosophy. Systems of this sort have not usually rested upon any observed facts, at least not in any great degree. They have been chiefly adopted because their fundamental propositions seemed "agreeable to reason." This is an apt expression; it does not mean that which agrees with experience, but that which we find ourselves inclined to believe. Plato, for example, finds it agreeable to reason that the distances of the celestial spheres[26] from one another should be proportional to the different lengths of strings which produce harmonious chords. Many philosophers have been led to their main conclusions by considerations like this; but this is the lowest and least developed form which the method takes, for it is clear that another man might find Kepler's theory, that the celestial spheres are proportional to the inscribed and circumscribed spheres of the different regular solids, more agreeable to *his* reason. But the shock of opinions will soon lead men to rest on preferences of a far more universal nature. Take, for example, the doctrine that man only acts selfishly—that is, from the consideration that acting in one way will afford him more pleasure than acting in another. This rests on no fact in the world, but it has had a wide acceptance as being the only reasonable theory.

This method is far more intellectual and respectable from the point of view of reason than either of the others which we have noticed. But its failure has been the most manifest. It makes of inquiry something similar to the development of taste; but taste, unfortunately, is always more or less a matter of fashion, and accordingly metaphysicians have never come to any fixed agreement, but the pendulum has swung backward and forward between a more material and a more spiritual philosophy, from the earliest times to the latest. And so from this, which has been called the *a priori* method, we are driven, in Lord Bacon's phrase, to a true induction. We have examined into this *a priori* method as something which promised to deliver our opinions from their accidental and capricious element. But development, while it is a process which eliminates the effect of some casual circumstances, only magnifies that of others. This method, therefore, does not differ in a very essential way from that of authority. The government may not have lifted its finger to influence my convictions; I may have been left outwardly quite free to choose, we will say, between monogamy and polygamy,[27] and, appealing to my conscience only, I may have concluded that the latter practice is in itself licentious.[28] But when I come to see that the chief obstacle to the spread of Christianity among a people of as high culture as the Hindoos has been a conviction of the immorality of our way of treating women, I cannot help seeing that, though governments do not interfere, sentiments in their development will be very greatly determined by accidental causes. Now, there are some people, among whom I must suppose that my reader is to be found, who, when they see that any belief of theirs is deter-

---

26 The positions of the sun, moon, planets, and stars (conceived as a concentric sequence of invisible spherical shells around the earth).

27 Monogamy means having only one spouse (or sexual partner) at a time; polygamy is the practice of having several spouses at once.

28 Lacking moral discipline.

mined by any circumstance extraneous to the facts, will from that moment not merely admit in words that that belief is doubtful, but will experience a real doubt of it, so that it ceases to be a belief.

To satisfy our doubts, therefore, it is necessary that a method should be found by which our beliefs may be caused by nothing human, but by some external permanency—by something upon which our thinking has no effect. Some mystics imagine that they have such a method in a private inspiration from on high. But that is only a form of the method of tenacity, in which the conception of truth as something public is not yet developed. Our external permanency would not be external, in our sense, if it was restricted in its influence to one individual. It must be something which affects, or might affect, every man. And, though these affections are necessarily as various as are individual conditions, yet the method must be such that the ultimate conclusion of every man shall be the same. Such is the method of science. Its fundamental hypothesis, restated in more familiar language, is this: There are real things, whose characters are entirely independent of our opinions about them; those realities affect our senses according to regular laws, and, though our sensations are as different as are our relations to the objects, yet, by taking advantage of the laws of perception, we can ascertain by reasoning how things really are; and any man, if he have sufficient experience and reason enough about it, will be led to the one true conclusion. The new conception here involved is that of reality. It may be asked how I know that there are any realities. If this hypothesis is the sole support of my method of inquiry, my method of inquiry must not be used to support my hypothesis. The reply is this: 1. If investigation cannot be regarded as proving that there are real things, it at least does not lead to a contrary conclusion; but the method and the conception on which it is based remain ever in harmony. No doubts of the method, therefore, necessarily arise from its practice, as is the case with all the others. 2. The feeling which gives rise to any method of fixing belief is a dissatisfaction at two repugnant propositions.[29] But here already is a vague concession

that there is some *one* thing to which a proposition should conform. Nobody, therefore, can really doubt that there are realities, or, if he did, doubt would not be a source of dissatisfaction. The hypothesis, therefore, is one which every mind admits. So that the social impulse does not cause me to doubt it. 3. Everybody uses the scientific method about a great many things, and only ceases to use it when he does not know how to apply it. 4. Experience of the method has not led me to doubt it, but, on the contrary, scientific investigation has had the most wonderful triumphs in the way of settling opinion. These afford the explanation of my not doubting the method or the hypothesis which it supposes; and not having any doubt, nor believing that anybody else whom I could influence has, it would be the merest babble for me to say more about it. If there be anybody with a living doubt upon the subject, let him consider it.

To describe the method of scientific investigation is the object of this series of papers. At present I have only room to notice some points of contrast between it and other methods of fixing belief.

This is the only one of the four methods which presents any distinction of a right and a wrong way. If I adopt the method of tenacity, and shut myself out from all influences, whatever I think necessary to doing this is necessary according to that method. So with the method of authority: the state may try to put down heresy by means which, from a scientific point of view, seem very ill-calculated to accomplish its purposes; but the only test *on that method* is what the state thinks; so that it cannot pursue the method wrongly. So with the *a priori* method. The very essence of it is to think as one is inclined to think. All metaphysicians will be sure to do that, however they may be inclined to judge each other to be perversely wrong. The Hegelian system[30] recognizes every

---

29   Two propositions which repel each other—which seem to be in conflict.

30   The system of philosophy developed by the important German philosopher G.W.F. Hegel (1770–1831). Peirce is thinking here of Hegel's dialectical view of the progress of both reason and history, in which one intellectual current (which Hegel calls a thesis) is faced with another opposing set of ideas, or antithesis, until the contradiction between the two is resolved in a synthesis. This synthesis is then faced with another

natural tendency of thought as logical, although it be certain to be abolished by counter-tendencies. Hegel thinks there is a regular system in the succession of these tendencies, in consequence of which, after drifting one way and the other for a long time, opinion will at last go right. And it is true that metaphysicians do get the right ideas at last; Hegel's system of Nature represents tolerably the science of that day; and one may be sure that whatever scientific investigation has put out of doubt will presently receive *a priori* demonstration on the part of the metaphysicians. But with the scientific method the case is different. I may start with known and observed facts to proceed to the unknown; and yet the rules which I follow in doing so may not be such as investigation would approve. The test of whether I am truly following the method is not an immediate appeal to my feelings and purposes, but, on the contrary, itself involves the application of the method. Hence it is that bad reasoning as well as good reasoning is possible; and this fact is the foundation of the practical side of logic.

It is not to be supposed that the first three methods of settling opinion present no advantage whatever over the scientific method. On the contrary, each has some peculiar convenience of its own. The *a priori* method is distinguished for its comfortable conclusions. It is the nature of the process to adopt whatever belief we are inclined to, and there are certain flatteries to the vanity of man which we all believe by nature, until we are awakened from our pleasing dream by some rough facts. The method of authority will always govern the mass of mankind; and those who wield the various forms of organized force in the state will never be convinced that dangerous reasoning ought not to be suppressed in some way. If liberty of speech is to be untrammeled[31] from the grosser forms of constraint, then uniformity of opinion will be secured by a moral terrorism to which the respectability of society will give its thorough approval. Following the method of authority is the path of peace. Certain non-conformities are permitted; certain others

(considered unsafe) are forbidden. These are different in different countries and in different ages; but, wherever you are, let it be known that you seriously hold a tabooed belief, and you may be perfectly sure of being treated with a cruelty less brutal but more refined than hunting you like a wolf. Thus, the greatest intellectual benefactors of mankind have never dared, and dare not now, to utter the whole of their thought; and thus a shade of *prima facie* doubt[32] is cast upon every proposition which is considered essential to the security of society. Singularly enough, the persecution does not all come from without; but a man torments himself and is oftentimes most distressed at finding himself believing propositions which he has been brought up to regard with aversion. The peaceful and sympathetic man will, therefore, find it hard to resist the temptation to submit his opinions to authority. But most of all I admire the method of tenacity for its strength, simplicity, and directness. Men who pursue it are distinguished for their decision of character, which becomes very easy with such a mental rule. They do not waste time in trying to make up their minds what they want, but, fastening like lightning upon whatever alternative comes first, they hold to it to the end, whatever happens, without an instant's irresolution. This is one of the splendid qualities which generally accompany brilliant, unlasting success. It is impossible not to envy the man who can dismiss reason, although we know how it must turn out at last.

Such are the advantages which the other methods of settling opinion have over scientific investigation. A man should consider well of them; and then he should consider that, after all, he wishes his opinions to coincide with the fact, and that there is no reason why the results of those three first methods should do so. To bring about this effect is the prerogative of the method of science. Upon such considerations he has to make his choice—a choice which is far more than the adoption of any intellectual opinion, which is one of the ruling decisions of his life, to which, when once made, he is bound to adhere. The force of habit will sometimes cause a man to hold on to old beliefs, after he is in a condition to see that they have no sound ba-

---

contradictory set of ideas, which is resolved into a further synthesis, and so on until rational perfection—a state of complete self-consciousness—is reached.

31   Freed from restriction, unhampered.

---

32   Doubt at first sight; initial doubt, which might or might not be removed by further investigation.

sis. But reflection upon the state of the case will overcome these habits, and he ought to allow reflection its full weight. People sometimes shrink from doing this, having an idea that beliefs are wholesome which they cannot help feeling rest on nothing. But let such persons suppose an analogous though different case from their own. Let them ask themselves what they would say to a reformed Mussulman[33] who should hesitate to give up his old notions in regard to the relations of the sexes; or to a reformed Catholic who should still shrink from reading the Bible. Would they not say that these persons ought to consider the matter fully, and clearly understand the new doctrine, and then ought to embrace it, in its entirety? But, above all, let it be considered that what is more wholesome than any particular belief is integrity of belief, and that to avoid looking into the support of any belief from a fear that it may turn out rotten is quite as immoral as it is disadvantageous. The person who confesses that there is such a thing as truth, which is distinguished from falsehood simply by this, that if acted on it will

carry us to the point we aim at and not astray, and then, though convinced of this, dares not know the truth and seeks to avoid it, is in a sorry state of mind indeed.

Yes, the other methods do have their merits: a clear logical conscience does cost something—just as any virtue, just as all that we cherish, costs us dear. But we should not desire it to be otherwise. The genius[34] of a man's logical method should be loved and reverenced as his bride, whom he has chosen from all the world. He need not contemn[35] the others; on the contrary, he may honor them deeply, and in doing so he only honors her the more. But she is the one that he has chosen, and he knows that he was right in making that choice. And having made it, he will work and fight for her, and will not complain that there are blows to take, hoping that there may be as many and as hard to give, and will strive to be the worthy knight and champion of her from the blaze of whose splendors he draws his inspiration and his courage.

---

33   Muslim.

34   The prevailing spirit or distinctive character.
35   Despise, show contempt for.

THOMAS KUHN
"Objectivity, Value Judgment, and Theory Choice"

Who Was Thomas Kuhn?

Thomas Kuhn's *The Structure of Scientific Revolutions* (first published in 1962) is the single most influential book in modern philosophy of science ... and indeed, in the opinion of some, is perhaps the most influential book published in the second half of the twentieth century.[1] In it, Kuhn presented a view of science

which seemed radically at variance with what most philosophers of science and scientists had previously supposed. Kuhn argued that most science—what he dubbed "normal science"—takes place against a background of unquestioned theoretical assumptions, which he called a *paradigm*. Typical scientists are

---

1   A report on the "most cited works of the twentieth century" issued by the Arts and Humanities Citation Index lists Lenin as the most cited author but *Structure*, by a fair margin, the most frequently mentioned

book. Kuhn's book is apparently treated with reverence inside the Washington Beltway: Al Gore claimed it as his favorite book, and both Bill Clinton and George Bush Sr. have praised its usefulness. *The Structure of Scientific Revolutions* has sold over a million copies and been translated into some twenty languages.

not, contrary to popular opinion, objective, skeptical, and independent thinkers: rather, according to Kuhn, they are community-minded conservatives who accept what they have been taught by their elders and devote their energies to solving puzzles dictated to them by their theories. Indeed, according to Kuhn, scientists habitually attempt to *ignore* research findings that threaten the existing paradigm. Occasionally, however, the pressures from anomalies—especially inexplicable experimental results—generated within that paradigm become such that a crisis occurs within the scientific community and it is necessary for a *paradigm shift* (a phrase first coined by Kuhn) to take place. These episodes in the history of science are what Kuhn called "revolutions." For example, to caricature Kuhn (who did not hold that paradigm shifts are caused entirely by the actions of single individuals), Galileo's (imagined) experiments—dropping wood and lead balls from the Leaning Tower of Pisa—caused the extinction of the Aristotelian theory that bodies fall at a speed proportional to their weight; Lavoisier's discovery of oxygen signaled the death knell for the older "phlogiston" paradigm of chemistry; Darwin's theory of natural selection overthrew ideas of a world governed by design; and Einstein's theory of relativity completely replaced Newtonian physics. Science, in other words, is "a series of peaceful interludes punctuated by intellectually violent revolutions." The old guard who worked within the previous paradigm then either undergo conversion to the new one, or simply die out and are replaced by younger scientists working in the new paradigm.

The most controversial and stimulating aspect of Kuhn's work has proved to be his claim that there can be no strictly rational reason to choose one new paradigm over another: that is, the adoption of scientific theories, according to Kuhn, is never and can never be a purely rational decision. According to the more extreme of Kuhn's adherents (though not—at least later in his career—Kuhn himself), this means that the logic and philosophy of science is to be replaced by the history and sociology of science: that is, science is best understood not as an ideally rational or logical enterprise, but as a sociological phenomenon. Furthermore, Kuhn has apparently held that successive scientific paradigms are *incommensurable*: scientists before and after a theoretical revolution essentially speak a different language and think in completely different ways, and so—since no one can think within two different paradigms at once—it is not possible for anyone to *compare* the two paradigms and see which is better. If this is the case, it seems to follow that we have no good reason to believe that the history of science is a story of progress or of the cumulative acquisition of scientific knowledge; the scientific revolutions which supplant one paradigm with another do not take us any closer to the truth about the way the world is, they simply replace one set of theoretical puzzles with a new incompatible set. The essay reprinted here, "Objectivity, Value Judgment, and Theory Choice," summarizes some of Kuhn's mature views on these topics.

Thomas Samuel Kuhn was born in Cincinnati, Ohio, in 1922, the son of an industrial engineer. He was educated in New York at a series of progressive, left-leaning schools—where, though bright, Kuhn by his own account felt anxious, isolated, and neurotic (feelings which apparently remained with him to some degree for the rest of his life)—and then in 1940 went to Harvard to take a degree in physics. His undergraduate degree completed in 1943, he joined the US army radar program as a physicist. Kuhn was assigned to work on radar profiles, first in the States and England, but was then sent to Europe in the wake of the Allied invasion—dressed in uniform so he would not be shot as a spy if captured behind enemy lines—to inspect captured German radar installations. He was present (by accident) when the victorious French general Charles de Gaulle entered Paris, and saw the German city of Hamburg after it had been flattened by Allied bombs.

After the war, Kuhn drifted into graduate work and received a PhD in physics from Harvard University in 1949. He remained at Harvard, teaching in the General Education in Science program which was aimed at giving students in the humanities and social sciences a background in natural science. However, in 1955 Kuhn was denied tenure at Harvard—on the grounds that he was insufficiently specialized in any particular academic discipline, either physics or history or philosophy—and he moved to the University of California at Berkeley, where in 1961 he became a full professor of the history of science. In 1964 Kuhn transferred to Princeton and then in 1979, after a divorce, moved again and settled at the Massachusetts Institute of Technology, where he remarried and taught until his retirement in 1991. He died in 1996.

What Is the Structure of This Reading?

Kuhn begins this paper by summarizing passages in *The Structure of Scientific Revolutions* about rational theory choice and progress in science, and claiming that his position on these matters has been seriously misunderstood by many of the book's critics. He then lays out what are sometimes known as his "five ways": five criteria, which are shared by scientists, for rational theory choice. However, he argues these five criteria are insufficient to determine the choice of one theory over another—scientists can only adopt or refuse to adopt a theory on the basis of partly *subjective* criteria. Kuhn then argues that this claim—that there is no single, shared algorithm available for theory choice in science—is a philosophically substantial finding, partly because, on Kuhn's view, there is no distinction to be made between the "contexts of discovery and justification." Furthermore, Kuhn insists, science could not properly function if there were some shared set of criteria that determined what any rational scientist must believe; instead, we should think of the five ways as *values* which influence theory choice rather than

rules which determine it. These five shared values are more or less permanent in the history of science, Kuhn goes on to claim, but they have no rational justification from outside of the practice of science, and furthermore they evolve and change with those practices. Finally, Kuhn addresses the sense in which the idiosyncratic factors that supplement the five ways in theory choice are 'subjective,' and reaffirms and clarifies his claim that paradigms are "incommensurable": that is, roughly, that two scientists who adopt different theories face communication barriers at least as extreme as those faced by two people who speak different languages.

Some Useful Background Information

1. A notion central to Kuhn's critique of the rationality of science is that of *incommensurability*. Two things are 'incommensurable' if they cannot be compared—if one cannot be said to be better, or truer, or more preferable than the other. For example, the number seven and the taste of apples are incommensurable: there is no scale of values on which they can both be compared. In the philosophy of science, two theories (or other linguistic systems) are said to be incommensurable if the claims of one cannot be stated in the language of the other. From this it follows also that there can be no neutral third language in which the claims of both theories can be stated and compared[2]—that is, there can be no neutral standpoint from which we can assess the theories and say that one is better than the other. And from *this*, it seems to be an inescapable conclusion that we cannot give any content to the notion that science is progressing—that scientific theories are be-

---

2 Suppose there were some theoretical language—call it theory C—which is capable of stating both the claims of theory A and those of theory B; then it would follow that A and B are not incommensurable, since the statements of A could be translated into C and those C-statements in turn could be translated into the language of B, and hence the claims of A could be stated in the terms of B (and vice versa).

coming closer approximations of the truth, for example—since we cannot any longer say that a later theory is better than an earlier one.

There are various reasons why one might think that scientific theories are incommensurable. One of the most influential arguments derives from a certain theory about how theoretical terms get their *meaning*. On this view (roughly), scientific terms like "electron" or "mass" do not, as ordinary words like "cow" and "yellow" may, get their meaning from being attached as labels to observable things in the world. (After all, we cannot *see* electrons, so how can we point to them in order to label them?) Instead, terms applied to theoretical entities get their meaning entirely from their *role in the theory*: for example, the meaning of the word "mass" is, roughly, *whatever it is* that performs the function that mass does in the mathematical equations which make up the theory. If all of this is right, then it seems to follow that *if you change the theory you also change the meanings of all the theoretical terms of that theory*. For example, mass plays a different role in Newton's theory than it does in relativity theory (e.g., mass is independent of velocity in classical mechanics but for Einstein mass increases as velocity does), and hence the word "mass" must mean something different in the two theories—that is, when Einstein talks about "mass" he is using a different language than when Newton talks about it, even though the words they use happen to look and sound the same.

2. Another notion of which Kuhn made influential use and which is often appealed to in arguments for incommensurability is the idea that all observation is "theory-laden." That is, it can be argued—and in fact is generally believed by philosophers of science—that it is impossible for a scientist to make any experimental observations of the world without relying upon certain theoretical assumptions, and furthermore that these observations *are changed* by those assumptions. For example, a scientist who uses equipment—such as a microscope, radio telescope, or fMRI machine—to make observations must rely upon many theoretical claims about the operation of that equipment, and what she believes she is seeing will depend upon how she believes the equipment operates. More fundamentally, it is thought that even unaided observations depend for their content upon the way a scientist categorizes or conceptualizes experience. For example, seventeenth-century chemists reported having *seen* phlogiston (a mythical substance) being emitted by burning objects as flames; a modern day chemist sees much the same phenomenon and observes a violent oxidation reaction. A medieval scientist observing the dawn would have *seen* a moving sun and a static earth; today's observer is aware that she is seeing the rotation of the earth carrying the sun into view. Finally, for many scientists and engineers trained in the Aristotelian science of the Middle Ages, projectiles were apparently *observed* to behave just as they were theoretically expected to—they rose into the air in a straight line until the force of their flight was overcome by the force of their weight, and then fell straight down to the ground; nowadays, *after* Newton has changed our theoretical framework, we observe that projectiles really have a parabolic trajectory.

One of the implications of this—or at least of the most radical versions of this thesis, sometimes called the collapse of the observation-theory distinction—is, once again, a kind of incommensurability. If all observation is infected by theory, the argument goes, then there can be no neutral body of data that can be used to evaluate competing theories. The observations recorded by scientists trained in theory *A* will support that theory because they see what they expect to see; meanwhile the experiments conducted by the partisans of theory *B* will support *their* theory; since all observations are theory-laden, there are no neutral experimental results available with respect to the two theories, and so no data that can legitimately be used to falsify one or confirm the other.

Suggestions for Critical Reflection

1. Kuhn quotes himself, from the *Structure of Scientific Revolutions,* as saying: "What better criterion [for which theory it is rational to adopt] could there be than the decision of the scientific group?" Do you agree with this claim? What better criterion *could* there be? If Kuhn is right about this, could the philosophy of science be replaced by the sociology of science (i.e., by the study of how groups of scientists come to consensus)?

2. What do you think is the philosophical value of studying the history of science? How much does the *actual* behavior of scientists show us about the ideal "scientific method"? In particular, do you think Kuhn establishes that the history of science reveals that there just *is* no completely rational method available to scientists?

3. Kuhn argues that not only do scientists possess no shared set of criteria for theory choice, but that science could not *survive* if there were a rational "scientific method" for confirming or discarding theories. Do you think he is right about this?

4. What do you think Kuhn made of the theories of science represented in this chapter by readings from Hempel and Popper? In what ways do you think his own account differs from theirs?

5. Both Hempel and, especially, Popper make a firm distinction between what Kuhn calls the context of discovery and the context of justification. How successful is Kuhn in arguing that there is no such distinction? What would be the implications if this distinction were collapsed?

6. Many critics have asserted that Kuhn's account of theory choice and paradigm shifts leaves no room for the notion that science *progresses* towards a closer and closer approximation to the *truth* about reality. On the basis of Kuhn's claims in this article, do you think that this is a fair criticism?

7. One unfriendly critic of Kuhn, James Franklin, has said the following: "The basic content of Kuhn's book [*The Structure of Scientific Revolu-* *tions*] can be inferred simply by asking: what would the humanities crowd *want* said about science? Once the question is asked, the answer is obvious. Kuhn's thesis is that scientific theories are no better than ones in the humanities.... [S]cience is all theoretical talk and negotiation, which never really establishes anything" (from *The New Criterion,* June 2000). Given what Kuhn says in this article, to what degree do you think that Franklin gets Kuhn right?

Suggestions for Further Reading

The first place to pursue Kuhn's ideas is, of course, his *The Structure of Scientific Revolutions* (University of Chicago Press, 1996). His most important papers are collected in two volumes: *The Essential Tension* (University of Chicago Press, 1977) and *The Road Since Structure: Philosophical Essays, 1970–1993* (University of Chicago Press, 2000), the second of which includes a lengthy autobiographical interview. Kuhn also published two books on case studies from the history of science: *The Copernican Revolution* (Harvard University Press, 1985) and *Black-Body Theory and the Quantum Discontinuity 1894–1912* (University of Chicago Press, 1987).

Currently the most authoritative book on Kuhn's philosophy is probably Paul Hoyningen-Huene's *Reconstructing Scientific Revolutions: Thomas S. Kuhn's Philosophy of Science* (University of Chicago Press, 1993). *Thomas Kuhn* by Alexander Bird (Princeton University Press, 2001) is also helpful. A dense, stimulating, rambling, and quite controversial attack on Kuhn (both his ideas and his person) is Steve Fuller's *Thomas Kuhn: A Philosophical History for Our Times* (University of Chicago Press, 2000). *Criticism and the Growth of Knowledge,* edited by Imre Lakatos and Alan Musgrave (Cambridge University Press, 1970), is an influential collection of articles on *The Structure of Scientific Revolutions,* with a reply from Kuhn, and *World Changes: Thomas Kuhn and the Nature of Science,* edited by Paul Horwich (MIT Press, 1993), is a more recent version along much the same lines. A collection called *Paradigms and Revolutions,* edited by Gary Gutting (University of Notre Dame Press, 1979), seeks to extend Kuhn's ideas to the humanities and social sciences.

"Objectivity, Value Judgment, and Theory Choice"[3]

In the penultimate chapter of a controversial book fifteen years ago, I considered the ways scientists are brought to abandon one time-honored theory or paradigm in favor of another. Such decision problems, I wrote, "cannot be resolved by proof." To discuss their mechanism is, therefore, to talk "about techniques of persuasion, or about argument and counterargument in a situation in which there can be no proof." Under these circumstances, I continued, "lifelong resistance [to a new theory] ... is not a violation of scientific standards.... Though the historian can always find men—Priestley, for instance[4]—who were unreasonable to resist for as long as they did, he will not find a point at which resistance becomes illogical or unscientific." Statements of that sort[5] obviously raise the question of why, in the absence of binding criteria for scientific choice, both the number of solved scientific problems and the precision of individual problem solutions should increase so markedly with the passage of time. Confronting that issue, I sketched in my closing chapter a number of characteristics that scientists share by virtue of the training which licenses their membership in one or another community of specialists. In the absence of criteria able to dictate the choice of each individual, I argued, we do well to trust the collective judgment of scientists trained in this way. "What better criterion could there be," I asked rhetorically, "than the decision of the scientific group?"[6]

A number of philosophers have greeted remarks like these in a way that continues to surprise me. My views, it is said, make of theory choice "a matter for mob psychology."[7] Kuhn believes, I am told, that "the decision of a scientific group to adopt a new paradigm cannot be based on good reasons of any kind, factual or otherwise."[8] The debates surrounding such choices must, my critics claim, be for me "mere persuasive displays without deliberative substance."[9] Reports of this sort manifest total misunderstanding, and I have occasionally said as much in papers directed primarily to other ends. But those passing protestations have had negligible effect, and the misunderstandings continue to be important. I conclude that it is past time for me to describe, at greater length and with greater precision, what has been on my mind when I have uttered statements like the ones with which I just began. If I have been reluctant to do so in the past, that is largely because I have preferred to devote attention to areas in which my views diverge more sharply from those currently received than they do with respect to theory choice.

What, I ask to begin with, are the characteristics of a good scientific theory? Among a number of quite usual answers I select five, not because they are ex-

---

3   This paper was originally given as the Machette Lecture delivered at Furman University in South Carolina in 1973. It was first published in *The Essential Tension: Selected Studies in Scientific Tradition and Change*, by Thomas Kuhn, Chicago: University of Chicago Press, 1977, pp. 320–339. Copyright © University of Chicago 1977.

4   Joseph Priestley (1733–1804) was an English scientist and theologian who discovered oxygen in 1774, though—in accordance with the terms of the then-current theory—he thought of it as "dephlogisticated air."

5   [Author's note] *The Structure of Scientific Revolutions*, 2d ed. (Chicago, 1970), pp. 148, 151–52, 159. All the passages from which these fragments are taken appeared in the same form in the first edition, published in 1962.

6   [Author's note] Ibid., p. 170.

7   [Author's note] Imre Lakatos, "Falsification and the Methodology of Scientific Research Programmes," in I. Lakatos and A. Musgrave, eds., *Criticism and the Growth of Knowledge* (Cambridge, 1970), pp, 91–195. The quoted phrase, which appears on p. 178, is italicized in the original.

8   [Author's note] Dudley Shapere, "Meaning and Scientific Change," in R.G. Colodny, ed., *Mind and Cosmos: Essays in Contemporary Science and Philosophy*, University of Pittsburgh Series in the Philosophy of Science, vol. 3 (Pittsburgh 1966), pp. 41–85. The quotation will be found on p. 67.

9   [Author's note] Israel Scheffler, *Science and Subjectivity* (Indianapolis, 1967), p. 81.

haustive, but because they are individually important and collectively sufficiently varied to indicate what is at stake. First, a theory should be accurate: within its domain, that is, consequences deducible from a theory should be in demonstrated agreement with the results of existing experiments and observations. Second, a theory should be consistent, not only internally or with itself, but also with other currently accepted theories applicable to related aspects of nature. Third, it should have broad scope: in particular, a theory's consequences should extend far beyond the particular observations, laws, or subtheories it was initially designed to explain. Fourth, and closely related; it should be simple, bringing order to phenomena that in its absence would be individually isolated and, as a set, confused. Fifth—a somewhat less standard item, but one of special importance to actual scientific decisions—a theory should be fruitful of new research findings: it should, that is, disclose new phenomena or unnoted relationships among those already known.[10] These five characteristics—accuracy, consistency, scope, simplicity, and fruitfulness—are all standard criteria for evaluating the adequacy of a theory. If they had not been, I would have devoted far more space to them in my book, for I agree entirely with the traditional view that they play a vital role when scientists must choose between an established theory and an upstart competitor. Together with others of much the same sort, they provide *the* shared basis for theory choice.

Nevertheless, two sorts of difficulties are regularly encountered by the men who must use these criteria in choosing, say, between Ptolemy's astronomical theory and Copernicus's,[11] between the oxygen and phlogis-

ton theories of combustion,[12] or between Newtonian mechanics and the quantum theory.[13] Individually the criteria are imprecise: individuals may legitimately differ about their application to concrete cases. In addition, when deployed together, they repeatedly prove to conflict with one another; accuracy may, for example, dictate the choice of one theory, scope the choice of its competitor. Since these difficulties, especially the first, are also relatively familiar, I shall devote little time to their elaboration. Though my argument does demand that I illustrate them briefly, my views will begin to depart from those long current only after I have done so.

Begin with accuracy, which for present purposes I take to include not only quantitative agreement but qualitative as well. Ultimately it proves the most nearly decisive of all the criteria, partly because it is less equivocal than the others but especially because predictive and explanatory powers, which depend on it, are characteristics that scientists are particularly unwilling to give up. Unfortunately, however, theories cannot always be discriminated in terms of accuracy. Copernicus's system, for example, was not more accurate than Ptolemy's until drastically revised by Kepler[14] more than sixty years after Copernicus's death.

---

10 [Author's note] The last criterion, fruitfulness, deserves more emphasis than it has yet received. A scientist choosing between two theories ordinarily knows that his decision will have a bearing on his subsequent research career. Of course he is especially attracted by a theory that promises the concrete successes for which scientists are ordinarily rewarded.

11 Ptolemy was a second-century CE astronomer from Alexandria, in Egypt, who based his astronomical theory on the belief that all heavenly bodies revolve around a stationary earth. Nicholas Copernicus (1473–1543)

was a Polish astronomer who advanced the competing theory that the earth and other planets revolve around the sun.

12 The former theory explains combustion as the violent chemical reaction of a substance with oxygen in the air around it; by contrast, the latter theory (which was current until the eighteenth century) postulated a volatile substance called phlogiston which is contained in all flammable materials and which is released as flame during combustion.

13 According to Newtonian theory, light (and other forms of what we now think of as electromagnetic energy) consisted in the mechanical motions of the particles in an all-enveloping, massless substance called "ether." Quantum theory is the modern scientific account of matter and energy; it is probabilistic rather than mechanical, and abandons the notion of a "medium" through which energy waves propagate.

14 Johannes Kepler (1571–1630), a German astronomer, is often considered the "father of modern astronomy"

If Kepler or someone else had not found other reasons to choose heliocentric astronomy, those improvements in accuracy would never have been made, and Copernicus's work might have been forgotten. More typically, of course, accuracy does permit discriminations, but not the sort that lead regularly to unequivocal choice. The oxygen theory, for example, was universally acknowledged to account for observed weight relations in chemical reactions, something the phlogiston theory had previously scarcely attempted to do. But the phlogiston theory, unlike its rival, could account for the metals' being much more alike than the ores from which they were formed. One theory thus matched experience better in one area, the other in another. To choose between them on the basis of accuracy, a scientist would need to decide the area in which accuracy was more significant. About that matter chemists could and did differ without violating any of the criteria outlined above, or any others yet to be suggested.

However important it may be, therefore, accuracy by itself is seldom or never a sufficient criterion for theory choice. Other criteria must function as well, but they do not eliminate problems. To illustrate I select just two—consistency and simplicity—asking how they functioned in the choice between the heliocentric and geocentric[15] systems. As astronomical theories both Ptolemy's and Copernicus's were internally consistent, but their relation to related theories in other fields was very different. The stationary central earth was an essential ingredient of received physical theory, a tight-knit body of doctrine which explained, among other things, how stones fall, how water pumps function, and why the clouds move slowly across the skies. Heliocentric astronomy, which required the earth's motion, was inconsistent with the existing scientific explanation of these and other terrestrial phenomena. The consistency criterion by itself, therefore, spoke unequivocally for geocentric tradition.

Simplicity, however, favored Copernicus, but only when evaluated in a quite special way. If, on the one

hand, the two systems were compared in terms of the actual computational labor required to predict the position of a planet at a particular time, then they proved substantially equivalent. Such computations were what astronomers did, and Copernicus's system offered them no labor-saving techniques; in that sense it was not simpler than Ptolemy's. If, on the other hand, one asked about the amount of mathematical apparatus required to explain, not the detailed quantitative motions of the planets, but merely their gross qualitative features—limited elongation, retrograde motion, and the like—then, as every schoolchild knows, Copernicus required only one circle per planet, Ptolemy two.[16] In that sense the Copernican theory was the simpler, a fact vitally important to the choices made by both Kepler and Galileo and thus essential to the ultimate triumph of Copernicanism. But that sense of simplicity was not the only one available, nor even the one most natural to professional astronomers, men whose task was the actual computation of planetary position.

Because time is short and I have multiplied examples elsewhere, I shall here simply assert that these difficulties in applying standard criteria of choice are typical and that they arise no less forcefully in twentieth-century situations than in the earlier and better-known examples I have just sketched. When scientists must choose between competing theories, two men fully committed to the same list of criteria for choice may nevertheless reach different conclusions. Perhaps they interpret simplicity differently or have different convictions about the range of fields within which the consistency criterion must be met. Or perhaps they agree about these matters but differ about the relative weights to be accorded to these or to other criteria when several are deployed together. With divergences of this sort, no set of choice criteria yet proposed is of any use. One can explain, as the

---

for his formulation of three fundamental laws of planetary motion.

15   "Heliocentric" means centered on the sun; "geocentric" means centered on the earth.

16   In the Ptolemaic system, celestial orbits are described by "epicycles": that is, the orbits of the sun and planets form small circles, the centers of which move around the circumference of a larger circle centered on the earth. For the Copernican system, of course, each planet's orbit is described by a single (elliptical) circle with the sun at its center.

historian characteristically does, why particular men made particular choices at particular times. But for that purpose one must go beyond the list of shared criteria to characteristics of the individuals who make the choice. One must, that is, deal with characteristics which vary from one scientist to another without thereby in the least jeopardizing their adherence to the canons that make science scientific. Though such canons do exist and should be discoverable (doubtless the criteria of choice with which I began are among them), they are not by themselves sufficient to determine the decisions of individual scientists. For that purpose the shared canons must be fleshed out in ways that differ from one individual to another.

Some of the differences I have in mind result from the individual's previous experience as a scientist. In what part of the field was he at work when confronted by the need to choose? How long had he worked there; how successful had he been; and how much of his work depended on concepts and techniques challenged by the new theory? Other factors relevant to choice lie outside the sciences. Kepler's early election of Copernicanism was due in part to his immersion in the Neoplatonic and Hermetic[17] movements of his day; German Romanticism[18] predisposed those it affected toward both recognition and acceptance of

energy conservation; nineteenth-century British social thought had a similar influence on the availability and acceptability of Darwin's concept of the struggle for existence. Still other significant differences are functions of personality. Some scientists place more premium than others on originality and are correspondingly more willing to take risks; some scientists prefer comprehensive, unified theories to precise and detailed problem solutions of apparently narrower scope. Differentiating factors like these are described by my critics as subjective and are contrasted with the shared or objective criteria from which I began. Though I shall later question that use of terms, let me for the moment accept it. My point is, then, that every individual choice between competing theories depends on a mixture of objective and subjective factors, or of shared and individual criteria. Since the latter have not ordinarily figured in the philosophy of science, my emphasis upon them has made my belief in the former hard for my critics to see.

What I have said so far is primarily simply descriptive of what goes on in the sciences at times of theory choice. As description, furthermore, it has not been challenged by my critics, who reject instead my claim that these facts of scientific life have philosophic import. Taking up that issue, I shall begin to isolate some, though I think not vast, differences of opinion. Let me begin by asking how philosophers of science can for so long have neglected the subjective elements which, they freely grant, enter regularly into the actual theory choices made by individual scientists? Why have these elements seemed to them an index only of human weakness, not at all of the nature of scientific knowledge?

One answer to that question is, of course, that few philosophers, if any, have claimed to possess either a complete or an entirely well-articulated list of criteria. For some time, therefore, they could reasonably expect that further research would eliminate residual imperfections and produce an algorithm able to dictate rational, unanimous choice. Pending that achievement, scientists would have no alternative but to supply subjectively what the best current list of objective criteria still lacked. That some of them might still do so even with a perfected list at hand would then be

17   Neoplatonism is a school of thought—originating in the third century CE, and influential in medieval and Renaissance philosophy—which fused Plato's philosophy with religious doctrines, and which sees the universe as an emanation from an omnipresent, transcendent, unchanging One. Hermeticism, which was also popular during the Renaissance, involves allegiance to the doctrines found in a collection of occult writings on magical and religious topics which were (wrongly) thought to be the texts of an ancient Egyptian priesthood.

18   Romanticism was a late eighteenth-century movement which reacted against the rationalism of the Enlightenment by embracing spontaneity, imagination, emotion, and inspiration. Among its themes was the belief that reality is ultimately spiritual, and that knowledge of nature cannot be achieved by rational and analytic means but only through a kind of intuitive absorption into the spiritual process of nature.

an index only of the inevitable imperfection of human nature.

That sort of answer may still prove to be correct, but I think no philosopher still expects that it will. The search for algorithmic decision procedures has continued for some time and produced both powerful and illuminating results. But those results all presuppose that individual criteria of choice can be unambiguously stated and also that, if more than one proves relevant, an appropriate weight function is at hand for their joint application. Unfortunately, where the choice at issue is between scientific theories, little progress has been made toward the first of these desiderata[19] and none toward the second. Most philosophers of science would therefore, I think, now regard the sort of algorithm which has traditionally been sought as a not quite attainable ideal. I entirely agree and shall henceforth take that much for granted.

Even an ideal, however, if it is to remain credible, requires some demonstrated relevance to the situations in which it is supposed to apply. Claiming that such demonstration requires no recourse to subjective factors, my critics seem to appeal, implicitly or explicitly, to the well-known distinction between the contexts of discovery and of justification.[20] They concede, that is, that the subjective factors I invoke play a significant role in the discovery or invention of new theories, but they also insist that that inevitably intuitive process lies outside of the bounds of philosophy of science and is irrelevant to the question of scientific objectivity. Objectivity enters science, they continue, through the processes by which theories are tested, justified, or judged. Those processes do not, or at least need not, involve subjective factors at all. They can be governed by a set of (objective) criteria shared by the entire group competent to judge.

I have already argued that that position does not fit observations of scientific life and shall now assume that that much has been conceded. What is now at issue is a different point: whether or not this invocation of the distinction between contexts of discovery and of justification provides even a plausible and useful idealization. I think it does not and can best make my point by suggesting first a likely source of its apparent cogency. I suspect that my critics have been misled by science pedagogy or what I have elsewhere called textbook science. In science teaching, theories are presented together with exemplary applications, and those applications may be viewed as evidence. But that is not their primary pedagogic function (science students are distressingly willing to receive the word from professors and texts). Doubtless *some* of them were *part* of the evidence at the time actual decisions were being made, but they represent only a fraction of the considerations relevant to the decision process. The context of pedagogy differs almost as much from the context of justification as it does from that of discovery.

Full documentation of that point would require longer argument than is appropriate here, but two aspects of the way in which philosophers ordinarily demonstrate the relevance of choice criteria are worth noting. Like the science textbooks on which they are often modelled, books and articles on the philosophy of science refer again and again to the famous crucial experiments: Foucault's pendulum,[21] which demonstrates the motion of the earth; Cavendish's demonstration of gravitational attraction;[22] or

---

19   Things lacking but needed or desired.

20   [Author's note] The least equivocal example of this position is probably the one developed in Scheffler, *Science and Subjectivity*, chap. 4.

21   This experiment was first performed in 1851 by the French physicist Jean Bernard Léon Foucault (1819–1868) in order to show that the earth spins around its axis. The oscillations of a weight swinging from a very long wire can be observed to slowly rotate (clockwise in the Northern hemisphere and anticlockwise in the Southern); however the pendulum itself must be moving in a straight line, since there is no outside force interrupting its movement; therefore, since the path of the pendulum seems to rotate with respect to the ground and yet we know that the pendulum is not rotating, it must be the *ground* which is spinning.

22   Henry Cavendish (1731–1810) used a sensitive torsion balance to measure the value of the gravitational constant G and this allowed him to estimate the mass of the Earth for the first time. Cavendish's experimental apparatus involved a light, rigid six-foot long rod, suspended from a wire, and having two small metal spheres attached to the ends of the rod. When the rod

Fizeau's measurement of the relative speed of sound in water and air.[23] These experiments are paradigms of good reason for scientific choice; they illustrate the most effective of all the sorts of argument which could be available to a scientist uncertain which of two theories to follow; they are vehicles for the transmission of criteria of choice. But they also have another characteristic in common. By the time they were performed no scientist still needed to be convinced of the validity of the theory their outcome is now used to demonstrate. Those decisions had long since been made on the basis of significantly more equivocal evidence. The exemplary crucial experiments to which philosophers again and again refer would have been historically relevant to theory choice only if they had yielded unexpected results. Their use as illustrations provides needed economy to science pedagogy, but they scarcely illuminate the character of the choices that scientists are called upon to make.

Standard philosophical illustrations of scientific choice have another troublesome characteristic. The only arguments discussed are, as I have previously indicated, the ones favorable to the theory that, in fact, ultimately triumphed. Oxygen, we read, could explain weight relations, phlogiston could not; but nothing is said about the phlogiston theory's power or about the oxygen theory's limitations. Compari-

sons of Ptolemy's theory with Copernicus's proceed in the same way. Perhaps these examples should not be given since they contrast a developed theory with one still in its infancy. But philosophers regularly use them nonetheless. If the only result of their doing so were to simplify the decision situation, one could not object. Even historians do not claim to deal with the full factual complexity of the situations they describe. But these simplifications emasculate by making choice totally unproblematic. They eliminate, that is, one essential element of the decision situation that scientists must resolve if their field is to move ahead. In those situations there are always at least some good reasons for each possible choice. Considerations relevant to the context of discovery are then relevant to justification as well; scientists who share the concerns and sensibilities of the individual who discovers a new theory are ipso facto[24] likely to appear disproportionately frequently among that theory's first supporters. That is why it has been difficult to construct algorithms for theory choice, and also why such difficulties have seemed so thoroughly worth resolving. Choices that present problems are the ones philosophers of science need to understand. Philosophically interesting decision procedures must function where, in their absence, the decision might still be in doubt.

That much I have said before, if only briefly. Recently, however, I have recognized another, subtler source for the apparent plausibility of my critics' position. To present it, I shall briefly describe a hypothetical dialogue with one of them. Both of us agree that each scientist chooses between competing theories by deploying some Bayesian algorithm[25] which permits him to compute a value for $p(T,E)$,

---

is twisted, the torsion of the wire exerts a force which is proportional to the angle of rotation of the rod, and Cavendish carefully calibrated his instrument to determine the relationship between the angle of rotation and the amount of torsional force. He then brought two large lead spheres near the smaller spheres attached to the rod: since all masses attract, the large spheres exerted a gravitational force upon the smaller spheres and twisted the rod a measurable amount. Once the torsional force balanced the gravitational force, the rod and spheres came to rest and Cavendish was able to determine the gravitational force of attraction between the masses.

23 Armand-Hippolyte Fizeau (1819–1896) is best known for experimentally determining the speed of light, and showing that different media (such as still water, moving water, and air) can affect the speed of propagation of light and sound.

24 *Ipso facto* means "by that very fact."

25 Thomas Bayes (1702–1761) was an English clergyman who developed an influential theorem for calculating the probability of a hypothesis given a certain body of evidence. According to this theorem, in its simplest form, the probability of the hypothesis is the product of a) its prior probability (i.e., its probability before the evidence) and b) the probability of the evidence being as it is given the hypothesis, divided by the prior probability of that evidence. That is, $p(T,E) = p(T) \times (p(E,T)/p(E))$.

i.e., for the probability of a theory T on the evidence E available both to him and to the other members of his group at a particular period of time. "Evidence," furthermore, we both interpret broadly to include such considerations as simplicity and fruitfulness. My critic asserts, however, that there is only one such value of p, that corresponding to objective choice, and he believes that all rational members of the group must arrive at it. I assert, on the other hand, for reasons previously given, that the factors he calls objective are insufficient to determine in full any algorithm at all. For the sake of the discussion I have conceded that each individual has an algorithm and that all their algorithms have much in common. Nevertheless, I continue to hold that the algorithms of individuals are all ultimately different by virtue of the subjective considerations with which each must complete the objective criteria before any computations can be done. If my hypothetical critic is liberal, he may now grant that these subjective differences do play a role in determining the hypothetical algorithm on which each individual relies during the early stages of the competition between rival theories. But he is also likely to claim that, as evidence increases with the passage of time, the algorithms of different individuals converge to the algorithm of objective choice with which his presentation began. For him the increasing unanimity of individual choices is evidence for their increasing objectivity and thus for the elimination of subjective elements from the decision process.

So much for the dialogue, which I have, of course, contrived to disclose the non sequitur[26] underlying an apparently plausible position. What converges as the evidence changes over time need only be the values of p that individuals compute from their individual algorithms. Conceivably those algorithms themselves also become more alike with time, but the ultimate unanimity of theory choice provides no evidence whatsoever that they do so. If subjective factors are required to account for the decisions that initially divide the profession, they may still be present later when the profession agrees. Though I shall not here

argue the point, consideration of the occasions on which a scientific community divides suggests that they actually do so.

My argument has so far been directed to two points. It first provided evidence that the choices scientists make between competing theories depend not only on shared criteria—those my critics call objective—but also on idiosyncratic factors dependent on individual biography and personality. The latter are, in my critics' vocabulary, subjective, and the second part of my argument has attempted to bar some likely ways of denying their philosophic import. Let me now shift to a more positive approach, returning briefly to the list of shared criteria—accuracy, simplicity, and the like—with which I began. The considerable effectiveness of such criteria does not, I now wish to suggest, depend on their being sufficiently articulated to dictate the choice of each individual who subscribes to them. Indeed, if they were articulated to that extent, a behavior mechanism fundamental to scientific advance would cease to function. What the tradition sees as eliminable imperfections in its rules of choice I take to be in part responses to the essential nature of science.

As so often, I begin with the obvious. Criteria that influence decisions without specifying what those decisions must be are familiar in many aspects of human life. Ordinarily, however, they are called not criteria or rules, but maxims, norms, or values. Consider maxims first. The individual who invokes them when choice is urgent usually finds them frustratingly vague and often also in conflict one with another. Contrast "He who hesitates is lost" with "Look before you leap," or compare "Many hands make light work" with "Too many cooks spoil the broth." Individually maxims dictate different choices, collectively none at all. Yet no one suggests that supplying children with contradictory tags like these is irrelevant to their education. Opposing maxims alter the nature of the decision to be made, highlight the essential issues it presents, and point to those remaining aspects of the decision for which each individual must take responsibility himself. Once invoked, maxims like these alter the nature of the decision process and can thus change its outcome.

Values and norms provide even clearer examples of effective guidance in the presence of conflict and

---

26 A *non sequitur* is something that does not follow, e.g., a conclusion that does not logically follow from the premises.

equivocation. Improving the quality of life is a value, and a car in every garage once followed from it as a norm. But quality of life has other aspects, and the old norm has become problematic. Or again, freedom of speech is a value, but so is preservation of life and property. In application, the two often conflict, so that judicial soul-searching, which still continues, has been required to prohibit such behavior as inciting to riot or shouting fire in a crowded theater. Difficulties like these are an appropriate source for frustration, but they rarely result in charges that values have no function or in calls for their abandonment. That response is barred to most of us by an acute consciousness that there are societies with other values and that these value differences result in other ways of life, other decisions about what may and what may not be done.

I am suggesting, of course, that the criteria of choice with which I began function not as rules, which determine choice, but as values, which influence it. Two men deeply committed to the same values may nevertheless, in particular situations, make different choices as, in fact, they do. But that difference in outcome ought not to suggest that the values scientists share are less than critically important either to their decisions or to the development of the enterprise in which they participate. Values like accuracy, consistency, and scope may prove ambiguous in application, both individually and collectively; they may, that is, be an insufficient basis for a *shared* algorithm of choice. But they do specify a great deal: what each scientist must consider in reaching a decision, what he may and may not consider relevant, and what he can legitimately be required to report as the basis for the choice he has made. Change the list, for example by adding social utility as a criterion, and some particular choices will be different, more like those one expects from an engineer. Subtract accuracy of fit to nature from the list, and the enterprise that results may not resemble science at all, but perhaps philosophy instead. Different creative disciplines are characterized, among other things, by different sets of shared values. If philosophy and engineering lie too close to the sciences, think of literature or the plastic arts. Milton's failure to set *Paradise Lost* in a Copernican universe does not indicate that he agreed with Ptolemy but that he had things other than science to do.

Recognizing that criteria of choice can function as values when incomplete as rules has, I think, a number of striking advantages. First, as I have already argued at length, it accounts in detail for aspects of scientific behavior which the tradition has seen as anomalous or even irrational. More important, it allows the standard criteria to function fully in the earliest stages of theory choice, the period when they are most needed but when, on the traditional view, they function badly or not at all. Copernicus was responding to them during the years required to convert heliocentric astronomy from a global conceptual scheme to mathematical machinery for predicting planetary position. Such predictions were what astronomers valued; in their absence, Copernicus would scarcely have been heard, something which had happened to the idea of a moving earth before. That his own version convinced very few is less important than his acknowledgment of the basis on which judgments would have to be reached if heliocentricism were to survive. Though idiosyncrasy must be invoked to explain why Kepler and Galileo were early converts to Copernicus's system, the gaps filled by their efforts to perfect it were specified by shared values alone.

That point has a corollary which may be more important still. Most newly suggested theories do not survive. Usually the difficulties that evoked them are accounted for by more traditional means. Even when this does not occur, much work, both theoretical and experimental, is ordinarily required before the new theory can display sufficient accuracy and scope to generate widespread conviction. In short, before the group accepts it, a new theory has been tested over time by the research of a number of men, some working within it, others within its traditional rival. Such a mode of development, however, *requires* a decision process which permits rational men to disagree, and such disagreement would be barred by the shared algorithm which philosophers have generally sought. If it were at hand, all conforming scientists would make the same decision at the same time. With standards for acceptance set too low, they would move from one attractive global viewpoint to another, never giving traditional theory an opportunity to supply equivalent attractions. With standards set higher, no one satisfying the criterion of rationality would be inclined to try out the new theory, to articulate it in ways which showed its fruitfulness or displayed its accuracy and scope. I doubt that science would survive the change. What from one viewpoint may seem the looseness and imperfection of choice criteria conceived as rules may, when the same criteria are seen as values, appear an indispensable means of spreading the risk which the introduction or support of novelty always entails.

Even those who have followed me this far will want to know how a value-based enterprise of the sort I have described can develop as a science does, repeatedly producing powerful new techniques for prediction and control. To that question, unfortunately, I have no answer at all, but that is only another way of saying that I make no claim to have solved the problem of induction. If science did progress by virtue of some shared and binding algorithm of choice, I would be equally at a loss to explain its success. The lacuna[27] is one I feel acutely, but its presence does not differentiate my position from the tradition.

It is, after all, no accident that my list of the values guiding scientific choice is, as nearly as makes any difference, identical with the tradition's list of rules dictating choice. Given any concrete situation to which the philosopher's rules could be applied, my values would function like his rules, producing the same choice. Any justification of induction, any explanation of why the rules worked, would apply equally to my values. Now consider a situation in which choice by shared rules proves impossible, not because the rules are wrong but because they are, as rules, intrinsically incomplete. Individuals must then still choose and be guided by the rules (now values) when they do so. For that purpose, however, each must first flesh out the rules, and each will do so in a somewhat different way even though the decision dictated by the variously completed rules may prove unanimous. If I now assume, in addition, that the group is large enough so that individual differences distribute on some normal curve, then any argument that justifies the philosopher's choice by rule should be immediately adaptable to my choice by value. A group too small, or a distribution excessively skewed by external historical pressures, would, of course, pre-

vent the argument's transfer.[28] But those are just the circumstances under which scientific progress is itself problematic. The transfer is not then to be expected.

I shall be glad if these references to a normal distribution of individual differences and to the problem of induction make my position appear very close to more traditional views. With respect to theory choice, I have never thought my departures large and have been correspondingly startled by such charges as "mob psychology," quoted at the start. It is worth noting, however, that the positions are not quite identical, and for that purpose an analogy may be helpful. Many properties of liquids and gases can be accounted for on the kinetic theory[29] by supposing that all molecules

---

27   Hole or gap.

28   [Author's note] If the group is small, it is more likely that random fluctuations will result in its members' sharing an atypical set of values and therefore making choices different from those that would be made by a larger and more representative group. External environment—intellectual, ideological, or economic— must systematically affect the value system of much larger groups, and the consequences can include difficulties in introducing the scientific enterprise to societies with inimical values or perhaps even the end of that enterprise within societies where it had once flourished. In this area, however, great caution is required. Changes in the environment where science is practiced can also have fruitful effects on research. Historians often resort, for example, to differences between national environments to explain why particular innovations were initiated and at first disproportionately pursued in particular countries, e.g., Darwinism in Britain, energy conservation in Germany. At present we know substantially nothing about the minimum requisites of the social milieux within which a sciencelike enterprise might flourish.

29   The kinetic theory is a theory of the thermodynamic behavior of matter, especially the relationships among pressure, volume, and temperature in gases. Among its central notions are that temperature depends on the kinetic energy of the rapidly moving particles of a substance, that energy and momentum are conserved in all collisions between particles, and that the average behavior of the particles in a substance can be deduced by statistical analysis.

travel at the same speed. Among such properties are the regularities known as Boyle's and Charles's law.[30] Other characteristics, most obviously evaporation, cannot be explained in so simple a way. To deal with them one must assume that molecular speeds differ, that they are distributed at random, governed by the laws of chance. What I have been suggesting here is that theory choice, too, can be explained only in part by a theory which attributes the same properties to all the scientists who must do the choosing. Essential aspects of the process generally known as verification will be understood only by recourse to the features with respect to which men may differ while still remaining scientists. The tradition takes it for granted that such features are vital to the process of discovery, which it at once and for that reason rules out of philosophical bounds. That they may have significant functions also in the philosophically central problem of justifying theory choice is what philosophers of science have to date categorically denied.

What remains to be said can be grouped in a somewhat miscellaneous epilogue. For the sake of clarity and to avoid writing a book, I have throughout this paper utilized some traditional concepts and locutions about the viability of which I have elsewhere expressed serious doubts. For those who know the work in which I have done so, I close by indicating three aspects of what I have said which would better represent my views if cast in other terms, simultaneously indicating the main directions in which such recasting should proceed. The areas I have in mind are: value invariance, subjectivity, and partial communication. If my views of scientific development are novel—a matter about which there is legitimate room for doubt—it is in areas such as these, rather than theory choice, that my main departures from tradition should be sought.

---

30 Boyle's law, formulated by Robert Boyle in 1662, is the principle that, at a constant temperature, the volume of a confined ideal gas varies inversely with its pressure. Charles's law, discovered by French scientist J.A.C. Charles in 1787, states that the volume of a fixed mass of gas held at a constant pressure varies directly with the absolute temperature.

Throughout this paper I have implicitly assumed that, whatever their initial source, the criteria or values deployed in theory choice are fixed once and for all, unaffected by their participation in transitions from one theory to another. Roughly speaking, but only very roughly, I take that to be the case. If the list of relevant values is kept short (I have mentioned five, not all independent) and if their specification is left vague, then such values as accuracy, scope, and fruitfulness are permanent attributes of science. But little knowledge of history is required to suggest that both the application of these values and, more obviously, the relative weights attached to them have varied markedly with time and also with the field of application. Furthermore, many of these variations in value have been associated with particular changes in scientific theory. Though the experience of scientists provides no philosophical justification for the values they deploy (such justification would solve the problem of induction), those values are in part learned from that experience, and they evolve with it.

The whole subject needs more study (historians have usually taken scientific values, though not scientific methods, for granted), but a few remarks will illustrate the sort of variations I have in mind. Accuracy, as a value, has with time increasingly denoted quantitative or numerical agreement, sometimes at the expense of qualitative. Before early modern times, however, accuracy in that sense was a criterion only for astronomy, the science of the celestial region. Elsewhere it was neither expected nor sought. During the seventeenth century, however, the criterion of numerical agreement was extended to mechanics, during the late eighteenth and early nineteenth centuries to chemistry and such other subjects as electricity and heat, and in this century to many parts of biology. Or think of utility, an item of value not on my initial list. It too has figured significantly in scientific development, but far more strongly and steadily for chemists than for, say, mathematicians and physicists. Or consider scope. It is still an important scientific value, but important scientific advances have repeatedly been achieved at its expense, and the weight attributed to it at times of choice has diminished correspondingly.

What may seem particularly troublesome about changes like these is, of course, that they ordinarily occur in the aftermath of a theory change. One of the objections to Lavoisier's new chemistry[31] was the roadblocks with which it confronted the achievement of what had previously been one of chemistry's traditional goals: the explanation of qualities, such as color and texture, as well as of their changes. With the acceptance of Lavoisier's theory such explanations ceased for some time to be a value for chemists; the ability to explain qualitative variation was no longer a criterion relevant to the evaluation of chemical theory. Clearly, if such value changes had occurred as rapidly or been as complete as the theory changes to which they related, then theory choice would be value choice, and neither could provide justification for the other. But, historically, value change is ordinarily a belated and largely unconscious concomitant of theory choice, and the former's magnitude is regularly smaller than the latter's. For the functions I have here ascribed to values, such relative stability provides a sufficient basis. The existence of a feedback loop through which theory change affects the values which led to that change does not make the decision process circular in any damaging sense.

About a second respect in which my resort to tradition may be misleading, I must be far more tentative. It demands the skills of an ordinary language philosopher, which I do not possess. Still no very acute ear for language is required to generate discomfort with the ways in which the terms "objectivity" and, more especially, "subjectivity" have functioned in this paper. Let me briefly suggest the respects in which I believe language has gone astray. "Subjective" is a term with

---

31   Antoine Laurent Lavoisier (1743–1794) isolated the major components of air and water, disproved the phlogiston theory by determining the role of oxygen in combustion, and organized the classification of chemical compounds upon which the modern system is based. He formulated the concept of an element as being a simple substance that cannot be broken down by any known method of chemical analysis, and he showed that although matter changes state during a chemical reaction its mass remains the same, thus leading him to propose the law of conservation of matter. Lavoisier was executed during the Reign of Terror after the French Revolution.

several established uses: in one of these it is opposed to "objective," in another to "judgmental." When my critics describe the idiosyncratic features to which I appeal as subjective, they resort, erroneously I think, to the second of these senses. When they complain that I deprive science of objectivity, they conflate that second sense of subjective with the first.

A standard application of the term "subjective" is to matters of taste, and my critics appear to suppose that that is what I have made of theory choice. But they are missing a distinction standard since Kant when they do so. Like sensation reports, which are also subjective in the sense now at issue, matters of taste are undiscussable. Suppose that, leaving a movie theater with a friend after seeing a western, I exclaim: "How I liked that terrible potboiler!" My friend, if he disliked the film, may tell me I have low tastes, a matter about which, in these circumstances, I would readily agree. But, short of saying that I lied, he cannot disagree with my report that I liked the film or try to persuade me that what I said about my reaction was wrong. What is discussable in my remark is not my characterization of my internal state, my exemplification of taste, but rather my *judgment* that the film was a potboiler. Should my friend disagree on that point, we may argue most of the night, each comparing the film with good or great ones we have seen, each revealing, implicitly or explicitly, something about how he *judges* cinematic merit, about his aesthetic. Though one of us may, before retiring, have persuaded the other, he need not have done so to demonstrate that our difference is one of judgment, not taste.

Evaluations or choices of theory have, I think, exactly this character. Not that scientists never say merely, I like such and such a theory, or I do not. After 1926 Einstein said little more than that about his opposition to the quantum theory. But scientists may always be asked to explain their choices, to exhibit the bases for their judgments. Such judgments are eminently discussable, and the man who refuses to discuss his own cannot expect to be taken seriously. Though there are, very occasionally, leaders of scientific taste, their existence tends to prove the rule. Einstein was one of the few, and his increasing isolation from the scientific community in later life shows how very limited a role taste alone can play in theory choice. Bohr,[32] unlike Einstein, did discuss the bases for his judgment, and he carried the day. If my critics introduce the term "subjective" in a sense that opposes it to judgmental—thus suggesting that I make theory choice undiscussable, a matter of taste—they have seriously mistaken my position.

Turn now to the sense in which "subjectivity" is opposed to "objectivity," and note first that it raises issues quite separate from those just discussed. Whether my taste is low or refined, my report that I liked the film is objective unless I have lied. To my judgment that the film was a potboiler, however, the objective-subjective distinction does not apply at all, at least not obviously and directly. When my critics say I deprive theory choice of objectivity, they must, therefore, have recourse to some very different sense of subjective, presumably the one in which bias and personal likes or dislikes function instead of, or in the face of, the actual facts. But that sense of subjective does not fit the process I have been describing any better than the first. Where factors dependent on individual biography or personality must be introduced to make values applicable, no standards of factuality or actuality are being set aside. Conceivably my discussion of theory choice indicates some limitations of objectivity, but not by isolating elements properly called subjective. Nor am I even quite content with the notion that what I have been displaying are limitations. Objectivity ought to be analyzable in terms of criteria like accuracy and consistency. If these criteria do not supply all the guidance that we have customarily expected of them, then it may be the meaning rather than the limits of objectivity that my argument shows.

Turn, in conclusion, to a third respect, or set of respects, in which this paper needs to be recast. I have assumed throughout that the discussions surrounding theory choice are unproblematic, that the

facts appealed to in such discussions are independent of theory, and that the discussions' outcome is appropriately called a choice. Elsewhere I have challenged all three of these assumptions, arguing that communication between proponents of different theories is inevitably partial, that what each takes to be facts depends in part on the theory he espouses, and that an individual's transfer of allegiance from theory to theory is often better described as conversion than as choice. Though all these theses are problematic as well as controversial, my commitment to them is undiminished. I shall not now defend them, but must at least attempt to indicate how what I have said here can be adjusted to conform with these more central aspects of my view of scientific development.

For that purpose I resort to an analogy I have developed in other places. Proponents of different theories are, I have claimed, like native speakers of different languages. Communication between them goes on by translation, and it raises all translation's familiar difficulties. That analogy is, of course, incomplete, for the vocabulary of the two theories may be identical, and most words function in the same ways in both. But some words in the basic as well as in the theoretical vocabularies of the two theories—words like "star" and "planet," "mixture" and "compound," or "force" and "matter"—do function differently. Those differences are unexpected and will be discovered and localized, if at all, only be repeated experience of communication breakdown. Without pursuing the matter further, I simply assert the existence of significant limits to what the proponents of different theories can communicate to one another. The same limits make it difficult or, more likely, impossible for an individual to hold both theories in mind together and compare them point by point with each other and with nature. That sort of comparison is, however, the process on which the appropriateness of any word like "choice" depends.

Nevertheless, despite the incompleteness of their communication, proponents of different theories can exhibit to each other, not always easily, the concrete technical results achievable by those who practice within each theory. Little or no translation is required to apply at least some value criteria to those results. (Accuracy and fruitfulness are most immediately applicable, perhaps followed by scope. Consistency

---

32 Niels Bohr, a Danish physicist, made basic contributions to the theory of atomic structure between 1913 and 1915 and received a Nobel prize in 1922 for this work. His model of the atom made essential use of quantum theory: he suggested that electrons in an atom move in orbits, and that when an electron moves to another orbit it gives off or absorbs a quantum of radiation.

and simplicity are far more problematic.) However incomprehensible the new theory may be to the proponents of tradition, the exhibit of impressive concrete results will persuade at least a few of them that they must discover how such results are achieved. For that purpose they must learn to translate, perhaps by treating already published papers as a Rosetta stone[33] or,

---

[33]   The Rosetta stone is a black basalt tablet discovered in 1799 by French troops near Rosetta, a northern Egyptian town in the Nile River delta. It can be seen in the British Museum in London and bears an inscription written in three different scripts—Greek, Egyptian hieroglyphic, and Egyptian demotic. This inscription provided the key to the code of (the hitherto baffling) Egyptian hieroglyphics.

often more effective, by visiting the innovator, talking with him, watching him and his students at work. Those exposures may not result in the adoption of the theory; some advocates of the tradition may return home and attempt to adjust the old theory to produce equivalent results. But others, if the new theory is to survive, will find that at some point in the language-learning process they have ceased to translate and begun instead to speak the language like a native. No process quite like choice has occurred, but they are practicing the new theory nonetheless. Furthermore, the factors that have led them to risk the conversion they have undergone are just the ones this paper has underscored in discussing a somewhat different process, one which, following philosophical tradition, it has labelled theory choice.

HELEN LONGINO

"Can There Be a Feminist Science?"

Who Is Helen Longino?

Helen E. Longino (born 1944) has been perhaps the most influential philosopher to apply contemporary feminist approaches to epistemology and philosophy of science. As an undergraduate, she majored in literary studies, moving to logic and philosophy of science for her graduate work at Johns Hopkins University. During the 1960s and 70s, she was active in anti-war and feminist political action movements. As a faculty member at Mills College, Rice University, and University of Minnesota, she was strongly influential in establishing women's studies courses and programs. At present, she teaches in the philosophy department at Stanford University.

Some Useful Background Information

Longino's target for feminist criticism is the long-held and (for a long time) universal view that the most

important feature of good science is its *objectivity*—which was taken to mean that scientific practice, when working right, should be utterly uninfluenced by any values of the scientist, or of his culture or society—any values, that is, other than the internal scientific values of care in observation, honesty, thoroughness, and so on. The idea here was that nature itself—the external facts—should determine what's taken to be true by scientists.

Nobody thinks that real science always works this way: there are numerous high-profile examples brought to light of outright fraud, or unconscious bias, the result of what the scientist himself or the source of his funding, or the dominant culture, hopes to find. But the traditional view counts these as bad science. A very moderate feminist critique of science has, for decades, pointed out how male bias is among the factors that can make for bad science in this sense. Feminists point to scientific studies like these: a study of the causes of heart-attack which studied only males as subjects, blithely considering their conclusions to be applicable to all humans; a study of societal dynamics which looked only at traditional male activities and roles; a study of cognitive abilities that rated subjects on the basis of typically male abilities, concluding with the intellectual inferiority of women.

But this is not Longino's critique.

What Is the Structure of This Reading?

Longino begins by mentioning various sorts of feminist approaches to science that her article will not take. Her subject will instead be a feminist critique of the idea that science should be impersonal, objective, and value-free; feminists, she argues, offer an alternative that makes for better science.

After a number of preliminaries, she reveals her central argument: that confirmation in science often essentially involves background assumptions, and that these assumptions are sometimes not merely established by simple observation or common sense, but are rather tied in with "contextual values"—not mere internal rules of science, but personal, social, or cultural values.

Common Misconceptions

1. Longino does not argue that there are typically feminine characteristics that should be represented more in scientific investigations. She does not reject this view wholesale; she merely argues that this is not what she will talk about.
2. Neither does Longino argue here for a position that some readers, seeing that this is a feminist treatment of scientific practice, might expect: that the current male science gets things all wrong, and that a replacement female science would do better. She mentions that her aim is not to replace one "absolutism" by another.

Suggestions for Critical Reflection

1. Explain in your own words exactly what the difference between "contextual" and "constitutive" values in science is. Do you think that a real distinction can be made here? Do you think that

it's a good idea to try to allow input from the latter, but not from the former?
2. Longino argues that the input of "constitutive values" is sometimes inevitable. But she concludes from this that inquiry with this sort of input is "perfectly respectable." Do you think that follows?
3. Try to imagine a story about *scientifically respectable* theory-testing that includes a significant input of "contextual values." If you have studied science, you may know a bit of the real history of the field that illustrates this. What are the "contextual values" that play a part here?
4. Now try to imagine (or come up with a real example) of such testing where the input of "contextual values" made the scientific procedure unacceptable, invalid. Do you think there's a difference between instances of acceptable and unacceptable value-input science?
5. Explain how Longino uses her example of the study of the influence of sex hormones. What is the "background assumption" she thinks was at work in this study? Why does Longino think that this is connected to particular personal, cultural, or societal values? Is she right? What would have made for a better study? Do you think that a "value-free" inquiry here would have been an improvement? or that it would have been even possible?
6. A central, simple, definition of feminism sees it as a movement to counter discrimination and injustice toward women. What else might be involved in feminism as an intellectual commitment? Can you see why Longino's view of science is properly conceived of as feminist? Explain why you think it is or isn't.
7. Longino does not advocate replacement of scientifically harmful "androcentric" values by supposedly scientifically superior feminist ones. What, exactly, does she advocate?

Suggestions for Further Reading

A good place to start reading more by Longino is on-line: "The Social Dimensions of Scientific Knowledge," *The Stanford Encyclopedia of Philosophy (Fall 2008 Edition)*, Edward N. Zalta (ed.) <http://plato.stanford.

edu/archives/fall2008/entries/scientific-knowledge-social/>. Other articles by her are "Feminist Epistemology" *Blackwell Guide to Epistemology*, John Greco and Ernest Sosa, eds. (Blackwell, 1999), pp. 327-353; and "Cognitive and Non-Cognitive Values in Science: Rethinking the Dichotomy" *Feminism, Science, and the Philosophy of Science,* Lynn Hankinson Nelson and Jack Nelson, eds. (Kluwer, 1996), 39-58. Her books: *Science as Social Knowledge: Values and Objectivity in Scientific Inquiry* (Princeton University Press, 1990) and *The Fate of Knowledge* (Princeton University Press, 2002). She discusses examples further in Helen Longino and Ruth Doell, "Body, Bias, and Behaviour: A Comparative Analysis of Reasoning in Two Areas of Biological Science" *Signs: Journal of Women in Culture and Society* 9/2 (1983), pp. 206-227.

There has been a great deal written in the past few decades on this subject. A good place to find a variety of important short readings is in any of these anthologies: *Feminist Epistemologies*, Linda Alcoff and Elizabeth Potter, eds. (Routledge, 1993); *A Mind of One's Own: Feminist Essays on Reason and Objectivity*, Louise Antony and Charlotte Witt, eds., (Westview, 1993); *Discovering Reality: Feminist Perspectives in Epistemology, Metaphysics, Methodology and Philosophy of Science,* Sandra Harding and Merrill Hintikka, eds. (Reidel, 1983); *Engendering Rationalities*, Nancy Tuana and Sandra Morgen, eds. (SUNY Press, 2001); and *Feminism and Science,* Nancy Tuana, ed. (Indiana University Press, 1989).

"Can There Be a Feminist Science?"[1]

This paper explores a number of recent proposals regarding "feminist science" and rejects a content-based approach in favor of a process-based approach to characterizing feminist science. Philosophy of science can yield models of scientific reasoning that illuminate the interaction between cultural values and ideology and scientific inquiry. While we can use these models to expose masculine and other forms of bias, we can also use them to defend the introduction of assumptions grounded in feminist political values.

I

The question of this title conceals multiple ambiguities. Not only do the sciences consist of many distinct fields, but the term "science" can be used to refer to a method of inquiry, a historically changing collection of practices, a body of knowledge, a set of claims, a profession, a set of social groups, etc. And as the sciences are many, so are the scholarly disciplines that seek to understand them: philosophy, history, sociology, anthropology, psychology. Any answer from the perspective of some one of these disciplines will, then, of necessity, be partial. In this essay, I shall be asking about the possibility of theoretical natural science that is feminist and I shall ask from the perspective of a philosopher. Before beginning to develop my answer, however, I want to review some of the questions that could be meant, in order to arrive at the formulation I wish to address.

The question could be interpreted as factual, one to be answered by pointing to what feminists in the sciences are doing and saying: "Yes, and this is what it is." Such a response can be perceived as question-begging, however. Even such a friend of feminism as Stephen Gould dismisses the idea of a distinctively feminist or even female contribution to the sciences. In a generally positive review of Ruth Bleier's book, *Science and Gender*, Gould (1984) brushes aside her connection between women's attitudes and values and the interactionist science she calls for. Scientists (male, of course) are already proceeding with wholist[2] and interactionist[3] research programs. Why, he implied, should women or feminists have any particular, distinctive, contributions to make? There is not masculinist and feminist science, just good and

---

1   *Hypatia*, Vol. 2, No. 3, 1987, pp. 51–64.

2   Wholists reject the assumption, made by positivists, that observation is independent from theory, and claim that confirming or disconfirming observations cannot be specified independently of the theory they are supposed to confirm or disconfirm.

3   This is the view, taken from a theoretical position in sociology, that derives social processes—in this case, the practice of science—from human interaction.

bad science. The question of a feminist science cannot be settled by pointing, but involves a deeper, subtler investigation.

The deeper question can itself have several meanings. One set of meanings is sociological, the other conceptual. The sociological meaning proceeds as follows. We know what sorts of social conditions make misogynist science possible. The work of Margaret Rossiter (1982) on the history of women scientists in the United States and the work of Kathryn Addelson (1983) on the social structure of professional science detail the relations between a particular social structure for science and the kinds of science produced. What sorts of social conditions would make feminist science possible? This is an important question, one I am not equipped directly to investigate, although what I can investigate is, I believe, relevant to it. This is the second, conceptual, interpretation of the question: what sort of sense does it make to talk about a feminist science? Why is the question itself not an oxymoron, linking, as it does, values and ideological commitment with the idea of impersonal, objective, value-free, inquiry? This is the problem I wish to address in this essay.

The hope for a feminist theoretical natural science has concealed an ambiguity between content and practice. In the content sense the idea of a feminist science involves a number of assumptions and calls a number of visions to mind. Some theorists have written as though a feminist science is one of the theories which encode a particular world view, characterized by complexity, interaction and wholism. Such a science is said to be feminist because it is the expression and valorization[4] of a female sensibility or cognitive temperament. Alternatively, it is claimed that women have certain traits (dispositions to attend to particulars, interactive rather than individualist and controlling social attitudes and behaviors) that enable them to understand the true character of natural processes (which are complex and interactive).[5] While propo-

nents of this interactionist view see it as an improvement over most contemporary science, it has also been branded as soft—misdescribed as non-mathematical. Women in the sciences who feel they are being asked to do not better science, but inferior science, have responded angrily to this characterization of feminist science, thinking that it is simply new clothing for the old idea that women can't do science. I think that the interactionist view can be defended against this response, although that requires rescuing it from some of its proponents as well. However, I also think that the characterization of feminist science as the expression of a distinctive female cognitive temperament has other drawbacks. It first conflates feminine with feminist. While it is important to reject the traditional derogation of the virtues assigned to women, it is also important to remember that women are *constructed* to occupy positions of social subordinates. We should not uncritically embrace the feminine.

This characterization of feminist science is also a version of recently propounded notions of a 'women's standpoint' or a 'feminist standpoint' and suffers from the same suspect universalization that these ideas suffer from. If there is one such standpoint, there are many: as Maria Lugones and Elizabeth Spelman spell out in their tellingly entitled article, "Have We Got a Theory for You: Feminist Theory, Cultural Imperialism, and the Demand for 'The Woman's Voice,'" women are too diverse in our experiences to generate a single cognitive framework (Lugones and Spelman 1983). In addition, the sciences are themselves too diverse for me to think that they might be equally transformed by such a framework. To reject this concept of a feminist science, however, is not to disengage science from feminism. I want to suggest that we focus on science as practice rather than content, as process rather than product; hence, not on feminist science, but on doing science as a feminist.

The doing of science involves many practices: how one structures a laboratory (hierarchically or collectively), how one relates to other scientists (competitively or cooperatively), how and whether one engages in political struggles over affirmative action. It extends also to intellectual practices, to the activities of scientific inquiry, such as observation and reasoning. Can there be a feminist scientific inquiry?

---

4   To valorize something is to enhance its value, usually artificially, or to assign a value to it.

5   [Author's note] This seems to be suggested in Bleier (1984), Rose (1983) and in Sandra Harding's (1980) early work.

This possibility is seen to be problematic against the background of certain standard presuppositions about science. The claim that there could be a feminist science in the sense of an intellectual practice is either nonsense because oxymoronic as suggested above or the claim is interpreted to mean that established science (science as done and dominated by men) is wrong about the world. Feminist science in this latter interpretation is presented as correcting the errors of masculine, standard science and as revealing the truth that is hidden by masculine 'bad' science, as taking the sex out of science.

Both of these interpretations involve the rejection of one approach as incorrect and the embracing of the other as the way to a truer understanding of the natural world. Both trade one absolutism for another. Each is a side of the same coin, and that coin, I think, is the idea of a value-free science. This is the idea that scientific methodology guarantees the independence of scientific inquiry from values or value-related considerations. A science or a scientific research program informed by values is *ipso facto* "bad science." "Good science" is inquiry protected by methodology from values and ideology. This same idea underlies Gould's response to Bleier, so it bears closer scrutiny. In the pages that follow, I shall examine the idea of value-free science and then apply the results of that examination to the idea of feminist scientific inquiry.

II

I distinguish two kinds of values relevant to the sciences. Constitutive values, internal to the sciences, are the source of the rules determining what constitutes acceptable scientific practice or scientific method. The personal, social and cultural values, those group or individual preferences about what ought to be, I call contextual values, to indicate that they belong to the social and cultural context in which science is done (Longino 1983c). The traditional interpretation of the value-freedom of modern natural science amounts to a claim that its constitutive and contextual features are clearly distinct from and independent of one another, that contextual values play no role in the inner workings of scientific inquiry, in reasoning and observation. I shall argue that this construal of the distinction cannot be maintained.

There are several ways to develop such an argument. One scholar is fond of inviting her audience to visit any science library and peruse the titles on the shelves. Observe how subservient to social and cultural interests are the inquiries represented by the book titles alone! Her listeners would soon abandon their ideas about the value-neutrality of the sciences, she suggests. This exercise may indeed show the influence of external, contextual considerations on what research gets done/supported (i.e., on problem selection). It does not show that such considerations affect reasoning or hypothesis acceptance. The latter would require detailed investigation of particular cases or a general conceptual argument. The conceptual arguments involve developing some version of what is known in philosophy of science as the underdetermination thesis, i.e., the thesis that a theory is always underdetermined by the evidence adduced in its support, with the consequence that different or incompatible theories are supported by or at least compatible with the same body of evidence. I shall sketch a version of the argument that appeals to features of scientific inference.

One of the rocks on which the logical positivist program foundered was the distinction between theoretical and observational language. Theoretical statements contain, as fundamental descriptive terms, terms that do not occur in the description of data. Thus, hypotheses in particle physics contain terms like "electron," "pion," "muon," "electron spin," etc. The evidence for a hypothesis such as "A pion decays sequentially into a muon, then a positron" is obviously not direct observations of pions, muons and positrons, but consists largely in photographs taken in large and complex experimental apparati: accelerators, cloud chambers, bubble chambers. The photographs show all sorts of squiggly lines and spirals. Evidence for the hypotheses of particle physics is presented as statements that describe these photographs. Eventually, of course, particle physicists point to a spot on a photograph and say things like "Here a neutrino hits a neutron." Such an assertion, however, is an interpretive achievement which involves collapsing theoretical and observational moments. A skeptic would have to be supplied a complicated argument linking the elements of the photograph to traces left by particles and these to particles themselves. What counts as theory and what as data in a pragmatic sense change over time, as some ideas and experimental procedures come to be securely embedded in a particular framework and others take their place on the horizons. As the history of physics shows, however, secure embeddedness is no guarantee against overthrow.

Logical positivists and their successors hoped to model scientific inference formally. Evidence for hypotheses, data, were to be represented as logical consequences of hypotheses. When we try to map this logical structure onto the sciences, however, we find that hypotheses are, for the most part, not just generalizations of data statements. The links between data and theory, therefore, cannot be adequately represented as formal or syntactic, but are established by means of assumptions that make or imply substantive claims about the field over which one theorizes. Theories are confirmed via the confirmation of their constituent hypotheses, so the confirmation of hypotheses and theories is relative to the assumptions relied upon in asserting the evidential connection. Conformation of such assumptions, which are often unarticulated, is itself subject to similar relativization. And it is these assumptions that can be the vehicle for the involvement of considerations motivated primarily by contextual values (Longino 1979, 1983a).

The point of this extremely telescoped argument is that one can't give an a priori specification of confirmation that effectively eliminates the role of value-laden assumptions in legitimate scientific inquiry without eliminating auxiliary hypotheses (assumptions) altogether. This is not to say that all scientific reasoning involves value-related assumptions. Sometimes auxiliary assumptions will be supported by mundane inductive reasoning. But sometimes they will not be. In any given case, they may be metaphysical in character; they may be untestable with present investigative techniques; they may be rooted in contextual, value-related considerations. If, however, there is no a priori way to eliminate such assumptions from evidential reasoning generally, and, hence, no way to rule out value-laden assumptions, then there is no formal basis for arguing that an inference mediated by contextual values is thereby bad science.

A comparable point is made by some historians investigating the origins of modern science. James Jacob (1977) and Margaret Jacob (1976) have, in a series of articles and books, argued that the adoption of conceptions of matter by 17th century scientists like Robert Boyle was inextricably intertwined with political considerations. Conceptions of matter provided the foundation on which physical theories were developed and Boyle's science, regardless of his reasons for it, has been fruitful in ways that far exceed his imaginings. If the presence of contextual influences were grounds for disallowing a line of inquiry, then early modern science would not have gotten off the ground.

The conclusion of this line of argument is that constitutive values conceived as epistemological (i.e., truth-seeking) are not adequate to screen out the influence of contextual values in the very structuring of scientific knowledge. Now the ways in which contextual values do, if they do, influence this structuring and interact, if they do, with constitutive values has to be determined separately for different theories and fields of science. But this argument, if it's sound, tells us that this sort of inquiry is perfectly respectable and involves no shady assumptions or unargued intuitively based rejections of positivism. It also opens the possibility that one can make explicit value commitments and still do "good" science. The conceptual argument doesn't show that all science is value-laden (as opposed to metaphysics-laden)—that must be established on a case-by-case basis, using the tools not just of logic and philosophy but of history and sociology as well. It does show that not all science is value-free and, more importantly, that it is not necessarily in the nature of science to be value-free. If we reject that idea we're in a better position to talk about the possibilities of feminist science.

III

In earlier articles (Longino 1981, 1983b; Longino and Doell 1983), I've used similar considerations to argue that scientific objectivity has to be reconceived as a function of the communal structure of scientific inquiry rather than as a property of individual scientists. I've then used these notions about scientific methodology to show that science displaying masculine bias is not *ipso facto* improper or 'bad' science;

that the fabric of science can neither rule out the expression of bias nor legitimate it. So I've argued that both the expression of masculine bias in the sciences and feminist criticism of research exhibiting that bias are—shall we say—business as usual; that scientific inquiry should be expected to display the deep metaphysical and normative[6] commitments of the culture in which it flourishes; and finally that criticism of the deep assumptions that guide scientific reasoning about data is a proper part of science.

The argument I've just offered about the idea of a value-free science is similar in spirit to those earlier arguments. I think it makes it possible to see these questions from a slightly different angle.

There is a tradition of viewing scientific inquiry as somehow inexorable. This involves supposing that the phenomena of the natural world are fixed in determinate relations with each other, that these relations can be known and formulated in a consistent and unified way. This is not the old "unified science" idea of the logical positivists, with its privileging of physics. In its "unexplicated" or "pre-analytic" state, it is simply the idea that there is one consistent, integrated or coherent, true theoretical treatment of all natural phenomena. (The indeterminacy principle of quantum physics is restricted to our understanding of the behavior of certain particles which themselves underlie the fixities of the natural world. Stochastic[7] theories reveal fixities, but fixities among ensembles rather than fixed relations among individual objects or events.) The scientific inquirer's job is to discover those fixed relations. Just as the task of Plato's philosophers was to discover the fixed relations among forms and the task of Galileo's scientists was to discover the laws written in the language of the grand book of nature, geometry, so the scientist's task in this tradition remains the discovery of fixed relations however conceived. These ideas are part of the realist tradition in the philosophy of science.

It's no longer possible, in a century that has seen the splintering of the scientific disciplines, to give such a unified description of the objects of inquiry.

But the belief that the job is to discover fixed relations of some sort, and that the application of observation, experiment and reason leads ineluctably to unifiable, if not unified, knowledge of an independent reality, is still with us. It is evidenced most clearly in two features of scientific rhetoric: the use of the passive voice as in "it is concluded that ..." or "it has been discovered that ..." and the attribution of agency to the data, as in "the data suggest...." Such language has been criticized for the abdication of responsibility it indicates. Even more, the scientific inquirer, and we with her, become passive observers, victims of the truth. The idea of a value-free science is integral to this view of scientific inquiry. And if we reject that idea we can also reject our roles as passive onlookers, helpless to affect the course of knowledge.

Let me develop this point somewhat more concretely and autobiographically. Biologist Ruth Doell and I have been examining studies in three areas of research on the influence of sex hormones on human behavior and cognitive performance: research on the influence of pre-natal, *in utero*, exposure to higher or lower than normal levels of androgens and estrogens on so-called 'gender-role' behavior in children, influence of androgens (pre- and post-natal) on homosexuality in women, and influence of lower than normal (for men) levels of androgen at puberty on spatial abilities (Doell and Longino, forthcoming).

The studies we looked at are vulnerable to criticism of their data and their observation methodologies. They also show clear evidence of androcentric bias[8]—in the assumption that there are just two sexes and two genders (us and them), in the designation of appropriate and inappropriate behaviors for male and female children, in the caricature of lesbianism, in the assumption of male mathematical superiority. We did not find, however, that these assumptions mediated the inferences from data to theory that we found objectionable. These sexist assumptions did affect the way the data were described. What mediated the inferences from the alleged data (i.e., what functioned as auxiliary hypotheses or what provided auxiliary hypotheses) was what we called the linear model—the assumption that there is a direct one-way causal

6   Normative means having to do with a value—a prescribed norm.

7   Probabilistic.

8   I.e., a bias in favor of the male point of view.

relationship between pre- or post-natal hormone levels and later behavior or cognitive performance. To put it crudely, fetal gonadal hormones organize the brain at critical periods of development. The organism is thereby disposed to respond in a range of ways to a range of environmental stimuli. The assumption of unidirectional programming is supposedly supported by the finding of such a relationship in other mammals; in particular, by experiments demonstrating the dependence of sexual behaviors—mounting and lordosis[9]—on peri-natal hormone exposure and the finding of effects of sex hormones on the development of rodent brains. To bring it to bear on humans is to ignore, among other things, some important differences between human brains and those of other species. It also implies a willingness to regard humans in a particular way—to see us as produced by factors over which we have no control. Not only are we, as scientists, victims of the truth, but we are the prisoners of our physiology.[10] In the name of extending an explanatory model, human capacities for self-knowledge, self-reflection, self-determination are eliminated from any role in human action (at least in the behaviors studied).

Doell and I have therefore argued for the replacement of that linear model of the role of the brain in behavior by one of much greater complexity that includes physiological, environmental, historical and psychological elements. Such a model allows not only for the interaction of physiological and environmental factors but also for the interaction of these with a continuously self-modifying, self-representational (and self-organizing) central processing system. In contemporary neurobiology, the closest model is that being developed in the group selectionist approach to higher brain function of Gerald Edelman and other researchers (Edelman and Mountcastle 1978). We argue that a model of at least that degree of complexity is necessary to account for the human behaviors studies in the sex hormones and behavior research

---

9   Arching the spine backwards or downwards, which is a sexual response in some mammals (such as cats and mice).

10   [Author's note] For a striking expression of this point of view see Witelson (1985).

and that if gonadal hormones function at all at these levels, they will probably be found at most to facilitate or inhibit neural processing in general. The strategy we take in our argument is to show that the degree of intentionality involved in the behaviors in question is greater than is presupposed by the hormonal influence researchers and to argue that this degree of intentionality implicates the higher brain processes.

To this point Ruth Doell and I agree. I want to go further and describe what we've done from the perspective of the above philosophical discussion of scientific methodology.

Abandoning my polemical mood for a more reflective one, I want to say that, in the end, commitment to one or another model is strongly influenced by values or other contextual features. The models themselves determine the relevance and interpretation of data. The linear or complex models are not in turn independently or conclusively supported by data. I doubt for instance that value-free inquiry will reveal the efficacy or inefficacy of intentional states or of physiological factors like hormone exposure in human action. I think instead that a research program in neuro-science that assumes the linear model and sex-gender dualism will show the influence of hormone exposure on gender-role behavior. And I think that a research program in neuroscience and psychology proceeding on the assumption that humans do possess the capacities for self-consciousness, self-reflection, and self-determination, and which then asks how the structure of the human brain and nervous system enables the expression of these capacities, will reveal the efficacy of intentional states (understood as very complex sorts of brain states).

While this latter assumption does not itself contain normative terms, I think that the decision to adopt it is motivated by value-laden considerations—by the desire to understand ourselves and others as self-determining (at least some of the time), that is, as capable of acting on the basis of concepts or representations of ourselves and the world in which we act. (Such representations are not necessarily correct, they are surely mediated by our cultures; all we wish to claim is that they are efficacious.) I think further that this desire on Ruth Doell's and my part is, in several ways, an aspect of our feminism. Our preference for a neurobiological model that allows for agency, for the efficacy of intentionality, is partly a validation of our (and everyone's) subjective experience of thought, deliberation, and choice. One of the tenets of feminist research is the valorization of subjective experience, and so our preference in this regard conforms to feminist research patterns. There is, however, a more direct way in which our feminism is expressed in this preference. Feminism is many things to many people, but it is at its core in part about the expansion of human potentiality. When feminists talk of breaking out and do break out of socially prescribed sex-roles, when feminists criticize the institutions of domination, we are thereby insisting on the capacity of humans—male and female—to act on perceptions of self and society and to act to bring about changes in self and society on the basis of those perceptions. (Not overnight and not by a mere act of will. The point is that we act.) And so our criticism of theories of the hormonal influence or determination of so-called gender-role behavior is not just a rejection of the sexist bias in the description of the phenomena—the behavior of the children studied, the sexual lives of lesbians, etc.—but of the limitations on human capacity imposed by the analytic model underlying such research.[11]

While the argument strategy we adopt against the linear model rests on a certain understanding of intention, the values motivating our adoption of that understanding remain hidden in that polemical context. Our political commitments, however, presuppose a certain understanding of human action, so that when faced with a conflict between these commitments and a particular model of brain-behavior relationships we allow the political commitments to guide the choice.

The relevance of my argument about value-free science should be becoming clear. Feminists—in and out of science—often condemn masculine bias in the sciences from the vantage point of commitment to a value-free science. Androcentric bias, once

identified, can then be seen as a violation of the rules, as "bad" science. Feminist science, by contrast, can eliminate that bias and produce better, good, more true or gender free science. From that perspective the process I've just described is anathema. But if scientific methods generated by constitutive values cannot guarantee independent from contextual values, then that approach to sexist science won't work. We cannot restrict ourselves simply to the elimination of bias, but must expand our scope to include the detection of limiting and interpretive frameworks and the finding or construction of more appropriate frameworks. We need not, indeed should not, wait for such a framework to emerge from the data. In waiting, if my argument is correct, we run the danger of working unconsciously with assumptions still laden with values from the context we seek to change. Instead of remaining passive with respect to the data and what the data suggest, we can acknowledge our ability to affect the course of knowledge and fashion or favor research programs that are consistent with the values and commitments we express in the rest of our lives. From this perspective, the idea of a value-free science is not just empty, but pernicious.

Accepting the relevance to our practice as scientists of our political commitments does not imply simple and crude impositions of those ideas onto the corner of the natural world under study. If we recognize, however, that knowledge is shaped by the assumptions, values and interests of a culture and that, within limits, one can choose one's culture, then it's clear that as scientists/theorists we have a choice. We can continue to do establishment science, comfortably wrapped in the myths of scientific rhetoric, or we can alter our intellectual allegiances. While remaining committed to an abstract goal of understanding, we can choose to whom, socially and politically, we are accountable in our pursuit of that goal. In particular we can choose between being accountable to the traditional establishment or to our political comrades.

Such accountability does not demand a radical break with the science one has learned and practiced. The development of a "new" science involves a more dialectical evolution and more continuity with established science than the familiar language of scientific revolutions implies.

---

11 [Author's note] Ideological commitments other than feminist ones may lead to the same assumptions and the variety of feminisms means that feminist commitments can lead to different and incompatible assumptions.

In focusing on accountability and choice, this conception of feminist science differs from those that proceed from the assumption of a congruence between certain models of natural processes and women's inherent modes of understanding.[12] I am arguing instead for the deliberate and active choice of an interpretive model and for the legitimacy of basing that choice on political considerations in this case. Obviously model choice is also constrained by (what we know of) reality, that is, by the data. But reality (what we know of it) is, I have already argued, inadequate to uniquely determine model choice. The feminist theorists mentioned above have focused on the relation between the content of a theory and female values or experiences, in particular on the perceived congruence between interactionist, wholist visions of nature and a form of understanding and set of values widely attributed to women. In contrast, I am suggesting that a feminist scientific practice admits political considerations as relevant constraints on reasoning, which, through their influence on reasoning and interpretation, shape content. In this specific case, those considerations in combination with the phenomena support an explanatory model that is highly interactionist, highly complex. This argument is so far, however, neutral on the issue of whether an interactionist and complex account of natural processes will always be the preferred one. If it is preferred, however, this will be because of explicitly political considerations and not because interactionism is the expression of "women's nature."

The integration of a political commitment with scientific work will be expressed differently in different fields. In some, such as the complex of research programs having a bearing on the understanding of human behavior, certain moves, such as the one described above, seem quite obvious. In others it may not be clear how to express an alternate set of values in inquiry, or what values would be appropriate. The first step, however, is to abandon the idea that scrutiny of the data yields a seamless web of knowledge. The second is to think through a particular field and try to understand just what its unstated and fundamental assumptions are and how they influence the course of inquiry. Knowing something of the history of a field is necessary to this process, as is continued conversation with other feminists.

The feminist interventions I imagine will be local (i.e., specific to a particular area of research); they may not be exclusive (i.e., different feminist perspectives may be represented in theorizing); and they will be in some way continuous with existing scientific work. The accretion of such interventions, of science done by feminists as feminists, and by members of other disenfranchised groups, has the potential, nevertheless, ultimately to transform the character of scientific discourse.

Doing science differently requires more than just the will to do so and it would be disingenuous to pretend that our philosophies of science are the only barrier. Scientific inquiry takes place in a social, political and economic context which imposes a variety of institutional obstacles to innovation, let alone to the intellectual working out of oppositional and political commitments. The nature of university career ladders means that one's work must be recognized as meeting certain standards of quality in order that one be able to continue it. If those standards are intimately bound up with values and assumptions one rejects, incomprehension rather than conversion is likely. Success requires that we present our work in a way that satisfies those standards and it is easier to do work that looks just like work known to satisfy them than to strike out in a new direction. Another push to conformity comes from the structure of support for science. Many of the scientific ideas argued to be consistent with a feminist politics have a distinctively non-production orientation.[13] In the example discussed above, thinking of the brain as hormonally programmed makes intervention and control more likely than does thinking of it as a self-organizing complexly interactive system. The doing of science, however, requires financial support

---

12   [Author's note] Cf. note [5], above.

13   [Author's note] This is not to say that interactionist ideas may not be applied in productive contexts, but that, unlike linear causal models, they are several steps away from the manipulation of natural processes immediately suggested by the latter. See Keller (1985), especially Chapter 10.

and those who provide that support are increasingly industry and the military. As might be expected they support research projects likely to meet their needs, projects which promise even greater possibilities for intervention in and manipulation of natural processes. Our sciences are being harnessed to the making of money and the waging of war. The possibility of alternate understandings of the natural world is irrelevant to a culture driven by those interests. To do feminist science we must change the social and political context in which science is done.

So: can there be a feminist science? If this means: is it in principle possible to do science as a feminist?, the answer must be: yes. If this means: can we in practice do science as feminists?, the answer must be: not until we change present conditions.

Notes

I am grateful to the Wellesley Center for Research on Women for the Mellon Scholarship during which I worked on the ideas in this essay. I am also grateful to audiences at UC Berkeley, Northeastern University, Brandeis University and Rice University for their comments and to the anonymous reviewers for *Hypatia* for their suggestions. An earlier version appeared as Wellesley Center for Research on Women Working Paper #63.

References

Addelson, Kathryn Pine. 1983. The man of professional wisdom. In *Discovering reality*, ed. Sandra Harding and Merrill Hintikka. Dordrecht: Reidel.

Bleier, Ruth. 1984. *Science and gender*. Elmsford, NY: Pergamon.

Doell, Ruth, and Helen E. Longino. N.d. *Journal of Homosexuality*. Forthcoming.

Edelman, Gerald, and Vernon Mountcastle. 1978. *The mindful brain*. Cambridge, MA: MIT Press.

Gould, Stephen J. 1984. Review of Ruth Bleier, *Science and gender. New York Times Book Review*, VVI, 7 (August 12): 1.

Harding, Sandra. 1980. The norms of inquiry and masculine experience. In *PSA 1980*, Vol. 2, ed. Peter Asquith and Ronald Giere. East Lansing, MI: Philosophy of Science Association.

Jacob, James R. 1977. *Robert Boyle and the English Revolution, A study in social and intellectual change*. New York: Franklin.

Jacob, Margaret C. 1976. *The Newtonians and the English Revolution, 1689-1720*. Ithaca, NY: Cornell University Press.

Keller, Evelyn Fox. 1985. *Reflections on gender and science*. New Haven, CT: Yale University Press.

Longino, Helen. 1979. Evidence and hypothesis. *Philosophy of Science* 46 (1): 35-56.

———. 1981. Scientific objectivity and feminist theorizing. *Liberal Education* 67 (3): 33-41.

———. 1983a. The idea of a value free science. Paper presented to the Pacific Division of the American Philosophical Association, March 25, Berkeley, CA.

———. 1983b. Scientific objectivity and logics of science. *Inquiry* 26 (1): 85-106.

———. 1983c. Beyond "bad science." *Science, Technology and Human Values* 8 (1): 7-17.

Longino, Helen, and Ruth Doell. 1983. Body, bias and behavior. *Signs* 9 (2): 206-227.

Lugones, Maria, and Elizabeth Spelman. 1983. Have we got a theory for you! Feminist theory, cultural imperialism and the demand for "the woman's voice." *Hypatia 1*, published as a special issue of *Women's Studies International Forum* 6 (6): 573-581.

Rose, Hilary. 1983. Hand, brain, and heart: A feminist epistemology for the natural sciences. *Signs* 9 (1): 73-90.

Rossiter, Margaret. 1982. *Women scientists in America: Struggles and strategies to 1940*. Baltimore, MD: Johns Hopkins University Press.

Witelson, Sandra. 1985. An exchange on gender. *New York Review of Books* (October 24).

Philosophical Puzzles and Paradoxes

INTRODUCTION

Paradoxes and puzzles have played an important role in philosophy since the beginning of philosophical thought. They make us question our beliefs and pre-suppositions—often very basic ones. They don't always make us reject what we had taken for granted, but they do always subject it to scrutiny from a new and fascinating direction.

A paradox is an argument that appears to derive an absurd or obviously false conclusion by entirely valid reasoning from clearly acceptable premises. Sometimes philosophers argue that a premise is, despite appearances, actually false, or that the reasoning is actually invalid. Sometimes they argue that the premises and reasoning are fine, but the conclusion is true. Sometimes philosophers simply don't know what to do about a paradox. Any of these reactions is surprising, and may be of deep philosophical importance.

Puzzles are questions that seem like they ought to have a satisfying answer—but apparently do not. Philosophical reactions here include arguments for an (unobvious) solution, claims that there's something wrong with the unanswerable question in the first place, or, again, just puzzlement. Again, any of these reactions is surprising and can be instructive.

The puzzles and paradoxes presented here are almost all very well-known and widely discussed in the philosophical literature. We'll often include a brief indication of how, in general, philosophers have reacted. We have not included very much discussion of philosophical reactions, or bibliographies, but you won't have any trouble finding these on the Internet. We have also little to say about philosophical implications. What we aim at here is to give you enough of an introduction to each puzzle or paradox to stimulate your own philosophical intelligence—to get you to think about these brain-twisters on your own—and

we're confident you'll often find this engaging, enlightening, and fun.

BARBER PARADOX

Imagine a town in which there's a (male) barber who shaves all the men who don't shave themselves, and only those men. Does he shave himself? The answer can't be yes—because he doesn't shave men who shave themselves. The answer can't be no—because he does shave all the men who don't shave themselves. This paradox is resolved by concluding that there can't be a town with a barber who is the way we're trying to imagine.

BERTRAND'S BOX PARADOX

Imagine three boxes, each containing two drawers. In one box, both drawers contain a gold coin. (Call this box GG.) In another box, both drawers contain a silver coin. (Call this box SS.) In the third box, one drawer has a gold coin, the other has a silver. (Call this box GS.) You pick a box at random, open one drawer, and find a gold coin. What's the probability the other drawer in that box contains a silver coin? (Stop now and try to answer.)

Here's how most people reason. You've got a gold coin, so that means that the box you picked isn't SS. It's equally likely—50%—to be GG or GS. So the likelihood that the other coin is silver is 50%.

But that's wrong. What you've got might be (1) drawer G of GS; (2) drawer G1 of GG; (3) drawer G2 of GG. The probability of each of these is equal:

33%. So the probability the other drawer has a silver coin is the probability of outcome (1): 33%.

BLACKMAIL PARADOX

It's neither illegal nor immoral to ask somebody for money. It's neither illegal nor immoral to threaten to expose somebody's theft. But it's both illegal and immoral to ask somebody for money, threatening that if you don't get the money, you'll expose their theft.

This is a paradox only if you accept the principle that if it's not illegal (or immoral) to do X, and it's not illegal (or immoral) to do Y, then it's not illegal (immoral) to do X and Y. But that's clearly a false principle. There are plenty of counter-examples. It's not illegal (or immoral) for example to drink, or to drive, but it is illegal to drink-and-drive (and probably immoral too, because of the increased risk of a damaging accident).

What is illegal (and immoral) in the blackmail case is not merely doing both actions—I might threaten to expose your theft, and also, unconnectedly, ask you for money—but to do both with a particular connection between them. What connection? What's the general principle here?

BURIDAN'S ASS

Imagine an ass (come on now, we mean a donkey) who is very hungry and very thirsty, and is placed equidistant between equal quantities of hay and water. If we assume that the ass is determined to choose by a variety of factors (more hungry or thirsty?; which hunger/thirst remover is nearer?; which is larger?), since all these are equal, nothing would cause the ass to go to one or the other; so it would stay stuck in the middle and starve to death.

Some philosophers argue that because this could never happen, decisions (even from an ass) cannot be fully determined in this fashion: there must be an arbitrary—free—element that's at least capable of resolving ties. (This free element is supposedly of primary importance in human decisions.) Others argue, however, that this sort of paralysis between equally attractive options could happen, but rarely does because such perfect equality is so uncommon.

THE CIRCLE THAT'S A STRAIGHT LINE

As the radius of a circle gets larger and larger, the curvature of the circle gets less and less. A circle with infinite radius would thus be a straight line!

Sometimes it's said that we should accept this odd result, and that it's just one of the odd things that happen when infinite magnitudes are imagined. (See, for example, the St. Petersburg Paradox, below.) Others point out that this would be true only if space is Euclidian—which it isn't, in fact.

CURRY'S PARADOX

Consider this sentence, which we'll call 'S':

If S is true, then Santa Claus exists.

Is S true? Well, suppose for the moment it is. Now we have the antecedent of the true conditional statement S, so the consequent follows: Santa Claus exists. When we assume S is true we derive Santa Claus exists, and this is the standard way to prove the truth of a conditional statement. So we've just proven If S is true then Santa Claus exists. But this is Statement S; so it follows that Santa Claus exists.

What's wrong here is not a matter of whether you're a Santa-believer or not. It's that this kind of reasoning can be used to prove any arbitrary proposition. What has gone wrong? Briefly, we can see the problem here as one of many odd consequences of allowing self-referential statements. (Statement S mentions itself.) See also, among others, Grelling's Paradox and The Liar Paradox.

DETERRENCE PARADOX

Think back to when the cold war between the US and the USSR was raging. Both countries had hundreds of nuclear warheads aimed at each other's cities. Each warned the other that the other's first strike would result in massive retaliation, in which hundreds of cities would be devastated and millions of innocent civilians killed and injured.

The aim here on both sides was preventing war, and in hindsight it seems we can say it was an astoundingly successful strategy. It's hard to find any other instances in history in which a face-off between powerful armed enemies did not result in major war.

But there are other moral considerations to raise here besides the morally laudable aim of preventing war. When one side threatens retaliation, it is announcing its intention to commit an absolutely horrible act. Is an intention to commit a hugely immoral act under certain circumstances itself immoral, even though—thankfully—those circumstances never come about?

Imagine that back then accidentally or on purpose the USSR bombed one or more US cities. Then what? The US would have had to choose whether to go forward with its threatened massive and unspeakably horrible retaliation on the USSR. That would have been in itself hugely immoral—it would have made things much worse than they already were, and would have been completely without any possible good effect. (At that point, nobody would have been deterred from anything.) If the US government had had any shred of morality left at that point, it would not have retaliated.

But surely the Soviet planners knew that the US people would have been thinking this way, and in fact would not have retaliated. (And vice versa: the US planners knew this about the Soviets.) If so, everyone would have known that all the threats of retaliation were empty.

To give retaliation-threats some force, in a situation like this, there would have to be some mechanism that unleashed retaliation automatically, no matter what the attacked side wanted to do then. (This is the "Doomsday Machine" imagined in the great movie *Doctor Strangelove*.) But then, having suffered a first strike from side B, horrible, useless, immoral retaliation would be unavoidable, whatever side A did—and they set it up to be this way!

GRELLING'S PARADOX

A couple of definitions:

- an adjective is homological if it describes itself.
- an adjective is heterological if it doesn't.

The adjective 'short' is homological because it's short. The adjective 'German' is heterological: it's not German—it's English.

Now consider the adjective 'heterological.' Which category does it go into? Is it heterological? If it is, then it doesn't describe itself; but if 'heterological' doesn't describe it, then it isn't heterological. So if it is heterological, then it isn't.

Is it then homological? If it is, then it does describe itself, but if 'heterological' describes itself, then it isn't homological. So if it is homological, then it isn't.

Either way, we get a self-contradiction. Another paradox resulting from self-reference; this one was formulated in 1908 by German mathematician Kurt Grelling. (See Russell's Paradox, below, which is analogous.)

GRUE (GOODMAN'S NEW RIDDLE OF INDUCTION)

Definitions:

- Time T is midnight on New Year's Eve at the end of the year 2020.
- X is grue provided that (a) it's T or earlier, and X is green; or (b) it's later than T, and X is blue.
- X is bleen provided that (a) it's T or earlier, and X is blue; or (b) it's later than T, and X is green.

All the emeralds we've seen so far have been green, so (because it's not yet T), they've also been grue. Ordinary scientific reasoning predicts the future on the basis of past observation, so we predict that after T, emeralds will still be green. But this sort of reasoning also predicts that after T emeralds will still be grue. But after T, something that's still green won't be grue any longer—it will have turned bleen overnight! It order to stay grue, it would have to turn blue.

A common reaction to this problem is to try to explain why 'grue' and 'bleen' are illegitimate properties to do science with. But what's wrong with them? The way we have defined them, they seem unlike regular color properties, in that their definitions include mention of time. Scientists who wanted to see whether things stayed grue around time T would have to keep checking their watches. But note that this is just a matter of the way we've been putting things. We could just as well have taken 'grue' and 'bleen' as the real color properties, and defined 'blue' and 'green' in terms of these, plus time T. (See if you can produce these definitions.) And a grue/bleen perceiving scientist would look at an emerald at time T, and might say, without consulting a watch, 'Yep, it stayed grue okay!' or 'Jeez! It suddenly turned bleen!'

HARMING THE DEAD

Imagine your best friend gives you a shirt which you hate, but you wear occasionally when you see her, so as not to insult. If she knew you hated it, she'd be upset, and you don't want that. But now your friend has died. You still think very kindly of her memory, but is it okay to throw away that awful shirt now? The answer seems to be yes. After all, the only morally relevant thing here is that you not hurt her feelings. That would be harming her. But after death, people can't be harmed.

But now consider other things that might be done to "harm the dead." Suppose you maliciously do what you can to destroy the good reputation of someone now dead. A lot of people think that there's something wrong with this. But what? Sometimes it's thought that the morality of actions regarding others isn't all a matter of helping or harming them, because this never applies to the dead. So what other moral considerations are relevant for "dealing with" dead people? and why?

HERACLITUS' PARADOX

The paradox associated with this ancient Greek philosopher is the claim that you can't step into the same river twice. Why not? Because at every instant, the water that makes up this section of the river (or the river as a whole, for that matter), changes.

What this shows, of course, is that identical water is not the basis for the same river. What then is? Note that the same sort of question might be raised with regard to the "same" anything, which (almost) always changes, to some small or large degree, over time.

HOTEL INFINITY

(HILBERT'S HOTEL)

David Hilbert was a pioneer in the mathematical treatment of infinity. He illustrated one way that notion introduces strange results by asking us to imagine a hotel with an infinite number of rooms, all completely booked for the night. A traveler arrives, asking for a room—a request that would be denied by an ordinary completely-booked hotel—but in Hilbert's Hotel, matters are easily solved: the guests in room 1 are asked to move to room 2, while those in room 2, move to room 3, and those in 3 to room 4, and so on. This leaves room 1 empty for the arrivals.

HYPOTHETICAL DESIRE

PARADOX

If you're right-handed, you'd probably assent to this:

If I have to lose an arm, I want to lose my left arm.

Now imagine that, unfortunately, the antecedent of this conditional (hypothetical statement) becomes true: you have to lose one arm. Given the truth of the conditional, it follows by very elementary logic that You want to lose your left arm. But wait! That's hardly true. You don't want to lose either arm! Is this a counter-example to the very basic logical principle called modus ponens: If P then Q; P; therefore Q?

Instead of rejecting modus ponens, it has been suggested, we might understand that original proposition not as "If P then I want X," but rather, "I want: (If P then X)." From P and the latter, X does not follow. But now we need a logic to distinguish hypothetical desires from desires for hypotheticals.

LIAR PARADOX

(EPIMENIDES' PARADOX)

Suppose Fred says, "I'm lying right now." Is he telling the truth? Well, telling the truth isn't lying, so he isn't lying. But what he says is that he is lying, so if he's telling the truth he is lying. On the other hand, if he's not telling the truth, then ... well the same kind of self-negating puzzle emerges. Turns out the assumption that Fred's statement is true and that it's false both imply self-contradictions.

There are many versions of this sort of paradox. Another one frequently seen is the Postcard Paradox: on one side of a postcard, it says, "What's written on the other side is false." On the other side, it says, "What's written on the other side is true." See if you can work out how there isn't any way to assign truth and falsity here.

And another variant is this book title:

> There Are Two Errors in the
> the Title of this Book

The Liar Paradox is one of the most basic and oldest versions of a self-referential paradox. It's sometimes called the Epimenides' Paradox, after the ancient Cretan philosopher who wrote that all Cretans (probably intending to exclude himself) were liars. There has been a great deal written ever since in the attempt to try to cope with self-reference. One major tack has been to try to find a way in principle to rule out self-reference (without making arbitrary restrictions).

LOTTERY PARADOX

Imagine a lottery that will randomly draw one winning ticket from a million tickets. It's unreasonable to believe that the ticket you hold—number 439,664—will win, and you believe it won't win. But it's also unreasonable to believe that number 439,665 will win, and to believe that 439,666 will win, and so on, for every one of the million tickets. So for each of the tickets, you completely reasonably believe it won't win. But you also believe, completely reasonably again, that one of the million will win. So your set of a million and one completely reasonable beliefs is inconsistent.

One sort of reply points out that ground-floor inconsistency of belief requires a belief that P and a belief that not-P; but that's not what we have here, unless we believe a principle of agglomeration: that if you believe Q and you believe R, then you do (or should) believe (Q and R). Some sort of principle of this type is very attractive, but perhaps needs to yield here.

MONTY HALL PARADOX

Loosely based on the TV gameshow of which Monty Hall was the emcee, the question is this:

You're presented with three doors, and told that one hides a valuable car, the other two each a worthless goat. You pick a door at random. Then Monty, the emcee, knowing what's behind the other two, picks one that hides a goat, and opens it, revealing the contents. Now he asks you: do you want to stick to your door or switch to the contents of the remaining closed door?

This widely-publicized problem got wrong answers from a huge variety of people including many mathematicians. They reasoned: you've picked (say) Door A: Door C is opened to reveal a goat. Now it's 50/50 whether the car is behind your door or behind door B. If there's any advantage to sticking to door A (e.g., you're offered $100 to stay put) you should do so; but otherwise there's no reason to stay put or switch.

The correct (but widely disbelieved) answer is this: there's 1/3 probability that Door A, the one you picked first, has the car, thus 2/3 that the car is behind one of Door B or Door C. Monty knows what's back there, and he picks one of (or the only) door hiding a goat (say Door C) and opens it. But there's still a 2/3 chance that a door you haven't picked—only Door B now—has the car; and a 1/3 chance that Door A has it. So you'll double your chances by switching.

(See also the related Bertrand's Box Paradox, above.)

MORAL LUCK

Fred and Barney are both at a party at Wilma's house, and both of them are drinking way more than they should, given that each will be driving himself home. When the booze runs out and Wilma kicks both of them out, they each get in their cars, and attempt to drive to their homes. They're barely capable of steering effectively, and both frequently swerve onto the wrong side of the road. Fred is stopped by the police half-way home, and is charged (and eventually convicted) of driving under the influence. He pays a large fine, and has his license suspended for a year. Barney is unlucky, however: while driving on the opposite side of the road, his car collides head-on with one coming the other way, killing its driver. Barney is convicted of second-degree murder, and is sentenced to a very long jail term.

What Fred and Barney did was significantly similar. Both drank far too much at the party, given that they intended to drive themselves home. Both drove themselves, at great risk, despite knowing that they had drunk too much. Both were swerving all over the road. The difference was merely a matter of luck: Fred didn't crash into anything, and the property and persons of others were unharmed, but unluckily for Barney, an oncoming car just happened to be there just where he swerved off of his side of the road.

Everyone feels that Barney's more to blame than Fred is, and that his much more severe legal punishment was entirely justified. But the difference between his case and Fred's was entirely out of either's control: one was comparatively lucky, the other wasn't. How can we distribute moral blame and judicial punishment differently on the basis of this sort of luck (or un-luck)? But we do it all the time.

NEWCOMB'S PARADOX

Imagine a really smart computer, able to predict people's responses almost perfectly having been fed information about their personality and background. This computer presents you with a choice involving two boxes, Box A and Box B. You can choose to take either the contents of Box B alone, or else what's in Box A plus what's in Box B. In Box A there is $10,000, and it's transparent, so you can see the big pile of $100 notes sitting inside. The contents of Box B, you're told, however, depends on the computer's prediction of what you're going to do. If it has predicted that you'll take Box B alone, it has already put $1 million in Box B. If it has predicted that you'll take Box A plus Box B, it has put nothing into Box B. Should you take what's in Box B alone, or what's in both boxes? There are two lines of reasoning that attempt to answer this question.

(1) At the time you must decide, the computer has already set up what's in Box B—maybe nothing or maybe $1 million. Anyway, your decision won't cause a change in what's in there. You can take whatever's in Box B alone, or else that plus the $10,000 in Box A. Maybe there's a million in Box B, maybe nothing; either way, you'd get $10,000 more by taking both boxes, so do it.

(2) The computer, remember, is almost always right in its predictions. That means that if you take both boxes, it almost certainly has predicted that, and put nothing in Box B, and you'll get $10,000. But if you take just Box B, it almost certainly has predicted that, and put $1 million in Box B, so you'll get a million. Go with the probabilities. Take just Box B.

This interesting problem has resulted in a lot of response. Reactions are divided between advocating strategy (1) and advocating strategy (2), and there are interesting implications for decision theory about which strategy might be the right one.

OMNISCIENCE PROOF OF GOD'S EXISTENCE

God is often conceived of as omniscient—that is, all-knowing. That means that He knows everything that's the case. Maybe we'd like to express that fact this way:

For all propositions P (P is true if and only if God knows that P).

The trouble is that this seems to presuppose the existence of God, so atheists wouldn't accept it. Let's reformulate it more neutrally:

For all propositions P (P is true if and only if, if God existed, God would know that P).

That sounds unexceptionable. Now, if that's true for all propositions, it's true in particular for the proposition, God exists. So we can infer:

'God exists' is true if and only if, if God existed, God would know that he exists.

Consider the second part of that sentence:

if God existed, God would know that he exists.

Nobody, it seems—atheist or believer—could deny this. After all, if anybody exists, he'd know that he exists, right?

But when you have a true sentence made of two parts connected by 'if and only if,' and when one of those parts is true, it follows that the other is true. So from the truth of the second part of that sentence, we can validly infer the truth of the first part:

'God exists' is true.

Or, putting the same thing more briefly,

God exists.

The reason there has to be something wrong in this reasoning is not that there isn't any God. The reason is that we appear to be pulling a proof of God's existence out of thin air—something atheists and believers alike should be suspicious of. What, exactly, has gone wrong here?

THE PREFACE

If you find out that what you say or believe is inconsistent, you shouldn't rationally continue to say or believe that: you should try to fix it, right? It's irrational to allow to stand what you know is an inconsistent set of statements one makes or beliefs one has, right? Wrong and wrong. Here's why.

Often one finds in the preface of a book the modest statement that the book surely contains errors, but that these are the fault of the author, not of the numerous people thanked for help in writing the book.

Now consider the set of sentences consisting of everything stated in book B, including the statement in its preface, "There's at least one error in here." It's logically impossible that this whole set is true. Here's why. If the preface-statement is true, then there's at least one false statement elsewhere in the set. But if the preface is false, then again the whole set isn't true. That set is what logicians call a logically inconsistent set: one such that it's logically impossible that everything in it is true.

Never mind about books and their prefaces. Everyone who is a clear thinker and who doesn't have inappropriately and ridiculously inflated views about his own omniscience knows that some of his many beliefs—one hopes not many, but some anyway—must be false. This is a rational thing to believe. Rational, but rendering one's whole belief set logically inconsistent.

PRISONER'S DILEMMA

You and your buddy are arrested for a major crime; the police know you both did it, but have evidence only good enough for convictions on a rather trivial charge. So they put you two in separate cells, and offer you a deal: your sentence will depend on whether or not you confess, implicating yourself and the other guy, and on what your buddy does when offered the same deal. The following chart summarizes how this works, specifies the years in jail you will serve under all four eventualities.

	He confesses	He stays silent
You confess	7 years	1 year
You stay silent	10 years	3 years

The best outcome for you is confession—if he stays silent. But he's offered the same deal, so his best deal is confession, while you stay silent. And if both of you confess, you'll both be badly off.

It seems that what's best for both of you would be to both keep quiet; you'd each get your second-best possible outcome, but you'd both avoid other possible disasters. If there were a way of making an enforceable and effective deal that both of you would keep silent, this would be good. But there isn't.

Under the circumstances, then, it seems that the most rational thing for you to do is to confess. Whatever he does, you'll come out better than if you stayed silent. This, however, is the most rational choice for the other guy as well. So if both of you do what's rational, both will get seven years in jail— next to the worst of the four possibilities. It seems that there's something irrational about doing what's most rational.

This little story can be taken as a simplified model for a wide range of social situations: competition vs. cooperation between individuals, and between nations. Psychologists and social and ethical philosophers have had a lot to say about it.

PROTAGORAS' PARADOX

The famous ancient Greek philosopher Protagoras taught law to Euathlus, with the agreement that Euathlus would pay Protagoras tuition fees if he won his first case; but if he lost, he wouldn't have to pay. Euathlus finishes his education, sets himself up as a lawyer, but for some reason takes on no cases. Finally, Protagoras gets fed up, and sues Euathlus for the money.

Protagoras points out that he's suing for the fees, so if he wins, Euthalus would have to pay, and if he loses, Euthalus wouldn't have to. But Euathlus reminds the court of the contract for payment: if he wins his first case, he pays the tuition; if he loses he doesn't. And this, of course, is his first case.

So who is right?

(Also called The Lawyer, Euathlus, the Paradox of the Court.)

THE QUESTION PARADOX

An angel visits the Annual Meetings of the American Philosophical Association, and tells the philosophers there that they will be given the gift of asking God exactly one question, and that God in His omniscience will answer it.

There is a good deal of debate about what is the one question to ask. "What is the meaning of life?" is ruled out as too vague, and as very likely to have an unsatisfying answer. "How do you best remove red wine stains from a light-colored carpet?" is a question whose answer many philosophers have an interest in, but in the end it's thought too trivial for such a great opportunity. There's some enthusiasm for asking "What is the most important question we could ask, and what is its answer?" but there's a worry this might be counted as two questions. A logician suggests they avoid this potential difficulty by converting this to one question: "What is the ordered pair consisting of (a) the most important question that could be asked and (b) the answer to that question?"

The angel appears, is asked this question, and five minutes later returns with God's answer: "The most important question you could ask is 'What is the ordered pair consisting of (a) the most important question that could be asked and (b) the answer to that question?' and the answer to that question is what I'm saying now."

RAVEN PARADOX

This famous paradox challenges two seemingly obvious assumptions: (1) that scientific generalizations are confirmed by observation of instances of them (e.g., that 'All ravens are black' is confirmed a little every time an additional black raven is observed); and (2) that if some observation O confirms generalization G, and G is logically equivalent to H, then O must also confirm H (because, after all, when two statements are logically equivalent, they say the same thing—anything that makes one true (or false) does the same to the other).

G: All non-black things are non-ravens is logically equivalent to H: All ravens are black. The observation of a yellow pencil confirms G, but it surely does not seem to confirm H. (Otherwise H would be confirmed by the uncountable number of observations of non-black non-ravens everyone makes all the time.)

Maybe, on the other hand, you might want to insist that that pencil does confirm (to an extremely tiny degree) the raven generalization. Or else, you might want to explore the idea that scientific confirmation is not at all merely a simple matter of observations of instances of a generalization.

RUSSELL'S PARADOX

Think of a class in the technical sense involved here as a collection of things that share a common attribute. Some classes are not members of themselves: the class of poodles, for example, is not itself a poodle.

Call these classes non-self-inclusive. Some classes are members of themselves: examples are the class of non-poodles (which is itself not a poodle), or the class of things with more than five members, which itself has more than five members. Call these classes self-inclusive.

Now consider the class of non-self-inclusive classes. It contains poodles, planets, and so on, but is it a member of itself? Try two answers:

YES: but since it's the class of non-self-inclusive classes, if it's a member of itself, then it's non-self-inclusive, so it doesn't include itself.

NO: but if it's not in there, it must be in the class of self-inclusive classes; so it does include itself.

Bertrand Russell discovered this paradox in 1901, and shortly thereafter told the great logician Frege about it. Frege realized that this paradox showed that two very basic axioms used in his book on formal logic, about to be published, were inconsistent. There has been a great deal of consideration about the implications of Russell's Paradox ever since. (See Grelling's Paradox, above, which is analogous.)

RUSSELL'S PROOF OF GOD'S EXISTENCE

The next time you're driving around, take a look at the first license plate number you see: it's EJR 036 (or whatever). What are the odds against seeing exactly that license plate number, out of all the possible ones, just then? They're minuscule, one out of several million or more. It's a miracle! God must exist.

This "proof" was cooked up by Bertrand Russell, who was a well-known atheist and of course had his tongue firmly planted in his cheek. Of course this goes no way toward proving God's existence. But the interesting question it raises is: why exactly is seeing that license plate not a hugely unlikely—almost miraculous—event?

SAYING WHAT YOU MEAN

Can you say, "Gloob! Gloob! Gloob!" but mean, It's snowing in Tibet? No? Why not?

SHIP OF THESEUS

According to ancient Greek legend, Theseus kept repairing the ship of which he was captain while at sea, replacing, one at a time, old rotten planks with new sound ones. When this process was complete, there was not a single bit of the ship that was there at the start of the voyage. Is the ship Theseus returned in the same one as the one he started out in? If yes, then how come? If no, then what happened to the old one?

In the seventeenth century, Thomas Hobbes added a wrinkle to this story by imagining further that Theseus kept all the old rotten lumber, and eventually a (pretty useless) ship was constructed out of this. At that point there are two ships: the one made of new, sound lumber, and the one made of rotten old planks. Which is the one Theseus began his voyage in?

SIMPSON'S PARADOX

In basketball, you get two points for a basket shot from closer in, 3 points from further out. The following table lists successes/attempts at 2- and 3-point shots made during a season by two players, Wilt Jordan and Michael Chamberlain:

	Jordan	Chamberlain
2 pt	200 / 400: 50%	440 / 950: 46.3%
3 pt	80 / 320: 25%	30 / 190: 15.8%

As you can see, Jordan's average is better at scoring on attempted 2-point shots and 3-point shots. That implies that Jordan is better at making shots altogether, right? Wrong. Here are the totals:

Jordan	Chamberlain
280 / 720: 38.9%	470 / 1140: 41.2%

Check the arithmetic yourself: there's no trick here. This sort of counterintuitive result is quite common in statistics. It was brought to wide attention by a mathematician named E.H. Simpson.

SORITES' PARADOX

A person 7 feet high is definitely tall. Subtract a ¼ inch from this, and consider a person 6 feet 11¾ inches high: that person is definitely tall too. Now imagine a series of subtractions, each of ¼ inch; is there a height H in this series such that a person of height H is tall, but a person of height (H–¼") is not tall? It seems not. If you think there is, try to specify that height, and see if you can get anyone to agree with you. But if there is no such H, then we can keep subtracting ¼", and still have the height of a tall person; so reach the obviously false conclusion that a person 3 feet high is tall. What has gone wrong here?

There are practical (mis)applications of this fallacious reasoning. Someone considering one more little sip of beer before driving home can believe correctly that one more little sip won't make any difference in his driving ability. But this is true of each little sip in a series in which, at some point, the drinker has become completely disabled.

A lot of thought has been given to how to rethink matters to locate and fix the mistake in reasoning of this sort.

'Sorites', pronounced so-RIGHT-eez, is Greek for heap (another traditional name for this paradox); a very early version imagined starting with one grain of sand—clearly not a heap—and reasoning that adding one additional grain never transformed a non-heap into a heap. Another traditional example reasons that removal of just one hair from a head cannot transform a non-bald head into a bald one.

THE SPECIOUS PRESENT

Your third birthday party does not exist—now. Nothing in the past exists. Neither does anything in the future. All that exists is the present.

Now consider apparently present facts: the cat is on the mat, Cleveland is in Ohio, Jupiter is the largest planet. Each of these has a time span, with a past and (we'd expect) a future component. But the past and future components, as we've seen, don't exist. Well, what about the present component? How long does that last? If it has any non-zero duration, then part of it is non-existent, in the past or in the future. Anything that's completely present must have a zero duration. But here's the problem: something that lasts for zero time is nothing at all. So the supposedly zero-duration present doesn't exist either. It apparently follows that nothing exists.

Obviously this reasoning is mistaken. But it's no easy job to figure out exactly where. In the process of considering this, in any case, we can get clearer on some things we would never otherwise consider, some basic presuppositions about duration and existence.

ST. PETERSBURG PARADOX

When you're playing a game of chance, a fair bet is the amount of money you should pay to play, expecting to come out even in the long run. (Of course, casinos never offer a fair bet in this sense—they need to make a profit on you.)

You calculate a fair bet by summing the products of multiplying the probability of each outcome times the payoff given that outcome. Imagine a coin flip that would pay you $1 for heads, $2 for tails. Each outcome has a probability of .5, so the fair bet is (.5 × $1) + (.5 × $2). This equals $1.50.

Now consider the St. Petersburg Game. You flip a fair coin counting the number of flips till it comes up tails, when the game ends. Call the number of flips in a finished game n; the payoff is then 2^n. (A run of three heads then a tails would thus have n = 4, and a payoff of $16.)

What's the fair bet for St. Petersburg? The probability that n = 1 is 1/2; its payoff is $2. The probability that n = 2 is 1/4; its payoff is $4. The probability that n = 3 is 1/8; its payoff is $8. And so on. You can see where this is going. The sum of (1/2 × $2) + (1/4 × $4) + (1/8 × $8) and so on equals $1 + $1 + $1 + $1 and so on. The fair bet is an infinite amount of money! In other words, any finite amount you pay to play each game will be smaller than your eventual winnings, if you play long enough.

Of course, you'd probably run out of money to bet before you had an enormous win; or the casino would close, or you'd die. This is not a practical plan. But it does, probability theorists think, raise important theoretical questions about the ideas taken for granted in thinking about fair bets on chance events.

THE THOMSON LAMP

This is an imaginary light-fixture. You push a button to turn it on, and in ½ of a minute, it turns itself off; then after another ¼ of a minute, it turns back on again, then after another ⅛ of a minute, it turns back off, and so on. Imagine (contrary, perhaps, to the laws of physics) that it can do this switching an infinite number of times. It doesn't take a great deal of mathematical skill to sum this series, and determine that the whole series will finish exactly one minute after you start it. The question is: at the end of this minute, will the lamp be on or off? (or, bizarrely, neither or both?)

This kind of peculiar event has been treated extensively in the literature, where it's sometimes called a supertask.

THE TIME AND THE PLACE

OF A MURDER

On December 2, 2002, Bob is visiting a tourist attraction, the Four Corners Monument, located at the only point in the US where four states come together and you can stand with one foot overlapping all four states (should that sound exciting to you). Bob notices his enemy Bart standing nearby, pulls out his gun, and shoots Bart in the foot. Police apprehend Bob, and Bart is taken to hospital, and eventually dies of his wound.

Bob is guilty of murder, but where did it take place? Bob was standing in Arizona when he shot Bart, but about eighteen inches of his right arm, with the gun in hand, extended east into New Mexico. Bart was standing north of Bob, in Utah, but his foot, when it was shot, was slightly over the state line, and was in Colorado. Did the murder take place where Bob was? And was that in Arizona or New Mexico (or both)? Or did it take place where Bart was? And was that in Utah or Colorado (or both)? Or maybe the murder took place in all four states?

Bart's medical condition deteriorated despite treatment, and he died in hospital in early January. This raises questions about timing. Did the murder take place when Bart was shot, in December, or when he died, the following January? Or maybe it was a spread-out event, taking about a month to happen? Imagine you're the police officer at the press conference in December, following Bob's apprehension. You're asked, "Was that murder?" What's the answer: "Not yet!" because Bart was still alive? But when he dies in January, does that retroactively transform the shooting, done the previous month, into murder? Or was it murder all along, though given Bart's survival through December, nobody knew it yet?

How these questions are answered may have practical bearing: the location questions if the laws regarding murder are different in each of the four states; the timing question if there's a change in law to take place on January 1. A court may have to decide these answers. Notice however that there don't seem to be any facts that could be discovered that would determine the right answers. We already know all the relevant facts, and they don't add up to any answers. Would the answers to these questions then be a matter of totally arbitrary decision?

TIME TRAVEL

The main paradox involved here involves the question about whether a time traveler could change the past. For example, could you, on Tuesday, go back to Monday, and move that coffee cup away from the edge of the table, so that it didn't get knocked off and break? This is hard to understand. We start by supposing that it's Tuesday, and the coffee cup did break on Monday. Then, supposedly, you go back and prevent this; but then does it happen that on Tuesday that the coffee cup didn't break earlier? Do those pieces of coffee-cup in the trash suddenly disappear? Or were they never there in the first place?

This sort of science-fiction story is familiar: Fred goes back 60 years, finds his grandfather aged 15, and tries to kill him. If Fred succeeds, then he wouldn't have been born, but then who went back in time and killed grandpa? Some philosophers argue that this doesn't show that time travel is inherently self-contradictory, but rather that no matter what else you accomplish when going back in time, you won't kill your grandfather when he was a teenager, because— simply put—it didn't happen!

TRAGEDY OF THE COMMONS

A commons is a piece of land in the center of a town which traditionally was publicly owned and reserved for shared use. Sometimes all the livestock owners in the town were allowed to graze their animals on this land. When grazed by too many animals, however, the grass could not grow back, and the land was ruined for this use.

The problem here is that it's clearly to each individual herder's self-interest to graze as many animals as he could on the commons. It would be highly unlikely that putting just his few animals there would overload an otherwise sustainable grass crop; if the land was already overloaded by general use, and the grass crop was headed for extinction, it would still be to each herder's interest to get as much as he could out of it, before it became useless.

The generalized problem illustrated here is that in many situations, when individuals act in their own undoubted rational self-interest, a shared general resource will ultimately be depleted, contrary to anyone's interest. What's at issue here is very much like the problem raised, above, by the Prisoner's Dilemma.

TREASURE-HUNTER PARADOX

Years ago, the CBC interviewed a historian who was researching treasure-hunting in Nova Scotia, where the numerous islands and hidden coves gave pirates an ideal place to bury their treasure. Of the many attempts to find buried treasure, a few had actually found it; the historian reported that a very large proportion of successful diggers had deepened holes made by previous searchers. The earlier searches had stopped just short of success. So the interviewer asked the historian what advice to give future treasure-hunters, on the basis of this information. The historian hesitated for a moment, then replied that he guessed that they should dig a little deeper than they do.

TRISTRAM SHANDY

This is the name of the hero of the novel bearing his name. In the novel, he has undertaken to write his autobiography, but he writes so slowly that he takes a year to cover only one day of his life. That means, as time goes on, he'll fall more and more behind. Bertrand Russell, however, pointed out in an influential study of infinity, that paradoxically if Shandy would live for an infinite length of time, despite falling further and further behind at any moment, he'd nevertheless be able to finish his work. One of the many paradoxes of infinity.

TROLLEY PROBLEM

You're standing next to trolley tracks, and see an out-of-control trolley fast approaching. Five people are tied to the tracks farther down, and would die when the trolley gets there; but you can throw a switch which would steer the trolley instead on to another track where only one person would die.

Some philosophers react to this story (introduced by Philippa Foot and widely discussed) that one is not morally permitted to throw the switch, because that would amount to killing the one person on the alternate track; one must, then, accept the (nevertheless horrible) outcome of the death of the five, because that's not the result of your wrongdoing. Killing is wrong; allowing to die is under some circumstances permitted.

Other philosophers, however, have the strong reaction that all that's relevant here is that you have the choice of five dying, or just one; so you must throw the switch: they deny that the difference between acting and refraining from acting has any moral significance.

TWO ENVELOPES PARADOX

You're presented with two sealed envelopes, a red and a blue one, and told that one contains twice the amount of money as the other; but you can't tell which is which. You pick the red one, at random. But before opening it, you're offered the option of swapping it for the blue one. Should you take that option?

At first glance, it seems that it's a matter of indifference whether you swap or not. But consider this reasoning: Call the amount of money in the red envelope (whatever that is) M. It's 50% probable that the blue envelope contains $\frac{1}{2} \times M$, and 50% probable it contains $2 \times M$. So it's equiprobable that swapping would increase your payoff by M, or decrease it by $\frac{1}{2}$ M. Swapping is a good bet. It's probably advantageous for you to swap.

Now, imagine that the reasoning convinces you, and you agree to swap, and exchange envelopes. Now you hold the blue envelope. But now you're offered the option of swapping again, back to the red one. You reason this way: Call the amount of money in the blue envelope (whatever that is) N. It's 50% probable that the red envelope contains ½ × N, and 50% probable it contains 2 × N. So it's equiprobable that swapping would increase your payoff by N, or decrease it by ½ N. Swapping is a good bet. It's probably advantageous for you to swap. So you swap again.

But it's clear that something has gone wrong here. It's impossible that this could go on and on, with your reasoning telling you that every time that each swap adds to your advantage. That can't be. Okay, it's clear that somewhere there's a mistake in your reasoning: but where?

There's a variant of the Two-Envelopes Paradox called the Two-Wallet Game. Here's how this works. You and a friend are drinking in a bar, and he suggests this game. You both put your wallets on the table, and whoever's wallet has less money in it gets the money that's in the other's wallet. (Neither of you has any idea of how much is in the others' wallet, or in your own.)

You reason: Call the amount of money in my wallet (whatever it is) A, and call the amount of money in Buddy's wallet B. It's equally likely that A is less than B, or more. So there's a 50% probability that A is more than B, and I'd lose A. But it's 50% probability that I'd win B—if B was larger than A. So if I won, what I'd win is more than what I'd lose if I lost. The game is favorable to me.

Buddy, of course, is reasoning the same way. It can't be that this game is favorable to both players. Both of you have made a mistake, and maybe you have the feeling that it's the same sort of mistake that showed up in the reasoning about the envelope switch.

UNEXPECTED (SURPRISE) HANGING (OR EXAM) PARADOX

On Friday, your algebra teacher announces that there will be a surprise quiz during one of the classes next week—'surprise' meaning that you won't be able to figure out when it will take place before the class starts in which it is given.

You reason: there are classes on Monday, Wednesday, and Friday. If the test were on Friday, we'd know that in advance—after class on Wednesday—because there was no test on Monday or Wednesday, and it had to be on one of those three days. So a Friday quiz wouldn't be a surprise. It can't be on Friday.

So it must be on Monday or Wednesday. But if it were on Wednesday, we'd know that in advance—after class on Monday; as we've already figured out, so since it wasn't on Monday, it would have to be on Wednesday. So a Wednesday quiz wouldn't be a surprise. It can't be on Wednesday.

So it must be on Monday, the only remaining possibility. But we can figure that out—know already that it has to be Monday. But that wouldn't be a surprise then.

So a surprise quiz under these conditions is impossible.

This is a very perplexing paradox because it's perfectly clear that there can be a surprise quiz, and so there has to be an error in the reasoning above. But philosophers have had some trouble finding a persuasive account of what has gone wrong.

Does this addition to the story help you figure out what's wrong? Having done all the reasoning above, you show up in Monday's algebra class, and the teacher hands out the quiz. "But!" you object, "But! But!" The teacher says, "Surprise!!"

(A nastier version of the same story involves the surprise timing of the hanging of a condemned man.)

UNINTERESTING NUMBERS

Consider what we'll call interesting numbers—positive integers with special facts or associations attached to them. 1 is surely an interesting number: it's the number of gods believed in by many religions, the smallest prime number, etc. 2 is also interesting: it's the smallest even number. 3 is the number of blind mice, of little pigs, of bears Goldilocks met, etc. 4 is the July date celebrated as the US national holiday. 5 is the number of fingers on one hand. Probably you can think of something that sets apart 6, 7, 8, 9, 10, and more, and makes them interesting. What then is the smallest uninteresting number? Hard to say, but let's suppose that it's 2,693, a number associated with no facts whatsoever. Oh but wait: there is something that makes this number stand out: it's the smallest uninteresting number, so it's interesting after all. (A contradiction?) Okay, anyway, let's keep looking. How about 2,694 then? If that's the smallest uninteresting number, that's an interesting fact about it. And so on, as high as you care to go. So we've proven that every number is interesting, right?

What's foolish about this reasoning?

VOTER'S PARADOX (1)

In the most common sort of election, the candidate wins who receives more votes than the others; and there are special procedures in the regulations concerning ties.

Voters often want to see their candidate get a large number of votes, win or lose, but we'll ignore this for our purposes, and consider only what's by far the chief motivation for voting: you want your candidate to win. Regarding this motivation, your vote can make a difference if, without it, your candidate would be tied for first place, or if your vote creates a tie.

Now, consider the chances of either of these happening in an election with more than a handful of voters. A statistics professor estimates that a tied congressional election might be expected to occur in the US once approximately every 400 years. It is overwhelmingly unlikely that your vote will make a difference in this and in almost every other sort of election.

So why vote? Your chances of being hit by lightning on the way to the polling station are probably greater than the chance of making a difference.

VOTER'S PARADOX (2)

Confusingly sometimes known by the same name as the one just considered, this one shows that under certain circumstances, voting is not a way to produce a rational general will out of individual preferences.

Consider this simple case: There are three candidates for a position, A, B, and C, and three voters, 1, 2, and 3. The three voters each have preferences among the candidates, in this order:

voter 1: prefers A to B, and B to C

voter 2: prefers B to C, and C to A

voter 3: prefers C to A, and A to B

A simple vote in which each voted for his/her preferred candidate would result in a tie: one vote for each of A, B, and C, and no decision.

Let's try a series of votes to see in general what preferences the voters have when considering only two of the three. Vote first on A and B: 1 and 3 prefer A to B; only 2 disagrees. Good so far. Now let's compare B and C: 1 and 2 prefer B to C.

So now we have majority votes preferring A to B, and B to C. Does that mean that the general will is best served by ranking them in the order A, B, C, giving the victory to A, with C coming in third? To make sure, let's compare A and C: 2 and 3 both prefer A to C. Whoops.

ZENO'S PARADOXES

Zeno of Elea was a fifth-century BCE Greek philosopher who is now known for having created a number of paradoxes involving motion, plurality, and change. Nine of these are known today, on the basis of quotation or discussion by other philosophers; we'll briefly look at the three best-known of them.

On the surface, Zeno's paradoxes seem like silly denials of the obvious, but really they are, in Russell's words, "immeasurably subtle and profound" explorations of problems involved in our presuppositions about time, space, motion, and so on.

Achilles and the Tortoise is the most famous of Zeno's paradoxes. Suppose speedy Achilles is in a race with a tortoise. Achilles can run much faster than the tortoise, so the latter is given a head start, beginning farther down the track than Achilles. The race begins, and Achilles very soon runs to the place the tortoise started from; but by then the tortoise has run (or waddled) on to a point a little further on. So then Achilles continues running till he gets to this second point, but by then the tortoise has gone on to a third point. And so on. No matter how many times Achilles catches up to where the tortoise just left, he hasn't caught up with him. Conclusion: he can never catch up.

This conclusion is obviously false, and modern mathematics (given the figures for the speed of each, and the head-start distance) can tell us exactly when Achilles will catch up—and pass—the tortoise. But then what has gone bad in this reasoning? This is a hard question to answer. (Note, by the way, the connection between this item and what's discussed above in the Thomson Lamp section.)

The Racecourse is closely related to the first Achilles paradox. Here Zeno concentrates simply on Achilles' run down the racecourse, ignoring the tortoise. Can Achilles reach the end of the course? To do so, he must first reach the half-way point; then, having gotten there, he must travel half of the remaining portion, arriving at the point ¾ of the way down the field; then he must again cover half the remaining distance, arriving at the ⅞ point; and so on and so on. There's an endless series of smaller and smaller runs he must make, and at the end of each run in the series there's still some distance to go. So he can never get to the end of the field. (This paradox is also often called The Dichotomy.)

The Arrow. Consider an arrow flying through the air. At any one moment—a dimensionless point in time, with zero duration—it's in exactly one well-defined space, which is not moving. At another moment, it's in another motionless space, not moving. There isn't any moment during its flight when this is not true. So how can it be moving?

Philosophical Lexicon

INTRODUCTION

Philosophy, having been around the longest of any academic discipline, has accumulated what may be the longest list of technical jargon terms. These are useful shorthand for philosophers already familiar with these words, but they can provide stumbling-blocks for students. We've included here a rather minimal dictionary of the more common philosophical terms, including some that occur in the readings in this volume, and others that don't.

This is a revised and severely shortened version of a much more inclusive philosophical lexicon: *The Philosopher's Dictionary*, by Robert M. Martin (Broadview Press).

LEXICON

abstract / concrete entities / ideas Abstract entities are supposed not to be locatable in space or time, not perceptible, without causes or effects, necessarily existing. Putative examples are properties, universals, sets, geometrical figures, and numbers. Something is, by contrast, concrete when it is particular and spatially and temporally locatable—perhaps material. There's a long history of philosophical argument about the reality of certain abstracta. Clearly some of them aren't real, for example, the average American family, with its 2.6 children. Reification is mistakenly taking something to be real that's merely abstract; this sort of reasoning is known as the fallacy of misplaced concreteness.

There's a good deal of historical debate about whether we can even have abstract ideas at all. We experience only particulars, so ab-stract ideas were a problem for the classical empiricists, who thought that every idea was a copy of an experience. Plato and others argued that we must have innate abstract ideas, not originating with sensation, in order to be able to classify the particulars.

act / agent moralities Some moral philosophers think that the basic sort of thing ethics evaluates is the worth of actions people do (act morality); others think that what's basic to moral theory is the worth of the person who acts (agent morality). Kant argued that good actions were those done by people with the right sort of motives, so his ethical theory is one species of agent morality; another species is virtue ethics. The utilitarians held that the basic kind of ethical reasoning evaluates actions (via their consequences), whatever the motives or moral worth of the people who do them, so their ethics is a variety of act morality.

action at a distance The effect that one thing can have on another that it is not touching and to which it is not connected by something in-between. Gravitation is an example. Some philosophers and scientists—e.g., Leibniz—thought that this was impossible. One way they tried to explain gravitation is to suppose that bodies that gravitationally attract each other are connected by some intervening invisible thing that fills the space between them and transfers the gravitational force.

action theory The branch of philosophy that considers questions about action. Examples of these are: What differentiates an action from other movements? Can there be actions that are refrainings from acting? Where does an action end and its consequences begin? What sort of explanation is suitable for actions?

Moral questions (about, for example, acts / omissions) and the questions of free will and responsibility are sometimes included in action theory.

acts / omissions An act is doing something, by contrast with an omission (or refraining), which is merely failing to do something. Some philosophers think that there can be a moral difference between these even when they have the same motives and outcome.

a fortiori (Latin: "from what is stronger") Means 'with even stronger reason', 'even more so'. "You owe thanks to someone who lets you use his car for a day. So a fortiori, you should really be grateful to Fred, who let you have his car for a whole month."

agent An agent is one who can perform a genuine intentional action, and who is thus morally responsible for what he/she does. This excludes people, for example, who are unable to perceive relevant facts, or who can't reason about consequences.

agent / event causation Often it is thought that causes and effects must be events. But if our actions are caused by other events, then how can we be responsible for them? It's sometimes argued that the cause of an action is not an event but rather the agent who did it.

agnosticism is in general the position that one does not, maybe cannot, know the truth or falsity of statements in some area—that there is insufficient reason to believe either. This term is used most frequently regarding religion, to contrast with theism and atheism (which are confident that we know that God does / doesn't exist).

alienation Estrangement, separation. Hegel discussed the possibility of human estrangement from the natural world. The existentialists thought that our alienation from nature and from each other was an important and inevitable part of the human condition. In Marx, 'alienation' means the separation from the products of our labor (as employees, we don't own what we produce) as well as from society and from ourselves.

altruism 1. Generosity. 2. The philosophical position that one ought to act for the benefit of others; contrast with egoism.

analogy / disanalogy An analogy is a similarity of two things. Reasoning from (or by) analogy—'analogical argument'—concludes that because two things share one or more characteristics, they share another; e.g., that because others show external behavior similar to one's own, others must have a similar internal life. A disanalogy is a difference between compared things; disanalogies between things reduce the strength of an argument from analogy.

analysis Some things are capable of being understood in terms of their component parts; analysis takes them apart into their simpler elements. Some twentieth century anglophone philosophers took analysis of concepts to be the job of philosophy. What is to be analyzed is called the analysandum, and what provides the analysis is called the analysans.

analytic / synthetic Kant called a judgment analytic when the "predicate was contained in the subject"; thus, for example, the judgment that all bachelors are unmarried is analytic because the subject ('bachelors') "contains" the predicate ('unmarried'). Later philosophers preferred to make this distinction in terms of sentences and meanings: a sentence is analytic when the meaning of the subject of that sentence contains the meaning of the predicate: 'unmarried' is part of the definition of 'bachelor'. So an analytic sentence is one that is true merely because of the meanings of the words. 'It's snowing or it's not snowing' is true merely because of the meaning of the words 'or' and 'not', so perhaps we should count this as analytic too. But since the relevant words in this case are "logical" words, this sentence is more particularly known as a logical truth. A synthetic truth is a sentence that is true, but not merely because of the meaning of the words. 'Pigs don't fly' is true partially because of the meaning of the words, of course: if 'pigs' meant 'woodpeckers', then that sentence would be false. But since the definition of 'pig' tells us nothing about flying, this sentence is not true merely because of the meaning of the words. One can speak also about analytically false sentences, for example, 'There exists a married bachelor'. Analytic sentences are necessarily true, and may (sometimes) be known a priori; but Kant argued that there are also synthetic a priori statements. Quine argued that the analytic / synthetic distinction is not a good one, because one cannot distinguish between matters of meaning of the words of a sentence and matters of fact.

ancient philosophy Ancient philosophy began in primitive form, we suppose, in prehistory; the earliest Western philosopher of whose work we have a historical account is Thales (c. 580 BCE.). The end of this period is often marked by the beginning of medieval philosophy, with the work of Augustine (about 400 CE).

antecedent conditions The events or states of affairs that come before a given event and that cause it, or are necessary or sufficient (See necessary / sufficient conditions) for it to happen.

a priori / a posteriori Two different ways in which something might be known to be true (or false). It can be known a priori if it can be known before—that is, or independently of—sense-experience of the fact in question. It can be known a posteriori if it can be known after—that is, on the basis of—sense-experience of the fact. One can know that all bachelors are unmarried a priori; one doesn't need to observe even one bachelor to know this is true. In this case (but perhaps not in all cases) a priori knowledge is possible because what's known is a conceptual truth or because the sentence that expresses this truth is analytic or logically true. Kant argued that certain a priori truths (for example, that every event has a cause) were not conceptual or analytic.

argument An argument in ordinary talk is a debate, especially a heated one. But in philosophical usage, an argument is one or more statements (called 'premises'; singular 'premise' or 'premiss') advanced in order to support another statement (the conclusion). Thus philosophers need not get angry when they argue. Premises actually support a conclusion only when there is the appropriate sort of logical connection between the premises and the conclusion. In deductive arguments, the conclusion must be true given the truth of the premises; in an inductive argument, the truth of the premises makes the conclusion more probable. Any deductive argument in which the premises really do have the appropriate logical connection with the conclusion is called a 'valid' argument; in invalid arguments, this connection is lacking. A valid argument may, however, fail to support its conclusion because one or more of its premises is false—for example: All pigs fly. All flying things are lighter than air. Therefore all pigs are lighter than air. This argument is valid, but it fails to convince because both of its premises are false. An argument with at least one false premise is called 'unsound'; a sound argument is a valid argument all of whose premises are true. A sound argument provides a proof of its conclusion (though in logic it's often said that a proof is provided merely when the argument is valid).

argument from illusion / hallucination The argument (against naïve realisms) that the existence of perceptual illusions and hallucinations shows that we really directly perceive only sense-data and not an independent world.

artificial intelligence An area of study in computer science and psychology that involves building (or imagining) machines, or programming computers, to mimic certain complex intelligent human activities. The creation of a program that can play chess at a high level is one of its successes. Artificial intelligence might shed light on what human mentality is like, and its successes and failures enter into arguments about materialism.

artificial / natural language A natural language is one used by some actual group of people, that has developed on its own, culturally and historically. An artificial language is one developed for some purpose—examples are computer languages and symbolic logic.

association of ideas One thought produces another: when you think about shoes, maybe this drags along the thought of socks. Associationism was the view that this sort of thing is at the core of our mental life, and that its laws constitute a scientific cognitive psychology.

atheism Atheists believe that God doesn't exist, and (sometimes) that religious practice is foolish, or that the morality fostered by religion is wrong. Because atheism has been so unpopular, atheistic philosophers have sometimes disguised their views. Lucretius and Hume were probably atheists. Russell was open about his atheism, and got into trouble for it. Not every religion includes the belief in God—Buddhism, for example, is sometimes said to be an atheistic religion. Atheism contrasts with theism, the view that God does exist, and with agnosticism, the view that there isn't any good reason to believe either that God exists or that He doesn't.

atomism The view that things are composed of elementary basic parts. From ancient times onward physics was often atomistic (though what's now called an 'atom' is no longer regarded as a basic component—contemporary physicists think that much smaller parts might be basic).

automata These are (arguably) mindless devices that imitate the intelligent and goal-directed actions of people—robots, for example. Descartes thought that animals were automata—merely physical "mechanisms" without mind.

autonomy / heteronomy Autonomy is self-governance—the ability or right to determine one's own actions and beliefs. Some ethical theories see the respect for autonomy as a central ethical principle. Heteronomy is its opposite: dependence on others.

average / total utilitarianism Utilitarianism needs to specify how to understand the greatest good for the greatest number of people. Is the measure of the worth of a society the average utility of its members, or the total utility?

axiom / postulate / posit An axiom is a statement regarded as obviously true, used as a starting point for deriving other statements. An axiomatic theory is one that is based on axioms. Non-axiomatic theories don't have such basic statements. 'Postulate' (as a noun) is often used to mean the same thing, though sometimes it refers only to such statements within a particular theory, while axioms are basic and obvious statements common to many theories (for example, the basic laws of logic). The verb 'to postulate' means the act of postulation—assumption, often of the existence of something, for theoretical purposes. A posit is an assumption, especially some thing assumed to exist; to posit something is to assume it.

basic statement The truth or falsity of some statements is determined by appeal to some others (by means of logic or scientific method, for example), but some philosophers think that there must be a starting point: basic statements. Whether there are basic statements, what they are, and why they are acceptable, are all controversial questions.

behaviorism Early in the twentieth century, many psychologists decided that introspection was not a good basis for the science of the mind; instead they advocated reliance on subjects' external, observable behavior. Methodological (psychological) behaviorism is the view that only external behavior should be investigated by science. Metaphysical or analytical behaviorism is the philosophical view that public behavior is all there is—that this is what we're talking about when we refer to mental events or characteristics in others, and even in ourselves. This is a form of materialism.

best of all possible worlds A phrase associated with Leibniz, who believed that God, being perfectly good, knowing, and powerful, could not have created anything less than perfect; thus this world (despite how it sometimes appears) is the best of all possible worlds.

bioethics The ethics involved in various sorts of biology-related activities, mostly centering on medical matters, where subjects for debate include, for example, abortion, genetic control, euthanasia, and in vitro fertilization.

biting the bullet What philosophers are said to do when they choose to accept the unlikely counterintuitive consequences of their position, rather than taking them as counterexamples. The phrase supposedly arose because biting down on something would help with the pain of surgery without anaesthetic.

bodily interchange This is what would happen if the same person existed at one time in one body and at another time in another body, for example, through reincarnation, or through a variety of science-fiction techniques such as brain or memory transplant. The topic is important in religious contexts and in thought experiments about personal identity.

bourgeoisie / proletariat Names of the two social /economic classes important in Marx's analysis. The former is the capitalist class—employers, financiers, landlords, etc., though more generally now the bourgeoisie is taken to include middle class wage earners as well. The latter is the working class.

bundle theory In general, the view of classical empiricists who argued that things are nothing more than bundles of properties, and that there is no need to think of substrata (underlying substance). The phrase most often refers to Hume's bundle theory of personal identity: we don't perceive a continuing self, so our self-idea must refer to an introspectible continuously changing "bundle" of different mental events.

burden of proof When there is a disagreement, it's sometimes the case that one side has the burden of proof, that is, it is expected to prove its case, and if it can't, the other wins by default. It may be the side with the position that is surprising, or unorthodox, or that runs counter to other well-accepted beliefs.

calculus An abstract system of symbols, aimed at calculating something. One can call each symbol-system of symbolic logic a 'calculus': for example, the sentential and quantifier calculi. The system for calculating probabilities is called the 'probability calculus'. Some philosophers think of the various sciences as interpreted calculi; a calculus is interpreted (given a "valuation") when its symbols are given meaning by relating them to things in the real world; uninterpreted, it is just a bunch of symbols with syntax but no semantics. 'The calculus' names a branch of mathematics independently developed by Leibniz and Newton during the late seventeenth century.

casuistry The determination of right and wrong by reasoning involving general principles applied to particular cases. Because religious casuists sometimes reasoned in overly complex ways to silly conclusions, this word has come to have disparaging overtones.

categorical / hypothetical imperative Kant's distinction. An imperative is a command. 'Categorical' means absolute—not dependent on particular aims or circumstances; 'hypothetical' means relative to, depending on, particular aims or circumstances. Thus, 'Tell the truth' is a categorical imperative, but 'If it is to everyone's benefit, tell the truth' and 'If you want others to trust you, tell the truth' are hypothetical imperatives. Kant argued that hypothetical imperatives could give useful practical advice, but do not express the standards of morality, which are expressed only by categorical imperatives. He argued further that there is one command central to all morality—the categorical imperative: Act in a way such that the general rule behind your action could consistently be willed to be a universal law. He argued that this was equivalent to saying that others should be treated as ends, never as means only.

category mistake A claim that's absurd because it makes an ascription completely inappropriate to the category of the object in question. To claim that the number 7 is faster than the number 8 is to assert this kind of absurdity. Gilbert Ryle introduced this term arguing that the standard Cartesian view of mind/body dualism committed this kind of mistake.

causal theories A variety of theories that make the notion of cause basic in some way. The causal theory of knowledge proposes, as a condition of 'P knows that x', that P's belief be causally connected in some appropriate way to the fact that x. The causal theory of perception points out that a "blue sensation" is one normally caused by a blue thing, and tries to avoid sense-data by explaining that what is happening when there is no blue thing there is that the sensation is one that would have been caused by a blue thing, were the situation normal. Functionalism is a causal theory of mind. The causal theory of meaning / reference makes the meaning / reference of terms a matter of the causal connections their uses have with the external world.

causation The relation that holds between a cause and its effect. Also called 'causality'. Long-standing philosophical problems are concerned with the nature of cause, and how we find out about it. Hume skeptically argued that we perceive no "power" in causal connections, and that when we say that x causes y, we're only saying that things of x-sort regularly precede things of y-sort. Critics object that this fails to distinguish between causal connections and mere accidental but universal regularities.

cause-of-itself (Latin: causa sui) Narrowly, a thing that causes itself to exist (or to be the way it is). God is commonly thought to be the only thing that is capable of this. But because causes are supposed to precede their effects, a cause-of-itself would (problematically) have to precede its own existence. Thinking of cause in an older way, as explanation, perhaps avoids this difficulty, but has its own problems: how can something provide the explanation for its own existence?

certainty A belief is called 'certain' in ordinary talk when it is believed very strongly, or when one is unable to think, or even imagine, that it might be false. Philosophers often don't want to rely on a subjective and psychological test for certainty, and demand proof that some belief really is beyond rational doubt. Some philosophers think that all our knowledge must have a certain foundation. 'Moral certainty' means sufficiently warranted to justify action; 'metaphysical certainty' means warranted not merely by fallible perception of particulars, but rather by some presumably more reliable reasoning about all being; 'logical certainty' is the extremely strong warrant we get for a proposition which is in some sense a truth of logic.

ceteris paribus (Latin: "other things being equal") This is used in comparing two things while assuming they differ only in the one characteristic under consideration. For example, it could be said that, ceteris paribus, a simple theory is better than a complicated one; though if everything else is not equal—if, for example, the simpler theory has fewer true predictions—then it might not be better.

circular reasoning / definition A definition is (viciously) circular (and thus useless) when the term to be defined, or a version of it, occurs in the definition; for example, the definition of 'free action' as 'action that is freely done'. (Viciously) circular reasoning defends some statement by assuming the truth of that statement; e.g.: "Why do you think what the Bible says is true?" "Because the Bible is the Word of God." "How do you know that it is the Word of God?" "Because it says so in the Bible, and everything there is true." Some philosophers argue that not all circles are vicious, and that some sorts of circular reasoning are acceptable—"virtuously circular"—for example, when the circle is wide enough. A dictionary, for example, must be circular, defining words in terms of other words; but this is okay. Circular reasoning is also known as 'begging the question'. Careless speakers sometimes think that this means 'raising the question'; it doesn't. Begging the question is sometimes called by its Latin name, 'petitio principii'.

cognitive / emotive meaning The former is what a sentence states—what makes it true or false. The latter is its "expressive" content—the speaker's feelings that it communicates, rather than any beliefs. Some theories of ethical statements hold that they have emotive, but no cognitive, meaning.

cognition The operations of the mind; sometimes particularly believing and awareness; sometimes, more particularly, the mental process by which we get knowledge.

cognitive science A recently-developed discipline combining philosophers, psychologists, and computer scientists, devoted to providing theories of cognition.

cognitivism / noncognitivism Cognitivism is the position that something can be known. Ethical cognitivism is the view that ethical statements are statements about (supposed) facts and thus are true or false, and might be known to be true or false. This is opposed to the noncognitivist position that ethical statements are not knowable. A species of ethical noncognitivism is emotivism, which argues that ethical statements are expressions of approval or disapproval (like 'Hooray for that!'), or invitations to action (like 'Please do that!') and are thus neither true nor false, and not knowable.

coherence / incoherence A set of beliefs or sentences is coherent when it fits together in a logical way—that is, when everything in the set is consistent, or when the items in it confirm others in it. A set in which one item would be false, or probably false, given the truth of others is not coherent (is incoherent).

collectively / distributively What applies to a group collectively applies to it as a whole only, i.e., not to its individual members (not distributively). The atoms that constitute a pig collectively, but not distributively, outweigh a fly.

collective responsibility The controversial idea that a group or nation or culture can bear responsibility as a whole for bad acts: for example, the whole German nation for Nazi atrocities.

commensurability / incommensurability Different things are commensurable when they can be measured on the same scale. Utilitarians sometimes assume that different people's different pleasures are commensurable on a common scale of utilites; but it has been argued that there's no way to make sensible quantity comparisons. Another example of supposed incommensurability is in the comparison of science and religion: some philosophers think that it's foolish to criticize religious statements using the criteria of scientific adequacy.

common sense 1. Until the eighteenth century or so, this term named the supposed mental faculty which combined input from different senses to give us a unified idea of an external object, combining, for example, the smell, taste, look and feel of a peach. 2. More recently, it has come to mean the mental faculty which all people are supposed to possess "in common," for knowledge of basic everyday truths. This is sometimes taken to answer skeptical doubts about the obvious truths that there exists an external world, other minds, etc. The eighteenth-century Scottish "common sense philosophers" relied heavily on this notion as a vindication of ordinary views and a refutation of skepticism.

communitarianism Advocates the position in social philosophy that the rights of individuals are not basic—that groups, or society as a whole, can have rights that are not constituted by or based on the individual rights of the members of those groups, and that these group rights may override claims to individual rights. Fascism is a rather extreme example of communitarianism. Communitarianism is a form of holism in social theory; the contrast is with individualism.

compatibilism Any philosophical position that claims that two things are compatible (they can both exist at once), most referring to the view that free will and determinism are compatible—that is, that people's actions are (sometimes) free even though they are fully causally determined. Compatibilists argue that we're not free when we're acting under compulsion (that is, forced to act), but that this is a different thing from the action's being determined or caused.

compulsion An action is said to be done under compulsion (also known as 'constraint' or 'coercion') when it is "forced" by internal or external circumstances, and thus the doer of that action can't be held morally responsible for doing it. If you steal something, for example, because someone is forcing you to do it at gunpoint, or because you are a kleptomaniac, that doesn't make your action any better, but it does mean that you're not to blame. Compatibilists about free will argue that compulsion makes one unfree and not responsible, but that ordinary actions are causally determined but not compelled in this sense.

concept May refer to the ability to categorize things; thus to say that someone has the concept of duck is to say that that person can sort things correctly into ducks and non-ducks. A concept is sometimes distinguished from a percept, which is a particular mental item had while sensing a particular thing. A concept, then, may be thought to be a generalization or abstraction from one or many percepts. Thus a percept is sometimes considered a particular idea, and a concept a general or abstract idea.

conceptual scheme The most general framework of someone's view of the world—a structured system of concepts that divide that person's world into kinds of things. It has sometimes been supposed that two people's conceptual schemes might differ so much that one would never be able to understand or translate what the other said.

conceptual truth A statement that is true merely because of the nature of the concepts that make it up. The fact that all bachelors are unmarried is a conceptual truth, because the concept of being a bachelor involves being unmarried. Compare: snow is white is not a conceptual truth, because being white, despite being true of snow, is not part of the concept of snow. We can imagine, consistent with our concept of snow, that snow is always green. (Substitute 'word' for 'concept' in this definition, and it turns into the definition of 'analytic truth'.)

confirmation / disconfirmation / verification / falsification Confirmation is the collection of evidence for a statement. Because there might be some evidence for a false statement, a statement might be confirmed though false. Collecting evidence that a statement is false is called 'disconfirmation'. 'Verification' means 'confirmation' and 'falsification' means 'disconfirmation', though one tends to speak of a statement as having been verified (or falsified) only if the statement is really true (or false), and has been shown to be so by the evidence. Confirmation theory is the attempt to give a general account of what counts as confirmation.

conscience This is the sense of right and wrong that is sometimes supposed to be a way of knowing moral facts, perhaps through a reliable internal "voice" or moral sense-perception, or a faculty of moral intuition.

consciousness 1. The state that we are in when awake: mental events are going on. 2. Awareness of something. (You aren't usually conscious of the position of your tongue.) 3. = mind (though it might be that the mind exists even while we are asleep or not aware of anything). The fact that we are conscious is supposed by some to distinguish people from machines and other non-living things, and perhaps from (at least the lower) animals.

consequentialism The position that people's actions are right or wrong because of their consequences (their results). This sort of ethical theory also called 'teleological', is contrasted with deontological theories—those that hold that results of actions are morally irrelevant. Thus, for example, a deontologist might think that lying is always wrong just in itself, whereas a consequentialist might think that lying is morally permissible in those circumstances in which the lie results in good consequences overall.

consistency A set of statements is consistent if it is logically possible that all the statements in that set are true. It is inconsistent if this is not possible—if one statement contradicts another, or if a contradiction results from reasoning from the set. The set consisting of this one statement 'It's raining and it's not raining' is inconsistent, because this statement is self-contradictory.

contingency To say that a statement is contingent is to say that it is neither necessary nor impossible. Metaphysical contingency is contrasted with what must be true or false; logical contingency is contrasted with logical truth / falsity.

contra-causal freedom It's sometime argued that a free action—one we're responsible for—could only be one that is not caused by previous events. Libertarians believe that some of our actions are free because contra-causal.

contradiction / contrary Two statements are contradictories when the truth of one logically requires the falsity of the other, and the falsity of one requires the truth of the other—in other words, when it is impossible that both are true, and it is impossible that both are false. 'It's raining' and 'It's not raining' are contradictory: exactly one of them must be true. Two statements are contraries when it is impossible that they are both true, though they might both be false. 'No pigs fly' and 'All pigs fly' are contraries, not contradictories. It is logically impossible that both of them are true, though they both might be false (were it the case that some, but not all, pigs fly). One can also call a self-contradiction a 'contradiction'.

cosmological argument for God's existence Given that every natural event has a cause, an apparently unacceptable infinite chain of past events would follow—unless there were an initial uncaused (supernatural) cause, identified with God. A very commonly encountered argument, with versions dating back at least to Plato. It's also commonly known as the first-cause argument.

counterexample An example intended to show that some general claim is false. Reasoning by counterexample is frequently a useful philosophical tactic for arguing against some position. (Also called 'counterinstance'.)

counterfactual A counterfactual (also called a 'counterfactual conditional' or a 'contrary-to-fact conditional') is a conditional statement whose antecedent is false. The subjunctive is used in English counterfactuals: 'If Fred were here, you wouldn't be doing that'. (This is properly said only when Fred isn't here.) One important and controversial area in modern logic is concerned with the truth-conditions for counterfactuals. A powerful and widely accepted way of understanding counterfactuals uses the notion of possible worlds: a counterfactual is true when the consequent is true in the nearest possible world (i.e., a world as much as possible like ours) in which the antecedent is true.

covering law A general law applying to a particular instance. The covering law theory (or "model") of explanation (also called the 'Deductive-Nomological' or 'D-N' theory) says that a particular event is explained by providing one or more covering laws that, together with particular facts, imply the event. For example, we can explain why a piece of metal rusted by appealing to the covering law that iron rusts when exposed to air and moisture, and the facts that the metal is iron, and was exposed to air and moisture.

criterion A test or standard for the presence of a property, or for the applicability of a word, or for the truth or falsity of a proposition. This word is singular; its plural is 'criteria'.

crucial experiment This is an experiment whose outcome would provide a central or conclusive test for the truth or falsity of some position or scientific hypothesis. Sometimes called, in Latin, 'experimentum crucis'.

decision theory The largely mathematical theory of decision-making. Generally includes some way of evaluating desirability of outcomes and their probabilities when not certain.

deconstructionism A skeptical and frequently anti-intellectual postmodern movement which seeks to interpret texts and the positions held in them by "deconstructing" them—showing their incoherence, the hidden and often contradictory presuppositions, prejudices, motives, and political aims behind them.

de dicto / de re (Latin: "about what's said" / "about a thing") A de re belief is a belief considered with respect to the actual thing that it's about. Thus, if someone mistakenly thinks that the moving thing in the sky he's looking at is a satellite, whereas it's actually a meteor, then he has the de re belief that a meteor is moving in the sky—more clearly: about that meteor, he believes it's moving in the sky above him. But he has the de dicto belief that a satellite is moving in the sky above him. Philosophers speak also of a distinction between de dicto and de re necessity. It is de re necessary of the number of planets that it is larger than five (because nine is necessarily larger than five); but it is de dicto contingent, because there might have been only three planets.

deduction / induction 1. In an outdated way of speaking, deduction is reasoning from the general to the particular, and induction is reasoning from the particular to the general. 2. Nowadays, this distinction between kinds of reasoning is made as follows: correct ("valid") deductive reasoning is reasoning of the sort that if the premises are true, the conclusion must be true; whereas correct inductive reasoning supports the conclusion by showing only that it's more probably true. Examples:

Deduction: No pigs fly; Porky is a pig; therefore, Porky doesn't fly.
Induction: Porky, Petunia, and all the other pigs observed in a wide variety of circumstances don't fly; therefore no pigs fly.

These examples in fact fit definition 1; but here are examples of deduction according to definition 2 that do not fit definition 1:

No pigs fly; therefore all pigs are non-flying things.
Porky doesn't fly; Porky is a pig; therefore not all pigs fly.

A common form of induction works by enumeration: as support for the conclusion that all A's are B's, one lists many examples of A's that are B's.

defeasible Means 'defeatible', in the sense of 'capable of being overruled'. A driver's license confers a defeasible right to drive, for example, because under certain circumstances (e.g., when he is drunk) the holder of a valid license would nevertheless not be allowed to drive. A defeasible proposition is one that can be overturned by future evidence.

definiens / definiendum A definiendum (Latin: "to be defined") is a word or phrase to be defined, and the definition is the definiens (Latin: "defining thing").

degrees of perfection argument for God's existence One of many different forms of this argument: Comparative terms describe degrees of approximation to superlative terms. Nothing would count as falling short of the superlative unless the superlative thing existed. Ordinary things are less than perfect, so there must be something completely perfect; and what is completely perfect is God. Objection: Comparative terms do not imply the existence of a superlative instance. For example, the existence of people who are more or less stupid does not imply that someone exists who is maximally, completely, perfectly stupid.

deism A form of religious belief especially popular during the Enlightenment. Deists practice "natural religion"—that is, they rely on reason, distrusting faith, revelation, and the institutional churches. They believe that God produced the universe with its laws of nature, but then left it alone to operate solely by these laws. Deism seems incompatible with some aspects of conventional religion, for example, with the notion of a loving God, or with the practice of prayer.

denotation / connotation The denotation or reference of a word is what that word refers to—the thing in the world that it "names." The connotation or sense of a word is, by contrast, its meaning. Synonymous with 'extension / intension'. A word can have connotation but no denotation: 'unicorn' has meaning but no reference. Note that the philosophical use of 'connotation' is different from the ordinary one, in which it refers not to what a word means, but to more or less distant associations it has; for example, the word 'roses' may carry the connotation of romance to many people. A connotative definition is one that gives the characteristics shared by all and only the objects to which the term refers; often a definition by genus / species. A denotative definition defines by identifying the denotation—for example, by pointing out or listing several things to which the word applies.

deontic Means 'having to do with obligation'. Deontic logic is that branch of modal logic dealing with connections of sentences saying what one ought to do, must do, is permitted to do, etc.

derivation A method for proving deductive validity, in which one moves from premises to succeeding steps using accepted rules of inference, eventuating at the conclusion. There are other methods of proof; for example, in sentential logic, the truth table.

determinism The view that every event is necessitated by previous causes, so that given its causes, each event must have existed in the form it does. There is some debate about how (and whether) this view can be justified. The view that at least some events are not fully caused is called 'indeterminism'. Determinism is often taken to be a presupposition of science; Kant thought it was necessary; but quantum physics says that it is false. One of the main areas of concern about determinism arises when it is considered in connection with free will.

deterrence A motive for punishment: that threatening punishment can prevent future occurrences of undesirable acts. (Other competing theories of punishment attempt to justify it as retribution or rehabilitation.) So one may try to justify jailing criminals by claiming that the threat of similar jailing will discourage them and others from future crime. One may even successfully deter crime by framing the innocent. Deterrence as a national defense policy attempts to prevent other nations' aggression by threatening them with massive (perhaps nuclear) retaliation. The moral status of deterrence is controversial. Preventing war is of course a good thing, but is threaten-

ing deterrence justified when it involves the willingness to go through with really horrible retaliation?

dialectic Sometimes this word refers to a style of philosophical discourse most famously due to Plato, involving dialogue: claims, counterclaims, and logical argument. (A contrasting style is rhetoric.) In Kant, dialectical reasoning fallaciously attributes external existence to objects internal to our minds. In Hegel, Marx, and other Continental philosophers, the Dialectic is the interplay of contradictory forces supposed to be a central principle of metaphysical and social existence and change.

divine command theory The ethical theory which explains morality as what is commanded by God. It is often argued that this has things backwards: God commands it because it is right, not vice versa.

double effect The doctrine of double effect holds that, although it is always wrong to use a bad means to a good end, one may act to bring about a good result when also knowingly bringing about bad results, under the following conditions: 1) The bad result is not caused by the good result—both are caused by the action (thus 'double effect'); (2) there's no way of getting the good result without the bad; 3) the good result is so good that it's worth accepting the bad one.

For example, a dentist is allowed to drill, and thus cause some pain (the bad result) for the sake of dental improvements (the good result), since these conditions hold—most notably (1): the pain doesn't cause the improvement; both are results of the drilling.

This principle is associated with Catholic morality, and has been applied most frequently in contexts of medical ethics. It is disputed by some philosophers, who sometimes argue that the distinction between double effect and bad means / good end is artificial and not morally relevant.

doxastic Means 'pertaining to belief', as in 'doxastic state', 'doxastic principle' (for justifying beliefs).

dualism Dualists hold that there are two sorts of things that exist, neither of which can be understood in terms of the other—often, in particular, mental and physical. Other sorts of dualism distinguish the visible and invisible, the actual and the possible, God and the universe, etc. The contrast here is with monism.

egalitarianism The view that people are equal—that they are entitled to equal rights and treatment in society, or to equal possessions or satisfactions.

egoism, ethical / psychological Psychological egoism is the position that people in fact act only in their own interests. It's sometimes argued that even the most generous act is done for the doer's own satisfaction; but this might simply be a way of saying that even the most generous act is motivated—something nobody would deny. Ethical egoism is the position that I (or people in general) ought to act only in my (their) own interests.

emotivism A position in meta-ethics that holds that ethical utterances are to be understood not as statements of fact that are either true or false, but rather as expressions of approval or disapproval, and invitations to the listener to have the same reactions and to act accordingly. Thus emotivists emphasize the "emotive meaning" of ethical utterances, denying that they have cognitive meaning. Emotivists can nevertheless agree that evaluative utterances have some "descriptive content": when I say this is a good apple, I express my approval, but also describe it as having certain characteristics on which my approval rests: that it is, for example, not worm-infested.

empirical This means having to do with sense-experience and experiment. Empirical knowledge is knowledge we get through experience of the world; thus it is a posteriori. An empirical concept is one that is not innate; it can be developed only through experience.

empiricism The position (usually contrasted with rationalism) that all our concepts and substantive knowledge come from sense experience. Empiricists deny that there are innate concepts. While they grant that certain kinds of trivial knowledge (of conceptual, analytic, and logical truths) can be gained by reason alone, independently of experience, they deny the existence of the synthetic a priori.

end in itself 1. Something sought for its own sake; an intrinsic good. 2. Someone is seen as an end in him / herself when that person's aims are seen as having value just because they are that person's aims. Treating people as ends in themselves is respecting their aims, and refraining from thinking of, or using, that person merely as a means to your aims.

ends / means A long-standing controversy in ethics is whether one might be permitted to use bad means to a good end: does the end justify the means? For example, is it permitted to lie to someone if everyone will be better off in the long run as a result? Extreme opponents of consequentialism sometimes hold that no action that is bad in itself is ever permitted no matter how good the consequences. Notice that this means that telling a little lie would not be justified even if it would prevent the destruction of the earth. A more moderate view merely warns against actions which are so bad in themselves that the good consequences do not overwhelm this badness.

Enlightenment The Enlightenment was a cultural and philosophical movement of the seventeenth and eighteenth centuries whose chief features were a belief in rationality and scientific method, and a tendency to reject conventional religion and other traditions. The Age of Enlightenment is also known as the 'Age of Reason'.

enthymeme An argument with some steps left unstated but understood. All pigs are sloppy eaters, so Porky is a sloppy eater is an enthymeme, leaving unsaid Porky is a pig.

epiphenomenalism A variety of dualism in which mental events are just "by-products" of physical ones: physical events cause mental ones, but not vice versa. Analogy: the noise your car makes is caused by the mechanical goings-on inside, but it has no effect on them.

epistemic Having to do with knowledge. Epistemic logic is that branch of modal logic dealing with relations between sentences involving 'knows', 'believes', etc.

epistemology Theory of knowledge: one of the main branches of philosophy. Among the central questions studied here are: What is the difference between knowledge and mere belief? Is all (or any) knowledge based on sense-perception? How, in general, are our knowledge-claims justified?

essence / accident The essential characteristics of something are the ones that it must have in order to be what it is, or the kind of thing it is. It is essential, for example, for a tree to be a plant—if something was not a plant, it could not be a tree. By contrast, a tree that in fact is thirty-three meters high could still be a tree if it weren't that height; thus this characteristic is accidental. (Note that 'accident' and 'accidental' don't have their ordinary meanings in this philosophical use.) Some philosophers think that the essence / accident distinction does not concern the real characteristics of something, but is only a consequence of the words we apply to them: being a plant is said to be an essential characteristic of a tree only because it's part of the definition of 'tree'. But essentialist philosophers believe in real, objective essences.

ethics The general philosophical study of what makes things good or bad, right or wrong. Often the following areas of study are distinguished within ethics: (1) Descriptive ethics: the discovery of what ethical views particular societies in fact have; and speculative anthropological theorizing about the origin and function of these views; (2) Normative ethics: theorizing about what the basic principles are that might serve systematically to distinguish right from wrong. (3) Applied ethics: the normative ethics of particular areas or disciplines: medical ethics, business ethics, computer ethics ... . (4) Meta-ethics: the study of the meaning of moral language and the possibility of ethical knowledge.

'Morality' and 'ethics' (and 'moral' and 'ethical') are usually used as synonyms, though 'ethics' is more frequently generally used as the name of the philosophical study of these matters. Philosophers usually avoid the tendency in ordinary talk to restrict the word 'ethics' to an official code of acceptable behavior in some area (as in 'professional ethics').

ethnocentric Someone is ethnocentric who regards the views or characteristics of his / her own race or culture as the only correct or important ones. Other "-centric" words have arisen by analogy: eurocentric, logocentric, phallocentric for example.

euthanasia Mercy killing, the intentional bringing-about or hastening of the death of someone, presumably for his own good, when his life is judged not to be worth continuing, typically when that person is suffering from an untreatable, fatal illness causing horrible unavoidable pain or suffering. Voluntary euthanasia is done at the expressed wish of that person; this wish is not expressed in the case of involuntary euthanasia (for example, when the person has mentally deteriorated beyond the point of being able to express, or perhaps even to have, coherent wishes). Passive euthanasia involves refraining from providing life-prolonging treatment to someone suffering from a fatal condition; active euthanasia is killing, for example, by administering a fatal injection. Ethical opinion is deeply divided concerning euthanasia. Some who argue in favor of its permissibility would accept it only when voluntary, and/or only when passive.

expected utility / value The expected utility (or expected value) of an action is calculated by multiplying the utility (or value) of each possible result of that action by its probability, and adding up the results. For example, consider this betting game: you get $10 if a random draw from a deck of cards is a spade; and you pay $4 if it's any other suit. Assuming the utility of each dollar is 1, to calculate the expected utility of this game we add: [.25 (probability of a spade) x 10 (the utility if it's a spade)] + [.75

(the probability of a non-spade) x -4 (the utility of a non-spade)]. Since (.25 x 10) + (.75 x -4) = 2.5 - 3 = -.5, the game thus has an expected utility of -.5, so you'll average 50 cents loss per play in the long run. One (controversial) theory for rational decision-making advocates maximizing expected utility, so you should not play this game. (But if you enjoy gambling, this has to be figured in too, and might make it worthwhile.)

explanans / explanandum An explanandum (Latin: "to be explained") is something that is being explained: what does the explaining is the explanans (Latin: "explaining thing").

explanation An explanation answers the question 'Why?' and provides understanding; sometimes it also provides us with the abilities to control, and to predict (and retrodict) the world. This is fairly vague, and philosophers have tried to provide theories of explanation—to give a general account of how explanations work, and what makes some good and some bad. One important account is the covering law model. One (but only one) sort of explanation is causal: we explain something by saying what its causes are. Sometimes, instead, we explain by telling what something is made of, or by giving reasons for human actions, as in some explanations in history.

externalism / internalism A variety of related doctrines. Meta-ethical externalism holds that the fact that something is good does not by itself automatically supply the motivation for someone to do it; in addition, motivation ("external" to the mere belief about goodness) must be supplied; internalism is the view that the judgment that something is good itself guarantees or includes the motivation to do it. As a theory of mind, externalism is the view that to specify the "content" of a belief one must refer to the external facts or objects that the belief is about.

fallacy An argument of a type that may seem correct but in fact is not. (Thus, not just any mistaken argument should be called 'fallacious'.) Formal fallacies are mistakes in reasoning that spring from mistakes in logical form; their persuasiveness springs from their similarity, on first glance, to valid forms. Informal fallacies spring instead from ambiguities in meaning or grammar, or from psychological tendencies to be convinced by reasons that are not good reasons.

fatalism The position that our futures are inevitable, whatever we do—that events are "fated" to happen. It's important to distinguish this from determinism, which claims merely that our futures are determined. A determinist who is not a fatalist thinks that our futures are not inevitable—they depend on what we do.

feminism The name of various philosophical—especially ethical, social, and political—theories and social movements that see elements of our society as unjust to and exploitative of women. Feminists often advocate equality under the law and equal economic status for women; but many go further, arguing in favor of preferential treatment for women to counteract past injustices. Sometimes they find male bias and male patterns of thought in many areas of our personal, social, and intellectual lives. Recent developments are feminist theories of the self, of knowledge, and of science.

formal In philosophy this means pertaining to structure (as opposed to content); or rigorous and rule-governed.

foundationalism The position that there is a particular sort of statement (sometimes thought to be indubitable) from which all other statements comprising a system of belief should be derived. There are foundationalist theories of knowledge, of ethics, etc.

free will To say that we have free will (or freedom) is to say that our decisions and actions are sometimes entirely (or at least partially) "up to us"—not forced or determined by anything internal or external to us. We can then either do or not do—we have alternatives. It seems that this is necessary for responsibility for our actions. But if determinism is true, then our actions and "decisions" are determined by previous causes, themselves determined by still earlier causes, and ultimately whatever we decide or do is determined by events that happened a long time ago, and that are not up to us. Thus, it seems that determinism is incompatible with free will. There are three main responses to this apparent problem: (1) Hard determinists accept determinism, which they take to rule out free will. (2) Libertarians accept free will. They think that this means determinism is false, at least for some human events. Both libertarianism and hard determinism are incompatibilist; that is, they hold that the freedom of an act is incompatible with its being determined. (3) Soft determinists are compatibilists, in that they attack the reasoning above, and argue that our actions might be determined, but also free in some sense—that a determined action might nevertheless be up to the doer, and one that the doer is morally responsible for—when it's determined but not compelled.

functional A functional definition defines by giving the typical use of the kind of thing, or its typical cause-and-effect relations with other things; a functional explanation explains something by its function, for example, telling what use the pancreas is in the body, or a social ritual in a particular society. A functional kind is defined by causes and effects (and not, for example, by shape or physical make-up). Functionalism centrally argues that a kind of thing is a functional kind. In philosophy of mind, functionalists argue that mental kinds are functional kinds.

generalization A statement about a group of things, or about everything in a particular category (contrasted with a 'particular statement / proposition'); or the process of reasoning that arrives at one of these. Inductive logic studies the principles of deriving them from particular instances; the rule in deductive logic for deriving one is called universal generalization. An ethical generalization is a rule everyone should follow; Kant argued that the right action was the one whose maxim could be generalized.

general will What is desired by, or desirable for, society as a whole; sometimes taken to be the appropriate justification for government policy. This notion can be problematic when it is taken to mean something other than what's revealed by majority vote or unanimity.

hedonism The advocacy of pleasure as the basic good; philosophical hedonists often distinguish between the "higher" (sometimes = mental or spiritual) and the "lower" pleasures (the merely sensual), making the former more important. Psychological hedonism claims that people in fact seek only pleasure; ethical hedonism claims that people ought to seek pleasure (or only pleasure).

holism / individualism In philosophical use, holism involves the claim that certain sorts of things are more than merely the sum of their parts—that they can be understood only by examining them as a whole; contrasted with individualism. In social science and history, for example, holists argue that one can't explain events on the basis of individual people's actions, because these get their significance only in a society. Semantic holism insists that words and sentences get their meaning only through their relationships with all other words and sentences. Holism about living things refuses to see them merely as the sum of their non-living parts. Methodological individualism is the method in sociology of investigating social facts by discovering facts about individual people. Individualism in ethics emphasizes individual rights and freedoms, contrasting with communitarianism.

hypothesis A tentative suggestion that may be merely a guess or a hunch, or may be based on some sort of reasoning; in any case it needs further evidence to be rationally acceptable as true. Some philosophers think that all scientific enquiry begins with hypotheses.

idea / impression An "idea" is, in general, any thought or perception in the mind. Platonic forms are sometimes called 'ideas'. In Hume, ideas are the faint imprint left on the mind by impressions, which are the mental events one has as the immediate result of, and while, using one's senses (= sense-data); ideas may be called up later in the absence of sensation. Empiricists believe that all ideas are copies of impressions.

idealism In the philosophical sense of this word, it's the view that only minds and their contents really or basically exist. Its competitors are materialism and dualism.

ideal observer theory A theory of ethics that attempts to explain what is really good as what would be chosen by an ideal observer—that is, someone who would have all the relevant information, and who would not be misled by particular interests or biases.

identity 1. Your identity is what you are—what's important about you, or what makes you different from everyone else. 2. Two different things might be said to be 'identical' when they are exactly alike in some characteristics; this is sometimes called qualitative identity. 3. Object a and object b are said to be (strictly or numerically or quantitatively) identical when a and b are in fact the same thing—when 'a' and 'b' are two different names or ways of referring to exactly the same object. 4. Identity (over time) is the relation between something at one time and that same thing at another time: they are said to be two temporal stages (or time-slices) of the same continuing thing.

identity theory of mind The view that each mental state is really a physical state, probably of the brain. Often identity theorists believe in addition in the type-identity of mental and physical states.

illusion / hallucination / delusion Illusions and hallucinations are "false" perceptual experiences—ones that lead, or could lead, to mistakes about what is out there. A hallucination is the apparent perception of something that does not exist at all (as in dreaming, mirages, drug-induced states). An illusion is the incorrect perception of something that does exist. A delusion is a perception that actually results in a false belief; illusions and hallucinations can delude, but often do not. The argument from illusion draws epistemological conclusions from the existence of these things.

imagination Sometimes philosophers have used this word to refer to the faculty of having images—mental pictures.

immaterialism 1. The view that some things exist that are not material: that are not made of ordinary physical stuff, but of mental or spiritual—immaterial stuff instead. This is the denial of materialism. The most extreme form of immaterialism is the view that no material things exist: this is idealism. 2. The view that objects are merely collections of qualities, without a substratum to hold them together. If one thinks of qualities as essentially mental perceptions, then this is a species of immaterialism in sense 1.

immediate / mediate In its more technical philosophical sense 'immediate' means 'without mediation'—that is, 'directly'. In this sense, for example, philosophers ask whether external things are sensed immediately, or mediated by the sensing of internal images. An immediate inference is one performed in one step, needing only a single use of only one rule, for example, when Q is inferred from (P and Q).

immorality / amorality The first means 'contrary to morality'; the second, 'without morality'. Someone who knows about moral rules but intentionally disobeys them or rejects them is immoral; someone who doesn't know or think about morality is amoral. Amorality is typical of small children; immorality of adults.

incorrigibility / corrigibility 'Corrigibility' means 'correctibility'. Something is incorrigible when it is impossible to correct it, or when it is guaranteed correct. Some philosophers have thought that our beliefs about our own mental states are incorrigible. For example, if you sincerely believe that you are now feeling a pain, how could you be wrong?

indubitability / dubitability 'Dubitable' means 'doubtable'. Dubitable statements are not just ones we are psychologically capable of doubting, but ones about which even highly fanciful and unlikely doubts might be raised, doubts that no one in his/her right mind would seriously have. Thus Descartes thought that because our senses might be fooled, information from them was dubitable. He then went on to try to discover what sort of belief was really indubitable: about which it could be proven that no doubt can be raised.

inference / implication / entailment 1. Implication (also known as entailment) is a logical relation that holds between two statements when the second follows deductively from the first. The first is then said to 'imply' (or 'entail') the second. Be careful not to confuse these with 'inference', which is something that people do, when they reason from one statement to another. A rule of inference is an acceptable procedure for reasoning from one set of statements of a particular form to another statement. 2. Sometimes a sentence 'implies' what it doesn't literally state. For example, if I said "Fred is now not robbing banks," I imply that at one time he was robbing banks. This is sometimes called conversational or contextual implicature, or pragmatic implication, to distinguish it from logical implicature.

infinite regress A sequence (of definition, explanation, justification, cause, etc.) that must continue backwards endlessly. For example, if every event must have a cause, then a present event must be caused by some past event; and this event by another still earlier, and so on infinitely. Sometimes the fact that reasoning leads to an infinite regress shows that it is faulty. One then calls it a vicious regress.

informal / formal logic The latter is that kind of logic that relies heavily on symbols and rigorous procedures much like those in mathematics; it concentrates on reasoning that is correct because of syntax. Only a small fraction of the ordinary sorts of reasoning we do can be explained this way, and there is a vast scope for informal logic, which analyzes good and bad arguments semantically, and relies less heavily on symbols and mathematics-style procedures.

informed consent Agreement based on sufficient knowledge of relevant information; relevant especially to medical ethics. It's widely agreed that informed consent by the patient is necessary for all medical procedures, but problems arise here: how much information is enough? What should be done when the patient is unable to understand the information or to make a rational choice?

innateness A belief, concept, or characteristic is innate when it is inborn—when it doesn't come from experience or education—though experience may be thought necessary to make conscious or actualize something that is given innately. An argument for the innateness of something is that experience is not sufficient to produce it in us.

in principle Contrasted with 'in fact' or 'in practice'. Philosophers talk about things we can do in principle, meaning that we could do them if we had the time or technology, or if other merely practical difficulties did not stand in the way. For example, we can verify the statement 'There is a red pebble lying on the north pole of Mars' in principle, though at the moment we can't test this by observation. In principle, we can count to one trillion, because we know the rules for doing it, though in fact we lack the patience and wouldn't live long enough anyway.

intentionality Sometimes this refers to what's true of things done on purpose—intentionally. But in contemporary usage in philosophy of mind, it usually refers to aboutness—the power of referring to or meaning real or imagined external objects. It's sometimes argued that this is a necessary, unique, and essential characteristic of mental states.

interactionism A form of mind / body dualism. It holds that mind and body can interact—that is, that mental events can cause physical events (e.g., when your decision to touch something causes your physical hand movement) and that physical events can cause mental events (e.g., when a physical stimulation to your body causes a mental feeling of pain). A standard objection to this commonsense position is that it's hard to see how this sort of causal interaction could take place, since the mental and the physical work according to their own laws: how could an electrical impulse in a (physical) nerve cell cause a non-physical pain in a mind?

intrinsic / inherent / instrumental / extrinsic Something has intrinsic value when it is valuable for its own sake and not merely as a means to something else. Pleasure, for example, is intrinsically valuable. Something by contrast has instrumental value when it is valuable as a means to some other end. The value of money is primarily instrumental. An intrinsic or inherent or natural right is one people have permanently or essentially, because of the very nature of a person. An extrinsic right is one people have only temporarily, or one they don't have unless they are granted it.

introspection The capacity for finding things out about oneself by "looking inward"—by direct awareness of one's own mental states. You might find out that you have a headache, for example, by introspection. This is contrasted with the way someone else might find this out, by observing your outward behavior—your groaning, holding your head, etc. Sometimes called 'reflection'.

intuition A belief that comes immediately, without reasoning, argument, evidence; before analysis (thus 'preanalytic'). Some philosophers think that certain intuitions are the reliable, rational basis for knowledge of certain sorts. Some beliefs that arise immediately when we perceive are the basis of our knowledge of the outside world (though perceptual intuitions are not always reliable). Our ethical intuitions are sometimes taken to be the basis and the test of ethical theories. Intuitionism is any theory that holds that intuition is a valid source of knowledge.

is / ought problem Clearly what is is sometimes different from what ought to be; but can one infer the latter from the former? Some philosophers hold that you can't: no matter how detailed an account you have of how things are, they don't imply how things ought to be. But

ethical naturalists and other objectivists typically claim that they do, because ethical facts are facts too. The supposed is / ought gap is also known as the fact-value gap.

lawlike statements Statements which have the logical form of laws whether they are true or not. Part of the philosophy of science is the attempt to specify the logic of lawlike statements.

law of the indiscernibility of identicals The supposed law of metaphysics (associated with Leibniz, thus also called 'Leibniz's law') that says that if x and y are identical—that is, if x is y—then x and y are indiscernible (share all the same properties). Distinguish this from its reverse, the law of the identity of indiscernibles: if x and y are indiscernible, then they are identical. Imagine two things that are alike in every detail: they even occupy the same space at the same time. Why then think of them as two? Wouldn't there really be only one thing?

libertarianism 1. The position that some of our actions are free in the sense of not being caused. 2. The political position that people have a strong right to political liberty. Thus libertarians tend to object to restrictive laws, taxes, the welfare state, and state economic control. A more specific variety of (traditional) liberalism, though nowadays this position tends to be espoused by some of those who are called 'conservatives'.

logic Loosely speaking, logic is the process of correct reasoning, and something is logical when it makes sense. Philosophers often reserve this word for reasoning norms covered by various particular theories of inference, justification, and proof. Traditional logic was fairly narrowly restricted, concentrating on the syllogism. Nowadays, symbolic deductive and inductive logics cover a much wider area, but far from the totality of reasoning.

logical form The form of a sentence is its general structure, ignoring the particular content it has. For example, If it's Tuesday, then I'm late for class and If Peru is in Asia, then Porky is a frog have the same overall logical form (if P then Q). The sort of logic that works by exhibiting, often in symbolic notation, the logical form of sentences is called 'formal logic'.

logical positivism A school of philosophy (also known as "logical empiricism"), subscribed to by many twentieth-century English-speaking philosophers. Impressed by empiricism and by the success and rigor of science, the logical positivists advocated that philosophers avoid speculation about matters only science and experience could settle; if a sentence was not scientifically verifiable or a matter of logical truth or conceptual truth, it was nonsense and should be discarded (the verifiability criterion). Ethical statements were thought not verifiable, so without literal meaning: they were sometimes thought merely to be expressions of feelings of approval or disapproval.

logical truth / falsity A sentence is logically true (or false) when it is true (or false) merely because of its logical structure. Examples: All ducks are ducks. Either it's raining or it's not raining. These should be distinguished from analytic truths / falsehoods, which are true / false merely because of the meaning of their words: for example, All fathers are male. Logical truths / falsehoods are also called logically necessary / impossible sentences, but these should also be distinguished from (metaphysically) necessary truths / falsehoods (see necessary / contingent truth): those that must be true or false. 'Tautology' is sometimes used as a synonym for 'logical truth', though in ordinary talk a tautology is something that says the same thing twice. Thus, It's raining and it's raining is a tautology in the ordinary sense, though not in the philosophers' sense (since it might be false). Sentences that are neither logically true nor logically false—that are merely true or false—are said to be logically contingent (or logically indeterminate).

materialism As a philosophical term, this refers to the position that all that exists is physical. (Synonym: physicalism.) Materialists about mind sometimes argue that apparently non-physical things like the soul or mind or thoughts are actually material things. Central-state materialists identify mental events with physical events central in the body (i.e., in the nervous system). Eliminative materialists, however, think that categorizing things as mental is altogether a mistake (like believing in ghosts).

matter of fact / relation of ideas Hume's distinction. He seems to have meant that a matter of fact is a contingent state of affairs, to be discovered a posteriori; a relation of ideas is a conceptual or analytic or logical truth, which can be known a priori.

medieval philosophy The dividing lines between ancient, medieval, and modern philosophy are rough, but it's often said that medieval philosophy starts with Augustine (c. 400), and ends just before Descartes (c. 1600).

meta- This prefix often means 'beyond', or 'about', so thinking about meta-x is (sometimes) thinking about the structure or nature of x. Examples of its use are 'meta-language' and 'meta-ethics'; it is used differently, however, in 'metaphysics'.

metaphysics One of the main branches of philosophy, having to do with the ultimate components of reality, the types of things that exist, the nature of causation, change, time, God, free will.

mind-body problem What is the relation between mental and physical events? Is one sort of event reducible to the other? Are mental events merely a sort of bodily event? Or are they distinct? If so, how are they connected?

modal statements are (roughly speaking) the ones that are not straightforward assertions, and have complexities involved in the logic of their relations (studied in modal logic), their confirmation, etc. The basic kind of modal statements are those affirming necessity and possibility; but also considered in this category are belief, tense, moral, counterfactual, causal, and lawlike statements.

modern philosophy The borderline between medieval philosophy and modern philosophy is rough, but it is usually said that Descartes was the first modern philosopher (around 1600). The era of modern philosophy can be said to extend through the present, though it's often taken to end around the beginning of the nineteenth century, or later with the advent of postmodernism.

monism A monistic metaphysics is the belief that there is one basic kind of thing in existence. Monists about mind deny dualism (belief in two irreducible substances, mind and matter). Nowadays most monists are materialists, but historically, many were idealists (believing that this one kind of stuff was basically mental).

monotheism / polytheism / pantheism Monotheism is the belief in one (and only one) God. Polytheism is the belief in many gods. Pantheism is the belief that God somehow exists in everything, or that everything is God.

moral argument for God's existence One version of this argument: There is a real objective difference between right and wrong, but the only way to make sense of this is to think of it as arising from a divine moral order. So the existence of morality shows that God exists.

moral realism The view that there are real, objective, knowable moral facts.

moral sense theory The idea that we have a way of "sensing" the objective moral properties, on the analogy of the way we can sense the property of redness using our eyes. Moral sensation would clearly be a very different kind of sensation, however; what is the sense organ involved? Is it at all reliable?

mutatis mutandis (Latin: "having changed the things that were to be changed") Philosophers say things like "This case is, mutatis mutandis, like the other," meaning that the two cases are alike except for certain details—that one can derive one case from the other by making the appropriate substitutions or changes.

mutually exclusive / jointly exhaustive Mutually exclusive sets do not overlap each other in membership. For example, each of these sets: mammals, birds, fish, reptiles, amphibians, is exclusive of the others, since nothing belongs to more than one of them. The list is jointly exhaustive of vertebrates, since every vertebrate is included in these categories. It is mutually exclusive and jointly exhaustive because every vertebrate is included in exactly one of these categories.

mystical experience argument for God's existence The existence and nature of the mystical experiences some people have are sometimes taken to show God's existence. One criticism of this argument is that even though having this experience sometimes provides a compelling motivation for belief, it's not reliable evidence.

mysticism A variety of religious practice that relies on direct experience which is often taken to be a union with God or with the divine ground of all being. The content of these experiences is often taken to be ineffable, but we are told that they produce enlightenment or bliss. Mystics often advocate exercises or rituals designed to induce the abnormal psychological states in which these experiences occur.

naïve realism What's supposed to be the ordinary view about perception: that it (usually) reveals external objects to us directly, the way they really are. The implication is that this "naïve" view is overturned by philosophical sophistication. Also called common-sense realism or direct realism.

naturalism This term names the view that everything is a natural entity, and thus to be studied by the usual methods of natural science. Naturalistic or "naturalizing" theories in philosophy try to apply ordinary scientific categories and methods to philosophical problems. Philosophers have proposed naturalized epistemology, philosophy of mind, and ethics.

natural kind Some philosophers think that some of the ways we divide the world into kinds correspond to the way nature really is divided—they "cut nature at the joints." Classically, a natural kind is a kind that things belong to necessarily: thus, human being is a natural kind because Fred is necessarily human; but living within fifty miles of the Empire State Building is not: Fred might move further away; or, if he doesn't he might have. Some contemporary thinkers hold that natural kinds are the ones that support certain modal implications needed in science; but others argue that there are no natural kinds—all kinds are artificial human creations.

natural law There are several philosophically relevant senses of this phrase: 1. A law of nature—i.e., a formulation of a regularity found in the natural world, the sort of thing science discovers. 2. A principle of proper human action or conduct, taken to be God-given, or to be a consequence of "human nature"—our structure or function. In this sense, there are "natural law" theories in ethics and in political philosophy. 3. The view that the validity of the laws of a legal system depends on their coherence with God-given or otherwise objective morality.

necessary / contingent truth A necessary truth is one that could not possibly be false; a contingent truth could be false but isn't, just as a matter of fact. Some philosophers think that the necessity or contingency of some fact is a metaphysical matter—is a matter of the way the external world is—but others hold that this difference is merely a matter of the way we think or talk about the world—that a truth taken to be necessary is merely a conceptual or logical or analytic truth. A necessary truth is also called a necessity, a contingent truth a contingency, and a necessary falsehood an impossibility.

necessary / sufficient condition x is a sufficient condition for y when: if x is true, then y must also be true—that x can't exist without y. This is the same as saying: x can't be without y. x is a necessary condition for y when: if y is true, then x must also be true. In other words, y can't be without x. If you can't have either without the other, then x and y are both necessary and sufficient for each other.

nomic Means 'having to do with law'. A nomic regularity is distinguished from a mere (accidental) regularity or coincidence, in that the first represents a law of nature. One way this difference is explained is by saying that a nomic regularity supports counterfactuals: it's not only the case that all A's are B's, but it's also the case that if something were an A, it would be a B. [synonym: 'nomological']

norm / normative A norm is a standard. 'Normative' means prescribing a norm. When somebody says, "We think abortion is wrong," that statement may be descriptive—informing you what a group's views are, or normative—morally condemning abortion.

obligation Generally, something one morally must do, a synonym for 'duty'. What one must do is perhaps not all there is to morality. Some good things are supererogatory—above and beyond the call of duty—great if you do them, but nobody would blame you if you didn't.

omni- Many (not all) religious thinkers take God to be omnibenevolent—totally, perfectly good; omnipotent—all-powerful, able to do anything; omnipresent—everywhere at once, or influential in everything; and omniscient—all-knowing.

ontological argument for God's existence A variety of arguments that rely on the concept of God to prove His existence. In the best-known version it is supposed that part of the concept of God is that He is perfect: since something would not be perfect if it did not exist, it follows that God exists.

ontology The philosophical study of existence or being. Typical questions are: What basic sorts of things exist? What are the basic things out of which others are composed, and the basic relations between things?

operational definition Defines by giving an account of the procedures or measurements used to apply the word. For example, one might describe weighing procedures and outcomes to define 'weight'.

operationalism / instrumentalism Operationalism is the view that scientific concepts should have operational definitions, and that any terms not definable in this way should be eliminated from science as meaningless. Instrumentalists are operationalists who are explicitly anti-realists about theoretical entities. They say that electrons, for example, don't really exist; electron-talk is about nothing but what's observable.

ordinary language philosophy A branch of twentieth-century philosophy that held that philosophical problems arose because of confusions about, or complexities in, ordinary language, and might be solved (or dissolved) by attention to the subtleties of actual talk.

overdetermination An event is overdetermined when two or more events have happened, each of which is individually a sufficient condition for it. Thus someone's death is overdetermined when he is given a fatal dose of poison and then shot through the heart.

parallelism Because of the difficulties in interactionism some philosophers were led to the belief that mind and body events don't cause each other, but just run along independently; they are coordinated, however, perhaps inexplicably, or maybe because God sets them up in advance (occasionalism) to run in parallel, like two clocks set in advance to chime the hour simultaneously.

Pascal's wager is Blaise Pascal's famous argument for belief in God: Belief in God might result in infinite benefit—eternal salvation—if He exists, while we risk only a little—wasting some time, and foregoing some pleasures forbidden to believers—if He doesn't. Conversely, disbelief might result in infinite harm—eternal damnation—if He exists, or could provide a tiny benefit if we were right. So even if there isn't any evidence one way or the other, it's a very good bet to believe.

paternalism Paternalistic action provides for what is taken to be someone's good, without giving that person responsibility for determining his/her own aims or actions. It arises from a sort of benevolence plus lack of trust in people's ability to decide what's to their own benefit or to act for their own real long-range good. Some critics of paternalism argue that the only way to determine someone's good is to see what that person chooses. Some argue that respect for individual autonomy means that we shouldn't interfere even when someone is

choosing badly. This issue arises most importantly in political theory and medical ethics, since governments and physicians often act paternalistically.

patriarchy Societal and familial institutions are patriarchal when they systematically embody male dominance over women: when they arrange things so that men hold power and women do not. Feminists emphasize the widespread incidence of patriarchal institutions in historical and contemporary families and societies.

perception In its broadest use, this means any sort of mental awareness, but it's more often used to refer to the awareness we get when using the senses.

person Philosophers sometimes use this word in such a way that persons do not necessarily coincide with living human organisms. The idea here is that a person is anything that has special rights (for example, the right to life, or to self-determination) or special dignity or worth. Sometimes it's held that some humans (e.g., those in a permanent coma) are not persons in this sense, or that some higher animals are.

personal identity 1. What makes you you. Is it your body, your mind, your personality, your memories, or something else? 2. What makes this person now the same person as that one, earlier. Is it a continuing body, or mind, or personality, or that this later stage remembers the experiences that happened to the earlier one?

phenomenalism Phenomenalists believe (on the basis, for example, of the argument from illusion) that all we're ever aware of is appearances or sense-data, the mental events we have when using our senses. Accepting the empiricist rule that we're entitled to believe in only what's given by our senses, they deny the existence of external objects independent of perception. Ordinary "objects" like tables and chairs are thus thought to be collections of these appearances—actual and perhaps possible ones.

phenomena / noumena Philosophers sometimes use 'phenomenon' in the ordinary sense, referring merely to something that happens, but often it's used in a more technical way, referring to a way things seem to us—to something as we perceive it. Noumena are, by contrast, things-in-themselves—things as they really are. These are unavailable to the senses, but perhaps rationally comprehensible; though Kant argued that they are unknowable.

pluralism Pluralist theories argue for a multiplicity of basic kinds. To be a pluralist about value is to believe that there are many incompatible, but equally valid, value systems.

positivism The philosophy associated with Auguste Comte, which holds that scientific knowledge is the only valid kind of knowledge, and that anything else is idle speculation. Sometimes this term is loosely used to refer to logical positivism, which is a twentieth-century outgrowth of more general nineteenth-century positivism.

possible worlds This world—the collection of all facts—is the actual world. The set of possible worlds includes the actual world plus non-actual worlds—ones in which one or more things are not as they actually are, but might have been.

postmodernism Various late twentieth-century movements, in general characterized by a rejection of foundationalism, an interest in textual interpretation and deconstruction, antagonism to analytic philosophy, rejection of the goals of the Enlightenment, tendency to perspectivism, denial of the applicability of the concepts of reality, objectivity, truth.

poststructuralism A postmodern view, thought of as a successor to structuralism. Holds in general that the meaning of words is their relation to other words (in a "text"), not their relation to reality; that human activity is not lawlike, but understood through its relations to power and the unconscious.

pragmatism A largely American school of philosophers who emphasized the relevance of the practical application of things, their connections to our lives, our activities and values, demanding instrumental definitions of philosophically relevant terms, and urged that we

judge beliefs on the basis of their benefit to the believer.

pre-Socratics The ancient Greek philosophers before Socrates, that is, of the sixth and fifth centuries BCE. Their thought is the earliest recorded Western philosophy.

presupposition A necessary condition for the truth of a statement, assumed beforehand by the speaker, but not itself stated. The speaker of 'The present king of France is bald' assumes that there is a present king of France. Because there isn't, the statement is not true, but is it false, or rather inappropriate and lacking a truth value?

prima facie (Latin: "at first appearance") Based on the first impression: what would be true, or seem to be true in general, before we have additional information about a particular case. Prima facie duties are what we're in general obliged to do, but that might not turn out to be obligatory in particular cases. Prima facie evidence can be overridden by contrary considerations.

primary / secondary qualities Locke (and others) argued that some characteristics we perceive are really as perceived in external objects (the primary qualities), whereas others (the secondary qualities) don't exist as perceived in the real world, but are just powers of external objects to produce ideas in us which don't resemble what's out there. Something's dimensions are supposed to be primary, but its color secondary.

privileged access Supposedly a special way you alone can find out about the contents of your mind. Other people need to infer what's in your mind from your external behavior, but you can discover your mental states directly.

problem of evil A problem for religious believers: God is supposed to be all-powerful, benevolent, and all-knowing. Evil is what is bad for us, so God must eliminate all evil. But there clearly is evil. So a God with all of these features does not exist.

problem of induction Everyone believes that the basic regularities we have observed in the past will continue into the future; this principle is called the principle of induction or the principle of the uniformity of nature. Note however that it would be circular to justify this principle by our past experience. How then to justify it?

problem of other minds If only your mind and its contents can be "perceived" directly only by you, this raises the problem of what ground (if any) you have for thinking that anyone else has a mind, and is not, for example, just a body with external appearance and behavior much like yours.

proposition This term has been used in a confusing variety of ways. Sometimes it means merely a sentence or a statement. Perhaps the most common modern use is the one in which a proposition is what is expressed by a (declarative) sentence: an English sentence and its French translation express the same proposition, and so do Seymour is Marvin's father and Marvin's male parent is Seymour.

propositional attitudes These are our mental states which are, so to speak, directed at propositions. For example, toward the proposition It will snow on Christmas, one can have the propositional attitude of wishing (I wish that it would snow on Christmas), believing, fearing, and so on. Compare these with mental states which are not directed at propositions: feeling happy, enjoying an ice cream, remembering Mama.

punishment Must punishment be unpleasant? Then a judicial sentence of not-unpleasant corrective therapy wouldn't be punishment. Must punishment be given in response to a previous bad act? Then a jail sentence given to an innocent person, either by mistake or to set an example for future wrongdoers, wouldn't count as punishment.

A continuing philosophical problem is the attempt to justify the existence of punishment. The deterrence and rehabilitation theories claim punishments are justified when they have good effects: for example, the prevention of future bad acts through the deterrent threat of punishment to others, or the reform of the wrongdoer. Retributivists claim that such uses of punishment are immoral, and that punishment is justified for wrongdoers merely because wrongdoing demands it—because it's justice—or a restoration of the moral order—to inflict punishment on wrongdoers.

pure reason 1. Pure reason is often taken to be reason working on its own, as contrasted with practical reason which connects facts with desires and yields conclusions about what we ought to do. 2. Pure reason is sometimes spoken of in contrast to empirical reason; thus it's a priori reasoning, supposedly independent of what we get from the senses.

qua (Latin: as) Means considered as (such and such). Usage example: "He is investigating hip hop qua social phenomenon, not qua music."

qualia 1. = characteristics (old-fashioned use). 2. = sense-data. 3. The characteristics of sensations (of sense-data), distinguished from characteristics of things sensed; for example, the flavor of an apple, as tasted, or the feel of a headache. The existence of qualia is sometimes supposed to be a problem for functionalism.

quality / attribute / property These words are synonyms. They each mean a characteristic of something. Some philosophers argue that a thing cannot be composed entirely of qualities; there must be something else, the thing itself, which these are qualities of, in which these qualities are said to "inhere".

rationalism Broadly, any philosophical position which makes reasoning or rationality extra-important. More particularly the view, contrasted with empiricism, that reason alone, unaided by sense experience, is capable of reliable and substantive knowledge; rationalists also tend to believe in innate ideas. Sometimes by "the rationalists" one means the modern continental rationalists, notably Descartes, Leibniz, and Spinoza.

rational self-interest Acting from self-interest is seeking one's own benefit. Some philosophers have sometimes argued that sometimes one can achieve this only by fulfilling some interests of others too; so they argue that rational self-interest often involves more than narrow selfishness.

realism / antirealism Realists hold views (in a variety of philosophical areas) that some sort of entity has external existence, independent of the mind; anti-realists think that that sort of entity is only a product of our thought.

reasons / causes You sometimes have reasons for doing something, but is this to be understood causally? That is, does that mean that there is a special sort of cause for your action? One reason to think that reasons are not causes is that talk about reasons often mentions the future, but a cause of x must occur before x does.

recursive Something (for example, a definition or a function) is recursive when it is to be applied over and over again to its own previous product. For example, one can define 'integer' by saying that 0 is an integer, and if x is an integer, then x + 1 is an integer. Thus, applying the second part of this definition to the first, 1 is an integer, applying the second part to this result, 2 is an integer, and so on.

reduction To reduce some notion is to define (or analyze) it in terms of others, and thus to eliminate it from the list of basic entities in the field under discussion. Reductionism about some notion is the idea that that notion can be reduced—can be given a reductive analysis.

reflective equilibrium A goal sometimes thought to guide the construction of theories. A theory is in reflective equilibrium when the basic general principles of the theory square with the particular facts the theory is supposed to explain. We start with beliefs about particulars, and construct some general principles to explain these. Alterations might then be made in other beliefs about particulars when they conflict with the principles, or in the principles when they conflict with beliefs about particulars.

reification The mistaken way of thinking about some abstract notion as if it were a real thing.

relational / intrinsic properties A property is intrinsic if things have that property in themselves, rather than in relation to other things. Thus being 100 meters tall is an intrinsic property, but being the tallest building in town is a relational property, because this is relative to the heights of other buildings in town.

relativism / absolutism Relativists argue that when certain views vary among individual people and among cultures (cultural relativism) there is no universal truth: there is instead, only "true for me (or us); false for you (or them)." This contrasts with absolutism (sometimes called objectivism): the position that there is an objectively right view. The most common relativist views concern morality (ethical relativism).

Renaissance The period (fourteenth through sixteenth century) characterized by the diminution of the authority of the Church in favor of a new humanism, and the rapid growth of science.

representationalism Theories that hold that mental contents—thoughts, perceptions, etc.—represent reality. If these representations are the only thing directly available to the mind, how do we know that the external world is actually being represented—and what it is really like?

retrocausation "Backward" causation, in which the effect occurs before the cause. The possibility of retrocausation is debatable.

retrodiction Means 'prediction backwards'—"prediction" of the past. A historian might retrodict, for example, on the basis of certain historical documents, that a battle took place centuries ago at a certain location. This retrodiction can be confirmed by present evidence, for example, by artifacts of war dug up at that site.

rights You are said to have a right to do or have something when it is thought that nobody should be allowed to keep you from it. Thus, we can speak of a right to property, or to vote, or to life. Having a right to do something doesn't mean you must or even ought to do it, but merely that you're allowed to do it if you want. Utilitarians might be able to justify according certain rights, but usually rights-theorists insist that a right is independent of utility:

that someone morally can exercise a genuine right even if it is contrary to the general welfare. An inalienable right is a right that one cannot give up or get rid of. A civil right is a right that is (or ought to be) guaranteed and enforced by government. Conventional rights are rights produced or guaranteed by society (by government or agreement, or just by custom). Natural rights, on the other hand, are rights we are supposed to have just because we are human (perhaps because they are God-given).

rigid designator A rigid designator is a term that refers to the same thing in every other possible world in which it exists. It's often thought that proper names are rigid designators, but definite descriptions aren't—they're non-rigid.

self-consciousness In philosophical use, this may mean the sort of knowledge one has of one's self that one gets by adopting the perspective that others might have of one; or else the sort of self-awareness one gets by introspection.

self-contradiction A statement is self-contradictory when it asserts and denies the same thing (It's raining and it's not raining), or when it's logically false. An inconsistent set is self-contradictory. Sometimes (more loosely) a statement that is analytically false is called a self-contradiction.

semantics / syntax / pragmatics These terms name aspects of language and the study of these aspects. Semantics is that part of language which has to do with meaning and reference. Syntax has to do with grammar or logical form. Syntax, then, can tell you whether a sentence is formed correctly (for example, 'Is the on but but' is not formed correctly), but cannot tell you what a correctly formed sentence means, or what conditions would make it true. Pragmatics concerns the relations between bits of language and their uses by language-users.

sense-data The data of the senses—what they give us: the internal event or picture or representation we get when perceiving external objects—or sometimes, as when we dream or hallucinate, even in their absence. A straight stick half under water looks bent; we then have a bent sense-datum, the same sort of internal picture we would have if we saw a bent stick out of water. The argument from illusion is supposed to show that all we really directly (immediately) perceive are sense-data, and that we only infer external objects from these.

simple / complex ideas A complex idea is one that can be analyzed into simpler ideas. Brother, for example, names a complex idea that is "composed" of the ideas of male and sibling; but green perhaps names a simple idea.

skepticism The view that knowledge in some area is not possible. The Skeptics were a group of (skeptical!) Greek philosophers. Skeptics often don't really doubt the truth of the belief about which they are skeptical: their central claim is that we don't have justification for that belief.

slippery slope A form of moral reasoning in which it is argued that some act or practice is undesirable not because it's bad in itself, but because its acceptance will or might lead to a series of other acts that differ from each other in small ways, and eventuate in something clearly bad. It might be argued, for example, that a city's allowing street vendors on one corner isn't in itself bad, but this might gradually lead to more and more permissiveness, resulting eventually in the clogging of city sidewalks by all sorts of undesirables.

social contract A way of justifying the legitimacy of a ruler or government, or the restrictions imposed by government or by moral rules, on the basis of an agreement (whether explicit or tacit or merely hypothetical) of the people involved. It is supposed that people agree (or would agree) to these restrictions because of the resulting long-range benefits to everyone. This agreement is called a 'social contract'. Thinking about this social contract is usually intended (by contractarians) to provide not an actual history of the origin of these rules, but rather a justification of their existence and of their binding force.

solipsism The position that the self is the only thing that can be known, or, more extremely, that one's own mind is the only thing that exists in the universe. Nobody sane ever believed this latter view, but it is philosophically interesting to try to refute it.

state of nature The condition of human societies—typically but not invariably thought to be unpleasant—before the invention of governmental or conventional rules regulating conduct, typically held to justify such invention.

Stoicism The views of the Stoics, an ancient Greek and Roman school. They held that virtue is the highest good, and stressed control of the passions and indifference to pleasure and pain (thus the ordinary use of 'stoic').

straw man Straw man argument or reasoning (or "setting up a straw man") is a bad form of reasoning in which one argues against some position by producing and refuting a false and stupid version of that position.

structuralism Wide-ranging and controversial largely French twentieth-century philosophical school of thought. Its central idea is that cultural phenomena should be understood as manifesting unchanging and universal abstract structures or forms; their meaning can be understood only when these forms are revealed.

subjective / objective Whether something is objective—a feature of the real external mind-independent world, or subjective—in our minds only—is a perennial and pervasive topic in all areas of philosophy. Examples: ethical subjectivism, for example, holds that our ethical "judgments" reflect our own feelings only, not facts about externals. Aesthetic subjectivism puts beauty (and other aesthetic properties) in the eye of the beholder.

substance Any basic, independently existing entity or subject; the stuff of which things are made. Thought sometimes to be unavailable to our senses, but conceptually necessary as that which "underlies" or "supports" characteristics we can sense, and as that which is responsible for things existing through time despite changes in characteristics. Dualists believe there are two substances: (1) physical (material, corporeal, or extended substance), making up physical things, that to which material qualities (size and shape, weight or mass, etc.) apply; (2) mental (immaterial or incorporeal), what mental or spiritual things are made of, and to which characteristics such as thinking, feeling, desiring apply.

supervenience Things of kind A supervene on things of kind B (the 'supervenience base') when the presence or absence of things of kind A is completely determined by the presence or absence of things of kind B; there can be no difference of sort A without a difference in sort B (though there may be differences in B without differences in A). A clear example is the supervenience of the biological on the microphysical: things have biological properties in virtue of their microphysical properties, and there can be no biological difference without a microphysical difference. It is sometimes thought that ethical properties, and mental properties, supervene on the physical.

tabula rasa (Latin: "blank slate") The term is associated with Locke; he and others opposed to innateness think that at birth our minds have no concepts or beliefs in them—they are "blank slates" that will get things "written" on them only after, and by, sense experience.

teleological argument for God's existence Arguments based on the apparent goal-directedness of things in nature. A common version: Living things are adapted to their environment—they are built in complex and clever ways to function well in their surroundings. This could not have happened merely by the random and mechanical processes of nature. They must have been constructed this way, with their functions in mind, by a creator much more clever and powerful than humans; thus they are evidence for God's existence. The usual reply to this argument is that Darwinian evolutionary theory provides a scientific account of how these things arose merely by the mechanical processes of nature, so one need not posit something unseen and supernatural to account for them.

teleology The study of aims, purposes, or functions. Much ancient philosophical and scientific thought saw teleology as a central principle of things, and a very important basis for explanation. Teleology is much less important in contemporary thought, but philosophers are still interested in what teleology remains (for example, scientific talk about what the pancreas is for, or about the function of individual species in the ecosystem). Teleological ethics sees the aim of actions—good results—as the basic concept, from which the notions of right action and good person can be derived.

theism Belief in the existence of at least one god; often, however, more narrowly monotheism—the belief in just one God. The contrast here is with atheism.

theory Scientists and philosophers do not mean "just a guess" by the word theory. A theory here is a system of interrelated statements designed to explain a variety of phenomena. Sometimes a theory is distinguished from a law or set of laws insofar as a theory postulates the existence of unseen theoretical entities.

thought experiment A state of affairs or story we are asked to imagine to raise a philosophical question, or to illustrate or test some philosophical point. For example, imagine that the brains of two people were interchanged; what you would then say about the location of the two might have implications for the principles of personal identity. (Sometimes encountered in its German translation, *Gedankenexperiment*.)

transcendental The most general philosophical usage of this term applies to any idea or system that goes beyond some supposed limit. The word is most often encountered, however, in connection with transcendental idealism, the name of Kant's system; he produced transcendental arguments that were supposed to show truths beyond the evidence of our senses, as necessary presuppositions of any rational experience or thought.

twin-earth An imaginary planet almost exactly like our Earth, commonly referred to in philosophical thought-experiments. Suppose, for example, that rivers and oceans on twin-earth are filled with XYZ, not H_2O, though the two are (except by chemists) indistinguishable. Then when on twin-earth Twin-John asks for "water" in his scotch, does this mean the same as in English?

type / token Two different things that are both of a certain sort are said to be two tokens of one type. Thus, in the sentence 'The cat is on the mat' there are six word tokens, but only five word types. Token physicalism is the view that each particular mental event is identical with (the same thing as) a particular physical event (e.g., a brain event). Type physicalism (sometimes known as the type-type identity theory) adds that each kind of mental event is also a kind of physical event. Functionalists tend to be token physicalists but not type physicalists. Identity theorists tend to be type physicalists. Anomalous monism admits token identity, but denies type identity.

underdetermination Something is underdetermined by a set of conditions if these conditions don't determine how (or that) it will exist. Thus, the striking of a match underdetermines its lighting because it's not sufficient. Language behavior underdetermines a translation manual when different equally adequate translation manuals can be constructed for that behavior. Scientific theory is underdetermined by empirical evidence when two rival hypotheses are both consistent with all the evidence.

universalizability True of a particular action when it can be universalized—that is, when the rule behind it can consistently or reasonably be conceived of as a universal law (one that could apply to everyone). The test of consistent rational universalizability is roughly what Kant thought to be the test of ethically right action. The test of practical universalizability (not Kant's test) is perhaps what we apply when we think morally about some action by evaluating the consequences if everyone were to do that sort of thing.

universals These are "abstract" things—beauty, courage, redness, etc. The problem of universals is whether these exist in the external world. Thus, one may be a realist or anti-realist about universals. Plato's theory of forms is an early and well-known realism about universals; the empiricists are associated with anti-realism. Nominalism is a variety of anti-realism that claims that only particulars exist, and that such abstractions are merely the result of the way we talk.

utilitarianism Utilitarians think that the moral worth of any action can be measured by the extent to which it provides valued results—usually pleasure or happiness—to the greatest number of people. Thus, their general moral principle is the principle of utility, also known as the 'greatest happiness principle': "Act so as to produce the greatest happiness for the greatest number of people." Act utilitarians hold that moral thinking evaluates each act, in context, separately; rule utilitarians argue that morality is concerned with general rules for action, and that a particular action is right if it is permitted or recommended by a moral code whose acceptance in the agent's society would maximize utility, even if that act in particular does not.

utility In utilitarianism, this means the quantity of value or desirability something has. Often it is thought that the utility of something can be given a number (the quantity of "utiles" it possesses), and utilities can be compared or added.

vacuous Means 'empty'. In logic, the statement All A's are B's is understood to be equivalent to For all x, if x is an A then x is a B. Suppose there aren't any A's at all. Then it's always false that any x is an A: but this makes the conditional, if x is an A then x is a B true. It follows, then, that if there aren't any A's, all statements of the form All A's are B's are true. So, for example, because there aren't any unicorns, the statement All unicorns are mammals is true, and so is All unicorns are non-mammals. This strange kind of truth is called vacuous truth.

vagueness In a technical logician's sense, a term is vague whose application involves borderline cases: thus, 'tall' is vague, because there are some people who are clearly tall, some clearly not tall, and some who are in a borderline area, and are not clearly tall or not tall.

verifiability A statement is verifiable when there exist (at least in principle) procedures that would show that it is true or false. 'In principle' is added here because there do not need to be procedures actually available now or ever, as long as we can imagine what they are. So, for example, the statement There is a planet on a star seven million light years from here is unverifiable given our current (and perhaps future) technology, but because we can imagine what would be evidence for its truth or falsity, it is verifiable in principle.

virtue Moral excellence or uprightness; the state of character of a morally worthwhile person. The virtues are those character traits that make for a good person. Some philosophers think that virtue, not good states of affairs or right action, is the central notion in ethics: thus virtue ethics.

zombies These are, of course, the walking dead of horror movies, starring also in the problem of absent qualia which haunts functionalism. In this thought experiment, we are to imagine that zombies show normal stimulus-response connections, but no qualia—no consciousness. The functionalist would have to grant them mentality; this is supposed to show what's wrong with functionalism.

IMAGE CREDITS

Line drawing portraits by Rose McNeil:

Nelson Goodman
Carl Hempel
Thomas Kuhn
G.E. Moore
Karl Popper
Wesley Salmon

Author images contributed by their respective authors:

Lorraine Code
Edmund Gettier

ACKNOWLEDGMENTS

The publisher has made every attempt to locate the authors of the copyrighted material or their heirs and assigns, and would be grateful for information that would allow correction of any errors or omissions in subsequent editions of the work.

Berkeley, George. *Three Dialogues Between Hylas and Philonous*. 3rd edition (revised), 1734.

Code, Lorraine. "Is the Sex of the Knower Epistemologically Significant?" Chapter 1 of *What Can She Know?: Feminist Theory and the Construction of Knowledge*; pp. 1–26. Copyright © 1991 by Cornell University. Used by permission of the publisher, Cornell University Press.

Descartes, René. *Meditations on First Philosophy*, 1641. Translated and edited by John Cottingham. Copyright © 1996 Cambridge University Press; pp. 9–62. Reprinted with the permission of Cambridge University Press.

Gettier, Edmund. "Is Justified True Belief Knowledge?" *Analysis* 23, June 1963; pp. 121–123. By permission of Oxford University Press.

Goodman, Nelson. "The New Riddle of Induction" reprinted by permission of the publisher from *Fact, Fiction, and Forecast* by Nelson Goodman, pp. 59–83, Cambridge, MA: Harvard University Press. Copyright © 1979, 1983 by Nelson Goodman.

Hempel, Carl G. "Scientific Inquiry: Invention and Test." From *Philosophy of Natural Science*, 1st Edition, © 1967; pp. 10–15. Reprinted by permission of Pearson Education, Inc., Upper Saddle River, NJ.

Hume, David. *Enquiry Concerning Human Understanding*. 1748; 1777.

Kant, Immanuel. *Critique of Pure Reason*. Translated by Norman Kemp Smith, 1929, Basingstoke, Hants: Palgrave, pp. 41–62. Copyright © 1929; revised edition 1933. Reproduced with permission of Palgrave Macmillan.

Kuhn, Thomas. "Objectivity, Value Judgment and Theory Choice." From *The Essential Tension: Selected Studies in Scientific Tradition and Change*. University of Chicago Press, 1977; pp. 320–339. Copyright © University of Chicago 1977.

Locke, John. *An Essay Concerning Human Understanding* was first published in 1690. The excerpts given here are from the sixth edition of 1710.

Longino, Helen. "Can There Be a Feminist Science?" *Hypatia* Volume 2, Issue 3, 1987; pp. 51–64.

Moore, G.E. "Proof of an External World." *Proceedings of the British Academy*. Volume 25, 1939; pp. 273–300. Reprinted with the kind permission of Dr. Thomas Baldwin, Literary Executor to G.E. Moore.

Peirce, C.S. "The Fixation of Belief." From *Illustrations of the Logic of Science, Popular Science Monthly* 12, November 1877; pp. 1–15.

Popper, Karl. "Science: Conjectures and Refutations." Chapter 1 of *Conjectures and Refutations: The Growth of Scientific Knowledge*, 5th revised edition. London: Routledge, 1989, pp. 33–59. Copyright © University of Klagenfurt/Karl Popper Library.

Russell, Bertrand. From Chapters 1 to 3 of *The Problems of Philosophy*. © Bertrand Russell, 1967. By permission of Oxford University Press.

Salmon, Wesley. "Unfinished Business: The Problem of Induction." *Philosophical Studies* Volume 33, Number 1, January 1978; pp. 1–19. With kind permission from Springer Science+Business Media.

SOURCES FOR QUOTATIONS

CHAPTER 1

Plato, *Apology*. In Plato *Complete Works*, ed. John M. Cooper (Indianapolis: Hackett, 1997) this quote appears on page 33.

Immanuel Kant, "An Answer to the Question: What is Enlightenment?" In Kant, *Practical Philosophy*, ed. Mary J. Gregor (Cambridge: Cambridge University Press, 1996) this quote appears on page 17.

Bertrand Russell, *The Problems of Philosophy* (Oxford: Oxford University Press, 1912), 93–94.

CHAPTER 2

Descartes

René Descartes, *Discourse on the Method*, Part 1. In *The Philosophical Writings of Descartes*, ed. Cottingham, Stoothoff and Murdoch (Cambridge: Cambridge University Press, 1985) the quote is in Volume I, page 115.

René Descartes, *Rules for the Direction of the Mind*, Rule Four. In *The Philosophical Writings of Descartes*, *ibid.*, the quote is in Volume I, page 19.

René Descartes, *Principles of Philosophy*, Part 64. In *The Philosophical Writings of Descartes*, *ibid.*, the quote is in Volume I, page 247.

René Descartes, *Principles of Philosophy*, Part 51. In *The Philosophical Writings of Descartes*, *ibid.*, the quote is in Volume I, page 210.

Bernard Williams, "Introduction" to Descartes' *Meditations on First Philosophy*, trans. John Cottingham (Cambridge: Cambridge University Press, 1996), vii.

John Cottingham, *The Cambridge Companion to Descartes*, ed. John Cottingham (Cambridge: Cambridge University Press, 1992), 1.

David Hume, *An Enquiry Concerning Human Understanding*, ed. Selby-Bigge and Nidditch (Oxford: Clarendon Press, 1975), 153.

Elizabeth Anscombe, "The First Person," in S. Guttenplan (ed.) *Mind and Language: Wolfson College Lectures 1974* (Oxford: Oxford University Press, 1975), 45–65.

Locke

P.H. Nidditch, "Introduction" to *An Essay Concerning Human Understanding* (Oxford: Oxford University Press, 1975), vii.

Kant

Immanuel Kant, *Critique of Practical Reason*, ed. Mary Gregor (Cambridge: Cambridge University Press, 1997), 133.

Immanuel Kant, *Critique of Pure Reason*, ed. Norman Kemp Smith (New York: Palgrave, 192), 24–25.

Russell

Bertrand Russell, *Autobiography* (London: George Allen & Unwin, 1967), Volume I, 145.

Moore

Gilbert Ryle, "G.E. Moore," in his *Collected Papers* (London: Hutchinson, 1971), Volume I, 270–271.

CHAPTER 3

Hume

Bertrand Russell, "The Metaphysician's Nightmare" in *Nightmares of Eminent Persons* (London: Simon & Schuster, 1955).

Goodman

Hilary Putnam, "Preface," to *Fact, Fiction, and Forecast* (Cambridge, MA: Harvard University Press, 1983), vii.

Hempel

Richard Jeffrey, "Preface," to Hempel's *Selected Philosophical Essays*, ed. Jeffrey (Cambridge: Cambridge University Press, 2000), ix.

Popper

Peter Medawar, BBC Radio 3, 28 July 1972.

John Eccles, *Facing Reality* (New York: Springer-Verlag, 1970).

Peirce

Peirce, "How to Make Our Ideas Clear" (1878). In *The Essential Peirce*, ed. Houser and Kloesel (Bloomington: Indiana University Press, 1992) the quote is on page 132.

Using 0,685 tons of Rolland Enviro100 Print instead
of virgin fibres paper reduces your ecological footprint of:

 12 trees

 11,334 gal. US of water
32 days of water consumption

 1,433 lbs de déchets
29 waste containers

 3,724 lbs CO2
emissions of 1 car per year

 18 MMBTU
83,755 60W light bulbs for one hour

11 lbs NOx
emissions of one truck during 34
days